Vocal Health and Pedagogy

About the Author

Robert T. Sataloff, M.D, DMA is Professor of Oto-laryngology at Jefferson Medical College, Thomas Jefferson University; Chairman of the Department of Otolaryngology—Head and Neck Surgery of the Allegheny University Hospitals, Graduate; Adjunct Professor, University of Pennsylvania, Department of Otorhinolaryngology—Head and Neck Surgery; and Adjunct Professor of Otolaryngology—Head and Neck Surgery at Georgetown University; on the Faculties of the Academy of Vocal Arts and the Curtis Institute of Music; Conductor of the Thomas Jefferson University Choir and Orchestra; Director of the Jefferson Arts-Medicine Center; and Chairman of the Board of Directors of the Voice Foundation and of the American Institute for Voice and Ear Research. Dr. Sataloff is also a professional singer and singing teacher. He holds an undergraduate degree from Haverford College in Music Theory and Composition, a medical degree from Jefferson Medical College, received a Doctor of Musical Arts in Voice Performance from Combs College of Music, and completed his Residency in Otolaryngology—Head and Neck Surgery at the University of Michigan. He also completed a Fellowship in Otology, Neurotology, and Skull Base Surgery at the University of Michigan. He is Editor-in-Chief of the *Journal of Voice*, Editor-in-Chief of the *Journal of Occupational Hearing Loss*, on the Editorial Board of the *Journal of Singing*, *Medical Problems of Performing Artists*, and *Ear, Nose & Throat Journal*, and on the Editorial Review Boards of many major otolaryngology journals in the United States. Dr. Sataloff has written over 400 publications, including 17 textbooks. His medical practice is limited to care of the professional voice and to neurotology-skull base surgery. Dr. Sataloff's books include:

Sataloff J, Sataloff RT, Vassallo LA. *Hearing Loss*. Philadelphia, Pa: JB Lippincott; 1980.

Sataloff RT, Sataloff J. *Occupational Hearing Loss*. New York, NY: Marcel Dekker; 1987.

Sataloff RT, Brandfonbrener A, Lederman R. *Textbook of Performing Arts Medicine*. New York, NY: Raven Press; 1991.

Sataloff RT. *Embryology and Anomalies of the Facial Nerve*. New York, NY: Raven Press; 1991.

Sataloff RT. *Professional Voice: The Science and Art of Clinical Care*. New York, NY: Raven Press, 1991.

Sataloff RT, Titze IR. *Vocal Health and Science*. Jacksonville, Fla: The National Association of Teachers of Singing; 1991.

Gould WJ, Sataloff RT, Spiegel JR. *Voice Surgery*. St. Louis, Mo: CV Mosby C; 1993.

Sataloff RT, Sataloff J. *Occupational Hearing Loss*. 2nd ed. New York, NY: Marcel Dekker; 1993.

Mandel S, Sataloff RT, Schapiro S. *Minor Head Trauma: Assessment, Management and Rehabilitation*. New York, NY: Springer-Verlag; 1993.

Sataloff RT, Sataloff J. *Hearing Loss*. 3rd ed. New York, NY: Marcel Dekker; 1993.

Rubin J, Sataloff RT, Korovin G, Gould WJ. *The Diagnosis and Treatment of Voice Disorders*. New York, NY: Igaku-Shoin Medical Publishers, Inc; 1995.

Rosen DC, Sataloff RT. *Psychology of Voice Disorders*. San Diego, Calif: Singular Publishing Group, Inc; 1997.

Sataloff RT: *Professional Voice: The Science and Art of Clinical Care*. 2nd ed. San Diego, Calif: Singular Publishing Group, Inc; 1997.

Sataloff, RT. *Vocal Health and Pedagogy*. San Diego, Calif: Singular Publishing Group, Inc; 1998.

Sataloff RT, ed. *Voice Perspectives*. San Diego, Calif: Singular Publishing Group, Inc; 1998.

Sataloff RT, Brandfonbrener A, Lederman R. eds. *Arts Medicine*. 2nd ed. San Diego, Calif: Singular Publishing Group, Inc; 1998.

Sataloff RT, Hawkshaw MJ. *Chaos in Medicine*. San Diego, Calif: Singular Publishing Group, Inc; 1998.

Vocal Health and Pedagogy

Robert Thayer Sataloff, M.D., D.M.A.

Professor of Otolaryngology—Head and Neck Surgery
Jefferson Medical College
Thomas Jefferson University

Chairman, Department of Otolaryngology—Head and Neck Surgery
Allegheny University Hospitals, Graduate

Adjunct Professor, Department of Otorhinolaryngology—Head and Neck Surgery
The University of Pennsylvania

Adjunct Professor, Department of Otolaryngology—Head and Neck Surgery
Georgetown University School of Medicine

Director, Jefferson Arts-Medicine Center

Faculty, The Curtis Institute of Music

Faculty, The Academy of Vocal Arts

Chairman, The Voice Foundation

Chairman, American Institute
for Voice and Ear Research
Philadelphia, Pennsylvania

SINGULAR PUBLISHING GROUP, INC.
SAN DIEGO · LONDON

Singular Publishing Group, Inc.
401 West A Street, Suite 325
San Diego, California 92101-7904

Singular Publishing Ltd.
19 Compton Terrace
London N1 2UN, UK

Singular Publishing Group, Inc., publishes textbooks, clinical manuals, clinical reference books, journals, videos, and multimedia materials on speech-language pathology, audiology, otorhino-laryngology, special education, early childhood, aging, occupational therapy, physical therapy, re-habilitation, counseling, mental health, and voice. For your convenience, our entire catalog can be accessed on our website at **http//www.singpub.com.** Our mission to provide you with materials to meet the daily challenges of the everchanging health care/educational environment will remain on course if we are in touch with you. In that spirit, we welcome your feedback on our products. Please telephone **(1-800-521-8545)**, fax **(1-800-774-8398)**, or e-mail **(singpub@mail.cerfnet.com)** your comments and requests to us.

Typeset in 10/12 Palatino by So Cal Graphics
Printed in the United States of America by McNaughton and Gunn

Library of Congress Cataloging-in-Publication Data

Sataloff, Robert Thayer,
    Vocal health and pedagogy / Robert Thayer Sataloff.
       p.   cm.
    An abridged version of the author's: Professional voice, 2nd ed.,
1997 with some new materials added.
    Includes bibilographical references and index.
    ISBN 1-56593-963-8 (soft cover : alk. paper)
    1. Voice disorders. 2. Voice—Care and hygiene. 3. Voice
culture. 4. Voice—Physiological aspects. I. Sataloff, Robert
Thayer Professional voice. 1997. II. Title.
    [DNLM: 1. Voice Disorders—therapy. 2. Voice. 3. Voice Training.
WV 500 S2525v 1998]
RF510.S283 1998
616.85'5—dc21
DNLM/DLC
for Library of Congress
                                                              97-42658
                                                                CIP

Contents

Preface

Vocal Health and Pedagogy was written as a companion book to *Professional Voice: The Science and Art of Clinical Care*, Second Edition. When I wrote the first edition of *Professional Voice: The Science and Art of Clinical Care*, which was published in 1991, I had hoped that it would be used not only as a medical text, but also for courses in vocal pedagogy and speech-language pathology. Although teachers in these fields found the book useful and helpful, only a few were comfortable using it in their courses because of the cost to their students (approximately $100.00). Now that the book has expanded from 33 chapters in the first edition to 68 chapters in the second edition, the cost of the book has tripled; and it has become virtually inaccessible to an important segment of the audience for whom it was written. Consequently, *Vocal Health and Pedagogy* has been written to make at least some of the information available and affordable for students.

Many of the 31 chapters in *Vocal Health and Pedagogy* come directly from *Professional Voice: The Science and Art of Clinical Care*, Second Edition, with little or no modification, although color figures have been converted to black and white in the interest of cost. Chapters were selected for inclusion based on their applicability to voice pedagogy courses in music schools and voice courses in speech-language pathology programs. Much of the detailed medical and surgical information in *Professional Voice: The Science and Art of Clinical Care*, Second Edition, has been drastically condensed or omitted. The result provides enough medical information to help readers understand the medical approach to voice problem analysis, standards of care in evalua-

tion and diagnosis, and substantial information about many of the most common and troublesome medical problems that afflict voice users. The information is more than enough help for readers to avoid preventable medical problems, and be "educated consumers" when they or their students consult a laryngologist. A few medical chapters have been retained in their entirety because their information is particularly complex and important to voice use and teaching. Chapter summaries and self-test questions have been added for the convenience of students and their professors.

Chapters on voice science including Anatomy and Physiology also have been included in their entirety. A new chapter has been added on the Physics of Sound. This book also retains the important chapters on Voice Therapy, and the Teaching of Singing and Acting Techniques for Patients with Vocal Injuries.

In educational settings, it is the author's hope that *Vocal Health and Pedagogy* will be used in conjunction with *Professional Voice: The Science and Art of Clinical Care*, Second Edition. Ideally, the longer book should be available as a library reference; and I believe it would be particularly valuable to anyone teaching courses in which *Vocal Health and Pedagogy* is used as a student text. *Professional Voice: The Science and Art of Clinical Care*, Second Edition, should also be useful as a reference for teachers or performers who develop voice problems and seek more extensive information. As a convenience, the Contents pages and Preface from *Professional Voice: The Science and Art of Clinical Care*, Second Edition, are included in this book for easy reference.

Preface to the Second Edition of
Professional Voice: The Science and Art of Clinical Care

(The Companion Text to *Vocal Health and Pedagogy*)

Professional Voice: The Science and Art of Clinical Care, Second Edition, is written primarily for physicians. Like the first edition, it is also intended to be useful for speech-language pathologists, voice teachers, performers, and anyone interested in voice. The book provides practical understanding of most specialized aspects of clinical care of professional voice users. Because voice is a new subspecialty of otolaryngology, there are few comprehensive texts available in which the interested otolaryngologist can find this information conveniently compiled. The first edition of this book has been used widely and seems to have been helpful in facilitating good clinical care and providing a basis from which new ideas and research have developed. It has proven similarly useful to speech-language pathologists whose training programs still rarely provide instruction in professional voice care and include virtually no training on how to work with the speaking voices of professional singers. Singing teachers and singers have also used the book not only in the study of voice pedagogy, but also as a practical reference on voice care.

The second edition is designed to be useful in similar ways. However, a great deal of new information has been included. The book is more than twice as long as the first edition and includes many topics not covered in the first book. Many of them have been added to the second edition in response to the inquiries of readers of the first edition. Every effort has been made to make this book comprehensive, yet accessible. It includes most of the subjects I have considered important enough to write about in the past, many new subjects never addressed in voice literature, and a few chapters republished for the reader's convenience from *Voice Surgery* (C.V. Mosby, Chicago, Illinois, by Wilbur James Gould, Robert T. Sataloff, and Joseph R. Spiegel) which is out of print. I am indebted once again to the National Association of Teachers of Singing for permission to use freely material from my "Laryngoscope" articles which appear in every issue of *The NATS Journal* (now *The Journal of Singing*). I am also grateful to MedQuest, Ltd. for per-

mission to republish the color pictures from my monthly column in the *Ear, Nose and Throat Journal.*

As a compendium of information about care of the professional voice, this book naturally includes information of practical value for the singer, actor, or other professional voice user. In fact, most of the material presented has been included in my courses on voice pedagogy taught at the Academy of Vocal Arts and the Curtis Institute of Music since 1980, as well as in courses for physicians. Voice students, singing teachers, acting-voice trainers, and others report having found this information valuable in augmenting their traditional teaching approaches, understanding healthy functioning of the voice, recognizing voice dysfunction early, knowing when to refer, and knowing how to assess the quality of medical care rendered. It also appears that students trained with this information appreciate the importance of and techniques for maintaining vocal health; and they seem to spend less time sick, injured, or in a physician's office (especially for preventable problems) than their colleagues without such training.

The **Introductory** chapter of the second edition provides an overview of modern voice medicine, and a brief historical overview of its development from the time of Hippocrates. **Chapter 2** is a classic treatise on the history of the larynx and voice over the centuries. **Chapter 3** is a new chapter which summarizes what little is known about the genetics of voice disorders. **Chapter 4**, which also did not appear in the first edition, reviews the latest concepts in laryngeal embryology. **Chapter 5** provides a detailed understanding of the complex function of the cricoarytenoid joint. This unique contribution is not available elsewhere in the literature. **Chapter 6** crystallizes clinically relevant anatomy and physiology of phonation. This chapter has been expanded to contain considerably more anatomical information which has proven valuable for surgeons, as well as new anatomic findings that were unknown at the time of the first edition. In **Chapter 7**, Dr. Ronald Baken presents an exceptionally lucid overview of the physiology of phonation. In

Chapter 8, Sundberg offers an elegant summary of his classic research on vocal tract resonance. Understanding this information is essential for healthcare professionals and for performers. **Chapter 9** deals with the exciting new field of nonlinear dynamics (Chaos) and its implications for understanding voice. **Chapters 10 and 11** provide in-depth information on special aspects of the medical history important in caring for singers and actors. The same information is relevant to a voice teacher when first evaluating a new student. **Chapters 12 and 13** detail state-of-the-art physical examination and clinical laboratory assessment for patients with voice disorders. All of these chapters have been revised and updated, but major changes have been made especially in the chapter on the clinical voice laboratory. Many of the recommendations and much of the equipment discussed in the first edition are obsolete; and the current chapter includes the latest information on clinical laboratory assessment. **Chapter 14** discusses in detail the important subject of laryngeal electromyography. The clinical relevance of laryngeal EMG has really been recognized only in the last few years. **Chapter 15** reviews the effects of age on the voice, including not only anatomic and physiologic changes, but also special considerations for children, teenagers, and aging professional voice users which were not discussed in the first edition. **Chapter 16** is a review of the problem of hearing loss in singers and the importance of music as a source of occupational hearing loss. Numerous references have been added in this edition. **Chapter 17** is a new chapter on ophthalmologic considerations in performers. Visual problems can be significant impairments in professional singers and actors. **Chapter 18** provides additional details on new techniques in eye surgery to restore vision, stressing advantages and disadvantages of refractive surgery for performers. **Chapter 19** on endocrine disorders that may affect the voice has also been completely rewritten and expanded. Much more information has been included, especially on female hormones and their effects on the voice. **Chapter 20** is a new chapter on the important subject of breast cancer and its implications for singers. **Chapter 21** on psychological factors in voice disorders has been extensively rewritten and expanded to include new information not appreciated or known at the time of the first edition. This information is important to anyone caring for the voice, and psychological information of particular importance to voice surgeons and others responsible for rehabilitation following vocal fold injury is stressed. **Chapter 22** on gastroesophageal reflux laryngitis has been completely rewritten and markedly expanded. It is now a comprehensive discussion of the management of reflux

disease, and it includes a lengthy literature review. This chapter also contains new, excellent illustrations which make the subject much more understandable to nonclinical readers. **Chapter 23** on Halitosis and **Chapter 24** on Obesity required only minor updating. **Chapter 25** is an extraordinary and scholarly new discussion of nutrition and its implications for general and vocal health, a subject never addressed comprehensively in previous books or chapters on voice care. **Chapter 26** on bodily injuries and their effects on the voice has been modified slightly, and complemented by the addition and expansion of subsequent chapters. **Chapter 27** provides a review of current concepts in arts-medicine and hazards of nonvoice performance including such activities as dance and playing wind instruments. **Chapter 28** is a new chapter on principles of seating and the problems associated with improper seating which can adversely affect performance especially during long choral rehearsals. In some cases, seating may be an important factor that contributes to choral voice abuse. **Chapter 29** on allergy has been substantially updated and expanded. Supplemental information on immunology has been included. **Chapter 30** discusses respiratory dysfunction in singers and includes the latest findings on the ARIAS syndrome (airway reactivity induced asthma in singers). **Chapter 31** discusses the consequences of pollution on voice function. **Chapters 32 and 33** cover pyrotechnics. These chapters define many of the terms used in pyrotechnics and introduce readers to the techniques used in pyrotechnics and the chemicals to which vocalists may be exposed through theatrical special effects. They include a glossary of terms used by specialists who create pyrotechnic effects. **Chapter 34** covers the important subject of theatrical fog. This topic has sparked debate and controversy, but most physicians and performers have had little scientific knowledge or information on which to base judgments. This chapter addresses a scientific approach to evaluating problems of theatrical fog and provides a valuable overview on this subject. **Chapter 35** is a greatly expanded review of infectious and inflammatory diseases with laryngeal manifestations. This information should be useful for all voice care providers, and should be of great interest to internists and family practitioners, as well. **Chapter 36** on sinusitis, **Chapter 37** on AIDS, and **Chapter 38** on chronic fatigue syndrome are all new, in-depth chapters on subjects of particular interest and importance to professional voice users. **Chapter 39** reviews current thinking on the need for and techniques of voice rest. **Chapter 40** on medications is completely rewritten and now contains an extensive discussion on drugs and their effects on the voice. **Chapter 41** has been retained because of its popularity among readers. It provides suggestions for medications which may be taken with a performer when he or she is traveling for extended periods of time, epecially when traveling in other countries. **Chapter 42** includes information on neurological disorders with emphasis on evaluation and treatment of many conditions including paralysis, paresis, tremor, and myasthenia gravis. **Chapter 43** is devoted to laryngeal dystonia (spasmodic dysphonia). It also contains information which was not included in the first edition. The chapter from the first edition on Structural and Neurological Disorders and Surgery of the voice has been replaced by four extensive and comprehensive chapters that cover the subjects much more thoroughly and practically. **Chapter 44** reviews structural disorders such as nodules, cysts, and polyps. **Chapter 45** is devoted to the particularly interesting and career-threatening problem of vocal fold hemorrhage. **Chapter 46** explores the challenging problem of vocal fold scar and the latest concepts in its treatment. **Chapter 47** is Dr. Hans von Leden's review of The History of Phonosurgery. Although this chapter has been published previously, these insights by the man who first proposed the term "phonosurgery" provide unique perspective. In **Chapter 48,** Zeitels expands on the history of microlaryngeal surgery including surprisingly advanced roots in the 19th century. **Chapter 49** is an extensive chapter on endoscopic and external voice surgery, including indications and techniques. This chapter, and the two chapters that follow, should be of special interest to otolaryngologic surgeons because of the detailed information included on various surgical judgments and approaches. **Chapter 50** is essentially a photo atlas of surgical pathology and provides insights into delicate microsurgical technique. **Chapter 51** reviews special concerns and considerations for professional voice users undergoing facial plastic surgery. **Chapter 52** on laryngeal trauma and **Chapter 53** on laryngeal cancer are comprehensive reviews that include detailed descriptions of surgical principles and methods. **Chapters 54** and **55** introduce the problems of voice abuse and the role of the speech-language pathologist in care of the professional voice user. The late Carol Wilder's classic chapter has been retained. **Chapter 56** on voice therapy has been modified, rewritten, and updated extensively. This chapter and the related appendixes provide detailed information for speech-language pathologists about techniques for treating professional voice users, including singers. **Chapter 57,** Increasing Vocal Effectiveness, presents techniques for public speakers and reviews the many practical considerations that may enhance or ruin speaking performance. In **Chapter 58,** Richard Miller offers

a sage perspective on the implications of voice science for modern singing teachers. This chapter has been modified slightly from the first edition. **Chapter 59** provides an extensive discussion on the role of the singing voice specialist and an overview for physicians and speech-language pathologists on the teaching of singing in general. This substantially revised chapter, and the chapters on speech therapy and acting-voice training include specific exercises offered as examples and extensive practical guidance. **Chapter 60** reviews the use of modern scientific instrumentation to augment traditional approaches in the singing studio. Since several conservatories (such as Oberlin and Westminster Choir college) have already developed voice laboratories within their music departments, interest in technological enhancement of voice teaching has increased substantially. This chapter required only minor updating. **Chapter 61** is another unique chapter on a subject never covered in the medical literature and neglected almost as completely in music literature: choral pedagogy. Choral singing is extremely popular throughout the world, and many people with little or no training participate. It is not uncommon to encounter singers who have sustained vocal injury through choral music activities. Yet, there is little guidance for choral conductors (most of whom are not singers) on approaches to safe singing in the choral environment. This chapter addresses that important subject. To the best of our knowledge, **Chapter 62** is the first chapter ever published on the role of the acting-voice trainer in the medical milieu. This chapter describes new concepts and an exciting expansion of the voice care team. It includes an overview of approaches to voice training, and specific guidelines for acting-voice trainers working with injured voices. **Chapter 63** is another unprecedented chapter on muscle physiology and its implications for voice training.

Nurses contribute enormously to many medical practices. As the role of nursing care expands, their potential to contribute even more is almost unlimited. **Chapter 64** addresses our current thinking regarding nursing considerations in care of the professional voice. This subject has never been addressed in previous literature. The importance of outcome assessment as been highlighted by the medical profession at large, and by the National Institutes of Health, in particular. **Chapter 65** is a new chapter that provides an overview of outcome assessement techniques applied to vocal performance. Outcome assessment has received increasing attention for both scientific and economic reasons, and Benninger and co-workers provide perspective on this important topic. **Chapter 66** is also a novel chapter on impairment and disability considerations in voice disorders. The very term "professional voice" implies that if the voice is impaired, disability may occur. Heretofore, this important topic has not been addressed even in the AMA *Guides to the Evaluation of Permanent Impairment*. **Chapter 67** offers extrapolations into the future of voice care and research. The authors hope that our vision will serve not just as a predictor, but more importantly, as an encouragement for colleagues to join and help further the field of voice. **Chapter 68** remains unchanged, and provides a philosophical perspective on the importance to physicians of studying the voice and the arts. The appendixes of the book should also be particularly useful. They include a summary of the phonetic alphabet in five languages, clinical history and examination forms, a special history form translated into 15 languages, sample reports from a clinical voice evaluation, voice therapy exercise lists, and an extensive multidisciplinary glossary. The second edition of the book is also enhanced by the inclusion of a large number of color photographs and illustrations.

Every effort has been made to maintain the style and continuity of the book throughout. Although the interdisciplinary expertise of numerous contributors has been recruited in the preparation of this text, I have authored or co-authored 49 of the 68 chapters, and carefully edited the rest. Because this book has the concept (and hopefully the continuity) of a single-author text with generous input from colleagues, rather than an edited text with numerous authors each writing chapters independently, it should provide nonrepetitious, consistent reading from cover to cover.

Like the first edition, the second edition of *Professional Voice: The Science and Art of Clinical Care* is intended as a readable text for students, vocalists, teachers, and residents. It is also designed as a practical guide to clinical treatment for practicing physicians, singing voice specialists, acting-voice trainers, speech-language pathologists, and as a ready reference for anyone interested in the care of the professional voice. In addition, this text is designed to serve as a companion text and faculty resource to be used in conjunction with a new student text *Vocal Health and Pedagogy*. The contributors and I hope that this new, inexpensive and shorter book, used in conjunction with *Professional Voice: The Science and Art of Clinical Care* (2nd ed.) will facilitate dissemination of this important information among students and performers who need it so much.

Robert Thayer Sataloff, M.D., D.M.A.

Contents of the Second Edition of
Professional Voice: The Science and Art of Clinical Care

(The Companion Text to *Vocal Health and Pedagogy*)

Acknowledgments

I am particularly indebted to the colleagues in my practice who have been so helpful during the writing of this and other books. Special gratitude goes to Mary Hawkshaw for her help editing the manuscript, and to Helen Caputo for her expert and critical transcription.

Contributors

Ronald J. Baken, Ph.D.
New York Eye and Ear Infirmary
New York, New York

Margaret M. Baroody, M.M.
Singing Voice Specialist
Voice Technician
American Institute for Voice and Ear Research
Philadelphia, Pennsylvania

Linda M. Carroll, M.S.
Speech-Language Pathologist and
Singing Voice Specialist
Doctoral Student, Teachers College
Columbia University
Voice Consultant
Department of Otolaryngology
Lenox Hill Hospital
New York, New York

John R. Cohn, M.D., F.C.C.P.
Clinical Associate Professor of Medicine
Clinical Assistant Professor of Pediatrics
Jefferson Medical College
Thomas Jefferson University
Philadelphia, Pennsylvania

Carolyn A. Dennehy, Ph.D.
Biological Sciences
University of Northern Colorado
Greeley, Colorado

Kate A. Emerich, B.M., M.S., CCC-SLP
Speech-Language Pathologist
Singing Voice Specialist
American Institute for Voice and Ear Research
Philadelphia, Pennsylvania

Sharon L. Freed, M.F.A.
Acting-Voice Trainer
American Institute for Voice and Ear Research
Philadelphia, Pennsylvania

Pamela H. Pilch, J.D.
University of Michigan Law School
Ann Arbor, Michigan

Mary Hawkshaw, R.N., B.S.N., CORLN
Otolaryngologic Nurse-Clinician
American Institute for Voice and Ear Research
Philadelphia, Pennsylvania

Reinhardt J. Heuer, Ph.D.
Speech-Language Pathologist
Senior Voice Researcher
American Institute for Voice and Ear Research
Philadelphia, Pennsylvania

Cheryl A. Hoover, PA-C, D.M.A.
Physician Assistant
Department of Otolaryngology—Head and Neck
Surgery
Allegheny University Hospitals, Graduate
American Institute for Voice and Ear Research
Philadelphia, Pennsylvania

Steven Mandel, M.D.
Clinical Professor of Neurology
Thomas Jefferson University
Philadelphia, Pennsylvania

Richard Miller, D.H.L.
Professor of Singing
Director, Otto B. Schoepfle Vocal Arts Laboratory
Oberlin, Ohio

S. H. Miller, R.D.
Registered Dietitian
Nutrition Services
Newton Wellesley Hospital
Newton Lower Falls, Massachusetts

Kathe S. Perez, M.A., CCC-SLP
University of Colorado Health Sciences Center
Doctoral Student
University of Boulder, Colorado
Department of Communication Disorders and Speech
Sciences
Boulder, Colorado

Bonnie N. Raphael, Ph.D.
Professor of Dramatic Art
University of North Carolina
Chapel Hill, North Carolina

Deborah Caputo Rosen, R.N., Ph.D., CORLN
Medical Psychologist
Bala Cynwyd, Pennsylvania

Rhonda K. Rulnick, M.A., CCC-SLP
Speech-Language Pathologist
American Institute for Voice and Ear Research
Philadelphia, Pennsylvania

Joseph Sataloff, M.D., D.Sc.
Professor
Department of Otolaryngology—Head and Neck
Surgery
Thomas Jefferson University
Philadelphia, Pennsylvania
President
Hearing Conservation Noise Control, Inc.
Bala Cynwyd, Pennsylvania

Robert T. Sataloff, M.D., D.M.A.
Professor
Department of Otolaryngology—Head and Neck
Surgery
Thomas Jefferson University
Chairman, Department of Otolaryngology—Head
and Neck Surgery
Allegheny University Hospitals, Graduate
Adjunct Professor of Otolaryngology
Georgetown University
Adjunct Professor
Department of Otorhinolaryngology—Head and
Neck Surgery
The University of Pennsylvania
Chairman, Board of Directors
The Voice Foundation
Chairman, American Institute for Voice and Ear
Research
Faculty, Academy of Vocal Arts
Faculty, The Curtis Institute of Music
Philadelphia, Pennsylvania

Keith G. Saxon, M.D.
Adjunct Professor
Performing Arts Medicine
University of Michigan School of Music
Ann Arbor, Michigan
President, Saxon Medical, Inc.
Liberty, Missouri

Carole M. Schneider, Ph.D.
School of Kinesiology and Physical Education
University of Northern Colorado
Greeley, Colorado

Brenda J. Smith, D.M.A.
Assistant Professor of Music (Voice)
Manatee Community College
Bradenton, Florida

Joseph R. Spiegel, M.D., F.A.C.S.
Associate Professor
Department of Otolaryngology—Head and Neck
Surgery
Thomas Jefferson University
Vice-Chairman, Department of Otolaryngology—
Head and Neck Surgery
Allegheny University Hospitals, Graduate
American Institute for Voice and Ear Research
Philadelphia, Pennsylvania

Johan Sundberg, Ph.D.
Professor, Department of Speech Communication
and Music Acoustics
Royal Institute of Technology
Stockholm, Sweden

Hans von Leden, M.D.
Consultant in Otolaryngology
Los Angeles, California

Carol N. Wilder, Ph.D. (Deceased)
Former Professor of Speech Science
Teachers College
Columbia University
New York, New York

Dedication

To my wife Dahlia Mishell Sataloff and twin sons
Benjamin Harmon Sataloff and Johnathan Brandon Sataloff

Introduction

Robert Thayer Sataloff

The importance of the human voice in modern society cannot be overstated. It is the primary instrument through which most of us project our personalities and influence our compatriots. Professional voice users constitute an ever-increasing segment of our population, and their need for expert care has inspired new interest in understanding the function and dysfunction of the human voice. The new information revealed through the work of physicians and voice scientists is valuable not only for medical care of ill or injured patients, but also for voice professionals and their teachers during the course of their daily activities. Understanding the anatomy and physiology of phonation, how the voice works, and how it is fixed when it fails, helps guide healthy teaching and provides performers with information that helps them avoid illness and injury. Consequently, performers and teachers should become as familiar as possible with medical and scientific insights, technique, and technology, and should expand their practical applications in the studio and on the concert stage.

Professional voice users provide exciting challenges and special responsibilities for physicians and other health care professionals. Professional voice users include not only singers and actors, but also attorneys, politicians, clergy, educators (including some physicians), telephone receptionists, and others. Although they span a broad range of vocal sophistication and voice needs, they share a dependence on vocal endurance and quality for their livelihoods. However, the vocal needs of performing artists are especially great. In this book, we emphasize the problems of professional actors and especially singers, because they are the Olympic athletes of the voice world. Their extreme anatomic, physiologic, and therapeutic demands tax our clinical and research skills, but what we learn from them is applicable to the care

of all voice patients. In most cases, mastery of the science and art of caring for professional singers provides the physician with sufficient expertise to treat other professional voice users as well, so long as the physician takes the trouble to really understand the special needs and problems associated with various voice-dependent professions.

Voice problems may arise from laryngeal or systemic disease, trauma, or improper treatment. The consequences of voice dysfunction may be devastating, and, if permanent (or even temporary) vocal problems result from suboptimal medical care, they may result in substantial claims for damages. Possibly spurred by the striking increase in litigation, but largely to provide good medical care for its own sake, a great many physicians have recently turned their attention to professional voice care. Interdisciplinary research has resulted in new understanding and technology that have improved the standard of practice of laryngologists, speech-language pathologists, singing teachers, and acting-voice trainers. It is no longer sufficient for a physician to glance at a singer's vocal folds with a laryngeal mirror and continuous light and declare, "Your cords are fine. It must be the way you sing." Similarly, it is no longer sufficient to say, "The voice sounds bad," or "The voice sounds better," anymore than we would tolerate such vagueness in describing hearing.

Although physicians are frequently called on to care for singers and other voice professionals, most doctors still have little or no training in sophisticated analysis and treatment of subtle problems of the voice. Voice disorders are complex. Initially, voice complaints may seem vague and subjective, especially to health care professionals unfamiliar with the jargon of singers and actors. However, accurate diagnosis and rational treatment may be achieved through systematic inquiry based on understanding of the anatomy, physiology, psychology, and psychoacoustics of voice production. More thorough understanding of voice is valuable not only in caring for voice problems themselves, but also in providing good medical care by recognizing systemic diseases that present with laryngeal manifestations. Just as otologists routinely diagnose diabetes and hypothyroidism that cause dizziness or fluctuating hearing loss, laryngologists should be alert to xerophonia as a sign of diabetes, muffling of the voice from hypothyroidism, fatigue from myasthenia gravis, and many other similar problems. Hypochondriasis is rare among serious singers and most other voice professionals. In general, failure to establish a diagnosis in a professional vocalist with a voice complaint is due to lack of expertise on the part of the physician rather than an imaginary complaint on the part of the singer or actor.

History

Fascination with the human voice has prompted study for centuries, as reviewed in Dr. Hans von Leden's classic chapter (*A Cultural History of the Larynx and Voice*) in this book. A brief overview helps put the evolution of voice medicine, and modern developments in voice care into perspective. In *Corpus Hippocraticum*, Hippocrates in the 5th century BC provided some of the earliest medical speculation on the workings of the voice, recognizing the importance of the lungs, trachea, lips, and tongue in phonation. Aristotle expanded knowledge on the scientific workings of the voice and commented on the close relationship between the voice and the soul, recognizing its importance in emotional expression. Claudius Galen, who practiced from 131 to 201 AD, is hailed as the founder of laryngology and voice science. He wrote an essay on the human voice (among his over 300 books) that is frequently referenced but has, unfortunately, been lost. He recognized the workings of the voice, described the larynx, recognized the importance of the brain in controlling phonation, and, for the first time, distinguished between speech and voice. Galen's work went virtually unchallenged for more than 15 centuries and some of it is still regarded as correct.

Major advancement did not come until the Renaissance and the writings of Leonardo di Vinci, particularly *Quaderni D Anatomia* in 1500. Additional important Renaissance writers who advanced knowledge of the voice included Andreas Vesalius, Bartolomeus Eustachius, and Fabricius Ab Aquapendente. Fabricius wrote three books on the larynx, including *De Larynge Vocis Instrumento*. Similar important advances

occurred in the East, particularly in the 9th century when Rhazes the Experienced, in Baghdad, described disorders of the voice and hoarseness and recommended respiratory and voice training. There are also excellent descriptions of voice production and disorders in the *Quanun*, written by Avicenna the Persian. The *Quanun* was a standard medical textbook for more than 500 years. Major additional advances occurred in the 18th century through the efforts of Giovanni Morgagni, who first related dysphonia to abnormalities in the larynx. Also in the 18th century, Antoine Ferrein described physiological experiments on animal and human cadaver larynges and coined the term "vocal cords," comparing them to the strings of an instrument, and Albrecht von Haller described the anatomy of vocal resonance. Later, Johannes Mueller in Germany described the mechanisms of vocal fold vibration. In the 19th century, Hermann von Helmholtz essentially started the experimental science of acoustics with experiments that are still considered valid. All the scientists mentioned above laid the foundation for the close liaison that has existed between physicians and singers.

However, the clear and widely recognized beginning of arts-medicine in the voice world dates from the time of Manuel Garcia, who was born in 1805. Garcia was a world-famous opera singer while in his teens. Although he was the son of an acclaimed singer and director, his probably faulty technique and extensive operatic singing sufficiently impaired his voice to cause him to retire while still in his 20s. Thereafter, he became a thoughtful, effective, and famous teacher and was made Professor of Singing at the Conservatoire de Paris at the age of 30. In 1854, Garcia bought a dental mirror and invented the technique of indirect laryngoscopy using the sun as his light source. The laryngeal mirror is still the basic tool for visualizing vocal folds and is used daily by otolaryngologists. Garcia closely observed larynges with his new tool and presented his findings before the Royal Society of Medicine in 1855. He was considered the greatest singing teacher of his age, and on his 100th birthday in 1905 he was honored by physicians, music teachers, and scientists from all over the world.

Voice medicine continued to develop slowly throughout the first seven decades of the 20th century. In recent decades, increasing interest and new technology have generated unprecedented activity within a number of disciplines. Since 1971, laryngologists, voice scientists, physicists, computer scientists, speech-language pathologists, singing teachers, acting teachers, voice coaches, singers, actors, and other professionals have met at the Voice Foundation's week-long annual Symposium on Care of the Professional Voice. At this unique meeting, formerly held at the Juilliard School of Music and now located in Philadelphia, experts have gathered to report their research and share their ideas. The resultant interdisciplinary understanding and cooperation have produced great advances and even greater promise for future understanding. These activities have rendered care of the professional voice the most advanced discipline within the new speciality of arts-medicine. They have also inspired numerous successful interdisciplinary publications, including the *Journal of Voice*. This important journal abandons traditional specialty boundaries and brings together in one peer-reviewed journal, with international distribution, articles of high quality on all subjects relating to the voice.

In many ways, the status of voice care is still analogous to that of otology 30 years ago. Until recently, voice evaluation was reminiscent of ear examinations with a head mirror instead of a microscope or whispered voice tests instead of audiograms. In many places, it still is. Fortunately, expert research has led to greater understanding of the voice and development of instrumentation for sophisticated assessment and quantitative analysis to facilitate clinical management and research. Although efforts have focused largely on professional singers and actors, the knowledge they have accrued has advanced our understanding of voice in general and has substantially modified the state-of-the-art in clinical care of all persons with voice disorders. Still, the field is new. The first extensive article in the English medical literature intended to teach clinicians how to approach professional singers was not published until 1981,[1] and the first major American general textbook of otolaryngology containing a chapter on care of the professional voice was not published until 1986.[2] The first modern comprehensive textbook in English on medical care of the professional voice was not published until 1991 (the first edition of this text).[3] However, it should be remembered that although these contributions in English helped signal the arrival and acceptance of voice as a subspecialty, there were noteworthy predecessors that discussed voice, and some even touched on the type of professional voice user.[4-10]

The importance of interdisciplinary voice care to the evolution of modern voice care cannot be overemphasized. Although there were a few scattered collaborations in the 19th and 20th centuries, the first formal, academically based interdisciplinary voice clinic in the United States of America was established by Drs. Hans von Leden and Paul Moore at Northwestern University Medical School in 1954. These pioneers, a laryngologist and a speech-language pathologist, established a clinic in which they saw patients simultaneously, sharing insights and optimizing patient care. They separately continued this approach after Dr. von Leden moved to Los Angeles and Moore moved to the University of Florida in Gainesville, although it was not always possible for them to practice as closely with interdisciplinary colleagues "under one roof." This concept was expanded in Philadelphia in 1981 when the author (R.T.S.) hired a singing teacher and a speech-language pathologist as full-time employees in his medical practice. His expanded interdisciplinary voice team now includes two singing teachers, three speech-language pathologists, two psychologists, a voice scientist, an acting-voice trainer, and two otolaryngologic nurse-clinicians. It also includes the very close collaboration of arts-medicine colleagues located nearby including a pulmonologist, psychiatrist, neurologist, gastroenterologist, endocrinologist, ophthalmologist, and others. He anticipates further expansion of this interdisciplinary approach, because it has proven so valuable in advancing patient care and stimulating creative research.

Various other relevant works are listed in the citations above, in subsequent chapters in this book, and elsewhere.[11]

In the past few years, many new centers and academic training programs have acquired voice laboratories and begun practicing and teaching modern, advanced voice care, but more time will be required before state-of-the-art care is available in most geographical areas. At present, new understanding of special aspects of the history and physical examination of professional voice users has been supplemented by technological advances through voice analyses that are readily available to interested clinicians. Flexible fiberoptic laryngoscopy has been indispensable. The development and refinement of laryngeal stroboscopy are singularly important advancements. Strobovideolaryngoscopic evaluation of vocal fold behavior in slow motion allows diagnoses that are simply missed without it. Spectrography, electroglottography, electromyography, airflow analysis, and other techniques have also enhanced our ability to analyze and reliably treat voice disorders.

The knowledge acquired through medical and basic science research has advanced not only clinical care but also the teaching of voice. Modern singing and acting teachers and speech-language pathologists have acquired new scientific understanding of the voice and use their new knowledge to augment and refine their traditional approaches to voice training. This should lead to consistently healthier and more efficient voice training. There are many other fascinating potential implications as well. For example, to sing correctly is essentially an athletic endeavor. In this century, most athletic records have been broken. Often this has been the result of technological advancements, such as computer analysis of a runner's form using high-speed photography or stroboscopy. Through these and other methods, the marathon, pole vault, high jump, and swimming records of 50 years ago are barely qualifying marks for today's athletes. Similar principles have just begun to be applied to the proper training of the voice. It is tempting to speculate about the results. Perhaps, as in other athletic pursuits, we shall find that the healthy limits of human vocal potential are far greater than we think.

Discretion

The excitement and glamour associated with caring for a famous performer naturally tempts the physician to discuss his distinguished patient. However, this tendency must be tempered. It is not always in a singer's or actor's best professional interest to have it known that he has consulted a laryngologist, particularly for treatment of a significant vocal problem. Famous singers and actors are ethically and legally entitled to the same confidentiality we assure for our other patients.

In speech-language pathology, voice science, and academic music, sounds are designated using the International Phonetic Alphabet (IPA) (Appendix I). This is standard notation and will be used throughout this book. Readers should familiarize themselves with IPA notation and use it, because its meaning is well defined and widely understood.

References

1. Sataloff RT. The professional singer: science and art of clinical care. *Am J Otolaryngol*. 1981;2(3):251–266.
2. Sataloff RT. The professional voice. In: Cummings CV, Fredrickson JM, Harker LA, et al, eds. *Otolaryngology-Head and Neck Surgery*. St. Louis, Mo: CV Mosby; 1986;3:2029–2053.
3. Sataloff RT: *Professional Voice: The Science and Art of Clinical Care*. New York, NY: Raven Press; 1991.
4. Rush J. *The Philosophy of Human Voice*. 4th ed. Philadelphia, Pa: Lippincott, Grambo & Co.; 1855.
5. Punt NA. *The Singers' and Actors' Throat*. London: William Heinemann; 1952.
6. Brodnitz FS. Vocal rehabilitation. *Am Acad of Opth and Otolaryngol*. Minn: 1959.
7. Damste PH, Lerman JW. *An Introduction to Voice Pathology*. Springfield, Ma: Thomas; 1975.
8. Hirano M. *Clinical Examination of Voice*. Vienna-New York, NY: Springer Verlag; 1981.
9. Luchsinger R. *Handbuch der Stimm und Sprachheilkunde. Die Stimme und ihre störungen*. Vienna-New York, NY: Springer Verlag; 1: 1970.
10. Schonharl E. *Die Stroboskopie in der praktischen Laryngologie*. Stuttgart: George Thieme Verlag; 1960.
11. Sataloff RT. *Professional Voice: The Science and Art of Clinical Care*, 2nd ed. San Diego, Calif: Singular Publishing Group, Inc.; 1997.

2

Clinical Anatomy and Physiology of the Voice

Robert Thayer Sataloff

Anatomy

The anatomy of a professional voice user is not limited to the region between the suprasternal notch (top of the breast bone) and the hyoid bone (tongue bone). Practically all body systems affect the voice. The larynx receives the greatest attention because it is the most sensitive and expressive component of the vocal mechanism, but anatomic interactions throughout the patient's body must be considered in treating the professional voice. It is helpful to think of the larynx as composed of four anatomic units: skeleton, mucosa, intrinsic muscles, and extrinsic muscles. The glottis is the space between the vocal folds.

Larynx: Skeleton

The most important parts of the laryngeal skeleton are the thyroid cartilage, cricoid cartilage, and the two arytenoid cartilages (Fig 2–1). Intrinsic muscles of the larynx are connected to these cartilages. One of the intrinsic muscles, the thyroarytenoid, extends on each side from the arytenoid cartilage to the inside of the thyroid cartilage just below and behind the thyroid prominence ("Adam's apple"). The medial belly of the thyroarytenoid is also known as the vocalis muscle, and it forms the body of the vocal fold. The laryngeal cartilages are connected by soft attachments that allow changes in their relative angles and distances, thereby permitting alterations in the shape and tension of the tissues extended between them. The arytenoids are capable of complex motion. It used to be said that the arytenoids rock, glide, and rotate. More accurately, the cartilages are brought together in the midline and revolve over the cricoid,

moving inferiorly and anteriorly. It appears as if people use different strategies for approximating the arytenoids and that such strategies may influence a person's susceptibility to laryngeal trauma that can cause vocal process ulcers and laryngeal granulomas.

Larynx: Mucosa

The vibratory margin of the vocal folds is much more complicated than simply mucosa applied to muscle. It consists of five layers[1] (Fig 2–2). The thin, lubricated epithelium covering the vocal folds forms the area of contact between the vibrating vocal folds and acts somewhat like a capsule, helping to maintain vocal fold shape. The epithelium lining most of the vocal tract is pseudo-stratified ciliated columnar epithelium, typical respiratory epithelium involved in handling mucous secretions. The vibratory margin of the vocal fold is covered with stratified squamous epithelium, better suited to withstand the trauma of vocal fold contact. The superficial layer of the lamina propria, also known as Reinke's space, is made up of loose fibrous components and matrix. It contains very few fibroblasts and consists primarily of elastic fibers. The deep layer of the lamina propria is composed primarily of collagenous fibers and is rich in fibroblasts. The thyroarytenoid or vocalis muscle makes up the body of the vocal fold and is one of the intrinsic laryngeal muscles. The region of the intermediate and deep layers of the lamina propria is called the vocal ligament and lies immediately below Reinke's space.

Although variations along the length of the membranous vocal fold are important in only a few situations, the surgeon, in particular, should be aware that they exist. Particularly striking variations occur at the

5

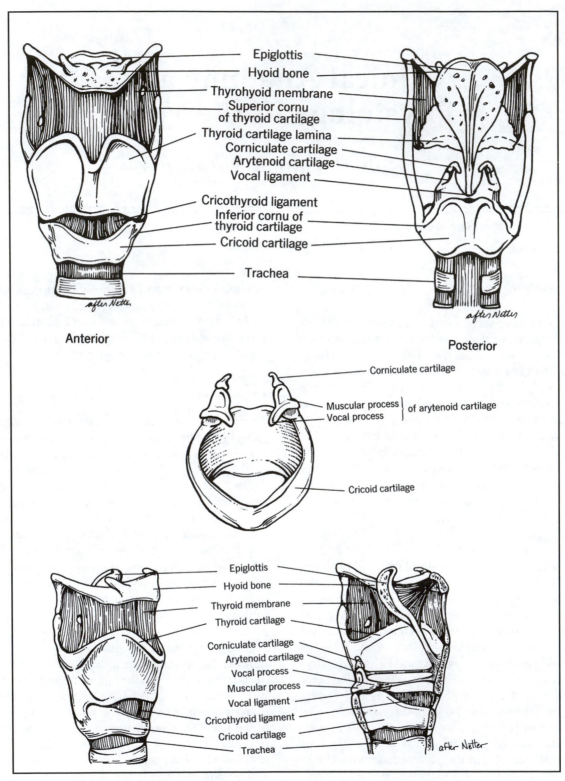

Epiglottis
Hyoid bone
Thyrohyoid membrane
Superior cornu
of thyroid cartilage
Thyroid cartilage lamina
Corniculate cartilage
Arytenoid cartilage
Vocal ligament
Cricothyroid ligament
Inferior cornu of
thyroid cartilage
Cricoid cartilage
Trachea

Anterior

Posterior

Corniculate cartilage

Muscular process } of arytenoid cartilage
Vocal process

Cricoid cartilage

Epiglottis
Hyoid bone
Thyroid membrane
Thyroid cartilage
Corniculate cartilage
Arytenoid cartilage
Vocal process
Muscular process
Vocal ligament
Cricothyroid ligament
Cricoid cartilage
Trachea

A

Fig 2–1. A. Cartilages of the larynx.

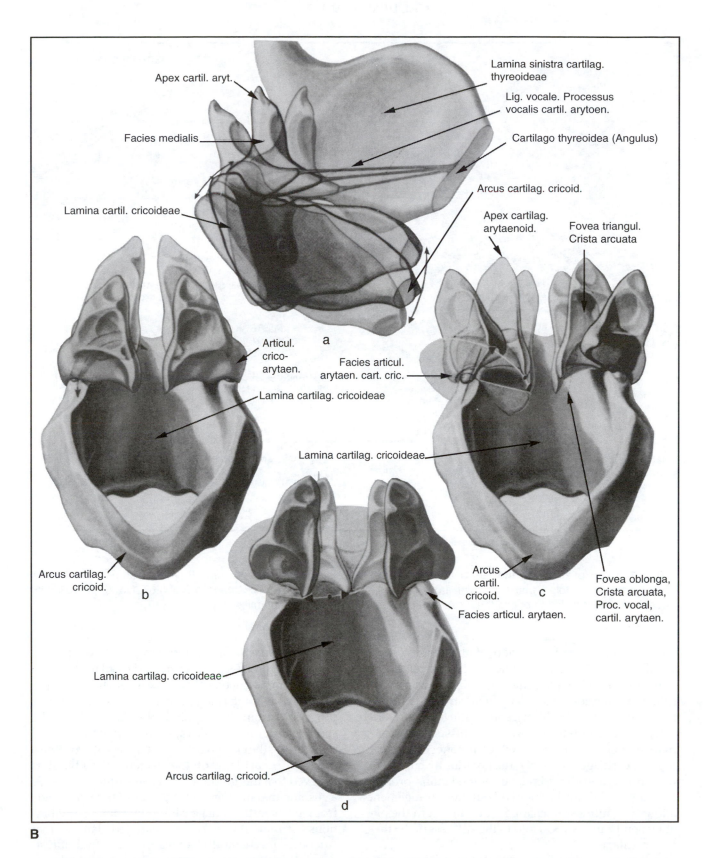

B

Fig 2–1. *(continued)* **B.** Schematic representation of position changes of laryngeal cartilages, illustrating the most extreme positions achieved by each. (From Pernkopf E. *Atlas of Topographical and Applied Human Anatomy.* Munich: Urban & Schwarzenberg; 1963, with permission.)

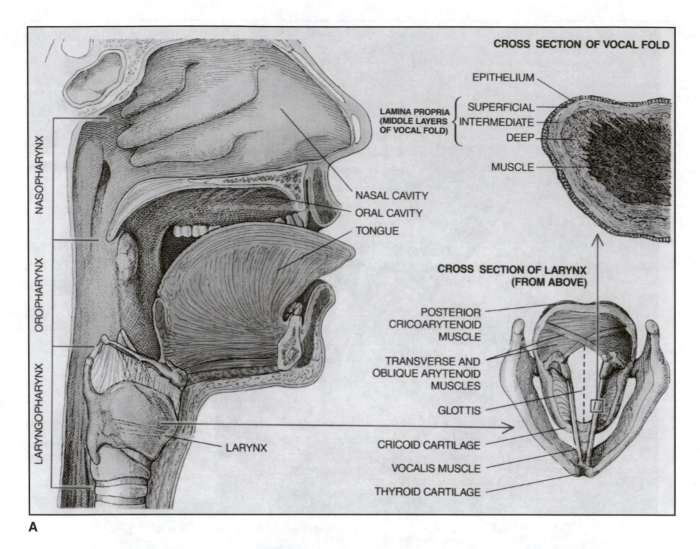

Fig 2–2 A. An overview of the larynx and vocal tract, showing the vocal folds, and the region from which the vocal fold was sampled to obtain the cross-section showing the layered structure. (From Sataloff, RT: The Human Voice. *Scientific American*, Vol. 267, No. 6, pp 108–115, 1992, with permission.)

anterior and posterior portion of the membranous vocal fold. Anteriorly, the intermediate layer of the lamina propria becomes thick, forming an oval mass called the anterior macula flava. This structure is composed of stroma, fibroblasts, and elastic fibers. Anteriorly, it inserts into the anterior commissure tendon, a mass of collagenous fibers, which is connected to the thyroid cartilage anteriorly, the anterior macula flava posteriorly, and the deep layer of the lamina propria laterally. As Hirano has pointed out, this arrangement allows the stiffness to change gradually from the pliable membranous vocal fold to the stiffness of the thyroid cartilage.[2]

A similar gradual change in stiffness occurs posteriorly where the intermediate layer of the lamina propria also thickens to form the posterior macula flava, another oval mass. It is structurally similar to the ante-

rior macula flava. The posterior macula flava attaches to the vocal process of the arytenoid cartilage through a transitional structure that consists of chondrocytes, fibroblasts and intermediate cells.[3] Thus, the stiffness progresses from the membranous vocal fold to the slightly stiffer macula flava, to the stiffer transitional structure, to the elastic cartilage of the vocal process, to the hyalin cartilage of the arytenoid body. It is believed that this gradual change in stiffness serves as a cushion that may protect the ends of the vocal folds from mechanical damage caused by contact or vibrations.[3] It may also act as a controlled damper that smoothes mechanical changes in vocal fold adjustment. This arrangement seems particularly well suited to vibration, as are other aspects of vocal fold architecture. For example, blood vessels in the vibratory margin come from posterior and anterior origins and

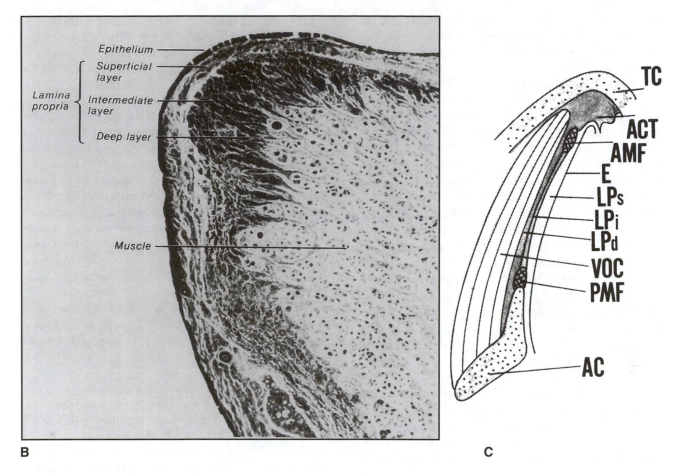

B

C

Fig 2–2 *(continued)* **B.** The structure of the vocal fold. (From Hirano M. *Clinical Examination of Voice.* New York: Springer-Verlag;1981:5, with permission.) **C.** Schematic representation of a horizontal section of the vocal fold. TC, thyroid cartilage; ACT, anterior commissure tendon; AMF, anterior macula flava; PMF, posterior macula flava; AC, ary-tenoid cartilage; E, epithelium; LP, lamina propria; s, superficial layer; i, intermediate layer; d, deep layer; VOC, vocalis muscle. (From Gray S, Hirano M, Sato K. Molecular and cellular structure of vocal fold tissue. In: Titze IR: *Vocal Fold Physiology.* San Diego: Singular Publishing Group, Inc; 1993:4, with permission.)

run parallel to the vibratory margin, with very few vessels entering the mucosa perpendicularly or from underlying muscle. The vibratory margin contains no glands that might interfere with the smoothness of vibratory waves. Even the elastic and collagenous fibers of the lamina propria run approximately parallel to the vibratory margin. The more one studies the vocal fold, the more one appreciates the beauty of its engineering.

Functionally, the five layers have different mechanical properties and may be thought of as somewhat like ball bearings of different sizes in allowing the smooth shearing action necessary for proper vocal fold vibration. The posterior two fifths (approximately) of the vocal folds are cartilagenous, and the anterior three fifths are membranous (from the vocal process forward) in adults. Under normal circumstances, most of the vibratory function critical to

sound quality occurs in the membranous portion.

Mechanically, the vocal fold structures act more like three layers consisting of the cover (epithelium and Reinke's space), transition (intermediate and deep layers of the lamina propria), and the body (the vocalis muscle). Understanding this anatomy is important because different pathologic entities occur in different layers and require different approaches to treatment. For example, fibroblasts are responsible for scar formation. Therefore, lesions that occur superficially in the vocal folds (such as nodules, cysts, and most polyps) should permit treatment without disturbance of the intermediate and deep layers, fibroblast proliferation, or scar formation.

In addition to the five layers discussed above, recent research has shown that there is a complex basement membrane connecting the epithelium to the superficial layer of the lamina propria.[4] The basement membrane is a multilayered, chemically complex structure. It gives rise to Type VII collagen loops which surround Type III collagen fibers in the superficial layer of the lamina propria (Fig 2–3). Knowledge of the basement membrane has already been important in changing surgical technique, as discussed later in this book. Additional research is likely to show its great importance in other matters such as the ability to heal following trauma, possibly the development of certain kinds of vocal fold pathology, and probably in histopathologic differential diagnosis.

The vocal folds may be thought of as the oscillator of the vocal mechanism.[5] Above the true vocal folds are tissues known as "false vocal folds." Unlike the true vocal folds, they do not make contact during normal speaking or singing. However, they may produce voice during certain abnormal circumstances. This phenomenon is called "dysphonia plica ventricularis." Until recently, the importance of false vocal folds during phonation was not appreciated. In general, they are considered to be used primarily for forceful laryngeal closure; and they come into play during pathological conditions. However, contrary to popular practice, surgeons should recognize that they cannot simply be removed without phonatory effects. The physics of airflow through the larynx is very complex, involving vortex shedding and sophisticated turbulence patterns that are essential to phonation. The false vocal folds provide a downstream resistance which is important in this process, and they probably play a role in vocal tract resonance, as well.

Larynx: The Intrinsic Muscles

Intrinsic muscles are responsible for abduction, adduction, and tension of the vocal folds (Figs 2–4 and 2–5). All but one of the muscles on each side of the larynx are innervated by one of the two recurrent laryngeal nerves. Because this nerve runs a long course from the neck down into the chest and back up to the larynx (hence, the name "recurrent"), it is easily injured by trauma, neck surgery, and chest surgery, especially on the left side of the body. Such injuries may result in abductor and adductor paralysis of the vocal fold. The remaining muscle, the cricothyroid muscle, is innervated by the superior laryngeal nerve on each side, which is especially susceptible to viral and traumatic injury. The recurrent and superior laryngeal nerves are branches of the tenth cranial nerve, or vagus nerve. The superior laryngeal nerve branches off the vagus high in the neck at the inferior end of the nodose ganglion. It divides into an internal and external branch. The external branch supplies the cricothyroid muscle. An extension of this nerve may also supply motor and sensory innervation to the vocal fold. The internal branch is primarily responsible for sensation in the mucosa above the level of the vocal fold, but it may also be responsible for some motor innervations of laryngeal muscles. The recurrent laryngeal nerves branch off the vagus in the chest. On the left, the nerve usually loops around the aortic arch. On the right, it usually loops around the brachycephalic artery. This anatomic relationship is usually, but not always, present; and non-recurrent recurrent nerves have been reported. There are interconnections between the superior and recurrent laryngeal nerves, particularly in the region of the interarytenoid muscle.

For some purposes, including electromyography, voice therapy, and surgery, it is important to understand the function of individual laryngeal muscles in greater detail. The muscles of primary functional importance are those innervated by the recurrent laryngeal nerve (thyroarytenoid, posterior cricoarytenoid, lateral cricoarytenoid, and interarytenoid or artenoideus) and superior laryngeal nerve (cricothyroid) (Figs 2–4, 2–5, and 2–6).

The thyroarytenoid muscle adducts, lowers, shortens, and thickens the vocal fold, rounding the vocal fold edge. Thus, the cover and transition are effectively made more slack, while the body is stiffened. Adduction from vocalis contraction is active, particularly in the membranous segment of the vocal folds. It tends to lower vocal pitch. The thyroarytenoid originates anteriorly from the posterior (interior) surface of the thyroid cartilage and inserts into the lateral base of the arytenoid cartilage from the vocal process to the muscular process. More specifically, the superior bundles of the muscle insert into the lateral and inferior aspects of the vocal process and run primarily in a horizontal direction. The antero-inferior bundles insert into the anterolateral aspect of the arytenoid cartilage from its tip to an area lateral to the vocal process. The most medial fibers run parallel to the vocal ligament. There are also cranial fibers that extend into the aryepiglottic fold. Anteriorly, the vertical organization of the muscle results in a twisted configuration of muscle fibers when the vocal fold is adducted. The thyroarytenoid is the third largest intrinsic muscle of the larynx. The thyroarytenoid muscle is divided into two compartments. The medial compartment is also known as the vocalis muscle. It contains a high percentage of slow twitch muscle fibers. The lateral compartment has predominantly fast twitch muscle fibers. One may infer that the medial compartment (vocalis) is specialized for phonation, while the lateral compartment (muscularis) is specialized for vocal fold adduction; but these suppositions are unproven.

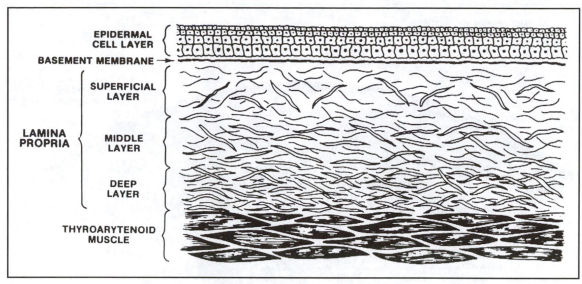

A

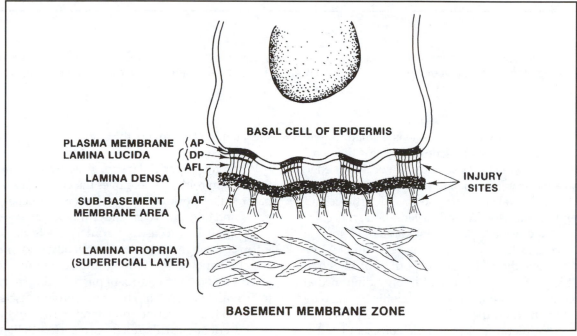

B

Fig 2–3. **A.** Structure of the vocal fold (not drawn to scale). The basement membrane lies between the epithelium and the superficial layer of the lamina propria. (From Gray S, Basement membrane zone injury in vocal nodules. In: Gauffin, J, Hammarberg B. *Vocal Fold Physiology*, Singular Publishing Group; 1991, with permission). **B.** Basement membrane zone. Basal cells are connected to the lamina densa by attachment plax (ap) in the plasma membrane of the epidermis. Anchoring filaments (afl) extend from the attachment plax through the sub-basal densa plate (dp) and attach to the lamina densa (dark single-layer, electron-dense band just beneath the basal cell layer). The sub-basement membrane zone consists of anchoring fibers (af) that attach to the lamina densa and extend into the superficial layer of the lamina propria. Type VII collagen fibers attach to the network of the lamina propria by looping around Type III collagen fibers. (From Gray S. Basement membrane zone injury in vocal nodules. In: Gauffin, J, Hammarberg B, eds. *Vocal Fold Physiology*. Singular Publishing Group; 1991, with permission).

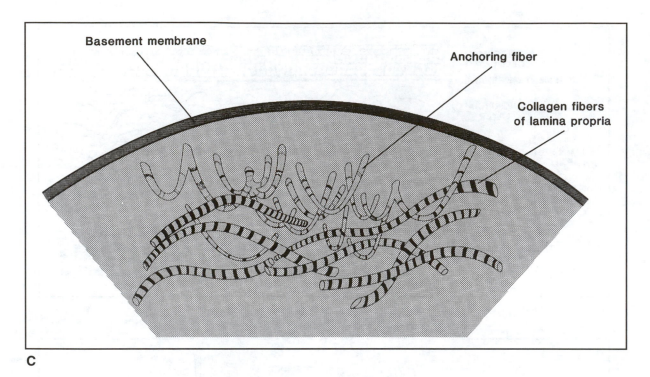

C

Fig 2–3. *(continued)* **C.** Type VII collagen anchoring fibers pass from the basement membrane, reinserting into it. Through the anchoring fiber loops pass Type III collagen fibers of the superficial layer of lamina propria (Courtesy Steven Gray).

The lateral cricoarytenoid muscle is a small muscle which adducts, lowers, elongates, and thins the vocal fold. All layers are stiffened, and the vocal fold edge takes on a more angular or sharp contour. It originates on the upper lateral border of the cricoid cartilage and inserts into the anterior lateral surface of the muscular process of the arytenoid. The interarytenoid muscle (arytenoideus, a medium sized intrinsic muscle) primarily adducts the cartilaginous portion of the vocal folds. It is particularly important in providing medial compression to close the posterior glottis. It has relatively little effect on the stiffness of the membranous portion. The interarytenoid muscle consists of transverse and oblique fibers. The transverse fibers originate from the lateral margin of one arytenoid and insert into the lateral margin of the opposite arytenoid. The oblique fibers originate from the base of one arytenoid and insert into the apex of the contralateral arytenoid.

The posterior cricoarytenoid muscle abducts, elevates, elongates, and thins the vocal fold by rocking the arytenoid cartilage posterolaterally. All layers are stiffened, and the edge of the vocal fold is rounded. It is the second largest intrinsic muscle. It originates over a broad area of the posterolateral portion of the cricoid lamina and inserts on the posterior surface of the muscular process of the arytenoid cartilage, forming a short tendon that covers the cranial aspect of the muscular process.

When the superior laryngeal nerve is stimulated, the cricothyroid muscle moves the vocal folds into the paramedian position. It also lowers, stretches, elongates, and thins the vocal fold, stiffening all layers and sharpening the vocal fold contour. It is the largest intrinsic laryngeal muscle. The cricothyroid muscle is largely responsible for longitudinal tension, a very important factor in control of pitch. Contraction tends to increase vocal pitch. The cricothyroid muscle originates from the anterior and lateral portion of the arch of the cricoid cartilage. It forms two bellies. The oblique belly inserts into the posterior half of the thyroid lamina and the anterior portion of the inferior cornu of the thyroid cartilage. The vertical (erect) portion inserts into the inferior border of the anterior lamina of the thyroid cartilage.

Intrinsic laryngeal muscles are skeletal muscles. All skeletal muscles are composed primarily of three types of fibers. Type I fibers are highly resistant to fatigue, contract slowly, and utilize aerobic (oxidative) metabolism. They have low glycogen levels, high levels of oxidative enzymes, and they are relatively small in diameter. Type IIA fibers use principally oxidative metabolism but contain both a high

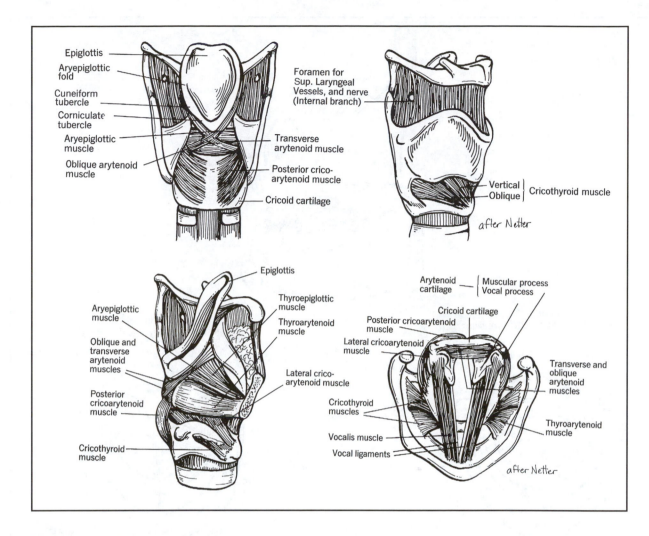

Fig 2–4. The intrinsic muscles of the larynx.

level of oxidative enzyme and glycogen. They contract rapidly but are also fatigue resistant. Type IIB fibers are the largest in diameter. They utilize aerobic glycolysis primarily, containing much glycogen but relatively few oxidative enzymes. They contract very quickly, but fatigue easily.

The fiber composition of laryngeal muscles differs from that of most larger skeletal muscles. Elsewhere, muscle fiber diameters are fairly constant, ranging between 60 and 80 microns. In laryngeal muscles, there is considerably more variability,[6,7] and fiber diameters vary between 10 microns and 100 microns, with an average diameter of 40–50 microns. Laryngeal muscles have a higher proportion of Type IIA fibers than most other muscles. The thyroarytenoid and lateral cricothyroid muscles are particularly specialized for rapid contraction. However, the laryngeal muscles

in general appear to have fiber distributions and variations that make them particularly well suited to rapid contraction with fatigue resistance.[8] In addition, many laryngeal motor units have multiple innervation. There appear to be approximately 20–30 muscle fibers per motor unit in a human cricothyroid muscle,[9] suggesting that the motor unit size of this laryngeal muscle is similar to that of extraocular and facial muscles.[10] In the human thyroarytenoid, 70–80% of muscle fibers have two or more endplates.[11] Some fibers have as many as five nerve endplates. Only 50% of cricothyroid and lateral cricoarytenoid fibers have multiple endplates, and multiple innervation is even less common in the posterior cricoarytenoid (5%). It is still not known whether one muscle fiber can be part of more than one motor unit (receive endplates from different motor neurons).[8]

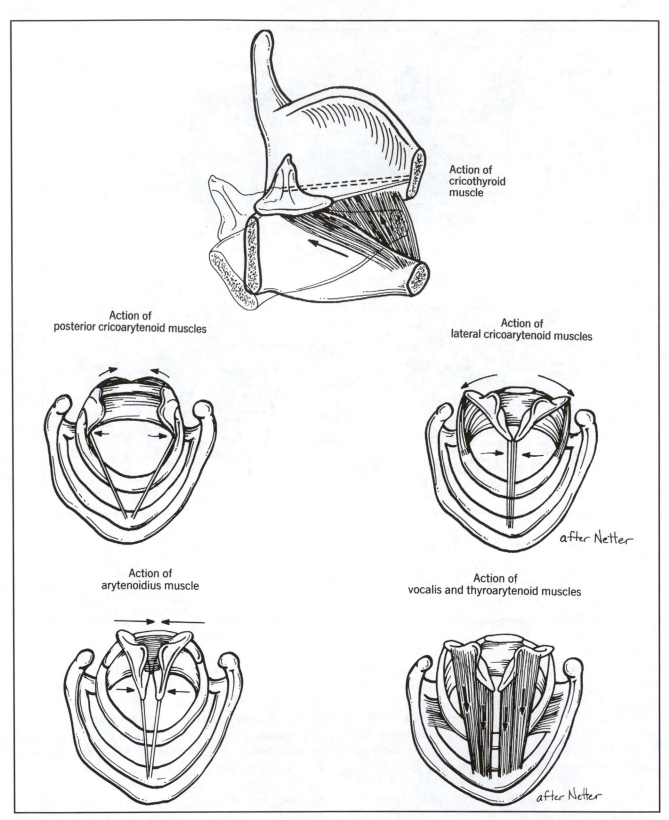

Action of
cricothyroid
muscle

Action of
posterior cricoarytenoid muscles

Action of
lateral cricoarytenoid muscles

after Netter

Action of
arytenoidius muscle

Action of
vocalis and thyroarytenoid muscles

after Netter

A

Fig 2–5. A. Action of the intrinsic muscles. In the bottom four figures, the directional arrows suggest muscle actions, but may give a misleading impression of arytenoid motion. These drawings should not be misinterpreted as indicating that the arytenoid cartilage rotates around a vertical axis.

The angle of the long axis of the cricoid facets does not permit some of the motion implied in this figure. However, the drawing still provides a useful conceptualization of the effect of individual intrinsic muscles, so long as the limitations are recognized. *(continued)*

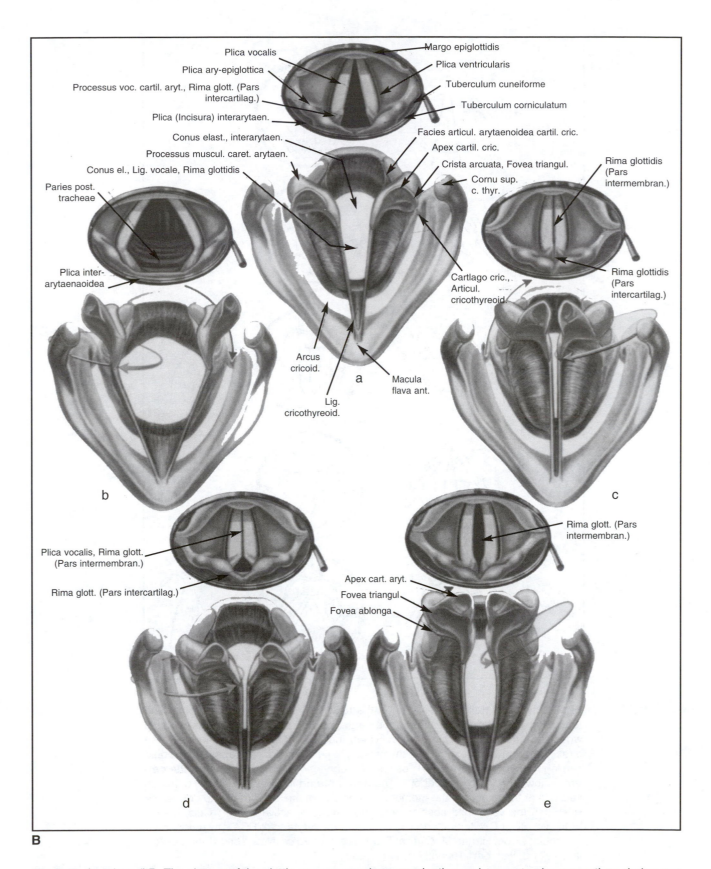

B

Fig 2–5. *(continued)* **B.** The shapes of the glottis as seen on mirror examination and on anatomic preparations during rest (a), inspiration (b), phonation (c), whispering (d), and falsetto singing (e). (From Pernkopf E. *Atlas of Topographical and Applied Human Anatomy.* Munich: Urban & Schwarzenberg; 1963, with permission.)

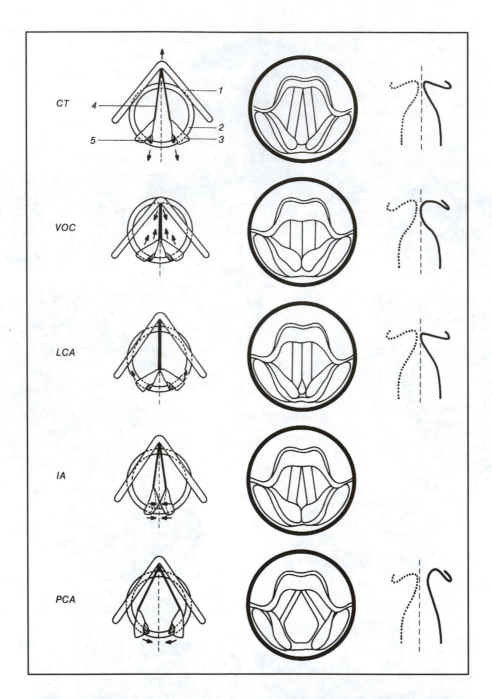

Fig 2–6. A schematic presentation of the function of the laryngeal muscles. The **left column** shows the location of the cartilages and the edge of the vocal folds when the laryngeal muscles are activated individually. The arrows indicate the direction of the force exerted. 1, thyroid cartilage; 2, cricoid cartilage; 3, arytenoid cartilage; 4, vocal ligament; 5, posterior cricoarytenoid ligament. The **middle column** shows the views from above. The **right column** illustrates contours of frontal sections at the middle of the membranous portion of the vocal fold. The dotted line illustrates the vocal fold position when no muscle is activated. CT, Cricothyroid; VOC, vocalis; LCA, lateral cricoarytenoid; IA, interarytenoid; PCA, posterior cricoarytenoid. (From Hirano M. *Clinical Examination of Voice.* New York: Springer-Verlag; 1981:8, with permission.)

Larynx: Extrinsic Muscles

Extrinsic laryngeal musculature maintains the position of the larynx in the neck. This group of muscles include primarily the strap muscles. Since raising or lowering the larynx may alter the tension or angle between laryngeal cartilages, thereby changing the resting lengths of the intrinsic muscles, the extrinsic muscles are critical in maintaining a stable laryngeal skeleton so that the delicate intrinsic musculature can work effectively. In the Western classically trained singer, the extrinsic muscles maintain the larynx in a relatively constant vertical position throughout the pitch range. Training of the intrinsic musculature results in vibratory symmetry of the vocal folds, producing regular periodicity. This contributes to what the listener perceives as a "trained" sound.

The extrinsic muscles may be divided into those below the hyoid bone (infrahyoid muscles) and those above the hyoid bone (suprahyoid muscles).

The *infrahyoid muscles* include the thyrohyoid, sternothyroid, sternohyoid, and omohyoid (Fig 2–7). The thyrohyoid originates obliquely on the thyroid lamina and inserts into the lower border of the greater cornu of the hyoid bone. Contraction brings the thyroid and hyoid closer together, especially anteriorly. The *sternothyroid muscle* originates from the first costal cartilage and posterior aspect of the manubrium of the sternum, and it inserts obliquely on the thyroid cartilage. Contraction lowers the thyroid cartilage. The *sternohyoid muscle* originates from the clavicle and posterior surface of the manubrium of the sternum, inserting into the lower edge of the body of the hyoid bone. Contraction lowers the hyoid bone. The inferior of the omohyoid originates from the upper surface of the scapula and inserts into the intermediate tendon of the *omohyoid* muscle. The superior belly originates from the intermediate tendon and inserts into the greater cornu of the hyoid bone. The omohyoid muscle pulls down on the hyoid bone, lowering it.

The *suprahyoid muscles* include the digastric, mylohyoid, geniohyoid, and stylohyoid. The posterior belly of the *digastric muscle* originates from the mastoid process and inserts into the intermediate tendon, which connects to the hyoid bone. The anterior belly originates from the inferior aspect of the mandible near the symphysis and inserts into the intermediate tendon. The anterior belly pulls the hyoid bone anteriorly and raises it. The posterior belly pulls the hyoid bone posteriorly and also raises it. The *mylohyoid muscle* originates from the inner aspect of the mandible (mylohyoid line) and inserts into a midline raphe with fibers from the opposite side. It raises the hyoid bone and pulls it anteriorly. The *geniohyoid muscle* originates

from the mental spine at the mental symphysis of the mandible and inserts on the anterior surface of the body of the hyoid bone. It raises the hyoid bone and pulls it anteriorly. The *stylohyoid muscle* originates from the styloid process and inserts into the body of the hyoid bone. It raises the hyoid bone and pulls it posteriorly. Coordinated interaction among the extrinsic laryngeal muscles is needed to control the vertical position of the larynx, as well as other conditions such as laryngeal tilt.

The Supraglottic Vocal Tract

The supraglottic larynx, tongue, lips, palate, pharynx, nasal cavity (Fig 2–2A), and possibly the sinuses shape the sound quality produced at the level of the vocal folds by acting as a resonator. Minor alterations in the configuration of these structures may produce substantial changes in voice quality. The hypernasal speech typically associated with a cleft palate and/or the hyponasal speech characteristic of severe adenoid hypertrophy are obvious. However, mild edema from an upper respiratory tract infection, pharyngeal scarring, or muscle tension changes produce less obvious sound alterations. These are immediately recognizable to a trained vocalist or astute critic, but they often elude the laryngologist.

The Tracheobronchial Tree, Lungs, and Thorax

The lungs supply a constant stream of air that passes between the vocal folds and provides power for voice production (Fig 2–8). Singers often are thought of as having "big chests." Actually, the primary respiratory difference between trained and untrained singers is not increased total lung capacity, as popularly assumed. Rather, the trained singer learns to use a higher proportion of the air in his or her lungs, thereby decreasing his or her residual volume and increasing respiratory efficiency.[12]

The Abdomen

The abdominal musculature is the so-called "support" of the singing voice, although singers generally refer to their support mechanism as their "diaphragm." The function of the diaphragm muscle in singing is complex, somewhat variable from singer to singer (or actor to actor). The diaphragm primarily generates inspiratory force. Although the abdomen can also perform this function in some situations,[13] it is primarily an expiratory-force generator. Interestingly, the diaphragm is co-activated by some performers during

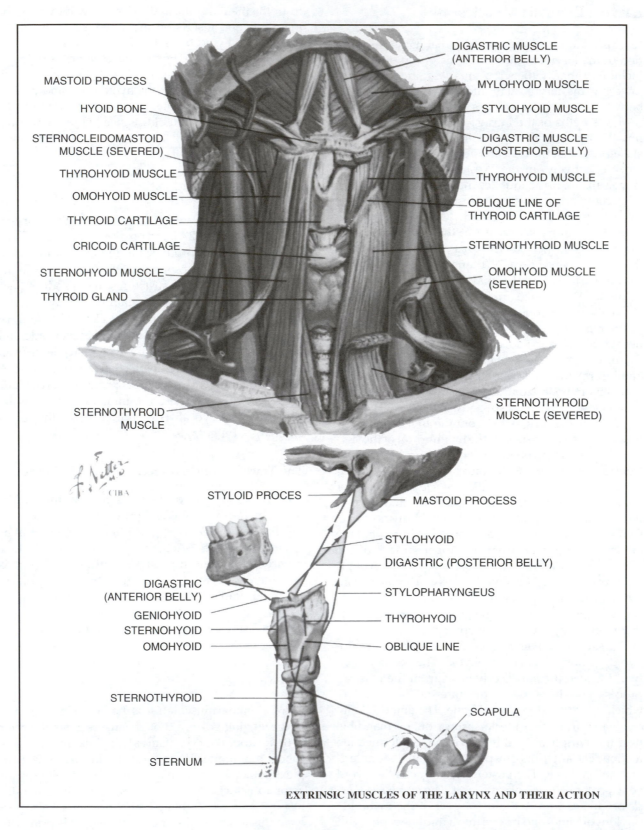

EXTRINSIC MUSCLES OF THE LARYNX AND THEIR ACTION

Fig 2–7. Extrinsic muscles of the larynx and their actions. (From The Larynx. *Clinical Symposia.* New Jersey: CIBA Pharmaceutical Company; 1964;16[3]: Plate 4, with permission.)

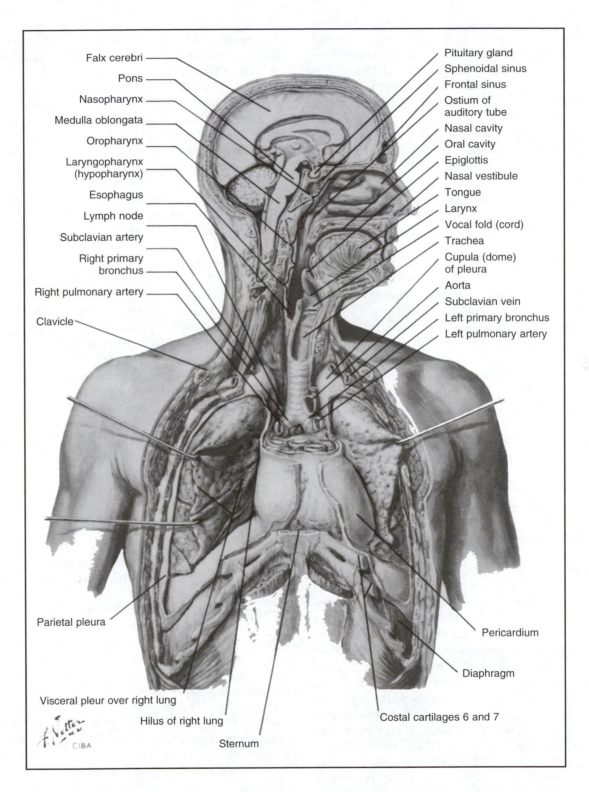

Falx cerebri
Pons
Nasopharynx
Medulla oblongata
Oropharynx
Laryngopharynx (hypopharynx)
Esophagus
Lymph node
Subclavian artery
Right primary bronchus
Right pulmonary artery
Clavicle

Pituitary gland
Sphenoidal sinus
Frontal sinus
Ostium of auditory tube
Nasal cavity
Oral cavity
Epiglottis
Nasal vestibule
Tongue
Larynx
Vocal fold (cord)
Trachea
Cupula (dome) of pleura
Aorta
Subclavian vein
Left primary bronchus
Left pulmonary artery

Parietal pleura
Pericardium
Diaphragm
Visceral pleur over right lung
Hilus of right lung
Costal cartilages 6 and 7
Sternum

Fig 2–8. The respiratory system, showing the relationship of supraglottic and infraglottic structures. The line marking the vocal fold actually stops on the false vocal fold. The level of the true vocal fold is marked by the arrow. The diaphragm is also visible in relation to the lungs, ribs, and abdomen muscles. (From The development of the lower respiratory system. *Clinical Symposia*. New Jersey: CIBA Pharmaceutical Company; 1975;27[4]: Plate 1, with permission.)

singing and appears to play an important part in fine regulation of singing.[14] Actually, the anatomy of support for phonation is quite complicated and not completely understood. Both the lungs and rib cage generate passive expiratory forces under many common circumstances. Passive inspiratory forces also occur. Active respiratory muscles working in consort with passive forces include the intercostal, abdominal wall, back, and diaphragm muscles. The principal muscles of inspiration are the diaphragm and external intercostal muscles.

Accessory muscles of inspiration include the pectoralis major, pectoralis minor, serratus anterior, subclavius, sternocleidomastoid; anterior, medial, and posterior scalenus; serratus posterior and superior, latissimus dorsi, and levatores costarum. During quiet respiration, expiration is largely passive. Many of the muscles used for active expiration (forcing air out of the lungs) are also employed in "support" for singing and acting. Muscles of active expiration either raise the intra-abdominal pressure forcing the diaphragm upward, or lower the ribs or sternum to decrease the dimension of the thorax, or both. They include the internal intercostals which stiffen the rib interspaces and pull the ribs down; transversus thoracis, subcostal muscles and serratus posterior inferior all of which pull the ribs down; and the quadratus lumborum which depresses the lowest rib. In addition, the latissimus dorsi, which may also act as the muscle of inspiration, is capable of compressing the lower portion of the rib cage and can act as a muscle of expiration, as well as a muscle of inspiration. The above muscles all participate in active expiration (and support). However, the *primary* muscles of active expiration are known as "the abdominal muscles." They include the external oblique, internal oblique, rectus abdominus, and transversus abdominus. The external oblique is a flat broad muscle located on the side and front of the lower chest and abdomen. Upon contraction, it pulls the lower ribs down and raises the abdominal pressure by displacing abdominal contents inward. It is an important muscle for support of singing and acting voice tasks. It should be noted that this muscle is strengthened by leg lifting and lowering, and other exercises, but is not developed effectively by traditional trunk curl sit-ups. Appropriate strengthening exercises of the external oblique muscles are often inappropriately neglected in voice training. The internal oblique is a flat muscle in the side and front wall of the abdomen. It lies deep to the external oblique. When contracted, the internal oblique drives the abdominal wall inward and lowers the lower ribs. The rectus abdominus runs parallel to the midline of the abdomen originating from the xiphoid process of the sternum and fifth, sixth, and seventh costal (rib)

cartilages. It inserts into the pubic bone. It is encased in the fibrous abdominal aponeurosis. Contraction of the rectus abdominus also forces the abdominal contents inward and lowers the sternum and ribs. The transversus abdominus is a broad muscle located under the internal oblique on the side and front of the abdomen. Its fibers run horizontally around the abdomen. Contraction of the transverse abdominus compresses the abdominal contents, elevating abdominal pressure.

The abdominal musculature receives considerable attention in vocal training. The purpose of abdominal support is to maintain an efficient, constant power source and inspiratory-expiratory mechanism. There is disagreement among voice teachers as to the best model for teaching support technique. Some experts describe positioning the abdominal musculature under the rib cage; others advocate distension of the abdomen. Either method may result in vocal problems if used incorrectly, but distending the abdomen (the inverse pressure approach) is especially dangerous, because it tends to focus the singer's muscular effort in a downward and outward direction, which is ineffective. Thus, the singer may exert considerable effort, believing he or she is practicing good support technique, without obtaining the desired effect. Proper abdominal training is essential to good singing and speaking, and the physician must consider abdominal function when evaluating vocal disabilities.

The Musculoskeletal System

Musculoskeletal condition and position affect the vocal mechanism and may produce tension or impair abdominal muscle function, resulting in voice dysfunction. Stance deviation, such as from standing to supine, produces obvious changes in respiratory function. However, lesser changes, such as distributing one's weight over the calcaneus rather than forward over the metatarsal heads (a more athletic position), alter the configuration of the abdominal and back musculature enough to influence the voice. Tensing arm and shoulder muscles promotes cervical muscle strain, which can adversely affect the larynx. Careful control of muscle tension is fundamental to good vocal technique. In fact, some teaching methods use musculoskeletal conditioning as the primary focus of voice training.

The Psychoneurological System

The psychological constitution of the singer impacts directly on the vocal mechanism. Psychological phenomena are reflected through the autonomic nervous system, which controls mucosal secretions and other functions critical to voice production. The nervous system is also important for its mediation of fine muscle control. This fact is worthy of emphasis, because minimal voice disturbances may occasionally be the first signs of serious neurologic disease.

Physiology

The physiology of voice production is exceedingly complex and will be summarized only briefly in this and the following two chapters. For more information, the reader is advised to consult other literature, including publications listed as Bibliography at the end of Chapter 4 and Suggested Reading List near the end of this book.

Volitional voice begins in the cerebral cortex. Complex interactions among centers for speech, and musical and artistic expression establish the command for vocalization. The "idea" of the planned vocalization is conveyed to the precentral gyrus in the motor cortex, which transmits another set of instructions to motor nuclei in the brainstem and spinal cord (Fig 2–9). These areas send out the complicated messages necessary for coordinated activity of the larynx, thoracic and abdominal musculature, and vocal tract articulators. Additional refinement of motor activity is provided by the extrapyramidal (cerebral cortex, cerebellum, and basal ganglion) and autonomic nervous systems. These impulses combine to produce a sound that is transmitted not only to the ears of listeners but also to those of the speaker or singer. Auditory feedback is transmitted from the ear through the brainstem to the cerebral cortex, and adjustments are made to permit the vocalist to match the sound produced with the intended sound. There is also tactile feedback from the throat and muscles involved in phonation that also undoubtedly helps in fine-tuning vocal output, although the mechanism and role of tactile feedback are not fully understood. In many trained singers, the ability to use tactile feedback effectively is cultivated because of frequent interference with auditory feedback by ancillary noise in the concert environment (such as an orchestra or band).

The voice requires interaction among the power source, vibrator, and resonator. The power source compresses air and forces it toward the larynx. The vocal folds close and open, permitting small bursts of air to escape between them. Numerous factors affect the sound produced at the glottal level, as discussed in greater detail in the next chapter. Among others, they include the pressure that builds up below the vocal folds (subglottal pressure), the amount of resistance to opening an airway presented by the vocal folds (glottal impedance), volume velocity of air flow at the glottis, and supraglottal pressure. The vocal folds do not vibrate like the strings on a violin. Rather, they separate and collide somewhat like clapping hands. The number of times they do so in any given second (ie, their frequency) determines the number of air puffs that escape. The frequency of glottal closing and opening is related to pitch. Other factors help determine loudness (such as subglottal pressure, glottal resistance, and amplitude of vocal fold displacement from the midline during each vibratory cycle). The sound created at the vocal fold level is a buzz, similar to the sound produced when blowing between two blades of grass. This sound contains a complete set of harmonic partials and is responsible in part for the acoustic characteristics of the voice. However, complex and sophisticated interactions in the supraglottic vocal tract may accentuate or attenuate harmonic partials, acting as a resonator (Fig 2–10). This portion of the vocal tract is largely responsible for the beauty and variety of the sound produced. Because of its complexity and importance, vocal tract resonance is explained in Chapter 5.

Interactions among the components of the voice are ultimately responsible for all the vocal characteristics we produce. Many aspects of the voice still await complete understanding and classification. Vocal range is reasonably well understood, and broad categories of voice classification are generally accepted (Fig 2–11). Other characteristics such as vocal register are controversial. Registers are expressed as quality changes within an individual voice. From low to high, they may include vocal fry, chest, middle, head, falsetto, and whistle, although not everyone agrees that all categories exist. The term modal register, used most frequently in speech, refers to the voice quality generally used by healthy speakers, as opposed to a low, gravelly vocal fry or high falsetto. Vibrato is a rhythmic variation in frequency and intensity. Its exact source remains uncertain, and its desirable characteristics depend on voice range and the type of music sung. It appears most likely that the frequency (pitch) modulations are primarily controlled by intrinsic laryngeal muscles, especially the cricothyroid and adductor muscles. However, extrinsic laryngeal muscles and muscles of the supraglottic vocal tract may also play a role. Intensity (loudness) variations may be caused by variations in subglottal pressure, glottal adjustments that affect subglottal pressure, secondary effect of the frequency

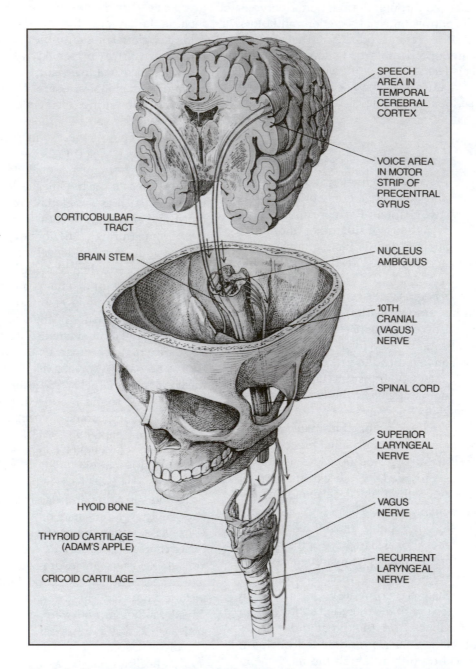

Labels in figure:

SPEECH AREA IN TEMPORAL CEREBRAL CORTEX

VOICE AREA IN MOTOR STRIP OF PRECENTRAL GYRUS

CORTICOBULBAR TRACT

BRAIN STEM

NUCLEUS AMBIGUUS

10TH CRANIAL (VAGUS) NERVE

SPINAL CORD

SUPERIOR LARYNGEAL NERVE

HYOID BONE

VAGUS NERVE

THYROID CARTILAGE (ADAM'S APPLE)

CRICOID CARTILAGE

RECURRENT LARYNGEAL NERVE

Fig 2–9. How the voice is produced. The production of speech or song, or even just a vocal sound, entails a complex orchestration of mental and physical actions. The idea for making a sound originates in the cerebral cortex of the brain—for example, in the speech area. The movement of the larynx is controlled from the voice area and is transmitted to the larynx by various nerves. As a result, the vocal folds vibrate, generating a buzzing sound. It is the resonation of that sound throughout the area of the vocal tract above the glottis—an area that includes the pharynx, tongue, palate, oral cavity and nose—that gives the sound the qualities perceived by a listener. Auditory feedback and tactile feedback enable the speaker or singer to achieve fine-tuning of the vocal output. (From Sataloff RT: The Human Voice. *Scientific American*, Vol. 267, No. 6, pp 108–115, 1992, with permission.)

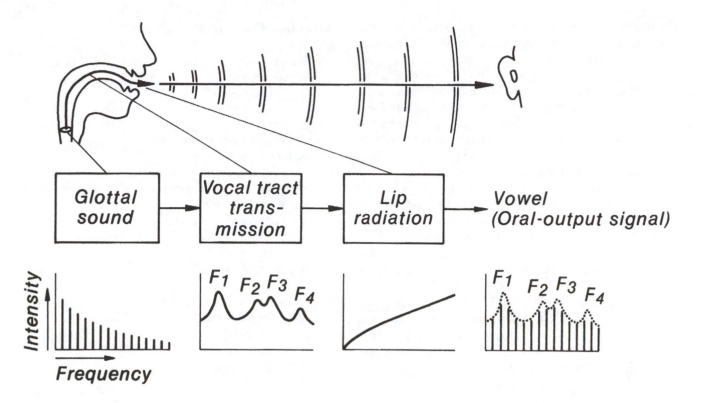

Fig 2–10. Some of the factors determining the spectrum of a vowel. (From Hirano M. *Clinical Examination of Voice*. New York: Springer-Verlag; 1981:67, with permission.)

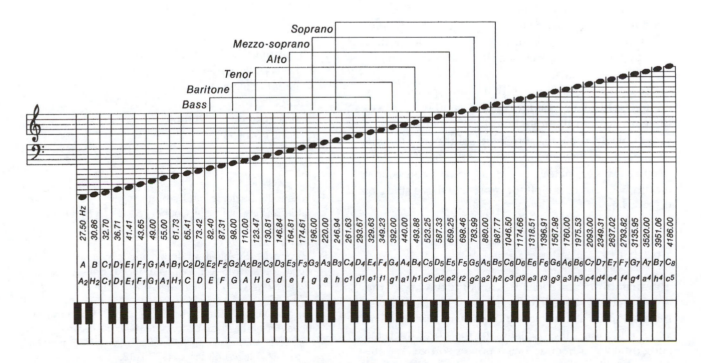

Fig 2–11. Correlation between a piano keyboard, pitch names (the lower in capital letters is used in music and voice research, and in this book), frequency, musical notation, and usual voice range. (From Hirano M. *Clinical Examination of Voice*. New York: Springer-Verlag; 1981:89, with permission.)

variation because of changes in the distance between the fundamental frequency and closest formant, or rhythmic changes in vocal tract shape that cause fluctuations in formant frequencies. When evaluating vibrato, it is helpful to consider the wave form of the vibrato signal, its regularity, extent and rate. The wave form is usually fairly sinusoidal, but considerable variation may occur. The regularity, or similarity, of each vibrato event to previous and subsequent vibrato events is greater in trained singers than in non-trained voice users. This regularity appears to be one of the characteristics perceived as a "trained sound." The vibrato extent corresponds to the amplitude of the vibrato wave form. Extent refers to deviation from the standard frequency (not intensity variation) and is usually less than, ±0.1 semitone in some styles of solo and choral singing. For most well-trained Western operatic singing, the usual vibrato extent at comfortable loudness is, ±0.5 to 1 semitones for singers in most voice classifications. Vibrato rate (the number of modulations per second) is generally 5 to 7. Rate may also vary greatly from singer to singer, and in the same singer. Vibrato rate can increase with increased emotional content of the material, and rate tends to decrease with older age (although the age at which this change occurs is highly variable). When variations from the central frequency become too wide, we perceive a "wobble" in the voice, and this is generally referred to as tremolo. It is not generally considered a good musical sound, and it is unclear whether it is produced by the same mechanisms responsible for normal vibrato. Ongoing research should answer many of the remaining questions.[15]

This chapter and the two that follow provide only enough information on terminology and workings of the voice to permit understanding of practical, every-day clinical problems and their solutions. The otolaryngologist, speech-language pathologist, singing teacher, singer, actor, or other voice professional would be rewarded well for more extensive study of voice science.

Summary

The anatomy of voice includes not only the larynx, but also all body systems. The larynx consists of a skeleton, mucosa, intrinsic muscles, and extrinsic muscles. The vocal folds form the oscillator of the vocal tract, the subglottic vocal tract acts as a power source, and the supraglottic vocal tract functions as a resonator. Complex interactions are responsible for voice production.

Review Questions

1. Intrinsic laryngeal muscles include all of the following except:
   a. thyroarytenoid
   b. thyrohyoid
   c. lateral cricoarytenoid
   d. posterior cricoarytenoid
   e. interarytenoid

2. Fibroblasts are scarce in which of the following layers of the vocal fold:
   a. superficial layer of the lamina propria
   b. intermediate layer of the lamina propria
   c. deep layer of the lamina propria
   d. the vocalis muscle

3. Under normal circumstances, the primary oscillator of the vocal tract is:
   a. the vocal folds
   b. the abdominal muscles
   c. the palate and nasal cavities
   d. the lungs

4. Individual vocal quality (timbre) is primarily determined by:
   a. the larynx
   b. the thorax
   c. the supraglottic vocal tract
   d. the abdomen

5. The primary abductor of the vocal fold is:
   a. thyroarytenoid
   b. lateral cricoarytenoid
   c. cricothyroid
   d. posterior cricoarytenoid
   e. none of the above

References

1. Hirano M. Structure and vibratory pattern of the vocal folds. In: Sawashima N, Cooper FS, eds. *Dynamic Aspects of Speech Production*. Tokyo: University of Tokyo Press, 1977:13–27.
2. Hirano M. Surgical anatomy and physiology of the vocal folds. In: Gould WJ, Sataloff RT, Spiegel JR, eds. *Voice Surgery*, St. Louis, MO: Mosby-Year Book; 1993: 135–158.
3. Hirano M, Yoshida T, Kurita S, et al. Anatomy and behavior of the vocal process. In: Baer T, Sasaki C, Harris K, eds. *Laryngeal Function in Phonation and Respiration*. Boston, College-Hill Press; 1987:1–13.
4. Gray S. Basement membrane zone injury in vocal nodules. In: Gauffin J, Hammarberg B, eds. *Vocal Fold Physiology: Acoustic, Perceptual and Physiologic Aspects of Voice*

Mechanics. San Diego: Singular Publishing Group; 1991:21–27.

5. Sundberg J. The acoustics of the singing voice. *Sci Am.* 1977; 236(3):82–91.

6. Brooke MH, Engle WK. The histographic analysis of human muscle biopsies with regard to fibre types. 1. Adult male and female. *Neurology,* 1969; 19:221–233.

7. Sadeh M, Kronenberg J, Gaton E. Histochemistry of human laryngeal muscles. *Cell Molec Biol.* 1981; 27:643–648.

8. Lindestad, P. *Electromyographic and Laryngoscopic Studies of Normal and Disturbed Vocal Function,* Stockholm: Suddinge University; 1994:1–12.

9. English ET, Blevins CE. Motor units of laryngeal muscles. *Arch Otolaryngol* 1969;89:778–784.

10. Faaborg-Andersen K. Electromyographic investigation of intrinsic laryngeal muscles in humans. *Acta Physiol Scand.* 1957(Suppl):41 .

11. Rossi G, Cortesina G. Morphological study of the laryngeal muscles in man: Insertions and courses of the muscle fibers, motor end-plates and proprioceptors. *Acta Otolaryngol* (Stockh). 1965;59:575–592.

12. Gould WJ, Okamura H. Static lung volumes in singers. *Ann Otol Rhinol Laryngol.* 1973;82:89–95.

13. Hixon TJ, Hoffman C. Chest wall shape during singing. In: Lawrence V, ed. *Transcripts of the Seventh Annual Symposium, Care of the Professional Voice.* New York: The Voice Foundation, 1978;1:9–10.

14. Sundberg J, Leanderson R, von Euler, C. Activity relationship between diaphragm and cricothyroid muscles. *J of Voice.* 1989; 3(3):225–232.

15. Dejonckere H, Hirano M, Sundberg J. *Vibrato.* San Diego, Calif.: Singular Publishing Group, Inc., 1995:1–149

3

An Overview of Laryngeal Function for Voice Production

Ronald J. Baken

It is common to call the larynx the vocal organ, implying that it is the place where the voice is produced. If by "voice" we mean the sound that reaches our ears, then, in the strict sense, nothing could be further from the truth. The larynx generates only the raw material, the basic waveform of voice, that must be modified and shaped by the vocal tract, the highly adjustable tube of the upper airway. The next chapter will consider that crucial shaping process. In this chapter, we shall concentrate on the laryngeal contribution alone. To keep things as clear and distinct as possible, we refer to it as the "vocal source signal."[1]

Some liken the vocal system to a wind instrument. The analogy is useful if it is clear that the instrument in question is brass, and *not* a woodwind. That is, despite the fact that we often (inexactly) speak of "laryngeal vibrations," the vocal folds do not vibrate like a reed at all. Actually they "chop" the airstream into short bursts of airflow. Thus, if the vocal system is analogous to a musical instrument, it is more like a trumpet, and the vocal folds correspond to the trumpeter's lips. The *vocal source signal* is similar to the sound a trumpeter would make with only a mouthpiece. The *voice*, in contrast, is the output from the trumpet's bell.

The Glottal Wave

Before examining the basic mechanisms by which the vocal source signal is produced, it will be worthwhile to take a brief look at the signal itself. In its most fundamental sense, it could be described as a patterned airflow through the glottis (the space between the vocal folds) like the airflow graphed in Fig 3–1. Driven by the pressure of the air in the lungs, the flow increases relatively gradually, reaches a peak, and then decreases suddenly until it stops. After a brief pause, the pattern repeats. This flow pattern is called the "glottal wave."

The sharp cutoff of flow is particularly crucial, because it is this relatively sudden stoppage of the air flow that is truly the raw material of voice. To understand why, think of an experience that you may have had with a poorly designed plumbing system. The faucet is wide open, and the water is running at full force. The tap is then quickly turned off. Water flow stops abruptly and there is a sudden THUMP! from the pipes inside the walls. (Plumbers call this "water hammer.") This happens because, in the simplest terms, the sudden cessation causes moving molecules of water to

---

[1]An effort has been made to keep this chapter as informal as possible in the conviction that what might be lost in rigor will be more than compensated by what is gained in understanding. When basic principles of physics are crucial, however, they are provided for the novice in interruptions of the main flow of the text that are labeled *Intermezzo*. These can be skipped by those already familiar with the concepts in question. Also, the common scholarly practice of citing references in the text has been abandoned so as to improve the flow of information and lessen the intimidation it might engender. The works listed in the Bibliography, however, will buttress the discussion and help satisfy the curiosity of those who may be encouraged to dig deeper.

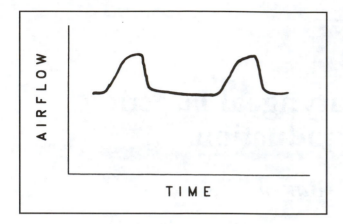

Fig 3–1. Two successive glottal waves. Increasing airflow is vertical.

collide with those ahead of them (like the chain-reaction collision caused when a car suddenly stops on a highway). This generates a kind of "shock wave." When the pipe is jolted by this shock, it moves, creating the vibrations in the air that we hear as a thump. The relatively sudden cutoff of flow that characterizes the glottal wave creates very much the same effect in the vocal tract. An impulse-like shock wave is produced that "excites" the vibration of the air molecules in the vocal tract. That excitation is the voice in its unrefined form.

The rate at which the shocks come is the *fundamental frequency* (F_0) of the voice and is measured in hertz (Hz). (One hertz equals one repetition per second.[2]) The time interval from the start of one cycle to the start of the next is called the *period* and is most conveniently measured in milliseconds. The intensity of phonation is related to the magnitude of the impulses. Now, any complex wave (such as the impulses that the larynx delivers into the vocal tract) is composed of a series of pure tones ("harmonics"), so the glottal source signal provides a palette of frequencies among which the rest of the vocal tract can select for creating the final vocal output.

This palette, or entire family, of frequencies is described as a *spectrum*. The spectrum's lowest tone is called the *fundamental*, and the rest of the tones are called *overtones*. The fundamental plus all of the overtones are called *partials*. Together, their frequencies form a *harmonic series*. The lowest partial is the fundamental. All of the other partials (each of which may be described as partial number N) have frequencies N times the fundamental. For example, the frequency of

the second partial is twice that of the fundamental. The third partial's frequency is three times that of the fundamental, and so on. In other words, the frequencies of the partial are integer multiples of the frequency of the fundamental.

Generating the Source Signal

We are now ready to explore how the glottal source signal is generated. The starring role in that performance definitely belongs to the vocal folds. The rest of the laryngeal structures (reviewed in the previous chapter) are, for our present purposes, essentially only stagehands that we can temporarily ignore.

Seen from the top, the vocal folds appear as whitish bands of tissue that stretch across the airway of the larynx. They join together and are attached to the inside of the thyroid cartilage in front, and each is anchored to an arytenoid cartilage at the rear. The arytenoid cartilages are capable of complex movements that cause the vocal folds to be brought into contact with each other along their length (approximated or adducted), or separated (abducted) to open the air passage for breathing. The space between the vocal folds is called the glottis. Since the vocal folds are movable, the *glottis* can be made quite large or reduced until its size is zero.

If we use special techniques (such as high-speed filming or stroboscopy) to observe vocal fold motion during phonation, we see the movements schematized in Fig 3–2. From an initial condition (Fig 3–2, A) in which the vocal folds are in complete contact (and the glottal size is, therefore, zero), they increasingly separate until the glottis attains some maximal size (Fig 3–2, D). The vocal folds then snap back to the midline, closing the glottis once again. In an average male voice, this cycle will repeat about 100 times each second. That is, the F_0 will be about 100 Hz. (Females have a higher F_0, on the order of 220 Hz.) Because the air in the lungs is under pressure, air is forced through the glottis during each glottal opening. The result is the patterned air flow of the glottal wave.

What causes this repeated opening and closing of the glottis, and how is its rate controlled? These have been central questions of voice research. Thanks to very rapid and significant advances in the past few years, we now understand quite a bit about what drives the phonatory process. What we know is derived from empirical studies by a large and international array of voice scientists (several of whom are cited in

[2]"Fundamental frequency" and "pitch" are related but not the same. F_0 is a physical attribute; pitch is a perception. One does not grow in a lock-step way with the other. The terminological confusion is not helped by the fact that engineers—whose work accounts for a significant fraction of the vocal research literature—typically refer to F_0 as "pitch"!

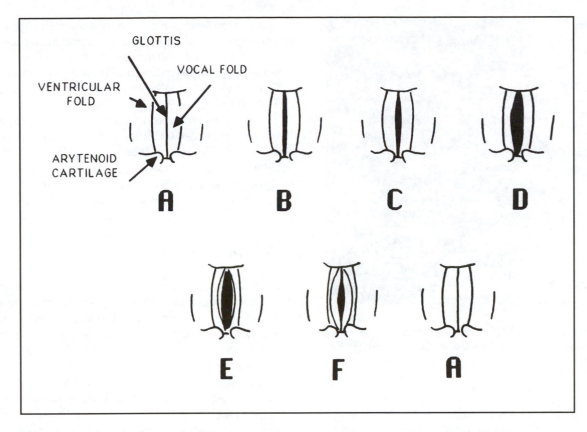

Fig 3–2. The glottal cycle as seen from above. Important anatomical landmarks are indicated.

the Bibliography) and from modern mathematical models of the phonatory process, especially those developed by Titze and Ishizaka. As with so much in the natural world, the mechanisms turn out to be both elegant (and simpler than we might have feared) and complex (and hence more complicated than we might have hoped). Although thorough study of the research literature is clearly essential for anyone intending seriously to pursue voice research, and examination of the available models is quite rewarding for those who have the advanced mathematical skills to follow them, we shall only be able to undertake a brief nonmathematical summary of the highlights of the vast store of information that is available. Readers who need to know more or are simply intrigued are urged and implored to delve much deeper.

To understand any of the finer details of the vocal process will require that we view the vocal folds in cross-section (rather than from the traditional viewpoint from above), examine a little bit of their fine structure, and consider a few things about the nature of air flow and pressure.

Structure of the Vocal Folds

The cross-section of a vocal fold in Fig 3–3 shows that it is basically divisible into two zones. Essentially, the vocal fold is built on the supporting mass of the thyroarytenoid muscle that runs along its length. This muscular region, which accounts for most of the bulk of the vocal fold, is referred to as the vocal fold *body*; but it would be a serious mistake to view the body as nothing more than a support for the overlying tissue. Contraction and relaxation of the thyroarytenoid muscle can significantly change its length, thickness, and stiffness. We shall see that these changes play a vital role in determining the characteristics of the vocal source signal.

The body of the vocal fold is wrapped in a layer called the *cover*. Its structure is actually quite complex, but the fine details need not concern us here. It is enough to understand that the cover's outer layer is formed by epithelial tissues (similar to the linings of the rest of the throat and to the upper layers of skin on the surface of the body), and that, under this epithelium, there is a network of fibers that, in some significant ways,

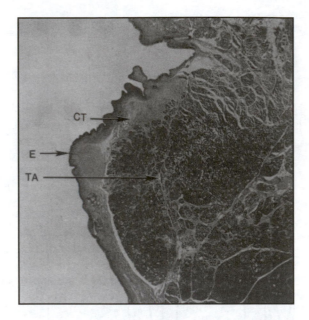

Fig 3–3. Cross-section of the human vocal folds. Courtesy of Dr. Joel C. Kahane, Memphis State University.

resemble rubber bands. The elastic network is particularly well formed near the edge of the upper portion of the vocal fold, where it constitutes the *vocal ligament*. This composite structure has very definite inherent mechanical properties, but, unlike the vocal fold body, those properties cannot normally be altered. The cover is attached relatively loosely. Like the skin on the back of one's hand, it is partially free to slide over the underlying vocal fold body. This mobility is important in phonation.

The Glottal Cycle

We are finally ready to examine the phonatory cycle in more meaningful detail. We shall assume that there is a supply of air in the lungs and that it has been pressurized (as it must be if phonation is to occur) to a level of perhaps 7 cm H_2O (a typical value).[3] The vocal folds are shown schematically in cross-section in Fig 3–4, and we shall consider their changing shape and posture as the vocal cycle progresses.

At the start of the cycle (Fig 3–4 A), the vocal folds are approximated. Note their cross-sectional shape: Each is a wedge, with a fairly flat surface on top and a sloping section below. The glottis at this stage is said to be "convergent"—it narrows from a relatively wide

space at the level of the lower surface of the vocal folds to no space at all higher up. The approximation of the vocal folds closes the airway; there is no flow. All the pressure of the air in the lungs acts on the sloping surface of the glottal walls. The pressure tends to push the vocal folds somewhat apart (Fig 3–4 B), and the separation grows wider and wider as the pressure continues to act (Fig 3–4 C). Finally, the pressure forces separation all the way to the upper surface of the vocal folds, and a glottal space appears (Fig 3–4 D). Air flow through the (partially) open glottis begins: the rising part of the glottal flow wave is now under way.

First Intermezzo

At this point, it might be useful to pause briefly to consider some basic facts about the physics of air flow and air pressure. The mathematical values and formulas will not be important to us, but the *concepts* are crucial to understanding the next events in the vocal cycle.

The energy available in the flow of any gas is stored in two forms. Everyday experience tells us that *pressure* represents one kind of energy storage. (Compressed air, for example, is commonly used to power machinery such as jackhammers.) Pressure represents what the physicist calls potential energy, energy waiting to be released to do work. The higher the pressure, the greater the *potential energy* available. Moving gas molecules have momentum, and that momentum also represents energy. So *motion* is the other form of energy storage. (The force against which one must struggle when walking into a very strong wind is produced by the moving air molecules releasing their momentum energy as they collide with you.) The energy of motion is called *kinetic* energy. The faster the gas molecules are moving, the greater is their kinetic energy.

Consider now the flow of air from the lower airway, through the constriction of the glottis, and into the wider space of the upper larynx just above the vocal folds. The diagram in Fig 3–5 represents this flow with the simplifying assumption that the tract has a uniform size except at the glottis, the shape of which has been made geometrically simpler.

Most basic to what will follow is the fact that the rate of air flow must be the same everywhere in the system. If, for example, 100 ml of air is entering the tube each second, then 100 ml/sec must be leaving it. (If not, the tube would soon either blow up and burst or empty itself of all air and generate a potent vacuum!) If the input and

---

[3] cm H_2O (read: centimeters of water) is the standard unit of pressure in vocal physiology. One cm H_2O is enough pressure to hold up a column of water 1 centimeter high.

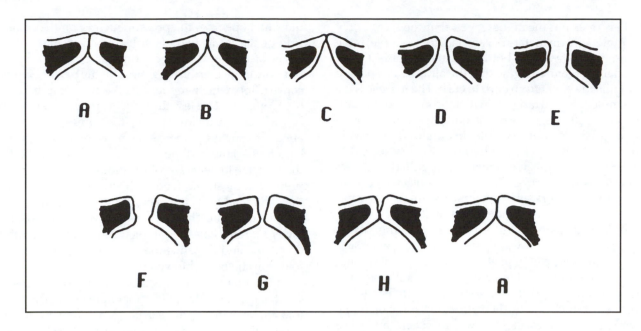

Fig 3–4. Movements of the vocal folds during phonation. The vocal folds are seen in cross-section.

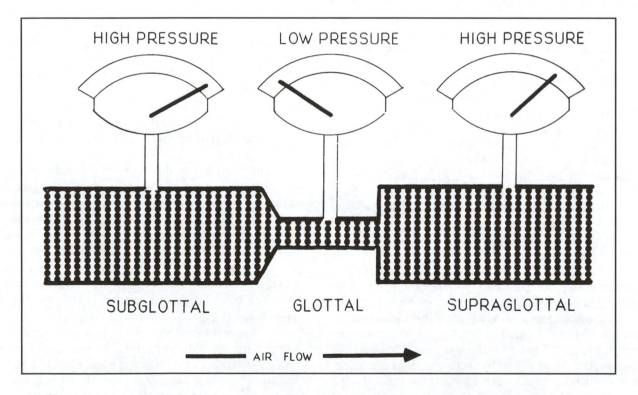

Fig 3–5. Pressure changes in the laryngeal airway, showing the Bernoulli effect. Pressure is sensed by gauges connected to the region below the glottis (subglottal), to the glottal space, and to the area just above the glottis (supraglottal). Air pressure within the glottis is lower than in the spaces above or below it.

output are the same, it must also be true that 100 ml of air moves past *every* point in the tube each second. Let us also remember that (all other things being equal) a given volume of air represents a given number of air molecules. Therefore, we can say that the same number of air molecules passes every point in the system every second.

This does not mean, however, that the *speed* of the air molecules (in meters per second, for example) is the same everywhere. The bottleneck at the glottis poses a special problem. Imagine that the air flow is a parade that fills the street from curb to curb. The marchers are air molecules, arranged in neat rows. Above and below the glottis, the street is quite spacious. In these regions, each row of molecules in the parade is so wide that only a few rows need to pass by every second in order to have a given number of individual marchers pass the spectators, so the rows of molecules do not have to move forward very quickly; just a few rows per second forward movement will do. Now the parade comes to the glottis—a narrowing of the parade route. The rows must become narrower, and fewer marchers can fit in each row, but, every second, the same number of marchers must still pass the parade watchers. (If fewer go by, the marchers to the rear will bunch up on them, creating a major traffic jam.) Since each row holds fewer marchers, and since the same number of marchers must pass every second, there is only one solution: the rows must pass more quickly. All the marchers in the glottal bottleneck have to speed up. When they return to the broader route above the vocal folds, they can all slow down again, but for the moment they must march in quickstep.

The moving air in the lower part of the larynx has a certain amount of energy. It is shared between its potential (pressure) and kinetic (speed of motion) energy, but its energy total is fixed. When the molecules speed up in the constriction, their kinetic energy increases. Such an increase would seem to imply that the total (potential + kinetic) energy would go up, but this cannot be. The total energy cannot increase, because one cannot create energy out of nothing. So, if the total must stay the same, and if the kinetic energy increases, then there is no way around it: The potential energy must decrease, which is another way of saying that the pressure must go down. Of course, when the air molecules reach the wider passage of the laryngeal region above the glottis and slow down again, their kinetic energy will decrease, and so their potential energy will be restored. What all of this means is that, if air is flowing through a narrow glottis, the pressure inside the glottal space will be less than the pressure in the wider spaces above the below it. This phenomenon (which is, of course, true for any constricted tube) is called the Bernoulli effect, and it plays an important role in the closing phase of the vocal cycle.

End of First Intermezzo

Now we can return to the vocal cycle, which we left in Fig 3–4 D with the glottis just barely open. In spite of the small opening, the pressure acting on the underside of the vocal folds is still operative, and so the edges of the vocal folds continue to be blown apart. But now there is an airflow through the narrow glottal constriction, which implies that the air pressure inside the glottis must be less than the air pressure above or below it. This relatively negative pressure has the effect of "sucking" the lower margins of the glottis back toward the midline. Also, having been pushed to the side, the lower walls of the glottis have been compressed, almost like foam rubber. The result is that they will tend to spring back, that is, to return to their original position. Therefore, as the cycle proceeds, the lower margins have begun their return to the midline (Fig 3–4 E and F), while the upper edges of the vocal folds are still being blown apart.

At this point, a new effect comes into play. Remember that the very edge of the upper portion of the vocal fold contains the highly elastic vocal ligament. As the edge of the vocal fold is pushed farther from the midline, the ligament is stretched more and more. Like a rubber band, the more it is stretched, the stronger is the tendency for it to snap back to its original shape. After a while, this restorative force begins to overcome the outward-pushing force of the air pressure (which, in any case, has been growing weaker as the approximation of lower portions of the folds increasingly pinches off the airflow). The upper portions of the vocal folds, therefore, begin to snap back toward the midline (Fig 3–4 G and H). Ultimately, the glottis will be restored to its original closed shape, and the cycle is ready to repeat.

Let us pause again, this time for a few observations on what has happened. One important consideration is that the motion of the vocal folds has been driven by a combination of *aerodynamic* forces (the lung pressure and the Bernoulli pressure) and the elastic (recoil) properties of the tissues. Hence, the mechanism just described is commonly called the *myoelastic aerodynamic* model of phonation. Another important fact is that the shape of the glottis, and, in particular, its convergence, has played an important role.

Even more interesting is the fact that the upper and lower portions of the vocal folds do not move in synchrony. The lower part is always somewhat ahead of the upper part: It begins to separate earlier, and it begins to return to the midline before the upper portion does. There is, in the more formal language of the vocal physiologists, a *vertical phase difference*. Although the reasons are far beyond the scope of our present discussion, it has been demonstrated that this phase difference is critical in maintaining normal phonation.

Finally, a careful examination of Fig 3–4 shows that a great deal of the vocal fold movement is accounted for by displacement of the mobile vocal fold cover and changes in its shape. (In fact, the rippling of the cover creates a "mucosal wave" that can be seen on the upper surface of the vocal fold during stroboscopic observation.) If there were no vocal fold cover (or its equivalent), normal phonation would not be possible.

Changing Vocal Fundamental Frequency and Amplitude

Several vocal characteristics can be voluntarily altered. The two most significant are F_0 and intensity. Their modification is important in speech and a *sine qua non* of singing.

Control of Vocal Fundamental Frequency

Changing the vocal F_0 means varying the rate at which the glottal wave repeats. The most efficient way of doing this is by modifying the mechanical properties of the vocal folds (although, as we shall see, it is also possible to change F_0 by altering the pressure of the air supply). The structure of the vocal fold, and its relationship to the rest of the larynx makes this fairly easy to accomplish by a number of means. We shall look at the most effective.

A reminder of a few anatomical facts is in order. Recall that the vocal folds stretch from the arytenoid cartilages (which are anchored to the back of the cricoid cartilage) at the rear, to the inside of the thyroid cartilage in front. The thyroid cartilage articulates with the cricoid cartilage in such a way that it can pivot, somewhat like the visor on a helmet. There is a muscle—the cricothyroid—that spans the gap from the thyroid to the cricoid cartilage in front. When it contracts, it pulls the two closer together. Because of the visor-like relationship of the thyroid and cricoid cartilages, contraction of the cricothyroid muscle causes the thyroid cartilage to pivot. Also, the thyroid cartilage will slide forward a bit. The result of these actions is diagrammed in Fig 3–6. Note that the net effect is to increase the distance from the arytenoid cartilages to the inside of the thyroid cartilage. Since the vocal folds must span the arytenoid-to-thyroid space, increasing this distance *stretches* the vocal folds and makes them *longer*.

These changes entail important modifications of the glottal cycle. First, if the vocal folds are longer, then

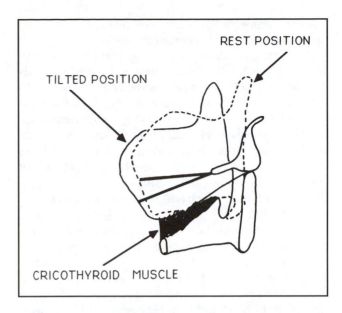

Fig 3–6. Contraction of the cricothyroid muscle causes the thyroid cartilage to rotate about its point of attachment to the cricoid cartilage. It is also pulled slightly forward. The result is to increase the length of the vocal folds, schematized here by *heavy straight lines*.

they present a greater surface area to the pressure in the airway just below them. That, in essence, makes the pressure more effective in separating the vocal folds during the opening phase of the cycle. The vocal folds, therefore, separate more quickly, shortening the cycle. A greater repetition rate, and hence a higher F_0, will be the result. But there is more. Stretching the vocal fold means that the elastic fibers of the vocal fold cover, and in particular the fibers of the vocal ligament, are stretched. The vocal ligament is like a rubber band, and stretching it has the same effect: The resulting increase in stiffness makes it snap back more quickly after being "plucked." Therefore, once the stretched vocal folds have been blown apart, they return more quickly to the midline, so increasing the stiffness of the vocal fold cover (by contracting the cricothyroid muscle) also shortens the cycle (increasing the repetition rate) and thereby contributes to the rise in F_0.

It is also possible to increase the stiffness of the vocal fold body by contracting the thyroarytenoid muscle (which, let us recall, *is* the body of the vocal fold) and having it pull against the stretching influence of the contracting cricothyroid muscle.[4] This increased con-

---

[4]To get a sense of the effect, rest your forearm and elbow on a table, relax your arm, and palpate your biceps muscle. Now (without letting your forearm rise from the table) contract your biceps ("make a muscle") and feel your biceps again. It is now much stiffer.

traction augments the stiffness of the vocal fold cover, and so it, too, helps to shorten the cycle.

Since the phonatory process is governed by aerodynamics as well as by biomechanics, it would be surprising if vocal F_0 could not also be changed by modifying the air pressure driving the cycle. Raising the pressure has the effect of increasing vocal intensity (to be discussed shortly), but, as any vocal artist is no doubt aware, there is a strong tendency for F_0 to increase as well. The exact basis of this effect has not been established for certain, but Titze has proposed a likely hypothesis, which has to do with the distance to which higher pressure drives the edge of the vocal fold from the midline. Several experiments have demonstrated that the vocal F_0 changes by about 4 or 5 Hz for every 1 cm H_2O change in the pressure operating on the vocal folds. For purposes of ordinary conversational speech, this amount of frequency change is not likely to be significant. However, implying as it does that the pitch of the vocal tone will rise as the loudness does, it is clearly of importance to singers, who will have to compensate to deal with it.

Control of Vocal Intensity

Vocal intensity[5] is a function of the amount of excitation that the glottal waves deliver to the air in the vocal tract. It is easy to see that, all other things being equal, the greater the amplitude of the glottal wave, the greater the resulting vocal tract excitation and hence the more intense the vocal signal. Raising the pressure of the air supply effectively increases the amount of air that is pushed through the glottis whenever it is open. That translates to a "taller" glottal flow wave. Hence, increased lung pressure translates to greater vocal intensity.

However, we learned earlier that it is the sudden cessation of the flow that bears the primary responsibility for setting the air of the vocal tract into acoustic vibration. The sharper the flow cutoff, the greater the vocal tract excitation will be and the more intense the resulting vocal signal. Greater vocal intensity is, in fact, associated with a much steeper decreasing phase of the glottal wave. This effect is achieved not only by the higher pressure, but also by voluntary changes in the biomechanics of the vocal folds that tend to resist the increase in air flow that the higher pressure would produce. So intensity increases are produced by a carefully regulated interaction of a higher driving pressure and an increased glottal resistance to flow.

Registers

To an outsider, there is probably no concept in the domain of the vocal arts that seems so contentious as that of vocal registers. Dozens and scores of different terms have been coined to describe subjective voice qualities, and the physiologic reality of almost every one of them as a voice register has been both the victim of vehement denial and the object of passionate defense.

Different registers sound different, to be sure. But variant acoustic impressions derive from changes in the way the vocal source signal is molded by the vocal tract as well as from differences in the vocal source signal itself. Because our concern here is solely with the source signal, we can simplify the problem of registers significantly by looking only at variations in laryngeal function. To keep the matter clear, let us agree to call the results of such differences *laryngeal registers*. We shall also impose the following requirements:

1. A laryngeal register must reflect a specific and distinct mode of laryngeal action. Vocal tract contributions are irrelevant.
2. A laryngeal register is produced across a contiguous range of fundamental frequencies.
3. The F_0 range of any given laryngeal register has little overlap with the F_0 range of any other register.

With these restrictions, only three distinct laryngeal registers have been verified. To avoid problems due to prior—and, frankly, often confused—terminology, and to reduce the influence of connotations commonly associated with older names, Hollien has suggested that we adopt completely new designations for these narrowly defined registers.

1. *Modal register* describes the laryngeal function in the range of fundamental frequencies most commonly used by untrained speakers (from about 75 to about 450 Hz in men; 130 to 520 Hz in women). The name, in fact, derives from the statistical term for "most common value." This register may include the musical "chest," "head," or "low," "mid," and "high" registers, depending on how these are defined.

2. *Pulse register* occurs in the F_0 range at the low end of the frequency scale (25 to 80 Hz in men; 20 to 45 Hz in women). The laryngeal output is perceived as pulsatile in nature. The term is broadly synonymous with "vocal fry," "glottal fry," or the musical term "strohbass."

---

[5]The relationship of vocal intensity and loudness is analogous to that of vocal F_0 and pitch. The former is a physical characteristic, the latter a perception, and the two are not exactly equivalent. We can measure intensity, but only judge loudness, which is influenced by many factors.

3. *Loft register* is employed at the upper end of the vocal continuum (275 to 620 Hz in men; 490 to 1,130 Hz in women). The name is intended to convey a sense of "upper reaches." In general, it corresponds to the older term "falsetto."

Modal register phonation is implicitly accepted as the norm, and, in fact, the glottal cycle we have been considering is that which characterizes it. Pulse and loft differ from modal register in the shape and tension to which the vocal folds are adjusted.

Pulse Register

As diagramed in Fig 3–7, pulse register phonation is accomplished with vocal folds that are rather massive in cross-section, a configuration that is achieved by freeing them of essentially all tension. (Laminagraphic studies by Allen and Hollien have suggested that the relaxation in the glottal region may be so complete that the ventricular folds may actually lie against the upper surface of the vocal folds. If this occurs, the effective mass of the vocal folds would obviously be increased enormously.) These two conditions—increased mass and reduced stretch—account for the very low fundamental frequencies associated with this laryngeal register. It takes longer for the vocal

folds to be blown apart, and, once moving laterally, their increased mass results in greater lateral momentum that sustains the abductory motion longer. The lack of tension implies a reduction of restoring (elastic) recoil, so the abductory motion is not opposed as vigorously, nor does closure, once it is finally under way, proceed as fast.

Pulse register phonation is associated with a very interesting pattern of vocal tract excitations, the results of which are also shown in Fig 3–7. Modal register glottal waves are relatively uniform in duration and amplitude, a fact that is reflected in the great similarity of the acoustic waves that they generate in the vocal tract. Pulse register, however, typically shows a pattern of weaker, shorter glottal waves alternating with larger and longer ones. The exact mechanisms that account for this behavior have yet to be demonstrated, but the phenomenon is so characteristic that some include its presence in the definition of this laryngeal register.

Loft Register

If pulse register represents an extreme in reduction of vocal fold tension, then loft register is just the opposite: Tension is increased to very high levels. The results are diagramed in Fig 3–7. The tension causes the vocal folds to be thinned to such an extent that they take the shape of mere shelves of tissue that may contact each other only over a small vertical distance. (In fact, it is a common observation that loft register phonation may be accomplished with no actual vocal fold contact at all.) A moment's reflection indicates that, under these conditions, vocal fold motion should be rapid but with a small excursion. The increased restorative forces associated with the higher tension cause the opening phase to be terminated early, and the recoil to the midline, driven by greater elasticity, will also be quite fast. On the whole then, loft register adjustment produces high vocal F_0, and the reduction in maximal glottic size generates only weak vocal tract excitations, associated with diminished vocal intensity.

Vocal Source Contributions to Voice Quality

Not all of what we hear in the voice is due to the shaping of the vocal source signal by the resonant and filtering actions of the vocal tract. Any product, after all, is a reflection of the raw material that created it, so some aspects of voice quality are bound to be inherent in the glottal wave itself (and, by inference, in the actions of the vocal folds). The time has now come to

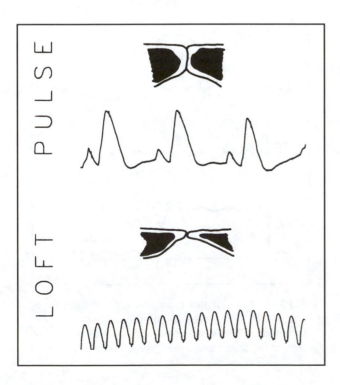

Fig 3–7. Vocal fold configuration and resulting waves in the pulse and loft register. The vocal folds are schematized in cross-section.

examine the vocal source signal in greater detail. To do so, we shall have to consider the *source spectrum*. Some readers may find it useful to pause for the second intermezzo.

Second Intermezzo

We begin with the somewhat startling statement that there really is no separate and distinct physical entity called sound. What we label by that name is simply our perception of changes in air pressure. The pressure changes must occur within a certain range of rates (about 20 to about 20,000 per second) and must be greater than a certain minimal size before we perceive them, but they are physically no different from the air pressure changes measured by a barometer.

The simplest possible way in which any variable—including air pressure—can change is referred to as "simple harmonic motion" and is depicted at the top of Fig 3–8, with pressure on the vertical axis and time

on the horizontal axis. The value of the pressure at any given point is proportional to the *sine* of its time location. Hence, this pattern is referred to as a *sine wave*. A sine wave can be almost completely characterized by its F_0 (repetition rate) and by the extent of its pressure change (amplitude).[6]

Very few sounds of the natural world are simple sine waves. Almost all are very much more complex, but a physical law known as the *Fourier theorem* tells us that any complex sound is composed of a series of sine waves of different frequencies and amplitudes. The reality of this statement is demonstrated in Fig 3–9, in which a complex wave is shown with the four sine wave components, which were added together to create it. (Dissecting a complex wave into its sine wave components is known as *Fourier analysis*.) If the repetition rate of the complex wave is perfectly regular, the wave is said to be *periodic*. In that case, all the component sine waves will be integer multiples of the complex wave's F_0. Such components are called *harmonics*. In Fig 3–9, the component sine waves have frequencies

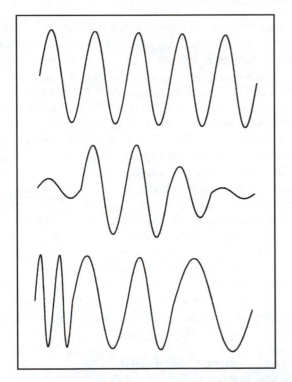

Fig 3–8. Sine waves represent the simplest form of pressure change. **Top:** Five sine wave cycles of equal period and amplitude. **Middle:** Waves of constant period but varying amplitudes. **Bottom:** Constant amplitude and variable period.

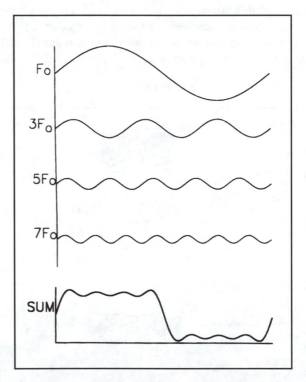

Fig 3–9. Any complex repetitive wave is the sum of a series of sine waves of different frequencies and amplitudes. The wave shown at the **bottom** is the sum of the four "harmonics" shown above it.

---

[6]There is another descriptor, known as the phase angle, that specifies the difference in starting times among two or more waves. When all three parameters—frequency, amplitude, and phase angle—are specified, we know all there is to know about a sine wave. The phase angle is unimportant to the present discussion, however.

of 1, 3, 5, and 7 times F_0; they are harmonic frequencies. Notice, however, that they have different amplitudes.

So, any complex wave could be expressed as a tabulation of component frequencies with their respective amplitudes, but such a list would hardly be easy to deal with. A better idea is to produce a graph of the information. We can do this by drawing lines along a frequency dimension wherever there is a component sine wave. The height of the line can represent the amplitude of the component. For the wave of Fig 3–10 A, such a graph would look like the plot in Fig 3–10 B. A plot of this type is known as an *amplitude spectrum*. It is nothing but a graphic summary of the components of a complex periodic wave.

Actually, because of the need to begin with simple cases, we have been a bit dishonest. We have behaved as if the wave that we considered as our example is perfectly periodic, that is, it was assumed to repeat with perfect precision and exactitude, each repetition a precise replica of every other. The spectrum of Fig 3–10 B is called a *line spectrum*, because it is composed of lines separated by empty space on the graph. (There are harmonic frequencies, and nothing else.) But a precisely periodic wave is not to be found in nature. There is always some noise, some irregularity of repetition.

Pure noise—a *totally* random wave, such as is shown in Fig 3–10 C—has no harmonics. It is composed of sine waves of any and all frequencies (at least within a specifiable range) having unpredictable amplitudes. Its spectrum does not have discrete lines: Since all frequencies are present, the lines fill in all available spaces on the graph, forming a *continuous spectrum*, as in Fig 3–10 D. If a signal is essentially periodic, but also has some noise or irregularity, its spectrum will be a combination of a line and a continuous spectrum: There will be some "fill in" between the harmonic lines.

End of Second Intermezzo

The Vocal Source Spectrum

The amplitude spectrum of an ideal (noise free) glottal wave is illustrated in Fig 3–11 (top). The regular spacing of the lines tells us that the components are har-

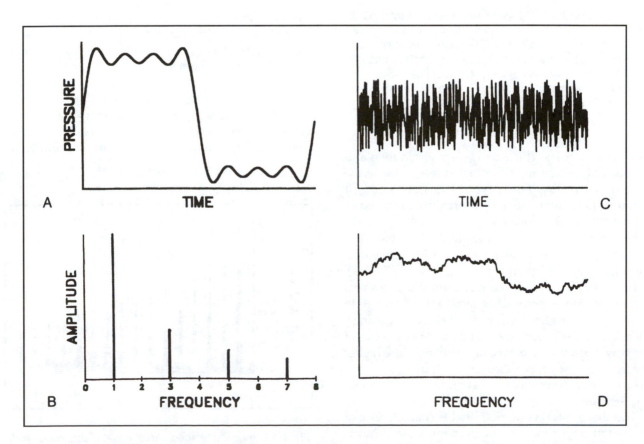

Fig 3–10. Amplitude spectra. The components of the complex wave of Fig 7–9 (redrawn in **A**) can be indicated in the *line spectrum* shown in **B**. Any purely periodic wave has a line spectrum. A random (noise) wave, such as the one shown in **C**, will have a *continuous spectrum*, like that of **D**.

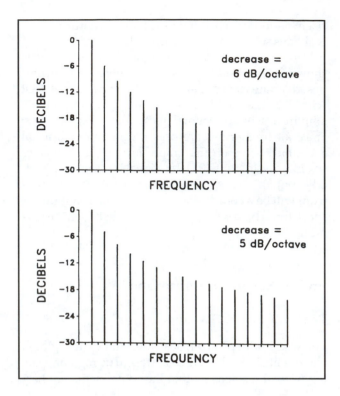

Fig 3–11. Spectra of the glottal wave. In the **upper spectrum**, the "roll-off" (decrease) in the amplitudes of the harmonic lines is at the rate of 6 dB/octave. This is typical of the voice at conversational intensity. Increasing intensity (or voluntary adjustment of the vocal folds) can strengthen the higher harmonics, resulting in a roll-off that is less steep, as in the **lower spectrum**.

monic frequencies. The orderly decrease in their amplitude with increasing frequency is referred to as the spectrum's *roll-off*. For a typical healthy voice, it amounts to an attenuation of approximately 6 dB per octave of frequency increase.

Let us take a moment and explore where the high-frequency harmonics come from. Consider the waveform we have used as an example (Fig 3–9 or 7–10 A). It has a sudden shift at its midpoint. Such a sharp movement represents a fairly rapid rate of change in the acoustic pressure. To generate such a quick change, there must be some among the sine wave components of the waveform that also have rapid change. The higher the frequency of a wave, the faster is its pressure variation, so rapid alterations in a wave translate to stronger high-frequency components in the wave's spectrum.

The sharp cutoff of air flow that is characteristic of the glottal wave now takes on even more significance. It is an important source of the high-frequency components of the glottal source spectrum. The sharper the cutoff becomes, the stronger those high-frequency compo-

nents should be. It is known that the cutoff becomes sharper as vocal intensity increases. It is also possible to sharpen the cutoff by adjusting the mechanical properties of the vocal folds. Also, of considerable importance to professional voice users, *stronger high harmonics give the voice a perceptually "brighter" sound.* Here, then, is one aspect of voice quality that derives directly from laryngeal adjustment.

Glottal Wave Irregularity

Examination of the amplitude spectrum of a real glottal wave (Fig 3–12) shows it to be different in two significant ways from the ideals we have examined so far. The harmonic lines are not nearly so sharp as we have pictured them thus far, and there is continuous energy that fills in part of the space between them. These differences are the result of two phenomena that we have avoided so far, but that are very much part of any real vocal signal: airflow turbulence and vibrational irregularity.

Turbulence

Air flow through the glottis is not perfectly smooth or (in the language of physics) "laminar." In other words, the air molecules do not all really move in straight lines, like the marchers in a parade. Whenever a flow is forced through a sufficiently narrow opening (like the glottis), there is always a certain amount of random movement or *turbulence*. Also, many individuals do not achieve complete phonatory closure. The arytenoid cartilages may fail to meet at the midline, or

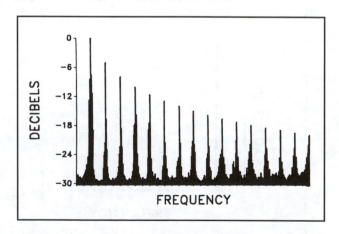

Fig 3–12. Amplitude spectrum of a real glottal wave. Note the thickening of the harmonic lines and the "fill" between them. These result from irregularity of the glottal vibration and airflow tubulence.

they may be angled in such a way that the posterior part of the glottis remains slightly open. In either case, there is often an open pathway by which air can travel around the glottis. This leakage is almost certain to be quite turbulent.

If some of the air molecules are moving in random directions, then there must be randomly oriented pressures acting on them. Since sound is nothing but pressure variation, these erratic pressures contribute randomness to the final acoustic product. That randomness, of course, is noise, and it adds its continuous spectrum characteristics to the line spectrum of the glottal pulsing, partially filling in the spaces between the harmonics.

What is the perceptual effect? Within reasonable limits, added noise in the spectrum produces a sensation of fuzzy softness to the sound, perhaps a velvety quality. A bit more turbulence might be heard as breathiness, or perhaps huskiness, and a lot of turbulence contributes to the perception of hoarseness.

Vibrational Irregularity

Glottal waves are imperfect not only because there are flow turbulences, but also because there is frequency and amplitude *perturbation*: Neither the frequency nor the amplitude of any two successive waves is ever likely to be precisely the same[7] (see Fig 3–13). The average differences are quite small: on the order of 40 μsec for period, and about 0.4 dB for amplitude. Still, if the F_0 and amplitude are varying, then the harmonics (which, let us recall, have frequencies that are integral multiples of F_0) must be varying. This results in thickening of the harmonic lines in the spectrum—an indication that the perturbation has introduced an uncertainty about what the exact frequency value of any given harmonic is.

Normal perturbation does not seem to be measurably lessened by attempts to control the voice or by vocal training. Its irreducibility stems from the fact that it reflects inherent instabilities and irregularities

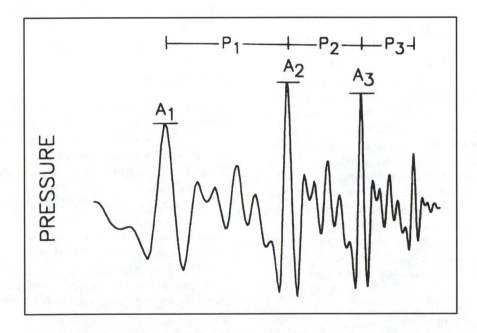

Fig 3–13. Perturbation as shown in the acoustic wave of a vowel. The difference between P(*eriod*), and P_2, and between P_2 and P_3 is called the *frequency perturbation* or *jitter*. The amplitude difference (A_1, A_2, A_3) is the *amplitude perturbation*, or *shimmer*. (For illustrative purposes, the differences shown here have been made greater than would be expected in a normal voice.)

---

[7]In the argot of everyday professional communication, frequency perturbation is referred to as *jitter*, amplitude perturbation as *shimmer*.

in the contractions of the muscles that control the vocal structures. It is not surprising, therefore, that it is one of the factors that give the voice a natural, humanlike quality (a fact appreciated by the creator of the "vox humana" stop on a pipe organ).

Coda

So, at least in outline, we have gone from two flaps of tissue blowing in the pulmonary wind to a palette of acoustic potentials ready to be refined into a baby's cry, a sports fan's cheer, a laborer's grunt, or a Verdi aria.

The voice may be a wondrous thing, but the process of voice production is neither mysterious nor inexplicable. In this chapter, we have been able to explore only the barest outline of the process by which voice is produced, just enough to get the reader started. (There is much that is not understood about laryngeal function, but there is very much that is.) It is obvious, however, that nothing more than perfectly ordinary laws of physics and common principles of physiology are involved.

The mystery, of course, enters with the art.

Summary

The voice is generated by the entire vocal tract, not just the larynx. The vocal source signal is a patterned air flow between the vocal folds. It is generated when subglottal pressure overcomes the forces holding the vocal folds together in the midline (adductory forces). The vocal folds then separate and then clap shut, producing sound. The frequency with which openings and closings occur responds to pitch. The amplitude of placement from the midline, and the characteristics with which vocal folds close, are related to the intensity of the voice. The pattern of vocal fold activity helps determine vocal register. Although much of voice quality is determined by the supraglottic vocal tract, the vocal source signal is also an important quality determinant.

Review Questions

1. A particularly important factor in creating vocal source signal is:
   a. a stringlike vibration of the vocal fold
   b. sudden stoppage of airflow between the vocal folds
   c. uninterrupted airflow between the vocal folds
   d. all of the above
   e. none of the above

2. The following muscle is dominant in control of fundamental frequency:
   a. thyroarytenoid
   b. lateral cricoarytenoid
   c. cricothyroid
   d. posterior cricoarytenoid
   e. interarytenoid

3. Phonation may be accomplished with no vocal fold contact in:
   a. modal register
   b. pulse register
   c. loft register
   d. all of the above
   e. none of the above

4. The vocal source signal is characterized by:
   a. peaks and valleys called "formants"
   b. orderly decrease in the amplitude of harmonics
   c. sine waves
   d. all of the above
   e. none of the above

5. The glottal waves of premiere singers are free of irregularities, giving rise to their "trained sound."
   a. true
   b. false

Bibliography

Of necessity, but unfortunately, this chapter could only touch on the highest of the high points of what is understood about laryngeal function. There is a great deal that the serious student of voice will want to know. This bibliography is intended to help in satisfying that desire.

The listing has been divided by topic to facilitate finding a source for whatever specific information is required. We hope readers will also be encouraged to browse, seeking items that strike a chord resonant with their interests.

Despite its length, this bibliography represents only a very small portion of what is available.

General Introductory Texts

Baken RJ. *Clinical measurement of speech and voice*. Boston: Little, Brown; 1987:518.

Bunch M. *Dynamics of the singing voice*. New York: Springer; 1982:156.

Daniloff R, Schuckers G, Feth L. *The physiology of speech and hearing*. Englewood Cliffs, NJ: Prentice-Hall; 1980:454.

Hirano M. *Clinical examination of voice*. New York: Springer; 1981:100.

Isshiki N. *Phonosurgery: theory and practice*. New York: Springer; 1989:233.

Titze IR: *The principles of voice production*, Englewood Cliffs, NJ: Prentice-Hall. In press.

Zemlin WR. *Speech and hearing science: anatomy and physiology*. Englewood Cliffs, NJ: Prentice-Hall; 1988:603.

Anatomy and Tissue Properties

Bach AC, Lederer RL, Dinolt R. Senile changes in the laryngeal musculature. *Arch Otolaryngol.* 1941;34:47–56.

Baken RJ, Isshiki N. Arytenoid displacement by simulated intrinsic muscle contraction. *Folia Phoniatrica.* 1977;29: 206–216.

Biondi S, Biondi-Zappala M. Surface of laryngeal mucosa seen through the scanning electron microscope. *Folia Phoniatrica.* 1974;26:241–248.

Gracco C, Kahane JC. Age-related changes in the vestibular folds of the human larynx: a histomorphometric study. *J Voice.* 1989;3:204–212.

Hast MH. Mechanical properties of the vocal fold muscle. *Practica Oto-Rhino-Laryngologica.* 1967;29:53–56.

Hirano M. Morphological structure of the vocal cord as a vibrator and its variations. *Folia Phoniatrica.* 1974;26:89–94.

Hirano M. Phonosurgery: basic and clinical investigations. *Otologia* (Fukuoka). 1975;21:239–440.

Hirano M. Structure of the vocal fold in normal and disease states. Anatomical and physical studies. In: Ludlow CL, Hart MO, eds. *Proceedings of the Conference on the Assessment of Vocal Pathology.* (ASHA Reports No. 11.) Rockville, MD: The American Speech-Language-Hearing Association;1981:11–30.

Hirano M, Kurita S, Sakaguchi S. Vocal fold tissue of a 104-year-old lady. *Ann Bull Res Inst Logopedics Phoniatrics.* 1988;22:1–5.

Hirano M, Matsuo K, Kakita Y, et al. Vibratory behavior versus the structure of the vocal fold. In: Titze IR, Scherer RC, eds. *Vocal Fold Physiology: Biomechanics, Acoustics and Phonatory Control.* Denver, CO: The Denver Center for the Performing Arts; 1983:26–39.

Kahane JC. Connective tissue changes in the larynx and their effects on voice. *J Voice.* 1987;1:27–30.

Kahane JC. Histologic structure and properties of the human vocal folds. *Ear, Nose Throat J* 1988;67:322–330.

Koike Y, Ohta F, Monju T. Hormonal and non-hormonal actions of endocrines on the larynx. *Excerpta Medica International Congress Series* 1969; 206:339–343.

Mueller PB, Sweeney RJ, Baribeau LJ. Senescence of the voice: morphology of excised male larynges. *Folia Phoniatrica.* 1985; 37:134–138.

Rossi G, Cortesina G. Morphological study of the laryngeal muscles in man: insertions and courses of the muscle fibres, motor end-plates and proprioceptors. *Acta Otolaryngol.* 1965;59:575–592.

Sataloff, R.T: The human voice, *Scientific American.* 1992; 267(6):108.

Sellars IE, Keen EN. The anatomy and movements of the cricoarytenoid joint. *Laryngoscope.* 1978;88:667–674.

F₀ and Intensity

Atkinson JE. Inter- and intraspeaker variability in fundamental voice frequency. *J Acoustic Soc Am.* 1976;60:440–445.

Bowler NW. A fundamental frequency analysis of harsh vocal quality. *Speech Monog.* 1964;31:128–134.

Coleman RF, Mabis JH, Hinson JK. Fundamental frequency-sound pressure level profiles of adult male and female voices. *J Speech Hearing Res.* 1977;20:197–204.

Colton RH, Hollien H. Phonational range in the modal and falsetto registers. *J Speech Hearing Res.* 1972;15:713–718.

Davis SB. Acoustic characteristics of normal and pathological voices, In: Lass NJ, ed. *Speech and Language: Advances in Basic Research and Practice.* vol. 1 . New York: Academic Press; 1979;271–335.

Dickopf G, Flach M, Koch R, Kroemer B. Varianzanalytische Untersuchungen zur Stimmfeldmessung. *Folia Phoniatrica.* 1988,40: 43–48.

Fairbanks G, Wiley JH, Lassman FM. An acoustical study of vocal pitch in seven- and eight-year-old boys. *Child Dev.* 1949; 0:63–69.

Fitch JL, Holbrook A. Modal vocal fundamental frequency of young adults. *Arch Otolaryngol.* 1970;92:379–382.

Gramming P, Akerlund L. Phonetograms for normal and pathological voices. In: Gramming P, ed. *The Phonetogram: an Experimental and Clinical Study.* Malmö, Sweden: University of Lund; 1988:117–132.

Gramming P, Sundberg J, Ternström S, et al. Relationship between changes in voice pitch and loudness. In: Gramming P, ed. *The Phonetogram: an Experimental and Clinical Study.* Malmö, Sweden: University of Lund; 1988:87–107.

Hacki T. Die Beurteilung der quantitativen Sprechstimmleistungen: Das Sprechstimmfeld im Singstimmfeld. *Folia Phoniatrica.* 1988;40:190–196.

Hiki S. Correlation between increments of voice pitch and glottal sound intensity. *J Acoust Soc Jpn.* 1967;23:20–22.

Hollien H, Jackson B. Normative data on the speaking fundamental frequency characteristics of young adult males. *J Phonetics* 1973;1: 117–120.

Hollien H, Massey K. A male-female coalescence model of vocal change. In: Lawrence VL, ed. *Transcripts of the Fourteenth Symposium: Care of the Professional Voice*, part I. New York: Voice Foundation; 1985:57–60a.

Hollien H, Paul P. A second evaluation of the speaking fundamental frequency characteristics of post-adolescent girls. *Lang Speech.* 1969;12:119–124.

Hollien H, Shipp T. Speaking fundamental frequency and chronologic age in males. *J Speech Hearing Res.* 1972;15: 155–159.

Linville SE. Maximum phonational frequency range capabilities of women's voices with advancing age. *Folia Phoniatrica.* 1987;39:297–301.

McGlone RE, Hollien H. Vocal pitch characteristics of aged women. *J Speech Hearing Res.* 1963;6:164–170.

Michel FJ, Hollien H, Moore P. Speaking fundamental frequency characteristics of 15, 16, and 17 year old girls. *Lang Speech.* 1966;9:46–51.

Mysak ED. Pitch and duration characteristics of older males. *J Speech Hearing Res.* 1959;2:46–54.

Pederson MF, Kitzing P, Krabbe S, Heramb S. The change of voice during puberty in 11 to 16 year old choir singers measured with electroglottographic fundamental frequency analysis and compared to other phenomena of puberty. *Acta Otolaryngol*. 1982;suppl 386:189–192.

Ramig LA, Ringel RL. Effects of physiological aging on selected acoustic characteristics of voice. *J Speech Hearing Res*. 1983;26:22–30.

Ramig LA, Scherer RC, Titze IR. Acoustic correlates of aging. *Recording Res Center Res Rep*. 1985;April:257–277.

Rauhut A, Stürzebecher E, Wagner H, Seidner W. Messung des Stimmfeldes. *Folia Phoniatrica*. 1979,31:119–124.

Robb MP, Saxman IH, Grant AA. Vocal fundamental frequency characteristics during the first two years of life. *J Acoust Soc Am*. 1989; 85:1708–1717.

Saxman JH, Burk KW. Speaking fundamental frequency characteristics of middle-aged females. *Folia Phoniatrica*. 1967;19:167–172.

Stone RE Jr. Ferch PAK. Intra-subject variability in F_0-SPLmin voice profiles. *J Speech Hearing Disord*. 1982;47: 123–134.

Stone RE Jr, Bell CJ, Clack TD. Minimum intensity of voice at selected levels within pitch range. *Folia Phoniatrica*. 1978; 30:113–118.

Perturbation

Beckett RL. Pitch perturbation as a function of subjective vocal constriction. *Folia Phoniatrica*. 1969;21:416–425.

Brown WS Jr, Morris RJ, Michel JF. Vocal jitter in young adult and aged female voices. *J Voice*. 1989;3:113–119.

Cavallo SA, Baken RJ, Shaiman S. Frequency perturbation characteristics of pulse register phonation. *J Commun Disord*. 1984;17:231–243.

Deal RE, Emanuel FW. Some waveform and spectral features of vowel roughness. *J Speech Hearing Res*. 1978;21: 250–264.

Higgins MB, Saxman JH. Variations in vocal frequency perturbation across the menstrual cycle. *J Voice*. 1989;3:233-243.

Horii Y. Fundamental frequency perturbation observed in sustained phonation. *J Speech Hearing Res*. 1979;22:5–19.

Horii Y. Jitter and shimmer in sustained vocal fry phonation. *Folia Phoniatrica*. 1985;37:81–86.

Horii Y. Vocal shimmer in sustained phonation. *J Speech Hearing Res*. 1980;23:202–209.

Iwata S, von Leden H. Pitch perturbations in normal and pathologic voices. *Folia Phoniatrica*. 1970;22:413–424.

Lieberman P. Perturbations in vocal pitch. *J Acoust Soc Am*. 1961;33:597–603.

Lieberman P. Some acoustic measures of the fundamental periodicity of normal and pathologic larynges. *J Acoust Soc Am*. 1963 35: 344–353.

Moore P, von Leden H. Dynamic variaiions of the vibratory pattern in the normal larynx. *Folia Phoniatrica*. 1958;10: 205–238.

Murry T, Large J. Frequency perturbation in singers. In: Lawrence V, ed. *Transcripts of the Seventh Symposium: Care of the Professional Voice*. New York: Voice Foundation; 1978:36–39

Orlikoff RF. Vocal jitter at different fundamental frequencies: a cardiovascular-neuromuscular explanation. *J Voice*. 1989;3:104–112.

Orlikoff RF, Baken RJ. Fundamental frequency modulation of the human voice by the heartbeat: preliminary results and possible mechanisms. *J Acoust Soc Am*. 1989;85: 888–893.

Ramig LA, Shipp T. Comparative measures of vocal tremor and vocal vibrato. *J Voice*. 1987;1:162–167.

Sorensen D, Horii Y. Frequency and amplitude perturbation in the voices of female speakers. *J Commun Disord*. 1983; 16:57–61.

Wilcox KA, Horii Y. Age and changes in vocal jitter. *J Gerontol*. 1980;35:194–198.

Control Mechanisms

Atkinson JE. Correlation analysis of the physiological factors controlling fundamental voice frequency. *J Acoust Soc Am*. 1978;63:211–222.

Baken RJ, Orlikoff RF. Changes in vocal fundamental frequency at the segmental level: control during voiced fricatives. *J Speech Hearing Res*. 1988;31:207–211.

Baken RJ, Orlikoff RF. The effect of articulation on fundamental frequency in singers and speakers. *J Voice*. 1987;1: 68–76.

Baken RJ, Orlikoff RF. Laryngeal and chest-wall responses to step-function changes in supraglottal impedance. *Folia Phoniatrica*. 1986;38:283.

Colton RH. Physiological mechanisms of vocal frequency control: the role of tension. *J Voice*. 1988;2:208–220.

Erickson D, Baer T, Harris KS. The role of the strap muscles in pitch lowering. In: Bless DM, Abbs JH, eds. *Vocal Fold Physiology: Contemporary Research and Clinical Issues*. San Diego, CA: College-Hill Press, 1983:279–285.

Faaborg-Andersen K. Electromyographic investigation of intrinsic laryngeal muscles in humans. *Acta Physiol Scand*. 1957; 41(suppl. 140):1–150.

Faaborg-Andersen K, Sonninen A. The function of the extrinsic laryngeal muscles at different pitch. *Acta Otolaryngol*. 1960;51:89–93.

Gay T, Hirose H, Strome M, Sawashima M. Electromyography of the intrinsic laryngeal muscles during phonation. *Ann Otol Rhinol Laryngol*. 1972;81:401–410.

Harvey N, Howell P. Isotonic vocalis contraction as a means of producing rapid decreases in F_0. *J Speech Hearing Res*. 1980;23:576–592.

Hast MH. Physiological mechanisms of phonation: tension of the vocal fold muscle. *Acta Otolaryngol*. 1966;62: 309–318.

Hirano M. Behavior of laryngeal muscles of the late William Vennard. *J Voice*. 1988;2:291–300.

Hirano M. The function of the intrinsic laryngeal muscles in singing. In: Stevens KN, Hirano M, eds. *Vocal Fold Physiology*. Tokyo: University of Tokyo Press; 1981:155–167.

Hirano M, Ohala J, Vennard W. The function of laryngeal muscles in regulating fundamental frequency and intensity of phonation. *J Speech Hearing Res*. 1969;12:616–628.

Hirano M, Vennard W, Ohala J. Regulation of register, pitch and intensity of voice. *Folia Phoniatrica*. 1970;22:1–20.

Hixon TJ, Klatt DH, Mead J. Influence of forced transglottal pressure changes on vocal fundamental frequency. *J Acoust Soc Am*. 1971;49 105.

Hollien H. Some laryngeal correlates of vocal pitch. *J Speech Hearing Res*. 1960;3:52–58.

Hollien H. Vocal fold thickness and fundamental frequency of phonation. *J Speech Hearing Res*. 1962;5:237–243.

Hollien H. Vocal pitch variation related to changes in vocal fold length. *J Speech Hearing Res*. 1960;3:150–156.

Hollien H, Colton RH. Four laminagraphic studies of vocal fold thickness. *Folia Phoniatrica*. 1969;21:179–198.

Hollien H, Curtis JF. Elevation and tilting of vocal folds as a function of vocal pitch. *Folia Phoniatrica*. 1962;14:23–36.

Hollien H, Moore GP. Measurements of the vocal folds during changes in pitch. *J Speech Hearing Res*. 1960;3:157–165.

Holmberg EB, Hillman RE, Perkell JS. Glottal airflow and transglottal air pressure measurements for male and female speakers in soft, normal, and loud voice. *J Acoust Soc Am*. 1988;84:511–529.

Horii Y. Acoustic analysis of vocal vibrato: a theoretical interpretation of data. *J Voice*. 1989;3:36–43.

Horii Y, Hata K. A note on phase relationships between frequency and amplitude modulations in vocal vibrato. *Folia Phoniatrica*. 1988;40:303–311.

Isshiki N. Regulatory mechanism of voice intensity variation. *J Speech Hearing Res*. 1964;7:17–29.

Isshiki N. Remarks on mechanism for vocal intensity variation. *J Speech Hearing Res*. 1969;12:665–672.

Isshiki N. Vocal intensity and air flow rate. *Folia Phoniatrica*. 1965;17:92–105.

Keenan JS, Barrett GC. Intralaryngeal relationships during pitch and intensity changes. *J Speech Hearing Res*. 1962;5:173–177.

Larson CL, Kempster GB. Voice fundamental frequency changes following discharge of laryngeal motor units. In: Titze IR, Scherer RC, eds. *Vocal Fold Physiology: Biomechanics, Acoustics and Phonatory Control*. Denver, CO: The Denver Center for the Performing Arts; 1983:91–103.

Leonard RJ, Ringel RL, Daniloff RG, Horii Y. Voice frequency change in singers and nonsingers. *J Voice*. 1987;1:234–239.

Lieberman P, Knudson R, Mead J. Determination of the rate of change of fundamental frequency with respect to subglottal air pressure during sustained phonation. *J Acoust Soc Am*. 1969;45:1537–1543.

Löfqvist A, Baer T, McGarr NS, Story RS. The cricothyroid muscle in voicing control. *J Acoust Soc Am*. 1989;85: 1314–1321.

Monsen RB, Engebretson AM, Vemula NR. Indirect assessment of the contribution of subglottal air pressure and vocal-fold tension to changes of fundamental frequency in English. *J Acoust Soc Am*. 1978;64:65–80.

Murry T, Brown WS Jr. Regulation of vocal intensity during vocal fry phonation. *J Acoust Soc Am*. 1971;49:1905–1907.

Niimi S, Horiguchi S, Kobayashi N. The physiological role of the sternothyroid muscle in phonation: an electromyographic observation. *Ann Bull Res Inst Logoped Phoniatr*. 1988;22:163–169.

Nishizawa N, Sawashima M, Yonemoto K. Vocal fold length in vocal pitch change. In: Fujimura O, ed. *Vocal Physiology: Voice Production, Mechanisms and Functions*. New York: Raven Press; 1988:75–52.

Ohala J, Hirano M, Vennard W. An electromyographic study of laryngeal activity in speech and singing. In: *Proceedings of the Sixth International Congress on Acoustics*. Tokyo, 1968:B-5–B-8.

Rubin HJ, LeCover M, Vennard W. Vocal intensity, subglottic pressure and air flow relationships in singers. *Folia Phoniatrica*. 1967;19:393–413.

Shin T, Hirano M, Maeyama T, et al. The function of the extrinsic laryngeal muscles. In: Stevens KN, Hirano M, eds. *Vocal Fold Physiology*. Tokyo: University of Tokyo Press; 1981:171–180.

Shipp T. Vertical laryngeal position during continuous and discrete vocal frequency change. *J Speech Hearing Res*. 1975;18:707–718.

Shipp T. Vertical laryngeal position in singers with jaw stabilized. In: Lawrence VL, ed. *Transcripts of the Seventh Symposium: Care of the Professional Voice, part I: The Scientific Papers*. New York: Voice Foundation; 1979:44–47.

Shipp T, McGlone RE. Laryngeal dynamics associated with voice frequency change. *J Speech Hearing Res*. 1971;14:761–768.

Shipp T, Morrissey P. Physiologic adjustments for frequency change in trained and untrained voices. *J Acoust Soc Am*. 1977;62:476–478.

Sundberg J, Askenfelt A. Larynx height and voice source: a relationship? In: Bless DM, Abbs JH, eds. *Vocal Fold Physiology: Contemporary Research and Clinical Issues*. San Diego, CA: College-Hill Press; 1983:307–316.

Tanaka S, Tanabe M. Experimental study on regulation of vocal pitch. *J Voice*. 1989;3:93–98.

Titze IR. Control of voice fundamental frequency. *Nat Assoc Teachers of Singing J*. 1988;November/December:6.

Titze IR. On the relation between subglottal pressure and fundamental frequency in phonation. *J Acoust Soc Am*. 1989;85:901–906.

Titze IR, Jiang J, Drucker DG. Preliminaries to the body-cover theory of pitch control. *J Voice*. 1987;1:314–319.

Tizte IR, Luschei ES, Hirano M. Role of the thyroarytenoid muscle in regulation of fundamental frequency. *J Voice*. 1989;3:213–224.

Registers

Allen EL, Hollien H. A laminagraphic study of pulse (vocal fry) register phonation. *Folia Phoniatrica*. 1973,25: 241–250.

Ametrano Jackson MC. The high male range. *Folia Phoniatrica*. 1987;39:18–25.

Colton RH. Spectral characteristics of the modal and falsetto registers. *Folia Phoniatrica*. 1972;24:337–344.

Colton RH. Vocal intensity in the modal and falsetto registers. *Folia Phoniatrica*. 1973;25:62–70

Gougerot L, Grémy F, Marstal N. Glottographie à large bande passante. Application à l'étude de la voix de fausset. *J Physiol*. 1960;52:823–832.

Hirano M, Hibi S, Sawada T. Falsetto, head, chest, and speech mode: an acoustic study with three tenors. *J Voice*. 1989;3:99–103.

Hollien H. On vocal registers. *J Phonet*. 1974;2:125–143.

Hollien H. Three major vocal registers: a proposal. In: Rigault A, Charbonneau R, eds. *Proceedings of the Seventh International Congress of Phonetic Sciences*. The Hague: Mouton, 1972;320–331.

Hollien H, Michel JF. Vocal fry as a phonational register. *J Speech Hearing Res*. 1968;11:600–604.

Hollien H, Brown WS Jr, Hollien K. Vocal fold length associated with modal, falsetto, and varying intensity phonations. *Folia Phoniatrica*. 1971;23:66–78.

Hollien H, Damsté H, Murry T. Vocal fold length during vocal fry phonation. *Folia Phoniatrica*. 1969;21:257–265.

Hollien H, Girard GT, Coleman RF. Vocal fold vibratory patterns of pulse register phonation. *Folia Phoniatrica*. 1977;29:200–205.

Hollien H, Moore P, Wendahl RW, Michel JF. On the nature of vocal fry. *J Speech Hearing Res*. 1966;9:245–247.

Kitzing P. Photo- and electroglottographic recording of the laryngeal vibratory pattern during different registers. *Folia Phoniatrica*. 1982;34:234–241.

McGlone RE. Air flow during vocal fry phonation. *J Speech Hearing Res*. 1967;10:299–304.

McGlone RE. Air flow in the upper register. *Folia Phoniatrica*. 1970;22:231–238.

McGlone RE, Brown WS Jr. Identification of the "shift" between vocal registers. *J Acoust Soc Am*. 1969;46:1033–1036.

McGlone RE, Shipp T. Some physiologic correlates of vocal-fry phonation. *J Speech Hearing Res*. 1971;14:769–775.

Murry T. Subglottal pressure and airflow measures during vocal fry phonation. *J Speech Hearing Res*. 1971;14: 544–551.

Murry T, Brown WS Jr. Subglottal air pressure during two types of vocal activity: vocal fry and modal phonation. *Folia Phoniatrica*. 1971;23:440–449.

Rohrs M, Pascher W, Ocker C. Untersuchungen über das Schwingungsverhalten der Stimmlippen in verschiedenen Registerbereichen mit unterschiedlichen stroboskopischen Techniken. *Folia Phoniatrica*. 1985;37: 113–118.

Roubeau C, Chevrie-Muller C, Arabia-Guidet C. Electroglottographic study of the changes of voice registers. *Folia Phoniatrica*. 1987;39:280–289.

Schutte HK, Seidner WW. Registerabhangige Differentzierung von Elektrogrammen. *Sprache-Stimme-Gehör*. 1988;12:59–62.

Titze IR. A framework for the study of vocal registers. *J Voice*. 1988;2:183–194.

Welch GF, Sergeant DC, MacCurtain F. Zeroradiographic-electrolaryngographic analysis of male vocal registers. *J Voice*. 1989;3:224–256.

Aerodynamics, Vocal Fold Movement, and Models

Baer T. Observation of vocal fold vibration: measurement of excised larynges. In: Stevens KN, Hirano M, eds. *Vocal Fold Physiology*. Tokyo: University of Tokyo Press; 1981: 119–132.

Baer T, Titze IR, Yoshioka H. Multiple simultaneous measures of vocal fold activity. In: Bless DM, Abbs JH, eds. *Vocal Fold Physiology: Contemporary Research and Clinical Issues*. San Diego, CA: College-Hill; 1983:227–237.

Biever DM, Bless DM. Vibratory characteristics of the vocal folds in young adult and geriatric women. *J Voice*. 1989; 3:120–131.

Brackett IP. The vibration of vocal folds at selected frequencies. *Annal Otol Rhinol Laryngol*. 1948;57:556–558.

Broad DJ. The new theories of vocal fold vibration. In: Lass NJ, ed. *Speech and language: Advances in Basic Research and Practice*. New York: Academic Press, 1979;2:203–257.

Cavagna GA, Camporesi EM. Glottal aerodynamics and phonation. In: Wyke B, ed. *Ventilatory and Phonatory Control Systems*. New York: Oxford University Press; 1974: 76–87.

Childers DG, Alsaka YA, Hicks DM, Moore GP. Vocal fold vibrations: an EGG model. In: Baer T, Sasaki C, Harris KS, eds. *Laryngeal Function in Phonation and Respiration*. Boston: Little, Brown; 1987:181–202.

Flanagan JL. Some properties of the glottal sound source. *J Speech Hearing Res*. 1958;1:99–116.

Gauffin J, Liljencrants J. Modelling the airflow in the glottis. *Ann Bull Res Inst Logoped Phoniatr*. 1988;22:39–50.

Hillman RE, Oesterle E, Feth LL. Characteristics of the glottal turbulent noise source. *J Acoust Soc Am*. 1983;74: 691–694.

Holmes, JN. The acoustic consequences of vocal-cord action. *Phonetica*. 1977;34:316–317.

Ishizaka K. Equivalent lumped-mass models of vocal fold vibration. In: Stevens, KN, Hirano M, eds. *Vocal Fold Physiology*. Tokyo: University of Tokyo Press; 1981:231–241.

Isogai Y Horiguchi S, Honda K, et al. A dynamic simulation model of vocal fold vibration. In: Fujimura O, ed. *Vocal Pphysiology: Voice Pproduction, Mechanisms and Functions*. New York: Raven Press; 1988:191–206.

Kitzing P, Sonesson B. A photoglottographical study of the female vocal folds during phonation. *Folia Phoniatrica*. 1974;26:138–149.

Kitzing P, Carlborg B, Löfqvist A. Aerodynamic and glottographic studies of the laryngeal vibratory cycle. *Folia Phoniatrica*. 1982;34:216–224.

Koike Y. Sub- and supraglottal pressure variation during phonation. In: Stevens KN, Hirano M, eds. *Vocal Fold Physiology*. Tokyo: University of Tokyo Press; 1981: 181–189.

Matsushita H. The vibratory mode of the vocal folds in the excised larynx. *Folia Phoniatrica*. 1975;27:7–18.

Monsen, RB, Engebretson AM. Study of variations in the male and female glottal wave. *J Acoust Soc Am*. 1977;62: 981–993.

Rothenberg M. Some relations between glottal air flow and vocal fold contact area. In: Ludlow CL, Hart MO, eds. *Proceedings of the Conference on the Assessment of Vocal Fold Pathology (ASHA Reports no. 11)*. Rockville, MD: American Speech-Language-Hearing Association; 1981:88–96.

Rothenberg M, Miller D, Molitor R. Aerodynamic investigation of sources of vibrato. *Folia Phoniatrica*. 1988;40: 244–260.

Saito S, Fukuda H, Kitahara S, Kokowa N. Stroboscopic observation of vocal fold vibration with fiberoptics. *Folia Phoniatrica*. 1978;30:241–244.

Schutte HK. Aerodynamics of phonation. *Acta Oto-rhino-laryngol Belg*. 1986; 40: 344–357.

Schutte HK, Miller DG. Transglottal pressures in professional singing. *Acta Oto-rhino laryngol Belg*. 1986;40: 395–404.

Sonesson B. On the anatomy and vibratory patterns of the human vocal folds. *Acta Otolaryngol*. 1960: suppl. 156: 44–67.

Stevens KN. Modes of vocal fold vibration based on a two-section model. In: Fujimura O, ed. *Vocal Physiology: Voice Production, Mechanisms and Functions*. New York: Raven Press; 1988:357–371.

Stevens KN. Physics of laryngeal behavior and larynx modes. *Phonetica*. 1977;34:264–379.

Stevens KN. Vibration modes in relation to model parameters. In: Stevens KN, Hirano M, eds. *Vocal Fold Pphysiology*. Tokyo: University of Tokyo Press; 1981:291–301.

Titze IR. Biomechanics and distributed-mass models of vocal fold vibration. In: Stevens KN, Hirano M, eds. *Vocal Fold Physiology*. Tokyo: University of Tokyo Press; 1981: 245–264.

Titze IR. The human vocal cords: a mathematical model. *Phonetica*. 1973;28:129–170.

Titze IR. On the mechanics of vocal fold vibration. *J Acoust Soc Am*. 1976;60:1366–1380.

Titze IR. Parameterization of the glottal area, glottal flow, and vocal fold contact area. *J Acoust Soc Am*. 1984;75: 570–580.

Titze IR. The physics of flow-induced oscillation of the vocal folds. I. Small-amplitude oscillations. *Record Res Center Res Rep*. 1985;April:1–49.

Titze IR, Talkin DT. A theoretical study of the effects of various laryngeal configurations on the acoustics of phonation. *J Acoust Soc Am*. 1979;66:60–74.

Neurology

Abo-el-Enein MA, Wyke B. Laryngeal myotatic reflexes. *Nature*. 1966;209:682–686.

Abo-el-Enein MA, Wyke B. Myotatic reflex systems in the intrinsic muscles of the larynx. *J Anat (Lond)*. 1966;100: 926–927.

Adzaku FK, Wyke B. Innervation of the subglottic mucosa of the lárynx and its significance. *Folia Phoniatrica*. 1979;31: 271–283.

Baer T. Reflex activation of laryngeal muscles by sudden induced subglottal pressure changes. *J Acoust Soc Am*. 1979;65:1271–1275.

Baken RJ. Neuromuscular spindles in the intrinsic muscles of a human larynx. *Folia Phoniatrica*. 1971;23:204–210.

Bowden REM. Innervation of intrinsic laryngeal muscles. In: Wyke B, ed. *Ventilatory and Phonatory Control Systems*. New York: Oxford University Press; 1974:370–381.

Kurozumi S, Tashiro T, Harada Y. Laryngeal responses to electrical stimulation of the medullary respiratory centers in the dog. *Laryngoscope*. 1971;81:1960–1967.

Larson CR. Brain mechanisms involved in the control of vocalization. *J Voice*. 1988;2:301–311.

Larson CR. The midbrain periaqueductal gray: a brainstem structure involved in vocalization. *J Speech Hearing Res*. 1985;28:241–249.

Larson CR, Kempster GB, Kistler MK. Changes in voice fundamental frequency following discharge of single motor units in cricothyroid and thyroarytenoid muscles. *J Speech Hearing Res*. 1987;30:552–558.

Larson CR, Wilson KE, Luschei ES. Preliminary observations on cortical and brainstem mechanisms of laryngeal control. In: Bless DM, Abbs JH, eds. *Vocal Fold Physiology:*

Contemporary Research and Clinical Issues. San Diego, CA: College-Hill Press; 1983:82–95.

Mallard AR, Ringel RL, Horii Y. Sensory contributions to control of fundamental frequency of phonation. *Folia Phoniatrica*. 1978;30:199–213.

Màrtensson A. Proprioceptive impulse patterns during contraction of intrinsic laryngeal muscles. *Acta Physiol Scand*. 1964;62:176–194.

Ortega JD, DeRosier E, Park S, Larson CR. Brainstem mechanisms of laryngeal control as revealed by microstimulation studies. In: Fujimura O, ed. *Vocal Physiology: Voice Production, Mechanisms and Functions*. New York: Raven Press; 1988:19–28.

Miscellaneous

Abitbol J, de Brux J, Millot G et al. Does a hormonal vocal cord cycle exist in women? Study of vocal premenstrual syndrome in voice performers by videostroboscopy-glottography and cytology on 38 women. *J Voice*. 1989;3:157–162.

Dmitriev LB, Chernov BP, Maslov VT. Functioning of the voice mechanism in double-voice Touvinian singing. *Folia Phoniatrica*. 1983;35:193–197.

Gossett CW Jr. Electromyographic investigation of the relationship of the effects of selected parameters on concurrent study of voice and oboe. *J Voice*. 1989;3:52–64.

Hamlet SL, Palmer JM. Investigation of laryngeal trills using the transmission of ultrasound through the larynx. *Folia Phoniatrica*. 1974;26:362–377.

Hicks DM, Childers DG, Moore GP, Alsaka J. EGG and the singers' voice. In: Lawrence VL, ed. *Transcripts of the Fourteenth Symposium: Care of the Professional Voice*. New York: The Voice Foundation; 1986:50–56c.

King AI, Ashby J, Nelson C. Laryngeal function in wind instruments: the brass. *J Voice*. 1989;3:65–67.

Murry T, Caligiuri MP. Phonatory and nonphonatory motor control in singers. *J Voice*. 1989;3:257–263.

Proctor DF. The physiologic basis of voice training. In: Bouhuys A, ed. *Sound Production in Man (Annals of the New York Academy of Sciences*; vol. 155). New York: New York Academy of Sciences; 1968:208–228.

Rosenberg AE. Effect of glottal pulse shape on the quality of natural vowels. *J Acoust Soc Am*. 1971;49:583–588.

Rubin J, Sataloff RT, Korovin G and Gould WJ: *The Diagnosis and Treatment of Voice Disorders*. New York, New York: Igaku-Shoin Medical Publishers, Inc; 1995.

Schutte HK. Efficiency of professional singing voices in terms of energy ratio. *Folia Phoniatrica*. 1984;36:267–272.

Silverman E-M, Zimmer CH. Effect of the menstrual cycle on voice quality. *Arch Otolaryngol*. 1978;104:7–10.

Sundberg J. The source spectrum in professional singing. *Folia Phoniatrica*. 1973;25:71–90.

Sundberg J. *The science of the singing voice*. Dekalb, Ill. Northern Illinois University Press; 1987.

Van Michel C. La courbe glottographique chez les sujects non entrainés au chant. *Comptes Rendus de la Société de Biologie*. 1968;1:583–585.

Vocal Tract Resonance

Johan Sundberg

The human voice organ consists of three parts,[1] as schematically illustrated in Fig 4–1. One part is the breathing apparatus, which acts as a compressor. It compresses the air contained in the lungs. The second is the vocal folds, which act as a proper sound generator. They chop the airstream from the lungs into a sequence of air pulses, which is actually a sound. Its sound is a buzz tone and contains a complete set of harmonic partials. The third part is the cavity system—the pharynx and mouth cavity, or the vocal tract. It acts as a resonator, or a filter, which shapes the sound generated by the vocal folds. In producing nasal sounds, the velum is lowered, supplementing the vocal tract resonator by the nasal cavity, called the nasal tract. Of the three parts—the breathing apparatus, the vocal folds, and the vocal tract—it is only the latter two that directly contribute to forming the voice timbre. In other words, the acoustic characteristics of the voice are determined by two factors, (a) the voice source (ie, the functioning of the vocal folds) and (b) the vocal tract. In this chapter, discussion focuses on the role of the vocal tract resonator.

The voice source passes through the vocal tract resonator, which thus shapes it acoustically. The nature of this shaping depends on the vocal tract configuration. As in phonetics and other voice sciences, the term *articulation* will be used to describe the change in the shape of the vocal tract. Also, the structures that we use in order to arrange the shape of the vocal tract in different ways will be called *articulators*. For example, the tongue is an articulator.

The vocal tract is a *resonator*. What, then, is a resonator? Actually, almost anything is a resonator: every system that can be compressed and has weight. The air column in the vocal tract is one of many examples.

Sound within a resonator decays slowly. If one hits a resonator, it will resound for a little while rather than

having the sound disappear immediately. This phenomenon of resounding is called *resonance*. In the vocal tract, the decay is rapid, but still it is possible to hear how a sound in the vocal tract decays. If one flicks one's neck above the larynx with a finger with closed glottis and open mouth, one can hear a quickly decaying tone; it sounds as when one hits an empty bottle or tin, which, incidentally, are other examples of resonators.

Another aspect of resonance is that a resonator applies very different conditions for sounds that try to pass through it. The frequency of the candidate sound makes all the difference. This is illustrated schematically in Fig 4–2. Sounds having certain frequencies pass through the resonator very easily, so that they are radiated with a high amplitude from the resonator. These preferred frequencies fit the resonator optimally, so to speak, and they are called resonance frequencies. It is tones with these resonance frequencies that resound in a struck resonator. In the case of the vocal tract resonator, however, the resonances are called *formants* and the resonance frequencies are called *formant frequencies*. Tones with frequencies in between these formant frequencies are attenuated more or less when they are transmitted through the resonator. They are not preserved when the resonator is struck.

These formants are of paramount importance to the voice sounds. They totally determine vowel quality, and they give major contributions to the personal voice timbre. In the vocal tract, there are four or five formants of interest. The two lowest formants determine most of the vowel color, while the third, fourth, and fifth are of greater significance to personal voice timbre.

We are very skilled in tuning our formant frequencies. We do this by changing the shape of the vocal tract (ie, by moving our articulators). In this way, the vocal tract may assume a great variety of shapes. The mandible is one articulator since it may be raised or

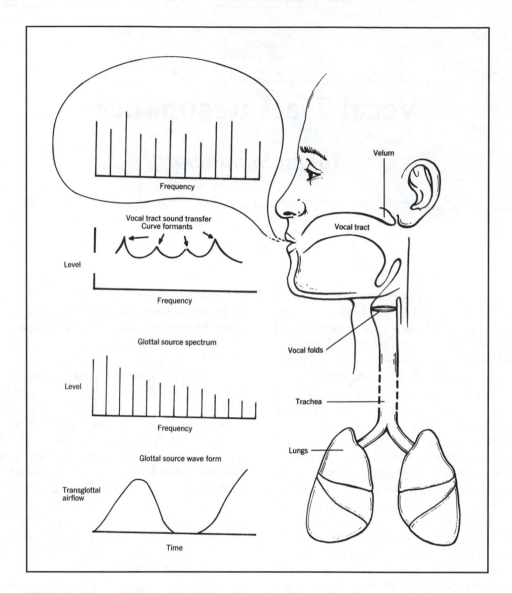

Fig 4–1. Schematic illustration of the voice organ. Generation of vocal sound.

lowered, thereby widening and narrowing the pharynx and narrowing and widening the mouth cavity. The tongue is another articulator because it may constrict the vocal tract at almost any position from the hard palate to the deep pharynx. The lip opening is a third articulator because it may be widened or narrowed, the larynx can be raised or lowered. The latter two variations also affect vocal tract length. Finally, the side walls of the pharynx can be moved, and by lowering the velum, the nasal tract can be included in the resonator system.

The length of the vocal tract affects all formant frequencies. Adult males have a tube length of about 17 to 20 cm. Assuming a cylindrical vocal tract shape of length of 17.5 cm, the formant frequencies occur at the odd multiples of 500 Hz: 500, 1500, 2500 . . . Hz.

Because of sex differences in vocal tract length, a similar articulatory configuration gives formant frequencies that are about 40% higher in children than in adult males. As adult females have shorter vocal tracts than adult males, their formant frequencies are on the average 15% higher than those of adult males.

The most common way of tuning formant frequencies is by adjusting the vocal tract shape. A reduction of the lip opening and a lengthening of the vocal tract by a lowering of the larynx or by protruding the lips lowers all formant frequencies. Similarly, constricting the vocal tract in the glottal region leads to an increase of the formant frequencies.

Some articulators are particularly efficient in tuning certain formant frequencies. The mandible, which expands the vocal tract in the lip region and constricts

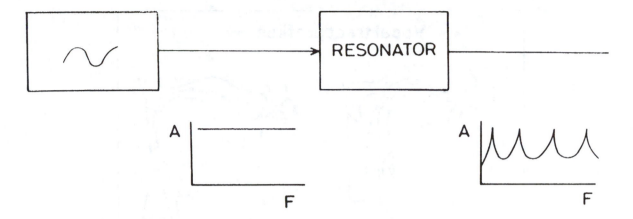

Fig 4–2. Schematic illustration of the phenomenon of resonance. If a sine wave of constant amplitude (A) sweeps from low to high frequency (F), the frequency-dependent sound transfer ability of the resonator imposes great variations in the amplitude. The amplitude culminates at the resonance frequencies.

it in the laryngeal region, raises the frequency of the first formant. In vowels produced by male adults, the first formant varies between approximately 200 and 800 Hz.

The second formant is particularly sensitive to the tongue shape. The second formant frequency in male adults varies within a range of approximately 500 and 2500 Hz.

The third formant is especially sensitive to the position of the tip of the tongue or, when the tongue is retracted, to the size of the cavity between the lower incisors and the tongue. In vowels produced by male adults, the third formant varies between approximately 1600 and 3500 Hz.

The relationships between the vocal tract shape and the fourth and fifth formants are more complicated and diffficult to control by particular articulatory means. However, they seem to be very dependent on vocal tract length and also on the configuration in the deep pharynx. In vowels produced by adult males, the fourth formant frequency is generally in the vicinity of 2500 to 4000 Hz, and the fifth, 3000 to 4500 Hz.

It is evident that the formant frequencies must have a great effect on the spectrum, as the vocal tract resonator filters the voice source (see Fig 4–1). The spectrum envelope of the voice source is smooth and slopes off at an average rate of approximately 12 dB per octave, if measured in airflow units. The spectrum of a radiated vowel, however, is characterized by peaks and valleys, because the partials lying closest to a formant frequency get stronger than adjacent partials in the spectrum. In this way, the vocal tract resonances form the vowel spectrum, hence the term formants. Recalling that formants are vocal tract resonances, we realize that it is by means of vocal tract resonance that we form vowels.

Various vowels correspond to different articulatory configurations attained by varying the positions of the articulators as illustrated in Fig 4–3. In the vowel /i:/ (as in heed), the tongue bulges so that it constricts the buccal part of the vocal tract. As a consequence of this, the first formant is low, while the second formant is high. In the vowel /u:/ (as in the word true), the first and second formant frequencies are both low, and in the vowel /a:/ (as in the Italian word *caro*), the first formant is high, and the second takes an intermediate position.

Fig 4–4 shows typical formant frequencies for various spoken vowels as produced by male adults. The "islands" in the figure imply that the vowel marked will result, provided the frequencies of the first and second formants remain within that island. For example, if the first and second formants are between 350 and 500 Hz, and 500 and 800 Hz, respectively, the vowel will be an /o:/. Note that the vowels are scattered along a triangular contour, the three corners of which are the vowels /i:/, /ʌ:/, and /u:/. The vowel /oe:/ (as in heard) is located in the center of the triangle.

Thus, the formant frequencies determine the vowel quality. Still, different individuals tune their formant frequencies a bit differently for the same vowel. For instance, it would be completely impossible for small children to bring their formant frequencies down to the values typically used by adult males; children's vocal tracts are simply not long enough. This is the reason the vowels are represented by islands rather than dots in the figure. The exact position of the two lowest formant frequencies for a given vowel depends on the individual morphology of the speaker's vocal tract, among other things, and also on the habits of pronunciation.

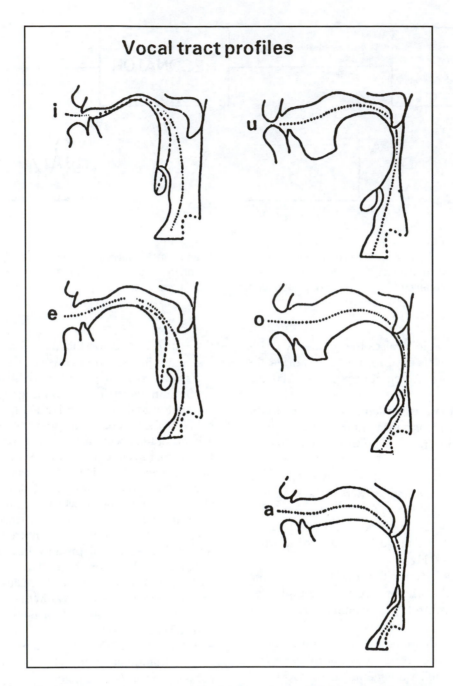

Fig 4–3. Tracings of X-ray profiles of the vocal tract showing articulatory configurations for some vowels (from Fant[5]).

Formant Frequencies in Singing

"Singer's Formant"

With regard to the loudest possible tone, it is remarkable that no clear difference was found between male singers and nonsingers when measured under identical conditions. This can be seen in Fig 4–5, which shows average maximum and minimum sound levels as functions of pitch frequency for professional male singers and nonsingers. Thus, the singers do not sing more loudly than nonsingers. Why, then, can we hear a singer so clearly even when he is accompanied by a loud orchestra?

The answer can be found in the spectral characteristics, which differ considerably between male singers and nonsingers. Moreover, vowels spoken and sung by male singers typically differ with regard to the

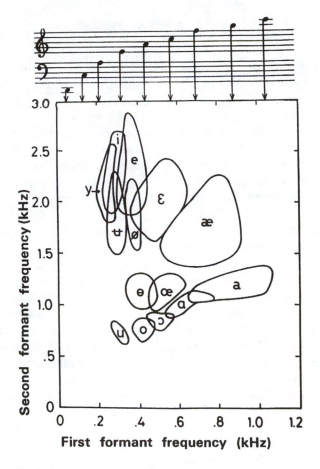

Fig 4–4. Typical values for the two lowest formant frequencies for various spoken vowels as produced by male adults. The first formant frequency is given in musical notation at the top.

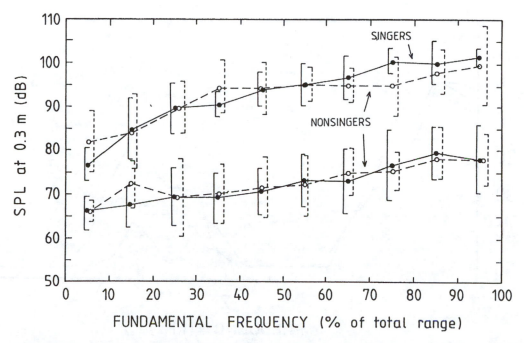

Fig 4–5. Average maximum and minimum sound pressure level (SPL) at 0.3 m distance in anechoic room as produced by 10 professional singers and 10 nonsingers. The bars represent ±1 standard deviation (from Gramming et al[6]).

spectrum charateristics. Fig 4–6 illustrates the most apparent difference, called the *singer's formant*. This is a prominent spectrum envelope peak appearing in the vicinity of 3 kHz in all vowel spectra sung by male singers and also by altos. It belongs to the typical features of sung vowels.

The level of this peak varies depending on the voice classification. It is somewhat lower for a bass and higher for a tenor. Sopranos, on the other hand, have a clearly lower spectrum level of this peak than the other categories. It appears that, in the case of the soprano, this peak is nothing but a perfectly normal third and fourth formant.

Regardless of voice category, the level of the singer's formant also varies with loudness of phonation, as illustrated in Fig 4–7. In the case shown in the figure, a sound pressure level (SPL) increase of 10 dB is accompanied by an increase of about 17 dB in the singer's formant. This effect derives from the voice source, the sound generated by the vocal fold vibrations.

The center frequency of the singer's formant varies, depending on the voice category. In bass singers, it is often found around 2.4 kHz; in baritones, near 2.6; in tenors, nearly 2.8; and in altos, near 3.0 kHz, but there are great individual variations. These frequency differences seem to contribute significantly to the timbre differences among these voice categories.

The presence of the singer's formant in the spectrum of a vowel sound is an advantage in that it helps the singer's voice to be heard through a orchestral accompaniment. In the spectrum of the sound from a symphony orchestra, the partials near 500 Hz tend to be loudest, and above this frequency region, the levels of the spectrum components decrease with rising frequency. This is illustrated by the long-term-average spectrum of orchestral music shown in Fig 4–8 where the slope above 500 Hz is about 9 dB/octave. Incidentally, normal speech appears to yield similar long-term-average spectrum characteristics. The perceptual point with a singer's formant is, then, to raise the spectrum envelope in a frequency range where the sound of the accompaniment offers only a moderate acoustic competition, so to speak.

How do singers generate this spectrum peak in all voiced sounds? The answer is "By resonance!" If it is assumed that the third, fourth, and fifth formants are close in frequency, thus forming a formant cluster, the singer's formant peak can be explained as an articulatory phenomenon that can be produced with a normal voice source. In Fig 4–9, formant frequency measurements compatible with this assumption for vowels sung by professional singers are compared with those typical for normal speech. As can be seen, the fifth formant in the sung vowels is lower than the fourth for-

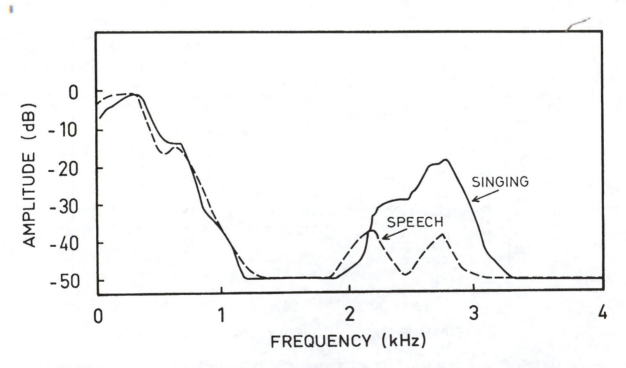

Fig 4–6. Illustration of the singer's formant, a prominent peak in the spectrum envelope appearing in the vicinity of 3 kHz in all vowel spectra sung by male singers and also by altos.

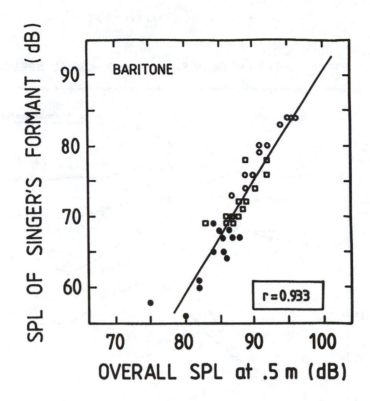

Fig 4–7. Level of the singer's formant as a function of loudness of phonation in a male singer (from Cleveland and Sundberg[7]).

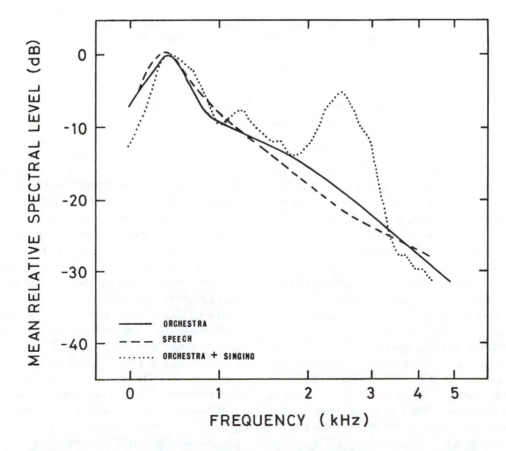

Fig 4–8. Long-term-average spectrum of normal speech and of orchestral music with and without a solo singer's voice.

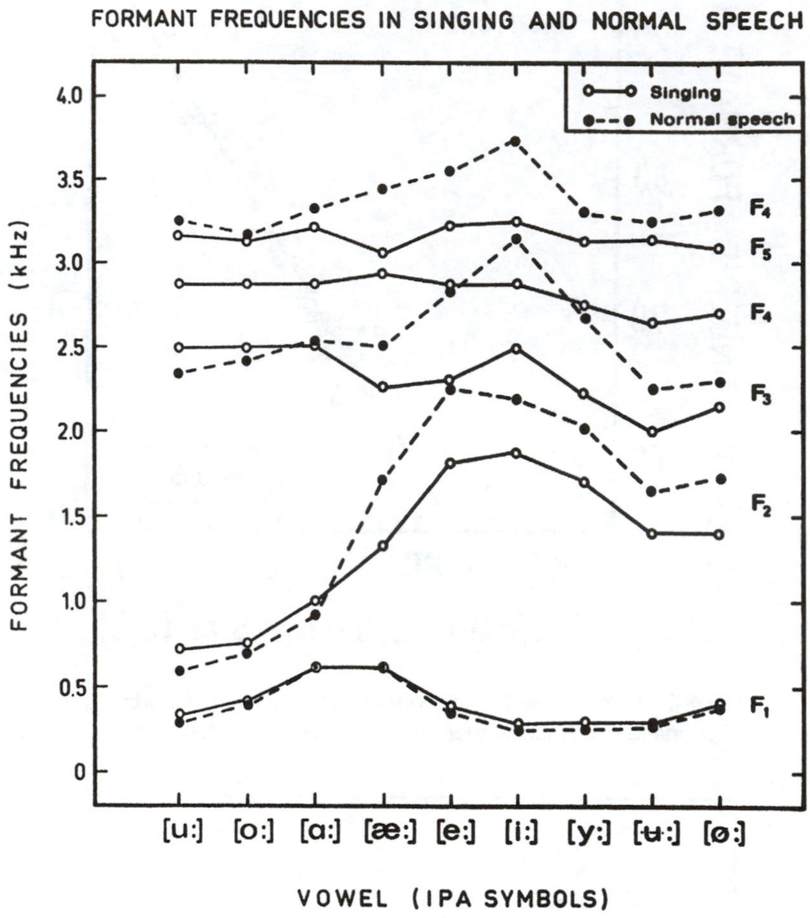

FORMANT FREQUENCIES IN SINGING AND NORMAL SPEECH

Fig 4–9. Average formant frequencies for Swedish vowels spoken normally and sung by professional male singers.

mant in the spoken vowels. Thus, five formants appear in the same frequency range as four formants in the spoken vowels. In the vicinity of the singer's formant, the density of formants is high in the sung vowels.

The acoustic consequence of clustering formants is that the spectrum partials in the frequency range of the cluster are enhanced in the radiated spectrum, as is illustrated in Fig 4–10. In other words, the singer's formant is compatible with the normal concept of voice production, provided a clustering of the higher formants is possible.

Experiments with acoustic models of the vocal tract showed that such a ring of formants can be attained if the pharynx is wide as compared with the entrance to the larynx tube. It seems that, in many singers, this is obtained by a lowering of the larynx. In this case, the larynx tube acts as a separate resonator with a resonance which can appear in the vicinity of 2.8 kHz.[2]

There also may be other, as yet unknown, ways of generating a singer's formant. A Chinese researcher,

S. Wang, found that, in Chinese singing and in the type of singing developed for medieval music, a singer's formant was produced without a lowering of the larynx. He hypothesized that the peak was produced by an acoustic interaction between the voice source and the tract resonator. However, as the criteria for the presence of a singer's formant in a voice are unclear, it is hard to decide if these types of voices possess a singer's formant or not.

The particular arrangements of the vocal tract that generate vowels with a singer's formant have certain consequences for the vowel quality, too. This is illustrated in Fig 4–9. We can see that the second and third formants of /i:/ are low, in fact, almost as low as in the German vowel /y:/. This is in accordance with the common observation that vowels are "colored" in singing. This coloring can be seen as a price the singer pays in order to buy his singer's formant.

Summarizing, we see that resonance is of a decisive relevance to singing, as it creates major characteristics

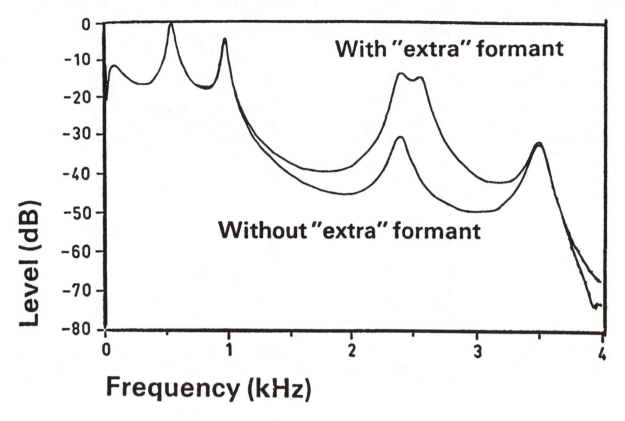

Fig 4–10. The effect of clustering of formants on the (idealized) spectrum envelope.

of the singing voice in the case of males and altos. It should be observed, however, that all of this resonance takes place in the vocal tract. It has not been possible to demonstrate any acoustic significance at all from the vibration sensations in the skull and face that one feels during singing. It seems that they are important to the control of articulation and phonation. In any event, they do not contribute directly to the filtering of the sound to any significant extent.

Super Pitch Singing

We just reviewed typical formant (or resonance) frequency differences between speech and singing in male singers and in altos. However, the formant frequency differences between spoken and sung vowels are much greater in the super pitch part of female singers. The reason for this seems to be the exceedingly high fundamental frequencies that occur in female singing. While a bass singer is not required to go higher than 330 Hz fundamental frequency (pitch E_4), the maximum for a high soprano may amount to no less than 1500 Hz (pitch F_6).

Let us now recall Fig 4–4, which showed the formant frequencies for various vowels. The scale for the first formant frequency was given in the usual frequency unit Hz, but also, at the top of the graph, in musical pitch symbols. From this, we can see that the super pitches in female singing are very high indeed, as compared with the normal frequency values of the first formant in most vowels. The first formant of /i:/ and /u:/ is about 250 Hz, and the highest value for the first formant in a vowel occurs at 900 Hz for the vowel /a:/.

It is difficult to determine formant frequencies accurately when the fundamental frequency is high. The spectrum partials of voiced sounds are equidistantly spaced along the frequency axis, as shown in Fig 4–11, since they form a harmonic series. This implies that the partials are densely spaced along the frequency axis only when fundamental frequency is low. In that case, the formants can easily be identified as spectrum envelope peaks. In the opposite case, such peaks are often impossible to discern, particularly if there is no partial near the formant frequency. It is certainly for this reason male voices have been analyzed much more often than female voices, although attempts have also been made to determine the formant frequencies in female singers.

Using various experimental techniques, efforts have been made to estimate formant frequencies in female singers. One method was to use external excitation of the vocal tract by means of a vibrator while

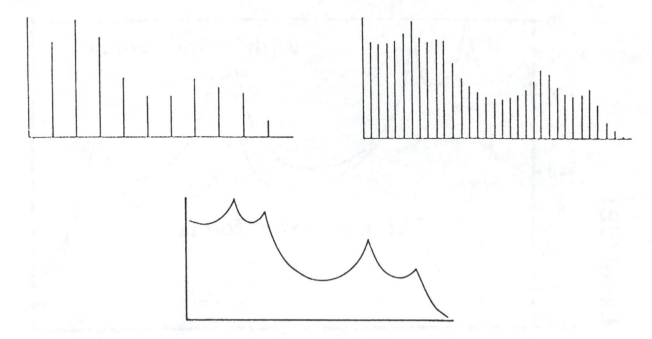

Fig 4–11. Illustration of the differing difficulty of determining formant frequencies in spectra with a high (**left**) and a low (**right**) fundamental frequency. Both spectra were generated using the same formant frequencies represented by the idealized spectrum envelope (**below**).

the professional soprano silently articulated a vowel. Another method was to take an x-ray picture of the vocal tract in profile while the singer sang different vowels at different pitches. For obvious reasons, the number of subjects in these studies had to be kept low, only one or two. Still, the results were encouraging in that they agreed surprisingly well. This supports the assumption that they are typical.

Some formant frequency values for soprano singers are shown in Fig 4–12. These results can be idealized in terms of lines, also shown in Fig 4–12, relating the first, second, third, and fourth formant frequencies to the fundamental frequency and to the formant frequencies in speech. The main principle seems to be as follows: As long as fundamental frequency is lower than the normal value of the vowel's first formant frequency, this formant frequency is used. At higher pitches, the first formant is raised with increasing fundamental frequency. In this way, the situation in which the frequency of the fundamental exceeds that of the first formant is avoided. With rising fundamental frequency, the second formant of front vowels is lowered, while that of back vowels is raised to a frequency just above the second spectrum partial; the third formant is lowered and the fourth is raised.

What articulatory means do the singers use to achieve these great pitch-dependent rearrangements of the formant frequencies? An articulatory tool that many female singers seem to recruit frequently for the purpose of tuning the first formant is the jaw opening. Formal measurements on some professional female singers' jaw openings have shown that, under controlled experimental conditions, it is systematically increased with rising fundamental frequency. This rule is illustrated in Fig 4–13, which shows the jaw opening of a professional soprano as a function of fundamental frequency. Within the pitch range covered by Fig 4–13, all vowels are produced with a jaw opening that increases with fundamental frequency. Even at the lowest fundamental frequency, the jaw openings are wider than those used for the spoken versions. This system applies to all vowels except /a:/, which is sung with a similar jaw opening throughout this range. However, the first formant frequency of this vowel is higher than the highest fundamental frequency used in this experiment.

Jaw opening is an excellent tool for the purpose of raising the first formant frequency, as mentioned. Other articulators can be recruited for the same purpose. One is the lip opening. By contracting the mouth corners, the vocal tract is shortened, so the frequencies of all formants will increase. The vocal tract can also be shortened by raising the larynx. At least some professional female singers take advantage of this tool for raising the first formant frequency. Fig 4–14 gives an example. It is interesting that most singing teachers regard such a pitch-dependent adaptation of larynx height as a mistake from a singing technique point of

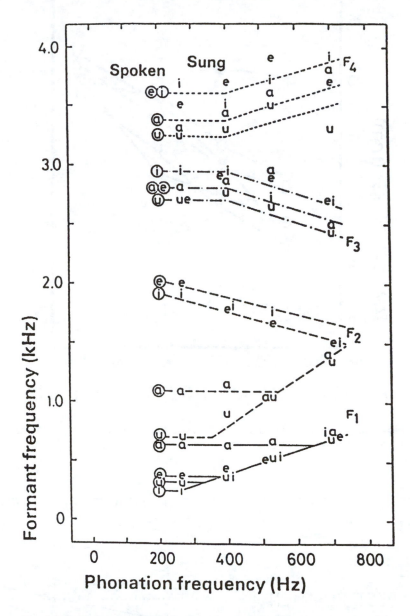

Fig 4–12. The vowel symbols show formant frequency estimates of the first, second, third, and fourth formant frequencies for various vowels as sung by a professional soprano. The *circled* vowel symbols represent the corresponding data measured when the vowels were pronounced by the same subject in a speech mode. The lines represent an idealization of how the formant frequencies changed with fundamental frequency.

view. Perhaps these teachers do not mean larynx elevation in general, but rather an elevation that is associated with an audible shift in the mode of phonation and vowel quality; in normal speech, a raised larynx is generally associated with a pressed type of phonation, screaming representing the extreme.

All of the pitch-dependent formant frequency changes illustrated in Fig 4–12 are not consequences merely of changes in jaw opening and larynx height. As shown in Fig 4–15, there are also considerable

changes in tongue shape. It appears that tongue shape changes rather abruptly with pitch. In the subject examined, the vowels /ɑ:/, /i:/, and /u:/ were all produced with very similar tongue shapes only at the fundamental frequency of 960 Hz (pitch B♭5). It is possible that the tongue shape differentiation is influenced by preceding and following consonants at these pitches. Still, with these wide jaw openings, a small difference in tongue shape is not likely to affect the formant frequencies to any great extent.

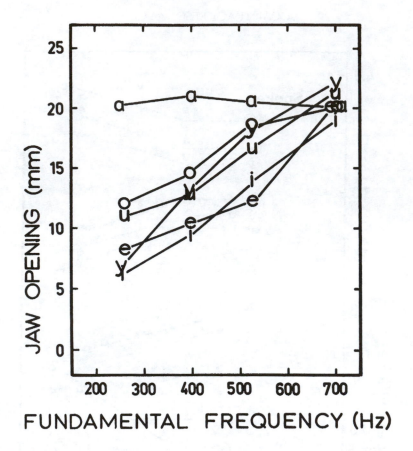

Fig 4–13. Jaw opening of a professional soprano singing the vowels indicated at various fundamental frequencies.

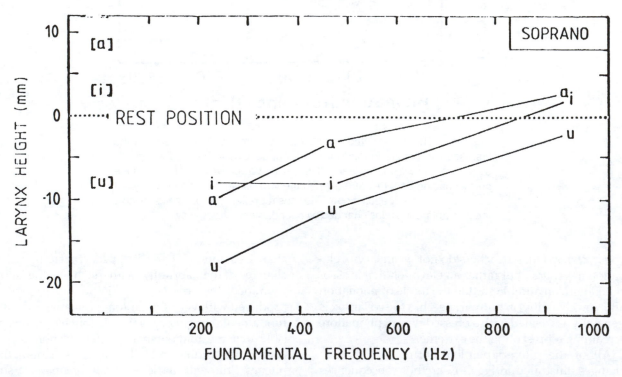

Fig 4–14. Vertical larynx position as determined from X-ray profiles of the vocal tract of a professional soprano singing the indicated vowels at various fundamental frequencies. Bracketed symbols refer to vowels spoken by the same subject.

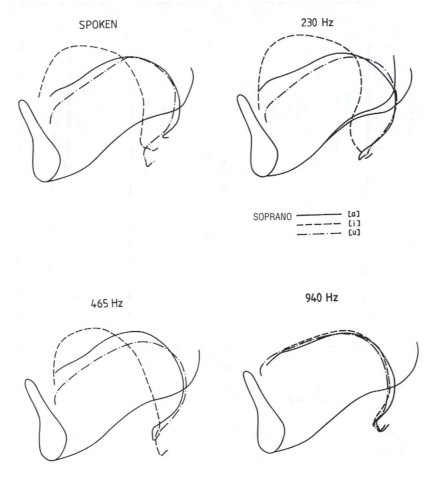

SPOKEN

230 Hz

SOPRANO ———— [ɑ]
------- [i]
—·—·— [u]

465 Hz

940 Hz

Fig 4–15. Midsagittal tongue contours as determined from X-ray profiles of the vocal tract of a professional soprano singing the indicated vowels at various fundamental frequencies shown (from Sundberg[2]).

This principle of tuning formant frequencies depending on the fundamental frequency has been found to be applied by soprano and tenor singers only. It probably is used also by other singers; all singers, except possibly basses, can encounter a situation where the first formant is lower in frequency than the fundamental prescribed by the composer. As the first formant frequency varies between vowels, the case depends on the vowel. In the highest range of baritone, the vowels /i:/, /y:/, and /u:/ would need pitch-dependent first formant frequencies. In the top part of an alto's range, all vowels except /a:/ and /æ:/ need modification of the first formant frequency. In such cases, it is likely that the other formant frequencies are modified in similar ways as in the case of sopranos.

The benefit of these arrangements of the formant frequencies is great. They imply that the sound level of the vowels increases enormously in some cases. Fig 4–16 shows the gain in sound level attained by means

of the pitch-dependent choice of formant frequencies that was shown in Fig 4–12. The gain is seen to amount to no less than 30 dB in some cases. This is a truly huge increase in sound level that the singer gains by sheer resonance.

Choral Singing

An often discussed question is to what extent choral singing requires the same vocal technique as solo singing. Choir directors tend to maintain that there are no important differences, while many singing teachers see huge differences.

As the singer's formant apparently serves the purpose of helping the individual singer's voice to be heard through a loud orchestral accompaniment, it can be hypothesized that the singer's formant is not indicated in choral singing. This hypothesis was supported by experiments in which male singers, experi-

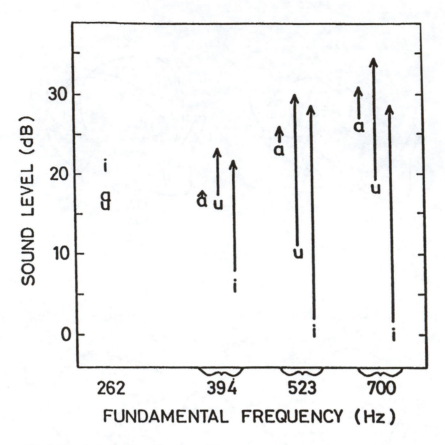

Fig 4–16. Gain in sound level at different fundamental frequencies resulting from the pitch-dependent choice of formant frequencies that were represented by the lines in Fig 4–11.

enced in both choral and soloistic performance, were asked to sing in a choral and in a soloistic framework.[3] For solo singing, they heard through earphones the piano accompaniment of a solo song that they were to sing. Similarly, for choir singing, they heard the sound of a choir they were asked to join. As shown in Fig 4–17A, the subjects had a singer's formant that was more prominent in solo than in choir singing, while the lowest spectrum partials, below the first formant, were weaker in solo singing. The higher level of the singer's formant in soloistic singing was associated with a denser clustering of the third, fourth, and fifth formant frequencies. The subjects, unlike average choral singers, were also excellent solo singers. It can be assumed that the differences between soloistic and choral singing are mostly greater than was revealed by this experiment.

The corresponding experiment was also performed with soprano subjects.[4] Disregarding the fact that it seems inadequate to speak of a singer's formant in soprano singing, the result was similar, as can be seen in Fig 4–17B; the mean spectrum level at 2 to 3 kHz was clearly higher when the singers sang in a solo mode.

This suggests that soprano singers also profit from high levels of the higher spectrum partials. This assumption was further supported by the fact that two opera sopranos of world fame were found to sing with a clearly higher level of the partials in the 2 to 4 kHz band than the singers who worked both as choral and solo singers (Fig 4–17C). These measurements seem to indicate that solo and choral singing differ slightly with respect to the vocal technique.

Overtone Singing

In some music cultures, a very special type of singing is practiced where voice pitch remains constant, as in a drone, while the musical interest is caught by the sounding of high overtones. Fig 4–18 shows an example of a vowel spectrum produced in this type of singing. The pitch perceived in these cases corresponded to the sixth and seventh partial, or a tone two octaves plus a fifth or a seventh above the fundamental. In view of the spectrum, this is not an unexpected finding. These partials are quite outstanding in the spectrum.

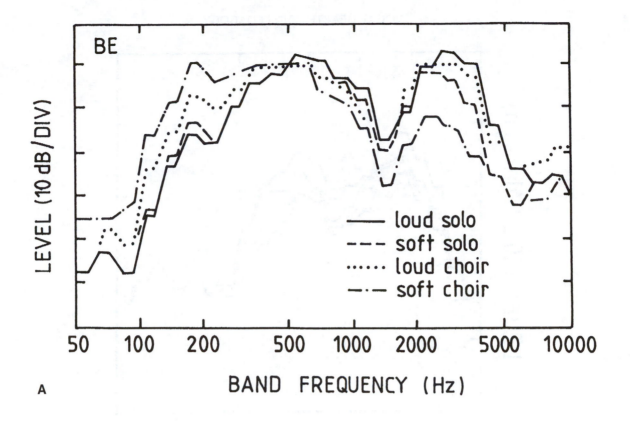

A

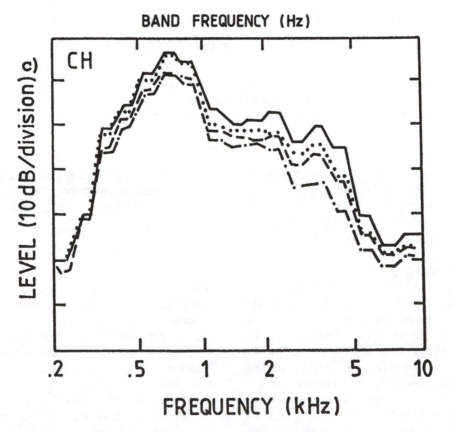

B

Fig 4–17. Long-term-average spectra of male (**A**) and female (**B**) singers singing as soloists as members of a choir. In **A** and **B** solid, dashed, dotted, and chain-dashed lines pertain to loud and soft solo, and loud and soft choral singing, respectively. (*continued*)

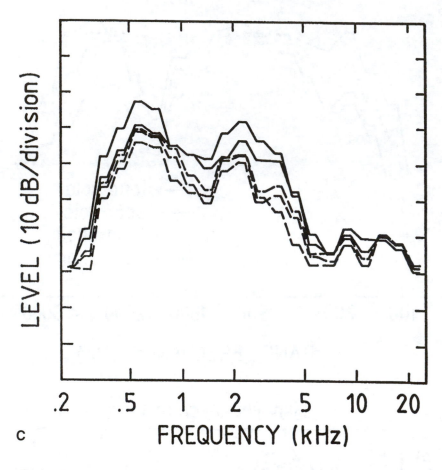

Fig 4–17. *(continued)* In **C**, the *solid curves* represent the spectra of two opera sopranos of international fame, and the *dashed curves* pertain to sopranos who sang professionally both as soloists and as choral singers.

The vocal technique behind such spectra seems based on formant tuning. The singers tune the second and third formants so that both are quite close to the partial to be enhanced. The other formants are carefully tuned to avoid enhancing any of the other partials. As a result, one single partial becomes much stronger than the others, so that its pitch stands out of the timbral percept. The articulatory tools used seem to be tongue shape and lip opening in the first place. The tongue tip is often raised, while the tongue body is pulled anteriorly or posteriorly. In addition, the voice source characteristics seem to be adjusted so that the fundamental is suppressed, presumably by shifting the type of phonation toward pressed phonation.

A more modest form of overtone singing is rather simple to practice and learn. The point is to keep the fundamental constant at a rather high frequency, say, 300 Hz, and then to vary articulation while changing the tongue shape and lip opening rhythmically in several steps between the /u:/ and the /i:/ positions. If the rhythmical pattern is repeated, the ear will soon catch individual overtones. Then, it is rather easy to moderate articulation to enhance the effect.

Head Resonance

We have discussed several examples of the enormous significance of resonance in singing. The only type of resonance dealt with has been the formants, the resonances of the vocal tract. No mention has been made of face or skull resonances. There is no doubt, however, that the voice sets up forceful vibrations in the structures limiting the voice organ, such as the chest wall, the throat, the face, and the skull. However, these vibrations are much too feeble to compete with the sound radiation from the open mouth. In other words, such vibrations do not contribute acoustically to the formation of vowel sounds. This is not to say that they cannot be used as a sign of a properly used voice organ.

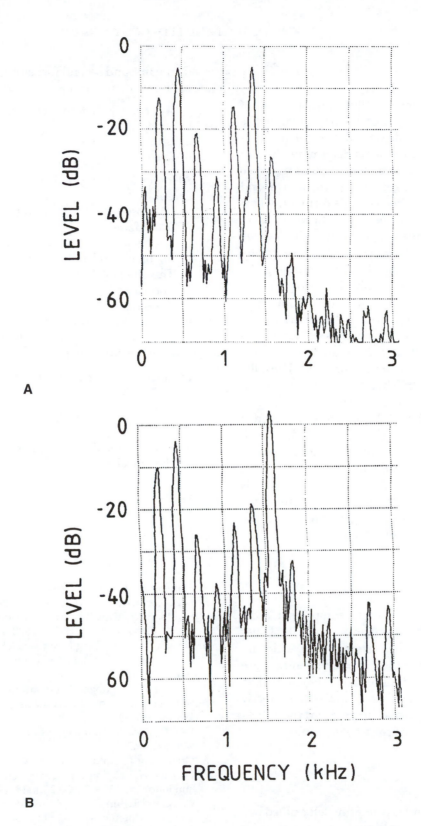

Fig 4–18. Vowel spectrum produced in two cases of overtone singing performed by one of the members of The Harmonic Choir. In **A**, the sixth harmonic partial was perceived as an extra tone in the spectrum, two octaves plus a fifth above the fundamental. In **B**, the seventh harmonic partial was perceived as an extra tone, two octaves plus a seventh above the fundamental.

Conclusions

The vocal tract resonances, called formants, are of paramount signifiance to voice and vowel quality. The two lowest formants decide what the vowel quality is going to be. The higher formants determine much of the personal voice characteristics, including voice classifcation. In male singers, the third, fourth, and fifth formants constitute the singer's formant, which helps the singer's voice to be heard through a loud accompaniment. In female high-pitched singing, the two first formants are tuned so that they optimally match the pitch frequency, thereby increasing the loudness of the voice considerably. It is also possible to play small articulatory games with formants and have them "show" individual partials to the listener.

However, the great relevance of vocal tract resonance to singing should not conceal the fact that there are other factors of major importance, too. Thus, the voice source, reflecting the chopped airstream through the vibrating glottis, is as decisive to voice quality as are the formants. On the one hand, the resulting great variability, of course, complicates the work of both singers and singing teachers. There are a great number of control parameters that the singer needs to bring under proper control. On the other hand, the rewards are great. The abundant timbre variability that may result certainly provides the singer with one of the potentially best musical instruments.

Summary

The human voice organ includes a compressor, oscillator, and resonator. The resonator acoustically shapes the voice source signal. The preferred frequencies are called the formant frequencies. Formants contribute to many things including timbre, vowel intelligibility, and audibility. The singer's formant is particularly important in allowing a voice to be heard over background noise, such as musical accompaniment.

Review Questions

1. Vocal quality (timbre) is primarily determined by:
   a. the voice source signal
   b. the shape of the sinuses
   c. chest size

   d. the first and second formants
   e. the third, fourth, and fifth formants

2. Vowel color is determined primarily by the two lowest formants.
   a. true
   b. false

3. All of the following are true about singers' formant except:
   a. It is a prominent spectrum envelope peak around 3000 Hz.
   b. The center frequency of the peak varies depending on voice classification.
   c. The singers' formant varies with loudness of phonation.
   d. The singers' formant helps audibility.
   e. The singers' formant may be used appropriately as a screening criterion when auditioning potential voice majors.

4. Production of a singers' formant requires lowering of the larynx.
   a. true
   b. false

5. The International Phonetic Alphabet (IPA) symbol for the vowel in "car" is:
   a. ah
   b. AH
   c. /a/
   d. /æ/

References

1. Sundberg J. *The Science of the Singing Voice*. DeKalb, Illinois: Northern Illinios University Press; 1987.
2. Sundberg J. Articulatory interpretation of the "singing formant." *J Acoust Soc Am*. 1974;55:838-844.
3. Rossing TD, Sundberg J, Ternstrom S. Acoustic comparison of voice use in solo and choir singing. *J Acoust Soc Am*. 1986;79:1975–1981.
4. Rossing TD, Sundberg J, Ternstrtom S. Acoustic comparison of soprano solo and choir singing. *J Acoust Soc Am*. 1987;82:830–836.
5. Fant G. *Acoustic Theory of Speech Production*. The Hague: Mouton; 1968.
6. Gramming P, Sundberg J, Ternstrom S, Leanderson, R, Perkins, W. Relationship between changes in voice pitch and loudness. *J Voice*. 1988;2(2):118–126.
7. Cleveland T, Sundberg J. Acoustic analysis of three male voices of different quality. In: Askenfelt A, Felicetti S, Jansson E, Sundberg J, eds. *Proceedings of Stockholm Music Acoustics Conference (SMAC 83). Vol 1*. Stockholm: Royal Swedish Academy of Music; 1983:143–156.

The Physics of Sound

Robert Thayer Sataloff

Fortunately, one need not be a physicist in order to function well in professions involved with hearing, sound, and music. However, a fundamental understanding of the nature of sound and terms used to describe it is essential to comprehend the language of otolaryngologists, audiologists, music acousticians, and engineers. Moreover, studying the basic physics of sound helps one recognize complexities and potential pitfalls in measuring and describing sound. These concepts are important to musicians interested in understanding concert hall acoustics, evaluating studies of risk from musical noise exposure, understanding the effects of vocal efficiency (like going from pressed to flow phonation), and other situations surrounding the professions above.

Sound

Sound is a form of motion. Consequently, the laws of physics that govern actions of all moving bodies apply to sound. Because sound and all acoustic conditions consistently behave as described by the laws of physics, we are able to predict and analyze the nature of a sound and its interactions. Sound measurement is not particularly simple. The study of physics helps us understand many practical aspects of our daily encounters with sound. For example, why does an audiologist or otologist use a different baseline for decibels in his office from that used by an engineer or industrial physician who measures noise in a factory? Why is it that when hearing at high frequencies is tested, a patient may hear nothing and then suddenly hear a loud tone when all the examiner did was move the earphone a fraction of an inch? Why is it when two machines are placed close together, each making 60 dB of noise, the total noise is not 120 dB?

Sound Waves

Sound is the propagation of pressure waves radiating from a vibrating body through an elastic medium. A vibrating body is essential to cause particle displacement in the propagating medium. An elastic medium is any substance or particles returned to their point of origin as soon as possible after they have been displaced. Propagation occurs because displaced particles in the medium displace neighboring particles. Therefore, sound travels over linear distance. Pressure waves are composed of areas of slightly greater than ambient air pressure compression and slightly less than ambient air pressure (rarefaction). These are associated with the bunching together or spreading apart of the particles in the propagating medium. The pressure wave makes receiving structures such as the eardrum move back and forth with the alternating pressure. For example, when a sound wave is generated by striking a tuning fork, by vocalizing, or by other means, the vibrating object moves molecules in air, causing them to be alternately compressed and rarefied in a rhythmical pattern. This sets up a chain reaction with adjacent air molecules and spreads at a rate of approximately 1100 ft/sec (the speed of sound). This is propagation of the pressure waves.

Sound requires energy. Energy is used to set a body into motion. The energy is imparted to particles in the propagating medium and is then distributed over the surface of the receiver (eardrum or microphone) in the form of sound pressure. Energy is equal to the square of pressure ($E = P^2$). However, we are unable to directly measure sound energy. Only the pressure exerted on the surface of a microphone can be quantified by sound-measuring equipment.

Characteristics of Sound Waves

Sound waves travel in straight lines in all directions from the source, decreasing in intensity at a rate inversely proportional to the square of the distance from their source. This is called the inverse-square law. This means that if a person shortens his distance from the source of a sound and moves from a position 4 feet away to only 2 feet from the source, the sound will be four times as intense rather than merely twice as intense. In practical application, this inverse-square law applies only in instances in which there are no walls or ceiling. It is not strictly valid in a room where sound waves encounter obstruction or reflection, and increasing the distance of a whisper or a ticking watch from the subject can rarely be truly accurate or reliable.

Sound waves travel through air more rapidly than through water. They are conducted through solids also at different speeds. An ear placed close to the iron rail of a train track will detect the approach of a train before the airborne sounds can reach the observer. Thus, sounds travel through different media at different speeds; the speed also varies when the medium is not uniform. However, sound waves are not transmitted through a vacuum. This can be demonstrated by the classic experiment of placing a ringing alarm clock inside a bell jar and then exhausting the air through an outlet. The ringing will no longer be heard when the air is exhausted, but it will be heard again immediately when air is readmitted. This experiment emphasizes the importance of the medium through which sound waves travel.

The bones of the head also conduct sounds, but ordinarily the ear is much more sensitive to sounds that are airborne. Under certain abnormal conditions, as in cases of conductive hearing loss, a patient may hear better by bone conduction than by air conduction. Such an individual can hear the vibrations of a tuning fork much better when it is held directly touching the skull than when it is held next to the ear but without touching the head.

Distortion of sound waves by wind is common. The effect also varies according to whether the wind blows faster near the ground or above it. When sound travels through the air and encounters an obstruction such as a wall, the sound waves can bend around the obstacle almost like water passing around a rock in a stream. The behavior of sound waves striking an object depends upon several factors, including wavelength. Sound waves may pass through an object unaffected, be reflected off the object, or may be partially reflected and partially passed through or around the object (shadow effect). Low-frequency sounds of long wavelength tend to bend (diffraction) when en-

countering objects, while diffraction is less prominent with sounds above 2000 Hz. The behavior of sound waves encountering an object also depends upon the nature of the object. The resistance of an object or system to the transmission of sound is called impedance. This depends upon a variety of factors such as mass reactants, stiffness reactants, and friction. The ability of an object to allow transmission of sound is called its admittance, which may be thought of as the opposite of impedance.

Components of Sound

A simple type of sound wave, called a pure tone, is pictured in Figure 5–1. This is a graphic representation of one and one-half complete vibrations or cycles, or periods, with the area of compression represented by the top curve and the area of rarefaction by the bottom curve. Although pure tones do not occur in nature, the more complicated sounds that we actually encounter are composed of combinations of pure tones. Understanding the makeup of this relatively simple sound helps us analyze more complex sounds. Fourier analysis is used to separate complex signals into their simple tonal components.

A pure tone has several important characteristics: One complete vibration consists of one compression and one rarefaction (Fig 5–2). The number of times such a cycle occurs in a given period of time (usually 1 second) is called frequency. Frequency is usually recorded in cycles per sound, or hertz. The perceptual correlate of frequency is pitch. In general, the greater the frequency, the higher the pitch, and the greater the intensity, the louder the sound. However, there is a difference between actual physical phenomena (such as frequency or intensity) and peoples' perceptions of them (pitch and loudness). A tuning fork is constructed so that it vibrates at a fixed frequency no matter how hard it is struck. However, although it will vibrate the same number of times per second, the prongs of the tuning fork will cover a greater distance when the fork is struck hard than when it is softly struck. We perceive this increased intensity as increased loudness. In the sine wave diagram of a pure tone, a more intense sound will have a higher peak and lower valley than a softer sound. Greater intensity also means that the particles in the propagating medium are more compressed. The height or depth of the sine wave is called its amplitude. Amplitude is measured in decibels (dB). It reflects the amount of pressure (or energy) existing in the sound wave.

Wavelength is the linear distance between any point in one cycle and the same point on the next cycle (peak to peak, for example). It may be calculated as the

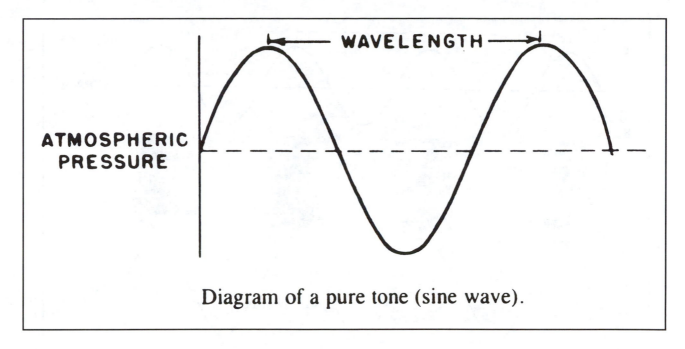

Diagram of a pure tone (sine wave).

Fig 5–1. Diagram of a pure tone (sine wave).

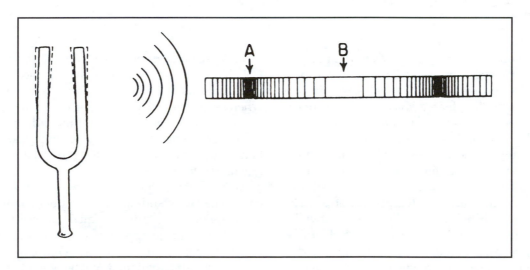

Fig 5–2. Areas of compression (A) and rarefaction (B) produced by a vibrating tuning fork.

speed of sound divided by the frequency. This is also one period. Wavelength is symbolized by the Greek letter lambda (λ) and is inversely proportional to frequency (Fig 5–3). This is easy to understand. If it is recalled that sound waves travel at about 1100 ft/sec, simple division tells us that a 1000-Hz frequency will have a wavelength of 1.1 ft/cycle. A 2000-Hz tone has a wavelength of about 6.5 inches. A 100-Hz tone has a wavelength of about 11 feet. The wavelength of a frequency of 8000-Hz would be 1100 divided by 8000, or

0.013 feet (about 1 inch). Wavelength has a great deal to do with sound penetration. For example, if someone is playing a stereo too loudly several rooms away, the bass notes will be clearly heard, but the high notes of violins or trumpets will be attenuated by intervening walls. Low-frequency sounds (long wavelengths) are extremely difficult to attenuate or absorb, and they require very different acoustic treatment from high-frequency sounds of short wavelengths. Fortunately, they are also less damaging to hearing.

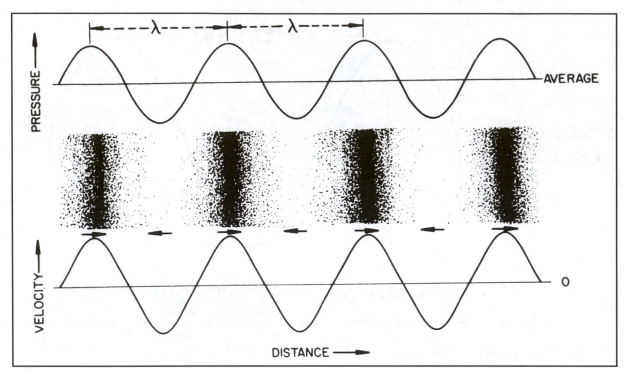

Fig 5–3. Diagram showing wavelength in relation to other components of a sound wave. (Adapted from Van Bergeijk.[1])

Any point along the cycle of the wave is its phase. Because a sine wave is a cyclical event, it can be described in degrees like a circle. The halfway point of the sine wave is the 180-degree phase point. The first peak occurs at 90 degrees, etc. The interaction of two pure tones depends on their phase relationship. For example, if the two sound sources are identical and are perfectly in phase, the resulting sound will be considerably more intense than either one alone (constructive inference). If they are 180 degrees out of phase, they will theoretically nullify each other and no sound will be heard (destructive interference) (Fig 5–4). This is the principle behind the concept of anti-sound, which is a sound generated to silence an unwanted sound that is equally loud but of opposite phase (180°) phase. Interaction of sound forces also depends upon other complicated factors such as resonance, which is affected by the environment and the characteristics of the receiver (such as the ear canal and ear).

Speech, music, and noise are complex sounds rather than pure tones. Most sounds are very complex with many different wave forms superimposed on each other. Musical tones are usually related to one another and show a regular pattern (complex periodic sound), whereas street noise shows a random pattern (complex aperiodic sound) (Fig 5–5).

It is somewhat difficult to accurately define noise, because so much of its meaning depends on its effect at any specific time and place, rather than on its physical characteristics. Sound in one instance or by one individual may be considered as very annoying noise, whereas on another occasion or to another observer the same sound may seem pleasant and undeserving of being designated "noise." For the purpose of this book, the term "noise" is used broadly to designate any unwanted sound.

An interesting aspect of sound waves is a phenomenon called the standing wave. Under certain circumstances, two wave trains of equal amplitude and frequency traveling in opposite directions can cancel out at certain points called "nodes." Figure 5–6 is a diagram of such a situation. It will be noted that when a violin string is plucked in a certain manner, at point "n" (node) there is no displacement. If this point falls at the eardrum, the listener will not be aware of any sound because the point has no amplitude and cannot excite the ear. This phenomenon occasionally occurs in hearing tests, particularly in testing at 8000 Hz and above. These higher frequencies are likely to be involved, because the ear canal is about 2.5 cm long and the wavelength of sound at such high frequencies is of the same order of magnitude. The point of maximum displacement is called the antinode.

Furthermore, when sound waves are produced within small enclosures, as when an earphone is placed over the ear, the sound waves encounter many

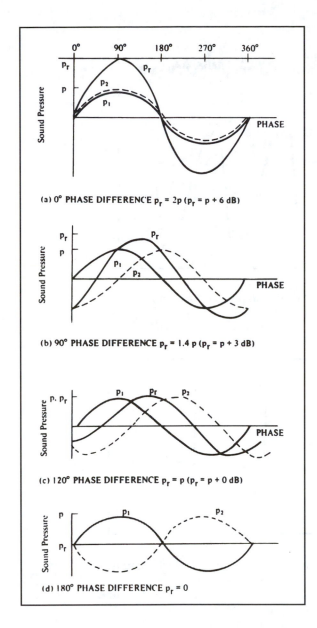

Fig 5–4. Combination of two pure tone noises (p₁ and p₂) with various phase differences.

ence of standing waves. During hearing testing, one often uses modulated or "warbled" tones to help eliminate standing wave problems that might result in misleading test results. Analogous but more complex problems may occur in acoustical environments such as concert halls.

In addition, resonant characteristics of the ear canal play a role in audition. Just like organ pipes and soda bottles, the ear may be thought of as a pipe. It is closed at one end and has a length of about 2.5 cm. Its calculated resonant frequency is approximately 3400 Hz (actually 3430 Hz if the length is exactly 2.5 cm and if the ear were really a straight pipe). At such a resonant frequency, a node occurs at the external auditory meatus (opening to the ear canal), and an antinode is present at the tympanic membrane, resulting in sound pressure amplification at the closed end of the pipe (ear drum). This phenomenon may cause sound amplification of up to 20 dB between 2000 and 5000 Hz. The resonance characteristics of the ear canal change if the open end is occluded, such as with an ear insert or muff used for hearing testing; and such factors must be taken into account during equipment design and calibration and when interpreting hearing tests.

The form of a complex sound is determined by the interaction of each of its pure tones at a particular time. This aspect of a sound is called a complexity and the psychological counterpart is timbre. This is the quality of sound that allows us to distinguish between a piano, oboe, violin, or voice all producing a middle "C" (256 Hz). These sound sources differently combine frequencies and consequently have different qualities.

Measuring Sound

The principal components of sound that we need to measure are frequency and intensity. Both are measured with a technique called scaling. The frequency scale is generally familiar because it is based on the musical scale, or octave. This is a logarithmic scale with a base of 2. This means that each octave increase corresponds to a doubling of frequency (Fig 5–7). Linear increases (octaves) correspond with progressively increasing frequency units. For example, the octave between 4000 and 8000 Hz contains 4000 frequency units, but the same octave space between 125 and 250 Hz contains only 125 frequency units. This makes it much easier to deal with progressively larger numbers and helps show relationships that might not be obvious if absolute numbers were used (Fig 5–8).

reflections and much of the sound at high frequencies is likely to be in the form of standing waves. Such waves often do not serve as exciting stimuli to the inner ear and no sensation of hearing is produced because of the absence of transmission of sound energy.

Sometimes, by simply holding the earphone a little more tightly or loosely to the ear in testing the higher frequencies, suddenly no sound may be produced at all when it should be loud, or a loud sound may be heard when a moment before there seemed to be no sound. This phenomenon occurs because of the pres-

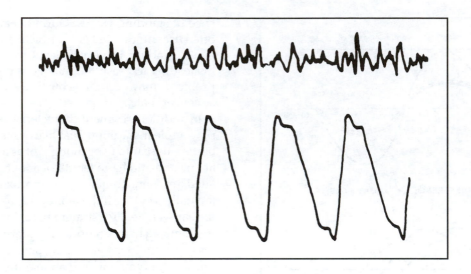

Fig 5–5. Upper graph, typical street noise. Lower graph, C on a piano.

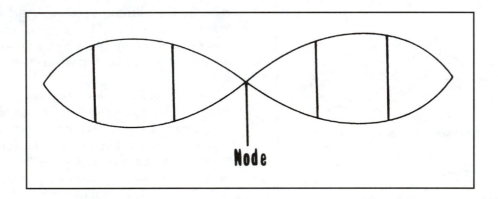

Fig 5–6. Diagram of a standing wave, showing the nodal point at which there is no amplitude.

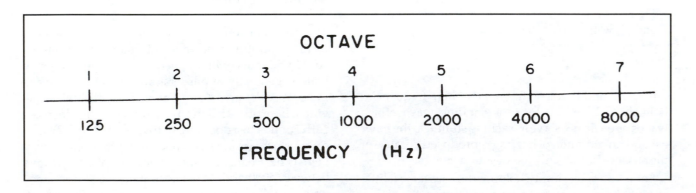

Fig 5–7. Scaling for octave notation of frequency levels.

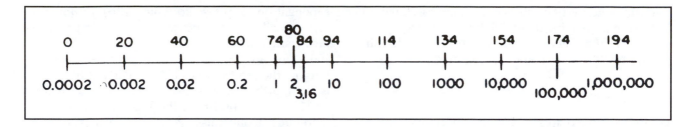

Fig 5–8. Decibel scaling (SPL). (After Lipscomb.[2])

Another reason for using an octave scaling was pointed out in the 19th century by psychophysicist Gustav Fechner. He noted that sensation increases as the log of the stimulus. This means that ever-increasing amounts of sound pressure are needed to produce equal increments in sensation. For example, loudness is measured in units called sones. Other psychoacoustic measures include the PHON scale of loudness level, and the MEL scale for pitch. The sone scale was developed by asking trained listeners to judge when a sound level had doubled in loudness relative to a 1000-Hz reference at 40 dB. Each doubling was called one sone. This is similar to doubling in pitch being referred to as one octave. One-sone increments correspond to approximately 10-dB increases in sound pressure, or about a 10-fold energy increase. So, in addition to being arithmetically convenient, logarithmic scaling helps describe sound more as we hear it.

In the kind of noise measurement done in industry, the chief concern is with very intense noise. In the testing of hearing, the primary concern is with very weak sounds, because the purpose is to determine the individual's thresholds of hearing. Accurate intensity measurement and a scale that covers a very large range are necessary to measure and compare the many intensities with which we have to work.

The weakest sound pressure that the keen, young human ear can detect under very quiet conditions is about 0.0002-μbar, and this very small amount of pressure is used as the basis or the reference level for noise measurements. This basis usually is determined by using a 1000-Hz tone (a frequency in the range of the maximum sensitivity of the ear) and reducing the pressure to the weakest measurable sound pressure to which the young ear will respond. In some instances, the keen ear under ideal conditions will respond to a pressure even weaker than 0.0002-μbar, but it is the 0.0002-μbar pressure that is used as a base.

Of course, sound pressures can be tremendously increased above the weakest tone. The usual range of audible sound pressures extends upward to about 2000-μbar, a point at which the pressure causes dis-

comfort and pain in the ears. Higher pressures can damage or even destroy the inner ear. Because this range (0.0002-μbar) is so great, the use of the microbar as a measurement of sound is too cumbersome.

Intensity

Measuring intensity or amplitude is considerably more complex than measuring frequency. Intensity is also measured on a logarithmic ratio scale. All such scales require an arbitrarily established zero point and a statement of the phenomenon being measured. Sound is usually measured in decibels. However, many other phenomena (such as heat and light) are also measured in decibels.

Decibels

The term "decibel" has been borrowed from the field of communication engineering, and it is the term most generally used to describe sound intensity. The detailed manner in which this unit was derived and the manner in which it is converted to other units is somewhat complicated and not within the scope of this book. However, a very clear understanding of the nature of the decibel and the proper use of the term is most valuable in understanding how hearing is tested and noise is measured.

A Unit of Comparison

The decibel is simply a unit of comparison, a ratio, between two sound pressures. In general, it is not a unit of measurement with an absolute value, such as an inch or a pound. The concept of the decibel is based on the pressure of one sound or reference level, with which the pressure of another sound is compared. Thus, a sound of 60 dB is a sound that is 60 dB more intense than a sound that has been standardized as the reference level. The reference level must be either implied or specifically stated in all sound measurement, for without the reference level, the expression of intensity in terms of decibels is meaningless. It would be the same as saying that something is "twice," without either implying or specifically referring to the other object with which it is being compared.

Two Reference Levels

For the purpose of this book, two important reference levels are used. In making physical noise measurements, as in a noisy industry or an orchestra hall, the base used is the sound pressure of 0.0002-µbar (one millionth of one barometric pressure or of one atmosphere), which is known as acoustical zero decibels. Sound-measuring instruments such as sound-level meters and noise analyzers are calibrated with this reference level. Several other terms have been used to describe acoustical zero. They include 0.0002 dyne/cm^2, 20 µN/m^2, and 20-µPA. Now, 0.0002-µbar has been accepted. When a reading is made in a room and the meter reads so many decibels, the reading means that the sound-pressure level in that room is so many decibels greater than acoustical zero. The designation SPL means that the measurement is sound-pressure level relative to 0.0002-µbar. When SPL is written, it tells us both the reference level and the phenomenon is being measured.

The other important reference level that is used in audiometry is known as zero decibels (0 dB) of hearing loss or average normal hearing. This level is not the same as that used as a base for noise measurement. Rather, it is known as hearing threshold level, or HTL. In the middle-frequency range (around 3000 Hz), it is 10 dB above the reference level known as acoustical zero. In testing hearing with an audiometer, 40-dB loss in hearing on the audiogram means that the individual requires 40 dB more of sound pressure than the average normal person to be able to hear the tone presented.

Since the baseline or reference level is different for the audiometer than it is for noise-measuring devices, it should be clear now that a noise of say 60 dB in a room is not the same intensity as the 60 dB tone on the audiometer. The noise will sound less loud because it is measured from a weaker reference level.

Formula for the Decibel

With these reference levels established, the formula for the decibel is worked out. To compare the two pressures, we have designated them as Pressure 1 and Pressure 2, with Pressure 2 being the reference level. The ratio can be expressed as P_1/P_2.

Another factor that must be taken into account is that in computing this ratio in terms of decibels, the computation must be logarithmic. A logarithm is the exponent or the power to which a fixed number or base (usually 10) must be raised in order to produce a given number. For instance, if the base is 10, the log of 100 is 2, because $10 \times 10 = 100$. In such a case, 10 is written with the exponent 2 as 10^2. Similarly, if 10 is raised to the fourth power and written as 10_4, the result is $10 \times 10 \times 10 \times 10$, or 10000; the logarithm of 10000 is, therefore 4. If only this logarithmic function is considered, the formula has evolved as far as dB = P_1/P_2. But it is not yet complete.

When the decibel was borrowed from the engineering field, it was a comparison of sound powers and not pressures and it was expressed in bels and not decibels. The decibel is 1/10 of a bel, and the sound pressure is proportional to the square root of the corresponding sound power. It is necessary, therefore, to multiply the logarithm of the ratio of pressures by 2 (for the square root relationship) and by 10 (for the bel-decibel relationship). When this is done, the decibel formula is complete and the decibel in terms of sound-pressure levels is defined thus:

$$dB = \frac{(20 \log P_1)}{P_2}$$

For instance, if the pressure designated as P_1 is 100 times greater than the reference level of P_2, substitution in the formula gives dB = $20 \times \log 100/1$. Since it is known that the log of 100 is 2 (as $10_2 = 100$), it can be seen that the formula reduces to dB = 20×2, or 40 dB. Therefore, whenever the pressure of one sound is 100 times greater than that of the reference level, the first sound can be referred to as 40 dB. Likewise, if P_1 is 1000 times greater, then the number of decibels would be 60, and if it is 10000 times greater, the number of decibels is 80. A few other relationships are convenient to remember. If sound intensity is multiplied by 2, sound pressure increases by 6 dB. If intensity is multiplied by 3.16 (the square root of 10), sound pressure increases by 10 dB. When intensity is multiplied by 10, sound pressure increases by 20 dB. These relationships can be seen clearly in Fig 5–8.

In actual sound measurement, if P_1 is 1-µbar, being a pressure of 1 dyne/cm^2, then the ratio is 1/0.0002, or 5000. By the use of a logarithmic table or a special table prepared to convert pressure ratios to decibels, the pressure level in such a case is found to be 74 dB, based on a reference level of 0.0002-µbar (Fig 5–8). Table 5–1 shows where a number of common sounds fall on this decibel scale in relation to a 0.0002-µbar reference level. This base level is used for calibrating standard sound-measuring instruments.

In audiometric testing, which uses a higher reference level than that for noise measurement, the tester

Table 5–1. The Physics of Sound at a Given Distance from Noise Source

	Environmental Decibels Re 0.0002 Microbar	
	-140-	
F-84 at take-off (80' From Tail)		
Hydraulic press (3')	-130-	
Large Pneumatic Riveter (4')		Boiler shop (Maximum level)
Pneumatic chipper (5')		
	-120-	
Multiple sand blast unit (4')		Jet engine test control room
Trumpet auto horn (3')		
Automatic punch press (3')	-110-	
Chipping hammer (3')		Woodworking shop
Cut-off saw (2')		Inside DC 6 Airliner
		Weaving room
Annealing furnace (4')	-100-	
Automatic lathe (3')		Can manufacturing plant
		Power lawn mower (Operator's ear)
Subway train (20')		Inside subway car
Heavy trucks (20')		
Train whistles (500')		Inside commercial jet
	-90-	
10 HP outboard (50')		
		Inside sedan in city traffic
Small trucks accelerating (30')		
	-80-	
Light trucks in city (20')		Garbage disposal (3')
		Heavy traffic (25' to 50')
Autos (20')		
	-70-	Vacuum cleaner
		Average traffic (100')
		Accounting office
Conversational speech (3')		Chicago industrial areas
	-60-	Window air conditioner (25')
15000 KVA, 115 KV Transformer 3 (200')		
	-50-	Private business office
Light traffic (100')		
		Average residence
	-40-	Quiet room
		Minimum levels for residential areas at night
	-30-	Broadcasting studio (Speech)
		Broadcasting studio (Music)
	-20-	Studio for sound pictures
	-10-	
Threshold of hearing—Young men 1000 to 4000 CPS		
	-0-	

does not need to concern himself or herself with additional mathematical formulas, because the audiometer used in testing is calibrated to take into account the increase above acoustical zero to provide the necessary reference level for audiometry of average normal hearing (0 dB of hearing loss).

Important Points

The important thing to remember is that the decibel is a logarithmic ratio. It is a convenient unit, because 1 dB approaches the smallest change in intensity between two sounds that the human ear can distinguish.

An important aspect of the logarithmic ratio is that as the ratio of the pressures becomes larger because the sound becomes more intense, the rate of increase in decibels becomes smaller. Even if the ratio of the pressures is enormous, such as one pressure being 10 million times that of another, the number of decibels by which this ratio is expressed does not become inordinately large, being only 140 dB. This is the principal reason for using the decibel scale. From the psychoacoustic aspect, it takes comparatively little increase in sound pressure to go from 0 to 1 dB, and the normal ear can detect this. However, when an attempt is made to increase the sound pressure from 140 to 141 dB, also an increase of 1 dB, which the ear can barely detect, it takes an increase of about 10 million times as much in absolute pressure.

A point to be remembered is that the effect of adding decibels together is quite different from that of adding ordinary numbers. For example, if one

machine whose noise has been measured as 70 dB of noise is turned on next to another machine producing 70 dB, the resulting level is 73 dB and not 140 dB. This is obtained as follows: When combining decibels, it is necessary to use an equation that takes into account that energy or power exerted by the sound sources, rather than the sound pressure exerted by this energy. The equation is:

$$dB_{power} = 10 \log_{10} \frac{E_1}{3_0}$$

where E_1 is known power (energy) and E_0 is the reference quantity
(there were two machines operating rather than one, resulting in a 2:1 ratio)

$$dB_{power} = 10 \log_{10} \frac{2}{1}$$

$$= (10)(0.3010) \text{ (the logarithm of 2 is 0.3010)}$$
$$= 3.01$$

Fig 5–9 is a chart showing the results obtained from adding noise levels. It may be used instead of the formulas. On this chart, it will be seen that if 70 db and 76 dB are being added, the difference of 6 dB is located on the graph, and this difference is found to produce an increase of 1 dB, which is added to the higher number. Therefore, the combined level of noise produced by the two machines is 77 dB above the reference level.

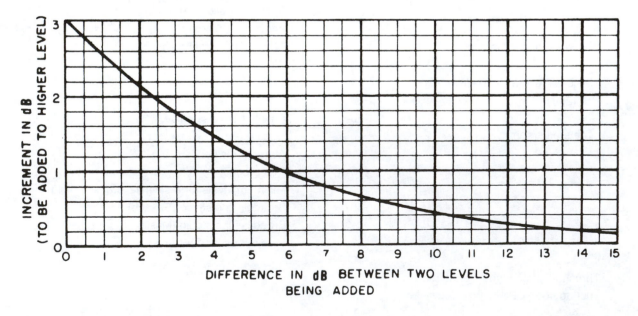

Fig 5–9. Results obtained from adding noise levels.

dBA Measurement

Most sound level meters that are used to measure noise levels do not simply record sound pressure level relative to 0.0002-μbar (dB SPL). Rather, they are generally equipped with three filtering networks: A, B, and C. Use of these filters allows one to approximate the frequency distribution of a given noise over the audible spectrum (Figs 5–10 and 5–11). In practice, the frequency distribution of a noise can be approximated by comparing the levels measured with each of the frequency ratings. For example, if the noise level is measured with the A and C networks and they are almost equal, then most of the noise energy is above 1000 Hz, because this is the only portion of the spectrum where the networks are similar. If there is a large difference between A and C measurements, most of the energy is likely to be below 1000 Hz. The use of these filters and other capabilities of sound level meters are discussed in other literature.[3]

The A network is now used when measuring sound to estimate the risk of noise-induced hearing loss, because it more accurately represents the ear's response to loud noise. It is not possible to describe a noise's damaging effect on hearing simply by stating its intensity. For instance, if one noise has a spectrum similar to that shown in curve A in Fig 5–10, with most of its energy in the low frequencies, it may have little or no effect on hearing. Another noise of the same overall intensity, having most of its sound energy in the higher frequencies (curve C), could produce substantial hearing damage after years of exposure. Examples of low-frequency noises are motors, fans, and trains. High-frequency noises are produced by sheet metal work, boiler making, and air pressure hoses. Although the human ear is more sensitive in the frequency range 1000 Hz to 3000 Hz than it is in the range below 500 Hz and above 4000 Hz (Fig 5–11), this frequency-specific differential sensitivity does not fully explain the ear's vulnerability to high-frequency sounds. Various explanations have been proposed involving everything from teleology to redundancy of low-frequency loci on the cochlea to cochlear shearing mechanics, but the phenomenon is not completely understood. Mechanisms of noise-induced hearing loss are discussed in other literature.[3]

Summary

Sound is a form of motion. Consequently, the laws of physics that govern all moving bodies apply to sound. Sound is the propagation of pressure waves radiating from the vibrating body through an elastic medium.

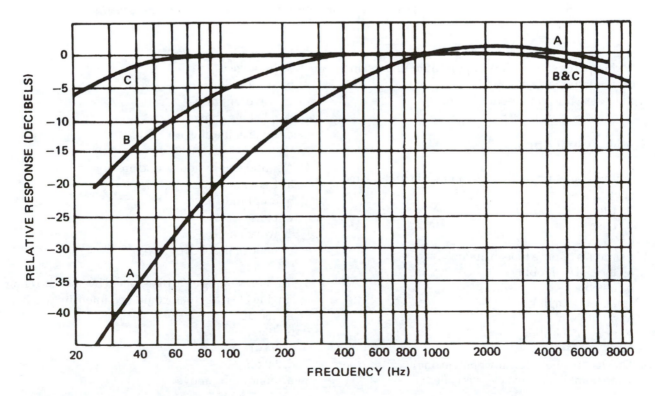

Fig 5–10. Frequency-response characteristics of a sound-level meter with A, B, and C weighting.

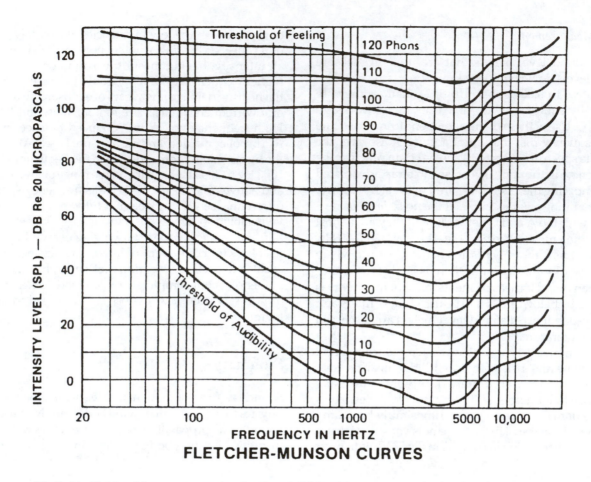

Fig 5–11. Fletcher-Munson curves showing the sensitivity of the ear to sounds of various frequencies.

Sound requires energy. It is important to understand various components of sound and the methodologies used to measure and describe them.

Review Questions

1. Sound waves travel through all media at the same speed.
   a. true
   b. false

2. Examples of pure tone include:
   a. the call of a robin
   b. an oboe
   c. falsetto singing
   d. all of the above
   e. none of the above

3. The distance between any point in one cycle and the same point in the next cycle is called:
   a. frequency
   b. amplitude
   c. wave length
   d. all of the above
   e. none of the above

4. A sound and its anti-sound are opposite in:
   a. frequency
   b. amplitude
   c. phase
   d. wavelength
   e. none of the above

5. If a choir singing at 90 dB is joined by a second choir singing at 90 dB, their combined intensity will be:
   a. 180 dB
   b. 106 dB
   c. 93 dB
   d. 90 dB
   e. none of the above

References

1. Van Bergeijk WA, Pierce JR, David EE. *Waves and the Ears.* New York, NY: Doubleday; 1960:44.

2. Lipscomb DM. Noise and occupational hearing impairment. *ENT-J.* 1980;59:13–23.

3. Sataloff RT, Sataloff J. *Hearing Loss,* 3rd ed. New York, NY: Marcel Dekker; 1993:371–402.

6

Patient History

Robert Thayer Sataloff

This chapter outlines the historical information collected by a physician in order to adequately evaluate and diagnose a professional voice user with vocal complaints. Essentially, the same questions are asked (or should be) by speech-language pathologists, singing teachers, and drama voice teachers when they start working with a new voice patient, client, or student. This chapter primarily discusses singers. Their vocal demands and astute self-analysis in many ways render them the most illustrative voice patients. The principles illustrated in assessing singers are applicable to other professional voice users, although the peculiar demands of each voice-dependent professional must be understood and investigated. It is also essential for professional voice users and teachers to understand the medical evaluation process and the importance of the questions asked. This allows the professional voice patient to organize his or her thoughts and be ready with the relevant information. It also provides the voice professional with some guidelines to help assess the thoroughness and adequacy of medical care. This chapter also includes an overview and preliminary discussion of many of the laryngeal and systemic conditions associated with voice dysfunction.

Extensive historical background is necessary for thorough evaluation of the singing voice, and the otolaryngologist who sees singers only occasionally cannot reasonably be expected to remember all the pertinent questions. Although some laryngologists feel that a lengthy inquisition is helpful in establishing rapport with professional singers, many of us who see a substantial number of singers per day within a busy practice need a thorough, but less time-consuming, alternative. A history questionnaire for professional singers can be extremely helpful in documenting all the necessary information, in assisting the singer sort

out and articulate his or her problems, and in saving the clinician time writing. The author has developed a questionnaire[1-3] that has proven helpful (Appendix IIA). The singer is asked to complete the form in the waiting room before seeing the doctor. An alternate questionnaire is used for professional voice users who are not singers (Appendix IIB). These questions may also be used by teachers and voice therapists.

No history questionnaire is a substitute for direct, penetrating questioning by the physician, teacher, or therapist. However, the direction of most useful inquiry can be determined from a glance at the questionnaire. Obviating the need for extensive writing permits the physician greater eye contact with the patient and facilitates rapid establishment of the close rapport and confidence that are so important in treating professional singers. The physician is also able to supplement his or her initial impressions and historical information from the questionnaire with seemingly leisurely conversation during the physical examination. The use of the historical questionnaire has substantially added to the efficiency, consistent thoroughness, and ease of managing these delightful, but often complex, patients. Use of a similar history questionnaire is recommended for singing teachers starting work with a new student and it may help the teacher identify potential problems that warrant medical referral. Astute teachers commonly represent the port of entry for a student into the medical system. In so doing, they often assist in identifying and treating important medical problems that can impair singing or that may result in disastrous vocal injury if left untreated. The same may be said for acting voice teachers and for speech-language pathologists, although most patients seeing a speech-language pathologist have already undergone medical evaluation.

How Old Are You?

Serious vocal endeavor may start in childhood and continue throughout a lifetime. As the vocal mechanism undergoes normal maturation, the voice changes. The optimal time to begin serious vocal training is controversial. For many years, most people advocated delay of vocal training and serious singing until near puberty in the female and after puberty and voice stabilization in the male. However, in a child with earnest vocal aspirations and potential, starting specialized training early in childhood is reasonable. Initial instruction should teach the child to vocalize without strain and avoid all forms of voice abuse. It should not permit premature indulgence in operatic bravado. Most experts agree that taxing voice use and singing during puberty should be minimized or avoided altogether, particularly by the male. Voice maturation (attainment of stable adult vocal quality) may occur at any age from the early teenage period to the fourth decade of life. The dangerous tendency for young singers to attempt to sound older than their vocal years frequently causes vocal dysfunction.

All components of voice production are subject to normal aging. Abdominal and general muscular tone frequently decrease, lungs lose elasticity, the thorax loses its distensibility, the mucosa of the vocal tract atrophies, mucous secretions change character, nerve endings are reduced in number, and psychoneurologic functions change. Moreover, the larynx itself loses muscle tone and bulk and may show depletion of submucosal ground substance in the vocal folds. The laryngeal cartilages ossify and the joints may become arthritic and stiff. Hormonal influence is altered. Vocal range, intensity, and quality may all be modified. Vocal fold atrophy may be the most striking alteration. The clinical effects of aging seem more pronounced in female singers, although vocal fold histologic changes may be more prominent in males. Excellent male singers occasionally extend their careers into their seventies or beyond.[4,5] However, some degree of breathiness, decreased range, and other evidence of aging should be expected in elderly voices. Nevertheless, many of the changes we typically associate with elderly singers (wobble, flat pitch) are due to lack of conditioning, rather than the inevitable changes of biological aging. These aesthetically undesirable concomitants of aging can often be reversed.[1]

What is Your Voice Problem?

Careful questioning as to the onset of vocal problems is needed to separate acute from chronic dysfunction. An upper respiratory tract infection will often send a patient to the physician's office, but penetrating inquiry may reveal a chronic vocal problem that is the patient's real concern, especially in singers and actors. Identifying acute and chronic problems before beginning therapy is important so that both patient and physician may have realistic expectations and optimal therapeutic selection.

The specific nature of the vocal complaint can provide a great deal of information. Just as dizzy patients rarely walk into the physician's office complaining of "rotary vertigo," voice patients may be unable to articulate their symptoms without guidance. They may use the term *hoarseness* to describe a variety of conditions that the physician must separate. *Hoarseness* is a coarse or scratchy sound most often associated with abnormalities of the leading edge of the vocal folds such as laryngitis or mass lesions. *Breathiness* is a vocal quality characterized by excessive loss of air during vocalization. In some cases, it is due to improper technique. However, any condition that prevents full approximation of the vocal folds can be responsible. Such causes include vocal fold paralysis, a mass lesion separating the leading edges of the vocal folds, arthritis of the cricoarytenoid joint, arytenoid dislocation, unilateral scarring of the vibratory margin, senile vocal fold atrophy, psychogenic dysphonia, malingering, and other conditions.

Fatigue of the voice is the inability to continue to speak or sing for extended periods without change in vocal quality and/or control. The voice may show fatigue by becoming hoarse, losing range, changing timbre, breaking into different registers, or exhibiting other uncontrolled aberrations. A well-trained singer should be able to sing for several hours without vocal fatigue. Fatigue is often caused by misuse of abdominal and neck musculature or "oversinging," singing too loudly, or too long. Vocal fatigue may also be a sign of general tiredness or serious illnesses such as myasthenia gravis.

Volume disturbance may manifest itself as the inability to sing loudly or the inability to sing softly. Each voice has its own dynamic range. Within the course of training, singers learn to sing more loudly by singing more efficiently. They also learn to sing softly, a more difficult task, through years of laborious practice. Actors and other trained speakers go through similar training. Most volume problems are secondary to intrinsic limitations of the voice or technical errors in voice use, although hormonal changes, aging, and neurologic disease are other causes. Superior laryngeal nerve paralysis impairs the ability to speak or sing loudly. This is a frequently unrecognized consequence of herpes infection ("cold sores") and may be precipitated by an upper respiratory tract infection.

Most highly trained singers require only about 10 minutes to half an hour to "warm up the voice." *Prolonged warm-up time*, especially in the morning, is most often caused by reflux laryngitis. *Tickling* or *choking* during singing is most often a symptom of abnormality of the vocal fold's leading edge. The symptom of tickling or choking should contraindicate singing until the vocal folds have been examined. *Pain* while singing can indicate vocal fold lesions, laryngeal joint arthritis, infection, or gastric acid irritation of the arytenoid region. However, pain is much more commonly caused by voice abuse with excessive muscular activity in the neck rather than an acute abnormality on the leading edge of a vocal fold. In the absence of other symptoms, these patients do not generally require immediate cessation of singing pending medical examination.

Do You Have Any Pressing Voice Commitments?

If a singer or professional speaker (eg, actor, politician) seeks treatment at the end of a busy season and has no pressing engagements, management of the voice problem should be relatively conservative and designed to assure long-term protection of the larynx, the most delicate part of the vocal mechanism. However, the physician and patient rarely have this luxury. Most often, the voice professional needs treatment within a week of an important engagement and sometimes within less than a day. Younger singers fall ill shortly before performances, not because of hypochondria or coincidence, but rather because of the immense physical and emotional stress of the preperformance period. The singer is frequently working harder and singing longer hours than usual. Moreover, he or she may be under particular pressure to learn new material and to perform well for a new audience. The singer may also be sleeping less than usual because of additional time rehearsing or because of the discomforts of a strange city. Seasoned professionals make their living by performing regularly, sometimes several times a week. Consequently, when they get sick, it is likely to precede a performance. Caring for voice complaints in these situations requires highly skilled judgment and bold management.

Tell Me About Your Vocal Career, Long-Term Goals, and the Importance of Your Voice Quality and Upcoming Commitments.

To choose a treatment program, the physician must understand the importance of the patient's voice in his or her long-term career plans, the importance of the upcoming commitment, and the consequences of canceling the engagement. Injudicious prescription of voice rest can be almost as damaging to a vocal career as injudicious performance. For example, although a singer's voice is usually his or her most important commodity, other factors distinguish the few successful artists from the multitude of less successful singers with equally good voices. These include musicianship, reliability, and "professionalism." Canceling a concert at the last minute may seriously damage a performer's reputation. Reliability is especially critical early in a singer's career. Moreover, an expert singer often can modify a performance to decrease the strain on his or her voice. No singer should be allowed to perform in a manner that will permit serious injury to the vocal folds, but in the frequent borderline cases, the condition of the larynx must be weighed against other factors affecting the singer as an artist. Special questions must be asked of people in other professions with high voice demands such as teaching (Appendix III).

How Much Voice Training Have You Had?

Establishing how long a singer or actor has been seriously performing is important, especially if his or her active performance career predates the beginning of vocal training. Active untrained singers and actors frequently develop undesirable techniques that are difficult to modify. Extensive voice use without training or premature training with inappropriate repertoire may underlie persistent vocal difficulties later in life. The number of years a performer has been training his or her voice may be a fair index of vocal proficiency. A person who has studied voice for one or two years is somewhat more likely to have gross technical difficulties than someone who has been studying for 20 years. However, if training has been intermittent or discontinued, technical problems are common, especially among singers. In addition, methods vary among voice teachers. Hence, a student who has had many teachers in a relatively brief period of time commonly has numerous technical insecurities or deficiencies that may be responsible for vocal dysfunction. This is especially true if the singer has changed to a new teacher within the preceding year. The physician must be careful not to criticize the patient's current voice teacher in such circumstances. It often takes years of expert instruction to correct bad habits.

All people speak more often than they sing, yet most singers report little speech training. Even if a singer uses the voice flawlessly while practicing and performing, voice abuse at other times can cause damage that affects singing.

Under What Kind of Conditions Do You Use Your Voice?

The Lombard effect is the tendency to increase vocal intensity in response to increased background noise.

A well-trained singer learns to compensate for this tendency and to avoid singing at unsafe volumes. Singers of classical music usually have such training and frequently perform with only a piano, a situation in which the balance can be well controlled. However, singers performing in large halls, with orchestras, or in operas early in their careers tend to oversing and strain their voices. Similar problems occur during outdoor concerts because of the lack of auditory feedback. This phenomenon is seen even more among "pop" singers. Pop singers are in a uniquely difficult position; often, despite little vocal training, they enjoy great artistic and financial success and endure extremely stressful demands on their time and voices. They are required to sing in large halls not designed for musical performance, amid smoke and other environmental irritants, accompanied by extremely loud background music. One frequently neglected key to survival for these singers is the proper use of monitor speakers. These direct the sound of the singer's voice toward the singer on the stage and provide auditory feedback. Determining whether the pop singer uses monitor speakers and whether they are loud enough for the singer to hear is important.

Amateur singers are often no less serious about their music than are professionals, but generally they have less ability to technically compensate for illness or other physical impairment. Rarely does an amateur suffer a great loss from postponing a performance or permitting someone to sing in his or her place. In most cases, the amateur singer's best interest is served through conservative management directed at long-term maintenance of good vocal health.

A great many singers who seek a physician's advice are primarily choral singers. They are often enthusiastic amateurs, untrained but dedicated to their musical recreation. They should be handled as amateur solo singers, specifically educated about the Lombard effect, and cautioned to avoid the excessive volume so common in a choral environment. One good way for a singer to monitor loudness is to cup a hand to his or her ear. This adds about 6 dB[6] to the singer's perception of his or her own voice and can be a very helpful guide in noisy surroundings. Young professional singers are often hired to augment amateur choruses. Feeling that the professional quartet has been hired to "lead" the rest of the choir, they often make the mistake of trying to accomplish that goal by singing louder than others in their sections. Such singers should be advised to lead their section by singing each line as if they were soloists giving a voice lesson to the two people standing beside them and as if there were a microphone in front of them recording their choral performance for their voice teacher. This approach usually not only preserves the voice, but also produces a better choral sound.

How Much Do You Practice and Exercise Your Voice?

Vocal exercise is as essential to the vocalist as exercise of other muscle systems is to the athlete. Proper vocal practice incorporates scales and specific exercises designed to maintain and develop the vocal apparatus. Simply acting or singing songs and giving performances without routine studious concentration on vocal technique is not adequate for the vocal performer. The physician should know whether the vocalist practices daily, whether he or she practices at the same time daily, and how long the practice lasts. Actors generally practice and warm up their voices for 10–30 minutes daily, although more time is recommended. Most serious singers practice for at least 1 to 2 hours per day. If a singer routinely practices in the late afternoon or evening but frequently performs in the morning (religious services, school classes, teaching voice, choir rehearsals, etc.), one should inquire into the warm-up procedures preceding such performances as well as cool-down procedures after voice use. Singing "cold," especially early in the morning, may result in the use of minor muscular alterations to compensate for vocal insecurity produced by inadequate preparation. Such crutches can result in voice dysfunction. Similar problems may result from instances of voice use other than formal singing. School teachers, telephone receptionists, sales people, and others who speak extensively also often derive great benefit from 5 or 10 minutes of vocalization of scales first thing in the morning. Although singers rarely practice their scales too long, they frequently perform or rehearse excessively. This is especially true immediately before a major concert or audition, when physicians are most likely to see acute problems. When a singer has hoarseness and vocal fatigue and has been practicing a new role for 14 hours a day for the last three weeks, no simple prescription will solve the problem. However, a treatment regimen can usually be designed to carry the performer safely through his or her musical obligations.

Do You Misuse or Abuse Your Voice During Singing?

A detailed discussion of vocal technique in singing is beyond the scope of this chapter. The reader is referred to other sources.[1] However, the most common technical errors involve excessive muscle tension in the tongue, neck, and larynx; inadequate abdominal support; and excessive volume. Inadequate preparation can be a devastating source of voice abuse and may result from limited practice, limited rehearsal of a difficult piece, or limited vocal training for a given role. The latter error is tragically common. In some situations, voice teachers are at fault, especially in competitive academic environments. Both singer and teacher must resist the impulse to show off the voice in works that are either too difficult for the singer's level of training or simply not suited to the singer's voice. Singers are habitually unhappy with the limitations of their voices. At some time or another, most baritones wish they were tenors and walk around proving they can sing high Cs in "Vesti la giubba." Singers with other vocal ranges have similar fantasies. Attempts to make the voice something that it is not, or at least that it is not yet, are frequently harmful.

Are You Aware of Misusing or Abusing Your Voice During Speaking?

Common patterns of voice abuse and misuse will not be discussed in detail in this chapter. They are covered elsewhere in this book and in other literature.[1] Voice abuse and/or misuse should be suspected particularly in patients who complain of voice fatigue associated with voice use, whose voices are worse at the end of a working day or week, and in any patient who is chronically hoarse. Technical errors in voice use may be the primary etiology of a voice complaint, or it may develop secondarily due to a patient's effort to compensate for voice disturbance from another cause.

Dissociation of one's speaking and singing voices is probably the most common cause of voice abuse problems in excellent singers. Too frequently, all the expert training in support, muscle control, and projection is not applied to a singers' speaking voice. Unfortunately, the resultant voice strain affects the singing voice as well as the speaking voice. Such damage is especially likely to occur in noisy rooms and in cars, where the background noise is louder than it seems. Backstage greetings after a lengthy performance can be particularly devastating. The singer usually is exhausted and distracted, the environment is often dusty and dry, and a noisy crowd is generally present. Similar conditions prevail at postperformance parties, where smoking and alcohol worsen matters. These situations should be avoided by any singer with vocal problems and should be controlled through awareness at other times.

Three particularly destructive vocal activities are worthy of note. Cheerleading requires extensive screaming under the worst possible physical and environmental circumstances. It is a highly undesirable activity for anyone considering serious vocal endeavor. This is a common conflict in younger singers because the teenager who is the high school choir soloist is often also student council president, yearbook editor, captain of the cheerleaders, and so on. Conducting, particularly choral conducting, can also be deleterious. An enthusiastic conductor, especially of an amateur group, frequently sings all four parts intermittently, at volumes louder than the entire choir, during lengthy rehearsals. Conducting is a common avocation among singers but must be done with expert technique and special precautions to prevent voice injury. Hoarseness or loss of soft voice control after conducting a rehearsal or concert suggests voice abuse during conducting. The patient should be instructed to record his or her voice throughout the vocal range singing long notes at dynamics from soft to loud to soft. Recordings should be made prior to rehearsal and following rehearsal. If the voice has lost range, control, or quality during the rehearsal, voice abuse has occurred. A similar test can be used for patients who sing in choirs, teach voice, or perform other potentially abusive vocal activities. Such problems in conductors can generally be managed by additional training in conducting techniques and by voice training, warm-up, and cool-down exercises. Teaching singing may also be hazardous to vocal health. It can be safely done but requires skill and thought. Most teachers teach while seated at the piano. Late in a long, hard day, this posture is not conducive to maintenance of optimal abdominal and back support. Usually, teachers work with students continually positioned to the right or left of the keyboard. This may require the teacher to turn his or her neck at a particularly sharp angle, especially when teaching at an upright piano. Teachers often demonstrate vocal works in their students' vocal ranges rather than their own, illustrating bad as well as good technique. If a singing teacher is hoarse or has neck discomfort, or his or her soft singing control deteriorates at the end of a teaching day (assuming that the teacher warms up before beginning to teach voice lessons), voice abuse should be suspected. Helpful modifications include teaching with a grand piano, sitting slightly sideways on the piano bench, or alternating student position to the right and left of the piano to facilitate better neck alignment. Retaining an accompanist so that the teacher can stand rather than teach from behind a piano, and many other helpful modifications, are possible.

What Kind of Physical Condition Are You in?

Speaking and singing are athletic activities that require good conditioning and coordinated interaction of numerous physical functions. Maladies of any part of the body may be reflected in the voice. Failure to exercise to maintain good abdominal muscle tone and respiratory endurance is particularly harmful in that deficiencies in these areas undermine the power source of the voice. Patients generally attempt to compensate for such weaknesses by using inappropriate muscle groups, particularly in the neck, causing vocal dysfunction. Similar problems may occur in the well-conditioned vocalist in states of fatigue. These are compounded by mucosal changes that accompany excessively long hours of hard work. Such problems may be seen even in the best singers shortly before important performances in the height of the concert season.

A popular but untrue myth holds that great opera singers must be obese. However, the vivacious, gregarious personality that often distinguishes the great performer seems to be frequently accompanied by a propensity for excess, especially culinary excess. This excess is as undesirable in the vocalist as it is in most other athletic artists and it should be prevented from the start of one's vocal career. Appropriate and attractive body weight has always been valued in the pop music world and is becoming particularly important in the opera world as this formerly theater-based art-form moves to television and film media. However, attempts to effect weight reduction in an established speaker or singer are a different matter. The vocal mechanism is a finely tuned, complex instrument and is exquisitely sensitive to minor changes. Substantial fluctuations in weight frequently cause deleterious alterations of the voice, although these are usually temporary. Weight reduction programs for people concerned about their voices must be carefully monitored and designed to reduce weight in small increments over long periods. A history of sudden recent weight change may be responsible for almost any vocal complaint.

Do You Have Allergy or Cold Symptoms?

Voice patients usually volunteer information about upper respiratory tract infections and "postnasal drip," but the relevance of other maladies may not be obvious to them. The physician must consequently seek out pertinent history. Acute upper respiratory tract infection causes inflammation of the mucosa, alters mucosal secretions, and makes the mucosa more vulnerable to injury. Coughing and throat clearing are particularly traumatic vocal activities and may worsen or provoke hoarseness associated with a cold. Postnasal drip and allergy may produce the same response. Infectious sinusitis is associated with discharge and diffuse mucosal inflammation, resulting in

similar problems, and may actually alter the sound of a voice, especially the patient's perception of his or her own voice. Laryngeal strain is often the result of futile attempts to compensate for disease of the supraglottic vocal tract whereby the patient tries to change the voice sound from abnormal to normal. The expert singer or speaker should compensate by monitoring technique by tactile rather than by auditory feedback or singing "by feel" rather than "by ear."

Do You Have Breathing Problems, Especially After Exercise?

Respiratory problems are especially important in voice patients. Even mild respiratory dysfunction may adversely affect the power source of the voice.[7,8] Occult asthma may be particularly troublesome.[9] A complete respiratory history should be obtained in most patients with voice complaints, and pulmonary function testing is often advisable.

Do You Have Jaw Joint or Other Dental Problems?

Dental disease, especially temporomandibular joint (TMJ) dysfunction, introduces muscle tension in the head and neck, which is transmitted to the larynx directly through the muscular attachments between the mandible and the hyoid bone, and indirectly as generalized increased muscle tension. These problems often result in decreased range, vocal fatigue, and change in the quality or placement of a voice. Such tension is often accompanied by excess tongue muscle activity, especially posterior pulling of the tongue. This hyperfunctional behavior acts through hyoid attachments to disrupt the balance between the intrinsic and extrinsic laryngeal musculature. TMJ problems are also problematic for wind instrumentalists and some string players including violinists. In some cases, the problems may actually be caused by instrumental technique. The history should always include information about musical activities including instruments other than the voice.

Have You Suffered Whiplash or Other Bodily Injury?

Various bodily injuries outside the confines of the vocal tract may have profound effects on the voice. Whiplash, for example, commonly causes changes in technique, with consequent voice fatigue, loss of range, difficulty singing softly, and other problems. Lumbar, abdominal, and extremity injuries may also affect voice technique and be responsible for the dysphonia that prompted the voice patient to seek medical attention.

Do You Have Morning Hoarseness, Bad Breath, Excessive Phlegm, a Lump in Your Throat, or Heartburn?

Reflux laryngitis is especially common among singers and trained speakers because of the high intraabdominal pressure associated with proper support and because of lifestyle. Singers frequently perform at night. Many vocalists refrain from eating before performances because a full stomach can compromise effective abdominal support. They typically compensate by eating heartily at postperformance gatherings late at night and then go to bed with a full stomach. Chronic arytenoid mucosa and vocal fold irritation by reflux of gastric secretions may occasionally be associated with dyspepsia or pyrosis. However, the key features of this malady are bitter taste and halitosis on awakening in the morning, a dry or "coated" mouth, often a scratchy sore throat or a feeling of a "lump in the throat," hoarseness, and the need for prolonged vocal warm-up. The physician must be alert to these symptoms and ask about them routinely; otherwise, the diagnosis will often be overlooked because people who have had this problem for many years or a lifetime do not even realize it is abnormal.

Do You Have Trouble With Your Bowels or Abdomen?

Any condition that alters abdominal function, such as muscle spasm, constipation, or diarrhea, interferes with support and may result in a voice complaint. These symptoms may accompany infection, anxiety, various gastroenterological diseases, and other maladies.

Do You or Your Blood Relatives Have Hearing Loss?

Hearing loss is often overlooked as a source of vocal problems. Auditory feedback is fundamental to speaking and singing. Interference with this control mechanism may result in altered vocal production, particularly if the person is unaware of the hearing loss. Distortion, particularly pitch distortion (diplacusis) may also pose serious problems for the singer. This appears to be due not only to aesthetic difficulties in matching pitch, but also to vocal strain which accompanies pitch shifts.[10] This subject is covered in greater detail in Chapter 11.

Are You Under Particular Stress or in Psychological Therapy?

The human voice is an exquisitely sensitive messenger of emotion. Highly trained voice professionals learn to control the effects of anxiety and other emotional stress on their voices under ordinary circumstances. However, in some instances this training may break down or a performer may be inadequately prepared to control the voice under specific stressful conditions. Preperformance anxiety is the most common example, but insecurity, depression, and other emotional disturbances are also generally reflected in the voice. Anxiety reactions are mediated in part through the autonomic nervous system and result in a dry mouth, cold clammy skin, and thick mucous secretions. These reactions are normal, and good vocal training coupled with assurance that no abnormality or disease is present generally overcomes them. However, long-term, poorly compensated emotional stress and exogenous stress (from agents, producers, teachers, parents, etc.) may cause substantial vocal dysfunction and may result in permanent limitations of the vocal apparatus. These conditions must be expertly diagnosed and treated. Hypochondriasis is uncommon among professional singers, despite popular opinion to the contrary.

Recent publications have highlighted the complexity and importance of psychological factors associated with voice disorders.[11,12] A more comprehensive discussion of this subject is presented in Chapter 20. It is important for the physician to recognize that psychological problems may not only cause voice disorders, but they may also delay recovery from voice disorders that were entirely organic in etiology. Professional voice users, especially singers, have enormous psychological investment and personality identifications associated with their voices. A condition that causes voice loss or permanent injury often evokes the same powerful psychological responses seen following the death of a loved one. This process may be initiated even when physical recovery is complete, following an incident (injury or surgery) that makes the vocalist realize that voice loss is possible, a "brush with death." It is essential for laryngologists and voice professionals to be aware of these powerful factors and properly manage them if optimal therapeutic results are to be expeditiously achieved .

Do You Have Problems Controlling Your Weight? Are You Excessively Tired? Are You Cold When Other People Are Warm?

Endocrine problems warrant special attention. The human voice is extremely sensitive to endocrinologic changes. Many of these are reflected in alterations of fluid content of the lamina propria just beneath the laryngeal mucosa. This causes alterations in the bulk and shape of the vocal folds and results in voice change. Hypothyroidism[13–17] is a well-recognized cause of such voice disorders, although the mechanism is not fully understood. Hoarseness, vocal fatigue, muffling of the voice, loss of range, and a sensation of a lump in the throat may be present even with mild hypothyroidism. Even when thyroid function tests results are within the low normal range, this diagnosis should be entertained, especially if thyroid stimulating hormone levels are in the high normal range or are elevated. Thyrotoxicosis may result in similar voice disturbances.[17]

Do You Have Menstrual Irregularity, Cyclical Voice Changes Associated With Menses, Recent Menopause, or Other Hormonal Changes or Problems?

Voice changes associated with sex hormones are commonly encountered in clinical practice and have been more thoroughly investigated than have other hormonal changes. Although a correlation appears to exist between sex hormone levels and depth of male voices (higher testosterone and lower estradiol levels in basses than in tenors),[18] the most important hormonal considerations in males occur during puberty.

When castrato singers were in vogue, castration at about age 7 or 8 resulted in failure of laryngeal growth during puberty and voices that stayed in the soprano or alto range and boasted a unique quality of sound.[19] Failure of a male voice to change at puberty is uncommon today and is often psychogenic in etiology.[20] However, hormonal deficiencies such as those seen in cryptorchidism, delayed sexual development, Klinefelter's syndrome, or Fröhlich's syndrome may be responsible. In these cases, the persistently high voice may be the complaint that causes the patient to seek medical attention.

Voice problems related to sex hormones are more common in female singers. Although vocal changes associated with the normal menstrual cycle may be difficult to quantify with current experimental techniques, they unquestionably occur.[1,21–24,25] Most of the ill effects are seen in the immediate premenstrual period and are known as laryngopathia premenstrualis. This common condition is caused by physiologic, anatomic, and psychologic alterations secondary to endocrine changes. The vocal dysfunction is characterized by decreased vocal efficiency, loss of the highest notes in the voice, vocal fatigue, slight hoarseness, and some muffling of the voice. It is often more apparent to the singer than to the listener and these symptoms tend to be more troublesome for singers than for speakers. Submucosal hemorrhages in the larynx are common in the premenstrual period.[22] In many European opera houses, singers used to be excused from singing during the premenstrual and early menstrual days ("grace days"). This practice is not followed in the United States and is no longer in vogue in most European countries. Premenstrual changes cause significant vocal symptoms in approximately one third of singers. Although ovulation inhibitors have been shown to mitigate some of these symptoms in some women (about 5%)[23] (Personnel Communication, Christine Carroll through Hans von Leden, 1992), birth control pills may deleteriously alter voice range and character even after only a few months of therapy.[25–28] When oral contraceptives are used, the voice should be closely monitored. Under crucial performance circumstances, oral contraceptives may be used to alter the time of menstruation, but this practice is justified only in unusual situations. Symptoms very similar to laryngopathia premenstrualis occur in some women at the time of ovulation.

Pregnancy frequently results in voice alterations known as laryngopathia gravidarum. The changes may be similar to premenstrual symptoms or may be perceived as desirable changes. In some cases, alterations produced by pregnancy are permanent.[29–30] Although hormonally induced changes in the larynx and respiratory mucosa secondary to menstruation and pregnancy are widely discussed in the literature, there are few references to the important alterations in abdominal support. Uterine muscle cramping associated with menstruation causes pain and compromises abdominal support. Abdominal distension during pregnancy also interferes with abdominal muscle function. Any high performance voice user whose abdominal support is substantially compromised should be discouraged from performing until the abdominal impairment is resolved.

Estrogens are helpful in postmenopausal speakers and singers but generally should not be given alone. Sequential replacement therapy is the most physiologic regimen and generally should be used under the supervision of a gynecologist. Under no circumstances should androgens be given to female singers even in small amounts, if any reasonable therapeutic alternative exists. Clinically, these drugs are most commonly used to treat endometriosis. Androgens cause unsteadiness of the voice, rapid changes of timbre, and lowering of the fundamental frequency (masculinization).[31–36] These changes are usually permanent.

We have recently seen increasing abuse of anabolic steroids. In addition to their many other hazards, these medications may alter the voice. They are (or are closely related to) male hormones and are thus capable of producing masculinization of the voice. Lowering of the fundamental frequency and coarsening of the voice produced in this fashion are generally irreversible.

Other hormonal disturbances may also produce vocal dysfunction. In addition to the thyroid gland

and the gonads, the parathyroid, adrenal, pineal, and pituitary glands are included in this system. Also, other endocrine disturbances may alter voice as well, such as pancreatic dysfunction may cause xerophonia (dry voice), as in diabetes mellitus. Thymic abnormalities can lead to feminization of the voice.[37]

Have You Been Exposed to Environmental Irritants?

Any mucosal irritant can disrupt the delicate vocal mechanism. Allergies to dust and mold are commonly aggravated during rehearsals and performances in concert halls, especially older theaters and concert halls, because of numerous curtains, backstage trappings, and dressing room facilities that are rarely thoroughly cleaned. Nasal obstruction and erythematous conjunctivae suggest generalized mucosal irritation. The drying effects of cold air and dry heat may also affect mucosal secretions, leading to decreased lubrication, a "scratchy" voice, and tickling cough. These symptoms may be minimized by nasal breathing, which allows inspired air to be filtered, warmed, and humidified. Nasal breathing, whenever possible, rather than mouth breathing is proper vocal technique. While the performer is backstage between appearances or during rehearsals, aspiration of dust and other irritants may be controlled by wearing a protective mask such as those used by carpenters, or a surgical mask, that does not contain fiberglass. This is especially helpful when sets are being constructed in the rehearsal area.

A history of recent travel suggests other sources of mucosal irritation. The air in airplanes is extremely dry and airplanes are noisy.[38] One must be careful to avoid loud talking and to maintain good hydration and nasal breathing during air travel. Environmental changes can also be disruptive. Las Vegas is infamous for the mucosal irritation caused by its dry atmosphere and smoke-filled rooms. In fact, the resultant complex of hoarseness, vocal "tickle," and fatigue is referred to as "Las Vegas voice." A history of recent travel should also suggest jet lag and generalized fatigue, which may be potent detriments to good vocal function.

Environmental pollution is responsible for the presence of toxic substances and conditions daily encountered. Inhalation of toxic pollutants may adversely affect the voice by direct laryngeal injury, by causing pulmonary dysfunction that results in voice maladies, or through impairments elsewhere in the vocal tract. Injested substances, especially those that have neurolaryngologic effects may also adversely affect the voice. Nonchemical environmental pollutants such as noise can cause voice abnormalities as well. Laryngologists and voice professionals should be familiar with the laryngologic effects of the numerous potentially irritating substances and conditions found in the environment.[39] We must also be familiar with special pollution problems encountered by performers. Numerous materials used by artists to create sculptures, drawings, and theatrical sets are toxic and have adverse voice effects. In addition, performers are routinely exposed to chemicals encountered through stage smoke and pyrotechnic effects.[40–42] Although it is clear that some of the "special effects" result in serious laryngologic consequences, much additional study is needed to clarify the nature and scope of these occupational problems.

Do You Smoke, Live With a Smoker, or Work Around Smoke?

The deleterious effects of tobacco smoke are indisputable. Anyone concerned about the health of his or her voice should not smoke. Smoking causes erythema, mild edema, and generalized inflammation throughout the vocal tract. Both smoke itself and the heat of the cigarette appear to be important. Marijuana produces a particularly irritating, unfiltered smoke that is directly inhaled, causing considerable mucosal response. Voice patients who refuse to stop smoking marijuana should at least be advised to use a water pipe to cool and partially filter the smoke. Some vocalists are required to perform in smoke-filled environments and may suffer the same effects as the smokers themselves. In some theaters, it is possible to place fans upstage or direct the ventilation system so as to create a gentle draft toward the audience, clearing the smoke away from the stage. "Smoke eaters" installed in some theaters are also helpful.

Have You Noted Voice or Bodily Weakness, Tremor, Fatigue, or Loss of Control?

Even minor *neurological disorders* may be extremely disruptive to vocal function. Specific questions should be asked to rule out neuromuscular and neurological diseases such as myasthenia gravis, Parkinson's disease, tremors, other movement disorders; spasmodic dysphonia, multiple sclerosis, central nervous system neoplasm; and other serious maladies that may be present with voice complaints.[7,43]

What Medications and Other Substances Do You Use?

A history of alcohol abuse suggests the probability of poor vocal technique. Intoxication results in incoordination and decreased awareness, which undermine vocal discipline designed to optimize and protect the voice. The effect of small amounts of alcohol is controversial. Although many experts oppose its use because of its vasodilatory effect and consequent mucosal alteration, many people do not seem to be adversely affected by small amounts of alcohol such as a glass of wine with a meal. However, some people have mild sensitivities to certain wines or beers. Patients who develop nasal congestion and rhinorrhea after drinking beer, for example, should be made aware that they probably have a mild allergy to that particular beverage and should avoid it before voice commitments.

Patients frequently acquire antihistamines to help control "postnasal drip" or other symptoms. The drying effect of antihistamines may result in decreased vocal fold lubrication, increased throat clearing, and irritability leading to frequent coughing. Antihistamines may be helpful to some voice patients, but they must be used with caution.

When a voice patient seeking the attention of a physician is already taking antibiotics, it is important to find out the dose and the prescribing physician, if any, as well as whether the patient frequently treats himself or herself with inadequate courses of antibiotics which are often supplied by colleagues. Singers, actors, and other speakers sometimes have a "sore throat" shortly before important vocal presentations and start themselves on inappropriate antibiotic therapy, which they generally discontinue after their performance.

Diuretics are also popular among some performers. They are often prescribed by gynecologists at the vocalist's request to help deplete excess water in the premenstrual period. They are not effective in this scenario because they cannot diurese the protein-bound water in the laryngeal ground substance. Unsupervised use of these drugs may cause dehydration and consequent mucosal dryness.

Hormone use, especially use of oral contraceptives, must be specifically mentioned during the physician's inquiry. Women frequently do not mention them when asked whether they are taking any medication. Vitamins are also frequently not mentioned. Most vitamin therapy seems to have little effect on the voice. However, high-dose vitamin C (5 to 6 g/day), which some people use to prevent upper respiratory tract infections, seems to act as a mild diuretic and may lead to dehydration and xerophonia.[44]

Cocaine use is common, especially among pop musicians. This drug can be extremely irritating to the nasal mucosa, causes marked vasoconstriction, and may alter the sensorium, resulting in decreased voice control and a tendency toward vocal abuse.

Many pain medications (including aspirin and ibuprofen), psychotropic medications, and other medications may be responsible for voice complaint. Laryngologists and voice professionals must be familiar with the laryngologic effects of the many substances medically and recreationally ingested.[45]

Do Any Foods Seem to Affect Your Voice?

Various foods are said to affect the voice. Traditionally, singers avoid milk and ice cream before performances. In many people, these foods seem to increase the amount and viscosity of mucosal secretions. Allergy and casein have been implicated, but no satisfactory explanation has been established. Restriction of these foods from the diet before a voice performance may be helpful in some cases. Chocolate may have the same effect and should be similarly viewed. Chocolate also contains caffeine which may aggravate reflux or cause tremor. Voice patients should be asked about eating nuts. This is important not only because some people experience effects similar to those produced by milk products and chocolate, but also because they are extremely irritating if aspirated. The irritation produced by aspiration of even a small organic foreign body may be severe and impossible to correct rapidly enough to permit performance. Highly spiced foods may also cause mucosal irritation. In addition, they seem to aggravate reflux laryngitis. Coffee and other beverages containing caffeine also aggravate gastric reflux and may alter secretions and necessitate frequent throat clearing in some people. Fad diets, especially rapid weight reducing diets, are notorious for causing voice problems. Lemon juice and herbal teas are considered beneficial to the voice. Both may act as demulcents, thinning secretions, and may very well be helpful. Eating a full meal before a speaking or singing engagement may interfere with abdominal support or may aggravate upright reflux of gastric juice during abdominal muscle contraction.

Did You Undergo Any Surgery Prior to the Onset of Your Voice Problems?

A history of laryngeal surgery in a voice patient is a matter of great concern. It is important to establish exactly why the surgery was done, by whom it was done, whether intubation was necessary, and whether voice therapy was instituted pre- or postoperatively if the lesion was associated with voice abuse (vocal nodules). If the vocal dysfunction that sent the patient to the physician's office dates from the immediate postoperative period, surgical trauma must be suspected.

Otolaryngologists frequently are asked about the effects of tonsillectomy on the voice. Singers especially may consult the physician after tonsillectomy and complain of vocal dysfunction. Removal of tonsils certainly can alter the voice.[46,47] Tonsillectomy changes the configuration of the supraglottic vocal tract. In addition, scarring alters pharyngeal muscle function, which is meticulously trained in the professional singer. Singers must be warned that they may have permanent voice changes after tonsillectomy; however, these can be minimized by dissecting in the proper plane to lessen scarring. The singer's voice generally requires 3 to 6 months to stabilize or return to normal after surgery. As with any procedure for which general anesthesia may be needed, the anesthesiologist should be advised preoperatively that the patient is a professional singer. Intubation and extubation should be performed with great care and the use of nonirritating plastic rather than rubber endotracheal tubes is ideal.

Surgery of the neck, such as thyroidectomy, may result in permanent alterations in the vocal mechanism through scarring of the extrinsic laryngeal musculature. The cervical (strap) muscles are important in maintaining laryngeal position and stability of the laryngeal skeleton, and they should be retracted rather than divided whenever possible. A history of recurrent or superior laryngeal nerve injury may explain a hoarse, breathy, or weak voice. However, in rare cases even a singer can compensate for recurrent laryngeal nerve paralysis and have a nearly normal voice.

Thoracic and abdominal surgery interfere with respiratory and abdominal support. After these procedures, singing and projected speaking should be prohibited until pain has subsided and healing has occurred sufficiently to allow normal support. Abdominal exercises should be instituted before resumption of vocalizing. Singing and speaking without proper support are often worse for the voice than not using the voice for performance at all.

Other surgical procedures may be important factors if they necessitate intubation or if they affect the musculoskeletal system so that the person has to change stance or balance. For example, balancing on one foot after leg surgery may decrease the effectiveness of the support mechanism.

Summary

In evaluating a new patient or student, many questions must be answered to determine vocal health and habits. Appropriate inquiry includes information about not only the larynx, but all body systems. Information about concerts and performing habits, professional and avocational activities, and stress are also relevant.

Review Questions

1. Prolonged warm-up time most commonly indicates:
   a. vocal nodules
   b. vocal polyps
   c. reflux laryngitis
   d. vocal fold hemorrhage
   e. none of the above

2. Common sources of voice abuse include:
   a. speaking in cars
   b. conducting
   c. teaching singing
   d. all of the above
   e. none of the above

3. Which of the following adversely affects the ability to "support" a sung tone?
   a. asthma
   b. menstrual cramps
   c. faulty technique
   d. all of the above
   e. none of the above

4. Irreversible voice changes due to hormones are most likely to be encountered:
   a. in a premenstrual period
   b. following the use of birth control pills
   c. following use of androgens
   d. following cortisone injections
   e. all of the above

5. It is most important to avoid which of the following whenever possible, and especially prior to heavy voice use commitments:
   a. antibiotics
   b. cortisone products
   c. aspirin
   d. Tylenol
   e. asthma medication

References

1. Sataloff RT. Efficient history taking in professional singers. *Laryngoscope*. 1984;94:1111–1114.
2. Sataloff RT. *Professional Voice: The Science and Art of Clinical Care*. 2nd ed. San Diego, Calif: Singular Publishing Group, Inc; 1997:1–1069.
3. Rubin JS, Sataloff RT, Korovin G, Gould WJ. *Diagnosis and Treatment of Voice Disorders*. New York, NY: Igaku-Shoin; 1995:1–525.

4. von Leden H. Speech and hearing problems in the geriatric patient. *Am Geriat Soc*. 1977;25:422–426.

5. Ackerman R, Pfan W. Geronlologische Untersuchungen zur Strungpanfalligkeit der Sprechstimme bei Berufssprechern. *Folia Phoniatr*. 1974;25:95–109.

6. Schiff M. Comment at the Seventh Symposium on Care of the Professional Voice. New York, NY: The Juilliard School; June 15 and 16, 1978.

7. Sataloff RT. *Professional Singers: The Science and Art of Clinical Care*. New York, NY: Raven Press; 1991:77–79, 159–178.

8. Spiegel JR, Cohn JR, Sataloff RT, Fish JE, Kennedy K. Respiratory function in singers: medical assessment, diagnoses, treatments. *J Voice*. 1988;2(1):40–50.

9. Cohn JR, Sataloff RT, Spiegel JR, Fish JE, Kennedy K. Airway reactivity-induced asthma in singers (ARIAS). *J Voice*. 1991;5(4):32–337.

10. Sundberg J, Prame E, Iwarsson J. Replicability and accuracy of pitch patterns in professional singers. In: *Vocal Fold Physiology: Controlling Chaos and Complexity*. San Diego, Calif: Singular Publishing Group, Inc; 1995:291–306.

11. Rosen DC, Sataloff RT. Psychological aspects of voice disorders. In: Rubin J, Korovin G, Sataloff RT, Gould WJ, eds. *Diagnosis and Treatment of Voice Disorders*. New York, NY: Igaku-Shoin Medical Publishers; 1995:491–501.

12. Rosen DC, Sataloff RT. *Psychology of Voice Disorders*. San Diego, Calif: Singular Publishing Group, Inc; 1997.

13. Ritter FN. The effect of hypothyroidism on the larynx of the rat. *Ann Otol, Rhinol Laryngol*: 1964;67:404–416.

14. Ritter FN. Endocrinology. In: Paparella M, Shumrick D, eds. *Otolaryngology*. Philadelphia, Pa: WB Saunders; 1973;1:727–734.

15. Michelsson K, Sirvio P. Cry analysis in congenital hypothyroidism. *Folia Phoniatr*. 1976;28:40–47.

16. Gupta OP, Bhatia PL, Agarwal MK, Mehrotra ML, Mishr SK. Nasal pharyngeal and laryngeal manifestations of hypothyroidism. *Ear Nose Throat J*. 1977;56(9):10–21.

17. Malinsky M, Chevrie-Muller, Cercean N. Etude clinique et electrophysiologique des alterations de la voix au cours des thyrotoxioses. *Ann Endocrinol*. (Paris). 1977;38:171–172.

18. Meuser W, Nieschlag E. Sexual hormone und Stimmlage des Mannes. *Deutsch Medekalischen Wochenschrieben*. 1977;102:261–264.

19. Brodnitz F. The age of the castrato voice. *J Speech Hear Disord*. 1975;40:291–295.

20. Brodnitz F. Hormones and the human voice. *Bull NY Acad Med*. 1971;47:183–191.

21. Schiff M. The influence of estrogens on connective tissue. In: Asboe-Hansen G, eds. *Hormones and Connective Tissue*. Copenhagen: Munksgaard Pres, 1967:282–341.

22. Lacina V. Der Einfluss der Menstruation auf die Stimme der Singerinnen. *Folia Phoniatr*. 1968;20:13–24.

23. Wendler J. Zyklusabhangige Leistungsschwankungen der Stimme und ihre Beeinflussung durch Ovulationshemmer. *Folia Phoniatr (Basel)*. 1972;24(4):259–277.

24. von Gelder L. Psychosomatic aspects of endocrine disorders of the voice. *J Comm Disord*. 1974;7:257–262.

25. Dordain M. Etude Statistique de l'influence des contraceptifs hormonaux sur la voix. *Folia Phoniatr*. 1972;24:86–96.

26. Pahn V, Goretzlehner G. Stimmstörungen durch hormonale Kontrazeptiva. *Zentralb Gynakol*. 1978;100:341–346.

27. Schiff M. "The pill" in otolaryngology. *Trans Amer Acad Ophthalmol Otolaryngol*. J–F; 1968;72:76–84.

28. Brodnitz F. Medical care preventive therapy (panel). In: Lawrence VL, *Transcripts of the Seventh Annual Symposium: Care of the Professional Voice*. New York, NY: The Voice Foundation; 1978;3:86.

29. Flach M, Schwickardi H, Simen R. Welchen Einfluss haben Menstruation and Schwängerschaft auf die augsgebildete Gesangsstimme? *Folia Phoniatr*. 1968;21:199–210.

30. Deuster CV. Irreversible Stimmstörung in der Schwängerschaft. *Hals Nase Ohren*. 1977;25:430–432.

31. Damste PH. Virilization of the voice due to anabolic steroids. *Folia Phoniatr*. 1964;16:10–18.

32. Damste PH. Voice changes in adult women caused by virilizing agents. *J Speech Hearing Disord*. 1967;32:126–132.

33. Saez FS. Recepteurs d'androgenes: mise en evidence dans la fraction cytosolique de muqueuse normale et d'epitheliomas pharyngolarynges humains. *C Royal Acad Science*. (Paris); 1975;280:935–938.

34. Vuorenkoski V, Lenko HL, Tjernlund P, Vuorenkoski L, Perheentupa J. Fundamental voice frequency during normal and abnormal growth, and after androgen treatment. *Arch Dis Child*. 1978;53:201–209.

35. Arndt HJ. Stimmstörungen nach Behandlung mit Androgenen und anabolen Hormonen. *München Medikalischen Wochenschreiben*, 1974;116:1715–1720.

36. Bourdial J. Les troubles de la voix provoques par la therapeutique hormonale androgene. *Ann Otolaryngol*. (Paris); 1970;87:725–734.

37. Imre V. Hormonell bedingte Stimmstörungen. *Folia Phoniatr*. 1968;20:394–404.

38. Feder RL. The professional voice and airline flight. *Otolaryngol Head Neck Surg*. 1984;92(3):251–254.

39. Sataloff RT. The impact of pollution on the voice. *Otolaryngol Head Neck Surg*. 1992;106(6):701–705.

40. Opperman DA. Pyrotechnics in the entertainment industry: an overview. In: Sataloff RT, ed. *Professional Voice: The Science and Art of Clinical Care*. 2nd ed. San Diego, Calif: Singular Publishing Group, Inc; 1997:393–402.

41. Rossol M. Pyrotechnics: health effects. In: Sataloff RT, ed. *Professional Voice: The Science and Art of Clinical Care*. 2nd ed. San Diego, Calif: Singular Publishing Group, Inc; 1997:407–411.

42. Herman H, Rossol M. Artificial fogs and smokes. In: Sataloff RT ed. *Professional Voice: the Science and Art of Clinical Care*. 2nd ed. San Diego, Calif: Singular Publishing Group, Inc; 1997:413–427.

43. Aronson AE. *Clinical Voice Disorders*. 3rd ed. New York, NY: Thieme; 1990:70–193.

44. Lawrence VL. Medical care for professional voice (panel). In: Lawrence VL, ed. *Transcripts from the Annual Symposium: Care of the Professional Voice.* New York, NY: The Voice Foundation; 1978;3:17–18.

45. Sataloff RT, Rosen DC, Hawkshaw M. Medications: effects and side-effects in professional voice users. In: Sataloff RT, ed. *Professional Voice: The Science and Art of Clinical Care.* 2nd ed. San Diego, Calif: Singular Publishing Group, Inc; 1997:453–465.

46. Gould WJ, Alberti PW, Brodnitz F, Hirano M. Medical care preventive therapy (panel). In: Lawrence VL, ed. *Transcripts of the Seventh Annual Symposium, Care of the Professional Voice.* New York, NY: The Voice Foundation; 1978;3:74–76.

47. Wallner LJ, Hill BJ, Waldrop W. Voice changes following adenotonsillectomy. *Laryngoscope.* 1968;78:1410–1418.

7

Special Patient History Considerations Relating to Members of the Acting Profession

Bonnie N. Raphael

Individuals who act for a living are a breed unto themselves. Many of the same attributes that make them exciting and electric onstage—high levels of habitual energy; ability to bring to the surface and communicate a large range of strong emotions; high degree of sensitivity, awareness, and concentration—make them susceptible to functional voice difficulties. Moreover, because so many of them rely on their vocal capabilities to do their work, any interference with their vocal effectiveness can be both frightening and highly intimidating.

Physicians and speech-language pathologists who work with actors must augment their standard patient histories to include additional questions relevant to both diagnosis and treatment. For example, many actors find they must supplement their income with "survival jobs"; in addition to whatever acting they are doing, many work as waiters and waitresses, taxicab drivers, receptionists, part-time teachers or babysitters, tour guides, or sales personnel. When a stage actor is a member of Actors' Equity Association ("Equity"), he or she can be called in for up to 8 hours per day, 6 days a week. (This does not include time spent learning lines; taking classes in singing, dancing, dialects, acting, fencing, and the like; research the actor may have to do on a particular role; etc.). Non-union stage actors may be working even longer hours for less money *and* may be holding down another job at the same time in order to make ends meet. Furthermore, the vast majority of working stage and film actors are hired for one show or one film at a time. Even as they rehearse and perform in their current projects, part of their energies must be devoted to finding their next employment.

It is important to ascertain what kind of acting each actor is doing—proscenium stage, theatre in-the-round, camera work (television and film), voiceover work (often requiring a number of different voices in quick succession), cabaret or club work, musical acting or "straight" performance, demanding character work, and so on. It is also important to find out whether the actor has been trained vocally or has learned how to use the voice by watching other actors and engaging in self-directed trial and error.

When an actor describes his or her symptoms to a physician or voice therapist, he or she may do so in a deceptively beautiful voice. As a result, the physician or speech-language pathologist may suspect either hypochondria or preopening night nervousness instead of understanding that many actors know their voices well enough and are sensitive enough to the sound and sensation of their voices to be the first to know that something is wrong. In a questionnaire study conducted at the Denver Center for the Performing Arts, a significant number of professional actors considered the following factors indicative of voice malfunction: general physical fatigue, throat fatigue, tightness or constriction, strain or tension, a greater awareness of the voice and the mechanism, greater effort needed to produce and sustain voice, reduction in functional pitch range, and greater difficulty in producing higher pitches.[1] Such factors may not be immediately discernible to anyone but the actor. For these reasons the criteria according to which the voice is evaluated need to be different for the actor than for the average voice patient.

A number of special circumstances make the work and life-style of actors particularly conducive to the development of voice difficulties:

1. Professional actors work hard and long. As stated earlier, a professional actor who is an Equity member is expected to work an 8-hour day during rehearsals (with one or two 10-out-of-12-hour days during technical rehearsals) and could conceivably be rehearsing his or her next show while performing a current show in the evenings. Actors who are doing workshop productions just to be seen by potential agents and producers or who are working at non-union theaters will be paid very little, if anything at all, and are typically holding down other work at the same time.

2. Professional actors often engage in a great deal of travel and in a series of temporary living arrangements. Many will be "jobbed in" for the run of a single show. Many will use their one day off per week to travel from the theater at which they are employed to a number of different places for auditions for their next jobs. This life-style often necessitates living in hotels or rooming houses. A number of actors who are members of touring companies will appear night after night in single performances in different theaters and travel by bus all day to their next destination. Temperature, relative humidity, altitude, irritants, allergens, and the like are in constant flux as a result.

3. Every actor must adjust vocal production to meet the particular needs of a number of different performance spaces. Theaters can range in size from that of a 99-seat proscenium house to a 2,500-seat stadium or even larger. Certain theaters are wonderfully designed to provide acoustics quite salutary to the speaking voice, whereas others provide absolute nightmares for even the best-trained actor. Projection of the voice is a concept that involves certain absolutes and a large number of variables that are related to different playing spaces. Furthermore, many actors change rehearsal spaces, change theaters during the run of a show, or even tour extensively, making these adjustments far more frequent. Technical skill at such changes is essential to the maintenance of good vocal production.

4. Many actors have personalities that a physician or speech-language pathologist might describe as volatile or emotional. In addition to a habitual energy level that is quite high by most standards, actors perform roles that very frequently involve out-of-the-ordinary life experiences. Plays are most typically written about people in crisis or transition. Actors are trained to get in touch with their emotions, to give over to the "given circumstances" of the plays in which they appear. (In "MacBeth," for example, young Malcolm discovers that his wife and children have been murdered . . . In "The Winter's Tale" Leontes believes that his wife is having an affair with his very dear friend . . . In "King Lear," the title character makes his final entrance howling, with the body of his daughter in his arms . . .) Simulating this broad range of emotions may produce volatility and vulnerability not only onstage but offstage as well.

5. The vocal demands made on actors' voices can be abusive. Even basic, nonfrills acting frequently necessitates vocal production that explores a wider than usual range—in terms of loudness, pitch, rhythm, and vocal quality. When one adds to this the demands of characterization (ie, the character being played by the actor may age during the course of the play from early 20s to late 70s; the character may be suffering from any number of illnesses, disabilities, or psychological aberrations; the actor may be playing two or three or more characters in the same show), the term "transformational actor" or "vocal athlete" becomes aptly descriptive. To create the illusion of illness or duress or high emotion, the actor may modify breathing or tighten the shoulders and jaw or constrict the voice, any of which may be harmful to the vocal mechanism. In addition, within the given circumstances of the play, the actor may be required to laugh hysterically or sob or scream or shriek or cough or choke or even "die." Although trained and experienced actors may be able to do this with relative impunity, there is a price to be paid for this extraordinary behavior. Last but certainly not least, many times, the actor is doing this work over a great deal of aural competition—there may be thunder in the background, a storm raging, music playing underneath spoken dialogue, the sounds of swords hitting shields or battle cries, the march of an approaching army—or even the constant hum and vibration of a theater's ventilation system—the siren of a passing ambulance—the roar of a passing airplane. The actor must find a way to ensure that his or her voice is dominant and the competition remains background to the ear of the audience. Not surprisingly, in the study previously cited,[1] actors reported that the three factors most consistently contributing to vocal strain and fatigue are long working hours, screaming or shouting onstage, and having to speak over high levels of background noise and/or music.

6. A series of potential occupational hazards complicate the actor's work even further. The wearing of certain costumes may restrict the actor's physical mobility so much that vocal production is affected. For example, ruffs, high collars, and heavy capes can produce difficulties, as can artificial beards and artificial moustaches, which are glued to the actor's skin. Actors may be asked to wear half or even full masks while they speak. They may be wearing makeup that limits facial mobility (eg, artificial scars) or prosthetic devices

(to change the look of the teeth or jawline), that make projection and articulation more difficult. Similarly, the scene may call for the presence of large amounts of onstage smoke, which the actor inhales before and while he or she performs. Add to this the ever-present stage dust (in the canvas on the flats, in the curtains, and in the costumes), that ongoing use of various sprays (to hold the hair in place, to set the makeup, to keep the costumes stain- and static-free) and it is clear that the hazards are ongoing and plentiful.

7. There is tremendous competition in the acting profession. Actors benefit greatly from being known as cooperative, professional, willing to go the extra mile. Typically, the actor has a real desire to please—an agent, a director, a critic—that will make him or her reticent to "take it easy" during rehearsals or performances. Many fear they will lose their jobs if they refuse to scream or to smoke a cigarette onstage or to shout over unfair competition. Most do not feel they are in a sufficiently secure position professionally to make demands or even requests for any modification of stage business.

8. The actor who has achieved success or popularity has done so by selling an image very closely connected with an identifiable vocal sound. Even if he or she knows that the sound is not ideal from a physiological or an aesthetic point of view, giving it up may be perceived as career-threatening, foolhardy, or professional suicide. A physician or speech-language pathologist must be clear and communicative with actor-patients, while at the same time being extremely aware of the ramifications of any significant vocal change in that individual.

Many actors will not seek the services of an otolaryngologist or a speech-language pathologist except as a last resort. They would rather tough it out or wait for this "cold" to pass. Consequently and unfortunately, this often means that they do not set foot in the office until the damage is already quite severe and the poor habits deeply entrenched.

Physicians and speech-language pathologists whom actors admire most are those who know about the exigencies of the actor's life and really care about the actor as both a patient and a performer. Such physicians and speech-language pathologists will take the time to come see the actor in action, on location whenever possible. Such physicians and speech-language pathologists will recommend treatment and/or therapy that makes sense to the actor and is compatible with and achievable within the confines of his or her professional needs and life-style. These physicians and speech-language pathologists will communicate with actors in a voice that sounds as if they, too, value a good, healthy, projectable sound, and in a language that the actor can understand and embrace rather than fear and reject. Such physicians and speech-language pathologists show both an interest in and a willingness to work directly with theatre and film teachers, coaches, and directors. Results can be astounding and "dramatic," but only if the actor is a willing contributor to the healing process rather than a frightened and intimidated victim of medical jargonese, inflexibility, insensitivity, or ignorance. Fortunately, with the rapid advance of voice medicine, more and more interested and specially trained physicians and speech-language pathologists are undergoing specialized training, and major improvements in quality of care are beginning to take place.

Summary

Actors encounter many special stresses and problems that may affect voice function. It is important to know the amount of training an actor has received, the specific nature of the acting environment, and vocational and avocational activities outside the theater. Health care providers and voice teachers must be familiar with the special requirements and vocal hazards associated with the acting profession.

Review Questions

1. Most professional actors support themselves through the theater, performances, and teaching and do not have to work in unrelated jobs.
   a. true
   b. false

2. Which of the following often requires the use of different voices in quick succession?
   a. theater in-the-round
   b. television
   c. voiceover
   d. cabaret
   e. proscenium stage

3. Actors Equity protects actors against working for more than 8 hours per day.
   a. true
   b. false

4. A good actor is able to maintain consistent technique, pitch, and loudness, and avoids vocal adjustments regardless of theater size.
   a. true
   b. false

5. Which of the following constitutes a potential vocal
   hazard?
   a. makeup
   b. theater acoustics
   c. costumes
   d. all of the above
   e. none of the above

References

1. Raphael BN, Scherer RC. Repertory actors' perceptions
   of the voice in relation to various professional conditions. In: Lawrence V, ed. *Transcripts of the Fourteenth
   Symposium: Care of the Professional Voice.* New York, NY:
   The Voice Foundation; 1985:124–130.

8

Physical Examination

Robert Thayer Sataloff

A comprehensive history frequently reveals the cause of a voice problem even before a physical examination is performed. However, a specialized physical examination, including objective assessment of voice function, is essential.[1–3] This includes a complete ear, nose, and throat examination; examination of a singer during the act of singing, or a professional speaker during a mock performance; slow motion evaluation of the vocal folds using strobovideolaryngoscopy; and quantitative measures of voice function. A physical examination other than the head and neck is also often indicated, particularly neurological and pulmonary examinations. Generally, only otolaryngologists subspecializing in voice care have all the equipment and team collaborators necessary for optimal comprehensive assessment. Many of the new technological devices used in the voice laboratory have interestingly proven extremely helpful adjuncts to traditional voice teaching, as well.

Complete Ear, Nose, and Throat Examination

Examination of the ears must include assessment of hearing acuity. Even a relatively slight hearing loss may result in voice strain as a singer tries to balance his or her vocal intensity with that of associate performers. Similar effects are encountered among speakers, but they are less prominent in the early stages of hearing loss. This is especially true of hearing losses acquired after vocal training has been completed. The effect is most pronounced with sensorineural hearing loss. Diplacusis makes vocal strain even worse. With conductive hearing loss, patients tend to speak or sing more softly than appropriate rather than too loudly, and this is less harmful.

During an ear, nose, and throat examination the conjunctiva and sclera should be routinely observed for erythema that suggests allergy or irritation, for pallor that suggests anemia, and for other abnormalities such as jaundice. These observations may reveal the problem reflected in the vocal tract even before the larynx is visualized.

The nose should be assessed for patency of the nasal airway, character of the nasal mucosa, and nature of secretions, if any. A singer who is unable to breathe through the nose because of anatomic obstruction is forced to breathe unfiltered, unhumidified air through the mouth. Pale gray allergic mucosa or swollen infected mucosa in the nose suggests abnormal mucosa elsewhere in the respiratory tract.

Examination of the oral cavity should include careful attention to the tonsils and lymphoid tissue in the posterior pharyngeal wall, as well as to the mucosa. Diffuse lymphoid hypertrophy associated with a complaint of "scratchy" voice and irritative cough may indicate infection. The amount and viscosity of mucosal and salivary secretions should also be noted. Xerostomia is particularly important. Dental examination should focus not only on oral hygiene but also on the presence of wear facets suggestive of bruxism. Bruxism is a clue to excessive tension and may be associated with dysfunction of the temporomandibular joints, which should also be routinely assessed. Thinning of the enamel of the central incisors in a normal or underweight patient may be a clue to bulimia. However, it may also result from excessive ingestion of lemons, which some singers eat to help thin their secretions.

The neck should be examined for masses, restriction of movement, excess muscle tension, and scars from prior neck surgery or trauma. Laryngeal vertical mobility is also important. For example, tilting of the larynx produced by partial fixation of cervical muscles cut during previous surgery may produce voice dysfunction, as may fixation of the trachea to overlying neck skin. Particular attention should be paid to the thyroid gland. Examination of posterior neck muscles and range of motion should not be neglected. The cranial nerves should also be examined. Diminished fifth nerve sensation, diminished gag reflex, palatal deviation, or other mild cranial nerve deficits may indicate cranial polyneuropathy. Post-viral infectious neuropathies may involve the superior laryngeal nerve and cause weakness, fatigability, and loss of range and projection in the voice. The recurrent laryngeal nerve is also affected in some cases. More serious neurologic disease may also be associated with such symptoms and signs.

Laryngeal Examination

Examination of the larynx begins when the patient enters the physician's office. The range, ease, volume, and quality of the speaking voice should be noted. Technical voice classification is beyond the scope of most physicians. However, the physician should at least be able to discriminate substantial differences in range and timbre such as between bass and tenor or alto and soprano. More detailed definitions of voice classification may be found elsewhere.[3] Although the correlation between speaking and singing voices is not perfect, a speaker with a low comfortable bass voice who reports that he is a tenor may be misclassified and singing inappropriate roles with consequent voice strain. This judgment should be deferred to an expert, but the observation should lead the physician to make the appropriate referral. Excessive volume or obvious strain during speaking clearly indicates that voice abuse or misuse is present and may be contributing to the patient's voice complaint.

Any patient with a voice problem should be at least examined by indirect laryngoscopy. Judging voice range, quality, or other vocal attributes by inspection of the vocal folds is not possible. However, the presence or absence of nodules, mass lesions, contact ulcers, hemorrhage, erythema, paralysis, arytenoid erythema (reflux), and other anatomic abnormalities must be established. Erythema of the laryngeal surface of the epiglottis is often associated with frequent coughing or clearing of the throat or with muscular tension dysphonia and is caused by direct trauma from the arytenoids during these maneuvers. A mirror or laryngeal telescope may provide a better view of the posterior portion of the vocal folds than is obtained with flexible endoscopy.

Fiberoptic laryngoscopy can be performed as an office procedure and allows inspection of the vocal folds in patients whose vocal folds are difficult to visualize indirectly. In addition, it permits observation of the vocal mechanism in a more natural posture than does indirect laryngoscopy. In the hands of an experienced endoscopist, this method may provide a great deal of information about both speaking and singing techniques. The combination of a fiberoptic laryngoscope with a laryngeal stroboscope may be especially useful. This system permits magnification, photography, and detailed inspection of vocal fold motion. Sophisticated systems that permit fiberoptic strobo-videolaryngoscopy are currently commercially available. They are an invaluable asset for routine clinical use. The video system also provides a permanent record, permitting reassessment, comparison over time, and easy consultation with other physicians. A refinement not currently commercially available is stereoscopic fiberoptic laryngoscopy, accomplished by placing a laryngoscope through each nostril, fastening the two together in the pharynx, and observing the larynx through the eyepieces.[4] This method allows visualization of laryngeal motion in three dimensions. However, it is primarily practical in a research setting. Rigid endoscopy with anesthesia may be reserved for the rare patient whose vocal folds cannot be adequately assessed by other means or for patients who need surgical procedures to remove or biopsy laryngeal lesions. In many cases this may be done with local anesthesia, avoiding the need for intubation and the traumatic coughing and vomiting that may occur even after general anesthesia administered by mask. Coughing after general anesthesia may be minimized by using topical anesthesia in the larynx and trachea. However, topical anesthetics may act as severe mucosal irritants in a small number of patients. They may also predispose the patient to aspiration in the postoperative period. If a patient has had difficulty with a topical anesthetic administered in the office, it should either be continuously used or not at all in the operating room. When used in general anesthesia cases, topical anesthetics should be applied at the end of the procedure. Thus, if inflammation occurs in response to the anesthetic, it will not interfere with the performance of the microsurgery. Postoperative duration of topical anesthetic effect is also optimized when it is applied at the conclusion of surgery. The author has had the least difficulty with 4% Xylocaine.

Objective Tests

Reliable, valid, objective analysis of the voice is extremely important, and is an essential part of a comprehensive physical examination. It is as invaluable to the otolaryngologist as audiometry is to the otologist.[3,5] Familiarity with some of the measures currently available is helpful.

Strobovideolaryngoscopy

Strobovideolaryngoscopy is the single most important technologic advance in diagnostic laryngology with the possible exception of fiberoptic laryngoscopy. Stroboscopic light allows routine slow-motion evaluation of the mucosal cover layer of the leading edge of the vocal fold. This state-of-the-art physical examination permits detection of vibratory asymmetries, structural abnormalities, small masses, submucosal scars, and other conditions that are invisible under ordinary light.[3,6,7] For example, in a patient who has a poor voice after laryngeal surgery and a "normal-looking larynx," stroboscopic light often reveals adynamic segments that explain the problem even to an untrained observer (such as the patient). The stroboscope is also extremely sensitive in detecting changes caused by fixation from small laryngeal neoplasms in patients who are being followed for leukoplakia or after laryngeal irradiation. Documentation of the procedure by coupling stroboscopic light with the video camera allows later reevaluation by the otolaryngologist or other health care providers.

A relatively standardized method of subjective assessment of videostroboscopic pictures is in wide clinical use,[8,9] allowing comparison of results among various physicians and investigators. Characteristics assessed include fundamental frequency, symmetry of bilateral movements, periodicity, glottal closure, amplitude, mucosal wave, presence of nonvibrating portions, and other unusual findings (such as a tiny polyp). In addition, objective frame-by-frame computer analysis is also possible, and it is now practical because of the program developed by Dr. Peak Woo and included in the software with the stroboscope (Model #RLS 9100) produced by Kay Elemetrics, Inc., Pine Brook, New Jersey.

Other Techniques to Examine Vocal Fold Vibration

Other techniques used to examine vocal fold vibration include ultra-high-speed photography, electroglottography (EGG), photoelectroglottography, and ultrasound glottograpy, and most recently, videokymography.[10] Ultra-high-speed photography provides images similar to those provided by strobovideolaryngoscopy but requires expensive, cumbersome equipment and delayed data processing. Electroglottography (EGG) uses two electrodes on the skin of the neck above the thyroid laminae. A weak, high-frequency voltage is passed through the larynx from one electrode to the other. Opening and closing of the vocal folds varies the transverse electrical impedance, producing variation of the electrical current in phase with vocal fold vibration. The resultant tracing is called an electroglottogram. It traces the opening and closing of the glottis and can be compared with stroboscopic images.[11] Electroglottography allows objective determination of the presence or absence of glottal vibrations and easy determination of the fundamental period of vibration and is reproducible. It more accurately reflects the glottal condition during its closed phase. Photoelectroglottography and ultrasound glottography are less useful clinically.[12]

Measures of Phonatory Ability

Objective measures of phonatory ability are among the easiest and most readily available to the otolaryngologist, are helpful in treatment of professional vocalists with specific voice disorders, and are quite useful in assessing the results of surgical therapies. Maximum phonation time is measured with a stopwatch. The patient is instructed to sustain the vowel /A/ for as long as possible after deep inspiration, vocalizing at a comfortable frequency and intensity. The frequency and intensity may be determined and controlled by an inexpensive frequency analyzer and sound level meter. The test is repeated three times and the greatest value is recorded. Normal values have been determined.[12] Frequency range of phonation is recorded in semitones and documents the vocal range from the lowest note in the modal register (excluding vocal fry) to the highest falsetto note. This is the *physiologic frequency range* of phonation and disregards quality. The *musical frequency range* of phonation measures lowest to highest notes of musically acceptable quality. Tests for maximum phonation time, frequency ranges, and many of the other parameters discussed later (including spectrographic analysis) may be preserved on a tape recorder for analysis at a convenient future time and used for pretreatment and post-treatment comparisons. Recordings should be made in a standardized, consistent fashion.

Frequency limits of vocal register may also be measured. The registers are (from low to high) vocal fry, chest, mid, head, and falsetto. However, classification of registers is controversial, and many other classifications are used. Although the classifications listed above are common among musicians, at present most voice scientists prefer a scheme that classifies registers as pulse, modal, and loft. Overlap of frequency among registers routinely occurs. Testing the speaking fundamental frequency often reveals excessively low pitch, an abnormality associated with chronic voice abuse and development of vocal nodules. This parameter may be objectively followed throughout a course of voice therapy. Intensity range of phonation (IRP) has proven a less useful measure than frequency range. It varies with fundamental frequency (which should be recorded) and is greatest in the middle frequency range. It is recorded in sound pressure level (SPL) re: 0.0002-μbar. For normal adults who are not professional vocalists and measuring at a single fundamental frequency, IRP averages 54.8 dB for males and 51 dB for females.[13] Alterations of intensity are common in voice disorders, although IRP is not the most sensitive test to detect them. Information from these tests may be combined in a fundamental frequency-intensity profile,[12] also called a phonetogram.

Glottal efficiency (ratio of the acoustic power at the level of the glottis to subglottal power) provides useful information but is not clinically practical because measuring acoustic power at the level of the glottis is difficult. Subglottic power is the product of subglottal pressure and airflow rate. These can be clinically determined. Various alternative measures of glottic efficiency have been proposed, including the ratio of radiated acoustic power to subglottal power,[14] airflow-intensity profile,[15] and ratio of the root mean square value of the AC component to the mean volume velocity (DC component).[16] Although glottal efficiency is of great interest, none of these tests is particularly helpful under routine clinical circumstances.

Aerodynamic Measures

Traditional pulmonary function testing provides the most readily accessible measure of respiratory function. The most common parameters measured include: (a) *tidal volume*, the volume of air that enters the lungs during inspiration and leaves during expiration in normal breathing, and (b) *functional residual capacity*, the volume of air remaining in the lungs at the end of inspiration during normal breathing. It may be divided into *expiratory reserve volume* (maximal additional volume that can be exhaled) and *residual volume* (the volume of air remaining in the lungs at the end of maximal exhalation); (c) *inspiratory capacity*, the maximal volume of air that can be inhaled starting at the functional residual capacity; (d) *total lung capacity*, the volume of air in the lungs following maximal inspiration; (e) *vital capacity*, the maximal volume of air that can be exhaled from the lungs following maximal inspiration; (f) *forced vital capacity*, the rate of air flow with rapid, forceful expiration from total lung capaci-

ty to residual volume; (g) *FEV₁*, the forced expiratory volume in 1 second; (h) *FEV₃*, the forced expiratory volume in 3 seconds; and (i) *maximal midexpiratory flow*, the mean rate of air flow over the middle half of the forced vital capacity (between 25% and 75% of the forced vital capacity).

For singers and professional speakers with an abnormality caused by voice abuse, abnormal pulmonary function tests may confirm deficiencies in aerobic conditioning or reveal previously unrecognized asthma.[17] Flow glottography with computer inverse filtering is also a practical and valuable diagnostic tool for assessing flow at the vocal fold level, evaluating the voice source, and imaging the results of the balance between adductory forces and subglottal pressure.[18,19] It also has therapeutic value.

The *spirometer*, readily available for pulmonary function testing, can be used for measuring airflow during phonation. However, it does not allow simultaneous display of acoustic signals, and its frequency response is poor. A *pneumotachograph* consists of a laminar air resistor, a differential pressure transducer, and an amplifying and recording system. It allows measurement of airflow and simultaneous recording of other signals when coupled with a polygraph. A *hot-wire anemometer* allows determination of airflow velocity by measuring the electrical drop across the hot wire. Modern hot-wire anemometers containing electrical feedback circuitry that maintains the temperature of the hot wire provide a flat frequency response up to 1 KHz and are clinically useful.[16]

The four parameters traditionally measured in analyzing the aerodynamic performance of a voice are: *subglottal pressure* (P_{sub}), *supraglottal pressure* (P_{sup}), *glottal impedance*, and *volume velocity of airflow at the glottis*. These parameters and their rapid variations can be measured under laboratory circumstances. However, their mean value is usually clinically determined as follows:

$$P_{sub} - P_{sub} = MFR \times GR$$

Where MFR is the mean (root mean square) flow rate and GR is the mean (root mean square) glottal resistance. When vocalizing the open vowel /A/, the supraglottic pressure equals the atmospheric pressure reducing the equation to:

$$P_{sub} = MFR \times GR$$

The mean flow rate is a useful clinical measure. While the patient vocalizes the vowel /A/, the mean flow rate is calculated by dividing the total volume of air used during phonation by the duration of phonation. The subject phonates at a comfortable pitch and loudness either over a determined period of time or for a maximum sustained period of phonation.

Air volume is measured by the use of a mask fitted tightly over the face or by phonating into a mouthpiece while wearing a noseclamp. Measurements may be made using a spirometer, pneumotachograph, or hot-wire anemometer. The normal values for mean flow rate under habitual phonation, with changes in intensity or register, and under various pathologic circumstances, have been determined.[12] Normal values are available for both adults and children. Mean flow rate is a clinically useful parameter to follow during treatment for vocal nodules, recurrent laryngeal nerve paralysis, spasmodic dysphonia, and other conditions.

Glottal resistance cannot be measured directly, but it may be calculated from the mean flow rate and mean subglottal pressure. Normal glottal resistance is 20 to 100 dyne seconds/cm^5 at low and medium pitches and 150 dyne seconds/cm^5 at high pitches.[14] *Subglottal pressure* is clinically less useful because it requires an invasive procedure for accurate measurement. It may be determined by tracheal puncture, transglottal catheter, or measurement through a tracheostoma using a transducer. Subglottal pressure may be approximated using an esophageal balloon. *Intratracheal pressure*, which is roughly equal to subglottal pressure, is transmitted to the balloon through the trachea. However, measured changes in the esophageal balloon are affected by intraesophageal pressure which is dependent on lung volume. Therefore, estimates of subglottal pressure using this technique are valid only under specific, controlled circumstances. The normal values for subglottal pressure under various healthy and pathologic voice conditions have also been determined by numerous investigators.[12]

The *phonation quotient* is the vital capacity divided by the maximum phonation time. It has been shown to correlate closely with maximum flow rate[20] and is a more convenient measure. Normative data determined by various authors have been published.[12] The phonation quotient provides an objective measure of the effects of treatment and is particularly useful in cases of recurrent laryngeal nerve paralysis and mass lesions of the vocal folds, including nodules.

Acoustic Analysis

Acoustic analysis of voice signals is both promising and disappointing. The skilled otolaryngologist, speech-language pathologist, musician, or other trained listener frequently infers a great deal of valid information from the sound of a voice. However, clinically useful technology for analyzing and quantifying subtle acoustic differences is still not ideal. In many ways, the tape recorder is still the otolaryngologist's most valuable tool for acoustic analysis. Recording a patient's voice under controlled, repeatable circumstances before, during, and at the conclusion of treatment allows both the physician and the patient to make a qualitative, subjective acoustic analysis. Objective analysis with instruments may also be made from recorded voice samples.

Care must be taken to use a standardized protocol, and utilizing sophisticated instrumentation that is available[3] may be valuable for both medical diagnosis and studio feedback. Acoustic analysis equipment can determine frequency, intensity, harmonic spectrum, cycle-to-cycle perturbations in frequency (jitter), cycle-to-cycle perturbations in amplitude (shimmer), harmonics-to-noise ratios, breathiness index, and many other parameters.

The DSP SONA-GRAPH Model 5500 (Kay Elemetrics, Pine Brook, New Jersey) is an integrated voice analysis system. It is equipped for sound spectrography capabilities. Spectrography provides a visual record of the voice. The acoustic signal is depicted using time (x axis), frequency (y axis), and intensity (z axis) shading of light vs dark. Using the bandpass filters, generalizations about quality, pitch, and loudness can be made. These observations are used in formulating the voice therapy treatment plan. Formant structure and strength can be determined using the narrow-band filters, of which a variety of configurations are possible. In clinical settings where singers and other professional voice users are routinely evaluated and treated, this feature is extremely valuable. A sophisticated voice analysis program (an optional program) may be combined with the Sona-Graph and is an especially valuable addition to the clinical laboratory. The voice analysis program (CSL, Kay Elemetrics) measures speaking fundamental frequency, frequency perturbation (jitter), amplitude perturbation (shimmer), harmonics-to-noise ratio, and provides a great number of other useful values. An electroglottograph (EGG) may be used in conjunction with the Sona-Graph to provide some of these voicing parameters. Examining the EGG waveform alone is possible with this setup, but its clinical usefulness has not yet been established. An important feature of the Sona-Graph is the long-term average (LTA) spectral capability which allows for analyzing longer voice samples (30–90 seconds). The LTA analyzes only voiced speech segments, and may be useful in screening for hoarse or breathy voices. In addition, computer interface capabilities (also an optional program) have solved many data storage and file maintenance problems.

In analyzing acoustic signals, the microphone may be placed at the level of the mouth or may be positioned in or over the trachea. We use airborne signals with a microphone near the mouth. Position should be standardized in each office or laboratory.[21] Various techniques are being developed to improve the usefulness of acoustic analysis. Because of the enormous amount of information carried in the acoustic signal, further refinements in objective acoustic analysis should prove particularly valuable to the clinician.

Laryngeal Electromyography

Electromyography requires an electrode system, an amplifier, an oscilloscope, a loudspeaker, and a recording system. Electrodes are placed transcutaneously into laryngeal muscles. It may be extremely valuable in confirming cases of vocal fold paresis, in differentiating paralysis from arytenoid dislocation, in distinguishing recurrent laryngeal nerve paralysis from combined recurrent and superior nerve paralysis, diagnosing other more subtle neurolaryngological pathologies, and documenting functional voice disorders and malingering. It is also recommended for needle localization when using botulinum toxin for treatment of spasmodic dysphonia and other conditions.

Laryngeal Evoked Brain Stem Response

Laryngeal evoked brain stem response (LBR) is a relatively new technique that shows promise for neurolaryngologic diagnostic purposes. The test assesses a laryngeal reflex which includes the internal branch of the superior laryngeal nerve, laryngeal loci in the brain stem, and recurrent and superior laryngeal nerves. Impulses from the superior laryngeal nerve pass through the nucleus of the tractus solitarium, the nucleus ambiguus, the nucleus of the vagus nerve, the retrofacial nucleus, and the nucleus of the reticular reformation. When the superior laryngeal nerve is electrically stimulated on one side, there are ipsilateral and bilateral adductor responses. Ludlow[22] showed an R1 and R2 response in the thyroarytenoid muscle after stimulation of the superior laryngeal nerve. R1 occurs ipsilaterally at a latency of 18 msec and R2 occurs bilaterally at 66–70 msec. This indicates that R2 is a polysynaptic bilateral response.

LBR can be clinically performed with an appropriate ABR device using equipment similar to that used for facial electroneuronography. The superior laryn-

geal nerve is stimulated using a bipolar surface electrode placed between the greater cornu of the hyoid bone and the superior cornu of the thyroid cartilage. Hooked wire electrodes can also be used instead of surface electrodes. Special techniques are necessary to refine the response, and LBR technique is still under development. In the near future, we anticipate greater sophistication of LBR technique and increasing recognition of its clinical value.

Imaging

Sophisticated imaging has greatly enhanced our ability to recognize the cause of many voice problems. CT (computerized tonography) scanning and MR (magnetic resonance) imaging are currently the two most important and widely used modalities. Details of imaging techniques will not be discussed in this book. Physicians caring for patients with voice problems should be familiar with the latest information in the radiologic literature, should demand the highest quality CT and MR studies, and should be familiar with special techniques such as 3-D CT (Fig 8–1) which may be extremely helpful under some circumstances.

Psychoacoustic Evaluation

Because the human ear and brain are the most sensitive and complex analyzers of sound currently available, many researchers have tried to standardize and quantify psychoacoustic evaluation. Unfortunately, even definitions of basic terms such as hoarseness and breathiness are still controversial. Psychoacoustic evaluation protocols and interpretations are not standardized. Consequently, although subjective psychoacoustic analysis of voice is of great value to the individual skilled clinician, it remains generally unsatisfactory for comparing research among laboratories or for reporting clinical results.

Evaluation of the Singing Voice

The physician must be careful not to exceed the limits of his or her expertise especially in caring for singers. However, if voice abuse or technical error is suspected, or if a difficult judgment must be reached on whether to allow a sick singer to perform, a brief observation of the patient's singing may provide invaluable information.

This is accomplished best by asking the singer to stand and sing scales either in the examining room or

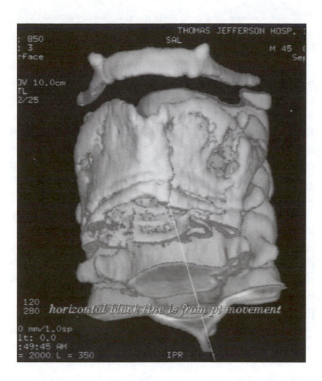

Fig 8–1. Three-dimensional CT of larynx, A-P (anterior-posterior) view illustrating vertical fracture (arrows).

Fig 8–2. Bimanual palpation of the support mechanism. The singer should expand posteriorly and anteriorly with inspiration. Muscles should tighten prior to onset of the sung tone.

in the soundproof audiology booth. Similar maneuvers may be used for professional speakers including actors (who can vocalize and recite lines), clergy and politicians (who can deliver sermons and speeches), and virtually all other voice professionals. The singer's stance should be balanced, with the weight slightly forward. The knees should be bent slightly and the shoulders, torso, and neck should be relaxed. The singer should inhale through the nose whenever possible allowing filtration, warming, and humidification of inspired air. In general, the chest should be expanded, but most of the active breathing is abdominal. The chest should not substantially rise with each inspiration, and the supraclavicular musculature should not be obviously involved in inspiration. Shoulders and neck muscles should not be tensed even with deep inspiration. Abdominal musculature should be contracted shortly before the initiation of the tone. This may be evaluated visually or by palpation (Fig 8–2). Muscles of the neck and face should be relaxed. Economy is a basic principle of all artforms. Wasted energy and motion and muscle tension are incorrect and usually deleterious.

The singer should be instructed to sing a scale (a five-note scale is usually sufficient) on the vowel /A/, beginning on any comfortable note. Technical errors are usually most obvious as contraction of muscles in the neck and chin, retraction of the lower lip, retraction of the tongue, or tightening of the muscles of mastication. The singer's mouth should be widely but comfortably open . When singing /A/, the singer's tongue should rest in a neutral position with the tip of the tongue lying against the back of the singer's mandibular incisors. If the tongue pulls back or demonstrates obvious muscular activity as the singer performs the scales, improper voice use can be confirmed on the basis of positive evidence (Fig 8–3). The position of the larynx should not substantially vary with pitch changes. Rising of the larynx with ascending pitch is also evidence of technical dysfunction (Fig 8–4). This examination gives the physician an opportunity to observe any dramatic differences between the quali-

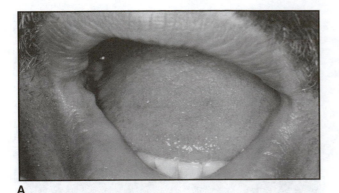

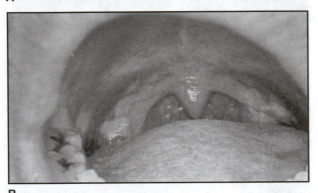

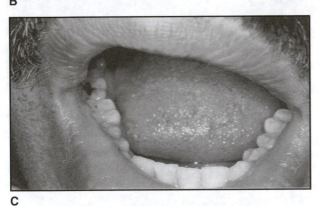

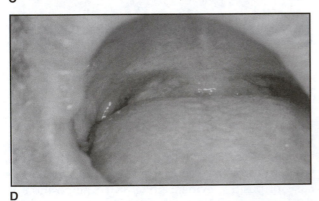

Fig 8–3. Proper relaxed position of the anterior (**A**) and posterior (**B**) portions of the tongue. Common improper use of the tongue pulled back from the teeth (**C**) and raised posteriorly (**D**).

ties and ranges of the speaking voice and the singing voice. A laryngeal examination summary has proved helpful in organization and documentation.[2]

Remembering the admonition not to exceed his or her expertise, the physician who examines many singers can often glean valuable information from a brief attempt to modify an obvious technical error. For example, deciding whether to allow a singer with mild or moderate laryngitis to perform is often difficult. On the one hand, an expert singer has technical skills that allow him or her to safely compensate. On the other hand, if a singer does not sing with correct technique and does not have the discipline to modify volume, technique, and repertoire as necessary, the risk of vocal injury may be substantially increased by even mild inflammation of the vocal folds. In borderline circumstances, observation of the singer's technique may greatly help the physician in making a judgment.

If the technique appears flawless, the physician may feel somewhat more secure in allowing the singer to proceed with performance commitments. Even good singers more commonly demonstrate technical errors when experiencing voice difficulties. In a vain effort to compensate for dysfunction at the vocal fold level, singers often modify their technique in the neck and supraglottic vocal tract. In the good singer, this usually means going from good technique to bad technique. The most common error involves pulling the tongue back and tightening the cervical muscles. Although this increased muscular activity gives the singer the illusion of making the voice more secure, this technical maladjustment undermines vocal efficiency and increases vocal strain. The physician may ask the singer to hold the top note of a five-note scale; while the note is being held, the singer may simply be told, "Relax your tongue." At the same time the physician points to the singer's abdominal musculature. Most good singers immediately correct to good technique. If they do, and if upcoming performances are particularly important, the singer may be able to perform with a reminder that meticulous technique is essential. The singer should be advised to "sing by feel rather than by ear," to consult his or her voice teacher, and conserve the voice except when it is absolutely necessary to use it. If a singer is unable to promptly correct from bad technique to good technique, especially if he or she uses excessive muscle tension in the neck and ineffective abdominal support, it is generally safer not to perform with even a mild vocal fold abnormality. With increased experience and training, the otolaryngologist may make

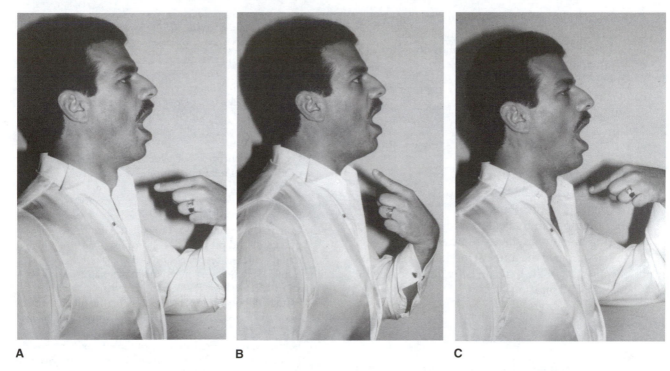

A B C

Fig 8–4. Larynx should remain in relatively constant position throughout scale (**A**). If it rises with ascending pitch (**B**) or lowers with descending pitch (**C**), technical error is present.

other observations that aid in providing appropriate treatment recommendations for singer patients. Once these skills have been mastered for the care of singers, applying them to other professional voice users is relatively easy, so long as the physician takes the time to understand the demands of the individual's professional, avocational, and recreational vocal activities.

If treatment is to be instituted, at least a tape recording of the voice is advisable in most cases and essential before any surgical intervention. The author routinely uses strobovideolaryngoscopy for diagnosis and documentation in virtually all cases as well as many of the objective measures discussed. Such testing is extremely helpful clinically and medicolegally.

Summary

Physical examination should include a thorough evaluation of the ears, nose, and throat; visualization of the vocal folds; and special examinations. Strobovideolaryngoscopy is particularly important because it provides slow motion assessment of the vibratory margin of the vocal fold. Objective voice measures are also extremely helpful to health care providers and singing teachers. All must be carefully documented (Appendix IV).

Review Questions

1. Performers tend to sing more loudly than usual without realizing it in the presence of:
   a. conductive hearing loss
   b. routine allergies
   c. occult sensorineural hearing loss
   d. all of the above
   e. none of the above

2. To determine the problem in a patient with hoarseness, the most important examination is:
   a. laryngeal mirror examination
   b. routine, transnasal fiberoptic laryngoscopy
   c. strobovideolaryngoscopy
   d. pulmonary function testing
   e. spectroscopic analysis

3. Techniques to examine vocal fold vibration include all of the following except:
   a. strobovideolaryngoscopy
   b. electroglottography
   c. ultra-high-speed photography
   d. spirometry
   e. videotomography

4. To help distinguish between vocal fold immobility caused by paralysis, and immobility caused by arytenoid dislocation, which of the following studies is especially helpful?
   a. spectroscopy
   b. electromyography
   c. pulmonary function testing
   d. flow glottography
   e. laryngeal evoked brain stem response testing

5. Tidal volume is:
   a. any volume of air that enters and leaves the lungs during normal breathing
   b. the volume of air that enters and leaves the lungs during breathing with extreme effort
   c. air remaining in the lungs at the end of inspiration
   d. the amount of air that can be exhaled following maximal inspiration
   e. none of the above

References

1. Sataloff RT. Professional singers: the science and art of clinical care. *Am J Otolaryngol*. 1981;2(3):251–266.
2. Sataloff RT. The professional voice: part II, physical examination. *J Voice*. 1987;1(2):191–201.
3. Sataloff RT. *Professional Voice: Science and Art of Clinical Care*. 2nd ed. San Diego, Calif: Singular Publishing Group, Inc; 1997.
4. Fujimura O. Stereo-fiberoptic laryngeal observation. *J Acous Soc Am*. 1979;65(12):70–72.
5. Sataloff RT, Spiegel JR, Carroll LM, Darby KS, Hawkshaw MJ, Rulnick RK. The clinical voice laboratory: practical design and clinical application. *J Voice*. 1990;4(3): 264–279.
6. Sataloff RT, Spiegel JR, Carroll LM, Schiebel BR, Darby SK, Rulnick RK. Strobovideolaryngoscopy in professional voice users: results and clinical value. *J Voice*. 1988;1(4): 359–364.
7. Sataloff RT, Spiegel JR, Hawkshaw MJ. Strobovideolaryngoscopy: results and clinical value. *Ann Otol Rhinol Laryngol*. 1991;100(9):725–727.
8. Hirano M. Phonosurgery: basic and clinical investigations. *Otologia*. 1975;21:239–442.
9. Bless D, Hirano M, Feder RJ. Video stroboscopic evaluation of the larynx. *Ear Nose Throat J*. 1987;66(7):289–296.
10. Svec J, Schutte H. Videokymography: high-speed lines scanning of vocal fold vibration. *J Voice*. 1996;10(2): 201–205.
11. Leclure FLE, Brocaar ME, Verscheeure J. Electroglottography and its relation to glottal activity. *Folia Phoniatr*. 1975;27:215.
12. Hirano M. *Clinical Examination of the Voice*. New York, NY: Springer-Verlag; 1981:1–98.
13. Coleman RJ, Mabis JH, Hinson JK. Fundamental frequency sound pressure level profiles of adult male and female voices. *J Speech Hear Res*. 1977;20:197.
14. Isshiki N. Regulatory mechanism of voice intensity variation. *J Speech Hear Res*. 1964;7:17–29.
15. Saito S. Phonosurgery, basic study on the mechanism of phonation and endolaryngeal microsurgery. *Otologia*. 1977;23:171.
16. Isshiki N. Functional surgery of the larynx. *Report of the 78th Annual Convention of the Oto-Rhino-Laryngological Society of Japan*. Fuokuoka, Japan: Kyoto University: 1977.
17. Cohn JR, Sataloff RT, Spiegel JR, Fish JE, Kennedy K. Airway reactivity-induced asthma in singers (ARIAS). *J Voice*. 1991;5(4):332–337.
18. Sundberg J. The acoustics of the singing voice. *Sci Am*. 1977;236(3):82–91.
19. Sataloff RT. The human voice. *Sci Am*. 1992; 267(6): 108–115.
20. Hirano M, Koike Y, von Leden H. Maximum phonation time and air usage during phonation. *Folia Phoniatr*. 1968;20:185.
21. Price DB, Sataloff RT. A simple technique for consistent microphone placement in voice recording. *J Voice*. 1988;2(3):206.
22. Ludlow CL, Pelt FV, Kohda J. Characteristics of late responses to superior laryngeal nerve stimulation in humans. *Ann Otol Rhinol Laryngol*. 1992;101:127–134.

9

Common Medical Diagnoses and Treatments in Professional Voice Users

Robert Thayer Sataloff

Introduction

There are numerous medical conditions that adversely affect the voice, some of which were discussed in chapter 6. Many have their origins primarily outside the head and neck. This chapter is not intended to be all inclusive, but rather to introduce some of the more common and important conditions found in professional voice users seeking medical care.

In the 2286 cases of all forms of voice disorders reported by Brodnitz in 1971,[1] 80% of the disorders were attributed to voice abuse or to psychogenic factors resulting in vocal dysfunction. Of these patients, 20% had organic voice disorders. Of women with organic problems, about 15% had identifiable endocrine causes. A much higher incidence of organic disorders, particularly reflux laryngitis and acute infectious laryngitis, is more commonly found in the author's practice.

Voice Abuse

Common patterns of voice abuse and misuse will not be discussed in detail in this chapter. They are covered elsewhere in this book and in other literature.[2] Voice abuse and/or misuse should be particularly suspected in patients who complain of voice fatigue associated with voice use, whose voices are worse at the end of a working day or week, and in any patient who is chronically hoarse. Technical errors in voice use may be the primary etiology of a voice complaint or may develop secondarily due to a patient's effort to compensate for voice disturbance from another cause.

Speaking in noisy environments, such as cars, airplanes, stock exchange, and factories, is particularly abusive to the voice. So are backstage greetings, post-performance parties, choral conducting, voice teaching, and cheerleading. With proper training, all of these activities can be done safely. However, most patients, surprisingly even singers, have little or no training for the speaking voice.

If voice abuse is caused by speech, treatment should be provided by a licensed, certified speech-language pathologist. In many cases, training the speaking voice also will greatly benefit singers not only by improving speech, but also by helping singing technique. Physicians should not hesitate to recommend such training, but it should be performed by an expert speech-language pathologist who specializes in voice. Many speech-language pathologists who are well trained in swallowing rehabilitation, articulation therapy, and other techniques are not expert in voice therapy.

Specialized singing training may also be helpful to some voice patients who are not singers and it is invaluable for patients who are singers. Initial singing training teaches relaxation techniques, develops muscle strength, and is symbiotic with standard speech therapy.

Abuse of the voice during singing is a complex problem. When voice abuse is suspected or observed in a patient with vocal complaints, he or she should be referred to a laryngologist who specializes in voice, preferably a physician affiliated with a voice care team.

Structural Abnormalties

Nodules

Nodules are callouslike masses of the vocal folds which are caused by vocally abusive behaviors and are a dreaded malady of singers. Occasionally, laryngoscopy reveals asymptomatic vocal nodules that do not appear to interfere with voice production; in such cases, the nodules should not be treated. Even some famous and successful singers have had untreated vocal nodules. However, in most cases nodules result in hoarseness, breathiness, loss of range, and vocal fatigue. They may be due to abusive speaking or singing. Voice therapy always should be tried as the initial therapeutic modality and will cure the vast majority of patients even if the nodules look firm and have been present for many months or years. Even apparently large, fibrotic nodules often shrink, disappear, or become asymptomatic with 6 to 12 weeks of voice therapy with good patient compliance. Even in those who eventually need surgical excision of the nodules, preoperative voice therapy is essential to prevent recurrence. Care must be taken in diagnosing nodules. It is almost impossible to accurately and consistently make the diagnosis without strobovideolaryngoscopy and good magnification. For example, without stroboscopy vocal fold cysts are commonly misdiagnosed as nodules; and treatment strategies are different for the two lesions. Vocal nodules are confined to the superficial layer of the lamina propria and are composed primarily of edematous tissue or collagenous fibers. Basement membrane reduplication is common. They are usually bilateral and fairly symmetrical.

Caution must be exercised in diagnosing small nodules in patients who have been actively singing. In many singers bilateral, symmetrical, soft swellings at the junction of the anterior and middle thirds of the vocal folds develop after heavy voice use. No evidence suggests that singers with such "physiologic swelling" are predisposed to development of vocal nodules. At present, the condition is generally considered to be within normal limits. The physiologic swelling usually disappears with 24 to 48 hours of rest from heavy voice use. The physician must be careful not to frighten the patient by misdiagnosing physiologic swellings as vocal nodules. Nodules carry a great stigma especially among singers and other voice professionals; and the psychologic impact of the diagnosis should not be underestimated. When nodules are present, these patients should be informed with the same gentle caution used in telling a patient that he or she has a life-threatening illness.

Submucosal cysts of the vocal folds are probably traumatic lesions that in many cases produce blockage of a mucous gland duct. However, they may also be congenital or occur from other causes. Cysts are ordinarily lined with thin squamous epithelium. Retention cysts contain mucus. Epidermoid cysts contain caseous material. Cysts are generally located in the superficial layer of the lamina propria. In some cases, they may be attached to the vocal ligament. They often cause contact swelling on the contralateral side and are usually initially misdiagnosed as nodules. They can usually be differentiated from nodules by strobovideolaryngoscopy when the mass is obviously fluid-filled. They may also be suspected when the nodule (contact swelling) on one vocal fold resolves with voice therapy while the mass on the other vocal fold does not resolve. Cysts may be discovered on one side (occasionally both sides) when surgery is performed for apparent nodules that have not resolved with voice therapy. The surgery should be performed superficially and with minimal trauma, as discussed later.

Polyps

Vocal *polyps*, another type of benign vocal fold mass, usually occur on only one vocal fold. They often have a prominent feeding blood vessel coursing along the superior surface of the vocal fold and entering the base of the polyp. The pathogenesis of polyps cannot be proven in many cases, but the lesion is thought to be traumatic and sometimes starts as a hemorrhage. Polyps may be sessile or pedunculated. They are typically located in the superficial layer of the lamina propria and do not involve the vocal ligament. In those arising from an area of hemorrhage, the vocal ligament may be involved with posthemorrhagic fibrosis that is contiguous with the polyp. Histological evaluation most commonly reveals collagenous fibers, hyaline degeneration, edema, thrombosis, and often bleeding within the polypoid tissue. Cellular infiltration may also be present. In some cases, even sizable polyps resolve with relative voice rest and a few weeks of low-dose steroid therapy (eg, Triamcinolone 4 mg twice a day). However, most require surgical removal. If polyps are not treated, they may produce contact injury on the contralateral vocal fold. Voice therapy should be used to assure good relative voice rest and prevention of abusive behavior before and after surgery. When surgery is performed, care must be taken not to damage the leading edge of the vocal fold, especially if a laser is used, as discussed later. In all laryngeal surgery, delicate microscopic section is now the standard of care. Vocal fold "stripping," a surgical approach formerly used for benign lesions, often resulted in scar and poor voice function. It is no longer an acceptable technique in most situations.

Granulomas

Granulomas usually occur in the cartilaginous portion of the vocal fold near the vocal process or on the medial surface of the arytenoid. They are composed of collagenous fibers, fibroblasts, proliferated capillaries, and leukocytes. They are usually covered with epithelium. They are actually chronic inflammatory tissue and not granulomas such as seen in tuberculosis or sarcoidosis. Laryngeal granulomas are associated with gastroesophageal reflux laryngitis and trauma (including trauma from voice abuse and from intubation). Therapy should include reflux control, voice therapy, and surgery if the granulomas do not promptly resolve.

Reinke's Edema

Reinke's edema is characterized by an "elephant ear," or floppy vocal fold appearance. It is also observed during examination in many nonprofessional voice users and is accompanied by a low, coarse, gruff voice. Reinke's edema is a condition in which the superficial layer of lamina propria (Reinke's space) becomes edematous. The lesion does not usually include hypertrophy, inflammation, or degeneration, although other terms for the condition include polypoid degeneration, chronic polypoid corditis, and chronic edematous hypertrophy. Reinke's edema is often associated with smoking, voice abuse, reflux, and hypothyroidism. Underlying conditions should be treated; however, the condition often requires surgery. The surgery should be performed only if there is a justified high suspicion of serious pathology such as cancer, if there is airway obstruction, or if the patient is unhappy with his or her vocal quality. For some voice professionals, abnormal Reinke's edema is an important component of the vocal signature. Although the condition is usually bilateral, surgery should generally be performed on one side at a time.

Sulcus Vocalis

Sulcus vocalis is a groove along the edge of the membranous vocal fold. The majority are congenital, bilateral, and symmetrical, although post-traumatic acquired lesions occur. When symptomatic, sulcus vocalis can be treated surgically.

Scar

Vocal fold scar results in fibrosis and obliteration of the layered structure of the vocal fold. It may markedly impede vibration and consequently cause profound dysphonia. Recent surgical advances have made this condition much more treatable than it used to be, but it is still rarely possible to restore voices to normal.[2]

Hemorrhage

Vocal fold hemorrhage is a potential disaster in singers. Hemorrhages resolve spontaneously in most cases with restoration of normal voice. However, in some instances, the hematoma organizes and fibroses,

resulting in a scar. This alters the vibratory pattern of the vocal fold and can result in permanent hoarseness. In specially selected cases, it may be best to avoid this problem through surgical incision and drainage of the hematoma.[2] In all cases, vocal fold hemorrhage should be managed with absolute voice rest until the hemorrhage has resolved and normal vascular and mucosal integrity have been restored. This often takes 6 weeks and sometimes longer. Recurrent vocal fold hemorrhages are usually due to weakness in a specific blood vessel. They may require surgical cauterization of the blood vessel using a laser or microscopic resection of the vessel.[2]

Papilloma

Laryngeal papillomas are epithelial lesions caused by human papilloma virus. Histology reveals neoplastic epithelial cell proliferation in a papillary pattern and viral particles. At the present time, symptomatic papillomas are treated surgically, although alternatives have been recommended to the usual laser vaporization approach.[2]

Cancer

A detailed discussion of *cancer of the vocal folds* is beyond the scope of this chapter. The prognosis for small vocal fold cancers is good, whether they are treated by radiation or surgery. Although it may seem intuitively obvious that radiation therapy provides a better chance of voice conservation than even limited vocal fold surgery, later radiation changes in the vocal fold may produce substantial hoarseness, xerophonia (dry voice), and voice dysfunction. From the standpoint of voice preservation, optimal treatments consequently remain uncertain.[3]

Prospective studies using objective voice measures and strobovideolaryngoscopy should answer the relevant questions in the near future. Strobovideolaryngoscopy is also valuable for follow-up of patients who have had laryngeal cancers. It permits detection of microscopic vibratory changes associated with infiltration by the cancer long before they can be seen with continuous light. Stroboscopy has been used in Europe and Japan for this purpose for many years. In the United States, the popularity of strobovideolaryngoscopy for follow-up of cancer patients has greatly increased in the last several years.[4]

The psychological consequences of vocal fold cancer can be devastating, especially in a professional voice user. They may be overwhelming for nonvoice professionals as well. These reactions are understandable and expected. In many patients, however, psychological reactions may be as severe following medically "less significant" vocal fold problems such as hemorrhages, nodules, and other conditions that do not command the public respect and sympathy afforded to a cancer. In many ways, the management of related psychological problems can be even more difficult in patients with these "lesser" vocal disturbances.

Vocal Fold Immobility

Vocal fold immobility may be caused by paralysis (no movement), paresis (partial movement), and arytenoid dislocation. Differentiating among these conditions is often more complicated than it appears at first glance. A comprehensive discussion is beyond the scope of this chapter and the reader is referred to other literature.[2] However, in addition to a comprehensive history and physical examination, evaluation commonly includes strobovideolaryngoscopy, objective voice assessment, laryngeal electromyography, and high resolution CT or MRI of the larynx. Most vocal fold motion disorders are amenable to treatment. Voice therapy should be used first in virtually all cases. Even in many patients with recurrent laryngeal nerve paralysis, voice therapy alone is often sufficient. When therapy fails to produce adequate voice improvement in the patient's opinion, surgical intervention is appropriate.

Infection and Inflammation

Upper Respiratory Tract Infection Without Laryngitis

Although mucosal irritation is usually diffuse, singers sometimes have marked nasal obstruction with little or no sore throat and a "normal" voice. If the laryngeal examination shows no abnormality, a singer with a "head cold" should be permitted to sing and advised not to try to duplicate his or her usual sound, but rather to accept the insurmountable alterations in self-perception caused by the change in the supraglottic vocal tract and auditory system. The decision as to whether performing under those circumstances is professionally advisable rests with the singer and his or her musical associates. The singer should be cautioned against throat clearing, as this is traumatic and may produce laryngitis. If a cough is present, medications should be used to suppress it.

Laryngitis With Serious Vocal Fold Injury

Hemorrhage in the vocal fold and mucosal disruption are *contraindications* to speaking or singing. When these findings are observed, medical treatment includes strict voice rest in addition to correction of any underlying disease. Vocal fold hemorrhage in skilled voice users is most commonly seen in premenstrual women using aspirin products. Severe hemorrhage with consequent mucosal scarring may result in permanent alterations in vocal fold vibratory function. In rare instances, surgical intervention may be necessary.

The potential gravity of these conditions must be stressed, because many people, especially performers including politicians and clergy, are reluctant to stop speaking or singing. At the present time, acute treatment of vocal fold hemorrhage is medically controversial. Most laryngologists allow the hematoma (blood clot) to resolve spontaneously. Because this sometimes results in an organized hematoma and scar formation requiring later surgery, some physicians advocate making an incision along the superior edge of the vocal fold and draining the hematoma in selected cases. Further study is ongoing to determine the optimal therapeutic approach.

Laryngitis Without Serious Vocal Fold Damage

Mild to moderate edema of the vocal folds may result from infectious or from noninfectious causes. In the absence of mucosal disruption or hemorrhage, they are not absolute contraindications to voice use. Noninfectious laryngitis commonly occurs in association with excessive voice use in preperformance rehearsals. It may also be caused by other forms of voice abuse and by mucosal irritation due to allergy, smoke inhalation, and other causes. Mucus stranding between the anterior and middle thirds of the vocal folds is often indicative of voice abuse. Laryngitis sicca is often indicative of voice abuse. Laryngitis sicca is associated with dehydration, dry atmosphere, mouth breathing, and antihistamine therapy. Deficiency of lubrication causes irritation and coughing and results in mild inflammation. If there is no pressing professional need for vocal performance, inflammatory conditions of the larynx are best treated with relative voice rest in addition to other modalities. However, in some instances, singing or acting may be permitted. The performer should be instructed to avoid all forms of irritation and to rest his or her voice at all times except during his or her warm-up and performance. Corticosteroids and other medications may be helpful. If mucosal secretions are copious, low-dose antihistamine therapy should still usually be avoided. Copious thin secretions are better the voice than scant, thick secretions or excessive dryness. The singer or actor with laryngitis must be kept well hydrated to maintain the desired character of mucosal lubrication.

Psychological support is crucial. It is often helpful for the physician to intercede on the singer's behalf and to convey "doctor's orders" directly to agents or theater management. Such mitigation of exogenous stress can be highly therapeutic. Infectious laryngitis is frequently indicative of a more severe infection which may be difficult to control in a short period of time. Indiscriminate use of antibiotics must be avoided. However, when the physician is in doubt as to the cause, and when a major performance is imminent, vigorous antibiotic treatment is warranted. In this circumstance, the damage caused by allowing progression of a curable condition is greater than the damage that might result from a course of therapy for an unproved microorganism while cultures are pending. When a major performance is not imminent, indications for therapy are the same as for the nonsinger.

Voice rest (absolute or relative) is an important therapeutic consideration in any case of laryngitis. When there are no pressing professional commitments, a short course of absolute voice rest may be considered, as it is the safest and most conservative therapeutic intervention. This means absolute silence and communication with a writing pad. The singer must be instructed not even to whisper, as this may be an even more traumatic vocal activity than speaking softly. Whistling through the lips also requires vocalization and should not be permitted. Absolute voice rest is necessary only for serious vocal fold injury such as hemorrhage or mucosal disruption. Even then, it is virtually never indicated for more than 7 to 10 days. There are some laryngologists who do not believe voice rest should be used at all. However, absolute voice rest for a few days may be helpful in patients with laryngitis, especially gregarious, verbal singers who find it difficult to moderate their voice use to comply with relative voice rest instructions. Voice rest is discussed elsewhere in the literature.[2] In many instances, considerations of economics and reputation militate against a recommendation for voice rest. Many factors must be considered in determining whether a given concert is important enough to justify the potential consequences.

Steam inhalations deliver moisture and heat to the vocal folds and tracheobronchial tree and are often useful. The anecdotal beneficial effects of steam inhalation are probably due to hydration of the mucosa and possible benefit to the nasal mucociliary flow, and to relaxation during periods of steam inhalation. The effects of steam on cold symptoms are controversial. Ophir end Alad demonstrated that steam improves nasal patency in patients with nasal congestion.[5] However, Forstall and co-workers found no benefit from steam inhalation on nasal congestion, nasal drainage, sneezing, and objective measures of nasal resistance.[6] Nevertheless, many singers and actors find steam inhalation subjectively useful and comforting. Steam may be obtained when traveling by running hot water in a bathroom sink, but this often results in general body overheating which may be uncomfortable and lead to chilling in cold climates. Controlled steam personal inhaler systems eliminate most of these disadvantages.

Ciliary function is important throughout the respiratory system and has been studied especially well in the nose. There is some evidence that nasal irrigations improve ciliary flow and benefit patients with postnasal drip, atrophic rhinitis, and chronic sinusitis,[7] and possibly patients with common cold symptoms.[8] There has also been recent interest in treatment of symptoms of upper respiratory infection and allergy with very high humidity. Such treatment depends on a device that delivers 100% water-saturated pressurized warm air (110° Fahrenheit, 43° Centigrade) directly to the nasal passages (Rhinotherm Eig Inc, Woodland Hills, Calif.).[9,10] Steam inhalation, nasal irrigation, and nasal insufflation must be considered as not having conclusively proven efficacy in performers, but they do appear to be helpful for some patients and to have no adverse effects. Gargling also has no proven efficacy, but it is probably harmful only if it involves loud, abusive vocalization as part of the gargling process. Ultrasonic treatments, local massage, psychotherapy, and biofeedback, in particular, must be expertly supervised if used at all. Voice lessons given by an expert teacher are valuable. When there is any question of technical dysfunction, the singer should be referred to his teacher. Even when there is an obvious organic abnormality, referral to a voice teacher is appropriate, especially for younger singers. There are numerous "tricks to the trade" that permit a singer safely to overcome some of the disabilities of mild illness. If a singer plans to proceed with a performance during an illness, he or she should not cancel a voice lesson as part of the relative voice rest regimen. Rather, a short lesson to assure optimum technique is extremely useful.

Sinusitis

Chronic inflammation of the mucosa lining the sinus cavities commonly produces thick secretions known as postnasal drip. Postnasal drip can be particularly problematic because it causes excessive phlegm which interferes with phonation, and because it leads to frequent throat clearing which may inflame the vocal folds. Sometimes chronic sinusitis is caused by allergies and can be treated with medications or immuno therapy. However, many medications used for this condition cause side effects that are unacceptable in professional voice users, particularly mucosal drying. When medical management is not satisfactory, functional endoscopic sinus surgery may be appropriate.

Acute purulent sinusitis is a different matter. It requires aggressive treatment with antibiotics, sometimes surgical drainage, treatment of underlying conditions (such as dental abscess), and occasionally surgery.[2]

Systemic Conditions

Aging

This subject is so important that it has been introduced in chapter 6, and is covered extensively in chapter 10.

Hearing Loss

Hearing loss is often overlooked as a source of vocal problems. Auditory feedback is fundamental to speaking and singing. Interference with this control mechanism may result in altered vocal production, particularly if the person is unaware of the hearing loss. Distortion, particularly pitch distortion (diplacusis), may also pose serious problems for the singer. This appears to be due not only to aesthetic difficulties in matching pitch, but also to vocal strain which accompanies pitch shifts.[11] In-depth discussion is not presented here as this subject is discussed in chapter 11.

Respiratory Dysfunction

Respiratory impairment is especially problematic for professional performers. The importance of "the breath" has been well recognized in voice pedagogy. Respiratory disorders are discussed at length in chapter 12.

Allergy

Because even mild allergies are more incapacitating to professional voice users than to others, and because allergy is so common, chapter 13 has been dedicated to this subject.

Gastroesophageal Reflux Laryngitis

Gastroesophageal reflux laryngitis is extremely common among voice patients, especially singers.[2] This is a condition in which the sphincter between the stomach and esophagus is inefficient, and acidic stomach secretions reach the laryngeal tissues causing inflammation. The most typical symptoms are hoarseness in the morning, prolonged vocal warm-up time, halitosis and a bitter taste in the morning, a feeling of a "lump in the throat," frequent throat clearing, chronic irritative cough, and frequent tracheitis or tracheobronchitis. Any or all of these symptoms may be present.

Heartburn is not common in these patients, so the diagnosis is often missed.

Physical examination usually reveals erythema (redness) of the arytenoid mucosa. A barium swallow radiographic study with water siphonage may provide additional information, but is not routinely needed. However, if a patient strictly complies with treatment recommendations and does not show marked improvement within a month, or if there is a reason to suspect more serious pathology, complete evaluation by a gastroenterologist should be carried out. Twenty-four hour pH monitoring of the esophagus and pharynx is often most effective in establishing a diagnosis. The results are correlated with a diary of the patient's activities and symptoms. Bulimia should also be considered in the differential diagnosis when symptoms are refractory to treatment and other physical and psychological signs are suggestive.[2]

The mainstays of treatment for reflux laryngitis are elevation of the head of the bed (not just sleeping on pillows), antacids, H-2 blockers or proton pump inhibitors, and avoidance of eating for 3 to 4 hours before going to sleep. This is often difficult for singers and actors because of their performance schedule, but if they are counseled about minor changes in eating habits (such as eating larger meals at breakfast and lunch), they can usually comply. Avoidance of alcohol, caffeine, and specific foods is beneficial. Medications that decrease or block acid production may be necessary and are further discussed in chapter 18. Laparoscopic Nissen fundoplication has proven extremely effective and should be considered a reasonable alternative to lifelong medication in this relatively young patient population.[12] This operation is performed through five small abdominal incisions. Using a laparoscope, the dysfunctional lower esophageal sphincter is repaired so that it works as a one-way valve, curing or markedly improving reflux, without a large incision in the belly.

It must be recognized that control of acidity is not the same as control of reflux. In many cases, acidity is provoked during singing because of the increased abdominal pressure associated with support. In these instances, it often causes excessive phlegm and throat clearing during the first 10 or 15 minutes of a performance or lesson, as well as other common reflux laryngitis symptoms including morning hoarseness, prolonged warm-up time, sore throats, cough, halitosis, recurrent upper respiratory infections, and frequent tracheitis or tracheobronchitis. Any or all of these symptoms may be present. It is associated with the development of Barrett's esophagus, esophageal carcinoma, and laryngeal carcinoma.[2]

Hormone Dysfunction

(See chapter 14).

Neurological Disorders

Neurological disorders affecting performance and voice are discussed in chapter 15.

Poor General Health

As with any other athletic activity, optimal voice use requires reasonably good general health and physical conditioning. Abdominal and respiratory strength and endurance are particularly important. If a professional voice user becomes short of breath from climbing two flights of stairs, he or she certainly does not have the physical stamina necessary for proper respiratory support for a speech, let alone a strenuous musical production. This deficiency usually results in abusive vocal habits used in vain attempts to compensate for the deficiencies.

General illnesses, such as anemia, mononucleosis, AIDS, chronic fatigue syndrome, or other diseases associated with malaise and weakness may impair the ability of vocal musculature to rapidly recover from heavy use and may also be associated with alterations of mucosal secretions. Other systemic illnesses may be responsible for voice complaints, particularly if they impair the abdominal muscles necessary for breath support. For example, diarrhea and constipation that prohibit sustained abdominal contraction may be reasons for the physician to prohibit a strenuous singing or acting engagement.

Any extremity injury, such as a sprained ankle, may alter posture and therefore interfere with customary abdominothoracic support. Voice patients are often unaware of this problem and develop abusive, hyperfunctional compensatory maneuvers in the neck and tongue musculature as a result. These technical flaws may produce voice complaints, such as vocal fatigue and neck pain, that bring the performer to the physician's office for assessment and care.

Anxiety

Good singers are frequently sensitive and communicative people. When the principal cause of vocal dysfunction is anxiety, the physician can often accomplish much by assuring the patient that no organic problem is present and by stating the diagnosis of anxiety reaction. The patient should be counseled that anxiety is normal and that recognition of it as the principal problem frequently allows the performer to overcome it. Tranquilizers and sedatives are rarely necessary and are undesirable because they may interfere with fine motor control. For example, beta-adrenergic blocking agents such as propranolol hydrochloride have became popular among performers for the treatment of preperformance anxiety. Beta-blockers are not recommended for regular use; they have significant effects on the cardiovascular system and many potential complications, including hypotension, thrombocytopenic purpura, mental depression, agranulocytosis, laryngospasm with respiratory distress, and bronchospasm. In addition, their efficacy is controversial. Although they may have a favorable effect in relieving performance anxiety, beta-blockers may produce a noticeable adverse effect on singing performance.[13] As the blood level of the drug established by a given dose of beta-blocker varies widely among individuals, initial use of these agents before performance may be particularly troublesome. In addition, beta-blockers impede increases in heart rate, which are needed as physiologic response to the psychologic and physical demands of performance. Although these drugs have a place under occasional, extraordinary circumstances, their routine use for this purpose not only is potentially hazardous but also violates an important therapeutic principle. Performers have chosen a career that exposes them to the public. If such persons are so incapacitated by anxiety that they are unable to perform the routine functions of their chosen profession without chemical help, this should be considered symptomatic of an important underlying psychologic problem. For a performer to depend on drugs to perform is neither routine nor healthy, whether the drug is a benzodiazepine, a barbiturate, a beta-blocker, or alcohol. If such dependence exists, psychologic evaluation should be considered by an experienced arts-medicine psychologist or psychiatrist. Obscuring the symptoms by fostering the dependence is insufficient. However, if the singer is on tour and will only be under a particular otolaryngologist's care for a week or two, the physician should not try to make major changes in his or her customary regimen. Rather, the physician should communicate with the performer's primary otolaryngologist or family physician to coordinate appropriate long-term care.

Since professional voice users constitute a subset of societies as a whole, all of the psychiatric disorders encountered among the general public are seen from time to time in voice professionals. In some cases, professionals voice users require modification of the usual psychological treatment, particularly with regard to psychotropic medications. Detailed discussion of this subject can be found elsewhere in the literature,[2] and in chapter 20.

When voice professionals, especially singers and actors, suffer a significant vocal impairment that results in voice loss (or the prospect of voice loss), they often go through a psychological process very similar to grieving.[14] In some cases, fear of discovering that the voice is lost forever may unconsciously prevent patients from trying to optimally use their voices following injury or treatment. This can dramatically impede or prevent recovery of function following a perfect surgical result, for example. It is essential that otolaryngologists, performers, and their teachers be familiar with this fairly common scenario; and it is ideal to include an arts-medicine psychologist and/or psychiatrist as part of the voice team.

Hypochondriasis

Hypochondriasis is uncommon among professional performers, partly because of the demands of their "show-must-go-on" profession. Psychogenic voice disorders, incapacitating psychological reactions to organic voice disorders, and other psychological problems are encountered commonly in young voice patients. They are discussed in other literature.[14]

Substance Abuse

The list of substances ingested, smoked, or "snorted" by many people is disturbingly long. Whenever possible, patients who care about vocal quality and longevity should be educated about the deleterious effects of such habits upon their voices and upon the longevity of their careers by their physicians and teachers. A few specific substances have already been discussed above and in chapter 18.

Other Conditions

Numerous other conditions could be included in this chapter. Some are discussed in subsequent chapters. For a more comprehensive discussion of the subjects covered above, the reader is referred to other literature.[2]

Medical Management for Voice Dysfunction

Medical management of many problems affecting the voice involves not only care prescribed by the otolaryngologist, but also voice therapy which is provided by an interdisciplinary team. The role in training of the principle members of the team are covered in detail in subsequent chapters. This chapter provides a brief introduction to their roles in the medical milieu.

Speech-Language Pathologist

An excellent speech-language pathologist is an invaluable asset in caring for professional voice users. However, otolaryngologists and singing teachers should recognize that, like physicians, speech-language pathologists have varied backgrounds and experience in treatment of voice disorders. In fact, most speech pathology programs teach relatively little about caring for professional speakers and nothing about professional singers. Moreover, few speech-language pathologists have vast experience in this specialized area; and no fellowships in this specialty exist. Speech-language pathologists often subspecialize. A speech-language pathologist who expertly treats patients who have strokes, stutter, have undergone laryngectomy, or have swallowing disorders will not necessarily know how to optimally manage professional voice users. The otolaryngologist must learn the strengths and weaknesses of the speech-language pathologist with whom he or she works. After identifying a speech-language pathologist who is interested in treating professional voice users, the otolaryngologist should work closely with the speech-language pathologist in developing the necessary expertise. Assistance may be found through otolaryngologists who treat large numbers of singers or through educational programs such as the Voice Foundation's Symposium on Care of the Professional Voice. In general, therapy should be directed toward vocal hygiene, relaxation techniques, breath management, and abdominal support.[2]

Speech (voice) therapy may be helpful even when a singer has no obvious problem in the speaking voice but significant technical problems singing. Once a person has been singing for several years, a singing teacher may have difficulty convincing him or her to correct certain technical errors. Singers are much less protective of their speaking voices. Therefore, a speech-language pathologist may be able to teach proper support, relaxation, and voice placement in rapid speaking. Once mastered, these techniques can be carried over fairly easily into singing through cooperation between the speech-language pathologist and singing teacher. This "back door" approach has been extremely useful. For the actor, coordinating speech-language pathology sessions with acting-voice lessons, and especially with training of the speaking voice provided by the actor's voice teacher or coach, is often helpful. In fact, we have found this combination so helpful that we have added an acting-voice trainer to our medical staff. Information from the speech-language pathologist, acting-voice trainer, and singing teacher should be symbiotic and should not conflict. If major discrepancies exist, bad training from one of the team members should be suspected and changes should be made.

Singing Voice Specialist

Singing voice specialists are singing teachers who have acquired extra training to prepare them for work with injured voices, in collaboration with a medical voice team. They are indispensable for singers.

In selected cases, singing lessons may also be extremely helpful to nonsingers with voice problems. The techniques used to develop abdomenothoracic strength, breath control, laryngeal and neck muscle strength, and relaxation are very similar to those used in speech therapy. Singing lessons often expedite therapy and appear to improve the outcome in some patients.

Otolaryngologists who frequently care for singers are often asked to recommend a voice teacher. This may put them in an uncomfortable position, particularly if the singer is already studying with someone in the community. Most physicians do not have sufficient expertise to criticize a voice teacher, and we must be extremely cautious about recommending that a singer change teachers. However, no certifying agency standardizes or ensures the quality of a singing teacher. Although one may be slightly more confident of a teacher associated with a major conservatory or music school or one who is a member of the National Association of Teachers of Singing (NATS), neither of these credentials assures excellence, and many expert teachers have neither affiliation. However, with experience, an otolaryngologist can ordinarily develop valid impressions. The physician should record the name of the voice teacher of every patient and observe whether the same kinds of voice abuse problems occur with disproportionate frequency in the pupils of any given teacher. The doctor should note whose pupils usually have few technical problems and are only seen for acute disease such as upper respiratory infection. Technical problems can cause organic abnormalities such as nodules; therefore, any teacher who has a high incidence of nodules among his or her students should be viewed with cautious concern. The physician should be particularly wary of teachers who are reluctant to allow their students to consult a doctor. The best voice teachers usually are quick to refer their students to a otolaryngologist if they hear anything disturbing in a student's voice. Similarly, voice teachers and voice professionals should compare information on the nature and quality of medical care received, and its success. No physician cures every voice problem in every patient, just as no singing teacher produces premiere stars from every student who walks through the studio. Nevertheless, voice professionals must be critical, informed consumers and accept nothing less than the best medical care.

After seeing a voice patient, the otolaryngologist should write a letter to the voice teacher (with the patient's permission) describing the findings and recommendations as he or she would to a physician, speech-language pathologist, or any other referring professional. An otolaryngologist seriously interested in caring for singers should take the trouble to talk with and meet local singing teachers. Taking a lesson or two with each teacher provides enormous insight as well. Regularly taking voice lessons is even more helpful. In practice, the otolaryngologist will usually identify a few teachers in whom he or she has particular confidence, especially for patients with voice disorders, and should not hesitate to refer singers to these colleagues, especially singers who are not already in training.

Pop singers may be particularly resistant to the suggestion of voice lessons, yet they are in great need of training. The physician should point out that a good voice teacher can teach a pop singer how to protect and expand the voice without changing its quality or making it sound "trained" or "operatic." It is helpful to point out that singing, like other athletic activities, requires exercise, warm-up, and coaching for anyone planning to enter the "big league" and stay there. Just as no major league baseball pitcher would play without a pitching coach and warm-up time in the bull pen, no singer should try to build a career without a singing teacher and appropriate strength and agility exercises. This approach has proved palatable and effective. Physicians should also be aware of the difference between a voice teacher and a voice coach. A voice teacher is essential and trains a singer in singing technique. A voice coach is responsible for teaching songs, language, diction, style, operatic roles, and so on, but is not responsible for exercise and basic technical development of the voice.

Acting-Voice Trainer

The use of acting-voice trainers (drama voice coaches) as members of the medical team is new.[2] This addition to the team has been extremely valuable to patients and other team members. Like singing-voice specialists, professionals with education in theater arts utilize numerous vocal and body movement techniques that not only enhance physical function, but also release tension and break down emotional barriers that may impede optimal voice function. Tearful revelations to the acting-voice trainer are not uncommon; and, like the singing teacher, this individual may identify psychological and emotional problems interfering with professional success that have been skillfully hidden from other professionals on the voice team and in the patient's life.

Others

A psychologist, psychiatrist, neurologist, pulmonologist, and others with special interest and expertise in arts-medicine are also invaluable to the voice team. Every comprehensive center should seek out such people and collaborate with them, even if they are not full-time members of the voice team.

Surgery

A detailed discussion of laryngeal surgery is beyond the scope of this chapter and can be found elsewhere.[2] However, a few points are worthy of special emphasis. Surgery for vocal nodules should be avoided whenever possible and should almost never be performed without an adequate trial of expert voice therapy, including patient compliance with therapeutic suggestions. A minimum of 6 to 12 weeks of observation should be allowed while the patient is using therapeutically modified voice techniques under the supervision of a speech-language pathologist and, ideally, a singing-voice specialist. Proper voice use rather than voice rest (silence) is correct therapy. The surgeon should not prematurely perform surgery for vocal

nodules under pressure from the patient for a "quick cure" and early return to performance. Permanent destruction of voice quality is a very real complication. Even after expert surgery, voice quality may be diminished by submucosal scarring, resulting in an adynamic segment along the vibratory margin of the vocal fold. This situation produces a hoarse voice with vocal folds that appear normal on indirect examination under routine light, although under stroboscopic light the adynamic segment is obvious. No reliable cure exists for this complication. Even large, apparently fibrotic nodules of long standing should be given a chance to resolve without surgery. In some cases the nodules remain but become asymptomatic and voice quality is normal. Stroboscopy in such patients usually reveals that the nodules are on the superior surface rather than the leading edge of the vocal folds during proper, relaxed phonation (although they may be on the contact surface and symptomatic when hyperfunctional voice technique is used and the larynx is forced down).

When surgery is indicated for vocal fold lesions, it should be limited as strictly as possible to the area of abnormality. Virtually no place exists for "vocal fold stripping" in professional voice users with benign disease. Submucosal resection through a laryngeal microflap used to be advocated; in fact, the technique was introduced and first published by this author.[15] Microflap technique involved an incision on the superior surface of the vocal fold, submucosal resection, and preservation of the mucosa along the leading edge of the vocal fold (Fig 9–1). The concept that led to this innovation was based on the idea that the intermedi-

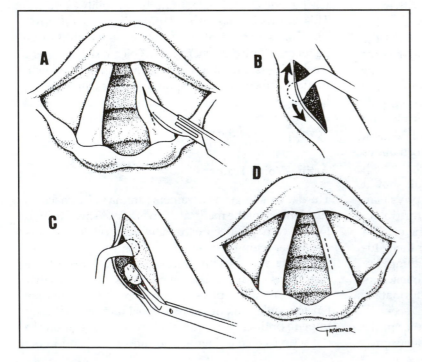

Fig 9–1. Microflap. In this technique, a superficial incision is made in the superior surface of the true vocal fold (A). Blunt dissection is used to elevate the mucosa from the lesion (B), minimizing trauma to the fibroblast-containing layers of the lamina propria. (C) Only pathologic tissue is excised under direct vision. (D) Mucosa is reapproximated without violating the leading edge.

ate layer of the lamina propria should be protected to prevent fibroblast proliferation, and it seemed reasonable to preserve the mucosa as a biological dressing. This technique certainly produced better results than vocal fold stripping. However, close scrutiny of outcomes revealed a small number of cases with poor results, and stiffness beyond the limits of the original pathology. Consequently, the technique was abandoned in favor of a mini-microflap, or of local resection strictly limited to the region of pathology[16] (Fig 9–2). Lesions such as vocal nodules should be removed to a level even with the vibratory margin rather than deeply into the submucosa. This minimizes scarring and optimizes return to good vocal function. Naturally, if concern about a serious neoplasm exists, proper treatment takes precedence over voice conservation. Surgery should be performed under microscopic control. Preoperative and postoperative objective voice

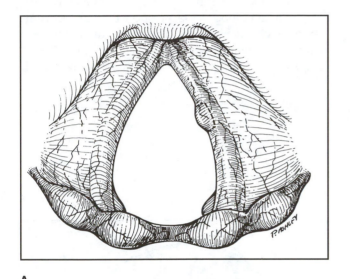

A

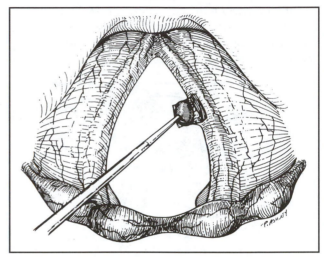

B

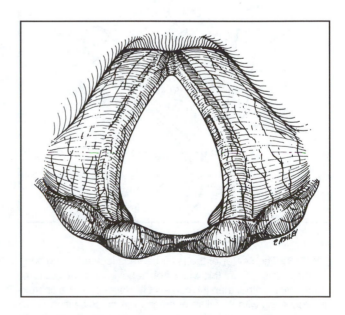

C   **D**

Fig 9–2. (A) In elevating a mini-microflap, the incision (dotted line) extends anterior, superior, and posterior to the lesion. (B) Using blunt dissection, the mass is gently separated from the lamina propria and reflected medially. (C) Enough mucosa is preserved to create a small mini-microflap. (D) The mini-microflap is replaced over the defect in the vibratory margin.

measures are essential to allow outcome assessment and self-critique. Only through such study can we improve surgical technique. Outcome studies are especially important in voice surgery since all of our technical pronouncements are anecdotal because there is no experimental model for vocal fold surgery (the human adult is the only species with a layered lamina propria). Lasers are an invaluable adjunct in the otolaryngologists' armamentarium, but they must be used knowledgeably and with care. Considerable evidence suggests that healing time is prolonged and the incidence of adynamic segment formation is higher with the laser on the vibratory margin than with traditional instruments. Two early studies raised serious concerns about dysphonia after laser surgery.[17,18] Such complications may result from using too low a

wattage, causing dissipation of heat deep into the vocal fold; thus high-power density for short duration has been recommended. Small spot size is also helpful. Nevertheless, many otolaryngologists caring for voice professionals avoid laser surgery in most cases pending further study. When biopsy specimens are needed, they should be taken before destroying the lesion with a lasers. If a lesion is to be removed from the leading edge, the laser beam should be centered in the lesions, rather than on the vibratory margin, so that the beam does not create a divot in the vocal fold (Fig 9–3). The CO_2 laser is particularly valuable for cauterizing isolated blood vessels responsible for recurrent hemorrhage. Such vessels are often found at the base of a hemorrhagic polyp (Fig 9–4). At the suggestion of Jean Abitbol, MD, the author has been placing a small

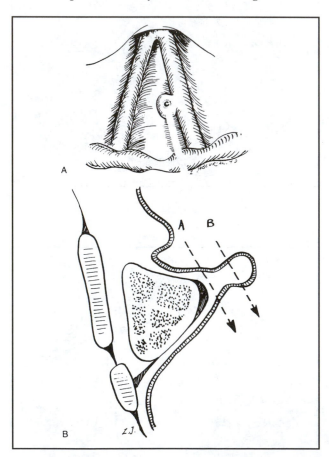

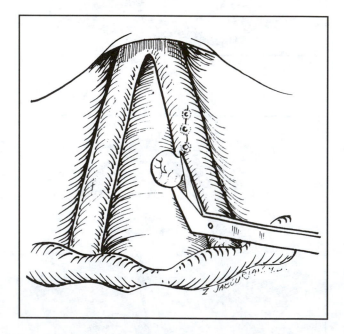

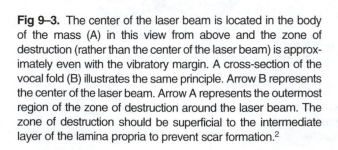

Fig 9–3. The center of the laser beam is located in the body of the mass (A) in this view from above and the zone of destruction (rather than the center of the laser beam) is approximately even with the vibratory margin. A cross-section of the vocal fold (B) illustrates the same principle. Arrow B represents the center of the laser beam. Arrow A represents the outermost region of the zone of destruction around the laser beam. The zone of destruction should be superficial to the intermediate layer of the lamina propria to prevent scar formation.[2]

Fig 9–4. The feeding vessel of a hemorrhagic polyp may be treated with 1-watt defocused laser bursts of short duration to cauterize the vessel and prevent recurrent hemorrhage. The polyp can then be removed from the leading edge with scissors, avoiding the risk of laser injury to the vibratory margin. Removal of the polyp using a laser is an acceptable alternative, although precautions must be taken as illustrated in Fig 9–3.[2]

piece of ice on the vocal fold immediately before and after laser use to dissipate heat and help prevent edema. No studies on the efficacy of this maneuver exist, and we need more clinical experience before drawing final conclusions, but the technique appears helpful.

Voice rest after vocal fold surgery is controversial. Although some otolaryngologists do not recognize its necessity at all, most physicians recommend voice rest for approximately 1 week, or until the mucosal surface has healed. Even after surgery, silence for more than 7 to 10 days is almost never necessary and represents a real hardship for many patients.[19]

Return to voice use following voice rest also must be done carefully. Whenever a professional voice user has been restricted from performing, return to performance should be accomplished in a progressive fashion and should be monitored. These precautions are particularly important in patients who have been on absolute voice rest. The strategy for return to voice use must be individualized, but the principles are the same as those applied for returning to athletic performance or instrumental music performance following injury. A baseball pitcher whose arm has been in a cast does not return to the starting rotation the day the cast is removed. The speed with which he returns depends upon the nature of the injury, length of time during which he has been casted, his age, physical condition,, performance demands (starting pitcher vs reliever who pitches one or two innings), and other factors. Similar issues must be considered in instrumentalists who are returning to play after injury, and in voice professionals.

Guidelines are based on anecdotal experience and not scientific research. The author routinely ends periods of voice rest by providing a brief voice therapy session to optimize speaking technique, minimize abuse and review vocal hygiene. The physician prescribes specific guidelines for voice use. For example, after a 1 week period of silence following voice surgery, the patient might be permitted to speak for 5 minutes per hour, with periods of phonation spread out over the hour (not 5 minutes in a row). The duration of phonation permissible will generally be increased within a few days following another voice therapy session, and, when appropriate, reexamination of the vocal folds by the laryngologist. The rapidity with which each patient returns to unlimited voice use depends upon the patient's technical skills, the duration of voice impairment, the speed with which the individual heals damage on the vibratory margin, and other factors. Although speaking and very limited singing exercises usually may be resumed within 1 to 2 weeks following surgery or injury, more vigorous singing exercises are generally delayed until strobo-

videolaryngoscopy reveals return of vibration to the vibratory margin of the vocal folds. As a very rough "rule of thumb," the time required for return to unrestricted performance is roughly the same as the period of rest. For example, if a person has undergone surgery and has been restricted from intensive singing practice for 6 weeks, it is safe and conservative to plan on another 6 weeks before the performer is rehabilitated and able to perform at full strength without restriction.

Too often, the otolaryngologist is confronted with a desperate singer whose voice has been "ruined" by vocal fold surgery, recurrent or superior laryngeal nerve paralysis, trauma, or some other tragedy. The cause is occasionally as simple as a dislocated arytenoid that can be reduced.[20,21] However, if the problem is an adynamic segment, decreased bulk of one vocal fold after "stripping," bowing caused by superior laryngeal nerve paralysis, or some other serious complication in a mobile vocal fold, great conservatism should be exercised. None of the available surgical procedures for these conditions is consistently effective. If surgery is considered at all, the procedure and prognosis should be realistically and pessimistically explained to the patient. The patient must understand that the chances of returning the voice to professional quality are very slim and that it may be made worse. Zyderm Collagen (Xomed) injection has been studied and is helpful in some of these difficult cases.[22] Collagen is not approved by the FDA for use in the vocal fold. If used at all, the material should be used under protocol and with Institutional Review Board approval. Collagen may be particularly helpful for small adynamic segments. New research with autologous collagen may expand its usefulness in the near future. In the author's opinion, at present the best technique for extensive vocal fold scarring is the recently introduced method of autologous fat implantation into the vibratory margin.[2] Voice professionals occasionally inquire about surgery for pitch alteration. Such procedures have been successful in specially selected patients (such as those undergoing sexchange surgery), but they do not consistently provide good enough voice quality and range to be performed on a professional voice user.[23]

Voice Maintenance

Prevention of vocal dysfunction should be the goal of all professionals involved in the care of professional voice users. Good vocal health habits should be encouraged in childhood. Screaming, particularly outdoors at athletic events, should be discouraged.

Promising young singers who join choirs should be educated to compensate for the Lombard effect. The youngster interested in singing should receive enough training to prevent voice abuse and should receive enthusiastic support for singing works suitable for his or her age and voice. Training should be continued during or after puberty, and the voice should be allowed to develop naturally without pressure to perform operatic roles prematurely.

Excellent regular training and practice are essential, and avoidance of irritants, particularly smoke, should be stressed early. Educating the singer with regard to hormonal and anatomic alterations that may influence the voice allows him or her to recognize and analyze vocal dysfunction, intelligently compensating for it when it occurs. The body is dynamic, changing over a lifetime, and the voice is no exception. Continued vocal education, training, and monitoring are necessary throughout a lifetime, even in the most successful and well-established singers. Vocal problems in premiere singers are commonly caused by cessation of lessons, excessive schedule demands, and other correctable problems, rather than by irreversible ravages of aging. Anatomical, physiological, and serious medical problems may affect the voices of singers of any age. Cooperation among the otolaryngologist, speech-language pathologist, acting-voice trainer, singing-voice teacher, and conductor provides an optimal environment for cultivation and protection of the vocal artist.

Conclusion

Many diagnoses and treatments are important in caring for voice patients. Those discussed in this chapter are among the most common. The exacting demands of a professional singer or actor, his or her acute ability to analyze the body's condition, and his or her professional athlete's need for a nearly perfect treatment result provide special challenges and gratification for physicians, speech-language pathologists, singing teachers, psychological professionals, and other health care providers. However, a great many voice patients who are not performers are also extremely dependent on voice quality and endurance for career advancement. Every patient with a voice complaint should consequently be treated as Luciano Pavarotti, James Earl Jones, or Barbra Streisand would be treated; and every voice evaluation should be systematically carried out until a diagnosis has been made on the basis of positive medical evidence. The emergence of interdisciplinary teams, advanced instrumentation, and voice laboratories has led to dramatic improvements in the standard of voice care. The rapid development of voice as a subspecialty promises continuing advances in the care of voice disorders.

Summary

A great many common medical conditions can affect the voices of professional voice users. These include voice abuse, structural abnormalities, infection and inflammation, systemic conditions, and others. All professionals responsible for voice training and care should be familiar with these common conditions and their appropriate management.

Review Questions

1. Nodules are usually all of the following except:
   a. bilateral (on both sides)
   b. solid
   c. treatable without surgery
   d. malignant
   e. cause of hoarseness

2. Granulomas are commonly:
   a. bilateral
   b. caused by reflux
   c. caused or aggravated by voice abuse
   d. all of the above
   e. none of the above

3. Absolute voice rest is generally necessary for:
   a. laryngitis
   b. vocal fold hemorrhage
   c. upper respiratory infections
   d. all of the above
   e. none of the above

4. In singers with reflux laryngitis, all of the following symptoms are commonly present except:
   a. prolonged warm-up time
   b. a "lump in the throat"
   c. heartburn
   d. frequent throat clearing
   e. bad breath

5. An ideal treatment for vocal nodules in most cases is:
   a. Absolute voice rest
   b. voice therapy
   c. surgery
   d. career changes

e. none of the above

References

1. Brodnitz F. Hormones and the human voice. *Bull NY Acad Med*. 1971;47:183–191.
2. Sataloff RT. *Professional Voice: Science and Art of Clinical Care*, 2nd ed. San Diego, Calif: Singular Publishing Group, Inc.; 1997:1–1069.
3. Gould WJ, Sataloff RT, Spiegel JR. *Voice Surgery*. St. Louis Mo: CV Mosby-Yearbook Inc.: 1993:307–338.
4. Arndt HJ. Stimmstörungen nach Behandlung mit androgenen und anabolen Hormonen. *Münch Med Wochenschr*. 1974;116:1715–1720.
5. Ophir D, Elad Y. Effects of steam inhalation on nasal patency and nasal symptoms in patients with the common cold. *Am J. Otolaryngol*. 1987;8(3):149–153.
6. Forstall GJ, MacKnin ML, Yen-Lieberman BR, Vander-Brug MS. Effect of inhaling vapor on symptoms of the common cold. *JAMA*. 1994;271(14):1109–1114.
7. Grossan M. Clinical measurement of mucociliary clearance. In: Gerald M. English, ed. *Otolaryngology* (rev. ed.). Philadelphia, PA: JB Lippincott Company; 1994; chap 7.
8. Grossan M. A device to aid nasal mucociliary flow. *ANL*. 1976;3:65–70.
9. Yersushalmi A, Karman S, Lwoff A. Treatment of perennial allergic rhinitis by local hyperthermia. *Proc Nat Acad Sci*. 1982;798:4766–4769.
10. Ophir D, Elad Y, Diev Z, et al. Effects of inhalated humidified warm air on nasal patency and nasal symptoms in allergic rhinitis. *Ann Allergy*. 1988;60:239–242.
11. Sundberg J, Prame E, Iwarsson J. Replicability and accuracy of pitch patterns in professional singers. In: Davis PJ, Fletcher NH: *Vocal Fold Physiology: Controlling Chaos and Complexity*. San Diego, Calif: Singular Publishing Group, Inc.; 1996:291–306.
12. Koufman J, Sataloff RT, Toohill R. Laryngopharyngeal reflux: consensus conference report. *J Voice*. 1996;10(3): 215–216.
13. Gates GA, Saegert J, Wilson N, Johnson L, Sheperd A, Hearnd EM. Effects of beta-blockade on singing performance. *Ann Otol Rhinol Laryngol*. 1985;94:570–574.
14. Rosen DC, Sataloff RT. *Psychology of Voice Disorders*. San Diego, Calif: Singular Publishing Group, Inc.; 1997:1–261.
15. Sataloff RT. The professional voice. In: Cummings CW, Frederickson JM, Harker LA, Krause CJ, Schuller DE, eds. *Otolaryngology—Head and Neck Surgery*. St. Louis, Mo: CV Mosby Yearbook, Inc.; 1986;3:2029–2056.
16. Sataloff RT, Spiegel JR, Heuer RJ, Baroody MM, Emerich KA, Hawkshaw M, Rosen DC. Laryngeal mini-microflap: a new technique and reassessment of the microflap saga. *J Voice*. 1995;9(2):198–204.
17. Abitbol J. Limitations of the laser in microsurgery of the larynx. In: Lawrence VL, ed. *Transactions of the Twelfth Symposium: Care of the Professional Voice*. New York, NY: The Voice Foundation; 1984.
18. Tapia RG, Pardo J, Marigil M, Pacivo A. Effects of the LASER upon Reinke's space and the neural system of the vocalis muscle. In: Lawrence VL, ed. *Transactions of the Twelfth Symposium: Care of the Professional Voice*. New York, NY: The Voice Foundation; 1983.
19. Sataloff RT. *Professional Voice: Science and Art of Clinical Care*, 2nd ed. San Diego, Calif: Singular Publishing Group, Inc.; 1997;453–456.
20. Sataloff RT, Feldman M, Darby KS, Carroll LM, Spiegel JR, Schiebel BR. Arytenoid dislocation. *J Voice*. 1986;1(4): 368–377.
21. Sataloff RT, Bough ID, Spiegel JR. Arytenoid diagnosis: diagnosis and treatment. *Laryngoscope*. 1994;104(10): 1353–1361.
22. Ford CN, Bless DM. Collagen injected in the scarred vocal fold. *J Voice*. 1988;1(1):116–118.

10

The Effects of Age on the Voice

Robert Thayer Sataloff,
Joseph R. Spiegel,
and Deborah Caputo Rosen

Anatomy and Physiology

Embryologically, the larynx develops most of its anatomical characteristics by the third month of fetal life. At birth, the thyroid cartilage and hyoid bone are attached to each other. The laryngeal skeleton then separates, and the slow process of ossification (cartilages turning to bone) begins. The hyoid bone starts to ossify by 2 years of age. The thyroid and cricoid cartilages ossify during the early 20s, and the arytenoid cartilages ossify in the late 30s. Except for the cuneiform and corniculate cartilages, the entire laryngeal skeleton is ossified by age 65. In the infant, the epiglottis is bulky and omega-shaped. It does not open to its normal adult configuration until puberty. The angle of the thyroid cartilage is about 110° in the male and 120° in the female at birth. These relationships also remain fairly stable until puberty. At birth, the larynx is high in the neck, resting at about the level of the third and fourth cervical vertebrae (C3 and C4). It descends to about the level of C6 by the age of 5 and continues gradual descent, lying at about the level of C7 between ages 15 and 20. Descent continues throughout life in both sexes. As the larynx descends, vocal tract length relationships change and average voice pitch tends to become lower. In infancy, the membranous and cartilaginous portions of the vocal folds are equal in length. By adulthood, the membranous portion accounts for approximately three fifths of vocal fold length. Total vocal fold length is 6 to 8 mm in the infant, but increases to 12 to 17 mm in the adult female, and to 17 to 23 mm in the adult male. The dimensions of all other aspects of laryngeal anatomy increase, as well.

First vocalizations sometimes occur prior to birth, although the birth cry is normally the first sound uttered. Its frequency averages about 500 Hz (one octave above middle C). At this time, laryngeal mobility is limited primarily to vertical movements, and the appearance of the larynx is very similar to that of primates (monkeys). As the child grows, mean fundamental frequency of speech (the predominant pitch of the speaking voice) drops gradually. By 8 years of age, it is approximately 275 Hz. Until puberty, male and female larynges are about the same size. During childhood, the physiologic frequency range (the highest and lowest sounds the child can produce) remains fairly constant. However, musical frequency range increases. That is, the child becomes able to produce musically acceptable sounds throughout an increasing percentage of his frequency range. Thus, between the ages of 6 and 16, the important developmental change is not absolute range (constant at about 2½ octaves) but rather improved control, efficiency, and quality. Recognizing this principle is helpful in structuring training of young voices to strengthen and take advantage of the natural developmental process, rather than concentrating too heavily and too early on exercises that are designed to stretch the extremes of range. Such exercises may be damaging, especially to fragile young voices.

Puberty provides particularly challenging problems for the young singer, as well as the singer's teacher and physician. Voice changes during puberty are caused by major alterations in laryngeal anatomy that occur coincident with the development of other secondary sex characteristics. Male vocal folds grow 4 to 11 mm, or as much as 60% in length, while female vocal folds grow 1.5 to 4 mm, or as much as 34%.[1] The connective tissue layers of the vocal fold develop progressively throughout childhood. The superficial and intermediate layers are well defined with a mature vocal ligament by age 16.[2]

The times of onset and duration of voice mutation vary somewhat from study to study and depend, to some extent, on the techniques used to measure and define voice change. Puberty usually begins between ages 8 and 15 in American females and between ages 9½ and 14 in American males. It is usually complete by age 12 to 16½ in females and by 13½ to 18 in males.[3] Voice mutation is most active between ages 12½ and 14, and is usually complete in both sexes by age 15.[4] Mutational voice usually lasts about 1½ years but can last as long as 3 years.[5] Voice mutation occurs because of laryngeal growth. The angle of the male thyroid cartilage decreases to 90°, while the female thyroid cartilage remains at 120°. In both sexes, the epiglottis flattens, grows, and elevates; laryngeal mucosa becomes stronger and thicker. During puberty, the female voice usually drops about 2.5 semitones and averages roughly 220 to 225 Hz when voice change is complete. The male voice drops approximately one octave, averaging about 130 Hz at age 18 years.[6]

The vocal tract is altered at many levels. The tonsil and adenoid tissues atrophy and partially disappear. This may relieve nasal obstruction and change oropharyngeal nasopharyngeal resonance. The basic contours of the pharynx can be fully developed as early as age 9, but the vocal tract continues to grow in length and circumference through puberty and into adulthood. Full growth is usually not complete until age 20 or 21. These changes can be demonstrated by examining the three lowest formant frequencies. Adult females average 12%, 17%, and 18% higher than adult males and prepubescent children average 20% higher than adult females.[7]

Dental development is completed during young adulthood and jaw alignment may change. Tongue position and mouth opening can be influenced by discomfort and limitations of the temporomandibular joint complex that develop as a result of dental malalignment or injury. Usually, it is best to address dental and orthodontic problems as early as possible, and when considering the voice as well, it is always advantageous to treat the underlying causes of poor vocal technique before injurious compensatory mechanisms develop.

The power source of the voice reaches its full potential as the chest enlarges and thoracic and abdominal musculature strengthens. In fact, muscular strength and stamina may peak during young adulthood and young singers and actors unfortunately often attempt to use these assets to compensate for inadequacies elsewhere in the vocal mechanism.

The Young Voice

Young voices have unique complexities and delicacies that make them exciting, challenging, and hazardous to care for. Their special problems are of interest not only to physicians, but also to voice teachers and speech-language pathologists. Arts medicine literature has shown new and welcome interest in aging voices,[8-15] but papers on the young voice have been less frequent and less expert than desirable. The subject was addressed in 1984 at the Voice Foundation's Thirteenth Symposium on Care of the Professional Voice,[16] and voice development is discussed in numerous standard speech-language pathology textbooks.[17-19] However, many basic, practical questions remain unanswered. It is important for all professionals who train and care for singers to understand as much as possible about the growth and development of the voice and to understand clearly anatomic and physiologic differences among children, adolescents, adults, and the elderly. Such knowledge should lead to optimal training and minimal risk of vocal injury.

The optimal time to begin vocal training remains controversial. Recently, new trends in education have introduced the concept of ear and voice training in early infancy. As most of the techniques suggested so far involve pitch matching and natural development of ear-voice coordination, they are unlikely to be harmful. The problems of vocal training for young school-aged children are more obvious to many of us who care for vocal disorders. They have been aggravated by the popularity of shows such as "Annie" and by the enthusiasm of preteens for various rock singers with abusive vocal habits. Children have constantly changing voices, with delicate muscles and fragile mucosa. Very few can tolerate the demands of prolonged "belting" or shouting several nights per week over a period of months or years without sustaining vocal injury. Certainly, it is possible and proper to train young voices to sing. Moreover, it is reasonable to begin this training as soon as a youngster shows a serious interest in and aptitude for voice performance. However, the training should be directed toward avoiding voice abuse and toward gradual development of vocal musculature and control. Erroneous technique early in childhood may underlie vocal difficulties throughout a lifetime by improperly developing muscles of singing. Once a muscle is contoured, it is extremely difficult to change its shape. Although the demands and opportunities of professional performance (such as "Annie") cannot be ignored, they should be met with compromises other than vocal destruction. For example, proper vocal training, frequent laryngeal examination, and multiple casting (several Annies who alternate appearances) may allow a successful production without injuring the star, or the many youngsters attempting to become the star. Classical musicians have shown greater sensitivity to the needs of young voices, usually limiting school and children's choir performances to appropriate repertoires. However, even among classical musicians, there is a dangerous tendency to ask children to perform works too difficult for their vocal ages. In addition, especially among boys' choirs, damage may be caused by encouraging a boy soprano or alto to maintain his treble voice beyond the initiation of voice change. Trying to force the voice up or down during this unstable period is potentially hazardous.

Voice training during puberty is especially problematic. For generations, voice teachers have believed that heavy voice use during the period of voice mutation and instability should be avoided. Although this tradition was born out of extensive experience rather than scientific experiment, there is much reason to believe its wisdom. Nevertheless, a controversial study purported to show that vigorous vocal training during voice change enhanced vocal development.[20] However, although the study raises interesting questions, other investigators who listened to the youngsters studied disagreed with the conclusions of the author and felt that the voices were injured rather than superior. Consequently, although the question remains open at the present time, the traditional warnings against heavy voice use during mutation should be followed. However, as with the problem of casting lead singers for "Annie," practical considerations must be addressed. For example, a junior high school music teacher is in no position to silence all changing voices. If this were done, there would be no one left to sing in the choir. There are safe ways to permit singing. Most of the abuses of the changing voice come from the youngster (usually male) forcing the voice down or up to avoid the embarrassment of voice breaks. If this behavior can be eliminated, safer singing results. One technique that the author (RTS) has found successful is to begin each rehearsal with exercises in which the youngsters are instructed to allow their voices to break. These exercises can be done as a chorus and individually. For the first few days, everyone laughs. Thereafter, the group is desensitized to the sound of breaking voices and accepts the natural voice change, and the students can be instructed to let their voices break naturally during songs. This produces a tolerable choral sound, and students can continue singing safely in whichever mode is most relaxed for any given note. Other such exercises and appropriate repertoire selection permit limited, safe singing, even during this particularly troublesome period of vocal development.

All the vocal health problems that occur in adults may occur in children. Most of them have been widely discussed in previous literature.[21–23] Voice abuse is especially common in children. Screaming may result in vocal nodules, hemorrhages, or other serious vocal cord problems. These habits are often associated with abusive vocal patterns among the child's parents and siblings. This problem is treated best with vocal education and therapy that involves the entire family and, if possible, the child's peer group. Although it is true that childhood vocal nodules usually resolve spontaneously at the time of puberty, excellent voice therapy and education may cure them much sooner and simultaneously develop good vocal habits that will last a lifetime.

Gastric reflux laryngitis also occurs in children. In fact, it even occurs in newborns and may be a cause of pneumonia in early childhood. As in adults, morning hoarseness, chronic cough (especially at night), and bad breath are often the most prominent symptoms. However, reflux in children may also present as recurrent vomiting, repeated respiratory infections, intractable asthma, or apnea (cessation of breathing) especially at night. Treatment with elevation of the head of the bed, antacids, and change in eating habits is usually effective.

Many other medical conditions may afflict children's voices. They include birth defects in the vocal folds, paralysis, infections, vocal fold polyps and cysts, asthma, which impairs respiratory support, and numerous other ailments.[24] Hormonal and psychological problems also occur in children and may manifest as abnormal voices. For this reason, any child, adolescent, or young adult with a persistently abnormal voice or failure of voice development deserves the same thorough investigation and diagnosis that we would provide for an adult professional voice user. In fact, it is sobering to remember that we never know which of these children will grow up to be the next bright light at the Metropolitan Opera Company.

Understanding the normal development of the human voice over time is important in recognizing vocal health and disease and in planning vocal training. The voice is complex and dynamic. Its special delicacy and rapid changes during youth warrant extreme care and respect. So long as we remember that children are children, and treat their voices within limits imposed by their bodies and minds, safe, educated singing should be possible at almost any age.

The Young Adult Voice

Young adults are inherently social, and as such, voice use is often vigorous, if not excessive and abusive. Social voice use must occasionally be curbed to "protect" the performance voice. This requires self-control, a sense of priorities, and a commitment to career, often underdeveloped qualities in the young adult. The advice to the sick or injured performer to "use your voice only when you're being paid for it" often cannot be followed because of other educational or employment commitments, but it should still be encouraged early.

The young adult performer has usually begun a career, but lacks experience, maturity, and confidence. It can be difficult for a young performer to understand the concept of a career-threatening injury or make career decisions that trade short-term gain for long-term productivity. Young performers must often be asked to distinguish between vocal pursuits that are fun, income generating, and those that have future implications (ie, an audition) in order to manage vocal use.

Early in their careers, performers will commonly work at one or more other jobs to supplement income. Sometimes these jobs will involve other professional voice pursuits such as religious choirs, wedding bands, or backup singing. However, other work, such as sales, telemarketing, teaching, and administration can also be quite vocally intensive. This "other work" must be accounted for when advising a young performer on restricting voice use and abuse, and is often the major indication for ongoing speech therapy.

The basic medical history, vocal history, and physical examination are not particularly specialized in the young adult. All of the techniques of laryngeal visualization and assessment, including strobovideolaryngoscopy, are utilized routinely. Young adults more commonly have a vigorous vagal response, especially to nasal stimulation. This can lead to lightheadedness and syncope during transnasal endoscopy. Additionally, young adults sometimes exhibit hyperactive or paradoxical reactions to usually benign medications such as the topical vasoconstrictors and anesthetics used in endoscopy. These reactions may include agitation, diaphoresis, nausea, blurred vision, and itching. They usually resolve quickly and spontaneously.

Most young adults are generally healthy and they are not at great risk for the chronic illnesses that commonly affect older age groups such as hypertension, heart disease, and chronic obstructive pulmonary disease (COPD). However, certain disease processes are more common in young adulthood. These include chronic or recurrent infection, allergies, substance abuse, gastroesophageal reflux laryngitis (common in all age groups), and other conditions discussed elsewhere in this book.

As a result of the propensity for voice overuse and abuse syndromes, vocal fold lesions such as edema, nodules, and submucosal cysts are common findings on laryngeal examination. Strobovideolaryngoscopy is invaluable for the accurate diagnosis of these vocal fold abnormalities.[25,26] The examiner must often use caution when reviewing the findings of the laryngeal examination with the young professional voice user. A diagnosis such as vocal nodules can have a devastating psychological effect because of worries over the possibility of a career-threatening problem, feelings of personal failure, and anger over requirements that may have contributed to a pattern of vocal abuse. The patient must be educated about the underlying causes of most vocal fold pathology, the transient nature of many such findings, and the potentially excellent response to relative voice rest, speech and singing voice therapy. It is critical to maintain voice use with the institution of appropriate guidance whenever possible. Long periods of total voice rest are virtually never indicated.

Muscle tension dysphonia (MTD) is commonly encountered as a component of the voice abuse complex. Using flexible transnasal laryngoscopy, MTD is seen in the supraglottic and pharyngeal musculature during phonation. In some cases, laryngeal hyperfunction is seen as a "substitute" for inadequate breath support. In other cases, MTD develops as a compensatory mechanism for a vocal injury or a vocal fold lesion. MTD is treated with speech and singing voice therapy.

The most serious potential vocal fold findings are those that can lead to permanent scarring, submucosal hemorrhages and mucosal tears. Traumatic vocal fold pathology occurs mainly secondary to severe vocal abuse, especially when the larynx is also irritated by concomitant upper respiratory infection (URI) or allergy. These lesions can also be seen as a direct result of coughing or a severe sneeze. Strobovideolaryngoscopy is critical to assess the integrity of the mucosal wave across the vocal fold and help judge the age and severity of the injury. In the early stages, absolute voice rest is recommended. When mucosal healing is documented by stroboscopy and some return of the vibratory motion is noted, return to voice use with appropriate therapeutic guidance is allowed. The presence or development of a mass lesion of the vocal fold usually indicates consideration of surgical intervention.

Surgical indications and technique are not specialized for patients in this age group compared to older adults. However, surgery under local or topical anesthesia with intravenous sedation is sometimes contraindicated due to the unpredictable and paradoxical medication reactions in this age group, as has been discussed previously. In patients with lesions related to voice abuse such as vocal nodules, most laryngologists are more conservative in suggesting surgery in young adults. Young singers and actors need time to respond to changes in vocal technique and speech patterns. The process of controlling all potential abusive activities and limiting excessive voice use develops with education, practice, and maturity. These abilities are also necessary for successful rehabilitation after voice surgery. Coordination of care between the laryngologist, speech-language pathologist and singing voice specialist is critical in determining the goals, results, and limitations of treatment before making any surgical recommendations. In patients with unilateral masses that show signs of permanence, such as hemorrhagic or epithelial cysts, fibrous nodules that persist after therapy, and papillomas, surgery must be considered. In many cases, a performer may be better able to tolerate a long hiatus from professional voice use early in a career when there are usually fewer professional commitments. However, the "breaks" that make or break a career also often come during this period. So, it is important to restore performance ability as soon as it is safe to do so. The return to performance may be delayed in a younger patient because of lack of vocal experience and the psychological response to surgical treatment.

Anxiety and depression, common disorders in our society as a whole, are exacerbated by the stress of performance and of general career issues. Additionally, young adults are often isolated and distant from their usual support system of family and friends. The first step in dealing with psychological factors affecting voice disorders is to provide a supportive atmosphere within the voice team. The patient should be provided with encouragement, and must feel assured of confidentiality. When necessary, referral to a psychologist or psychiatrist specializing in arts medicine is indicated for additional support and perhaps pharmacologic treatment.

Anorexia and bulimia occur primarily in adolescent and young adult women. The body image distortions in these patients can be worsened in performers with real issues about personal appearance. Eating disorders can affect the voice indirectly because of loss of muscle mass and general strength, and because of hormonal factors, but most importantly, they represent a threat to the patient's life and health. If eating disorders are suspected, psychiatric referral is mandatory.

All professional voice users require special consideration when presenting with vocal complaints. When evaluating young adult performers, the laryngologist must be aware of the physical changes occurring in the vocal tract and the psychosocial factors that may be influencing the patient. Assessment is carried out with consideration for the age-related prevalence of vocal abuse and medical problems such as allergy and chronic infections. Treatment is tailored to the special concerns of the performer and the limitations of some therapies in the younger age groups.

The Adult Voice

Throughout adult life, mean fundamental frequency of the speaking voice drops steadily, in females from about 225 Hz in the 20- to 29-year-old group to about 195 Hz in the 80- to 90-year-old group.[27] In males, fundamental frequency of the speaking voice drops until roughly the fifth decade, after which it rises gradually.[28] It is important to be aware of normal changes in the speaking voice, because unskilled conscious or unconscious attempts to alter the quality and frequency of the speaking voice often are abusive and may produce problems reflected in the singing voice. Interestingly, it appears as if many of these changes do not occur in trained voice professionals.

The Aging Voice

Like death and taxes, most people have considered aging changes in the voice inevitable. Indeed, as we get older, there are certainly fundamental changes in the body that often modify the sound of the singing voice. Typically, we are not surprised to hear breathiness, loss of range, change in the characteristics of vibrato, development of tremolo, loss of breath control, vocal fatigue, pitch inaccuracies, and other undesirable features in older singers. Although some of these alterations cannot be avoided in specific individuals, not all of them are manifestations of irreversible deterioration. In fact, as our understanding of the aging process improves, it is becoming more and more apparent that many of these changes can be forestalled or even corrected. Woo et al reached similar conclusions recognizing that "presbylarynges is not a common disorder and should be a diagnosis of exclusion made only after careful medical and speech evaluation."[29] As physicians and teachers, we need to look closer before concluding: "I can't help your voice; you're just getting older."

Aging

The aging process is being researched extensively because of the importance of aging to the heart, brain, and all other body systems. No natural process has greater impact on our lives. Much of the pioneering work is being performed by scientists who have dedicated their lives to this subject, such as Drs. Robert L. Ringel and Wojtek Chodzko-Zajko of Purdue University who discussed aging at the Voice Foundations Fifteenth Symposium: Care of the Professional Voice in 1986.[10] The author (RTS) also presented on this subject at the Voice Foundation's Twenty-fourth Symposium: Care of the Professional Voice in 1995.[31] We are beginning to learn much more about the aging voice by combining general knowledge about the aging process with specific knowledge about laryngeal aging, such as that provided through microscopic studies by scientists such as Dr. Joel Kahane at Memphis State University and Dr. Minoru Hirano in Kurume, Japan. This interdisciplinary approach helps us understand our perceptions of voices over the years and helps explain our recent observations that some "old" voices can be made "young" again.

Aging is a complex conglomeration of biological events that change the structure and function of various parts of the body. There are many theories of aging that focus on processes of individual cells, molecules responsible for the genetic transmission of our characteristics, and changes in various organ systems. The details of specific theories are beyond the scope of this chapter. However, their principles and solutions show great promise for clinical application not only in the physician's office, but also in the voice studio. All theories and approaches to study of the aging process recognize well-established and predictable changes throughout the body. Although various mechanisms are involved in causing these changes, the effects are remarkably similar among various organ systems. As body structure changes, so does performance. Aging is associated with deteriorating bodily functions. Among them are accuracy, speed, endurance, stability, strength, coordination, breathing capacity, nerve conduction velocity, heart output, and kidney function. Muscle and neural tissues atrophy, and the chemicals responsible for nerve transmission change. Ligaments atrophy and cartilages turn to bone (including those in the larynx). Joints develop irregularities that interfere with smooth motion. The vocal folds themselves thin and deteriorate, losing their elastic and collaginous fibers. This makes them stiffer and thinner and may correlate with voice changes often noted with aging. The vocal fold edge also becomes less smooth. The not-so-cheery picture is one of inevitable decline for all of us. However, the notion that this decline occurs gradually and progressively (linear senescence) is open to challenge. It appears possible that many of these functions can be maintained at a better level than expected until very near the end of life, perhaps allowing a high-quality singing or acting career to extend into or beyond the seventh decade.

We have not yet stated how old "old" is. One simply cannot categorize people on the basis of how long they have lived—their chronological age. Biological age is a more useful measure, taking into account the condition and functioning of each individual's body. The desired result is to slow biological aging while chronological age advances inexorably. Although the aging process is inevitable, there are great differences among individuals in the rate and extent of its bodily changes. Although more study is needed, physicians and voice teachers already have some tools for intervention to slow the effects of aging.

Intervention

Certain aspects of the aging process are relatively easy to control medically. For example, as female singers reach menopause, estrogen deprivation causes substantial changes in the mucous membranes that line the vocal tract, the muscles, and throughout the patient's body. These and other hormonal effects are frequently reflected in the voice but can be forestalled for many years through hormone replacement therapy. Dosage is best determined by checking estrogen levels prior to menopause. Preparations containing androgens should be avoided whenever possible because they can cause masculinization of the voice. However, treating physicians must be aware of contraindications to hormone replacement, especially if there is a history of other health problems such as breast cancer. Expert advice is always essential when weighing the risks and benefits of any treatment, including hormone replacement.

Systematically attacking the aging process in other areas is more novel and controversial. The bodily changes characteristic of aging are not unique. In many ways, they are identical to those seen in disease and in disuse such as prolonged bed rest or immobilization of a leg. In particular, muscle disuse causes loss of muscle fibers indistinguishable from that seen with advanced age. Exercise avoids or reverses many of these changes in the young, and it appears to have the same effect when the changes are caused by aging. Appropriate exercise may not only help maintain muscle function and coordination, but it should also help elsewhere in the vascular system, nervous system, and especially in the respiratory system. Proper nutrition and weight control are also important. Respiratory function normally decreases with advancing age. In particular, residual volume increases, with a consequent decrease in vital capacity, tending to undermine the primary respiratory improvements resulting from earlier voice training. So, as a singer's respiratory potential diminishes, it is essential that he or she remain as close as possible to optimum respiratory conditioning.

We find it helpful to think of each individual as having a performance range from his or her poorest performance to his or her optimal performance. Audiences have established a certain level of performance that is acceptable for a professional singer. At the age of 18, a singer with an excellent voice may perform at only 50% of his current potential. Yet, he may get away with it, because the condition of his body is above the acceptable performance standard. However, as a singer ages, his physical abilities deteriorate. If the singer still performs at only 50% of his new ability, he will fall below the acceptable performance standard. However, if, through appropriate training, exercise, medication, and other factors, he is able to get to 70, 80, or 90% of his potential performance level, he may maintain professionally acceptable performance standards for many decades. For this reason, in treating age-related dysphonia, we combine traditional voice therapy, singing training, acting voice techniques, and aerobic conditioning to optimize neuromuscular performance. In general, rehabilitation is sufficient to restore acceptable voice function and eliminate most of the acoustic characteristics perceived as "old." However, occasionally substantial tissue changes make it impossible for therapy and medical management alone to restore satisfactory voice, and some such patients may benefit from laryngeal surgery. Nevertheless, surgery is unnecessary for the vast majority of patients with age-induced dysphonia.

We are accustomed to thinking of older people as having greater latitude in most things by virtue of experience and in deference to their age. When we hear a 60-year-old tenor develop a "wobble," we write it off as "getting old" and are reluctant or embarrassed to challenge him, because, after all, he cannot help aging. We also often do not think of prescribing exercises such as swimming, walking, jogging, or other aerobic exercise for people with gray hair and a little extra weight. However, this reticence is unfair and unproductive. To the contrary, as lungs and thorax lose their elasticity and distensibility and abdominal muscle mass begins to deteriorate, it is all the more important for a professional voice user to be in peak physical condition. A singer whose respiratory and abdominal conditioning is not good enough to allow him or her to walk up a few flights of stairs without becoming winded probably is unable to maintain

good abdominal support throughout a recital or opera. When the power source of the voice is undermined in this way, excessive muscle use in the neck and tongue usually supervenes. Conditioning muscles gradually in a disciplined fashion under medical supervision restores good support. Regular vocal technical training can eliminate the tremolo and improve agility, accuracy, and endurance in the older singer just as it can in the beginner.

Other age-related medical changes may also be significant to vocal function in some people. Personality has been most commonly described in terms of a five-factor model: extroversion, emotional stability, agreeableness, conscientiousness, and culture. In their 1989 study, Peabody and Goldberg described the five replicable factors which emerge from factor analysis of a large number of personality traits.[32] In general, personality traits are quite stable after approximately age 30. It is useful for the physician to understand personality traits and their tendency for stability. These may be helpful in interpreting other psychological changes associated with aging. Certain mental disorders are more common in the elderly, including Alzheimer's disease, a disorder of memory and mood. Alzheimer's disease is a diagnosis that can only by made with certainty by post-mortem examination of the brain, which reveals characteristic neuritic plaques and neurofibrillary tangles. However, clinical observation, and decline in cognitive function documented by neuropsychological batteries over time, are commonly used to make a presumptive diagnosis. Impairments in cognitive function and other neurological sequelae are also seen in multi-infarct dementia which presents with increasing frequency correlated to age. Mood disorders, including major depression, are not unusual in the elderly and may account for significant decline in cognitive, affective, and behavioral function. In addition, elderly people have a higher incidence of risk factors associated with mental illness, including poverty, bereavement, isolation, sensory deficits, and physical illness. It should also be noted that older people perform differently on some psychodiagnostic tests, and such studies must be interpreted with great caution, especially when attempting to distinguish between dementia and expected mental changes such as benign senescent forgetfulness. In IQ testing of the elderly, research indicates that age-related decrements on tests such as the WAIS-R are primarily in the speed tests, measuring perceptual-motor skills. There are more often decrements in *fluid* abilities (such as reaction speed) than in *crystallized* abilities (such as fund of knowledge). Verbal ability is retained until very old age. With renorming of the WAIS-R to age-appropriate populations, IQ changes in the elderly are now clearly seen as functions of educational opportunity and health status.[33,34] Alterations in cognition, especially memory, and changes in personality secondary to mood disorders and delusionality may impair a person's ability to concentrate, consistently perform vocal tasks, and cooperate optimally with voice rehabilitation.

Sexual dysfunction is also common among the elderly. It is important to recognize that this is associated with alterations in the hormonal environment that may also affect vocal function. For example, in males, serum levels of testosterone decline along with sexual function. In women, post-menopausal levels of estrogen are low, although their effect on sexual function is less predictable. However, they are associated with changes in mucosal secretions and structure, and in mood. Physicians should be aware that estrogen-androgen medications are prescribed for sexual dysfunction in women. The androgens may cause irreversible masculinization of the voice, and their use should be avoided whenever possible, especially in professional voice users.

In addition to the endocrine problems discussed above, thyroid disease in the elderly deserves special mention. Both hyperthyroidism and hypothyroidism are notoriously difficult to diagnose during advanced age. The elderly patient with hypothyroidism frequently does not display the "typical" features encountered in younger people. These include mental slowing, loss of energy, neurotic behavior, hearing loss, weight gain, musculoskeletal discomfort, dry skin, changes in facial appearance, and other problems. The diagnosis in the elderly is often missed because of many of the symptoms may be inaccurately attributed to age. In addition, elderly patients often have other problems to which their difficulties are ascribed in the absence of clear diagnostic clues to hypothyroidism. Alterations in thyroid function frequently produce substantial changes in vocal quality including loss of range, efficiency, and "muffling" of the voice. These vocal derangements generally resolve when the thyroid abnormality is treated.

Oral cavity changes associated with aging may be particularly troublesome to singers. Loss of dentition may alter occlusion and articulation causing especially disturbing problems for professional voice users and wind instrumentalists. These difficulties may be avoided to some extent by having impressions made while dentition is still normal. Dentures that are more similar to the person's natural teeth can then be fashioned. Although salivary glands lose up to about 30% of their parenchymal tissue over a lifetime, salivary secretion remains adequate in most healthy, non-medicated people throughout life. However, changes in the oral mucosa are similar to those occurring in the skin (thinning and dehydration). They render oral mucosa in the elderly more suceptible to injury, and the sensation of xerostomia may be especially disturbing to singers. Oral cancers also comprise about 5% of all malignancies, and 95% of oral cancers occur in people over 40 years of age. Cancers in the head and neck may result in profound voice dysfunction.

Many other factors must also be taken into account in diagnosis and treatment of elderly patients. These include *coronary artery disease, cerebrovascular disease, hypertension, obesity, stroke, diabetes, cancer, diet, osteoporosis, hearing loss, vision loss, swallowing dysfunction, anemia, arthritis, neurological dysfunction including tremor, incontinence, gastrointestinal disorders,* and other conditions. All of these may have adverse effects on the voice either through action on the larynx or through impairment of the voice producing mechanism at another anatomical site.

Because older singers and actors may have considerably less natural reserve and resilience than youthful performers, we need to be particularly demanding with them. They cannot compensate for or tolerate weaknesses like teenagers, nor can they recover quickly from injuries to their vocal apparatus. However, with optimal physical and vocal conditioning, proper medical supervision of cardiac and respiratory function, and appropriate medication, weight control, and nutrition, it appears likely that a great many singers, actors and others may enjoy extra years or decades of performance that are gratifying both to them and to their audiences.

Summary

At birth, the larynx is high in the neck. It gradually descends throughout life. Laryngeal growth and change in vocal tract length are associated with changes in vocal quality. At puberty, the female voice usually drops two to three semitones, and the male voice drops about one octave. Special problems are associated with each age range from early childhood through the last years of life. With proper medical care, and appropriate repertoire, high quality, safe voice performance is possible at virtually any age.

Review Questions

1. At birth, the larynx is all of the following except:
    a. at about the level of C3
    b. equipped with vocal folds that are about 50% cartilaginous and 50% membranous

   c. about the same in size and shape in males and females
   d. well-ossified
   e. equipped with an omega-shaped epiglottis

2. Puberty occurs earlier in males.
   a. true
   b. false

3. Vocal polyps are an affliction of adults and are not encountered in children.
   a. true
   b. false

4. Presbylarynges (vocal aging) is a common cause of vocal weakness and can usually be accurately diagnosed using a laryngeal mirror.
   a. true
   b. false

5. Sexual dysfunction among the elderly is not usually associated with vocal problems, and the subject need not be discussed.
   a. true
   b. false

References

1. Kahane JC: Growth of the human prepubertal and pubertal larynx. *J Speech Hear*. 1982;25:226-455.
2. Hirano M, Kurita S, Nashashima T: The structure of the vocal folds. In: Hirano M (ed). *Vocal Fold Physiology*. Tokyo: University of Tokyo Press; 1991.
3. Lee PA. Normal ages of pubertal events among American males and females. *J Adoles Health Care*. 1980;1(1):26-29.
4. Thurman L, Klitzke CA: Voice education and health care for young voices. In: Benninger MS, Jacobson BH, Johnson AF, eds. *Vocal Arts Medicine: The Care and Prevention of Professional Voice Disorders*. New York: Thieme Medical Publishers; 1994:238.
5. Hagg U, Tarranger J. Menarche and voice change as indications of the pubertal growth spurt. *Acta Odontal Scand*. 1980;38(3):179-186.
6. Sataloff RT: Effects of age on the voice. In Sataloff RT, *Professional Voice: The Science and Art of Clinical Care*. New York: Raven Press, Ltd; 1991:143.
7. Sundberg J: *The Science of the Singing Voice*. DeKalb, Ill: Northern Illinois Press; 1987:102.
8. Sataloff RT. The aging voice. *NATS J*. 1987;44(1):20-21.
9. Hollien H. Old voices: what do we really know about them? *J Voice*. 1987;1:2-17.
10. Chodzko-Zajko WJ, Ringel RL. Physiological aspects of aging. *J Voice*. 1987;1:18-26.
11. Kahane JC, Connective tissue changes in the larynx and their effects on the voice. *J Voice*. 1987;1:27-30.
12. Ringel RL, Chodzko-Zajko WJ. Vocal indices of biological aging. *J Voice*. 1987;1:31-37.
13. Morris RJ, Brown WS. Age-related voice measures among adult women. *J Voice*. 1987;1:38-43.
14. Linville SE. Acoustic-perceptual studies of aging voice in women. *J Voice*. 1987; 1:44-48.
15. Huntley R, Hollien H, Shipp T. Influences of listener characteristics on perceived age estimates. *J Voice*. 1987; 1:49-52.
16. Lawrence VL, ed. *Transcripts of the thirteenth symposium: care of the professional voice*. Part II: Vocal Therapeutics: "Pediatric Laryngology." New York: The Voice Foundation; 1985:447-480.
17. Aronson AE. *Clinical Voice Disorders*. 2nd ed. New York: Thieme; 1985:43-45.
18. Wilson DK. *Voice Problems in Children*. 3rd ed. Baltimore: Williams & Wilkins; 1986;2-341.
19. Andrews ML, Summers A. *Voice Therapy for Adolescents*. Boston: College-Hill Press; 1988;1-202.
20. Blatt IM. Training singing children during the phases of voice mutation. *Ann Otol Rhinol Laryngol*. 1983;92(5, pt 1):462-468.
21. Sataloff RT. The professional voice, I. Anatomy and history. *J Voice*. 1987;1(1):92-104.
22. Sataloff RT. The professional voice, II. Physical examination. *J Voice*. 1987;1(2):191-201.
23. Sataloff RT. The professional voice, III. Common diagnoses and treatments. *J Voice*. 1987;1(3):283-292.
24. Rubin J, Sataloff RT, Korovin G, Gould WJ: *The Diagnosis and Treatment of Voice Disorders*. New York: Igaku-Shoin Medical Publishers, Inc; 1995.
25. Woo P, Colton R, Casper J, Brewer D: Diagnostic Value of Stroboscopic Examination in Hoarse Patients. *J Voice*. 1990;5:332-337.
26. Sataloff RT, Spiegel JR, Hawkshaw MJ: Strobovideolaryngoscopy: results and clinical value. *Ann Otol Rhinol Laryngol*, 1991;100:725-727.
27. McGlone R, Hollein H. Vocal pitch characteristics of aged women. *J Speech Hear Res*. 1963;6:164-170.
28. Hollein H, Shipp T. Speaking fundamental frequency and chronologic age in males. *J Speech Hear Res*. 1972; 15:155-169.
29. Woo P, Casper J, Colton R, Brewer D: Dysphonia in the aging: physiology versus disease. *Laryngoscope*. 1992; 102(2):139-144.
30. Special issue on vocal aging. *J Voice*. 1987;1(1):2-67.
31. Sataloff RT, Rosen DC, Hawkshaw M, Spiegel JR: The three ages of voice: the aging adult voice. *J Voice*. 1997; 11(2):156–160.
32. Peabody D, Goldberg LR: Some determinants of factor structures from personality trait descriptors. *J Pers Soc Psychol*, 1989;57:552-567.
33. Botwinic J: *Aging and Behavior*. New York: Springer-Verlag; 1978:22-30.
34. Anastasi A: *Psychological Testing*. 6th ed., New York: Macmillan Publishing; 1988:347-351.

11

Hearing Loss in Singers and Other Musicians

Robert Thayer Sataloff and Joseph Sataloff

Singers depend on good hearing to match pitch, monitor vocal quality, and provide feedback and direction for vocal adjustments during singing. The importance of good hearing has been underappreciated. While well-trained singers are usually careful to protect their voices, they may subject their ears to unnecessary damage and thereby threaten their musical careers. The ear is a critical part of the singer's "instrument." Consequently, it is important for singers to understand how the ear works, how to take care of it, what can go wrong with it, and how to avoid hearing loss from preventable injury.

Causes of Hearing Loss

The classification and causes of hearing loss have been described in detail in standard textbooks of otolaryngology, and previous works by the authors,[1,2] and they will be reviewed only briefly in this chapter. Hearing loss may be hereditary or non-hereditary, and either form may be congenital (present at birth) or acquired. There is a common misconception that hereditary hearing loss implies the presence of the problem at birth or during childhood. In fact, most hereditary hearing loss occurs later in life. All otolaryngologists know families whose members begin to lose their hearing in their third, fourth, or fifth decade, for example. Otosclerosis, a common cause of correctable hearing loss, often presents when people are in their twenties or thirties. Similarly, the presence of deafness at birth does not necessarily imply hereditary or genetic factors. A child whose mother had rubella during the first trimester of pregnancy or was exposed to radiation early in pregnancy may be born with a hearing loss. This is not of genetic etiology and has no predictive value for the hearing of the child's siblings or future children. Hearing loss may occur because of problems in any portion of the ear, the nerve between the ear and the brain, or the brain. Understanding hearing loss requires a basic knowledge of the structure of the human ear.

Anatomy and Physiology of the Ear

The ear is divided into three major anatomical divisions: the outer ear, the middle ear, and the inner ear.

The outer ear has two parts: (1) the trumpet-shaped apparatus on the side of the head, the *auricle* or *pinna*, and (2) the tube leading from the auricle into the temporal bone, the *external auditory canal*. The opening is called the *meatus*.

The *tympanic membrane*, or eardrum stretches across the inner end of the external ear canal, separating the outer ear from the middle ear. The middle ear is a small cavity in the temporal bone in which three auditory ossicles, the *malleus* (hammer), *incus* (anvil), and *stapes* (stirrup) form a bony bridge from the external ear to the inner ear (Fig 11–1). This bony bridge is held in place by muscles and ligaments. The middle ear chamber is filled with air and connects to the nasopharynx through the *eustachian tube*. The eustachian tube helps to equalize pressure on both sides of the eardrum.

The inner ear is a fluid-filled chamber divided into two parts: (1) the vestibular labyrinth, which functions as part of the body's balance mechanism, and (2) the *cochlea*, which contains thousands of minute,

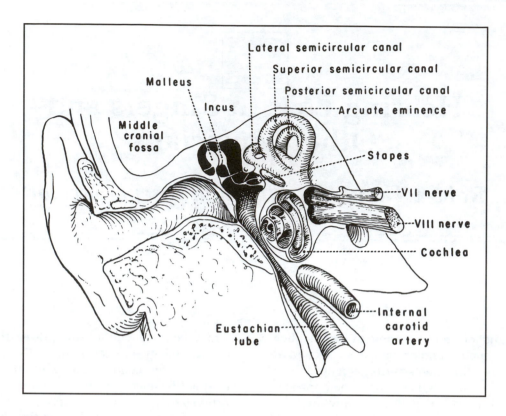

Fig 11–1. Cross-section of the ear. The semicircular canals are part of the balance system.

sensory, hairlike cells (Fig 11–2). The *organ of Corti* functions as the switchboard for the auditory system. The eighth cranial (acoustic) nerve leads from the inner ear to the brain, serving as the pathway for the impulses the brain will interpret as sound.

Sound creates vibrations in the air somewhat similar to the waves created when a stone is thrown into a pond. The pinna collects these sound waves and funnels them down the external ear canal to the eardrum. The sound waves cause the eardrum to vibrate. These vibrations are transmitted through the middle ear over the bony bridge formed by the malleus, incus, and stapes. The vibrations in turn cause the membranes over the openings to the inner ear to vibrate, causing the fluid in the inner ear to be set in motion. The motion of the fluid in the inner ear excites the nerve cells in the organ of Corti, producing electrochemical impulses that are transmitted to the brain along the acoustic nerve. As the impulses reach the brain, we experience the sensation of hearing.

Establishing the Site of Damage in the Auditory System

The cause of a hearing loss, like that of any other medical condition, is determined by carefully obtain-

ing a meaningful history, making a physical examination, and performing certain laboratory tests. In otology, hearing tests parallel the function of clinical laboratory tests in general medicine. When a hearing loss is classified, the point at which the auditory pathway has broken down is localized, and it is determined whether the patient's hearing loss is conductive, sensorineural, central, functional, or a mixture of these.

Details of the otologic history, physical examination, and test protocols are available in many otolaryngology texts. Medical evaluation of a patient with a suspected hearing problem includes a comprehensive history; complete physical examination of the ears, nose, throat, head, and neck; assessment of the cranial nerves, including testing the sensation in the external auditory canal (Hitselberger's sign), audiogram (hearing test); and other tests, as indicated. Recommended additional studies may include computed tomography, magnetic resonance imaging, dynamic imaging studies (SPECT, PET), specialized hearing tests (such as brain stem evoked response audiometry), tympanometry, central auditory testing, balance testing, and a variety of blood tests for the many systemic causes of hearing loss. All patients with hearing complaints deserve a thorough

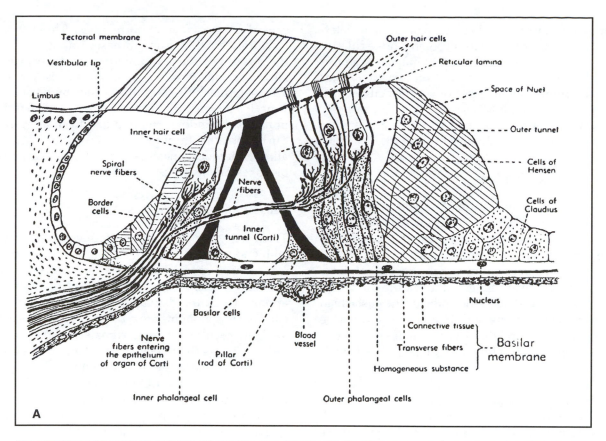

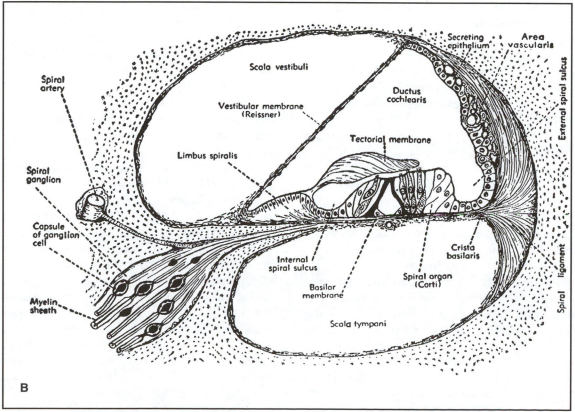

Fig 11–2. A cross-section of the organ of Corti. **A.** Low magnification. **B.** Higher magnification.

examination and comprehensive evaluation to determine the specific cause of the problem and to rule out serious or treatable conditions that may be responsible for the hearing impairment. Contrary to popular misconceptions, not all cases of sensorineural hearing loss are incurable. Therefore, "nerve deafness" should be assessed with the same systematic vigor and enthusiasm as conductive hearing loss.

Conductive Hearing Loss

In cases of conductive hearing loss, sound waves are not transmitted effectively to the inner ear because of some interference in the external canal, the eardrum, the ossicular chain, the middle ear cavity, the oval window, the round window, or the eustachian tube. For example, damage either to the middle ear, which transmits sound energy efficiently, or the eustachian tube, which maintains equal air pressure between the middle ear cavity and the external canal, could result in a mechanical defect in sound transmission. In pure conductive hearing loss, there is no damage to the inner ear or the neural pathway.

Patients diagnosed as having conductive hearing loss have a much better prognosis than those with sensorineural loss, because modern techniques make it possible to cure or at least improve the vast majority of cases in which the damage occurs in the outer or middle ear. Even if they are not improved medically or surgically, these patients stand to benefit greatly from a hearing aid, because what they need most is amplification. They are not bothered by distortion and other hearing abnormalities that may occur in sensorineural losses.

Conductive hearing loss may result from anything that completely blocks the outer ear or interferes with sound transmission through the middle ear. Outer ear problems include birth defects, total occlusion of the external auditory canal by wax, foreign body (such as a piece of cotton swab or ear plug), infection, trauma, or tumor. Large perforations in the tympanic membrane may also cause hearing loss, especially if they surround the malleus. However, relatively small, central perforations usually do not cause a great deal of hearing impairment. If someone with such a perforation has a 30 dB or 40 dB hearing loss, there is probably also a problem involving the ossicles. Middle ear dysfunction is the most common cause of conductive hearing loss. It may occur in many ways. The middle ear may become filled with fluid because of eustachian tube dysfunction. The fluid restricts free movement of the tympanic membrane and ossicles, thereby producing hearing loss. Middle ear conductive hearing loss may also be caused by ossicular abnormalities. These include fractures, erosion from disease, impingement by tumors, congenital malformations, and other causes. However, otosclerosis is among the most common. This hereditary disease afflicts the stapes and prevents it from moving in its normal pistonlike fashion in the oval window. Hearing loss from otosclerosis can be corrected through stapes surgery, a brief operation under local anesthesia, and it is usually possible to restore hearing.

Sensorineural Hearing Loss

The word *sensorineural* was introduced to replace the ambiguous terms *perceptive deafness* and *nerve deafness*. It is a more descriptive and more accurate anatomical term. The term sensory hearing loss is applied when the damage is localized in the inner ear. Useful synonyms are *cochlear* or *inner-ear hearing loss*. The cochlea has approximately 15,000 hearing nerve endings (hair cells). Those hair cells, and the nerve that connects them to the brain, are susceptible to damage from a variety of causes. *Neural hearing loss* is the correct term to use when the damage is in the auditory nerve proper, anywhere between its fibers at the base of the hair cells and the auditory nuclei. This range includes the bipolar ganglion of the eighth cranial nerve. Other common names for this type of loss are nerve deafness and *retrocochlear hearing loss*. These names are useful if applied appropriately and meaningfully, but too often they are used improperly.

Although at present it is common practice to group together both sensory and neural components, it has become possible in many cases to attribute a predominant part of the damage, if not all of it, to either the inner ear or the nerve. Because of some success in this area and the likelihood that ongoing research will allow us to differentiate between even more cases of sensory and neural hearing loss, we shall divide the terms and describe the distinctive features of each type. This separation is advisable because the prognosis and the treatment of the two kinds of impairment differ. For example, in all cases of unilateral sensorineural hearing loss, it is important to distinguish between a sensory and neural hearing impairment, because the neural type may be due to an acoustic neuroma which could become life-threatening. Those cases which we cannot identify as either sensory or neural and those cases in which there is damage in both regions we shall classify as sensorineural.

There are various and complex causes of sensorineural hearing loss, but certain features are characteristic and basic to all of them. Because the histories obtained from patients are so diverse, they contribute more insight into the etiology than into the classification of a case. Sensorineural hearing loss often involves not only loss of loudness but also loss of clarity. The hair cells in the inner ear are responsible for analyzing auditory input and instantaneously coding it. The auditory nerve is responsible for carrying this complex coded information. Neural defects such as acoustic neuromas (tumors of the auditory nerve) are frequently accompanied by severe difficulties in discriminating words, although the hearing threshold for soft sounds may not be so severely affected. Sensory deficits in the cochlea are often associated with distortion of sound quality, distortion of loudness (loudness recruitment), and distortion of pitch (diplacusis). Diplacusis poses particular problems for musicians because it may make it difficult for them to tell whether they are playing or singing correct pitches. This symptom is also troublesome to conductors. Keyboard players and other musicians whose instruments do not require critical tuning adjustments compensate for this problem better than singers, string players, and the like. In addition, sensorineural hearing loss may be accompanied by tinnitus (noises in the ear) and/or vertigo.

Sensorineural hearing loss may be due to a great number of conditions, including exposure to ototoxic drugs (including a number of antibiotics, diuretics, and chemotherapy agents), hereditary conditions, systemic diseases, trauma, and noise, among other causes. Most physicians recognize that hearing loss may be associated with a large number of hereditary syndromes[2,3] involving the eyes, kidneys, heart, or any other body system, but many are not aware that hearing loss also accompanies many very common systemic diseases. Naturally, these occur in musicians as well as others. The presence of these systemic illnesses should lead physicians to inquire about hearing and to perform audiometry in selected cases. Problems implicated in hearing impairment include Rh incompatibility, hypoxia, jaundice, rubella, mumps, rubeola, fungal infections, meningitis, tuberculosis, sarcoidosis, Wegener's granulomatosis, vasculitis, histiocytosis X, allergy, hyperlipoproteinemia, syphilis, hypothyroidism, hypoadrenalism, hypopituitarism, renal failure, autoimmune disease, coagulopathies, aneurysms, vascular disease, multiple sclerosis, infestations, diabetes, hypoglycemia, cleft palate and others.[2]

Prolonged exposure to very loud noise is a common cause of hearing loss in our society. Noise-induced hearing loss is seen most frequently in heavy industry. However, occupational hearing loss caused by musical instruments is a special problem, as discussed below.

Mixed Hearing Loss

For practical purposes, *a mixed hearing loss* should be understood to mean a conductive hearing loss accompanied by a sensory, neural (or a sensorineural) loss in the same ear. However, the clinical emphasis is on the conductive hearing loss, because available therapy is so much more effective for this disorder. Consequently, the otologic surgeon has a special interest in cases of mixed hearing loss in which there is primarily a conductive loss complicated by some sensorineural damage. In a musician, curing the correctable component may be sufficient to convert hearing from unserviceable to satisfactory for performance purposes.

Functional Hearing Loss

Functional hearing loss occurs as a condition in which the patient does not seem to hear or to respond, yet the handicap is not caused by any organic pathology in the peripheral or central auditory pathways. The hearing difficulty may have an entirely psychological etiology, or it may be superimposed on some mild organic hearing loss, in which case it is called a *functional* or a *psychogenic overlay*. Often, the patient has normal hearing underlying the functional hearing loss. A careful history usually will reveal some hearing impairment in the patient's family or some personally meaningful reference to deafness that generated the patient's psychogenic hearing loss. The important challenge for the clinician in such a case is to classify the condition properly, so that effective treatment can be initiated. Functional hearing loss occurs not only in adults, but also in children. This diagnosis should be considered whenever hearing problems arise in musicians under great pressure regardless of age, including young prodigies.

Central Hearing Loss (Central Dysacusis)

In central hearing loss, the damage is situated in the central nervous system at some point in the brain between the auditory nuclei (in the medulla oblongata) and the cortex. Formerly, central hearing loss was described as a type of "perceptive deafness," a term now obsolete.

Although information about central hearing loss is accumulating, it remains mysterious and complex. Physicians know that some patients cannot interpret or understand what is being said, and that the cause of the difficulty is not in the peripheral mechanism but somewhere in the central nervous system. In central hearing loss the problem is not a lowered pure-tone threshold, but the patient's ability to interpret what he or she hears. Obviously, it is a more complex task to interpret speech than to respond to a pure-tone threshold; consequently, the tests necessary to diagnose central hearing impairment must be designed to assess a patient's ability to handle complex information.

Psychological Consequences of Hearing Loss

Performing artists are frequently sensitive, somewhat high-strung people who depend on physical perfection in order to practice their crafts and earn their livelihoods. Any physical impairment that threatens their ability to continue as musicians may be greeted with dread, denial, panic, depression, or similar responses that may be perceived as exaggerated, especially by physicians who do not specialize in caring for performers. In the case of hearing loss, such reactions are common even in the general public. Consequently, it is not surprising that psychological concomitants of hearing loss in musicians are seen in nearly all cases.

Many successful performers are communicative and gregarious. Naturally, anything that impairs their ability to interact with the world causes problems similar to those seen in nonmusicians. However, in addition, their vocational hearing demands are much greater than those required in most professions. Therefore, musicians' normal reactions to hearing loss are often amplified by legitimate fears about interruption of their artistic and professional futures through hearing impairment. These concerns are encountered in musicians with hearing impairment regardless of the cause. The problems involved in accurately assessing the disability associated with such impairments are addressed below in the discussion of occupational hearing loss in musicians.

Performing artists have vocational hearing demands that are much greater than those required in most professions. They must be able to do more than simply understand conversational speech. They are required to accurately match frequencies over a broad range, including frequencies above those required for speech comprehension. Even mild pitch distortion (diplacusis) may make it difficult or impossible for musicians to play or sing in tune. Elevated high-frequency thresholds may lead to excessively loud playing at higher pitches, and to an artistically unacceptable performance, which may end the career of a violinist or conductor, for example. Consequently, it is extremely important for singers and

other musicians to be protected from hearing loss. However, the musical performance environment poses not only critical hearing demands, but also noise hazards. Review of the literature reveals convincing evidence that music-induced hearing loss occurs, but there is a clear need for additional research to clarify incidence, predisposing factors, and methods of prevention.

Occupational hearing loss is sensorineural hearing impairment caused by exposure to high-intensity workplace noise or music. This subject has been reviewed in detail elsewhere.[4]

It has been well established that selected symphony orchestra instruments, popular orchestras, rock bands, and personal stereo headphones produce sound pressure levels (SPLs) intense enough to cause permanent hearing loss. Such hearing loss may also be accompanied by tinnitus and may be severe enough to interfere with performance, especially in violinists. The violin is the highest pitched string instrument in routine use. The amount of hearing loss is related to the intensity of the noise, duration and intermittency of exposure, total exposure time over months and years, and other factors. Various methods have been devised to help protect the hearing of performers. For example, many singers and other musicians (especially in rock bands) wear ear protectors at least during practice. Noise levels in choral environments are also high, but their possible effects on hearing have not been studied yet. Singers should be aware of these hazards and avoid them or use hearing protection in noisy surroundings whenever possible. They should also be careful to avoid exposure to potentially damaging avocational noise such as loud music through headphones, chainsaws, snowmobiles, gunfire, motorcycles, and power tools.

For many years, people have been concerned about hearing loss in rock singers and other musicians exposed to intense noise from electric instruments, and in audiences who frequently attend rock music concerts. We have seen hearing loss in both of these populations, and similar problems in people who listen to music at very high volumes through earphones. Because of the obviously high intensity that characterizes rock music, hearing loss in these situations is not surprising. This situation raises serious concerns about prevention that are of compelling relevance to professional rock singers and other musicians whose livelihoods depend on their hearing. Clinical observations in the authors' practice suggest that the rock performance environment may be another source of asymmetrical noise-induced hearing loss, a relatively unusual situation since most occupational hearing loss is symmetrical. Rock singers and instrumentalists tend to have slightly greater hearing loss in the ear adjacent to the drum and cymbal, or the side immediately next to a speaker, if it is placed slightly behind the musician. Various methods have been devised to help protect the hearing of rock players. For example, most of them stand beside or behind their speakers, rather than in front of them. In this way, they are not subjected to peak intensities, as are the patrons in the first rows.

The problem of occupational hearing loss among classical singers and other musicians is less obvious, but equally important. In fact, in the United States, it has become a matter of great concern and negotiation among unions and management. Various reports have found an increased incidence of high-frequency sensorineural hearing loss among professional orchestra musicians as compared to the general public; and sound levels within orchestras have been measured between 83 dBA and 112 dBA, as discussed below. The size of the orchestra and the rehearsal hall are important factors, as is the position of the individual instrumentalist within the orchestra. Players seated immediately in front of the brass section appear to have particular problems, for example. Individual classical instruments may produce more noise exposure for their players than assumed.

Because many singers and instrumentalists practice or perform 4 to 8 hours a day (sometimes more), such exposure levels may be significant. An interesting review of the literature may be found in the report of a clinical research project on hearing in classical musicians by Axelsson and Lindgren.[5] They also found asymmetrical hearing loss in classical musicians, greater in the left ear. This is a common finding, especially among violinists. A brief summary of most of the published works on hearing loss in musicians is presented below.

In the United States, various attempts have been made to solve some of the problems of the orchestra musician, including placement of plexiglass barriers in front of some of the louder brass instruments, alteration in the orchestra formation, such as elevation of sections or rotational seating, changes in spacing and height between players, use of ear protectors, and other measures. These solutions have not been proven effective, and some of them appear impractical, or damaging to the performance. The effects of the acoustic environment (concert hall, auditorium, outdoor stage, etc.) on the ability of music to damage hearing have not been studied systematically. Recently, popular musicians have begun to recognize the importance of this problem and to protect themselves and educate their fans. Some performers are wearing ear protectors regularly in rehearsal, and

even during performance (*Time.* September 29, 1989:78). Considerable additional study is needed to provide proper answers and clinical guidance for this very important occupational problem. In fact, review of the literature on occupational hearing loss reveals that surprisingly little information is available on the entire subject. Moreover, all of it is concerned with instrumentalists, and no similar studies in singers were found.

Study of the existing reports reveals a variety of approaches. Unfortunately, neither the results nor the quality of the studies is consistent. Nevertheless, familiarity with the research already performed provides useful insights into the problem. In 1960, Arnold and Miskolczy-Fodor[6] studied the hearing of 30 pianists. Sound pressure level (SPL) measurements showed that average levels were approximately 85 dB, although periods of 92 db to 96 dB were recorded. The A-weighting network was not used for sound level measurements in this study. No noise-induced hearing loss was identified. The pianists in this study were 60 to 80 years of age; and, in fact, their hearing was better than normal for their age. Flach and Aschoff,[7] and later Flach,[8] found sensorineural hearing loss in 16% of 506 music students and professional musicians, a higher percentage than could be accounted for by age alone, although none of the cases of hearing loss occurred in students. Hearing loss was most common in musicians playing string instruments. Flach and Aschoff also noticed asymmetrical sensorineural hearing loss worse on the left in 10 of 11 cases of bilateral sensorineural hearing loss in instrumentalists. In one case (a flautist), the hearing was worse on the right. In 4% of the professional musicians tested, hearing loss was felt to be causally related to musical noise exposure. Histories and physical examinations were performed on the musicians and tests were performed in a controlled environment. This study also included interesting measurements of sound levels in a professional orchestra. Unfortunately, they are reported in DIN-PHONS, rather than dBA.

In 1968, Berghoff[9] reported on the hearing of 35 big band musicians and 30 broadcasting (studio) musicians. Most had performed for 15 to 25 years, although the string players were older as a group and had performed for as many as 35 years. In general, they played approximately 5 hours per day. Hearing loss was found in 40- to 60-year-old musicians at 8000 Hz and 10,000 Hz. Eight musicians had substantial hearing loss, especially at 4000 Hz. Five out of 64 (8%) cases were felt to be causally related to noise exposure. No difference was found between left and right ears, but hearing loss was most common in musicians who were sitting immediately beside drums, trumpets, or bassoons. Sound level measurements for wind instruments revealed that intensities were greater 1 m away from the instrument than they were at the ear canal. Unfortunately, sound levels were measured in PHONS. Lebo and Oliphant studied the sound levels of a symphony orchestra and two rock and roll orchestras.[10] They reported that sound energy for symphony orchestras is fairly evenly distributed from 500 Hz through 4000 Hz, but most of the energy in rock and roll music was found between 250 Hz and 500 Hz. The SPL for the symphony orchestra during loud passages was approximately 90 dBA. For rock and roll bands, it reached levels in excess of 110 dBA. Most of the time, music during rock performance was louder than 95 dB in the lower frequencies, while symphony orchestras rarely achieved such levels. However, Lebo and Oliphant made their measurements from the auditorium, rather than in immediate proximity to the performers. Consequently, their measurements are more indicative of distant audience noise exposure than that of the musicians or audience members in the first row. Rintelmann and Borus also studied noise-induced hearing loss in rock and roll musicians, measuring SPL at various distances from 5 ft to 60 ft from center stage.[11] They studied six different rock and roll groups in four locations and measured a mean SPL of 105 dB. Their analysis revealed that the acoustic spectrum was fairly flat in the low-and mid-frequency region and showed gradual reduction above 2000 Hz. They also detected hearing loss in only 5% of the 42 high school and college student rock and roll musicians they studied. The authors estimated that their experimental group had been exposed to approximately 105 dB (SPL) for an average of 11.4 hours a week for 2.9 years.

In 1970, Jerger and Jerger studied temporary threshold shifts (TTS) in rock and roll musicians.[12] They identified TTSs greater than 15 dB in at least one frequency between 2000 Hz and 8000 Hz in eight of nine musicians studied prior to performance and within 1 hour after the performance. Speaks and coworkers[13] examined 25 rock musicians for threshold shifts, obtaining measures between 20 and 40 minutes following performance. In this study, shifts of only 7 dB to 8 dB at 4000 and 6000 Hz were identified. TTSs occurred in about half of the musicians studied. Six of the 25 musicians had permanent threshold shifts. Noise measurements were also made in 10 rock bands. Speaks et al found noise levels from 90 dBA to 110 dBA. Most sessions were less than 4 hours, and actual music time was generally 120 to 150 minutes. The investigators recognized the hazard to hearing posed by this noise exposure. In 1972, Rintel-

mann, Lindberg, and Smitley studied the effects of rock and roll music on humans under laboratory conditions.[14] They exposed normal hearing females to rock and roll music at 110 dB SPL in a sound field. They also compared subjects exposed to music played continuously for 60 minutes with others in which the same music was interrupted by 1 minute of ambient noise between each 3 minute musical selection. At 4000 Hz, they detected mean TTS of 26 dB in the subjects exposed to continuous noise, and 22.5 dB in those exposed intermittently. Both groups required approximately the same amount of time for recovery. TTS sufficient to be considered potentially hazardous for hearing occurred in slightly over 50% of the subjects exposed to intermittent noise, and 80% of subjects subjected to continuous noise.

In 1972, Jahto and Hellmann[15] studied 63 orchestra musicians playing in contemporary dance bands. Approximately one third of their subjects had measurable hearing loss, and 13% had bilateral high frequency loss suggestive of noise-induced hearing damage. They also measured peak SPL of 110 dB (the A scale was not used). They detected potentially damaging levels produced by trumpets, bassoons, saxophones, and percussion instruments. In contrast, in 1974 Buhlert and Kuhl[16] found no noise-induced hearing loss among 17 performers in a radio broadcasting orchestra. The musicians had played for an average of 20 years and were an average of 30 years of age. In a later study, Kuhl[17] studied members of a radio broadcasting dance orchestra over a period of 12 days. The average noise exposure was 82 dBA. He concluded that such symphony orchestras were exposed to safe noise levels, in disagreement with Jahto and Hellmann. Zeleny et al[18] studied members of a large string orchestra with intensities reaching 104 to 112 dB SPL. Hearing loss greater than 20 dB in at least one frequency occurred in 85 of 118 subjects (72%), usually in the higher frequencies. Speech frequencies were affected in six people (5%).

In 1976, Siroky et al reported noise levels within a symphony orchestra ranging between 87 dBA and 98 dBA, with a mean value of 92 dBA.[19] Audiometric evaluation of 76 members of the orchestra revealed 16 musicians with hearing loss, 13 of them sensorineural. Hearing loss was found in 7.3% of string players, 20% of wind players, and 28% of brass players. All percussionists had some degree of hearing loss. Hearing loss was not found in players who had performed for fewer than 10 years but was present in 42% of players who had performed for more than 20 years. This study needs to be reevaluated in consideration of age-matched controls. At least some of the individuals reported have hearing loss not causally related to noise (such as those with hearing levels of 100 dB in the higher frequencies). In a companion report, Folprechtova and Miksovska also found mean sound levels of 92 dBA in a symphony orchestra with a range of 87 dBA to 98 dBA.[20] They reported that most of the musicians performed between 4 and 8 hours daily. They reported the sound levels of various instruments as seen in Table 11–1.

A study by Balazs and Gotze, also in 1976, agreed that classical musicians are exposed to potentially damaging noise levels.[21] The findings of Gryczynska and Czyzewski[22] supported the concerns raised by other authors. In 1977, they found bilateral normal hearing in only 16 of 51 symphony orchestra musicians who worked daily at sound levels between 85 dBA and 108 dBA. Five of the musicians had unilateral normal hearing; the rest had bilateral hearing loss.

In 1977, Axelsson and Lindgren studied factors increasing the risk for hearing loss in pop musicians.[23] They reported that aging, length of exposure per musical session, long exposure time in years, military service, and listening to pop music with head phones all had a statistically significant influence on hearing. They noted that the risk and severity of hearing loss increase with increasing duration of noise exposure, and increasing sound levels. In pop music, the exposure to high sound levels was felt to be limited in time, and less damaging low frequencies predominated.

Also in 1977, Axelsson and Lindgren published an interesting study[24] of 83 pop musicians and noted a significant incidence of hearing loss. They reanalyzed previous reports investigating a total of 160 pop musicians, which identified an incidence of only 5% hearing loss. In their 1978 study, Axelsson and Lindgren tested 69 musicians, 4 disk jockeys, 4 managers, and 6 sound engineers.[25] To have hearing loss, a subject had to have at least 1 pure-tone threshold exceeding 20 dB at any frequency between 3000 and 8000 Hz. Thirty-eight musicians were found to have sensorineural hearing loss. In 11, only the right ear was affected; in 5, only the left ear was affected. Thirteen cases were excluded because their hearing loss could be explained by causes other than noise. Thus, 25% of the pop musicians had sensorineural hearing loss probably attributable to noise. The most commonly impaired frequency was 6000 Hz, and very few ears showed hearing levels worse than 35 dB. After correction for age and other factors, 25 (30%) had hearing loss as defined above. Eleven (13%) had hearing loss defined as a pure-tone audiometric average greater than 20 dB at 3000, 4000, 6000, and 8000 kHz in at least one ear. Of these 11, 7 (8%) had unilateral hearing loss. The authors concluded that it seemed unlikely that sensorineural hearing loss would result from popular music presented at 95 dBA with interruptions, and with relatively short exposure durations and low frequency emphasis. Axelsson and Lindgren published further articles on the same study.[26,27] They also noted that TTS measurements in pop music environments showed less shift in musicians than in the audience. They also found that female listeners were more resistant to TTS than males.

In 1981, Westmore and Eversden[28] studied a symphony orchestra and 34 of its musicians. They recorded SPL for 14.4 hours. Sound levels exceeded 90 dBA for 3.51 hours and equaled or exceeded 110 dBA for 0.02 hours. In addition, there were brief peaks exceeding 120 dBA. They interpreted their audiometric testing as showing noise-induced hearing loss in 23 of 68 ears. Only 4 of the 23 ears had a hearing loss greater than 20 dB at 4000 Hz. There was a "clear indication" that orchestral musicians may be exposed to damaging noise. However, because of the relatively mild severity, they speculated that "it is unlikely that any musician is going to be prevented from continuing his artistic career." In Axelsson and Lindgren's 1981 study[5] sound level measurements were performed in two theaters, and 139 musicians underwent hearing tests. Sound levels for performances ranged from 83 dBA to 92 dBA. Sound levels were slightly higher in an orchestra pit, although this is contrary to the findings of Westmore.[28] Fifty-nine musicians (43%) had pure-tone thresholds worse than expected for their ages. French hornists, trum-

Table 11–1. Sound Levels of Various Instruments.

Instrument	Sound Level (in dBA)
Violin	84–103
Cello	84–92
Bass	75–83
Piccolo	95–112
Flute	85–111
Clarinet	92–103
French horn	90–106
Oboe	80–94
Trombone	85–114
Xylophone	90–92

Data from Folprechtova and Miksovska.[20]

peters, trombonists, and bassoonists were found to be at increased risk for sensorineural hearing loss. Asymmetric pure-tone thresholds were common in musicians with hearing loss, and in those still classified as having normal hearing. The left ear demonstrated greater hearing loss than the right, especially among violinists. Axelsson and Lindgren also found that the loudness comfort level was unusually high among musicians. Acoustic reflexes also were elicited at comparatively high levels, being pathologically increased in approximately 30%. TTSs were also identified, supporting the assertion of noise-related etiology.

Also, in 1983, Lindgren and Axelsson attempted to determine whether individual differences of TTS existed after repeated controlled exposure to noninformative noise, and to music having equal frequency, time, and sound level characteristics.[29] They studied 10 subjects who were voluntarily exposed to 10 minutes of recorded pop music on five occasions. On five other occasions they were exposed to equivalent noise. Four subjects showed almost equal sensitivity in measurements of TTS, and six subjects showed marked differences, specifically, greater TTS after exposure to the nonmusic stimulus. This research suggests that factors other than the physical characteristics of the fatiguing sound contributed to the degree of TTS. The authors hypothesized that these factors might include the degree of physical fitness, stress and emotional attitudes toward the sounds perceived. The authors concluded that high sound levels perceived as noxious cause greater TTS than high sound levels that the listener perceived as enjoyable.

In 1983, Karlsson and co-workers published a report with findings and conclusions substantially different from those of Axelsson and others.[30] Karlsson investigated 417 musicians, of whom 123 were investigated twice at an interval of 6 years. After excluding 26 musicians who had hearing loss for reasons other than noise, he based his conclusions on the remaining 392 case. Karlsson et al concluded that there was no statistical difference between the hearing of symphony orchestra musicians and that of a normal population of similar age and sex. Those data revealed a symmetric dip of 20 dB at 6000 Hz in flautists, and a 30 dB left high-frequency sloping hearing loss in bass players. Overall, a 5 dB difference between ears was also found at 6000 and 8000 Hz, with the left side being worse. Although Karlsson and co-workers concluded that performing in a symphonic orchestra does not involve an increased risk of hearing damage, and that standard criteria for industrial noise exposure are not applicable to symphonic music, their data are similar to previous studies. Only their interpretation varies substantially.

In 1984, Woolford studied SPLs in symphony orchestras and hearing.[31] Woolford studied 38 Australian orchestral musicians and measured SPLs using appropriate equipment and technique. He found potentially damaging sound levels, consistent with previous studies. Eighteen of the 38 musicians had hearing losses. Fourteen of those had threshold shifts in the area of 4000 Hz, and four had slight losses at low frequencies only.

Johnson et al studied the effects of instrument type and orchestral position on the hearing of orchestra musicians.[32] They studied 60 orchestra musicians from 24 to 64 years in age, none of whom had symptomatic hearing problems. The musicians underwent otologic histories and examinations and pure-tone audiometry from 250 Hz through 20,000 Hz. Unfortunately, this study used previous data from other authors as control data. In addition to the inherent weakness in this design, the comparison data did not include thresholds at 6000 Hz. There appeared to be a 6000 Hz dip in the population studied by Johnson et al, but no definitive statement could be made. The authors concluded that the type of instrument played and the position on the orchestra stage had no significant correlation with hearing loss, disagreeing with findings of other investigators. In another paper produced from the same study,[33] Johnson reported no difference in the high-frequency thresholds (9000 Hz to 20,000 Hz) between musicians and nonmusicians. Again, because he examined 60 instrumentalists, but used previously published reports for comparison, this study is marred. This shortcoming in experimental design is particularly important in high-frequency testing during which calibration is particularly difficult and establishment of norms on each individual piece of equipment is advisable.

In 1987, Swanson et al studied the influence of subjective factors on TTS after exposure to music and noise of equal energy,[34] attempting to replicate Lindgren and Axelsson's 1983 study. Swanson's study used two groups of subjects, 10 who disliked pop music, and 10 who liked pop music. Each subject was tested twice at 48-hour intervals. One session involved exposure to music for 10 minutes. The other session involved exposure to equivalent noise for 10 minutes. Their results showed that individuals who liked pop music experienced less TTS after music than after noise. Those who disliked the music showed greater TTS in music than in noise. Moreover, the group that liked pop music exhibited less TTS than the group that disliked the music. These findings support the notion that sounds perceived as offensive produce greater TTS than sounds perceived as enjoyable.

A particularly interesting review of hearing impairment among orchestra musicians was published by Woolford et al in 1988.[35] Although this report presents only preliminary data, the authors have put forward a penetrating review of the problem and interesting proposals regarding solutions, including an international comparative study. They concluded that among classical musicians the presence of hearing loss from various etiologies including noise has been established, that some noise-induced hearing impairments in musicians are permanent (although usually slight), and that efforts to reduce the intensity of noise exposure can be successful.

In addition to concern about hearing loss among performers, in recent years there has been growing concern about noise-induced hearing loss in audiences. Those at risk include not only people at rock concerts, but also people who enjoy music through stereo systems, especially modern personal headphones. Concern about hearing loss from this source in high school students has appeared to the lay press and elsewhere.[36,37] Because young music lovers are potentially performers, in addition to other reasons, this hazard should be taken seriously and investigated further.

In 1990, West and Evans studied 60 people aged 15 to 23 years at the University of Keele, looking for hearing loss caused by listening to amplified music.[38] They found widening of auditory band widths to be a sensitive, early indicator of noise- induced hearing loss that was detectable before threshold shift at 4000 or 6000 Hz occurred. They advocated the use of frequency resolution testing and high resolution Békésy audiometry for early detection of hearing impairment. West and Evans found that subjects extensively exposed to loud music were significantly less able to differentiate between a tone and its close neighbors. Reduced pitch discrimination was particularly common in subjects who had experienced TTS or tinnitus following exposure to amplified music.

In 1991, van Hees published an extensive thesis on noise-induced hearing impairment in orchestral musicians.[39] He agreed that noise levels were potentially damaging in classical and wind orchestras. Unlike other researchers, van Hees found it more useful to classify the instruments by orchestral zone, rather than by instrument or instrument group. However, he found a much greater incidence of hearing loss among both symphony and wind orchestra musicians than was reported in previous literature. He also did not find evidence of asymmetric hearing loss in violinists and cello players, in contrast to previous investigators.

In 1992, Camp and Horstman investigated sound exposure among instrumentalists during a performance of Wagner's Ring Cycle. Peak exposures ranging as high as 100 dBA to 104 dBA were measured in the orchestra pit, although measured dose for selected musicians ranged from only 20.2% to 46.1%. They also investigated the efficacy of free-standing clear plastic shields. Sound attenuation was found to be dependent on the position and angle of the ear and measuring equipment microphone relative to the shield. Attenuation up to 17 dB at high frequencies was noted in some cases. However, the free-standing plastic shields provided little or no attenuation unless they were placed within 7 inches of the ear.[40]

In 1995, Griffiths and Samaroo studied hearing sensitivity among professional pannists. The hearing of members of two steel pan orchestras was compared with a group of nonplaying control subjects in Trinidad. Four-hour noise dosimetry revealed time-weighted averages of 98 dBA in a small group indoor setting and at 113 dBA in a large group outdoor rehearsal. Compared with controls, the pannists had significantly poorer hearing at 2000, 3000, 4000, and 6000 Hz. Audiometric dips were found in 72% of the pannists studied.[41]

Review of these somewhat confusing and contradictory studies reveals that a great deal of important work remains to be done in order to establish the risk of hearing loss among various types of musicians, the level and pattern of hearing loss that may be sustained, practical methods of preventing hearing loss, and advisable programs for monitoring and early diagnosis. However, a few preliminary conclusions can be drawn. First, the preponderance of evidence indicates that noise-induced hearing loss occurs in both pop and classical musicians and is causally related to exposure to loud music. Second, in most instances, especially among classical musicians, the hearing loss is not severe enough to interfere with speech perception. Third, the effects of mild high-frequency hearing loss on musical performance have not been established. Fourth, it should be possible to devise methods to conserve hearing in performing artists without interfering with their performance. In 1991, Chasin and Chong reported on an ear protection program for musicians.[42] They provide an interesting discussion of the use of ear protectors in musicians, although several aspects of their paper are open to challenge. In particular, their assertion that some vocalists (particularly sopranos) have self-induced hearing loss caused by singing has not been substantiated. In a subsequent paper, Chasin and Chong proposed four environmental techniques to reduce the effect of music exposure on hearing.[43] They recommended that speakers and amplifiers should be elevated from the floor; treble brass instruments should be on risers; there should be 2 meters of unobstructed floor space in front of the orchestra; and small stringed instruments should have at least 2 meters of unobstructed space above them.

Legal Aspects of Hearing Loss in Singers and Musicians

The problem of hearing loss in musicians raises numerous legal issues, especially the implications of occupational hearing loss; and hearing has become an issue in some orchestra contracts. Traditionally, workers' compensation legislation has been based on the theory that workers should be compensated when a work-related injury impairs their ability to earn a living. Ordinarily, occupational hearing loss does not impair earning power (except possibly in the case of musicians and a few others). Consequently, current occupational hearing loss legislation broke new legal ground by providing compensation for interference with quality of life; that is, loss of living power. Therefore, all current standards for defining and compensating occupational hearing loss are based on the communication needs of the average speaker, and are usually compensated in accordance with the recommendations of the American Academy of Otolaryngology.[2] Because music-induced hearing loss appears to rarely affect the speech frequencies, it is not compensable under most laws. However, although a hearing loss at 3000, 4000, or 6000 Hz with preservation of lower frequencies may not pose a problem for a boiler maker, it may be a serious problem for a violinist. Under certain circumstances, such a hearing loss may even be disabling. Because professional instrumentalists require considerably greater hearing acuity throughout a larger frequency range, we must investigate whether the kinds of hearing loss caused by music are severe enough to impair performance. If so, new criteria must be established for compensation for disabling hearing impairment in musicians, in keeping with the original intent of the workers' compensation law.

There may also be legal issues unresolved regarding hearing loss not caused by noise in professional musicians. Like people with other disabilities, numerous federal laws protect the rights of those with hearing impairment. In the unhappy situation in which an orchestra must release a hearing impaired violinist who can no longer play in tune, for example, legal challenges may arise. In such instances, and in many other circumstances, an objective assessment process is in the best interest of performers and management. Objective measures of performance are already being used in selected areas for singers, and they have proven beneficial in helping the performer assess dispassionately certain aspects of performance quality and skill development. Such technologic advances will probably be used more frequently in the future to supplement traditional subjective assessment of performing artists for musical, scientific, and legal reasons.

Treatment of Occupational Hearing Loss in Singers and Musicians

For a complete discussion of the treatment of hearing loss, the reader is referred to other sources[1] and to standard otolaryngology texts. Most cases of sensorineural hearing loss produced by aging, hereditary factors, and noise cannot be cured. When they involve the speech frequencies, modern, properly adjusted hearing aids are usually extremely helpful. However, these devices are rarely satisfactory for musicians during performance. More often, appropriate counseling is sufficient. The musician should be provided with a copy of his or her audiogram and an explanation of its correspondence with the piano keyboard. Unless a hearing loss becomes severe, this information usually permits musicians to make appropriate adjustments. For example, a conductor with an unknown high-frequency hearing loss will call for violins and triangles to be excessively loud. If he or she knows the pattern of hearing loss, this error may be reduced. Musicians with or without hearing loss should routinely be cautioned against avocational loud noise exposure without ear protection (hunting, power tools, motorcycles, etc) and ototoxic drugs. In addition, they should be educated about the importance of immediate evaluation if a sudden change in hearing occurs. When diplacusis (pitch distortion) is present, compensation is especially difficult, especially for singers and string players. Auditory retraining may be helpful in some cases. Hopefully, electronic devices will be available in the future to help this problem, as well.

Summary

Good hearing is of great importance to musicians, but the effects on performance of mild high-frequency hearing loss remain uncertain. It is most important to be alert for hearing loss from all causes in performers, recognize it early, and treat it or prevent its progression whenever possible. Musical instruments and performance environments are capable of producing damaging noise. Strenuous efforts must be made to define the risks and nature of music-induced hearing loss in musicians, establish damage-risk criteria, and implement practical means of noise reduction and hearing conservation.

Singers depend on their hearing almost as much as they do on their voices. It is important not to take such valuable and delicate structures as the human ears for granted. For a singer to enjoy a long, happy, and successful career, like the voice, the ear must be understood and protected.

Review Questions

1. The following structures are contained in the middle ear, except:
   a. the stapes
   b. the malleus
   c. cochlea
   d. incus
   e. facial nerve

2. Hearing loss caused by chronic exposure to noise is typically conductive.
   a. true
   b. false

3. Music-induced hearing loss has been identified in:
   a. rock musicians
   b. violists
   c. flutists
   d. all of the above
   e. none of the above

4. Peak sound levels in a classical orchestra are not high enough to pose a risk to hearing.
   a. true
   b. false

5. Because of the nature of music, exposure to hazardous noise is unavoidable, and some hearing loss should be expected and accepted.
   a. true
   b. false

References

1. Sataloff J, Sataloff RT. *Hearing Loss*. 3rd ed. New York, NY: Marcel Dekker; 1993.
2. Sataloff RT, Sataloff J. *Occupational Hearing Loss*. 2nd ed. New York, NY: Marcel Dekker; 1993.
3. Konigsmark BW, Gorlin RJ. *Genetic and Metabolic Deafness*. Philadelphia, Pa: WB Saunders; 1976.
4. Sataloff RT, Sataloff JR. Hearing loss in musicians. *Amer J Otol*. 1991;12(2):122-127.
5. Axelsson A, Lindgren F. Hearing in classical musicians. *Acta Otolaryngol*. 1981;(suppl 377):3-74.
6. Arnold GE, Miskolczy-Fodor F. Pure-tone thresholds of professional pianists. *Arch Otolaryngol*. 1960;71:938-947.
7. Flach M, Aschoff E: Zur Frage berufsbedingter Schwerhörigkeit beim Musiker. *Z Laryngol*. 1966;45:595-605.
8. Flach M. Das Gehör des Musikers aus ohrenarztlicher Sicht. *Msch Ohr Hk*. 1972;9:424-432.
9. Berghoff F. Hörbeleistung und berufsbedingte Hörschädigung des Orchestermusikers mit einem Beitrag zur Pathophysiologie des Larmtraumatischen Hörschadens. 1968, Dissertation. Cited in Axelsson A, Lindgren F. Hearing in classical musicians. *Acta Otolaryngol*. 1981;(suppl 377):3-74.
10. Lebo CP, Oliphant KP. Music as a source of acoustic trauma. *Laryngoscope*. 1968;72(2):1211-1218.
11. Rintelmann WF, Borus JF. Noise-induced hearing loss in rock and roll musicians. *Arch Otolaryngol*. 1968;88:377-385.
12. Jerger J, Jerger S. Temporary threshold shift in rock- and-roll musicians. *J Speech Hear Res*. 1970;13:221-224.
13. Speaks C, Nelson D, Ward WD. Hearing loss in rock-and-roll musicians. *J Occup Med*. 1970;13:221-224.
14. Rintelmann WF, Lindberg RF, Smitley EK. Temporary threshold shift and recovery patterns from two types of rock and roll presentations. *J Acoust Soc Am*. 1972;51:1249-1255.
15. Jahto K, Hellmann H. Zur Frage des Larm- und Klangtraumas des Orchestermusikers. *Audiol Phoniat HNO*. 1972;20(1):21-29.
16. Buhlert P, Kuhl W. Höruntersuchungen im freien Schallfeld zum Altershörverlust. *Acustica*. 1974;31:168-177.
17. Kuhl W. Keine Gehörschädigung durch Tanzmusik, simfonische Musik und Maschinengeräusche beim Rundfunk. *Kampf dem Larm*. 1976;23(4):105-107.
18. Zeleny M, Navratilova Z, Kamycek Z, et al. Relation of hearing disorders to the acoustic composition of working environment of musicians in a wind orchestra. [Czech] *Cesk Otolaryngol*. 1975;24(5):295-299.
19. Siroky J, Sevcikova L, Folprechtova A, et al. Audiological examination of musicians of a symphonic orchestra in relation to acoustic conditions. [Czech] *Cesk Otolaryngol*. 1976;25(5):288-294.
20. Folprechtova A, Miksovska O. The acoustic conditions in a symphony orchestra. [Czech] *Pracov Lek*. 1978;28:1-2.
21. Balazs B, Gotze A. Comparative examinations between the hearing of musicians playing on traditional instruments and on those with electrical amplifications. [Czech] *Ful-orr-gegegyogyaszat*. 1976;22:116-118.
22. Gryczynska D, Czyzewski I. Damaging effect of music on the hearing organ in musicians. [Polish] *Otolaryngol Pol*. 1977;31(5):527-532.
23. Axelsson A, Lindgren F. Factors increasing the risk for hearing loss in "pop" musicians. *Scand Audiol*. 1977;6:127-131.

24. Axelsson A, Lindgren F. Does pop music cause hearing damage? *Audiology.* 1977;16:432-437.

25. Axelsson A, Lindgren F. Hearing in pop musicians. *Acta Otolaryngol.* 1978;85:225-231.

26. Axelsson A, Lindgren F. Horseln hos popmusiker. *Lakartidningen.* 1978;75(13):1286-1288.

27. Axelsson A, Lindgren F. Pop music and hearing. *Ear and Hearing.* 1981;2(2):64-69.

28. Westmore GA, Eversden ID. Noise-induced hearing loss and orchestral musicians. *Arch Otolaryngol.* 1982; 107:761-764.

29. Lindgren F, Axelsson A. Temporary threshold shift after exposure to noise and music of equal energy. *Ear and Hearing.* 1983;4(4):197-201.

30. Karlsson K, Lundquist PG, Olaussen T. The hearing of symphony orchestra musicians. *Scand Audiol.* 1983; 12:257-264.

31. Woolford DH. Sound pressure levels in symphony orchestras and hearing. Preprint 2104 (B-1), Australian Regional Convention of the Audio Engineering Society, Melbourne, September 25-27, 1984.

32. Johnson DW, Sherman RE, Aldridge J, et al. Effects of instrument type and orchestral position on hearing sensitivity for 0.25 to 20 kHZ in the orchestral musician. *Scand Audiol.* 1985;14:215-221.

33. Johnson DW, Sherman RE, Aldridge J, et al. Extended high frequency hearing sensitivity: a normative threshold study in musicians. *Ann Otol Rhinol Laryngol.* 1986;95:196-201.

34. Swanson SJ, Dengerink HA, Kondrick P, Miller CL. The influence of subjective factors on temporary threshold shifts after exposure to music and noise of equal energy. *Ear and Hearing.* 1987;8(5):288-291.

35. Woolford DH, Carterette EC, Morgan DE. Hearing impairment among orchestral musicians. *Music Percept.* 1988;5(3):261-284.

36. Gallagher G. Hot music, high noise, and hurt ears. *Hear J.* 1989;42(3):7-11.

37. Lewis DA. A hearing conservation program for high-school level students. *Hear J.* 1989;42(3):19-24.

38. West DB, Evans EF. Early detection of hearing damage in young listeners resulting from exposure to amplified music. *Br J Audiol.* 1990;28:89–103.

39. van Hees OS. *Noise induced hearing impairment in orchestral musicians.* Amsterdam, Holland: University of Amsterdam Press; 1991.

40. Camp JE, Horstman SW. Musician sound exposure during performance of Wagner's Ring Cycle. *Med Prob Perform Arts.* 1992;7:37–39.

41. Griffiths SK, Samaroo AL. Hearing sensitivity among professional pannists. *Med Prob Perform Arts.* 1995;10: 11–17.

42. Chasin M, Chong J. An in situ ear protection program for musicians. *Hearing Instr.* 1991;42(12):26–28.

43. Chasin M, Chong J. Four environmental techniques to reduce the effect of music exposure on hearing. *Med Prob Perform Arts.* 1995;10:66–69.

12

Respiratory Dysfunction

Joseph R. Spiegel, Robert Thayer Sataloff, John R. Cohn, and Mary Hawkshaw

Anyone who works with singers and actors has encountered the term "support." Although the laryngologist, speech-language pathologist, voice scientist, singing teacher, acting teacher, and performer may have slightly different understandings of the word, virtually everyone agrees that support is essential to efficient, healthy, professional voice production. Although singers and actors frequently use the term "diaphragm" synonymously with support, it is actually a combination of thoracic, rib cage, back, and abdominal muscle function. This support mechanism constitutes the power source of the voice and should generate a vector of force in the direction of the air column passing between the vocal folds. The diaphragm is an inspiratory muscle, of course, and represents only a portion of the support mechanism. Practitioners in all fields recognize that proper training of the thoracic and abdominal support mechanism is essential. Deficiencies in anatomy or technique, or diseases undermining the effectiveness of the abdominal musculature and respiratory system, often result not only in unacceptable vocal quality and projection, but also in abusive compensatory vocal behavior and laryngeal injury.

Breathing is a complex process. Voice scientists have struggled for years to break it down into component parts in order to study breathing more effectively. Basic research has provided insight into optimal methods of inspiration, prephonatory positioning of the chest and abdomen, and expiration. The knowledge acquired through scientific research has helped guide the speech-language pathologist, singing teacher, and acting teacher in modifying vocal behavior. It has helped reinforce some traditional practices and explained why others have often failed and should be abandoned.

Respiratory problems are especially problematic to singers and other voice professionals.[1] They also cause similar problems for wind instrumentalists, also by interfering with support. The effects of severe respiratory infection are obvious and will be discussed only briefly in this chapter. Restrictive lung disease such as that associated with obesity may impair support by decreasing lung volume and respiratory efficiency. Even mild obstructive lung disease can impair support enough to result in increased neck and tongue muscle tension and abusive voice use capable of producing vocal nodules. This scenario occurs with unrecognized asthma. This may be difficult to diagnose unless suspected, because such cases of asthma may be exercise-induced. Performance is a form of exercise. The singer will have normal pulmonary function clinically and may even have normal pulmonary function tests at rest in the office. He or she will also usually support well and sing with good technique during the first portion of a performance. However, as performance exercise continues, obstruction occurs. It is theorized that hyperventilation leads to impairment of pulmonary function, but it may also be that air trapping or other problems related to small airway changes lead to early fatigue. This effectively impairs support and results in abusive technique. When suspected, this entity can be confirmed through a methacholine challenge test. Treatment of the underlying pulmonary disease to restore effective support is essential to resolving the vocal problem. Treating asthma is rendered more difficult in professional voice users because of the need in some patients to avoid not only inhalers, but also drugs that produce even a mild tremor, which may be audible during soft singing. A skilled pulmonologist or allergist can usually tailor a satisfactory regimen.

147

Assessment

The respiratory system consists of the nose, nasopharynx, oropharynx, larynx, trachea, lungs, musculoskeletal thorax, and abdominal musculature. Its function is influenced by the overall health and fitness of the individual. Assessment and care of the entire respiratory system are essential.

Assessment of a professional voice user's respiratory complaints begins with a complete history and physical examination and is followed by appropriate laboratory testing. It is particularly important to identify the correct diagnosis in a singer, since empiric trials of "shotgun" treatments may have deleterious effects on the voice (ie, laryngeal inflammation encountered with some inhaled steroids, drying effects of antihistamines, etc.) and may adversely affect performance.

History

Evaluation begins with a complete history, emphasizing questions related to each portion of the respiratory tract. Symptoms may be constant or intermittent, have seasonal variation, be brought on or relieved by environmental changes (ie, exposure to animals, plants, dusty environments, etc.), relieved by medication, or associated with other symptoms. Many singers and actors are symptomatic only when they perform outdoors or in dusty buildings.

Questions regarding respiratory complaints begin with the nose. Has the patient noted obstruction, congestion, epistaxis, rhinorrhea, or postnasal drip? Does he have a history of nasal trauma? Trauma that leads to nasal obstruction may not involve a significantly displaced nasal fracture. Minor nasal trauma, especially in early life, can lead to severe intranasal deformities as facial growth progresses.

Throat dryness and pain during performance may be noted by singers with nasal obstruction. Complaints of swelling in the throat, dysphagia, odynophagia, otalgia, and hyponasality are found with obstructing lesions. Such complaints may also be due to causes other than primary pathology in the respiratory system such as gastroesophageal reflux.

Laryngeal complaints may be due to either primary lesions that obstruct breathing or dysfunction of the lower respiratory tract. Mass lesions can cause stridor, hoarseness, breathiness, diplophonia, or pain with use of the singing or speaking voice. Symptoms such as loss of vocal range or vocal fatigue may be due to either primary laryngeal lesions or inadequate airflow being produced by the lungs. Singers and actors may complain of stiffness or pain in the neck during or after rehearsal and performance. These symptoms are usually secondary to tension and may result from changes in technique to compensate for inadequate respiratory function. A history of a neck mass may indicate infection, laryngocele, neoplasm, or other serious pathology. However, occasionally the "mass" will turn out to be severe spasm of neck muscles. This is especially common after trauma such as whiplash and is often associated with severe vocal dysfunction.

Questions regarding breathing strength, support, and control are critical. Does the vocalist feel short of breath, and, if so, is it related to performance? Is there wheezing or chest tightness related to dyspnea? Is there a cough, and is this cough productive? Is there hemoptysis? Chest pain can be related to dyspnea, hard coughing, improper vocal technique, or other causes.

The history also investigates the patient's overall health. Nutritional status is evaluated, remembering that the presence of obesity or anorexia can affect the bellows action of the chest. Recent changes in weight or bowel habits and the presence of symptoms such as headache, fever, and night sweats are noted. Allergies and asthma are especially important, because of their direct effect on breathing. A history of abdominal hernias, symptoms of gastroesophageal reflux (throat clearing, thick mucus, intermittent hoarseness, halitosis, prolonged warm-up time, dyspepsia), neurologic weaknesses, paresthesia, and lesions of the extremities may lead the physician to the cause of the voice complaint.

The past medical history is evaluated first for previous pulmonary diseases including tuberculosis (especially in recent immigrants, immunosuppressed patients, and the inner city population), pneumonia, and environmental exposure to pulmonary irritants such as asbestos. Cardiac disease can directly influence respiratory function or can have indirect effects when it leads to exercise intolerance. Thyroid disease can have effects on both the general health of the patient and local compressive effects on the trachea.

The patient must be questioned about any drugs he or she is taking, including over-the-counter preparations. Propranolol, used by some performers to reduce anxiety, can exacerbate an underlying asthmatic condition.[2] Long-term antibiotic use can cause secondary infections with opportunistic organisms. Antihistamines and decongestants produce drying of the upper airway that can alter respiratory function.

Alcohol and tobacco use and dietary and sleeping habits also give an indication of the patient's general and respiratory health status. Cigarette smoking is the leading cause of respiratory disease in the United States and should be avoided by all professional voice users! Cigarette smoking by family members or in the workplace may also cause symptoms. Marijuana and cocaine are especially deleterious.

Specific questions about vocal training and technique are helpful in determining the diagnosis and the most appropriate treatment for the professional voice user.[3] The history and current level of vocal training, experience, and career goals provide an assessment of the patient's professional skill and needs. Particularly important is determining the date of the next critical performance or audition. Physicians who care for singers should also be aware of the basics of technique in both the singing and speaking voice.

Physical Examination

The patient is evaluated for obesity or lack of appropriate muscle mass. Affect is assessed for signs of anxiety or depression, which may affect breathing patterns.

A complete head and neck examination is required. The nose is examined during forceful inspiration for collapse of the critical nasal "valve" area, as well as for deformities that can lead to nasal obstruction. Mucosal inflammation, mass lesions, and the presence and quality of nasal secretions are noted.

Examination of the oral cavity reveals the level of dental hygiene, moisture of the mucosal surfaces, and motion of the tongue and soft palate. Mass lesions that can cause upper airway obstruction are noted. Patients with a history of adenoidectomy are evaluated for nasopharyngeal stenosis from excessive scar formation and for velopharyngeal incompetence.

The larynx is examined by indirect laryngoscopy, flexible laryngoscopy, or strobovideolaryngoscopy as the situation demands. Large obstructive mass lesions, severe mucosal edema, and recurrent nerve paralysis can usually be detected by mirror examination. Examination of the larynx in a singer is not complete without examination of the singing voice.[3] Posture during singing or acting, abdominal support, breath control, and the development of dyspnea while performing are assessed, and the voice is evaluated for range, hoarseness, breathiness, and fatigue. Assessment of voice technique and efficiency often reveals the etiology of the performer's complaints.

The chest is examined to evaluate rales, wheezes, rhonchi, and areas of hyper- and hypoaeration. Auscultation of the chest with forced expiration may accentuate wheezing not apparent during quiet breathing. Auscultation of the heart is performed to determine rate, rhythm, the presence of murmurs, or a pericardial friction rub. The abdomen is examined for masses, hernias, and muscle tone. Extremities are evaluated for weakness, level of sensation, and deformities. The neurologic examination must be complete.

Cranial nerve problems can affect the upper airway, whereas generalized problems of muscle weakness and loss of coordination can severely affect the thoracic and abdominal respiratory musculature.

Laboratory Tests

Rhinomanometry is considered the most useful test for quantifying nasal airflow before and after treatment.[4,5] However, variability among tests limits its clinical usefulness.[6,7] Additional research is needed to develop a more valid, reliable technique for assessing nasal function.

Airflow Rate Testing

Airflow rate testing determines the flow of air across the larynx during phonation. It is usually measured with a spirometer but can be evaluated more accurately with a pneumotachograph or hot-wire anemometer. The mean flow rate is defined as the total volume of air expired during phonation divided by the duration of the phonation. The average is 89 to 141 ml/sec and the normal range is 72 to 200 ml/sec.[8] There is no significant difference noted between males and females or between older children and adults.[9] The phonation quotient is defined as the vital capacity of the patient divided by the maximum time of phonation. The average for this test is 120 to 190 ml/sec with an upper limit of 200 to 300 ml/sec.[8] Both these determinates are used to evaluate laryngeal lesions that affect upper respiratory function. Lesions that cause glottic incompetence, reducing laryngeal efficiency (ie, vocal nodules, vocal fold paralysis), will lead to increased flow rates. Airflow testing is also useful for documenting the results of treatment for lesions such as nodules, a problem found frequently in professional voice users.[9,10]

Pulmonary Function Testing

The cornerstone of pulmonary function testing is spirometry. Various aspects of this important test are also discussed in chapter 8. Spirometry is based on the measurement of the forced vital capacity (FVC) and its components (Fig 12–1). The FVC is the quantity of air that is exhaled after the lungs are maximally filled (total lung capacity or TLC) and then forcefully emptied. This is plotted as a volume versus time curve. From this curve, the vital capacity (VC), forced expiratory volume in 1 sec (FEV_1), and maximal mid-expiratory flow rate (MMEFR, $FEF_{25-75\%}$) can be determined (Fig 12–2). The MMEFR is the volume of air expired between the 25% point of the FVC ($FEV_{25\%}$) and the

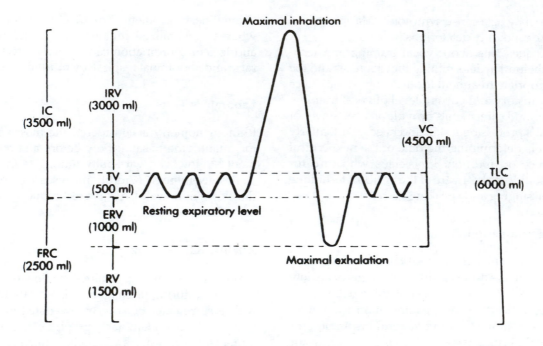

Fig 12–1. Lung volumes (normal adult averages). TLC, total lung capacity; VC, vital capacity; IC, inspiratory capacity; FRC, functional reserve capacity; TV, tidal volume; IRV, inspiratory reserve volume; ERV, expiratory reserve volume; RV, reserve volume.

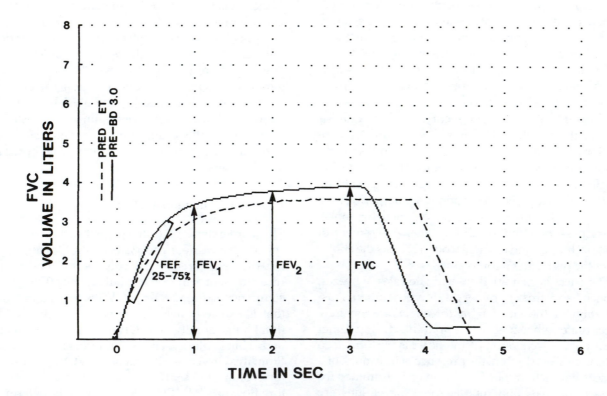

Fig 12–2. Volume vs. time spirometric tracing. FVC, forced vital capacity; FEV$_1$, FEV$_3$, forced expiratory volume in 1 and 3 sec, respectively; FEF$_{25-75\%}$; RV, reserve volume.

75% point of the FVC ($FEV_{75\%}$) divided by the time it takes to expire that volume. This measurement is the single most sensitive value in diagnosing obstructive pulmonary disease that can be measured with simple equipment.[11] The peak expiratory flow rate correlates well with normal functional limitations, but this is difficult to measure with conventional volume displacement spirometers.[12] Others use the ratio of FEV_1/FVC to quantitate the degree of airflow obstruction. The skill of the technician performing the test is critical in interpretation results, along with adherence to published guidelines.[13]

The computer-generated flow versus volume loop has become popular as a more sensitive means of evaluating ventilatory impairment. The computer measures the instantaneous flow at multiple points during a forced expiration followed by a forced inspiration and plots the instantaneous flow against the volume expired or inspired at each point on a continuous graph (Fig 12–3). This "loop" has a characteristic shape that

can be useful in detecting and characterizing pulmonary and laryngeal pathology.[14]

Spirometry is performed with the nose occluded and the patient making forceful expirations into the spirometer. The patient should complete three FVC trials with less than 5% variability in order to consider a test acceptable. Predicted normal values are determined from the height, weight, and sex of the patient. Blacks tend to have smaller lung volumes, so lower predicted values may be used. Normal values for the test subject are considered to be anything greater than or equal to 80%, or within 1.64 standard deviations of these predicted values.[15]

Patterns of pulmonary disease can be determined from both the standard spirometric plot and the flow-volume loop.[16] In obstructive disease, there are decreased flows represented by decreased FEV, and a decreased FEV_1/FVC ratio (Fig 12–4). A flow-volume loop will initially show increased convexity of the expiratory phase, while, with more severe obstruc-

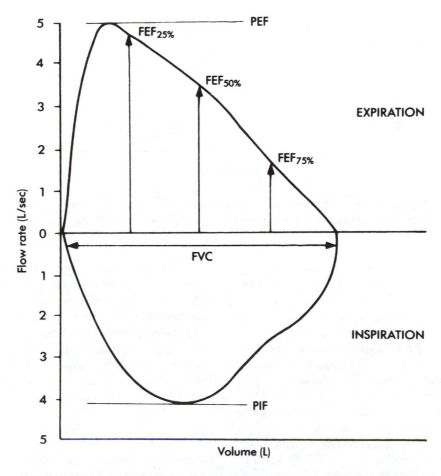

Fig 12–3. Flow vs. volume loop. PEF, peak expiratory flow; FEF, forced expiratory flow; FVC, forced vital capacity; PIF, peak inspiratory flow.

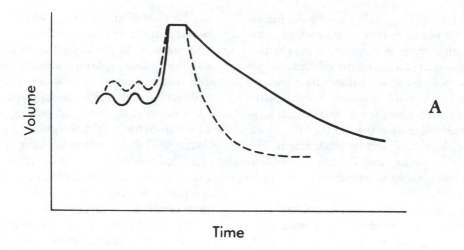

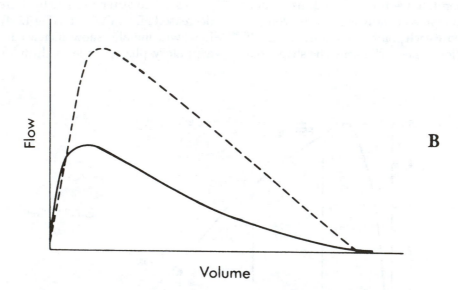

Fig 12–4. Spirometric pattern in obstructive disease. **A.** Volume vs. time curve. **B.** Flow vs. volume curve, expiratory phase. Normal, dotted line; abnormal, solid line.

tion, there may be loss of expiratory volume and flattening of both the inspiratory and expiratory phases. These characteristics can be variable, especially in the flow-volume loop, depending on the site and duration of the obstruction. Even when FEV_1 and FEV_1/FVC are normal, a decreased MMEFR can be noted in patients with asymptomatic asthma and in smokers. Patients with restrictive lung disease have decreased volumes but normal flow (Fig 12–5). Thus, the FEV_1 and FVC are proportionately decreased, causing the FEV_1/FVC ratio to be normal or even increased.

Determination of reversible obstructive pulmonary disease can be made if an increase of 12% is noted in the FVC and FEV, or 25% in the MMEFR after treatment with inhaled bronchodilators.[15] If the diagnosis is suspected but the test results are inconclusive or normal, a methacholine challenge may be performed using progressively greater concentrations of methacholine, with measurement of the FEV_1 and MMEFR after each dose. The test is completed when the FEV_1 is decreased by 20% or more.[17] This dose is called the $PD_{20}FEV_1$. Generally, nonasthmatic subjects will have a PD_{20} greater than 8 mg/ml of methacholine.[18] This measure of relative airway spasticity is particularly important in the diagnosis of mild asthma that is symptomatic under performance conditions.[19]

Diffusing Capacity

Diffusing capacity is the relative ability of oxygen to diffuse across the arteriole-alveolar membranes in the lung, although the matching of ventilation and perfusion may be of equal or greater importance. It is tested by measuring diffusion of inhaled carbon monoxide into

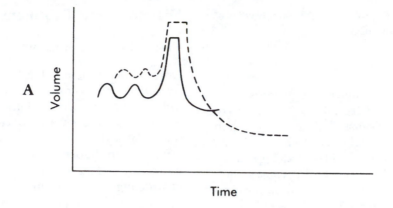

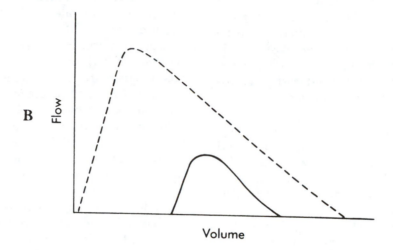

Fig 12–5. Spirometric pattern in restrictive disease. **A.** Volume vs. time curve. **B.** Flow vs. volume curve, expiratory phase. Normal, dotted line; abnormal, solid line.

the blood (DLco). This determination is useful in the evaluation of patients with interstitial lung disease and correlates with oxygen desaturation during exercise.[20]

Lung Volumes

TLC is measured indirectly by first determining functional reserve capacity (FRC) using an inert gas dilution technique, nitrogen washout, or body plethysmographic technique. Decreased TLC is the *sine qua non* of restrictive lung disease. Of interest, highly trained singers do not have substantially increased TLC but have improved their pulmonary efficiency by increasing FRC and reducing reserve volume (RV).[21]

Radiology

A chest radiograph should be obtained on every patient with persistent pulmonary complaints to rule out infectious or neoplastic disease. Patients with more common ailments such as asthma and bronchi-

tis generally have normal chest radiographs. When mass lesions or other significant pulmonary pathology is identified, more detailed evaluation is required.

Patients with nasal obstruction and acute or chronic sinonasal symptoms are evaluated first with plain radiographs of the sinuses. If extensive disease is suspected, computerized tomography using coronal sections will better define this region.

Other Tests

Arterial blood gas analysis (ABG) may be useful in the diagnosis of pulmonary disease. Appropriate stains of a sputum smear can provide important information in the diagnosis of infectious, allergic, and neoplastic pulmonary disease.

An electrocardiogram (ECG) and echocardiogram may assist in the diagnosis of dyspnea not readily explained by other studies. A complete blood count (CBC) may demonstrate anemia, which contributes to dyspnea, an increased white blood cell count, which may be a sign of infection, or eosinophilia, suggesting allergy or other systemic disease.

Allergy Testing

Allergy tests are used to confirm the diagnosis and assist in the treatment of allergic disease. Problems of allergies in singers are discussed at greater length in chapter 13. The most commonly used technique is skin testing, which can be performed by scratch, prick, or intradermal technique.[22,23] Prick testing causes minimal discomfort and can be used to determine the presence of allergy to specific substances rapidly. The intradermal injection of antigens is the most sensitive test for allergy. When properly performed, either test, but particularly the intradermal technique, can be used to rule out immediate and late phase allergic responses. Proponents of skin test-based therapy argue that it is the most sensitive and least expensive way to determine the presence of allergy and plan treatment.[24]

In recent years, a blood test for antigen-specific immunoglobulin E (IgE) to both inhaled and food antigens has become available. Originally done with a radioimmunoassay technique, the radioallergosorbent test (RAST),[25] it is now commonly performed as an enzyme-linked immunoabsorbent assay. These tests quantify the immunoglobulins responsible for the allergic reaction to each antigen. The proponents of RAST-based treatment, primarily otolaryngologists, contend that this precise measure of relative allergic response can be used to formulate individualized immunotherapy for the patient[26] and that RAST testing can be used to monitor the patient's response to therapy,[27] but this has not been demonstrated in controlled, randomized, blinded studies.

Endoscopy

Fiberoptic technology allows accurate visualization of the entire respiratory tract. Nasopharyngoscopy using a short, narrow fiberoptic endoscope is useful in defining internal nasal anatomy and in the diagnosis of pharyngeal and laryngeal obstruction. Mass lesions can be fully defined and their relationship to the vibrating edge of the vocal fold determined, especially when strobovideolaryngoscopy is also employed. Less obvious lesions such as arytenoid dislocation, vocal fold paresis, and scar are often much more apparent under stroboscopic light. Using bronchoscopy, mass lesions of the lower respiratory tract can be assessed clinically and, with the use of endobronchial biopsy, transbronchial biopsy, or brushings, can be identified pathologically.

Diagnosis and Treatment

Nasal Airway Obstruction

Obstruction of the nasal airway can be due to structural deformities, mass lesions, foreign bodies, or inflammation. Structural deformities usually involve deviation of the bony and/or cartilaginous nasal septum. Nasal deformity can also be complicated by inflammatory hypertrophy of the inferior turbinates and collapse of the external skeleton. Treatment of the obstructing nasal septum is surgical and involves resection and/or repositioning of the abnormal portions. It is suggested that the approach to surgery of the inferior turbinates be conservative in singers because long-term drying effects have occurred secondary to mucociliary disruption when extensive resection is performed.[28] Mass lesions are usually readily apparent on examination. After adequate radiologic assessment, sometimes including arteriography, most are removed surgically.

Inflammatory nasal obstruction may be infectious or allergic. Viral rhinitis is manifested by clear or mucoid rhinorrhea, postnasal drip, associated nasal obstruction, and other symptoms such as low-grade fever, sore throat, hoarseness, cough, myalgia, and malaise. Treatment is supportive with oral decongestants and hydration. When a patient has a crucial performance within 24 to 48 hr, intramuscular or oral steroids can be used to relieve many of the obstructive symptoms.

Allergic rhinitis usually involves the common "hay fever" symptoms of sneezing, itchiness, clear rhinorrhea, nasal obstruction, and associated complaints of allergic conjunctivitis. Symptoms may be related to geographical location, exposure to specific plants or wild life, changes in diet, and the general environmental aspects and ventilation systems of lodgings and concert halls. The diagnosis is assisted by specific allergy testing. Skin tests or RAST may be employed, but enhanced sensitivity, reduced cost, and speed make skin testing preferred for patients who do not have a contraindication. Skin testing is used almost exclusively in our evaluation of patients. When a single specific allergen can be defined, avoidance is the simplest solution. Removal of plants or pets, or taking precautions to avoid dust exposure within the home environment can yield dramatic improvement. Treatment of allergic rhinitis in a singer with multiple allergies by specific allergen immunotherapy is advisable. This involves weekly injections of increasing concentrations of a serum containing all the antigens to which the patient is allergic. This can provide relief from symptoms without the side effects from oral drug preparations or nasal sprays. The success of immunotherapy is enhanced by proper selection of patients and antigens and is limited by variable patient compliance, as well as other alternative mechanisms accounting for the patient's symptoms.

Multiple pharmaceutical preparations are available to alleviate symptoms for patients who cannot fully avoid their allergic stimulus and are not candidates for immunotherapy. Topical steroid sprays (eg, flunisolide, beclomethasone) can reduce nasal symptoms; and, in proper doses, these steroids are safe.[29] Cromolyn sodium topical spray reduces allergic response in the mucosa, probably at least partly by stabilizing the mast cell membrane. It may be effective in preventing allergic nasal symptoms and has few significant local side effects.[30] Oral decongestant/antihistamine preparations can reduce most symptoms significantly, but the side effects of drying of the mucosal membranes and sedation, and the development of tolerance, limit the use of these medications in vocal performers. Parenteral and oral steroids rapidly reduce the edema associated with the allergic response without these side effects. In an acute obstructive phenomenon they are necessary to maintain the airway. However, long-term use should be avoided because of the many potential serious side effects.

Sinusitis can cause partial or total nasal obstruction and can exacerbate an asthmatic condition.[31] Major symptoms are mucopurulent rhinorrhea, postnasal drip, facial pressure, retro-orbital headache, and fever. Radiologic confirmation of chronic inflammatory changes or opacification of the paranasal sinuses and documentation of pathologic bacteria on culture of the sinus are helpful. Treatment of the acute phase of this illness includes antibiotics for 2 to 3 weeks, oral and topical decongestants, and steam inhalations. Performance can usually be permitted. In chronic conditions, long-term antibiotics and treatment of any underlying conditions such as nasal obstruction blocking a sinus ostium, dental disease, or allergy are necessary. In persistent cases, surgical therapy of the paranasal sinuses may be required (see chapter 36).

Pharyngeal Obstruction

Most cases of pharyngeal obstruction are due to adenoid and palatine tonsil hypertrophy in the adolescent or young adult. The patient usually complains of nasal obstruction and chronic mouth breathing and may have a significant snoring history. The source of the obstruction is usually apparent on physical examination and can be confirmed with lateral neck radiographs. When the obstruction is secondary to an acute infection, it is treated with high-dose oral or parenteral antibiotics. When rapid increase in the size of

adenoids and tonsils is seen, mononucleosis should be considered, especially if there is associated cervical, axillary, or inguinal adenopathy. Adenoidectomy and tonsillectomy may be indicated in patients who have chronic symptomatic hypertrophy. Detailed examination of the palate is made prior to consideration of adenoidectomy. The presence of a submucous cleft, bifid uvula, or short palate can lead to significant hypernasality postoperatively.[32]

Laryngeal Obstruction

Laryngeal lesions significant enough to cause respiratory impairment will cause changes in the voice. Edema secondary to infection, allergy, gastroesophageal reflux, and voice abuse can lead to partial upper airway obstruction in rare, severe cases. Anatomic defects, trauma, neoplasm, and epiglottitis are more likely to cause airway problems. Diagnosis is generally made by laryngeal examination, except in cases of epiglottitis. Radiographs are helpful in some patients. The degree of respiratory dysfunction is determined by airflow testing and pulmonary function testing. Steroids may be effective in reducing edema quickly in most of these conditions and should be accompanied by treatment of the underlying problem. Lesions that alter the respiratory function of the larynx such as vocal fold paralysis/paresis, laryngeal webs, and arytenoid dislocation usually cause vocal impairment to a far greater degree than they impair respiratory function. However, some patients elect improvement of their voices through compensatory vocal techniques or surgery, which may leave them with an adequate voice and impaired respiratory function. Treatment of the respiratory problems that these lesions cause in singers is extremely difficult. Surgical intervention to reduce the upper airway obstruction often disturbs vocal quality. Optimizing pulmonary function to overcome laryngeal inefficiency is often the best approach.

Most obstructing laryngeal lesions will not persist long enough to cause severe upper airway obstruction requiring tracheotomy, because vocal impairment occurs early in their course. When a laryngeal mass is found, endoscopic removal may be necessary if the lesion is not amenable to other therapy. These masses should be removed using an operating microscope and meticulous microsurgical technique. Local anesthesia is used frequently in order to assess the surgical result during the procedure and avoid intubation, but excellent sedation by an anesthesiologist is necessary to keep the patient motionless even in cooperative patients. When general anesthesia is necessary, the laryngologist must take responsibility for protecting the larynx during intubation and extubation, and the most skilled anesthesiologist available should be used.

Pulmonary Lesions

Obstructive Conditions

The most common obstructive airway disease is asthma, affecting approximately 8 million people in the United States.[33] It is defined as reversible obstructive airway disease, in the absence of an alternative explanation such as heart failure. Classic asthma is manifested by paroxysms of dyspnea, wheezy respirations, chest tightness, and cough, although a chronic cough can be the only presenting symptom.[34] While it is usually allergic, the etiology can be nonallergic or mixed. Nonallergic groups of patients are usually older and may have symptoms associated with chronic infectious phenomena such as sinusitis or bronchitis. Symptoms can also be induced by exercise or exposure to cold air[35] or be associated with a triad including aspirin sensitivity and nasal polyps.[36] The diagnosis of asthma is made by history or by demonstrating an obstructive pattern on pulmonary function testing that is reversible with bronchodilators either acutely or with chronic treatment. Bronchoprovocation with methacholine may be necessary to demonstrate the presence of asthma in patients with normal pulmonary function. Additional testing such as chest radiography, pulse oximetry, arterial blood gasses, lung volumes, diffusion capacity, and noninvasive cardiac studies may be useful in ruling out other conditions and diagnosing the long-term sequelae of obstructive disease.

Airway reactivity induced asthma in singers (ARIAS) is a special form of exercise-induced asthma.[37] It is postulated that airway obstruction is caused by the hyperventilation of singing performance. Decreased airflow undermines support, creating problems similar to those seen with improper abdominal muscle use. The singer may become short of breath, or may simply note voice fatigue, decreased range, and impaired volume control. As in other conditions that impair the power source of the voice, compensatory efforts are common, including increased jaw tension, tongue retraction, and strap muscle hyperfunction. Treatment of the singing-induced asthma helps restore support for the singing voice and allows the singer to resume correct singing technique. In conjunction with singing lessons (and speech training when appropriate), voice symptoms usually disappear quickly.

The treatment of asthmatic conditions in singers is somewhat different from that of the general population. One must eliminate even mild airway reactivity in order to optimize respiratory function for performance. Inhaled steroids should be avoided if at all possible in singers because of the possibility of dysphonia from the propellant, steroid effects on the laryngeal musculature, or from Candida overgrowth.[38-40] Mild asthma can usually be treated with sustained release oral theophylline with an inhaled beta-2 agonist for acute attacks or before performing. Cromolyn sodium may also be useful in patients with exertion-induced problems just prior to strenuous voice use.[41,42] Appropriate allergen immunotherapy and inhaled cromolyn sodium are used in the care of allergic asthma and can reduce the need for bronchodilators. In more severe cases, an oral beta-2 agonist in addition to theophylline may be necessary. Steroids are effective in obtaining rapid control of asthmatic symptoms; however, they are usually reserved for severe acute exacerbations because of the side effects of prolonged use.

Chronic obstructive pulmonary disease (COPD) is a general term that is applied to airway obstruction that is not fully reversible. The most common cause of COPD is cigarette smoking. It is manifested by either bronchitis or emphysema, although many patients have elements of both diseases. Patients with bronchitis have a chronic productive cough. In emphysema, there is destruction of alveolar membranes. Patients with bronchitis or emphysema may have severe obstructive changes on pulmonary function testing and an abnormal radiograph with increased lung volume due to air trapping. Exacerbations of bronchitis are treated with antibiotics. Otherwise, treatment is similar to that for asthma, but, because of the irreversibility of much of the airway disease, less response can be expected. In singers, hydration and cough suppressants reduce laryngeal trauma associated with coughing unless the pulmonary condition and need to clear secretions militate against the use of antitussives.

Another less commonly diagnosed cause of persistent pulmonary symptoms is gastroesophageal reflux. Vagal stimulation and chronic aspiration of gastric juice or particulate matter can result in chronic coughing, increased airway reactivity, or recurrent pneumonia.[43-48] There is evidence that reflux of gastric acid into the esophagus can increase airway reactivity even without reaching the larynx or lungs although results of studies of the addition of anti-reflux measures to the treatment of asthma have been mixed. Diagnosis is made by noting arytenoid and posterior glottic inflammation on laryngeal examination, reflux during radiologic upper gastrointestinal study, by esophagoscopy, and esophageal manometric testing with 24-hr esophageal pH monitoring. Acid levels should be measured specifically during singing. Treatment includes antacids, elevation of the head of the bed, and histamine-2 antagonists or proton pump inhibitors in severe cases. When medical treatment fails, surgical plication of the lower esophageal sphincter may be performed. Recently, laparoscopic fundoplication has decreased the morbidity of this procedure including disruption of important abdominal wall muscles.

Pneumonia presents special problems for the singer. It often takes longer than a singer realizes for lung function to return to normal. Singing too soon after such infections may result in vocal difficulties as attempts are made to compensate for minor deficiencies in the power source of the voice.

Restrictive Conditions

Restrictive lung disease can be divided into two groups. The first involves restriction of the chest bellows function. Weakness of the musculoskeletal support system is found in myasthenia gravis, Guillain-Barré syndrome, poliomyelitis, multiple sclerosis, spinal cord injury, and diaphragmatic paralysis. Additionally, massive obesity, kyphoscoliosis, and flail chest from thoracic trauma impair the function of the chest wall. A second group of restrictive lesions affects the pulmonary parenchyma and includes hypersensitivity pneumonitis, atelectasis, sarcoidosis, pulmonary fibrosis, pulmonary edema, pneumonia, neoplasm, drug reactions, and congestive heart failure. The diagnosis of restrictive respiratory impairment is confirmed by detailed pulmonary function testing. These patients have decreased lung volume with proportionately normal flow rates. The treatment of each of these syndromes is complex and not within the scope of this review. However, obesity is one cause of restrictive lung disease, and many singers have a significant weight problem. The effects of obesity on the voice have not been studied adequately; yet, there is no doubt that excessive weight can alter respiratory function. Restrictive pulmonary function due to excess weight has adverse effects on the endurance of a singer and probably on his or her lon-gevity as a performer. Obesity is also related to hypertension, diabetes, and other conditions that may actually shorten the performer's life. Finally, a restrictive pattern of pulmonary function in a previously healthy singer may indicate early neurologic or neuromuscular disease, and comprehensive evaluation is warranted whenever this finding appears.

Summary

Most singers and actors come to the laryngologist with complaints about changes in their voices; yet, many times the problem is not in the vocal folds but rather in the production of adequate airflow to drive the voice. Mild respiratory maladies such as cough or nasal congestion may not alter the voice primarily but can cause irritation or changes in technique that can impair vocal performance. Minor alterations in respiratory function that would go barely noticed in the general population can have significant effects on a professional voice user, causing vocal fatigue, loss of range, hyperfunctional abusive compensation, and other problems. Adequate knowledge of respiratory function and its disorders is essential to comprehensive care of the professional voice.

Much additional research about breathing and support is needed. Remembering that the end point of this research is the training and maintenance of healthy, beautiful professional voices, it is essential for voice scientists, voice teachers, and physicians to work together closely in clinical and basic research. Only through concerted efforts can we define the right questions and discover the right answers.

Review Questions

1. All of the following statements are true about asthma except:
   a. it impairs the support mechanism by obstructing the flow of air from the lungs
   b. it can be induced by exercise
   c. it can be induced by singing
   d. it is a form of restrictive lung disease
   e. in voice professionals, it should be primarily treated with inhalers

2. Which of the following may produce a restrictive pulmonary dysfunction?
   a. myasthenia gravis
   b. multiple sclerosis
   c. obesity
   d. all of the above
   e. none of the above

3. The leading cause of respiratory disease in the United States of America is:
   a. tuberculosis
   b. cigarette smoking
   c. air pollution
   d. asthma
   e. cancer

4. At the end of forced respiration, the air left in the lungs is known as:
   a. forced vital capacity

b. vital capacity

c. FEV_1

d. residual volume

e. none of the above

5. In young adults, pharyngeal obstruction is usually due to adenoids and palatine tonsil enlargement.
   a. true
   b. false

References

1. Spiegel JR, Sataloff RT, Cohn JR, Hawkshaw M. Respiratory function in singers: medical assessment, diagnoses and treatments. *J Voice.* 1988; 2(1):40–50.

2. Thorn GW, Adams RD, Braunwald E, et al, eds. *Harrison's Principles of Internal Medicine.* New York: McGraw-Hill; 1977:1215.

3. Sataloff RT. Professional singers: the science and art of clinical care. *Am J Otolaryngol.* 1981;2:251–266.

4. Mertz JS, McCaffrey TV, Kern EB. Objective evaluation of anterior septal surgical reconstruction. *Otolaryngol Head Neck Surg.* 1984;92:308–311.

5. Orgel HA, Meltzer EO, Kemp JP, Welch MJ. Clinical, rhinomanometric, and cytologic evaluation of seasonal allergic rhinitis treated with beclamethasone dipropionate as aqueous nasal spray or pressurized aerosol. *J Allergy Clin Immunol.* 1986;77:858–864.

6. McCaffrey TV, Kern EB. Clinical evaluation of nasal obstruction. *Arch Otolaryngol.* 1979;105:542–545.

7. Daubenspeck JA. Influence of small mechanical loads on variability of breathing pattern. *J Applied Physiol.* 1981;50:299–306.

8. Hirano M. *Clinical Examination of the Voice.* New York: Springer-Verlagwein; 1981.

9. Shigemori Y. Some tests related to the air usage during phonation. *Clin Invest Otol (Fukuoka).* 1977;23:138–166.

10. Tanaka S, Gould WJ. Vocal efficiency and aerodynamic aspects in voice disorders. *Ann Otol Rhinol Laryngol.* 1985;94:29–33.

11. Segall JJ, Butterworth BA. The maximal midexpiratory flow time. *Br J Dis Chest.* 1968;62:139–145.

12. Despas PJ, Leroux M, Macklem PT. Site of airway obstruction in asthma determined by measuring maximal expiratory flow breathing air and a helium-oxygen mixture. *J Clin Invest.* 1982;51:3235–3243.

13. Hyatt RE, Black LF. The flow-volume curve. *Am Rev Resp Dis.* 1973;107:191–199.

14. Standardization of Spirometry—1987 Update. Official Statement of the American Thoracic Society (approved by the ATS Board of Directors), March, 1987; Reed Gardner, Ph.D.(Chairman), John L. Hankison, Ph.D., Jack L. Clausen, M.D., Robert O, Crapo, M.D., Robert L. Johnson, Jr., M.D., Gary R. Epler, M.D., *American Rev Respir Dis.* 1987; 136:1285–1298.

15. Statement on spirometry: a report of the section on respiratory pathophysiology. *Chest.* 1983;83:547–550.

16. Sackner MA, ed. Diagnostic Techniques in Pulmonary Disease. New York: Marcel Dekker, 1980.

17. Chai H, Farr RS, Froehlich LA, et al. Standardization of bronchial inhalation challenge procedures. *J Allergy Clin Immunol.* 1975;56:323–327.

18. Malo JL, Pineau L, Carter A, Martin RR. Reference values of the provocative concentrations of methacholine that cause 6~ and 20% changes in forced expiratory volume in one second in a normal population. *Am Rev Resp Dis.* 1983;128:8–11.

19. Chatham M, Bleeker ER, Smith PL, et al. A comparison of histamine, methacholine, and exercise airway reactivity in normal and asthmatic subjects. *Am Rev Resp Dis.* 1982;126:235–240.

20. Martin L. Pulmonary *Physiology in Clinical Practice.* St. Louis: CV Mosby; 1987.

21. Gould WT, Okamura H. Static lung volumes in singers. *Ann Otol Rhinol Laryngol.* 1973;82:89–95.

22. Nelson HS. Diagnostic procedures in allergy. I. Allergy skin testing. *Ann Allergy.* 1983;51:411–418.

23. Practice and Standards Committee. American Academy of Allergy and Immunology position statement. *J Allergy Clin Immunol.* 1983;72:515–517.

24. Mangi RJ. Allergy skin tests: an overview. Otolaryngol Clin NA. 1985;18:719–723.

25. Nalebuff DJ. An enthusiastic view of the use of RAST in clinical allergy. *Immunol Allergy Pract.* 1981;3:77–87.

26. Fadal RG, Nalebuff DJ. A study of optimum dose immunotherapy in pharmacological treatment failures. *Arch Otolaryngol.* 1980;106:38–43.

27. Ali M. Serum concentration of allergen-specific IgG antibodies in inhalant allergy: effect of specific immunotherapy. *Am J Clin Pathol.* 1983;80:290–299.

28. Martinez SA, Nissen AJ, Stock CR, Tesmer T. Nasal turbinate resection for relief of nasal obstruction. *Laryngoscope.* 1983;93:871–875.

29. Parkin JL. Topical steroids in nasal disease. *Otolaryngol Head Neck Surg.* 1983;91:713–714.

30. Pelikan Z, Pelikan-Filipek M. The effects of disodium cromoglycate and beclomethasone dipropionate on the immediate response of the nasal mucosa to allergen challenge. *Ann Allergy.* 1982;49:283–292 .

31. McCaurin JG. A review of the interrelationship of paranasal sinus disease and certain chest conditions, with special consideration of bronchiectasis and asthma. *Ann Otol Rhinol Larvngol.* 1935;44:344–353.

32. Croft CB, Shprintzen RJ, Ruben RJ. Hypernasal speech following adenotonsillectomy. *Otolaryngol Head Neck Surg.* 1981;88:179–188.

33. Baum GC, Wolinsky E. *Textbook of Pulmonary Disease.* Boston: Little, Brown; 1983.

34. Corraa WM, Braman SS, Irwin RS. Chronic cough as the sole presenting manifestation of bronchial asthma. *N Eng J Med.* 1979;300:633–637.

35. Strauss RH, McFadden ER, Ingram RH, Jaeger JJ. Enhancement of exercise-induced asthma by cold air. *N Engl J Med.* 1977;297:743–747.

36. Spector SL, Wangaard CH, Farr RS. Aspirin and concomitant idiosyncrasies in adult asthmatic patients. *J Allergy Clin Immunol.* 1979;64:500–506.

37. Cohn JR, Sataloff RT, Spiegel JR, Fish JE & Kennedy K. Airway reactivity—induced asthma in singers (ARIAS), *J Voice.* 1991;5(4):332–337.

38. Watkins KL, Ewanowsk SJ. Effects of aerosol corticosteroids on the voice: triamcinolone acetonide and beclomethasone dipropionate. *J Speech Hearing Res.* 1985;28:301–304.

39. Toogood JH, Jennings B, Greenway RW, Chuang L. Candidiasis and dysphonia complicating beclomethasone treatment of asthma. *J Allergy Clin Immunol.* 1980;65:145–153.

40. Williams AJ, Baghat MS, Stableforth DE, et al. Dysphonia caused by inhaled steroids: recognition of a characteristic laryngeal abnormality. *Thorax.* 1983;38:813–821.

41. Gimeno F, vanVeenen R, Steenhuis EJ, Berg WCH. Comparison of disodium cromoglycate, terbutaline and thiazinamium in the prevention of exercise-induced asthma and its relation to non-specific bronchial responsiveness. *Respiration.* 1985;48:108–115.

42. Tullett WM, Tan KM, Wall RT, Patei KR. Dose-response effect of sodium cromoglycate pressurized aerosol in exercise induced asthma. *Thorax.* 1985;40:41–44.

43. Davis MV. Relationship between pulmonary disease, hiatal hernia, and gastroesophageal reflux. *NY State J Med.* 1972;72:935–938.

44. Mansfield LE, Stein MR. Gastroesophageal reflux and asthma: a possible reflex mechanism. *Ann Allergy.* 1978;41:224–226.

45. Barish CF, Wu WC, Castell DO. Respiratory complications of gastroesophageal reflux. *Arch Intern Med.* 1985;145:1882–1888.

46. Larrain A, Carrasco E, Galleguillos R, Sepulveda R, Pope CE: Medical and surgical treatment of nonallergic asthma associated with gastroesophageal reflux. *Chest.* 1991; 99(6):1330–1335.

47. Sontag SJ, O'Connell S, Khandewal S, Miller T, Nemchausky B, Schnell TG, Serlovsky R. Most asthmatics have gastroesophageal reflux with or without bronchodilator therapy. *Gastroenterology.* 1990;99(3):613–620.

48. Wesseling G, Brummer RJ, Wouters EFM, ten Velde GPM. Gastric asthma? No change in respiratory impedance during intraesophageal acidification in adult asthmatics. *Chest.* 1993; 104(6):1733–1736.

13

Allergy

John R. Cohn, Joseph R. Spiegel, Mary Hawkshaw, and Robert Thayer Sataloff

About one of every five persons in America has an allergic disease. *Allergy*, in simple terms, is a specific but abnormal response to substances that ordinarily do not adversely affect people. An allergic reaction may occur in response to something an individual inhales, ingests, has contact with, or is injected with. Symptoms range from mild to severe (even fatal) and may include upper respiratory (allergic rhinitis) and lower respiratory (asthma) complaints. Individuals may suffer seasonal bouts of allergic symptoms or may be ill perennially depending on what in their environment causes their hypersensitivity.

The human immune response is based on a complex, interrelated system of cells (primarily leukocytes) and cell products (enzymes, immunoglobulins, and complements). This system provides recognition and response to foreign substances (antigens) that contact the body or are ingested. Lymphocytes produce multiple classes of immunoglobulins that can be converted into specific antibodies targeting an antigen. After the immune response is initiated with the recognition of the antigen, the body's response is manifested by many different cellular and intracellular mediators (complements, prostaglandins, leukotrienes, interleukins). Coombs and Gell[1] classified the mechanisms of hypersensitivity into four classes. Type I hypersensitivity is mediated primarily by IgE and is exemplified by the common allergic phenomena of allergic rhinitis, anaphylactic shock, urticaria, and asthma. Type II hypersensitivity is mediated by IgG or IgM directed toward cell-bound antigens. Hemolytic anemia in the newborn is an example. Type III hypersensitivity involves immune complex diseases such as found in serum sickness. Type IV reactions are characterized by delayed cellular-mediated immunity, such as contact dermatitis.

Allergic individuals make abnormal amounts of antibodies, mostly of the IgE class, which are specific for the substances to which they are allergic.[2] Patients who have a genetic tendency to make specific IgE may react to a number of substances, and cross-reacting antibodies to related substances, such as to pollens from various grasses, may be present. In adults, most allergic reactions are to inhalant allergens, while food allergies are relatively rare. Allergic and certain nonallergic individuals may also be more sensitive to nonspecific irritants, such as strong odors, as well as to selected pharmacologic agents such as methacholine and histamine.[3] This chapter discusses the diagnosis and treatment of inhalant respiratory allergies only, because they are most likely to adversely affect singers and many other professionals. Upper respiratory tract allergies will be addressed here. Lower respiratory tract problems affecting singers, including the syndrome of Airway Reactivity Induced Asthma in Singers (ARIAS),[4] are discussed in chapter 12 and in a review.[5] Also, it should be remembered that allergies to ingested substances (including foods) may affect singers by thickening secretions and causing congestion; similar reactions may also occur from skin contact and other allergic exposures.

The mechanism of the allergic reaction is more complex than initially believed. The traditional explanation, including release of mediators from mast cells and basophils secondary to linkages between IgE on the cell surface and the allergen, has expanded to include a long list of intercellular messengers, cells, and mediators, all of which appear to play a role in the development of the allergic reaction. Additionally, neurogenic factors may also be involved.[6] The classic allergic reaction involves immediate hypersensitivity, with symptoms resulting from the release of histamine and other cell mediators noted within minutes. Of the four types of hypersensitivity reaction originally described by Coombs and Gell,[1] this is a type I hypersensitivity reaction. Late phase reactions, mediated by basophils and mast cells through other mediators such as prostaglandins and leukotrienes, can cause tissue inflammation for hours or days.[7]

Mild allergies are more incapacitating to professional voice users than to others because of their effect on the mucosal cover layer. If a singer has a short period of annual allergy and is able to control the symptoms well with medications that do not produce disturbing side effects, this approach is reasonable. When more sustained treatment is required, when medication side effects impair performance, or when relief is inadequate in the context of the voice user's increased demands, more extensive evaluation is required.

Signs and Symptoms

The term *allergic rhinitis*, commonly referred to as hay fever or rose fever, describes an array of allergic symptoms involving the eyes, ears, nose, and throat. In effect, these terms are misnomers, because flowering plants do not have wind-borne pollen, and most fall allergic symptoms are brought on by weeds such as ragweed and not hay. Identical symptoms may occur in the summer and winter in response to exposures to common allergens such as animal dander and dust mites. Symptoms include nasal congestion, sneezing, clear drainage from the nose; watery, itchy eyes; throat soreness and a sensation of the constant need for throat clearing (from postnasal drip); pain and/or pressure in the ears; and headache and fatigue. Professional voice users, especially singers, with mild allergies may present with subtle vocal complaints such as occasional voice breaks or vocal fatigue that may be the result of relative drying in the vocal tract. These symptoms are most commonly seasonal, when the grasses, trees, and weeds are pollinating. However, they may occur year round in some individuals. Pollinating seasons vary significantly across the United States, as do the allergens that are most problematic in each region.[8] This fact holds special importance for singers and actors who are commonly called on to travel often, sometimes weekly.

Allergies to dust and mold commonly are aggravated during rehearsals and performances in concert halls, especially older concert halls, because of the numerous curtains, backstage trappings, and dressing room facilities that are rarely cleaned thoroughly. Because many singers travel extensively, location is important to bear in mind when attempting to elicit an allergic history and when planning allergy treatment with regard to an upcoming performance schedule. Additionally, the history must include not only geographical location, but also details of recent working, living, and traveling environments.

Allergic rhinitis is one of the most common etiologies in the development of *chronic sinusitis*. Patients with chronic sinusitis suffer from nasal congestion, postnasal drainage, pressure headaches, and olfactory disturbances. Chronic sinusitis can also exacerbate asthma.

Evaluation

Although the history may provide the best clues for the diagnosis of allergy, it can also be misleading. Nasal examination classically reveals hypertrophied, boggy nasal mucosa with a pale bluish color. Clear rhinorrhea is often noted, but thicker secretions can be present if there is an element of chronic sinusitis or if there is relative dehydration. Allergic polyps are common in the nose and are usually found in the middle meatus or involving the middle turbinates. Polyps related to allergy are usually multiple, pale, yellowish, and firm. Most findings of allergic rhinitis can be seen on routine anterior rhinoscopy. However, nasal endoscopy can be used for more detailed intranasal examination, when necessary. Nasal examination performed before and after the application of topical mucosal decongestants (ie, phenylephrine, oxymetazolam) can help predict the patient's response to pharmacologic treatment.

In addition to the findings on nasal examination, other head and neck signs of allergic rhinitis include conjunctival irritation, periorbital ecchymosis ("allergic shiners"), serous otitis media, oral and pharyngeal drying, and lymphoid hypertrophy in Waldeyer's ring. On laryngeal examination, thick secretions with mucous stranding across the vocal folds, supraglottic edema, and vocal fold edema can be seen.

Radiologic testing is usually not necessary in the primary evaluation of allergic rhinitis. When sinusitis is suspected, a nonenhanced CT scan is the best single study to evaluate the paranasal sinuses. Plain sinus X-rays are useful to screen children and patients with acute sinusitis.

Allergy Testing

As previously stated, allergy evaluation begins with a detailed history of the patient's symptoms and exposures. Appropriate testing can then be performed to look for demonstrated atopy. Prick skin testing can rapidly screen for reactions to a number of allergens. It is the quickest and least expensive means of confirming allergic sensitization. Patients must be off most antihistamines for 5 days before skin testing can be performed. Astemizole (Hismanol) may interfere with skin test reactions for several months. Intradermal skin tests are the most sensitive way to look for signs of allergy. They may also provide a rapid answer, but they carry a higher risk of adverse reaction. Extremely rare fatalities have been associated with skin testing, which should be reserved for experienced practitioners who are prepared to treat the rare allergic reactions that occur.

Radioallergosorbent testing (RAST) can measure antigen-specific IgE levels to multiple antigen classes from a single blood specimen. RAST testing is more expensive but it is not altered by antihistamines. It is also not as sensitive as skin testing and requires at least a 1- to 2-day wait for results. It can be especially useful in patients with dermatologic conditions that make skin testing impossible. RAST testing has been used as a screening technique[9] to confirm the diagnosis of allergy, or as a basis for the development of immunotherapy,[10] but there is inadequate evidence to justify its use as a substitute for conventional skin testing.

Treatment

Pharmacologic Treatment

When used on a regular basis, topical nasal steroid sprays may provide adequate control of seasonal or perennial symptoms.[11] There are multiple preparations that require only once or twice daily usage (Table 13–1). Nasal and pharyngeal irritation is rare with these sprays, and there is no risk of significant systemic absorption at recommended dosages. Topical sodium cromolyn may also control allergic nasal airway disease with rare adverse effects, although in our experience it is less effective.

The primary disadvantage of topical nasal medications is failure to control ocular symptoms, which may accompany nasal complaints. Although less likely to impact negatively on the voice, ocular symptoms may produce considerable discomfort in the atopic singer whose nasal symptoms have been relieved by topical therapy. This may cause eye blinking, which gives an audience the false impression that the performer is nervous or uncomfortable. Eye irritation may also cause slight blurring of vision that may make it difficult to read music. Ocular cromolyn sodium is available as a 4% solution. As with nasal steroids and cromolyn, this is a prophylactic medication that requires regular use to provide effective relief. Alternatively, ketorolac tromethamine, a nonsteroidal anti-inflammatory drug (NSAID), may provide symptomatic relief of allergic ocular complaints. This drug may cause adverse reactions in patients allergic to salicylates (aspirin) and other NSAIDs, but it is unlikely to cause altered coagulation as with systemic NSAIDs. A variety of vasoconstrictor topical ocular preparations that may also be used for transient relief are available over the counter. Most of these preparations are contraindicated in users of soft contact lenses, and care should be taken to exclude other causes of eye pain, particularly when that is the sole complaint.

When topical preparations do not adequately control allergic rhinitis, oral antihistamines may be necessary. All antihistamines potentially cause drying of the mucosal surfaces of the upper and lower airway. This can be a critical problem for a professional voice user, because even mild relative drying may cause major problems affecting both vocal quality and vocal stamina. Additionally, most antihistamines also potentially cause some level of sedation, although over the past few years, new drugs with minimal sedative side effects have become available. Details of commonly used antihistamines and their sedative side effects can be found in Table 13–2.

Because antihistamines do not directly address the problem of nasal congestion, decongestants are com-

Table 13–1. Topical Nasal Preparations.

Drug	Trade Name	Dosing
Beclomethasone	Beconase, Vancenase	Twice daily
Budesonide	Rhinocort	Once or twice daily
Flunisolide	Nasalide	Twice daily
Triamcinolone acetonide	Nasacort	Once or twice daily
Cromolyn sodium	Nasalcrom	Two or four times daily

Table 13–2. Commonly Used Antihistamines.[12]

Generic Name	Trade Name	Sedative Effect
Alkylamines		
Chlorpheniramine	Chlor-trimeton	Mild
Dexchlorpheniramine	Polaramine	Mild
Brompheniramine	Dimetane	Mild
Triprolidine	Actidil	Mild
Ethylenediamines		
Tripelenamine	Pyribenzamine	Moderate
Methylpyrilene	Histadyl	Moderate
Ethanolamines		
Diphenhydramine	Benadryl	Marked
Carbinoxamine	Clistin	Moderate
Doxylamine	Decapryn	Moderate
Clemastine	Tavist	Mild
Azatadine	Trinalin	Moderate
Nonsedating		
Terfenadine	Seldane	Slight
Astemizole	Hismanol	Slight
Loratadine	Claritin	Slight

monly added to the medical regimen. Decongestants are often added to antihistamines to form combination preparations to both potentiate the mucosal drying effects and to take advantage of the stimulatory side effects of decongestants to counteract the sedation from the antihistamine. The newer, nonsedating antihistamines have also been combined with decongestants (Claritin-D). These products can provide excellent control of allergic nasal congestion with no risk of CNS sedation, but they can also cause mild stimulatory side effects such as insomnia and tachycardia.

The mucosal drying effects of both antihistamines and decongestants may be counteracted to some extent with mucolytic agents that liquefy mucus and increase the output of thin respiratory tract secretions. Guaifenesin is an excellent mucolytic expectorant. It is available as a single agent (Robitussin, Humibid) or combined with a decongestant (Entex-LA, Entex-PSE).

It is often necessary to experiment with several antihistamines, decongestants, or combinations in singers before finding a suitable balance in a singer between therapeutic effect and side effects. The clinician must be familiar with many different medications and drug classes, both to minimize side effects and because patients tend to develop tolerance to antihistamines with long-term use and may require changes in prescriptions. Professional voice users should generally avoid new medication shortly before a performance. Drugs are usually taken in small doses for short trial periods to determine both the level of allergy control and the effects on the vocal tract. If a singer obtains consistent control of allergic symptoms and does not suffer from excessive drying, sedation, or hyperstimulation, these medications can be used safely for both short- and long-term treatment.

Acute symptoms of allergic rhinitis are usually quite responsive to systemic steroids. Intramuscular or oral steroids can rapidly reverse allergic inflammation and can also result in mild mucosal drying and mild CNS stimulation. Steroids can be used to treat a singer or actor suffering an acute allergic "attack," or to rapidly initiate medical treatment because of a difficult upcoming performance schedule. In these instances corticosteroids are usually administered as either a single intramuscular injection or a rapidly weaning course taken orally over 3 to 5 days. There is no evidence that inhaled steroids reduce vocal fold edema, whether it results from allergic or infectious etiologies. The use of long-term systemic steroids in the treatment of most allergic patients is inappropriate.

Allergy-Directed Therapy

Singers may be particularly sensitive to both the effects of their underlying allergy and to the medications prescribed to control their disorder. For this reason, specific allergy-directed treatment is virtually always indicated. Serious singers should be referred to a physician with specialized training and expertise in the treatment of allergic disorders. The American Boards of Pediatrics and Internal Medicine supervise 2-year fellowship training programs in the evaluation and treatment of allergic diseases. Physicians who complete the fellowship successfully may sit for the certifying examination. Other medical specialties including otolaryngology also offer training in this area.

Appropriate testing is performed to look for demonstrated atopy. Once allergy is identified, avoidance measures provide a first step to limiting symptoms. It is well established that the less a patient is exposed to the allergens to which he or she is sensitized, the less difficulty he or she will have with unavoidable exposures. Environmental control may consist of measures such as providing air-conditioning in a performer's suite, or dust control in the home environment. Alteration in props may also be helpful, as demonstrated by a singer who experienced difficulty in a new role that included a feather boa as part of the costume. After skin testing confirmed the presence of feather allergy, symptoms resolved with the substitution of a synthetic boa.[13]

Immunotherapy injections may provide the best possible therapeutic modality for many professional voice users. They offer the opportunity for allergen-directed control of the allergic response with no worry about vocal tract side effects. Immunotherapy is based on the pattern of allergy and demonstrated specific sensitivity as determined by allergy testing. The patient receives injections of slowly increasing concentrations of various allergens at approximately weekly intervals. The mechanism by which allergen immunotherapy works is not known. It has been proposed that IgG antibodies develop and block the IgE molecules at the receptor sites on immune response cells, but a variety of physiologic responses have been demonstrated. Immunotherapy is effective in a majority of appropriately selected patients who complete the full dosing regimen.[14]

Summary

Allergic disease is a common problem and must not be overlooked in the evaluation of professional voice users who seek medical attention for complaints of change in their voice. Even complaints of mild nasal congestion or dry scratchy throat, which may not alter the voice primarily, can cause chronic irritation that may impair vocal performance. It is important to remember that symptoms of allergy are generally chronic, but they may be acute with a new specific exposure. They may vary in severity and sometimes, but not always, have seasonal variation. Understand-

ing the pathophysiology and immunology of allergy, as well as its diagnosis and treatment, is essential in providing comprehensive care to the professional voice user. An appreciation for allergy and its special implications for performers is important not only for physicians, but also for professional voice users and their teachers.

Review Questions

1. Type I hypersensitivity is primarily mediated by:
   a. IgA
   b. IgE
   c. IgG
   d. IgM
   e. none of the above

2. Contact dermatitis (inflammation of the skin) is an example of:
   a. Type I hypersensitivity
   b. Type II hypersensitivity
   c. Type III hypersensitivity
   d. Type IV hypersensitivity
   e. none of the above

3. Allergy tests are not affected by a patient's use of medications such as antihistamines.
   a. true
   b. false

4. For singers, appropriate allergy therapy may include:
   a. immunotherapy
   b. avoidance
   c. antihistamines
   d. all of the above
   e. none of the above

5. Long-term use of topical nasal steroids should be avoided in singers because of voice complications:
   a. true
   b. false

References

1. Coombs RRA, Gell PGH. Classification of allergic reactions responsible for clinical hypersensitivity and disease. In: Gell PGH, Coombs RRA, eds. *Clinical Aspects of Immunology*. Philadelphia, Pa: FA Davis; 1968:575–596.
2. Ishizaka T. Mechanisms of IgE-mediated hypersensitivity. In: Middleton E, Reed C, Ellis E, et al, eds. *Allergy Principles and Practice*. St Louis, Mo: Mosby Year-Book, Inc; 1988:71–93.

3. Cartier A, Bernstein IL, Burge PS, Cohn JR. Guidelines for bronchoprovocation in the investigation of occupational asthma: report of the subcommittee on bronchoprovocation for occupational asthma. *J Allergy Clin Immunol.* 1989;84:823–829.

4. Cohn JR, Sataloff RT, Spiegel JR, Fish JE, Kennedy K. Airway reactivity- induced asthma in singers (ARIAS). *J Voice.* 1990;5:332–337.

5. Cohn JR, Spiegel JR, Sataloff RT. Vocal disorders on the professional voice user: the allergist's role. *Ann Allergy Asthma Immunol.* 1995;74:363–375.

6. Kaliner M, Lemanske R. Rhinitis and asthma. *JAMA.* 1992;268(2):2807–2829.

7. Naclerio RM, Proud D, Togias AG. Inflammatory mediators in late antigen-induced rhinits. *N Eng J Med.* 1985; 313:65–67.

8. Lewis W, Vinay P, Zenger V. *Airborne and Allergic Pollen of North America.* Baltimore, MD: The Johns Hopkins University Press; 1983.

9. King WP. Efficacy of a screening radioallergosorbent test. *Arch Otolaryngol.* 1982;108:781–786.

10. Nalebuff DJ. In vitro-based allergen immunotherapy. In: Krause HF., ed. Otolaryngic Allergy and Immunology. Philadelphia, PA: WB Saunders; 1989:163-168.

11. Mabry RL. Pharmacotherapy with immunotherapy of the treatment of otolaryngic allergic. *ENT J.* 1990;69:63–71.

12. Fireman P. Allergic rhinitis. In: Bluestone CD, Stool SE, Scheetz MD, eds. *Pediatric Otolaryngology.* Philadelphia, Penna: WB Saunders; 1990;793–804.

13. Cohn JR, Sataloff RT. Boa constrictor. *Chest.* 1993;103:653.

14. Creticos PS. Immunotherapy with allergens. *JAMA.* 1992; 268:2834–2839.

Endocrine Dysfunction

Robert Thayer Sataloff,
Kate A. Emerich,
and Cheryl A. Hoover

Endocrine problems are worthy of special attention. The human voice is extremely sensitive to endocrinologic changes. Many of the voice changes are caused by alterations of fluid content beneath the vocal fold mucosa. Although the otolaryngologist can get a great deal of guidance from his or her clinical impression, and from laboratory tests such as thyroid function, dehydroepiandrosterone, androstenedione, cortisol, testosterone (total and free), estrogen, prolactin, 17-hydroxyprogesterone, and other tests, the value of a good endocrinologist interested in consulting in the care of professional voice users cannot be overestimated. As in other areas of professional voice care, recognizing abnormalities and prescribing therapy can be tricky. The endocrinologist who understands arts-medicine concerns can help with diagnosis, adjusting postmenopausal sex hormone replacement by clinical and laboratory monitoring, optimizing thyroid replacement, stabilizing serum hormone concentrations in women prone to cyclical vocal fold hemorrhage, and assisting laryngologists in many other difficult situations. Otolaryngologists are strongly encouraged to enlist the services of an interested consultant and to assist in his or her education in the special problems of professional voice users. Nevertheless, the laryngologist caring for voice patients must be familiar with the broad range of hormonal imbalances that may affect the voice in order to recognize them promptly and generate appropriate treatment and referrals.

Sex Hormones

Voice changes associated with sex hormones are encountered commonly in clinical practice and have been investigated more thoroughly than have most other hormonal changes. The most obvious and profound hormonal effects are physiologic and occur at the time of puberty. The consequences of changes in circulating hormone levels at this time are discussed in chapter 10, Effects of Age on the Voice. When castrato singers were in vogue, castration of males at about age 7 or 8 resulted in failure of laryngeal growth during puberty and voices that stayed in the soprano or alto range and boasted a unique quality of sound.[1] Failure of castrato voices to change was due to lack of the normal testosterone surge at puberty. This practice continued from the 16th century until 1903, when it was officially banned by Pope Pius X.[2]

Failure of a male voice to change at puberty is uncommon today, and usually is psychogenic. However, hormonal deficiencies such as those seen in cryptorchidism, delayed sexual development, Klinefelter's syndrome, or Fröhlich's syndrome may be responsible.[3] In these cases, the persistently high voice may be the complaint that brings the patient to medical attention. In some ways, these disorders mimic castration as it used to be performed. For example, patients with Klinefelter's syndrome become tall at puberty, and have long legs and gynecomastia. They have small testes that do not produce sperm. In some patients, the levels of circulating testosterone are very low, pubic hair is absent, and the voice remains soprano. These effects may be less prominent in some Klinefelter's syndrome patients in whom more testosterone is produced. Testosterone has been hypothesized as causally related to the increased incidence of coronary heart disease and atherosclerosis in men as compared with women. This suggests that there may have been at least some advantage to being a castrato. However, in an interesting study, Nieschlag and co-workers compared the life span of 50 famous castrati born between 1581 and 1858 with 50 equally famous, intact male singers born during the same period and found no trend toward increased longevity in castrati.[4] It should also be recognized that castration is still occasionally required therapeutically in adult males, particularly for treatment of prostate or testicular cancer. In such cases, the increase in fundamental frequency of the speaking voice that occurs physiologically with aging may be accelerated, but survival considerations must take precedence over vocal concern.

After puberty, hormone problems are encountered relatively uncommonly in men. Although there appears to be a correlation between sex hormone levels and depths of male voices (higher testosterone and lower estradiol levels in basses than in tenors),[5] the most important hormonal considerations in males occur during the maturation process. The most common

hormonal problems encountered in postpubertal males are probably those related to ingestion of anabolic steroids. In males, these drugs cause testicular atrophy, and they may cause lowering and coarsening of the voice in some cases. Females suffer even greater vocal problems ingesting anabolic steroids. Marked virilization of the voice is common and irreversible. Physicians must be familiar with these side effects since male hormones are not only used by women body builders, but are also prescribed by gynecologists for postmenopausal sexual dysfunction. Such treatments may substantially masculinize and age a voice and may end a vocal career. Risks must be weighed carefully against benefits before such medication is prescribed.

Voice problems related to sex hormones are encountered most commonly in female voice patients. Familiarity with the normal ovarian cycle is helpful in understanding these problems (see Fig 14–1). The cycle begins with the menstrual period and ends just

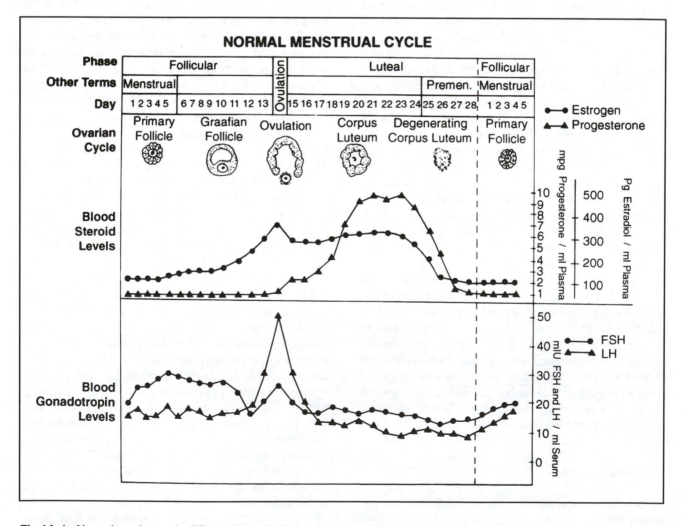

Fig 14–1. Normal ovarian cycle. FSH, follicle-stimulating hormone; LH, luteinizing hormone.

prior to the next menses. The first portion of the cycle is known as the *follicular phase*. It is characterized by gradually increasing levels of estrogen and low levels of progesterone. The follicular phase normally occupies the first 14 days of the cycle. During the ovulatory phase, progesterone remains low and estrogen peaks. The following 14 days are the *luteal phase*. Progesterone levels increase for the first half of luteal phase. Estrogen decreases but rises again slightly premenstrually.

Although voice changes associated with the normal menstrual cycle may be difficult to quantify, there is no question that they occur.[6–9] Most of the ill effects are seen in the immediate premenstrual period and are known as *laryngopathia premenstrualis*. This condition is common and is caused by physiologic, anatomic, and psychologic alterations secondary to endocrine changes. The vocal dysfunction is characterized by decreased vocal efficiency, loss of the highest notes in the voice, vocal fatigue, slight hoarseness, and some muffling of the voice, and it is often more apparent to the singer than to the listener. Submucosal hemorrhages in the larynx are common.[9] Singers used to be excused during the premenstrual and early menstrual days ("grace days"). This practice is not followed in the United States. Voice dysfunction similar to laryngopathia premenstrualis is also relatively common at the time of ovulation.

The cause of premenstrual (and midcycle) dysphonia remains incompletely understood. The premenstrual estrogen/progesterone combined activity causes vasodilatation by relaxing smooth muscles, thereby increasing blood volume. These changes result in engorgement of vocal fold blood vessels, and vocal fold edema. In addition, polysaccharides break down into smaller molecules in the vocal folds and bind water, increasing fluid accumulation. Aldosterone contributes to cyclical salt and water retention, as well.[10] Vasodilatation also causes changes in nasal patency, self-perception (audition), and possibly concentration (premenstrual syndrome). The premenstrual hormonal environment also decreases gastric motility. This effect may aggravate reflux and cause bloating, which can impair effective support. In addition, Abitbol et al,[11] in an elegant research paper, showed a strong correlation between premenstrual dysphonia and luteal insufficiency. They also demonstrated that the larynx is as dramatic a hormonal target organ as vaginal mucosa. In fact, epithelial smears from larynx and vagina at various times during the ovarian cycle are indistinguishable from one another. The incidence of premenstrual hoarseness is unknown, but anecdotally it appears to be significant in about one third of women. Although most authors and clinicians have been more impressed with premenstrual voice changes than with those occurring during midcycle, at least one author has suggested that voice changes occurring at the time of ovulation may actually be more prominent.[12]

Although ovulation inhibitors have been shown to mitigate some of these symptoms,[8] in some women (about 5%; C. Carroll MD and H. von Leden MD, personal communication, September, 1992.), birth control pills may deleteriously alter voice range and character even after only a few months of therapy.[13–16] When oral contraceptives are used, the voice should be monitored closely. Care must be taken to use oral contraceptives that contain no androgens. Medications marketed in the United States generally do not. However, androgen-containing oral contraceptives are still available in Europe and may cause permanent masculinization of the voice. Under crucial performance circumstances, oral contraceptives may be used to alter the time of menstruation, but this practice is justified only in unusual situations. In general, there is no effective treatment for these voice problems that does not carry significant drawbacks for singers and other professional voice users. However, when cyclical voice changes are incapacitating, endocrinologic assessment and appropriate hormonal therapy should certainly be considered.

The hormonal cycle is also associated with menstrual cramping, or dysmenorrhea. Cramps occur in approximately one half to three quarters of menstruating women, and about 10% are disabled for one to three days monthly.[17,18] Muscle cramping associated with menstruation causes pain and compromises abdominal contraction. This undermines support and makes singing or projected speech (acting and public speaking) difficult and potentially dangerous. Dysmenorrhea is also associated with diarrhea and low back pain, which further impair support. It may also be accompanied by fatigue, headache, dizziness, emesis, nausea, and agitation, all of which are distracting and potentially impair technique and performance. Although menstrual cramps are widely believed to be due to an imbalance between estrogen and progesterone prior to menstruation, it is clear that the pain is prostaglandin-mediated. Hence, prostaglandin inhibitors such as aspirin and ibuprofen are commonly prescribed for dysmenorrhea. The combination of such drugs with capillary fragility and other premenstrual changes puts a professional voice user at unacceptable risk of vocal hemorrhage, and medications that impair coagulation should be avoided.

The hormonal cycle is also associated in some women with premenstrual syndrome (PMS). The mood disorder may include emotional lability, depression, anxiety, irritability, decreased concentration ability, abdominal bloating, edema, nausea, diarrhea, palpitations, pain in various locations, water and salt retention, and other changes that may adversely affect voice performance. Insomnia commonly occurs, as well, and subsequent sleep deprivation may further impair voice function. There is no consistently good treatment for PMS, and medical regimens that include androgens should be avoided in voice professionals.

Menopause is also associated with insomnia and sleep deprivation, as well as hot flashes, emotional and psychological changes, genital atrophy, laryngeal mucosal changes, osteoporosis, cardiovascular disease, decreased libido, decreased concentration, and other alterations. Isenberger et al investigated the possible connections between the reproductive system and the singing voice. They studied singers with amenorrhea and found that common vocal complaints among these singers included a crack in the voice; an inability to make a smooth transition between chest and head voice; breathiness/weakness; an inability to phonate on certain pitches; a lack of flexibility or inability to sing certain scales and/or arpeggios quickly and easily; and an inability to adequately support tones.[19] These complaints are similar to those reported by singers studied during the premenstrual phase. In addition to the hormonal changes, women entering or in menopause also have to deal with age-related factors that affect the voice. They include decrease in lung power, atrophy of laryngeal muscles, stiffening of laryngeal cartilages, vocal fold thickening, virilization of the voice (due to hormonal changes), and a loss of elastic and collagenous fibers. The vocal correlates may include breathiness, decrease in overall vocal range (especially upper range), a change in characteristics of the vibrato, development of a tremolo, decreased breath control, vocal fatigue, and pitch inaccuracies. After menopause, voices typically drop in fundamental frequency because the ovary secretes little or no estrogen, but continues to secrete androgen. It should be remembered that cessation of menstrual periods is often a late sign of menopause. In female singers and actresses over the age of 35 to 40, it is helpful to obtain baseline estrogen levels. The author (RTS) prefers to ask women to identify the time during their cycle when their voices seem best. This is often during menses (athletic performance in runners and other athletes is also often best then, too). Hormone levels are obtained during the vocally optimal time of the month and recorded for later use in individualizing hormone replacement therapy. Hormone levels can then be monitored in consultation with an endocrinologist. The most prominent hormonal change is a 10- to 20-fold drop in estradiol levels.[20] In some cases, hypoestrogenic voice changes may precede interruption of menses, and it may be desirable to start estrogen replacement even before menstrual periods become irregular or stop. Estrogens are helpful in menopausal singers. Sequential replacement therapy using estrogen and progesterone is most physiologic and should be used under the close supervision of a gynecologist or endocrinologist and a laryngologist. Care must be taken to keep progesterone doses low, and this medication may even be omitted in some cases. There is still controversy regarding the length of time that estrogen replacement can be used safely. There are many benefits of estrogen replacement, including not only increased vocal longevity, but also avoidance of osteoporosis, cardiovascular disease, and other systemic problems. However, there are also potential risks, including a probable increased incidence of endometrial carcinoma and a questionable increased incidence of breast cancer. Studies investigating the effect of prolonged hormone use on breast cancer are particularly contradictory and controversial. They should be interpreted with great caution, with particular attention to the kind of estrogen used, doses, and methods of maintaining hormone levels. Many women have used estrogen replacement for decades without adverse affect. If there are no medical contraindications to estrogen replacement, after the singer has been fully informed regarding risks and benefits, there does not appear to be sufficient evidence at present to justify withholding or discontinuing the drugs. Conjugated estrogens (such as Premarin) should be used, and estradiol should be avoided. Medication doses should be minimized and adjusted according to serum estrogen levels, and close medical follow-up is mandatory. Through estrogen replacement and voice therapy/training, singing, speaking, and teaching careers can generally be prolonged for decades.

Under no circumstances should androgens be given to female singers, even in small amounts, if there is any reasonable therapeutic alternative. Clinically, these drugs are now used most commonly to treat endometriosis, decreased libido, or (illicitly) to enhance athletic performance. Androgens cause unsteadiness of the voice, rapid changes of timbre, and lowering of fundamental voice frequency.[21–26] The changes are irreversible. In the past, voices with androgenic damage have been considered "ruined." In our experience, voices are permanently altered, but not necessarily ruined. Through a slow, meticulous retraining process, it has been possible in some cases to return singers with androgenic voice changes to a professional singing career. However, their "new voice" has fewer high notes and fuller low notes than before androgen exposure. In rare instances, androgens may be produced by pathologic conditions such as ovarian or adrenal tumors, and voice alterations may be the presenting symptoms. Rarely, they may also be secreted during an otherwise normal pregnancy. The changes may be similar to premenstrual symptoms or may be perceived as desirable changes. In some cases, alterations produced by pregnancy are permanent.[27,28] Voice changes associated with pregnancy are known as *laryngopathia gravidarum*. In part, they are due to edema of the superficial layer of the lamina propria associated with markedly increased estrogen and progesterone levels that are present throughout pregnancy. Abdominal distention during pregnancy also interferes with abdominal muscle function. Any singer whose abdominal support is compromised substantially should be discouraged from singing until the abdominal disability is resolved. In some singers, this may occur as early as the fourth or fifth month, and some women can support adequately and may sing safely into the ninth month of pregnancy. The individual variations are due to the size and position of the uterus, the size of the woman, the severity of reflux that is commonly aggravated by decreased gastric motility and increased intraabdominal pressure during pregnancy, weight gain, and other factors.

Thyroid Hormones

The thyroid gland regulates protein synthesis and tissue metabolism through the production of thyroid hormones, under the control of thyroid-stimulating and thyrotropin-releasing hormones. Thyroid hormone is also necessary for numerous other normal functions, including growth.

Thyroid disorders are extremely common in clinical practice. It has been estimated that 1.4% of women in the United States have low thyroid function (hypothyroid), and approximately 4% of adult Americans have thyroid nodules.[29] Hypothyroidism is more common in the elderly and often produces symptoms mistaken for aging changes. In general, hypothyroidism causes lethargy, muscle weakness, weight gain, temperature intolerance, dry skin, brittle hair, constipation, menstrual irregularities, muscle cramps, neurological dysfunction, and dysphonia. Hypothyroidism is a well-recognized cause of voice disorders.[30–34] Hoarseness, vocal fatigue, muffling of the voice, loss of range, and a feeling of a lump in the throat may be present even with mild hypothyroidism. Even when thyroid function tests are within the low-normal range, this diagnosis should be considered, especially if thyroid-stimulating hormone levels are in the high-normal range or are elevated. Thyroid evaluation may also require other blood tests, ultrasound, uptake scans, fine needle biopsy, and additional studies not discussed in this book.

The mechanism of voice changes associated with hypothyroidism is not completely understood, especially in cases of mild hypothyroidism. More than 30 years ago, Ritter demonstrated an increased level of acid mucopolysaccharides submucosally in the vocal folds.[31] They probably act as an osmotic diuretic and increase fluid content in the lamina propria. This results in effectively increased vocal fold mass and decreased vibration. In some cases, Reinke's edema may be apparent. In severe hypothyroidism with myxedema, these changes are more profound and may be associated with decreased muscle strength and vocal fold paralysis. Treatment for hypothyroidism depends on the etiology. In most cases, if neoplasm is not present, thyroid replacement is sufficient. However, numerous functions (including voice) should be monitored closely; and otolaryngologists who do not work frequently with thyroid disease should certainly consider collaborative management with an endocrinologist.

Thyrotoxicosis may produce voice disturbances similar to those seen with hypothyroidism.[34] Mild hyperthyroidism does not usually cause voice problems. In advanced thyrotoxicosis, these changes may be due not only to submucosal vocal fold changes, but also to muscle weakness. Thyrotoxicosis may require complex therapeutic intervention, sometimes including medical thyroid ablation with radioactive iodine or total thyroidectomy.

It should also be remembered that the thyroid gland is anatomically related to the recurrent and superior laryngeal nerves. Structural thyroid disorders including goiter, tumor, and thyroiditis may interfere with the voice by causing vocal fold paralysis, impingement of the larynx or trachea, or impairment of vertical laryngeal motion. Similar problems may arise consequent to surgery of the thyroid gland.

Other Hormone Dysfunctions

Hormonal disturbances in other segments of the diencephalic-pituitary system may also result in vocal dysfunction. In addition to the thyroid and the gonads, the parathyroid, adrenal, pineal, and pituitary glands are included in this system. Other endocrine disturbances may alter the voice, as well. For example, thymic abnormalities can lead to feminization of the voice.[35] In addition, pancreatic dysfunction may result in xerophonia (dry voice) as occurs in patients with diabetes mellitus.

Because diabetes mellitus is so common, laryngologists must be particularly familiar with its laryngeal manifestations. In addition to the commonly recognized problems of polyuria, polydipsia, polyphagia, xerostomia, and xerophonia, diabetes is well known to cause microvascular disease and neuropathy. Microvascular occlusion results in tissue death, including muscle atrophy. Neuropathy leads to gradual loss of fine motor control, which may be noticed early by a professional voice user. In advanced states, neuropathy may even cause vocal fold paralysis. Neuropathy also involves the sensory nerves and can impair tactile information needed for voice control. In addition to causing other control problems, sensory deficits may impair or destroy the person's ability to sing "by feel" rather than "by ear" in noisy environments. In addition, diabetes mellitus is associated with an increased rate of infection, generalized fatigue, edema, and other health problems that impair voice function. It is common for the laryngologist attuned to laryngeal manifestations of systemic disease to be the first physician to diagnose diabetes, just as otologists commonly diagnosis diabetics who present with Ménière's syndrome. Maintenance of good vocal health, technique, and hygiene is essential in individuals with diabetes as is good general aerobic conditioning. Proper maintenance of blood glucose levels under the supervision of an endocrinologist is essential, although there is no convincing evidence that good control alters the development of microvascular or neuropathic changes.

Summary

Hormone imbalances and dysfunction commonly affect the voice; dysphonia may be the presenting symptom of serious systemic disease. Laryngologists must be constantly alert for hormonal dysfunction in patients with voice complaints. The collaboration with a skilled endocrinologist interested in the problems of singers and actors is invaluable.

Review Questions

1. The most profound hormonal effects are associated with:
   a. puberty
   b. premenses
   c. pregnancy
   d. menopause
   e. birth control pills

2. Irreversible voice changes are most likely the result of:
   a. laryngopathia premenstrualis
   b. laryngopathia gravidarum
   c. birth control pills
   d. anabolic steroids
   e. progesterone

3. Voice abnormalities due to sex hormones are not encountered in males.
   a. true
   b. false

4. Estrogen levels are highest:
   a. premenstrual
   b. during menses
   c. in the first half of the cycle
   d. at ovulation
   e. in the second half of the cycle

5. Hypothyroidism is associated with all of the following except:
   a. weight loss
   b. temperature intolerance
   c. muffling of the voice
   d. constipation
   e. muscle cramps

References

1. Brodnitz F. The age of the castrato voice. *J Speech Hearing Disord*. 1975;40:291–295.
2. Smith AM. Eunuchs and castrations: *JAMA* faces the music. JAMA 1991;266:655–656.
3. Brodnitz F. Hormones and the human voice. *Bull NY Acad Med*. 1971;47:183–191.
4. Nieschlag E, Nieschlag S, Behre HM. Lifespan and testosterone. *Nature*. 1993;366(18):21.
5. Meuser W, Nieschlag E. Sexuell Hormone und Stimmlage des mannes. *Deutsch Med Wochenschr*. 1977;102:261–264.
6. von Gelder L. Psychosomatic aspects of endocrine disorders of the voice. *J Commun Disord*. 1974;7:257–262.
7. Schiff M. The influence of estrogens on connective tissue. In: Asboe-Hansen G, ed. *Hormones and Connective Tissue*. Copenhagen: Munksgaard Press; 1967: 282–341.
8. Wendler J. Zyklusabhngige leistungsschwankungen der Stimme und ihre Beeinflussung durch Ovulationshemmen. *Folia Phoniatr*. 1972;24:259–277.
9. Lacina V. Der Einfluss der Menstruation auf die Stimme der Sngerinnen. *Folia Phoniatr*. 1968;20:13–24.
10. Rovisky JJ. Maternal physiology in pregnancy. In: Sciarro JJ ed. *Gynecology and Obstetrics*. Vol II. Philadelphia, PA: JB Lippincott; 1990:1–19.

11. Abitbol J, deBrux J, Millot G, et al. Does a hormonal vocal cord cycle exist in women? Study of vocal premenstrual syndrome in voice performers by videostroboscopy glottography and cytology on 38 women. *J Voice*. 1989;3:157–162.

12. Higgin MB, Saxman JH. Variations in vocal frequency perturbation across the menstrual cycle. *J Voice*. 1989;3:233–243.

13. Dordain M. Étude statistique de l'influence des contraceptifs hormonaux sur la voix. *Folia Phoniatr*. 1972;24:86–96.

14. Pahn V, Goretzlehner G. Stimmestörungen durch hormonale Kontrazeptiva. *Zentralb Gynakol*. 1978;100:341–346.

15. Schiff M. "The pill" in otolaryngology. *Trans Am Acad Ophthalmol Otolaryngol*. 1968;72:76–84.

16. Brodnitz F. Medical care preventive therapy (panel). In: Lawrence V, ed. *Transcripts of the Seventh Annual Symposium, Care of the Professional Voice*. New York, NY: The Voice Foundation; 1978:3:86.

17. Wentz AC. Dysmenorrhea, premenstrual syndrome and related disorders. In: Jones HW, Wentz AC, Burnett LS, eds. *Nowak's Textbook of Gynecology*. Baltimore, Md: Williams & Wilkins; 1988:240–262.

18. Andersch B, Milson I. An epidemiologic study of young women with dysmenorrhea. *Am J Obstet Gynecol*. 1982;144:655–660.

19. Isenberger H, Brown WS, Rothman H. Effects of menstruation on the singing voice. Part II: further developments in research. *Transcripts of the Twelfth Symposium: Care of the Professional Voice*. New York, NY: The Voice Foundation; 1983:117–123.

20. Khaw K. The menopause and hormone replacement therapy. *Post-graduate Med J*. 1992;68:615–623.

21. Damste PH, Virilization of the voice due to anabolic steroids. *Folia Phoniat*. 1964;16:10–18.

22. Damste PH. Voice changes in adult women caused by virilizing agents. *J Speech Hearing Disord*. 1967;32:126–132.

23. Saez S, Francoise S. Récepteurs d'androgènes: mise en évidence dans la fraction cytosolique de muqueuse normale et d'épithéliomas pharyno larynges humains. *C R Acad Sci* (Paris). 1975;280:935–938.

24. Vuorenkoski V, Lenko HL, Tjernlund, P Vuorenkoski L, Perheentupa J. Fundamental voice frequency during normal and abnormal growth, and after androgen treatment. *Arch Dis Child*. 1978;53:201–209.

25. Arndt HJ. Stimmestörungen nach Behandlung mit androgenen und anabolen Hormonen. *Münch Med Wochenschr*. 1974;116:1715–1720.

26. Bourdial J. Les troubles de la voix provoqués par la thérapeutique hormonale androgène. *Ann Otolaryngol (Paris)*, 1970;87:725–734.

27. Flach M, Schwickardi H, Simen R. Welchen Einfluss haben Menstruation und Schwängerschaft auf die augsgebildete Gesangsstimme? *Folia Phonatr*. 1968;21:199–210.

28. Deuster CV: Irreversible Stimmestörung in der Schwängerschaft. *HNO*. 1977;25:430–432.

29. Larson PR. The thyroid. In: Wyngaarden JB, Smith LH eds. *Cecil's Textbook of Medicine*. 18th ed. vol 2. Philadelphia, Pa: WB Saunders; 1988:1315–1344.

30. Ritter FN. The effect of hypothyroidism on the larynx of the rat. *Ann Otol Rhinol Laryngol*. 1964;67:404–416.

31. Ritter FN. Endocrinology. In: Paparella M, Shumrick D eds. *Otolaryngology*. vol 1. Philadelphia, Pa. WB Saunders; 1973:727–734.

32. Michelsson K, Sirvio P. Cry analysis in congenital hypothyroidism. *Folia Phoniat*. 1976;28:40–47.

33. Gupta OP, Bhatia PL, Agarwal MK, Mehrotra ML, Mishr, SK. Nasal pharyngeal and laryngeal manifestations of hypothyroidism. *Ear Nose Throat*. 1977;56(9):10–21.

34. Malinsky M et al. Étude clinique et électrophysiologique des altérations de la voix au cours des thyrotoxioses. *Ann Endocrinol (Paris)*. 1977;38:171–172.

35. Imre V. Hormonell bedingte Stimmestörungen. *Folia Phoniat*. 1968;20:394–404.

15

Neurologic Disorders Affecting the Voice in Performance

Robert Thayer Sataloff, Steven Mandel, and Deborah Caputo Rosen

The complex functions necessary for normal voice function require coordinated interactions among multiple body systems. Neurologic dysfunction that impairs control of these interactions commonly causes voice dysfunction. In fact, it is not unusual for voice disorders to be the presenting complaint in patients with neurologic disease. There have been substantial advances in our knowledge of neuroanatomy related to phonation, neurological diagnosis, and treatment of neurologically based voice disorders. It is essential for laryngologists to be familiar with current knowledge and thinking, and to be familiar with new concepts in neurolaryngology.

Neurolaryngology

Neurolaryngology is emerging as a new subspecialty. The first book in this field was published in 1992.[1] Although still in its infancy, the development of neurolaryngology is inevitable. In many ways, the field is analogous to neurotology. In 1960, there was no such field as neurotology. A few years later, Dr William House perfected the translabyrinthine approach for excision of acoustic neuromas. From this humble beginning, neurotology developed as one of the most sophisticated subspecialties in otolaryngology. It came to incorporate not merely elegant and complex surgical procedures, but also diagnostic and therapeutic advances in the management of inner ear, ear-brain interface, and central auditory system abnormalities. Such developments were made possible through the efforts of courageous and creative clinicians and close collaboration with colleagues in other fields such as neurology, neurosurgery, and basic science. Many of the scientists were trained in disciplines that seemed relatively far afield, at first. Biochemists, physicists, physiologists, engineers, and others grouped together at places like the House Ear Institute and the Kresge Hearing Research Institute. Their collaboration produced a vastly expanded understanding of the ear and its related structures, development of a new interdisciplinary subspecialty of physicians dedicated to neurotological problems, and dramatic advances in patient care. Neurolaryngology today stands where neurotology stood when Bill House was thinking seriously about resecting his first acoustic neuroma.

Just as the ear and hearing were fairly well understood 30 years ago, reasonable notions of how the voice works and modest understanding of the central pathways involved in volitional speech and other voice and speech functions exist. Yet, there are great gaps in both knowledge and application. The neuroanatomy and physiology of voice and speech are not fully appreciated and the interactions that constitute control mechanisms are largely undefined. Consequently, many neurogenic problems of voice and speech remain obscure. Even in conditions that are recognized as possibly neurological or neuromuscular in etiology, current treatment approaches seem every bit as crude as the acoustic neuroma surgery of the 1950s. For example, until the last few years spasmodic dysphonia was treated by surgical division of the recurrent laryngeal nerve. Injection with botulinum toxin appears to be an improvement. However, 10 years from now, poisoning muscles with botulinum may appear as barbaric as cutting recurrent laryngeal nerves, if the true nature of the disease process has been discovered. In fact, there are not even standardized surgical procedures for even the most clear-cut neurolaryngologic injury: traumatic recurrent laryngeal nerve paralysis. Reanastamosis or grafting of an injured facial nerve generally results in acceptable function. Why are the results so frequently unsatisfactory after similar procedures with laryngeal nerves? What can be done to restore function? These are fairly basic neurolaryngologic questions. They do not even begin to address issues such as restoration of voice control in people with more complex neurogenic dysfunction, or major surgical challenges such as laryngeal transplantation after laryngectomy, or neurological concomitants of professional voice training.

At this point, neurolaryngology presents many exciting questions, but not enough credible answers. However, given the kind of interdisciplinary interest and collaboration that nurtured neurotology, neurolaryngology promises to develop into an exciting, challenging, and enlightening subspecialty. This maturing field undoubtedly will answer many compelling clinical questions, raise as many exciting new questions, and augment the practice of laryngology as richly as neurotology has altered the practice of otology.

Neuroanatomy and Neurophysiology of Phonation

A comprehensive discussion of the neuroanatomy and neurophysiology of phonation is beyond the scope of this book, and knowledge is being added so quickly that this section would surely be out of date before publication if an all-inclusive discussion were attempted. The brief overview presented in chapter 5 is markedly oversimplified. For example, research has revealed clinically important information about periaquaductal gray matter control of respiration and phonation, premotor cortical control of voluntary respiration, unusual differences in afferent and efferent conduction speed for intercostal and abdominal muscles, effects of auditory feedback on phonation (particularly with regard to frequency), and many other subjects.[2]

Interest in laryngeal evoked brain stem responses (LBR) has emphasized the importance of laryngeal brain stem reflex pathways. For example, the superior laryngeal nerve has neural connections with the nucleus tractus solitarius, nucleus ambiguus, the retrofacial nucleus, the tenth nerve nucleus, and the nucleus of the reticular formation. There are also numerous subcortical and cortical regions involved in laryngeal motor regulation, and possibly involved in laryngeal reflexes. Involved structures appear to include the amygdala, thalamus, hypothalamus, and basal ganglia. This rais-

es the possibility of potentially useful, measurable middle and late latency LBR waves.

In addition, new research methods are resulting in many more discoveries about phonation, including neurological functions. Foremost among these new methodologies is the application of chaos, or nonlinear dynamic theory, to voice research and analysis. This new methodology has already provided clinically important insights, and it has enormous potential to improve our understanding of voice control, function, and dysfunction.[3,4] It is essential for the laryngologist to maintain familiarity with the latest literature in neuroanatomy and neurophysiology so that new scientific insights can be applied clinically as soon as possible. They have already changed the approach and treatment to some neurolaryngologic disorders, and many future refinements are anticipated in the near future.

Neurological Dysfunction and Voice

The remainder of this chapter is dedicated to a discussion of specific neurolaryngologic problems and their effects on voice. This chapter is not intended to be all-inclusive. Many of the more common and important topics have been selected for inclusion, but the reader is encouraged to consult other otolaryngologic, neurologic, and research literature for additional information.

Vocal Fold Paralysis

Vocal fold paralysis may be unilateral or bilateral, central or peripheral and it may involve the recurrent laryngeal nerve, superior laryngeal nerve, or both (Figs 15–1 through 15–4). The physician's first responsibility in any case of vocal fold paralysis it to confirm the diagnosis (visually, with strobovideolaryngoscopy, radiographically, electromyographically, or in other ways), being certain that the laryngeal movement impairment is not caused by arytenoid dislocation, cricoarytenoid arthritis, neoplasm, or other causes, and to determine the etiology.

The true incidence of vocal fold paralysis remains unknown.[5] However, the problem is encountered commonly in clinical practice. Thyroidectomy used to be considered among the most common causes of unilateral vocal fold paralysis. However, improvements in thyroid surgical techniques and the availability of electromyographical monitoring of vocal fold function have markedly decreased the incidence of this complication. Gillen and Benninger reviewed the etiology in 159 patients seen between 1985 and 1991.[6] They found paralysis due to miscellaneous causes (including idiopathic) in 33.9% of patients, nonlaryn-

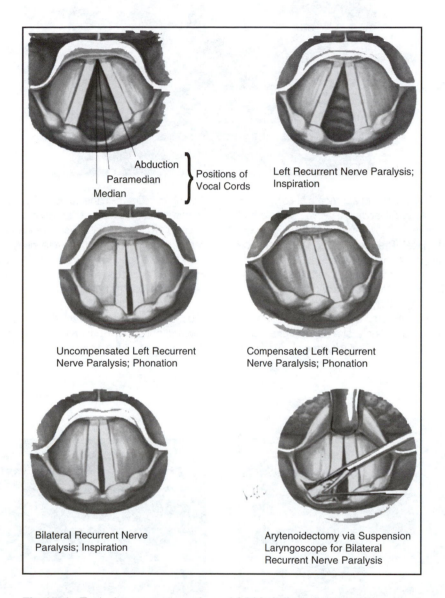

Abduction
Paramedian   } Positions of
Median   Vocal Cords

Left Recurrent Nerve Paralysis;
Inspiration

Uncompensated Left Recurrent
Nerve Paralysis; Phonation

Compensated Left Recurrent
Nerve Paralysis; Phonation

Bilateral Recurrent Nerve
Paralysis; Inspiration

Arytenoidectomy via Suspension
Laryngoscope for Bilateral
Recurrent Nerve Paralysis

Fig 15–1. Typical appearances of vocal fold in cases of recurrent laryngeal nerve paralysis. The illustration in the lower right-hand corner depicts endoscopic arytenoidectomy. This is one procedure to help reestablish an adequate airway for patients with bilateral vocal fold paralysis. However, it does so at the expense of vocal quality. (From The larynx. *Clinical Symposia.* Summit, NJ: CIBA Pharmaceutical Company; 1964: 16(3):Plate VII, © Copyright 1996. CIBA-GEIGY Corporation. Reprinted with permission from the C.I.B.A. Collection of Medical Illustrations, illustrated by Frank Netter, M.D. All rights reserved.)

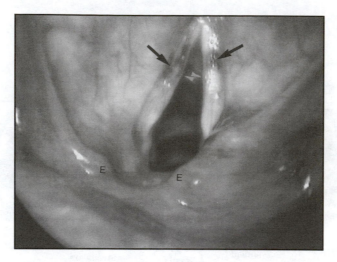

Fig 15–2. Forty-year-old woman with a 2-month history of sudden hoarseness. Right recurrent laryngeal nerve paralysis had been diagnosed. The position of the right vocal fold during abduction in this videoprint is typical. The vocal fold is in the paramedian position, and the height of the vocal process and vibratory margin is normal and the same as the mobile left side. However, this patient had other findings of interest. She had been struggling vocally to compensate for her paralyzed vocal fold. At the time of examination, there were small nodular swellings on both vocal folds *(white arrows)*. Most interestingly, she had bilateral, acute submucosal vocal fold hemorrhages *(black arrows)*. This is not the only case in which the authors have seen this problem, and it serves to illustrate the fact that voice disorders traditionally classified as "hypofunctional" (such as vocal paralysis) do not necessarily protect patients from severe injury from voice abuse. The authors have seen similar findings that occurred during therapy with forced adduction exercises (pushing) at other facilities. Incidental note was also made of arytenoid erythema *(E)*. In this case, it was due to voice abuse rather than reflux. Reflux rarely causes erythema this severe along the aryepiglottic folds and petiolus (not shown); but erythema in these regions is common with severe hyperfunction.

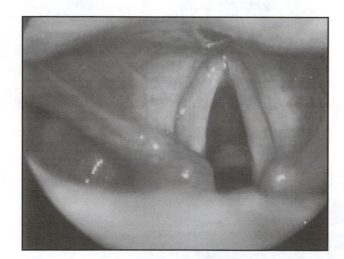

A

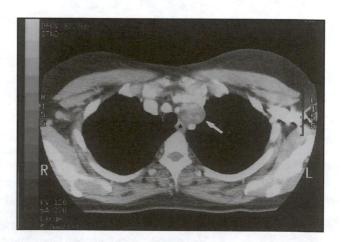

B

Fig 15–3. Videoprint from a 42-year-old teacher who had developed gradually progressive hoarseness and breathiness. **A.** The left vocal fold is abducted, bowed, and flaccid. It appeared short and its longitudinal tension did not increase normally with changes in pitch. A jostle sign was present (the left arytenoid moved passively when contacted by the right arytenoid). Laryngeal electromyography confirmed left recurrent laryngeal nerve paralysis with marked weakness of the superior laryngeal nerve. **B.** A CT scan revealed a left mediastinal mass *(white arrow)*, which proved to be a vagus nerve schwannoma.

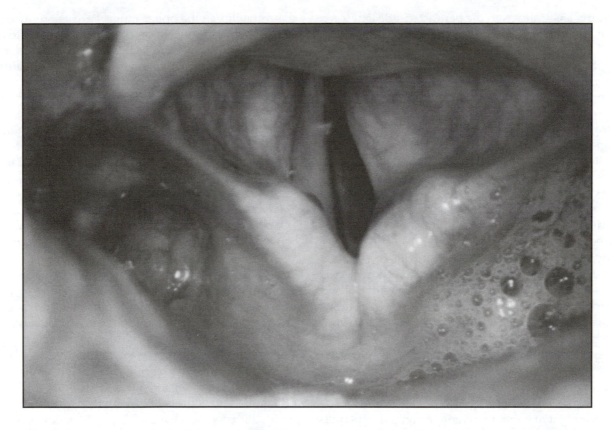

Fig 15–4. Appearance of total right superior and recurrent nerve paralysis, with prolapse of supraglottic tissues partially obscuring the abducted vocal fold, lower vertical position of the paralyzed vocal fold, and pooling of saliva in the right piriform sinus. This is another interesting case of vocal fold hemorrhage occurring in the presence of vocal fold paralysis. The submucosal hemorrhage extends throughout the superior surface of the right vocal fold.

geal malignancy in 24.5%, trauma and nonthyroid surgery in 22.7%, thyroidectomy in 10.1%, and neurologic disorders in 8.8%. These findings are consistent with the authors' experience. Patients more often present to the author (RTS) with paralysis related to thoracic surgery, cervical fusion, and endarterectomy than from thyroidectomy. The laryngologist must always keep in mind more unusual causes, such as cerebral vascular accidents, brainstem tumors, skull base tumors, multiple sclerosis, Lyme disease, and syphilis.

Patients with vocal fold paralysis deserve comprehensive evaluation. Strobovideolaryngoscopy and various objective evaluations are extremely helpful in diagnosis, treatment planning, and assessment of treatment efficacy. They are reviewed in previous chapters of this book, and in other publications.[5] Laryngeal electromyography is especially valuable in distinguishing paralysis from paresis, in confirming clinical infections, and in detecting abnormalities in other laryngeal nerve-muscle complexes that may be missed because of distortion related to the most severe injury. For example, in a total right recurrent nerve paralysis, a left

superior laryngeal nerve paresis will be considerably less obvious than usual. However, such information is important in designing optimal therapy.

Each vocal fold is moved by many intrinsic laryngeal muscles. These muscles permit adduction, abduction, and longitudinal tension of the vocal folds. The vocal folds are supplied by paired laryngeal nerves. The superior laryngeal nerves supply the cricothyroid muscle, which is the primary structure responsible for increasing longitudinal tension. Maintaining stretch of the vocal fold is extremely important for pitch control, volume, and stability during soft singing, especially from the upper midrange up. All of the other intrinsic muscles of the larynx are innervated by the recurrent laryngeal nerves. Paralysis or paresis may involve one or both vocal folds, although only one vocal fold is involved in the vast majority of cases. The superior laryngeal nerve, recurrent laryngeal nerve, or both may be affected. When the recurrent laryngeal nerve is paralyzed, the vocal fold appears to stand still, except for slight respiratory motion. However, longitudinal tension is maintained. So, the vocal folds are at the same level, and even the paralyzed side lengthens as pitch is increased. Consequently, if the normal vocal fold can cross the midline far enough to reach the paralyzed vocal fold, compensation is possible, and glottic closure and reasonably good phonation can be achieved. However, the normal vocal fold can only compensate in the horizontal plane. It cannot move superiorly or inferiorly to meet the injured side if superior laryngeal nerve paralysis is present and has resulted in differences in vocal fold height. After years, atrophy of the thyroarytenoid may occur, making even horizontal compensation more difficult.

When the superior laryngeal nerve is involved, longitudinal tension is impaired and the vocal fold is bowed, or sagging. Consequently, it lies in a lower plane, and compensation is difficult. This is especially true if both recurrent and superior laryngeal nerves are paralyzed, but problems occur even with isolated superior laryngeal nerve. Superior laryngeal nerve paralysis is relatively common, especially after a viral illnesses, particularly those accompanied by a cold sore or "fever blister." Often, paresis or even paralysis of the superior or recurrent laryngeal nerve can resolve spontaneously. Resolution may occur in a matter of days, or may take as long as 12 to 14 months, and medical treatment may help prevent prolonged or permanent dysfunction.

Briefly, if vocal fold paralysis appears to occur below the level of the nodose ganglion, complete evaluation from the skull base through the chest (including the thyroid) is essential. This localization usually can be made reliably in isolated unilateral recurrent laryngeal nerve paralysis. The voice is usually breathy and somewhat hoarse, but it varies among individuals from profoundly dysphonic to essentially normal. If the paralysis is complete (recurrent and superior) or if there are other neurological findings, intracranial studies should be performed, as well. Occasionally, central disease (such as multiple sclerosis) can produce unexpected neurologic signs, and, if no etiology is found after a recurrent laryngeal nerve has been worked up, addition of a magnetic resonance image (MRI) of the brain and other studies should be considered. Because of the seriousness of missing intracranial lesions, many physicians obtain an MRI of the brain and tenth cranial nerve (with enhancement) in all cases; and this practice certainly is not unreasonable. Superior laryngeal nerve paralysis is suspected when one vocal fold lags in adduction and when the larynx is tilted (usually toward the side of the lesion, and more prominently at high pitches). When it is complete, superior laryngeal nerve paralysis usually impairs volume and causes threadiness and crackling in the singer's midrange, and loss of the highest notes

and stability in the upper range. Paresis produces the same symptoms to a lesser degree. In addition to confirmation by electromyography the authors have found three clinical maneuvers particularly useful for making this condition more apparent. Repeated rapid phonation on /i/ with a complete stop between each phonation frequently causes increased vocal fold lag, as the pathologic side fatigues more rapidly than the normal side. Other rapidly alternating instances are also helpful, including /i/-/hi/-/i/-/hi/-/i/-/hi/... and /pʌ/-/tʌ/-/kʌ/-/pʌ/-/tʌ/-/kʌ/ .... The vocal fold lag is sometimes easier to see during whistling. Laryngeal posture during this maneuver provides particularly good visibility of rapid vocal fold motions. The third maneuver is a glissando, asking the patient to slide slowly from his or her lowest to highest note. The vocal process should be observed under continuous and stroboscopic light. If a superior laryngeal nerve is injured, longitudinal tension will not increase as effectively on the abnormal side, disparities in vocal fold length will be apparent at higher pitches, and the vocal folds may actually scissor slightly, with the normal fold being higher. Bilateral superior laryngeal nerve paralysis is often more difficult to diagnose and is probably frequently missed. Patients with this condition have a "floppy" epiglottis, rendering their larynges difficult to see. Their vocal quality, volume, and pitch range are impaired. It is often particularly helpful to confirm a clinical impression of bilateral superior laryngeal nerve paralysis through electromyography.

Treatment for *unilateral* vocal fold paralysis is designed to eliminate aspiration and improve voice. When there is no aspiration, treatment depends on the patient's need and desire for improved voice quality. It is well recognized that recovery of laryngeal nerve function is common if the injury was not caused by transection of the nerve. Even when the nerve is transected, some reinnervation may occur. Consequently, it is best to delay surgical intervention for approximately 1 year, if possible, unless the nerve is known to have been divided or resected. However, this does not mean that therapy should be delayed—only irreversible surgery should be! The collaboration of an excellent speech-language pathologist is invaluable.

Objective voice analysis and assessment by speech-language pathologists specializing in voice are helpful in virtually all patients with voice abnormalities. In people with unilateral vocal fold paralysis, initial assessment not only quantifies and documents vocal dysfunction but also explores a wide range of potentially useful compensatory strategies. Therapy should generally begin as soon as the diagnosis is made. The speech-language pathologist also identifies spontaneous compensatory behaviors that may be counterproductive. For example, although speech pathology textbooks generally classify and treat vocal fold paralysis as a *hypofunctional* disorder,[7,8] undesirable compensatory hyperfunctional behavior is common in these patients. This is responsible for most of the voice strain, neck discomfort, and fatigue that may accompany unilateral vocal fold paralysis. Such gestures can often be eliminated, even during the first assessment and trial therapy session, increasing vocal ease and endurance. Moreover, if the assessment reveals improved voice with a different pitch, training in safe pitch modification in combination with other techniques may also provide rapid improvement. Indeed, under good guidance, therapy sometimes produces astonishingly rapid improvements in voice quality despite persistence of the neurologic deficit. In any case, initial assessment is worthwhile to document vocal condition before surgery is considered and to get an estimate of how much the patient's voice can be improved without surgery.

Most often, initial assessment results in modest but noticeable improvement in voice quality and subjectively important improvement in ease and endurance. Generally, several therapy sessions are needed to optimize vocal function. The speech-language pathologist provides patients with educational information about the workings of phonation, their specific abnormality, and vocal hygiene. The importance of and rationale for therapy are also explained. Therapy is directed toward avoidance of hyperfunctional compensation and progressive development of optimal breathing, abdominal support, and intrinsic laryngeal muscle strength and agility. Training includes head and neck muscle relaxation exercises, aerobic conditioning, abdominal and thoracic muscle strength and control exercises, attention to respiration, and various voice exercises that build limb strength through multiple repetitions with light weights. Forced adduction exercises, often recommended in speech-language pathology texts,[7,8] such as pushing or pulling on chairs, must be avoided or monitored closely and used with extreme caution. Although such exercises are still in fairly common use, other techniques may be more effective and have less potential for harm. When available, traditional voice therapy combined with a few expert singing lessons may expedite improvement. This is akin to including jogging or running in a rehabilitation program aimed at improving limb strength for walking.

Like surgery, therapy is least successful in combined paralysis. In the majority of patients with unilateral vocal fold paralysis, therapy results in voice improvement. In many cases, the improvement is sufficient for the patients' needs. When patients have complied with voice therapy, improvements have

reached a plateau, and they feel that their voice quality is not satisfactory, surgery may be indicated.

If preoperative voice therapy has been optimal and if surgery has been successful, the postoperative voice therapy course should be short. Nevertheless, the patient is working with a "new voice." At least a few sessions with a speech-language pathologist generally will help the patient apply effective principles learned in preoperative therapy. It is particularly important for the voice therapist to monitor the patient, avoiding development of abusive habits and stressing the importance of vocal hygiene measures. At the conclusion of therapy, objective voice measures should be repeated.

If the patient is interested in optimizing voice quality, it is reasonable to continue therapy as long as it continues to produce voice improvement. This judgment is usually made jointly by the patient, speech-language pathologist, and laryngologist. In most patients who have had good preoperative voice therapy, this point is reached within 1 to 3 months after surgery.

Bilateral vocal fold paralysis creates much greater problems; this is true for bilateral recurrent, bilateral superior, or bilateral combined nerve paralysis, or combinations thereof. There is still no satisfactory treatment for bilateral recurrent nerve paralysis. Frequently, this condition leaves the patient in the uncomfortable position of choosing between good voice and tracheotomy, or good airway and bad voice. Therapy may provide some help to these patients, but it is rarely definitive. Hopefully, laryngeal pacing will be developed within the next few years and may provide a solution to these problems. If so, there will be an important role for the voice therapist, working with patients after pacemaker implantation.

Voice therapy is invaluable in the management of vocal fold paralysis. In all cases, the speech-language pathologist can provide detailed pre- and postoperative assessment. Such assessment is often of diagnostic value. It is also of great help to the surgeon for objectively evaluating the efficacy of treatments. In addition, voice therapy sometimes avoids the need for surgery, saving the patient from exposure to unnecessary surgical risks. Even when surgery eventually is required, preoperative voice therapy helps the patient while surgical decisions are pending, provides training for optimal postoperative phonation, and prepares the patient psychologically for surgery with the knowledge that everything possible has been done to avoid unnecessary operative intervention. This results in superior patient cooperation, motivation, and understanding through educated participation in the voice restoration process. The importance of preoperative voice therapy should not be overlooked in terms of both the art of medicine and medical legal prudence. Surgery for vocal fold paralysis is discussed in chapter 49 of *Professional Voice: The Science and Art of Clinical Care.*

Dysarthria

Dysphonia is voice disturbance, usually involving a problem at the level of the larynx. *Dysarthria* means imperfect articulation in speech. This little-understood condition is actually symptomatic of a group of disorders related to strength, speed, and coordination involving the brain and the nerves and musculature of the mouth, larynx, and the respiratory system as they relate to speech. Because of the importance of articulation in professional voice users, neurological problems that cause dysarthria may present initially as speech or voice complaints.

The causes of dysarthria can be vascular, metabolic, motor, traumatic, or infectious. Dysarthria is always clearly exhibited in speech and will commonly affect a person's voice training. It is never rooted in a language deficit.

The span of dysarthria is great. It can be acute, as in stroke; transient, as with a single episode of unknown cause; slowly progressive, as in neurologic disease, such as Parkinson's; or rapidly progressive, due to metabolic causes or infection.

Physicians should be familiar with neurogenic voice disorders, dysarthrias, and dysphonias. They should understand the diagnostic significance of each of the six types of dysarthria and their symptoms.[9,10] *Flaccid dysarthria* occurs in lower motor neurons in primary muscle disorders such as myasthenia gravis and tumors or strokes involving the brain stem nuclei. *Spastic dysarthria* is found in upper motor neuron disorders (pseudobulbar palsy) such as multiple strokes and cerebral palsy. *Ataxic dysarthria* is seen with cerebellar disease, alcohol intoxication, and multiple sclerosis. *Hypokinetic dysarthria* accompanies Parkinson's disease. Hypokinetic dysarthria may be spasmodic, as in the Gilles de la Tourette syndrome, or dystonic, as in chorea and cerebral palsy. *Mixed dysarthria* is seen in amyotrophic lateral sclerosis. Dysarthria may affect the tongue, lips, mandible, and phonation or respiration. When dysarthria involves the larynx, it affects phonation; when it involves the velopharynx, it affects resonance; and when it involves the tongue, lip, or mandibular area, it affects articulation. The classification above actually combines *dysphonic* and *dysarthric* characteristics, but it is very useful clinically.

In addition to the articulation dysfunctions described above, the clinician should be familiar with specific voice characteristics associated with various neurologic deficits. They can be elicited through careful examination including a variety of voice tasks (running speech, rapidly varying speech, sustained phonation, and other maneuvers). The type of voice associated with lesions producing flaccid dysfunction depends on the site of the lesion. Flaccid paralysis from a problem located high in the vagus nerve typically produces a very breathy, whispered voice with hypernasal resonance. A lower vagus nerve lesion (recurrent laryngeal nerve, below the nodose ganglion) produces no resonance defect, but a hoarse, breathy voice, associated with diplophonia. Spastic conditions due to lesions in the corticobulbar region of the brain bilaterally produce hypernasal resonance and a hoarse, strained voice. Combined spastic and flaccid signs occur when bilateral corticobulbar lesions are present in addition to tenth nerve paralysis. This combination results in hypernasal resonance, vocal flutter, and a strained voice with hoarseness and crackling from poorly controlled secretions on the vocal folds. Cerebellar lesions associated with ataxia usually do not affect resonance, but they cause vocal tremor and irregularities. Hoarseness and breathiness are not present typically. Parkinson's disease provides the classic example of hypokinetic dysfunction. It is associated with lesions in the basal ganglia and causes a soft, breathy voice with little pitch variability, but fairly normal resonance. Basal ganglia lesions are also responsible for dystonias and choreas. Dystonic disorders are frequently accompanied by a hoarse, strained voice with vocal arrests similar to those seen in adductor spastic dysphonia; and resonance may be hypernasal or normal. In chorea, vocal arrests are the most prominent vocal feature. Brain stem lesions produce two typical voice abnormalities. One is *essential (organic) tremor.* This condition involves a regular voice tremor occurring at a rate of approximately 7–10 times per second (although rates as slow as 4 per second may occur), with interruptions reminiscent of abductor or adductor spastic dysphonia. Visible tremor in the head or neck and elsewhere is common. The other is *action myoclonus,* in which rapid, machine gun-like voice arrests can be heard on sustained vocalization. In contrast, *palatopharyngeal myoclonus* produces regular voice arrests so slow that they may be missed in running speech without careful examination. They occur at about 1–4 times per second, and are associated with obvious myoclonic contractions of the larynx and related structures. This condition is believed to be due most commonly to lesions in the region of the dentate, red, and inferior olivary nuclei. Recognition of these disordered voice characteristics may lead the astute clinician to an early diagnosis of important and treatable neurological disease. The value of a comprehensive neurolaryngological evaluation cannot be overstated.[11,12]

Cranial nerve involvement with dysarthria is characterized by a disability in movement, referred to as *hypokinetic* (decreased movement), *kinetic* (altered movement), or *hyperkinetic* (increased movement). Hyperkinetic dysarthria causes increased tone or flow with lack of inhibition, known as dystonia or dyskinesia, that is, involuntary movements. The hypokinetic type will be exhibited as monotone and slowed speech.

Ataxic dysarthria, an irregular, articulatory breakdown in speech, is exhibited as excess stress the voice. Multiple sclerosis, with most commonly a young adult age of onset, can have ataxic dysarthria as one of the earliest signs. Ataxic dysarthria can also affect the tongue, causing it to appear to have decreased control, and affecting sounds heavily dependent on the tongue. Spinal nerves can also cause problems in phonation, if, for example, cervical nerves or muscles are affected or weakened. Flaccid dysarthria will present as an inability to move the mandible or as a drooping mouth. The unilateral type will involve drooping on one side; bilateral conditions will affect both sides.

Factors contributing to dysarthria are multifaceted. Some causal conditions are serious. Others are minor. Many are amenable to treatment. The observant voice care professional may be the first to recognize such a problem, by observing the person's smile, tongue movements, swallowing patterns, breathing patterns, and facial expressions. Can the person whistle? move the tongue in a wide range of motion? puff and inhale cheeks? Abnormalities in movement and/or inability to articulate may lead to early diagnosis of numerous serious problems.

Diagnosing neurological problems responsible for dysarthria can be complex. The physician considers the age of onset, type of speech abnormality, constancy versus intermittency, progression (slow, rapid or none), and other factors. When indicated, various tests are also helpful in determining the cause of the problem. In many cases, medications improve the condition and may even eliminate the dysarthria. In others, the physician's ability to determine the site of lesion permits guidance for the development of compensatory strategies that permit improved speaking and singing. The patient's response to medication and other treatment may also be helpful in confirming the diagnosis.

Spasmodic Dysphonia

Since spasmodic dysphonia is encountered only occasionally in professional voice users, the subject will be reviewed briefly in this chapter.

Spasmodic or spastic dysphonia is a term applied to patients with specific voice sounds as described below. These patients have a variety of diseases that produce the same vocal result. There are also many interruptions in vocal fluency that are incorrectly diagnosed as spasmodic dysphonia. It is important to avoid this error, because different types of dysphonia require different evaluations and carry different prognostic implications. Spasmodic dysphonia is subclassified into *adductor* or *abductor* types.

Adductor spasmodic dysphonia is characterized by hyperadduction of the vocal folds, producing an irregularly interrupted, effortful, strained staccato voice. It may be neurologic, psychogenic, or idiopathic in etiology, and its severity varies substantially among patients and over time. It is generally considered a focal dystonia. In many cases, the voice may be normal or more normal during laughing, coughing, crying, or other nonvoluntary vocal activities, or during singing. Adduction may involve the true vocal folds alone, or the false vocal folds and supraglottis may squeeze shut. Because of the possibility of serious underlying neurologic disease or association with other neurologic problems such as seen in Meige's syndrome (blepharospasm, medial facial spasm, and spasmodic dysphonia), a complete neurologic and neurolaryngological evaluation is required. Adductor spastic dysphonia may also be associated with spastic torticollis (wry neck) and extrapyramidal dystonia, although the condition was previously believed to be psychogenic.

Abductor spasmodic dysphonia is similar to adductor spasmodic dysphonia except that voice is interrupted by breathy, unphonated bursts, rather than constricted and shut off. Like adductor spasmodic dysphonia, various causes may be responsible. The abductor spasms tend to be most severe during unvoiced consonants, better during voiced consonants, and absent or least troublesome during vowels. Both abductor and adductor spastic dysphonia characteristically gradually progress, and both are aggravated by psychological stress.

After comprehensive evaluation to rule out organic causes, treatment for spasmodic dysphonia should include voice therapy. Adductor spastic dysphonia is much more common, and most therapy and surgical procedures have been directed at this form. Unfortunately, traditional voice therapy is often not successful. Speaking on inhalation has worked well in some cases. Patients who are able to sing without spasms but are unable to speak may benefit from singing lessons. The author (RTS) has used singing training as a basic approach to voice control and then bridging the singing voice into speech. In a few patients, medications such as Baclofen (Warner Chilcott) or Dilantin (Parke Davis) have also been helpful, but these patients are in the minority. When all other treatment modalities fail, various surgical techniques have been used. Recurrent laryngeal nerve section produces vocal fold paralysis and initially improves spastic dysphonia in many patients. However, there is a high incidence of recurrence. Other surgical techniques that alter vocal fold length and modify the thyroid cartilage may also be efficacious in selected cases. A new procedure that sections only the branch of the recurrent nerve to the thyroarytenoid muscle is particularly promising. However, the most encouraging treatment for patients disabled by severe spasmodic dysphonia is Botulinum toxin injection. At present, this is usually done with electromyographic guidance, and the technique produces temporary paralysis of selected muscles. This results in temporary relief or resolution of the spasmodic dysphonia. However, the injections need to be periodically repeated in most patients.

Vocal Tremor

Voice tremors require comprehensive neurologic evaluation. One of the most common causes is essential tremor, also know as *benign heredofamilial tremor*. This may be associated with tremors elsewhere in the body, or it may involve the voice only. Although a small number of patients will improve somewhat with medication, in most instances, this tremor cannot be treated effectively. Before making a diagnosis of essential tremor, however, it is important to rule out serious conditions such as cerebellar disease, Parkinson's disease, psychogenic tremor, thyrotoxicosis, or drug-induced tremor.

Parkinson's Disease

Parkinson's disease is one of the most common movement disorders affecting persons over age 55 today, with a prevalence of up to 1 in 1000. Parkinson's disease is a progressive movement disorder which is caused by degeneration of the substantia nigra resulting in decreased dopamine availability. The primary etiology of Parkinson's disease has not been determined. Depression has been reported in approximately 30% of patients with Parkinson's disease; and dementia has also been described.[13] As the disease progresses, patients experience increasing difficulty with verbal, speech, and motor skills. It causes rigidity, characteristic tremor, and movement disorders, including bradykinesia (slowed movement), hypokinesia (reduced movement), akinesia (difficulty initiating movement), gait difficulty, and postural instability.

Prosody, the melody of language, as it relates to pitch, loudness, and duration, are all eventually affected by Parkinson's disease. The person will often exhibit increased or prolonged silent hesitation with speech. Control of sentence duration can become impaired. The disorder can cause jaw problems which, in turn, may affect speech. In fact, jaw functioning is often within normal range, but the speed with which the jaw moves is greatly reduced. Additionally, reduced lip movements will also factor into voice performance. Parkinson's disease may also impact upon lung function, causing irregular chest wall movements while the individual performs vowel prolongation and syllable repetitive tasks. Nasal airflow will be affected, changing the individual's ability to produce nasal consonants.

The signs and symptoms are subtle in the early stages. Because Parkinson's does not progress quickly and is highly variable in its progression and staging, it may take up to 10 years to reach a stage in which the person is unable to function for normal daily activities. Performance impairment may come much sooner.

Time-tested, new, and experimental medications and treatments are available not to cure but to arrest the progression of this disease. Parkinson's disease is treated primarily by pharmacotherapy including anticholinergic medications, preparations of L-dopa (a dopamine agonist), and amantadine hydrochloride which stimulates the release of dopamine from the remaining intact dopaminergic neurons. Dopamine receptor agonists such as Parlodel, (bromocriptine HCl) MAO (monoamine oxidase) inhibitors and, occasionally, neuroleptic drugs are prescribed. These drugs have potential effects on mood, cognition, and perception. Surgical treatments have been used in some settings to decrease the symptoms of Parkinson's disease. These include lesioning specific areas of the brain (pallidotomy, thalatomy) and tissue implantation into the striatum. Other neurologic diseases mimic the symptoms of Parkinson's disease, but their descriptions are beyond the scope of this chapter. Specialized voice therapy has proven extremely effective in overcoming many of the voice and speech problems associated with later stages of the disease, as illustrated in extensive research by Dr Lorraine Ramig.[14–17]

Postpolio Syndrome

Postpolio syndrome may cause neuromuscular abnormalities beginning years after recovery from acute poliomyelitis.[18–20] Often, symptoms first develop nearly 30 years after an acute episode.[18] The syndrome is characterized by gradually declining muscle strength. Muscle biopsies and electromyography generally reveal signs of new and chronic denervation. The neurons lost are associated with disintegration of the terminals of individual nerve axons, rather than with loss of motor neurons as seen in amyotrophic lateral sclerosis. Cerebrospinal fluid analysis may show oligoclonal bands, but there is no evidence of in situ antibody production to polio virus at the time of diagnosis of post-polio syndrome.[18] Postpolio syndrome may include hoarseness. Of the three patients described recently, two had bilateral vocal fold paresis and one had unilateral abnormalities.[21]

Stuttering

Multiple areas of the nervous system can cause stuttering alone or in combination; and stuttering can be due to many causes, including developmental, psychogenic, and neurogenic. Developmental stuttering appears to be the most frequent, with onset usually early in life. However, when stuttering occurs in later life, it may be the presenting sign of a brain lesion and requires neurological evaluation before it can be ascribed to developmental or psychogenic causes.

Stuttering is also not a common problem among professional voice users and is discussed widely in speech-language pathology and neurology literature. It is interesting to note, however, that stuttering rarely affects the singing voice. Consequently, even people with severe stuttering in speech have had successful professional singing careers. Botulinum toxin has been tried as a treatment for some stutterers.

Myasthenia Gravis

Myasthenia gravis is a disease of the myoneural junction. Ordinarily, nerve endings release acetylcholine, which depolarizes the end plate of the muscle fiber, causing excitation and muscle contraction. In myasthenia gravis, the muscle fails to depolarize either because of insensitivity of the muscle end plate, a defect in acetylcholine released from the nerve ending, or both. Ordinarily, acetylcholine is destroyed rapidly by acetylcholinesterase. Myasthenia gravis occurs most commonly in women in their 20s and 30s and in men in their 50s and 60s. The prognosis is better in young women. Although muscles of swallowing, respiration, the limbs, and ocular muscles are involved most commonly, virtually all areas of the body may be affected by myasthenia. Localized disease is well recognized and may involve only one eye, for example. Myasthenia gravis may also be isolated to the larynx. This results in rapid voice fatigue, breathiness, moderate hoarseness, and loss of range. In professional voice users, voice dysfunction may also be the first

symptom the patient notices of more widely disseminated myasthenia.

Myasthenia gravis should be in the physician's differential diagnosis whenever the complaint of voice fatigue is present, although it is only rarely the cause. A history of weakness elsewhere in the body makes one more suspicious. Although the strobovideolaryngoscopic findings have not yet been reported in the literature, the authors have observed varying neurologic abnormalities in the larynx. For example, when myasthenia is suspected, patients are examined early in the morning when they are well rested. A mild laryngeal asymmetry may be noted, such as a lag in adduction of one vocal fold. The patient is then instructed to vocalize actively until marked fatigue develops and the strobovideolaryngoscopic examination is repeated. Changing abnormalities are observed, such as markedly slower adduction on the opposite side, bilateral failure of complete adduction, and other changes from the time of the examination at rest. In some people, the fluctuating neurological asymmetries are apparent almost immediately. Such patients may appear initially to have, for example, right superior laryngeal nerve paresis. A few minutes later during the same examination, the paresis may appear to have switched to the left side. This kind of fluctuation should make the laryngologist suspicious enough to order appropriate studies to rule out myasthenia gravis.

Laboratory and other tests assist the diagnosis. Blood should be evaluated for levels of antistriatal muscle antibody and antiacetylcholine receptor antibody. A Tensilon test is helpful. The voice should be fatigued prior to the Tensilon test and should be recorded before and during the test. Unless the consultant neurologist is used to working with the laryngologist in such cases, he or she should be warned that a Tensilon test has been requested. Most neurologists are not equipped to perform the test in the office routinely, although arrangements can be made easily with advanced warning. Imaging studies to rule out thymoma are required if the diagnosis is confirmed. Electromyography with repetitive stimulation tests often establishes the diagnosis. The disease can usually be treated well with pyridostigmine bromide (Mestinon) and long-term steroid therapy can usually be avoided. Careful training in speech and singing is essential, because nearly all professional voice users with this problem develop undesirable vocal habits in vain attempts to compensate for vocal impairment before the diagnosis is made. Good technique must be established in conjunction with disease control. In some instances, thymectomy is appropriate. Because of the risk of injury to the recurrent laryngeal nerves, it is best to avoid this procedure in professional voice users when possible.

Other Neurological Conditions Affecting Voice Performance

Many conditions that do not involve the larynx or even the vocal tract directly may adversely affect performance. Physicians must be familiar with the consequences of neurological dysfunction. Important conditions include not only major neurological problems such as quadriplegia, but also more common disorders such as headache, facial paralysis, dizziness, and other disorders that impair memory, concentration, and optimal athletic function.

Amyotrophic Lateral Sclerosis

Amyotrophic lateral sclerosis (ALS) is a degenerative, progressive, and fatal disease involving motor neurons of the cortex, brain stem, and spinal cord.[13,22] The etiology is unknown. Mean onset age is 56 years, and the disease is twice as common in men as in women. Vogel and Carter report that, in 50% of all cases, death occurs within 3 years after identification of the symptoms; approximately 10% of the patients survive up to 10 years, and some patients live as long as 20 years after diagnosis.[13] The entire body is eventually involved, and communication is impaired by a mixed spastic-flaccid dysarthria with severe compromise of speech intelligibility. A number of drugs have been tried in the treatment of ALS, but all have been disappointing. The initial therapeutic effects of the drugs are eventually overcome by the progression of the disease. Speech-language pathologists treat these patients with interventions designed to improve communication and instruction in the use of augmentative communication devices as the disease progresses. Prostheses for palatal lift and surgical interventions using pharyngeal flaps have also been used.

Multiple Sclerosis

Multiple sclerosis (MS) is a disease of the central nervous system that involves loss of myelin and lesions in the cerebral cortex, brain stem, cerebellum, or spinal tracts. The diagnosis of MS is based on history and the diagnostic appearance of the brain on magnetic resonance imaging. Cerebrospinal fluid may demonstrate abnormal immunoglobulin production, oligoclonal bands, or myelin breakdown products. The disease is characterized by exacerbations and remissions. Five to 10% of patients develop a more chronic progressive illness.[13] The cause of multiple sclerosis is unknown, but it is clearly an autoimmune disease in which the helper T-cells attack and destroy myelin. Unfortunately, early in the disease progression when neurologic

abnormalities are minimal, many of these patients are diagnosed as anxious, depressed, hypochondriacal, or somatosizing. Both sensory and motor abnormalities appear as the disease progresses. Speech may eventually manifest a mixed flaccid, spastic, and/or ataxic dysarthria.

There is currently no known cure for multiple sclerosis, and drug therapy focuses on reducing the number of attacks of demyelination or reducing the damage caused by each attack. Speech-language pathologists treat these patients to enhance intelligibility, and some patients may also undergo physical therapy for ataxia, tremor, and muscle weakness. Psychotherapy to address the associated depression, emotional lability, and occasional psychosis which may be the result of the disease or the drug therapy will be an integral part of these patients' treatments.

Huntington's Chorea

Huntington's disease (Huntington's chorea) is an inherited disorder characterized by degeneration in the striatum (the caudate and putamen). The defective gene is carried on chromosome four. Onset is usually between the ages of 25 and 45 years, with an average duration of 15 years. Death usually occurs in the middle-50s.[13] Symptoms include involuntary tics and twitching which gradually evolve into chorea with rapid, jerky, semipurposeful movements, usually in the extremities. In the later stages, the movements become grotesque contortions, and dementia develops and progresses. The disease is diagnosed by history, genetic findings, and characteristic abnormalities of CT and MRI of the brain. There is no cure, and drug therapy is offered for the suppression of involuntary movement. The drugs themselves commonly cause extra-pyramidal symptoms and may also produce tardive dyskinesia.

Gilles de la Tourette Syndrome

Gilles de la Tourette syndrome is a dual neurological and psychiatric diagnosis. It is often familial, and onset may be as early as the first year of life. The median age at onset is 7 years. Tourette's syndrome is characterized by multiple motor and one or more vocal tics which worsen intermittently during the life of the affected individual. They tend to become more intense in periods of stress. Obsessive-compulsive behaviors may also coexist. Patients with Tourette's syndrome sometimes have dysphagia with incoordination of swallow. Vocal tics include involuntary sounds such as grunts, clicks, yelps, barks, sniffs, coughs, screams, snorts, and coprolalia (the uttering of obscenities) which is present in up to 50% of cases.[13,22,23] Drug therapy utilized in the treatment of Tourette's syndrome includes neuroleptics, klonidine and pimozide. Patients with Tourette's syndrome usually benefit from stress management techniques since emotional overload often increases the frequency and intensity of the tics.

Cerebrovascular Accident

Cerebrovascular accident (CVA or stroke) is a sudden, rapid onset of a focal neurologic deficit caused by cerebrovascular disease. Blood supply to the brain is disrupted, resulting in damage which affects the function of the part of the brain nourished by the damaged blood vessel. There are two primary mechanisms for a CVA: cerebral ischemia from cerebral thrombosis or cerebral embolism, or intracranial hemorrhage. Some patients experience stroke-like symptoms which last for minutes or hours and then resolve. This is referred to as a transient ischemic attack (TIA). Strokes produce sudden loss of neurologic function including motor control, sensory perception, vision, language, visuo-spatial function, and memory.[13] CVAs cause a wide variety of communication difficulties including aphasia, dysarthria, and cognitive impairment. The features and extent of communication impairment depend on the site of lesion.

Treatment of CVA may include the use of thrombolytic agents to degrade clots, anticoagulants to prevent further clot formation, rehabilitative services including physical and occupational therapy, and speech-language therapy. Patients who have experienced CVA and their families require psychological support and care. This is ordinarily provided during the acute and rehabilitative phases of treatment. Neuropsychologists may perform formal testing batteries, prescribe and implement cognitive rehabilitation, and offer psychotherapy for treatment of the affective consequences associated with such significant changes in level of function.

Quadriplegia

Abdominal muscle support is essential for singing and acting. Therefore, it would seem that quadriplegia following a cervical fracture would end a professional singing career, and possibly an acting career. Sataloff et al described the rehabilitation of a quadriplegic professional singer in 1984.[24] Since that report, the singer has been able to continue a limited recording career and occasional public and television appearances, and he is now able to do so without the device which was designed for him. In studying this patient and other quadriplegic people deprived of voice support, frequent problems with voice fatigue and decreased volume, range, and projection are encountered. The degree of dysfunction and potential for rehabilitation are dependent particularly on the level of the lesion. Additional activity in therapy and research should provide greater insights into the best methods to help the voices of quadriplegic patients in general and to restore performance ability to quadriplegic professional voice users. In addition, quadriplegic patients provide scientists with an opportunity to observe the consequences of consistent, drastic reduction in the support mechanism.

Facial Paralysis in Singers and Actors

Facial paralysis is a relatively common affliction, and it can be devastating for a singer or actor. Facial paralysis creates cosmetic and functional deficits that may be extremely troublesome. Usually, the condition involves one side of the face. If the muscles cease working altogether, the condition is facial *paralysis*. If the muscles are merely weak, the condition is facial *paresis*. In this chapter, we will use the word paralysis to refer to complete paralysis or severe paresis. This condition results in drooping of one side of the face, inability to close the eye (which exposes it to dryness and injury), and incompetence of the corner of the mouth, which may cause drooling of liquids, and difficulty articulating some sounds.

One of the principal problems of facial paralysis is a widespread tendency in many sectors of the medical community to underevaluate the problem, and to misdiagnose it. In 1821, Sir Charles Bell studied the innervation of the facial musculature and named the motor nerve of the face the facial nerve. Soon, all conditions of facial paralysis came to be known as Bell's palsy. As time passed, the true cause of many cases of facial paralysis was discovered. *Bell's palsy* is now the name used to describe only cases of facial paralysis in which the cause cannot be determined. Unfortunately, many physicians still diagnose "Bell's palsy" without going through the comprehensive evaluation necessary to diagnose and treat important causes of facial paralysis. A proper evaluation includes a complete history; careful physical examination of the ears, nose, throat, neck, and parotid gland; at least a partial neurological examination; imaging studies (usually CT scan and MRI); hearing tests; electrical facial nerve tests; and blood tests. These tests are designed to detect the cause of the problem. If none is found, the condition may properly be called Bell's palsy. Patients with Bell's palsy always recover, at least partially; although recovery may take as long as a year. If the face remains paralyzed without recovery of facial function, the diagnosis of Bell's Palsy is generally wrong, and the true cause should be sought again.

There are many etiologies of facial paralysis, and this chapter will provide a brief overview of only a few of them. Facial paralysis can be *congenital*. That is, some people are born with paralysis of one side or both sides of the face. This problem may result from various causes ranging from syndromes to brain dysfunction to forceps trauma.[25] *Acquired* facial paralysis is much more common. Infection and inflammation are well established causes. The infection may be viral, particularly herpetic and is often associated with a herpetic cold sore or fever blister. This problem may also involve the hearing nerve, which runs in close proximity to the facial nerve. Viral or bacterial infections of the ear (otitis media) or brain (meningitis) also cause facial paralysis, as do Lyme disease and AIDS. Facial paralysis has also been associated with toxic effects from exposure to heavy metals such as lead, and the immunologic response after injections for tetanus, rabies, and polio. Metabolic conditions, including diabetes, hypothyroidism, and pregnancy, may precipitate facial paralysis, as well. So may blood vessel problems associated with vasculitis, some of which may accompany arthritis syndromes. Trauma is also an important cause of facial paralysis, particularly temporal bone fracture associated with motor vehicle accidents or falls, and surgical trauma (facial paralysis is a potential complication of ear, brain, or parotid gland surgery). Paralysis of any cranial nerve can be a presenting sign of a generalized neurological disorder. This must be suspected especially if more than one cranial nerve is involved.

In addition, facial paralysis may be the first presenting sign of a tumor. The tumor may be benign or malignant. It may occur anywhere along the course of the facial nerve, which starts in the brain stem, courses circuitously through the ear encased in a tight bony canal, exits the mastoid bone at the skull base, and spreads out along the face. Tumors of the facial nerve itself (facial neuromas) commonly present with facial paralysis. So do cancerous tumors of the middle ear, parotid gland, and upper neck. For this reason alone, if for no other, a thorough, systematic evaluation is required in any patient with facial paralysis until a diagnosis has been established with the greatest possible degree of certainty. Tumors, and many of the other conditions discussed above, are potentially treatable, if they are discovered soon enough.

Treatment for facial paralysis depends on the cause. If a specific disease or tumor is identified, it is treated appropriately; and in many cases facial function can be restored. If no cause is found, and the condition is truly Bell's palsy, various treatments are available. The medical specialists most involved in caring for facial paralysis are neurotologists. Most of us specializing in facial nerve disorders base our treatment recommendations for Bell's palsy on electrical testing of the facial nerve called, *electroneuronography*. Treatment may involve observation, use of high-dose steroids, or surgery. Surgery is always a last resort. However, it should be considered if electrical excitability decreases by 90% or more; if facial paralysis is sudden, total, and associated with severe pain; and in selected other situations. In general, if recovery from facial paralysis begins within 3 weeks, it is excellent and total. If recovery does not start until after 3 months, it is usually imperfect. In these cases, the nerve usually develops some degree of synkinesis, that is, inappropriate neuromuscular function caused by aberrant reinnervation. This results, for example, in a slight smiling of the lips when the person closes his or her eyes. "Crocodile tears" and "gustatory sweating" result similarly from misdirected nerve fibers that should have gone to salivary glands. Hence, when the person eats, tears fall from the eye, and the side of the face perspires. These problems can often be minimized with early, accurate diagnosis.

Headache

Headache is one of the most common complaints in American medicine. An estimated 10–20% of the population have suffered from severe headaches at one time, and approximately 8 to 12 million Americans have suffered from migraine headaches. An even larger number have a variety of additional headache complaints, including muscular tension headaches, and headaches from more serious sources. Even an occasional headache can be annoying, as most of us know. However, chronic, recurring headaches may be more than annoying. Headaches may interfere with concentration, impair a person's ability to memorize scores, distract the singer or actor enough to impair performance, and create many other impediments to a performing career, or any other occupation. They can certainly undermine the effectiveness of voice lessons or therapy, and headaches may be a common cause of absenteeism.

Although many headaches are secondary to stress, many serious causes also exist. Consequently, it is important for the voice professional with frequent and/or severe headaches to seek expert evaluation (usually a neurologist) and to pursue the tests necessary to achieve an accurate diagnosis. Fortunately, many headaches can be treated, usually with medications that do not impair performance. An overview of the most common, and most important causes of headaches is helpful in understanding the complexity and diversity of this problem.

The first step in the evaluation of a headache sufferer is to obtain the history. One must ascertain whether the headaches are of recent onset or of long duration. If they are of recent onset, one should ask what are the associated symptoms, such as blurring of vision, dizziness, numbness and tingling, and the localization of the headache. Is it associated with any nasal discharge? Does it occur as an explosion, suggesting a subarachnoid hemorrhage? Is there fever associated with the headache, which would indicate a meningitis? Has there been a history of any recent dental infections, ear infections, or recent viral illness? Has there been contact with other individuals who may have had headaches?

When headaches have been present for a long period of time, several questions need to be asked. Are they recurrent? Are they getting worse? Have there been any changes of personality? What brings on the headaches? Can they be associated with changes in body position or allergies?

One should question what brings on the headache, what may provide relief, associated symptoms, what treatment the patient has received, and special implications regarding the headache. Are there problems with work? Does it interfere with concentration, or bring on anxiety? Is the medication used to treat headaches intolerable because of tiredness, nausea, stomach upset, or difficulty concentrating?

What are the different types of headaches and the symptoms that may accompany them? Migraine headaches are episodic. They usually affect one side of the head, but the affected side can vary. They are pounding, frequently accompanied by nausea, and there can be visual changes. Patients may experience diarrhea, palpitations, or feelings of coldness. The pain may last for 48 hours and the scalp may be tender to the touch.

Classic migraines present with an aura preceding the headache by up to 30 minutes. This may be accompanied by scintillating scatoma where visual fields may be obscured or there may be spots before the eyes. There can also be diplopia or problems with speech, such as the inability to say words or transient paresis. The aura provides warning time during which medicines may be taken to ward off the headache.

In common migraines, the aura is not present. The implication for patients with common migraine is that there is no warning time during which one can take medication to abort the headache. Complicated migraine can be associated with attacks of blindness, hemiplegia, and aphasia. Migraine can lead to stroke with permanent neurological deficit. This can occur as part of a migraine attack or be precipitated by the use of ergotamine drugs.

Chronic daily headaches can be associated with prolonged tension or migraine headaches. Many of these headaches are precipitated by over-the-counter analgesics as part of a withdrawal syndrome. Opioids can be used inappropriately and this also can lead to withdrawal symptoms and ongoing headache complaints as a "drug withdrawal headache syndrome" leading to chronic daily headaches.

Cluster attacks occur generally at night, but can also occur during the day either at a regular time interval or randomly. The pain is usually around the eye on one side; but it then can spread to the jaw, shoulder, face, and neck. Patients have a tendency to walk around banging their heads and squeezing their scalps, as compared with migraine patients who cannot tolerate even the stimulation of a dimly lit room. These headaches can last up to 2 hours, can occur once or twice a day, or 10 times per day. They last for weeks to months, and then there is a remission for months or years. The patients' eyes may water, and they may feel as if their nose is blocked. This condition is eight times more common in males than in females. Some patients with cluster headaches can also have migraine headaches in combination. Other individuals can have episodic attacks of vertigo, tinnitus, and even deafness as associated manifestations of a cluster or a migraine headache. Some individuals can have speech disturbances or difficulty expressing themselves as part of a migraine attack. They may have dysarthria or slurring of words, difficulty reading, confusion, or experience transient pareses not followed by the headache. This is called migraine aura without headaches and is also thought to be a migraine equivalent.

Headaches can be related to exertion, sports, and even sexual intercourse. Many of these patients have either a history of migraine or a family history of migraine. Some exertion headaches can be benign, with the etiology obscure, or they may be seen in patients with brain tumors, subdural hematomas, and vascular malformations. Patients can have a cough headache. Once again, these can be benign or indicative of underlying masses or vascular malformations. Joggers or football players can have severe headaches, generally associated with the start of a fitness program. Coital cephalalgia has been described related to sexual activity. It can develop suddenly, occurring before and after intercourse, and is most commonly benign, although subarachnoid hemorrhage following orgasm has been reported.

Of great relevance for the singer and actor are allergic headaches. Migraine headaches can occur occasionally after eating or exposure to various drugs or allergens. It has been found that, in most patients who have allergies as well as migraine, the allergies do not cause the migraine, although occasionally the allergic rhinitis, thickening of the nasal membrane, and pressure within the sinuses can precipitate a migraine attack. Certain foods and beverages such as coffee, tea, chocolate, alcoholic beverages, hot dogs, Chinese foods, cheeses, or liver can bring about a migraine attack. Migraine headaches can also be precipitated by hypoglycemia, by not eating, and by withdrawal from caffeine.

Muscle contraction headaches, or tension headaches, are described as pressure in the head or a vise-like attack. They can be unilateral or bilateral. Patients may be under a great deal of stress and tend to abuse over-the-counter medication.

Headaches can occur from underlying cerebral problems, such as cerebrovascular disease. In subarachnoid hemorrhage, pain is described as very severe, generally the worst headache of their lives. The headache comes on suddenly, and only rarely evolves over hours. There may be problems with vision, including blurring of vision, or dull vision, confusion, or changes in the level of consciousness. On examination, there may be significant neck rigidity. This kind of headache requires immediate neurologic attention including CT scan studies and lumbar puncture.

Cerebral hemorrhages are frequently associated with hypertension. This headache may not be severe, but it is generally present in addition to more localized neurologic findings such as weakness, numbness, visual changes, unsteadiness, vertigo, and speech difficulties, out of proportion to the extent of the headache itself.

Headaches of infectious origin, including meningitis, usually proceed rapidly and develop over hours. They may be in the front or back portion of the scalp radiating to the neck, and they are increased with activity. They may also be associated with fever, nausea, vomiting, and confusion. Lumbar puncture is usually required as well as a CT scan.

Patients with AIDS and other HIV-related conditions can present with headaches, changes in mental status, or focal neurologic findings. This headache or a focal neurologic complaint can be the presenting symptoms of an opportunistic central nervous system infection or malignancy that requires urgent neurologic evaluation. The headache or the focal neurological complaint can be the presenting symptom.

Brain tumors have accompanying headache in 60–90% of individuals. The pain associated with this is dull, deep, aching, intermittent, and generally worse in the morning. Vomiting may also be associated. The pain is generally not as severe as the migraine headache. There might not be localization to the site of the underlying tumor. Postural changes may increase the episodic nature of the headache in some cases.

Intracranial pressure has been associated with increased headache in young individuals. The entity to be most considered is benign intracranial hypertension, or pseudotumor cerebrii. Patients may have headaches with visual disturbance such as blurring of vision, or double vision, and the headache may be present for several weeks, with more severe pain in the early morning. Diagnosis is made by CAT scan and lumbar puncture.

Following trauma, various types of headache syndromes can occur. For example, a patient can have postconcussion syndrome with headache, dizziness, cognitive difficulties, hypersensitivity to light and sound, anxiety, nervousness, and changes in libido. Trauma can induce migraine or even clusterlike headaches. Patients can have similar headaches with cervical whiplash (with or without underlying cervical disc disease) producing headaches that can begin in the occiput and radiate to the front portion of the scalp. One also has to be aware that even minor trauma can precipitate the development of a subdural hematoma. Subdural hematomas especially occur in those patients who are alcoholic or epileptic, or are taking anticoagulants, including aspirin.

There are several neuralgias one should consider when diagnosing headache. Patients with post-herpetic neuralgia (following herpes zoster infection) can develop facial pain which mimics tic douloureux or occipital neuralgia (pain in the back of the scalp), superior laryngeal neuralgia, or glossopharyngeal neuralgia (associated with syncope and cardiac arrhythmias). These patients develop symptoms such as pain in the throat (Fig 15–5) or ear with trigger zones within the tonsillar area or pharyngeal region. Pain may also be triggered by swallowing, speaking or singing. In some instances, patients with post-herpetic neuralgias have no recollection of ever having had a skin lesion. If symptoms are constant rather than intermittent, a structural cause must be sought diligently.

Headaches can occur secondary to ear infection. They can also be caused by tumors within the ear, acoustic neuromas, and even barotrauma from an air flight. Toxins and metabolic causes can occur secondary to acute mountain sickness. This has been estimated to occur in 50% of mountain hikers. Patients on a variety of medications can suffer from headaches, and headaches may also be associated with the consumption of various foods. Headaches can also occur secondary to substance withdrawal, alcohol withdrawal or consumption, dental pain, or endocrine conditions related to hypoglycemia, menses and menopause, birth control pills, or pituitary tumors. Headaches can be accompanied by seizure-like activity, and anemia, as well as more serious problems in some instances.

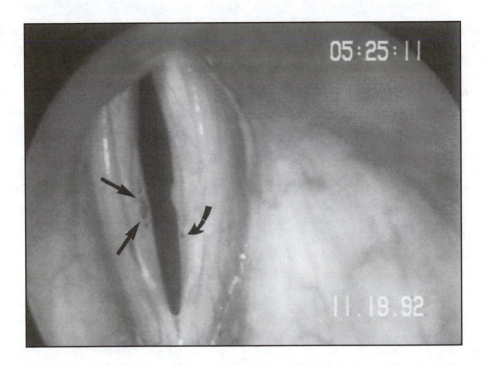

Fig 15–5. This videoprint came from a 35-year-old college professor who developed severe pain when speaking. The pain was localized in the larynx, and was severe enough to interfere with her ability to function as a college professor. It had started following an upper respiratory infection accompanied by laryngitis. The hoarseness resolved but the pain persisted. Vocal fold varicosities had been diagnosed elsewhere. Laser surgery had been recommended as a treatment for her pain. She came to us for a second opinion. Our examination revealed a small varicosity on her left vocal fold *(curved arrow)* and a cluster of varicosities with a surrounding blush on her right vocal fold *(straight arrows)*. However, vocal fold vibration was normal, and her voice was normal. We considered the varicosities asymptomatic. A diagnosis of atypical pain (probably postviral neuralgia) was established, and the patient was treated with Tegretol. No surgery was performed. Her pain disappeared promptly, returned when she stopped the medication because of planned pregnancy, and resolved again when Tegretol was resumed after delivery.

In summary, we need to recognize subtleties in the history of headaches, and their implication for either benign or serious origins. The headache itself, the underlying neurologic or other medical condition, and the treatment can lead to problems in daily performance, including voice performance. Headaches can also produce anxiety, which can lead to interference with a person's ability to function in competitive employment. Severe recurrent or persistent headache deserves thorough, expert evaluation, and should never be minimized or neglected.

Dizziness

Dizziness can affect anyone. Sometimes imbalance develops gradually. Sometimes, it can strike suddenly, even on stage. Loss of equilibrium is not only extremely frightening, but it can also impair a performer's ability to walk and move effectively for an indefinite period of time. Dizziness is often associated with ear problems. However, the ear is only one part of the balance system. Evaluation of disequilibrium disorders is extremely complex, and often not managed well.

The terms *dizziness* and *vertigo* are used by patients to describe a variety of sensations, many of which are not related to the vestibular system. It is convenient to think of the balance system as a complex conglomerate of senses that each send the brain information about one's position in space. Components of the balance system include the vestibular labyrinth, the eyes, neck muscles, proprioceptive nerve endings, cerebellum, and other structures. If all sources provide information in agreement, one has no equilibrium problem. However, if most of the sources tell the brain that the body is standing still, for example, but one component says that the body is turning left, the brain becomes confused and we experience dizziness. It is the physician's responsibility to systematically analyze each component of the balance system to determine which component or components are providing incorrect information, and whether correct information is being provided and analyzed in an aberrant fashion by the brain.

Typically, *labyrinthine dysfunction* is associated with a sense of motion. It may be true spinning, a sensation of being on a ship or of falling, or simply a vague sense of imbalance when moving. In many cases, it is episodic. Fainting, light headedness, body weakness, spots before the eyes, general light-headedness, tightness in the head, and loss of consciousness are generally not of vestibular origin. However, such descriptions are of only limited diagnostic help. Even some severe peripheral (vestibular or eighth nerve) lesions may produce only mild unsteadiness or no dizziness at all, such as seen in many patients with acoustic neuroma. Similarly, lesions outside the vestibular system may produce true rotary vertigo, as seen with trauma or microvascular occlusion in the brain stem, and with cervical vertigo.

Dizziness is a relatively uncommon problem in healthy individuals. In contrast to a 24% incidence of tinnitus, Sataloff et al found only a 5% incidence of dizziness in their study of 267 normal senior citizens.[26] However, the general population is not as healthy as this selected sample. Five to 10% of initial physician visits involve a complaint of dizziness or imbalance, accounting for over 11 million physician visits annually.[27] Dizziness is the most common reason for a visit to a physician in patients over 65 years of age. Approximately one third to one half of people age 65 and older fall each year, and the consequences can be serious.[28] Falls result in approximately 200,000 hip fractures per year, and this injury carries a 10% mortality rate. Falls are the leading cause of death by injury in persons over 75 years old. Dizziness is also a common consequence of head injury. Over 450,000 Americans suffer serious head injuries annually.[29] A majority of these persons complain of dizziness for up to 5 years following the injury, and many are disabled by this symptom.[30] Dizziness may also persist for long periods of time following minor head injury.[31]

However, causes of dizziness are almost as numerous as causes of hearing loss, and some of them are medically serious (multiple sclerosis, acoustic neuroma, diabetes, cardiac arrhythmia, etc.). Consequently, any patient with an equilibrium complaint needs a thorough examination. For example, although dizziness may be caused by head trauma, the fact that it is reported for the first time following an injury is insufficient to establish causation without investigating other possible causes.

It is important to pursue a systematic inquiry in all cases of disequilibrium not only because the condition is caused by serious problems in some patients, but also because many patients with balance disorders can be helped. Many people believe incorrectly that sensorineural hearing loss, tinnitus, and dizziness are incurable; but many conditions that cause any or all of these may be treated successfully. It is especially important to separate peripheral causes (which are almost always treatable) from central causes such as brain stem contusion in which the prognosis is often worse.

Vestibular disturbance may be suspected with a history of vertigo described as motion, particularly if associated with tinnitus, hearing loss, or fullness in the ear. However, even severe peripheral disease of the eighth nerve or labyrinth may produce vague unsteadiness rather than vertigo, especially when caused by a slowly progressive condition such as acoustic neuroma. Similarly, central disorders such as brain stem vascular occlusion may produce true rotary vertigo typically associated with the ear. Therefore, clinical impressions must be substantiated by thorough evaluation and testing.

One of the most common causes of peripheral vertigo is Ménière's disease. The vertigo is classically of sudden onset, comparatively brief in duration, and reocurs in paroxysmal attacks. During the attack it generally is accompanied by an ocean-roaring tinnitus, fullness in the ear, and hearing loss. Pitch distortion (diplacusis) is common and may cause significant problems for singers. Occasionally, there may be some residual imbalance between attacks, but this does not happen often. Similar symptoms may accompany inner-ear syphilis and certain cases of diabetes mellitus, hyperlipoproteinemia, or hypothyroidism.

Another type of vertigo associated with an abnormality in the inner ear is being recognized more frequently. In Benign Positional Paroxysmal Vertigo (BPPV), the attack often occurs briefly with sudden movements of the head. Classically, there is a slight delay in onset, and if the maneuver is repeated immediately after the vertigo subsides, subsequent vertiginous responses are less severe. It generally is not associated with deafness or tinnitus. The posterior semicircular canal is most often the source of the difficulty.

Therapy for this condition is symptomatic. Vestibular exercises help more than medications. When the condition is disabling, it may be cured surgically by dividing all or part of the vestibular nerve. In most cases, hearing can be preserved. If the problem can be localized with certainty to one posterior semicircular canal, an alternative surgical procedure called *singular neurectomy* may be considered. Benign positional paroxysmal vertigo must be distinguished from *cervical vertigo*. Cervical vertigo is another common cause of disequilibrium, especially following head or neck trauma, including whiplash. The condition is usually associated with neck discomfort, spasm in the posterior neck musculature, limitation of motion, and dizziness when turning or extending the head. Cervical vertigo is often misdiagnosed as BPPV. Although the symptoms may be similar, the treatments are different, and prescribing vestibular exercises for cervical vertigo patients may actually make symptoms worse. Certain viruses such as herpes classically produce vertigo by involving the peripheral end-organ. The attack usually is of sudden onset, associated with tinnitus and hearing loss, and it subsides spontaneously. In the absence of tinnitus and hearing loss, the virus is assumed to have attacked the nerve itself; this condition is called *vestibular neuritis*. Certain toxins also readily produce vertigo.

Whenever a patient complains of vertigo and there is evidence of chronic otitis media, it is essential to determine whether a cholesteatoma is present that is eroding into the semicircular canal and causing the vertigo. Vertigo can also be present with certain types of otosclerosis that involves the inner ear. In all such cases the specific cause of the vertigo should be determined, and whenever possible, proper therapy based on the specific cause should be instituted. Perilymph fistula as a cause of vertigo is particularly amenable to surgical treatment.

In cases in which the labyrinth has been completely destroyed on both sides, some patients develop oscillopsia. That is, the horizon bounces when they walk. This is a particularly disturbing symptom and is very difficulty to treat. Fortunately, it is uncommon.

Disequilibrium involving the central nervous system is an urgent problem and must be ruled out in every case, especially in cases in which it is associated with other symptoms outside the ear.

Certain symptoms strongly suggest that the cause of the vertigo must be sought in the central nervous system. If spontaneous nystagmus (flickering eye movement) is present and persists, the physicians should look for associated neurological signs such as falling. This is especially true if the condition has persisted for a long time. If the rotary vertigo is associated with a loss of consciousness, the physicians should suspect also that the vertigo originates in the central nervous or cardiovascular system. The association of intense vertigo with localized headache makes it mandatory to rule out a central brain lesion. Among the common central nervous system causes of vertigo are vascular crises, tumors of the posterior fossa, multiple sclerosis, epilepsy, encephalitis, and concussion.

The dizziness in a vascular crisis is of sudden onset and generally is accompanied by nausea and vomiting as well as tinnitus and deafness. This is a form of stroke. In many instances there is involvement of other cranial nerves.

It is also possible to have a much more discrete vascular defect in the vestibular labyrinth without an involvement of the cochlea. This usually results in an acute onset of severe vertigo. Recovery is rather slow, and the vertigo may persist as postural imbalance. The nystagmus may subside, but unsteadiness and difficulty in walking may continue much longer.

A still milder form of vascular problems related to dizziness occurs in hypotension and vasomotor instability. People with these problems have recurrent brief episodes of imbalance and instability, particularly after a sudden change of position such as suddenly arising from tying their shoelaces or turning quickly. Many such maneuvers are required during opera and theater performance. This condition requires evaluation and management by an internist and is potentially treatable by increased salt intake, sodium retention medications, and beta blockers.

In multiple sclerosis, vertigo is commonly a symptom, but it is rarely severe enough to confuse the picture with other involvement of the vestibular pathways. In epilepsy, vertigo occasionally may be a premonitory sensation before an epileptic attack, but unconsciousness usually accompanies the attack and helps to distinguish the condition.

A complaint of vertigo in post-concussion syndrome is extremely common. The vertigo usually is associated with movement of the head or the body, severe headache, and marked hypersensitivity to noise and vibration. The patients usually are jittery, tense, and very irritable.[30]

Basilar artery compression syndrome is another condition associated with head motion, particularly neck extension. It is due to compression of the basilar artery with resultant interference with blood flow to the brain stem. This diagnosis cannot be made with certainty without objective confirmation through arteriography or other tests.

Carotid sinus syndrome and psychic disturbances frequently produce vertigo that may be confused with vertigo of vestibular origin. Taking a careful history and testing the carotid sinus make it possible to distinguish these conditions.

Of special interest to the otologist is the dizziness that sometimes is associated with a lesion of the posterior cranial fossa and particularly with an acoustic neuroma. It is a standing rule in otology that, when a patient complaints of true vertigo, an acoustic neuroma must be ruled out. This is especially true when the vertigo is accompanied by a hearing loss or tinnitus in one ear. Vertigo is not always a symptom in all posterior fossa lesions, but when it occurs, a number of simple tests help to establish the possibility that a tumor is present.

Other occasional causes of dizziness include encephalitis, meningitis, direct head injuries, and toxic reactions to alcohol, tobacco, or other drugs such as streptomycin.

Evaluation of the dizzy patient is extremely involved and will not be reviewed in this chapter. It includes taking a complete history; a thorough physical examination including neurological assessment, blood tests, radiologic tests (such as CT, MRI, and SPECT); hearing tests; and balance tests. Otolaryngologists subspecializing in neurotology are particularly expert in the evaluation and treatment of balance disorders, although other specialists, particularly neurologists, are often involved, too. Many patients with disequilibrium can now be helped. In some cases, the problem can be cured. This treatment may involve medicine, surgery, physical therapy, or other modalities, depending on the cause of the problem.

When disequilibrium occurs in professional voice users, especially singers or actors, every effort must be made to determine its cause and cure or minimize the symptoms to avoid disturbing interference with performance, and potentially serious safety hazards during maneuvers on stage.

Summary

Numerous other neurologic disorders may affect voice performance. Familiarity with the latest concepts in neurolaryngology, clinical voice disorders, and a close working relationship between laryngologists and neurologists optimize treatment for the many patients with these troublesome problems.

Review Questions

1. Vocal fold paralysis is commonly caused by each of the following except:
   a. thyroidectomy
   b. other surgery
   c. unknown causes
   d. neurologic disorders
   e. voice abuse

2. After accurate diagnosis, the first step in the treatment of vocal fold paralysis is voice therapy.
   a. true
   b. false

3. A voice disturbance usually involving a problem at the level of the larynx is called:
   a. dysphonia
   b. dysarthria
   c. dysmetria
   d. dysgeusia
   e. dyspepsia

4. Parkinson's disease is typically characterized by:
   a. flaccid dysarthria
   b. spastic dysarthria
   c. hypokinetic dysarthria
   d. ataxic dysarthria
   e. mixed dysarthria

5. All of the following typically affect the neurologic motor function of the voice except:
   a. myasthenia gravis
   b. amyotrophic lateral sclerosis
   c. polio
   d. multiple sclerosis
   e. vocal nodules

References

1. Blitzer A, Brin M, Sasaki CT, Fahn S, Harris K, eds. *Neurologic Disorders of the Larynx*. New York, NY: Thieme Medical Publishers, Inc; 1992.
2. Davis P, Fletcher N, eds. *Vocal Fold Physiology: Controlling Chaos and Complexity*. San Diego, Calif: Singular Publishing Group; 1996.
3. Sataloff RT, Hawkshaw M, Bhatia R. Medical applications of chaos theory. In: Davis P, Fletcher N, eds. *Vocal Fold Physiology: Controlling Chaos and Complexity*. San Diego, Calif: Singular Publishing Group; 1996.
4. Sataloff RT, Hawkshaw MJ. *Chaos in Medicine: Source Readings*. San Diego, Calif: Singular Publishing Group; in press.
5. Benninger MS, Crumley RL, Ford CN, Gould WJ, Hanson DG, Ossoff RH, Sataloff RT. Evaluation and treatment of the unilateral paralyzed vocal fold. *Otolaryngol Head Neck Surg*. 1994;111(4):497–508.
6. Gillen J, Benninger MS. The changing etiology of vocal fold immobility. Presented at the Triologic Society, Middle Section Meeting; January, 1994; Ottawa, Ontario, Canada.
7. Aronson AE. *Clinical Voice Disorders*. 3rd ed. New York, NY: Thieme Medical Publishers, Inc; 1990:339–345.

8. Greene MCL, Mathieson L. *The Voice and Its Disorders.* 5th ed. London: Whurr Publishers; 1989:305–306.

9. Darley F, Aronson AE, Brown JR. Differential diagnosis of patterns of dysarthria. *J Speech Hearing Res.* 1969;12: 246–249.

10. Darley F, Aronson AE, Brown JR. Clusters of deviant speech dimensions in the dysarthrias. *J Speech Hearing Res.* 1969;12:462–496.

11. Rosenfeld DB. Neurolaryngology. *Ear Nose Throat J.* 1987;66(8):323–326.

12. Aronson AE. *Clinical Voice Disorders.* 2nd ed, New York: Thieme Medical Publishers, Inc; 1985:77–126.

13. Vogel D, Carter J. *The Effects of Drugs on Communication Disorders.* San Diego, Calif: Singular Publishing Group, Inc; 1995:30–90.

14. Ramig LO, Scherer RC. Speech therapy for neurologic disorders of the larynx. In: Blitzer A, Brin MF, Sasaki CT, Fahn S, Harris KS, eds. *Neurological Disorders of the Larynx.* New York, NY: Thieme Medical Publishers; 1992: 163–181.

15. Ramig LO. The role of phonation in speech intelligibility: a review and preliminary data from patients with Parkinson's disease. In: RD Kent, ed. *Intelligibility in Speech Disorders.* Philadelphia, Pa: John Benjamins Publishing Co; 1992:119–156.

16. Ramig LO, Scherer RC, Titze IR, Ringel SP. Acoustic analysis of voices of patients with neurologic disease: rationale and preliminary data. *Ann Otol Rhinol Laryngol.* 1988;97:164–172.

17. Ramig LO. Speech therapy for patients with Parkinson's disease. In: Koller W, Paulson G, eds. *Therapy of Parkinson's Disease.* New York, NY: Marcel Dekker; in press.

18. Dalakas MC, Elder G, Hallett M, et al. A long-term follow up study of patients with post-poliomyelitis neuromuscular symptoms. *N Engl J Med.* 1986;314:959–963.

19. Agre JC, Rodriquez JC, Taffel JA. Late effects of polio: critical review of the literature on NM Fx. *Arch Phys Med Rehab.* 1991;72:923–931.

20. Harmon RL, Agree JC. Electrodiagnostic findings in patients with poliomyelitis. *PMR Clinics of North Am.* 1994;8:559–569.

21. Hillel AD, Robinson L, Waugh P. Management of post-polio laryngeal weakness. Presented at the Pacific Voice Conference; October 20–21, 1995; San Francisco, Calif.

22. Andrews M. *Manual of Voice Treatment: Pediatrics through Geriatrics.* San Diego, Calif: Singular Publishing Group, Inc; 1995:268–270.

23. American Psychiatric Association. *Diagnostic Statistical Manual of Mental Disorders—IV.* Washington, DC: American Psychiatric Association. 1994:71–73.

24. Sataloff R T, Heuer RJ, O'Connor MJ. Rehabilitation of a quadriplegic professional singer. *Arch Otolaryngol.* 1984;110(10):682–685.

25. Sataloff RT. *Embryology and Anomalies of the Facial Nerve.* New York, NY: Raven Press; 1991.

26. Sataloff, J, Sataloff RT, Lueneberg W. Tinnitus and vertigo in healthy senior citizens with no history of noise exposure. *Amer. J. Otol.* 1987;8(2);87–89.

27. US Dept of Health and Human Services, Public Health Services; Washington, DC: 1978. National Center for Health Statistics Series 13, No. 56.

28. Jenkins HA, Furman JM, Gulya AJ, Honrubia V, Linthicum FH, Mirko A. Dysequilibrium of aging. *Otolaryngol Head Neck Surg.* 1989;100:272–282.

29. Head injury: hope through research. Washington, DC: US Dept of Health and Human Services; 1989. Publication NIH 84-2478.

30. Gibson WPR. Vertigo associated with trauma. In: Dix, ed. *Vertigo,* Somerset, NJ: John Wiley and Sons; 1984.

31. Mandel S, Sataloff RT, Schapiro S. *Minor Head Trauma: Assessment, Management and Rehabilitation.* Springer-Verlag; New York, NY: 1993.

16

Performing Arts-Medicine and the Professional Voice User: Risks of Non-Voice Performance

Robert Thayer Sataloff and Mary Hawkshaw

The developing specialty of arts-medicine is extremely valuable for voice professionals. It is useful for the physician caring for professional vocalists to be aware of developments in related fields.[1] Through the National Association of Teachers of Singing, the *Journal of Singing*, the *Journal of Voice*, The Voice Foundation Symposia, and many other sources, enlightened singing teachers have become familiar with recent advances in the care of professional voice users. Many of these arose out of interdisciplinary teamwork, and new insights have resulted in better methods of history taking, physical examination, objective voice measures, and wider availability of educational information about the voice. These have produced better informed, healthier singers. Although voice-medicine is the most advanced area of arts-medicine, there are several other specialties that may be helpful during a singing career. As singers must often be actors, dancers, pianists, and do other jobs as well, it is useful for singers and singing teachers to be aware of developments in related fields.

What Is Different About Arts-Medicine?

For physicians, arts-medicine and sports-medicine pose special interests, challenges, and problems. Traditional medical training has not provided the background necessary to address them well. Consequently, development of both fields has required understanding and interaction among physicians, performers (or athletes), and members of other disciplines. Such

cooperation and interaction have taken so long to develop because of language problems. For example, when a singer complains of a "thready midrange," most doctors do not know what he or she is talking about. To the traditional physician, if such a singer looks healthy and has "normal" vocal folds on mirror examination, he or she is deemed normal by the physician. Medicine in general enjoys a broad range of physical condition that is considered "normal." The biggest difference we encounter in arts and sports-medicine is the patient's sophisticated self-analysis and narrow definition of normal. In general, doctors are not trained to recognize and work with the last few percent of physical perfection. The arts-medicine specialist is trained to recognize subtle differences in the supranormal to near-perfect range in which the professional performer's body must operate. To really understand performers, physicians must either be performers themselves or work closely with performers, teachers, coaches, trainers, and specific paramedical professionals. In voice, this means a laryngologist working with a singing teacher, voice coach, voice trainer, voice scientist, speech-language pathologist, and often other professionals. In other fields, the specialties vary, but the principles remain the same.

Hand-Medicine

After voice-medicine, hand-medicine is the second most advanced specialty of arts-medicine. Like vocalists' problems, problems of pianists, violinists, harpists, and other instrumentalists who depend on their hands are treated best by a team. An arts-medicine hand clinic usually includes a hand specialist (usually a surgeon), physical therapist, radiologist, and perhaps music coaches, teachers, and trainers. Facilities are available to observe the musician while playing his or her instrument, as many problems are due to subtle technical quirks. Hand-medicine really catapulted arts-medicine to public prominence. A great many musicians have health problems. A self-completion questionnaire study of the 48 affiliate orchestras of the International Conference of Symphony and Opera Musicians (ICSOM)[2] resulted in return of questionnaires by 2,212 of the 4,025 professional musicians studied. Of the musicians responding, 82% reported medical problems, and 76% had a medical problem that adversely affected performance. Many of these musicians have problems caused or aggravated by musical performance. Yet, until the past few years, this was not widely known, and musicians were afraid to admit their difficulties for fear of losing work. Moreover, those who did seek medical attention usually were disappointed with the evaluation and results. World-class pianist Gary Graffman changed all of that almost single-handedly. When he developed difficulty controlling his right hand, he persevered until he found a physician who was willing to look at the possibility that his problem was caused by his piano playing. Together, they came to understand his overuse syndrome. When Graffman made his difficulties known to the general public and Leon Fleischer followed suit, thousands of musicians discovered they were not alone and began seeking help. Gradually, the medical profession has learned to provide the care they need. Moreover, far-sighted music schools like the Curtis Institute, which Graffman directs, are beginning to incorporate scientifically based practice and development techniques in their curricula.

Vague incomplete control over one's hands at the keyboard or on the strings is one of the primary symptoms of overuse syndrome. This often comes from excessive, ineffective practicing with unbalanced muscle development, which may result in nearly crippling problems that end an instrumentalist's career. Chronic pain is also a common concomitant symptom. In an early paper, Hochberg et al.[3] reported that the most common hand complaints among musicians were (in order): pain, tightening, curling (drooping or cramping), weakness, stiffness, fatigue, pins and needles, swelling, temperature change, and redness. They resulted in loss of control and decreased facility, endurance, speed, or strength; and tension. Many of the musicians with these problems had either stopped playing, altered their practice, or changed their fingering, technique, or repertoire. Some of them also had

related problems in their forearms, elbows, upper arms, or shoulders. Arts-medicine centers now provide accurate diagnosis and helpful treatment for most of the conditions that cause these problems, if they are diagnosed early. Hand problems are not limited to pianists, violinists, and harpists, of course. For example, clarinetists often develop pain in the right thumb from the weight of the instrument and the position used to hold it up.

Orthopedics and General Arts-Medicine

Like swimmer's shoulder and tennis elbow in sports-medicine, many instruments produce localized pain. Among the most common are cymbalist's shoulder, flutist's forearm, and guitarist's nipple. Brass players may develop problems in their lips, jaws, tongue, and teeth. Changes in tooth alignment, which may follow dental wear, work, or injury, also present special and potentially disabling problems for wind players in whom embouchure is critical. There are arts-medicine specialists in the field of dentistry who are especially skilled at handling such problems. Wind players may also develop pharyngoceles or laryngoceles that present as large airbags in the neck, which stand out as they play. They sometimes interfere with performance and require treatment.

Performance-related problems may also occur in other parts of the performer's body. For example, neck and back problems are almost routine in violinists and violists. Skin abrasions and even cysts requiring surgery occur under the left side of the jaw at the contact point of the instrument in many string players. Dermatologic problems also occur in flutists. Lower back pain is also a problem in many instrumentalists, especially in pianists who sit on benches without back support for 8 hours of practice. In many performers, such problems exist throughout a career. In established performers, they are often precipitated by illness or slight changes in technique of which the performer may be unaware. Skilled analysis in an arts-medicine center can now usually help.

Dance-Medicine

Ballet and modern dance are among the most demanding of all athletic pursuits. Various forms of popular and show dancing, and especially break dancing, also place enormous demands on the body. The stresses caused by unusual positions (such as dancing sur les pointes), hyperextension, and leaps and lifts result in injury. In young dancers, hip injuries are especially common. Ankle, foot, and lower leg problems are more common in older dancers. Even a mild muscle strain may interfere with performance for weeks or months and may produce minor technical changes that predispose to other injuries. Major injuries such as rupture of the Achilles tendon also occur. Stress fractures in the hips, legs, and feet, which cause persistent pain, are often missed on x-ray but can now be diagnosed early with computerized tomography or bone scan.

The aesthetic requirements of dance may result in other problems. Excessive weight loss, bulimia, and even anorexia are disturbingly common, although, in their most severe forms, they are usually encountered in students rather than in established dancers. However, the prevalence of malnutrition among classical dancers of all ages is most disturbing. Dancers also have other special problems that may be less obvious. Menarche (the age when the first menstrual period occurs) is approximately 2 years later among young dancers than it is in the general population. This is believed to be due to low body weight and extreme exercise and may be aggravated by malnutrition from weight loss. Amenorrhea (cessation of menstrual periods) is also common. The incidence of reversible infertility is also increased among female dancers. Vaginal yeast infections are also common because of the tights worn by ballet dancers. These and other problems of dancers are recognized immediately by physicians specializing in dance-medicine. Often, these are orthopedists who also are directors of sports-medicine centers. Participation by members of the arts-medicine clinic in the educational programs of dance schools and professional companies is already helping to avoid such problems for many dancers.

Respiratory Dysfunction in Wind Instrumentalists

Just as asthma may undermine support and impair a singer's technique (see chapter 12), pulmonary dysfunction can undermine a wind instrumentalist's support and result in lip dysfunction in brass players, and analogous problems in other musicians. Most of the patients we have cared for with such problems were trumpeters, but there were trombonists, flutists, oboists, and a clarinetist, as well. The most common complaints were fatigue during playing, lip and throat pain, loss of upper range, and loss of ability to sustain long notes. In some cases, embouchure was seriously impaired by rapid fatigue of lip muscles, asymmetry of muscle contraction, lip tremor, or apparent hypertrophy with nearly constant contraction; and some patients had been diagnosed as having lip dystonias. As in singers with similar performance problems, some of these instrumentalists appear to have developed performance dysfunctions because of pulmonary dysfunction, particularly unrecognized asthma. When the pulmonary condition is treated, performance ability generally improves. Anecdotal, unpublished reports indicate that other centers have had similar experiences. Because of the importance of reversible pulmonary dysfunction as a cause of performance impairment, and the fact that this association is not widely recognized, this preliminary report is presented to review the subject.

Performance using woodwind or brass musical instruments requires consistent control over the stream of expired air. This is also true for singers, in whom pulmonary and glottal aerodynamics have been studied more extensively. The importance of respiratory training and endurance for optimal playing and singing has been recognized widely within the musical community for generations. In fact, there is extensive pedagogical literature on similarities and differences in breathing requirements for singers and instrumentalists, and on the advisability of concurrent study of voice and wind instruments. The consensus is that optimal breathing technique and techniques of abdominal support are essentially the same for singers and most instrumentalists, despite specific differences in resistance, flow rate, and flow volume associated with reeds and mouthpieces of varying sizes.

Recent studies have also confirmed the importance of laryngeal activity and vocal tract shape in instrument playing.[4,5] Although such interactions have not been clearly documented until recently, they have been recognized for many years by musicians and are responsible for standard language in instrumental teaching, such as "play with an open throat." For example, in his study of breathing for instrumentalists, Eckberg[6] discusses the importance of proper breathing and pharyngeal relaxation. He states, "As your music teacher instructed you to 'use more air' and 'blow harder,' you may have subconsciously decided to protect that slowly developing embouchure from the overpowering air pressure by tightening your throat. But when you add resistance to the airflow by closing off the throat, you need to 'push' harder from the abdominal muscles—and with more push, the throat muscles constrict even tighter to keep the air from overblowing the embouchure. So it becomes a hopeless tension-producing cycle that can cause a thin, pinched-sounding tone and a limited range."

It is clear that the larynx plays a significant role in shaping the quality of sound for many instrumentalists, such as flutists during trills, trombonists, trumpeters, saxophonists, and others. Consequently, illness or technical abuses such as excessive constriction of neck muscles that cause laryngeal dysfunction (as demonstrated in singers) also appear to produce dysfunction among wind instrumentalists. This may be due in part to the fact that such conditions can alter intrapulmonic pressure and air flow.[7]

Breath support is fundamental in traditional training of wind and brass players, as well as singers. In singers, the oscillator of the musical "instrument" is the larynx, specifically the vibrating vocal folds. The resonator is the supraglottic vocal tract. For the instrumentalist, the lips and mouthpiece or reed constitute the oscillator, and the rest of the instrument itself is the resonator. The resonator is responsible for much of the quality or "timbre." The importance of the lungs, thorax, and abdominal muscles as the power source for sound production has been established for all wind instrumentalists and vocalists. Large muscle groups in these areas generate a vector of force that directs the expired air through the oscillator. Using more delicate muscles for fine control, the lips or vocal folds interrupt the stream of air to produce the desired sound. Abrupt, irregular, or uncontrolled changes in the flow of air require large compensatory muscular adjustments at the oscillator that interfere with controlled tone production, quality, and endurance. Moreover, if the column of air is not sufficiently constant and powerful to drive the instrument or voice, the performer usually attempts to compensate with excessive muscle contraction not only at the oscillator, but also elsewhere in the head or neck. This is observed most easily in singers as hyperfunctional activity in the face, jaw, and strap muscles, and tongue retraction.[8]

Similar changes occur in instrumentalists. Tightening of the lips, increased pressure of the mouthpiece against the mouth, and forceful biting of single-reed instruments are the most prominent changes. However, tongue retraction, tightening of neck muscles, and pharyngeal constriction also occur and appear to affect sound quality and the performer's endurance. These problems are also well recognized in music literature. Bouhouys notes that "the maintenance of a tone of constant pitch and loudness on a wind instrument requires a constant mouth pressure and a constant airflow rate."[9] Gradwell adds that trouble "starts for a musician if he has not taken in adequate air to last the phrase, as he now forces air out with his abdominal muscles and automatically the neck muscles will contract to help with the forced breathing. This causes strain, stiffens the shoulders, exhausts the player and of course ruins

the sound of the note he is playing."[10] Any condition that impairs respiratory function (such as asthma) may produce the same effects as if the performer had not taken in adequate air.

The effect of musical performance on pulmonary function remains uncertain in healthy patients,[11–13] although it appears that musical training probably produces little significant increase in total lung capacity but a higher tidal volume and lower residual lung volume. The adverse effects of respiratory dysfunction upon performers have been clearly established.[14]

Various conditions may undermine respiratory support and cause performance dysfunction, the most common being improper technique. In many performers, especially the elderly, lack of exercise and poor aerobic conditioning are responsible. The results are unfortunately often mistaken for irreversible changes associated with aging, resulting in the premature conclusion of salvageable performance careers. Respiratory disease is a particularly important cause of technical dysfunction in young singers and instrumentalists, as well as in performers who straining with inappropriate muscles in neck, face, and lips to compensate for deficient support by impaired breathing.

As discussed in chapter 12, the most common obstructive airway disease is asthma, affecting 8 million people in the United States.[15] The problems obstructive pulmonary disease creates for singers are now well recognized.[16] Our clinical observations suggest that the treatment of asthma in performers is somewhat different from that of the general population. The principles discussed for singers in the chapter on Respiratory Dysfunction are probably appropriate for wind instrumentalists, but studies on this population have not been done.

Psychiatry

Performance careers are stressful. The demand for daily perfection, public scrutiny, constant competition, critics, and old-fashioned stage fright may all exact a heavy toll. The additional strain on the performer and his or her family that accompanies an extensive tour may be particularly trying and often results in marital strife and/or divorce. Such problems are shared by many successful performers, and usually they can be kept under control. However, when the stress has become unmanageable or interferes excessively with the performer's life or artistic ability, the intervention of a professional may be appropriate. Fortunately, there are now psychologists and psychiatrists who have special skills and insight into these problems. Many of them are performers themselves. They can be most helpful in controlling the effects of these stresses, managing stage fright, overcoming writer's block, and in teaching the performer to regain sufficient control over his or her life to permit continuation of his or her career. This subject is covered in chapter 20. Most arts-medicine centers have access to psychological professionals with special interests in this area.

Other Arts-Medicine Problems

Many other special problems occur in performers. For example, hearing loss may be an occupational hazard for musicians. This occurs not only in rock musicians, but also in members of symphony orchestras. Rock musicians help avoid the problem by standing behind or beside their speakers rather than in front of them. Satisfactory solutions in the orchestra environment have not yet been advanced. Instrumentalists sitting in front of the brass section have particular problems. Certain instruments may actually cause hearing loss in the performers who play them. For example, the left ear of a violinist is at risk. Occupational hearing loss in general is a complex subject, and the special problems of hearing loss in musicians require a great deal more study, as discussed in chapter 11.

Bagpiper's disease, a little known problem within the medical profession, is also potentially serious. The skins used to make bagpipes are cured in glycerine and honey. Bags make an excellent culture medium for growth of bacteria and fungi. Chronic fungal pneumonias occur among bagpipers. They are usually caused by *Cryptococcus*, and occasionally by aspergillosis. Bagpipers may also develop a spastic, "hourglass" stomach, which makes frequent rumbling noises. Many other similar problems exist but are beyond the scope of this review. In addition to those already known, there is no doubt that many more will be recognized as sensitivity to performers increases.

Importance for Singers

Singers are often called on for performance functions other than singing. Both singers and their teachers should be aware of the potential hazards of nonvocal performance and should recognize signs of problems early. Fortunately, they can usually be corrected. However, if left unattended, they may worsen and interfere not only with playing and dancing but also with a singing career. Help is usually available through arts-medicine centers.

Education in Arts-Medicine

Arts-medicine is a newly established specialty that poses unique educational challenges. The field involves basic research and specialized clinical care for singers, instrumentalists, dancers, visual artists, and others who place unique demands on their bodies and minds and require function much closer to optimal than virtually any other patients in medicine. The demands on some performing artists are extraordinary. For example, in a study of 55 "sports" by a sports medicine center, ballet dancing was determined to be the most difficult and challenging.[17]

A great deal of information remains to be discovered in order to understand the anatomy, physiology, physics, and other fundamentals that allow efficient, healthy development of artists and rational clinical management by physicians and teachers of the arts. The research and clinical challenges are made more difficult by the fact that available information is scattered among diverse professions, each with its own literature, educational traditions, and institutions. Traditionally, even the language used by the various professions is incomprehensible to practitioners of fields now interacting through arts-medicine. Although recently there has been a substantial increase in basic research, in the opening of clinical "arts-medicine centers," in the development of scientifically based pedagogy courses within music schools, and in the publication of arts-medicine literature,[18–20] there are few places one can go to obtain the necessary training. At present, no academic programs or degrees are offered in "arts-medicine." To educate oneself, it is necessary to either obtain multiple degrees, which frequently require time and information not applicable to the student's goals, or to find informal "apprenticeships" to fill in gaps left by traditional educational categorization.

A couple of programs have been proposed to address these problems. Titze suggested a curriculum in vocology.[21] This program was conceived as a modification of the masters program in speech-language pathology. It combined techniques offered in theater arts and music with those traditionally taught in speech-language pathology programs. It is designed to optimize training in vocal habilitation and rehabilitation. For singing teachers who wish to become singing voice specialists, and who are willing to obtain a master's degree and clinical certification in speech-language pathology, the vocology program offers many advantages over most speech-language pathology programs. Vocology training has been initiated and is available at the University of Iowa.

Sataloff proposed a doctoral program in arts-medicine.[22] The degree was intended to assure and promote the development of academic excellence in arts medicine. The actual proposal had four tracks from which a student could choose: voice, hand, dance, or other. Although there was some overlap in the proposed curriculum, course requirements were different for each concentration. Detailed curriculum requirements were proposed, and considerable interest was generated. However, so far, no school has initiated such a program. Consequently, physicians and other health care providers must still find less efficient ways to educate themselves in this important, multifaceted specialty.

Summary

Many voice professionals also play instruments, dance, and are active in other performance activities. There are many risks and consequences of nonvoice performance that may affect the voice. Voice professionals and their teachers and therapists should be familiar with potential health consequences of all artist and performance activities, and especially those that are common among singers and actors including dance, string, and keyboard instrument playing and wind instrument performance.

Review Questions

1. In a dancer with persistent foot pain, a normal foot X-ray provides assurance that there is no stress fracture.
   a. true
   b. false

2. In young dancers, menarche (first menstrual period) occurs:
   a. at the normal time
   b. approximately 2 years earlier than normal
   c. approximately 2 years later than normal
   d. approximately 3 years earlier than normal
   e. none of the above

3. Playing a wind instrument is damaging to the vocal apparatus and should be forbidden in serious singers.
   a. true
   b. false

4. A patient with cryptococcus pneumonia and rumbling noises in his stomach is most likely:
   a. a trumpet player
   b. a flutist
   c. a singer
   d. a percussionist
   e. a bagpiper

5. What percentage of instrumentalists report medical problems that adversely affect performance?
   a. about 26%
   b. about 56%
   c. about 76%
   d. about 96%
   e. none of the above

References

1. Sataloff RT, Brandfonbrener AG, Lederman RJ. *Performing arts-medicine.* New York: Raven Press; 1991.
2. Fishbein M, Middlestadt SE, Ottati V, et al. Medical problems among ICSOM musicians: overview of a national survey. *Med Prob Perform Art.* 1988;3:1–8.
3. Hochberg FH, Leffert RD, Heller MD, Merriman L. Hand difficulties among musicians. *JAMA.* 1983;249(14):1869–1872.
4. King AL, Asby J, Nelson C. Laryngeal function in wind instrumentalists: the woodwinds. *J Voice.* 1988;1:365–367.
5. King AL, Asby J, Nelson C: Laryngeal function in wind instrumentalists: the woodwinds. Presented at the Seventeenth Symposium: *Care of the Professional Voice;* June 9, 1976; The Voice Foundation, New York.
6. Eckberg JC. Better breathing: The key to better playing. *Accent.* 1976;1:18–19, 1976.
7. Tanaka S, Gould WJ. Vocal efficiency and aerodynamic aspects in voice disorders. *Ann Otol Rhinol Laryngol.* 1985;94:29–33.
8. Sataloff RT: Professional singers, Part II. *J Voice.* 1987;1:191–201.
9. Bouhouys A. Pressure-flow events during wind instrument playing. *Ann NY Acad Scie.* 1968;155:266–268.
10. Gradwell J. Breathing for woodwind players. *Woodwind World.* 1974;8:17–37.
11. Gould WJ, Okamura H. Static lung volumes in singers. *Ann Otol.* 1973;82:89–95.
12. Schorr-Lesnick B, Teirstein AS, Brown LK, Miller A. Pulmonary function in singers and wind-instrument players. *Chest.* 1985;82:201–205.
13. Heller SS, Hicks WR, Root WS. Lung volumes in singers. *J Appl Physiol.* 1960;15:40–42.
14. Spiegel JR, Sataloff, Cohn JR, Hawkshaw M. Respiratory function in singers: medical assessment. *J Voice.* 1988;2:40–50.
15. Shigemorei Y. Some tests related to the air usage during phonation: Clinical investigations. *Otologia (Fukuoka).* 1977;23:138–166.
16. Cohn JR, Sataloff RT, Spiegel JR, Fish JE & Kennedy K. Airway reactivity-induced asthma in singers (ARIAS), *J Voice.* 1991;5(4):332–337.
17. Nicholas JA. Risk factors, sports medicine and the orthopedic system: an overview. *J Sports Med.* 1975;3:243–259.

18. *Journal of Voice*, published by Raven Press (New York, NY, USA).
19. *Medical problems of performing artists*, published by Hanley & Belfus (Philadelphia, Pa, USA).
20. Sataloff RT, Brandfonbrener A, Lederman RJ. *Textbook of Performing Arts Medicine*. New York: Raven Press; 1991.
21. Titze IR. Rationale and structure of a curriculum in vocology. *J Voice*. 1992;6(1):1–9.
22. Sataloff RT. Proposal for establishing a degree of doctor of philosophy in arts medicine. *J Voice*. 1992;6(1):17–21.

17

Nutrition and the Professional Voice User

Pamela L. Harvey and Susan H. Miller

Performers must understand why attention to their own nutritional status is specifically important to their lives and livelihoods. Laryngeal and vocal health cannot be separated from general health and longevity. Increasingly, health status has been linked to life-style choices, involving diet, smoking, and exercise.[1-3] Although singers and actors are frequently referred to as vocal athletes,[4] the nutritional status of singers has not received the attention in research or recommendations that other athletes have enjoyed.

Nutritional status is extremely important to the singer or actor who wants to be vital and energetic, maintain appropriate body weight, and remain well, resisting the colds and common maladies that often travel through an entire cast or choir. Through the power of targeted nutrition, the singer can begin to define his or her own health, not just as the absence of disease, but as the optimal functioning of the body's intricate systems. Seeking voice treatment may serve as the catalyst for making broad life-style changes as performers realize that they must stand up on their own behalf and begin to take care of themselves. This means taking care of the voice issues, and general health as well.

Stress and fatigue are endemic in performers. Grueling audition, rehearsal, and performance schedules, working second and third jobs, intense competition, and self-scrutiny may eventually take a toll on the performer's overall health. Performers are often overworked, overtired, and overextended. They often say, " I don't have time to be sick," reporting that the onset of their voice problem followed one of many upper respiratory infections. Without proper instruction and attention to nutrition and food choices, a performer's life-style demands can result in an unstable, inadequate nutritional status that invites illness.

Another hallmark of the performer's life-style is change. Changes in activity level require changes in diet, both with regard to the types of food selected and the total number of calories consumed. The nutritional needs of an actor in a rigorous lead role will be different from when that actor is a member of the chorus, or in a smaller or less strenuous role. Singing and acting are physically demanding activities. Like other athletes, the performer can benefit from a diet rich in complex carbohydrates, such as grains and pastas. These foods optimize the body's glycogen stores, leading to sustainable energy.[5]

The performer who is sweating profusely due to being cloaked in heavy costumes or rehearsing in a hot space should attend to replenishing fluids and minerals such as sodium, potassium, choride, and magnesium.[6] The traveling performer may stave off dehydration via extra water intake and avoid the frequent complaint of constipation by increasing fiber intake. The performer on tour should be advised to eat 3–4 servings of fresh fruit daily, contributing to both fluid and fiber intake.[7]

The remainder of this chapter will provide information on basic nutrition, relate recent research on laryngeal aging, and propose some suggestions on promoting general and vocal health through nutrition.

Basic Nutrition and Dietary Guidelines

Food is the fuel for life. Our bodies require food and its nutrients to sustain life and promote cell and tissue growth. Our nutritional requirements include the *macronutrients* (carbohydrates, proteins, and fats), the *micronutrients* (vitamins and minerals), and water.[8]

The Recommended Daily Allowances (RDA) for essential nutrients were established by the Food and Nutrition Board of the National Research Council in 1941. These levels were adopted to ensure satisfactory growth in children and considered to be adequate to meet the nutritional needs of a healthy individual over 2 years of age.[9] Many RDA levels were adopted to prevent deficiency diseases, such as scurvy, rickets, and beriberi. A listing of nutrients, their functions, food sources and RDA levels is presented in Table 17–1 at the end of this chapter.

For many years nutrition experts believed that as long as we ate three square meals a day, having a variety of foods from the four food groups (meats, dairy foods, fruits/vegetables and grains) we were meeting our body's needs. The four food groups were touted as total nutrition. These guidelines changed as a mass of evidence revealed that the American diet was contributing to escalating rates of heart disease and cancer.[10-14]

In April, 1992, the United States Department of Agriculture and National Institutes of Health revised the dietary suggestions by introducing the *Eating Right Pyramid*.[15] Figure 17–1 shows the current USDA Food Pyramid, an illustration of dietary guidelines for the type and amount of food to be eaten. The base of the pyramid, whole grains, should comprise the largest part of the diet, between 30% and 45%. Next, fruits and vegetables should comprise 20% to 30% of the diet. Meats and dairy products should each comprise approximately 10% of the diet. Fats, sweets, and oils should be used sparingly and comprise only about 5% of the diet.[15]

One shortcoming of the Food Pyramid should be noted. Although it speaks to the quantity of selections, it does not address the quality of those selections. For example, iceberg lettuce and spinach count equally as a serving of vegetables, though the dark leafy spinach would be more nutrient dense.

Unfortunately, the dietary guidelines put forth via the Food Pyramid are difficult for many people to follow. The Food Pyramid suggests 2–4 servings of fruit and 3–5 servings of vegetables—for many people this is more realistic as a weekly goal, not a daily reality. USDA statistics indicate that only 9% of Americans follow these guidelines[16] and one may predict that the percentage of performers eating the suggested diet is even lower.

The current typical American diet of highly processed, packaged food lacks many essential nutrients.[17-21] The average American eats only two servings of fruits and vegetables and nearly 100 grams of fat per day with a goal of no more than 30–40 grams per day.[22] Americans may accurately be described as the most overfed, yet under-nourished population in the world. Singers who eat this way should be advised that they may be trading their health for convenience.

Unfortunately, optimal nutrition is difficult to achieve even for those who do follow the Food Pyramid model. Our modern farming techniques produce food that is increasingly nutrient deficient.[23] We no longer rotate crops regularly, but grow the same produce year after year in soil that becomes increasingly depleted of many important minerals. Some studies suggest that conventionally grown fruits and vegetables have as much as 86% fewer minerals and trace minerals as organically grown produce.[24,25]

Recent Research in Nutrition

Because of nutrient depletion of the soil and the increased intake of processed food, the continuing

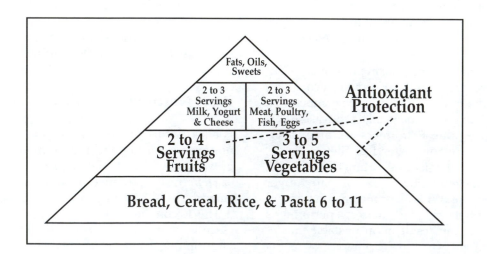

Fig 17–1. The United States Department of Agriculture Eating Right Pyramid[15]

decline of nutrition in the diet is occurring just as the value of achieving nutrient levels that exceed RDA recommendations is becoming established.[26] The last 5 years have seen an explosive growth in medical research regarding the relationship between nutrition, health, and disease. Globally, over 20,000 clinical studies have been initiated since 1990 to investigate this relationship. Pertinent studies can be conveniently reviewed through the Internet and informational software packages such as the Nutrition Infobase by Intelligent Health.[27]

Scientific exploration has revealed a number of benefits related to micronutrition. Among these benefits are slowing of some of the physiological aspects of aging,[28,29] enhanced athletic performance,[30,31] increased protection against many forms of cancers,[32-47] stronger defenses against cardiovascular disease,[48-58] reduction in neural tube birth defects,[59] protection from macular degeneration and cataracts,[60-62] and bolstering of the immune system.[63,64] As the science of nutrition matures and additional health benefits are revealed, the nutritional advice given to singers will expand and solidify. One can predict research will explore the nutritional status of healthy and injured singers and the inclusion of an informed nutritionist into the professional voice care team.

Free Radical Pathology and Antioxidant Defenses

Anyone investigating the cutting edge of anti-aging and disease prevention research encounters discussions of free radical oxidation.[65] A free radical is a molecule of oxygen that is missing an electron from one of its pairs of electrons.[66] Free radicals have been referred to as cellular renegades that go on a search-and-destroy mission attempting to steal an electron from a healthy molecule.[65]

Where do free radicals come from? We generate them ourselves through the biochemical processes that occur within the body as we metabolize oxygen.[67] The production of free radicals is increased with high intensity exercise, aging, stress, infection, or injury.[68-70] Free radicals are also generated by external sources such as cigarette smoke, air pollution, smog, food additives, stress, and pesticides.[71] Free radical oxidation may be of particular importance to performers because singing and acting are aerodynamic tasks that involve deep inhalations and large exchanges of oxygen.

By causing irregular cross-linking between molecules which leads to DNA damage,[72] cellular mutation

and death,[73] free radical pathology has been linked to the aging process in general and in many disease processes, including cancer, heart disease, diabetes, atherosclerosis, infectious diseases, arthritis, cerebrovascular disease, macular degeneration, cataracts, Parkinson's disease, and amyotrophic lateral sclerosis.[73-82] The connection to such a wide variety of disease processes suggests that free radicals are not peripheral players, but rather central characters in many human health problems.

The body resists free radical assault by manufacturing its own endogenous antioxidants (superoxide dismutase, catalase, and glutathione peroxidase), which have an extra electron to give up, thereby neutralizing free radicals.[83,84] Unfortunately, the body's exposure to free radicals has outstripped these endogenous resources.[85] Exogenous antioxidants are provided to the body through foods and supplements that contain the antioxidants vitamin C, vitamin E and beta carotene, which is converted to vitamin A in the body.[86]

The level of antioxidants needed to defend the body against the deleterious free radicals exceeds current RDA levels and can be achieved most conveniently through supplementation.[87] In the past, vitamin supplements were often recommended for the wrong reasons and without scientific support. However, the strength of the recent empirical evidence has influenced the thinking and recommendations of medical clinicians and researchers worldwide. Nutrition experts are now suggesting that "optimal" levels of the antioxidant micronutrients be established.[88] It should be noted these optimal levels have not been adopted by the Food and Drug Administration. Safe optimal levels are discussed in this chapter's section on supplementation and are included in the Table at the end of this chapter.

Physicians should be aware that many recent nutritional studies have been summarized in the popular press, so performers may have knowledge of the topic (*Time*, April 6, 1992; *The Wall Street Journal*, Sept. 5, 1993; Harvard Health Letter, April, 1995; Mayo Clinic Health Letter, August, 1993). For example, the "Berkeley Wellness Letter," the largest health newsletter in the world recently reversed an 18-year bias against nutritional supplements by stating "The accumulation of research in recent years has caused us to change our mind . . . the role these substances play in disease prevention is no longer a matter of dispute" (p. 1, University of California at Berkeley *Wellness Letter*, 10 [4], 1994).

Determining Nutritional Status

Physicians have routinely determined their patient's nutritional status via an oral history of eating habits and food preferences. Just as hearing testing and acoustic analysis of voice are now considered standard features of audiologic and phonatory assessment, objective measures of nutritional status are becoming more commonplace. Quantitative measures of nutrient levels in serum, urine, blood cells, or hair allow for documentation of the amount of nutrients present and are indicative of, at least, short-term nutritional status.[89]

Functional nutrition tests have emerged that provide a deeper understanding of nutritional status.[90,91] Examples of these functional tests are the Essential Metabolics Analysis (EMA), which assesses long-term functional nutrition status and related metabolic processes associated with particular nutrients, and Spectrox, which assesses the intracellular protective function of antioxidants against oxidative damage from free radicals.[92,93]

Even marginal nutrient deficiencies can be medically relevant since these deficiencies may affect the professional voice user's ability to resist disease and infection, recover from surgery, or withstand stress. The HANES I and II studies (Health and Nutrition Examination Survey) conducted by the Federal Government identified over 70% of the American population to be at risk for the clinical impact of long-term marginal dietary deficiencies.[11,12] By reviewing a patient's functional nutrient status in combination with physiological, pathological, environmental, life-style and dietary factors, the physician can pinpoint marginal nutritional deficits and make recommendations based on sound data.

Choosing Supplements

Over 80 million Americans spend billions of dollars annually on vitamin and mineral supplements (*Time*, April, 1992: 53-59). Over 90% of these people take a supplement without the direction of either a physician or nutritionist and may be taking the wrong supplement for the wrong reason in the wrong amount. By including state-of-the-art nutritional counseling within the medical practice, the physician can assist singers in taking responsibility for their own health, and provide a valuable and sought-after office service.

Singers should understand some underlying principles regarding supplementation. First, vitamins and minerals work synergistically, such that the balanced combination of two or more vitamins taken in appropriate amounts creates a stronger response.[94–96] For example, in order for bioflavanoids to work properly, they must be taken along with vitamin C; and calcium absorption is partially dependent on vitamin D intake. Generally speaking, a balanced multiple ingredient

formula of moderate dosages should be used rather than large doses of a single nutrient.

Performers should also understand that if a health problem emerges, they should not self-prescribe a supplement for an illness. If deficiencies are identified through testing, supplementation should be followed by posttreatment testing since some patients can consume large doses of nutrients and still be deficient if their intestinal absorption is poor. Singers should be counseled that supplementation is exactly that, a supplement. Singers typically understand and respond well to the analogy that wearing a seat belt does not give a driver permission to speed recklessly, just as taking a supplement does not excuse a poor diet.

Ideally, supplementation is individually tailored and based on family history, physical status, and functional nutritional testing. However, until performers are as familiar with their nutrient levels as they now are with their cholesterol and blood pressure levels, they (and their physicians) will need to choose from among the hundreds of commercially available products. One visit to the pharmacy or nutrition store is enough to give even the most informed performer a megadose of confusion. Physicians can assist their patients by staying well informed regarding the criteria for choosing quality supplementation.

A quality multivitamin multimineral supplement should meet the following criteria:

- contain RDA levels of most of the required micronutrients: 11 vitamins, 4 minerals, and 3 trace minerals. Additionally, many formulations now contain greater than RDA levels of the antioxidant vitamins, usually 400 IU of vitamin E, 500–1000 mg of vitamin C and 15 mg (25,000 IU) of beta carotene. Superior products may also contain such ingredients as anthocyanosides, antioxidants capable of crossing the blood-brain barrier, and glutathione, an intracellular antioxidant.[97]
- contain vitamin forms that are maximally absorbable.[98] Some singers may choose "all natural" vitamin forms, derived from whole foods, believing that these are more easily digested and assimilated than synthetic vitamins. Actually, bioavailability varies from nutrient to nutrient. For example, Ester-C,[99] a patented synthetic form of vitamin C is more quickly absorbed and is retained in the body longer than natural vitamin C (ascorbic acid) which is largely excreted in the urine.[100] Additionally, Ester-C has the advantage of being pH neutral. In contrast, the natural form of vitamin E (d-alpha tocopherol) is more biologically available than synthetic vitamin E (dl-alpha tocopherol).[101] Superior products may contain natural vitamin E in several forms: alpha, beta, gamma, and delta tocopherols. Vita-

mins should be of pharmaceutical purity and potency, rather than standard grade.

- contain minerals in a bioavailable form. Minerals can be difficult to absorb since in their natural form they are, just as their names suggest, tiny "pebbles" of zinc, copper, chromium, etc. Some multimineral formulas are chemically structured in chelated form. A chelate is formed when an organic molecule binds around the inorganic mineral atom. Superior chelates are formed in a process in which a mineral of low molecular weight is surrounded by an amino acid using a strong covalent bond, which prevents breakdown in gastric acid, allows for intestinal absorption, and facilitates transportation into the bloodstream.[102,103]
- provide ingredients via capsules rather than in a compressed pill, which may resist breakdown. Because the gelatin in most capsules is derived from a bovine source, strict vegetarians may prefer tablets. Both tablets and capsules should meet the US Pharmacopoeia XXIII requirements for disintegration and dissolution within 20–30 minutes.
- should be packaged in opaque containers, since supplements can be degraded by light exposure.

Evaluating and choosing a quality supplement can be time consuming and often requires contacting the manufacturer. Products that meet the above general criteria are available through Informed Nutrition Services.[104]

Supplements should be stored in a cool, dry place. Effective supplementation should be taken after meals, usually twice a day. This is because water soluble vitamins are not retained by the body and because adequate amounts of minerals cannot be supplied in a one-a-day form. A single pill attempting to contain RDA levels of minerals would simply be too large to swallow. It should be noted that although supplements cite RDA levels these are usually US RDA levels which are the upper ranges of the recommended dietary allowances set by the National Research Council.[105] To avoid confusion, new labeling laws, effective December, 1996, will require the term *daily value* or DV.

Nutrition Fact Food Labels

To further assist the public in making food choices, the Food and Drug Administration began requiring nutrition labeling on packaged food, as of May, 1994. The Nutritional Facts Label is shown in Fig 17–2.

The top portion of the label must indicate a realistic portion size and the number of servings per container. Calories per serving and calories from fat are then listed. By dividing the total calories (in this example, 90)

Nutrition Facts

Serving Size 1/2 cup (114g)
Servings Per Container 4

Amount Per Serving

Calories 90   Calories from Fat 30

	% Daily Value*
Total Fat 3g	**5%**
Saturated Fat 0g	**0%**
Cholesterol 0mg	**0%**
Sodium 300mg	**13%**
Total Carbohydrate 13g	**4%**
Dietary Fiber 3g	**12%**
Sugars 3g	
Protein 3g	

Vitamin A	80%	•	Vitamin C	60%
Calcium	4%	•	Iron	4%

* Percent Daily Values are based on a 2,000 calorie diet. Your daily values may be higher or lower depending on your calorie needs:

	Calories	2,000	2,500
Total Fat	Less than	65g	80g
Sat Fat	Less than	20g	25g
Cholesterol	Less than	300mg	300mg
Sodium	Less than	2400mg	2400mg
Total Carbohydrate		300g	375g
Fiber		25g	30g

Calories per gram:
Fat 9   •   Carbohydrates 4   •   Protein 4

Fig 17–2. The Nutrition Facts Label appears on all packaged foods as mandated by the Food and Drug Administration since May, 1994.

by the calories from fat (in this example, 30), one can determine the percentage of calories per serving from fat. In our example, the resultant number is 3, indicating that this food get 1/3 of its calories from fat. An answer of 5 or more indicates that the food gets 20% or less of its calories from fat and would be appropriate for those attempting to follow a low fat diet, as recommended by the USDA.

Labels promoting a *low fat* product must contain no greater than 3 g of fat per serving. A notable exemption to this rule was achieved by the dairy industry for the promotion of 2%, "low fat" milk which contains 5 g of fat per eight ounce serving. The low fat designation can be somewhat misleading. Looking at our pictured example, this product meets the low fat claim requirement since total fat per serving is 3 grams. However, as previously noted, this product gets over 30% of its calories from fat.

The remainder of the label provides information on the nutrient content of the food. Percent daily values are based on a 2000-calorie diet. Calorie requirements would be dependent on the singer's activity level, physical build, and metabolic rate, as well as goals such as weight gain or reduction. Thus, the singer's daily values may be higher or lower, secondary to specific calorie needs.

Products that claim to be "light" or "reduced fat" must have 50% less fat or one third fewer calories than their original counterparts. Again, this can be misleading. For example, light or reduced fat bacon, although much lower in fat than regular bacon, still receives 60%–70% of its calories from fat. Foods labeled as "healthy" have restrictions on cholesterol and sodium and must contain 10% of RDA levels of one or more of the following nutrients: vitamin A, vitamin C, protein, calcium, or iron. Products labeled as "natural" are unregulated by any agency. A juice, containing only 10% natural fruit juice and 90% water and sugar, can be labeled as "natural."

Fiber has no nutritional value but is extremely important to good health. Low fiber diets have been associated with colon cancer, gastrointestinal disorders, and constipation, while high fiber diets may prevent these disorders.[106] The daily goal for fiber intake is approximately 25–30 g. The average diet provides only 12–15 g of fiber. Fiber has several functions within the body. Fiber slows the absorption of sugar and breakdown of carbohydrates and helps to stabilize blood glucose levels. Adequate fiber intake promotes good intestinal function and elimination.

Singers and actors often eat on the run and should be counseled to read and accurately interpret food labels. Labeling, of course, only appears on packaged foods. Performers should realize that many of their most nutritious choices will be found in the produce section and will not contain labeling at all.

Food as Medicine

The use of food as medicine dates back to humankind's earliest curative efforts. Despite Hippocrates' suggestion in 426 BC, "Let food be thy medicine," the study of the medicinal benefits of food is considered among the most innovative frontiers in nutritional science. Advances in technology now allow researchers to accurately separate and identify substances in foods that have medicinal applications and to enhance many foods to boost nutritional value. Scientists have adopted the term *nutraceutical* to describe a food substance which provides medical or health benefits, including the prevention and treatment of disease.[107] Other terms that describe these foods are *pharmafoods, medicinal foods, prescriptive foods* or *FOSHU* or Foods with Specific Heath Uses.

Much of current neutraceutical research uses scientific methodology to explore traditional or folklore remedies for valid therapeutic benefits. Many mothers have used the principles of neutraceuticals as they have served up chicken soup to the child with a cold. Pharmafood research has revealed that chicken contains the amino acid cysteine, that is chemically similar to the expectorant drug acetylcysteine.[108] Further research demonstrated that chicken soup has an anti-inflammatory action that inhibits neutrophil chemotaxis—the process which attracts white blood cells to a site of inflammation.[109]

Other examples of neutraceutical research include studies on the possible disease-fighting capabilities of garlic and soy products. The allium vegetable garlic contains quercetin, cyanidin, and bioflavaniods, which have been found to inhibit cancer cell multiplication, lower serum cholesterol and triglyceride levels, and boost immune response.[110–112] Soy products contain a protease inhibitor, genistein, which has demonstrated the ability to neutralize the effects of some cancer-causing agents. Soy products also contain phytoestrogens, which may have particular importance in fighting breast and cervical cancer.[113–115]

Performers are probably much like the rest of the population, which is focusing its nutritional efforts on *avoidance* of food substances such as fat and cholesterol that may be detrimental to health. Neutraceutical research may change that focus to emphasizing the *inclusion* of specific food elements found to have health benefits. Information regarding neutraceuticals will likely increase as a result of the $20.5 million funding in 1993 by the National Cancer Institute for a "Designer Food Program."[116]

Vocal Longevity and Nutrition

What is known about vocal aging is an apparent overlay of general information about the aging process and specific information about the aging larynx. Generally, physiologic adaptations expected in aging include changes in cardiovascular characteristics, pulmonary function, hormonal balance, immune response, musculoskeletal integrity, and central nervous system function.[117] Specific to laryngeal function, age-related degenerative changes include muscle atrophy, ligament deterioration, ossification of the hyaline cartilages, slowing of neural transmission, and nerve conduction velocity.[118]

Many of these changes begin to be apparent during the fourth decade of life. Given the early onset and insidious progression of decline in these functions, it is important to recognize that certain life-style choices and vocal use patterns may either accelerate or retard this progression. While these changes may be inevitable, they are not abrupt. Data from nutrition research have indicated that we can be proactive and slow physiologic aging while chronological aging moves inexorably forward.

Vocal longevity will be achieved by attending to vocal health through healthy voice production, following a vocal hygiene program, and avoiding vocal injury—and not losing sight of the importance of general health. Performers are busy, goal-oriented people who will need instruction and encouragement to strive for optimum health.

Nutritional Goals for Performers

Before beginning any health improvement program, performers should obtain medical clearance from their personal physician. After a thorough discussion of the basic elements of nutrition and gaining an understanding of some of the current findings in nutritional science, performers should participate in determining, and then writing, their personal nutrition goals: Goals should be specific, measurable and time limited. Examples of these goals might be:

1. I will eat at least four servings of fruits and vegetables per day.
2. I will take a quality comprehensive antioxidant, vitamin, and mineral supplement.
3. When eating meat, I will have a portion that is smaller than my vegetable portion.
4. I will check the nutritional fact panel on packaged food.
5. I will choose foods that derive 20% or less of their calories from fat.
6. I will limit my fat intake to 30–40 g daily.
7. I will drink eight 8-ounce glasses of water daily.
8. I will eat 25–30 g of fiber daily.

Whatever a performer's age, he or she should understand that what he does now will significantly affect how he will look and feel (and possibly sound) in the years to come. Obtaining adequate nutrition via a healthy carbohydrate rich, low fat, high fiber diet should be the professional voice user's goal. However, due to travel, stress, and constantly changing schedules, most performers are unable to achieve this goal through diet alone. Quality supplementation can be a powerful ally for these singers, actors, and other voice professionals. Informed nutrition—combined with exercise—can create an optimal environment for the long-term health that is essential to an enduring career in voice performance.

Summary

It is important for performers and their teachers to understand why attention to nutrition is important to their voices, lives, and livelihoods. Laryngeal and vocal health cannot be separated from general health and longevity. We require macronutrients and micronutrients. Good health depends on a diet that provides the body with appropriate levels of both. Performers and their teachers should be familiar with basic nutritional requirements, methods of determining nutritional status, and signs of nutritional deficiencies.

Review Questions

1. Products that claim to be "light" or "reduced fat" provide less than 50% of their calories from fat.
   a. true
   b. false

2. The body resists free radical assault by creating:
   a. free conservatives
   b. antioxidants
   c. extra water
   d. all of the above
   e. none of the above

3. Quantitative measures of nutrient levels in hair may be helpful in determining nutritional status.
   a. true
   b. false

4. A quality multivitamin, multimineral supplement should meet all the of the following criteria except:
   a. contain RDA levels of most of the required micronutrients
   b. contain vitamins in absorbable forms
   c. contain bioavailable minerals
   d. provide ingredients in compressed pills
   e. prepackaged in opaque containers

5. Food may have medicinal effects.
   a. true
   b. false

Table 17–1. Nutrients—Their Functions, RDA Levels, and Food Sources.

Nutrient	Function	Requirements	Signs of Deficiency	Food Sources
Water/Fluids The body is 60% water by weight. Water is the primary component of all bodily fluids and is an essential nutrient.	Water is involved in every bodily function. It transports nutrients in and out of cells, removes toxins, and is necessary for all digestive, absorptive, circulatory, and excretory functions. Water is necessary for the utilization of water-soluble B-complex and C vitamins, and for maintaining proper body temperature.	Adults: three quarts per day. Recommended: Eight 8 ounce glasses taken at intervals throughout the day.	Pale yellow urine shows a healthy state of hydration. Dark or scanty urine, thirst, and dry mouth are early signs of dehydration.	Best: Pure and clean spring water. Avoid: Beverages containing caffeine, sodas, prepackaged punches, and colored drinks.
Complex Carbohydrates Complex carbohydrates are classified as sugars, starches, or fiber and contain many vitamins, minerals, and trace minerals essential to good health.	Complex carbohydrates are needed to regulate protein and fat metabolism. Carbohydrates provide the body with energy. They are needed for digestion and assimilation of food.	50–65% of total calories.	Lack of energy, exhaustion, mineral imbalances, breakdown of proteins in tissues.	Whole grains, vegetables, legumes (dried beans, peas), fruits.
Proteins Protein makes up about 20% of our body weight and is the primary component of muscle, hair, skin, and eyes. Proteins are composed of amino acids, 22 of which are essential for normal development. The body can make 14 of them; the other 8 must be obtained in the diet.	Protein is essential for growth and maintenance of body tissue. Protein is needed for the manufacture of hormones, antibodies, and enzymes. It provides the body with energy and heat and also maintains the acid/alkali balance.	15–25% of total calories. The recommendaton for daily intake is 0.8 g/kg of ideal body weight.	Weight loss, weakness, lack of appetite, edema, diarrhea, vomiting.	Complete proteins: milk, eggs, cheese, fish, meat, poultry, nuts, legumes. Combining grains and vegetables will also provide a complete protein.
Fatty Acids The body does require essential fatty acids (EFAs): linoleic, linolenic, and arachidonic. The typical American diet is deficient in EFAs but has too much saturated fat.	Fatty acids transport fat-soluble A, D, E, and K vitamins. EFAs help manage cholesterol, regulate body temperature, and control blood pressure. EFAs are essential for growth and development and healthy skin, hair, and nails. Fats are a form of energy reserve and insulation for the body.	10–20% of total calories	Skin, hair, and nail disorders; impaired metabolism of fats and fat-soluble vitamins. Symptoms of excess dietary fat are more common: obesity; high LDL: HDL cholesterol ratio: atherosclerosis; colon cancer, etc.	Best: cold-expeller pressed safflower, sunflower, canola, olive, flax, pumpkin oils. In moderation: saturated fats found in animal products such as meat and dairy products, tropical oils such as palm and coconut oil.

(continued)

212

Table 17–1. (continued)

Vitamin	Function	Recommended Daily Allowance—Optimum Levels	Signs of Deficiency	Food Sources
Fat Soluble Vitamins				
Beta Carotene (converts to Vitamin A)	*Known:* Strengthens mucous membranes, adrenal glands, and eyes. Promotes healthy skin and epithelial tissue *Possible:* May reduce the risk of heart disease, breast, lung, colon, cervical cancer; may retard macular degeneration	*Females:* 5000-25000 IU *Males:* 5000-25000 IU *Toxicity:* Vitamin A is best taken as beta carotene, which the body turns into vitamin A as needed and shows little potential for toxicity. About 10000-15000 IU will convert to approximately 5000 IU of Vitamin A. Preformed vitamin A, taken as Retinol or Palmitate, can build up to toxic levels when taken above 5000-10000 IU.	Night blindness; eye problems; increased susceptibility to infection; dry, bumpy skin.	Fish liver oil, dark green leafy vegetables, yellow fruits and vegetables, vitamin A fortified milk.
Vitamin D	*Known:* Supports bone and tooth growth, assists nervous system functions. Necessary for proper absorption of calcium, phosphorus, magnesium, and zinc. Supports the healthy functioning of the thyroid gland. *Possible:* May help prevent osteoporosis and kidney disease	*Females:* 400 IU *Males:* 400 IU *Toxicity:* 1000 IU	Bone and tooth problems. Nearsightedness and hearing loss	Fish liver oil, fortified milk and cereal, salmon, herring, sardines, butter, eggs. Sunshine is the best source.
Vitamin E	*Known:* helps prevent anemia and retrolental fibroplasia in premature infants. Possible: May reduce risk of colon, breast, and oral cancers, heart attack, and atherosclerosis. May slow the aging of cells and protect tissues from damage by pollutants.	*Females:* 12 IU-400 IU *Males:* 15 IU-400 IU *Toxicity:* 1200 IU	Dry skin.	Cold pressed vegetable, seed or nut oils. Nuts, seeds, or whole grains.
Vitamin K	*Known:* Essential for blood clotting. Necessary for bone formation.	*Females:* 65 mcg; *Males:* 80 mcg	Blood clotting difficulty.	Dark green leafy vegetables, liver, milk, yogurt, cold pressed corn and soy bean oils.

(continued)

Table 17–1. *(continued)*

Vitamins	Function	Recommended Daily Intake	Signs of Deficiency	Food Sources
Water Soluble Vitamins				
Vitamin B1 (Thiamine)	Supports healthy functioning of the heart, muscles, and nerves. Plays a role in the breakdown of carbohydrates and cellular production of energy.	*Females:* 1.5 mg–10 mg *Males:* 1.1 mg–10 mg No known toxicity	Fatigue, memory loss, irritability, insomnia, depression. Severe thiamine deficiency causes beriberi.	Wheat germ and bran, Brewer's yeast, blackstrap molasses, brown rice, pork, peas, spinach, nuts
Vitamin B2 (Riboflavin)	Plays a role in the breakdown and use of carbohydrates, fats, and proteins; helps cells use oxygen; involved in cellular energy production; supports the production of adrenal hormones; helps the body utilize other vitamins; supports the eyes, skin, and hair.	*Females:* 1.3 mg–10 mg *Males:* 1.7 mg–10 mg No known toxicity	Sensitivity or inflammation of mucous membranes of the mouth, cracks at the corners of the mouth, light-sensitivity, reddening of the eyes, dermatitis.	Brewer's yeast, organ meats, trout, mackerel, salmon, Nori seaweed, Brussels sprouts, asparagus, spinach
Vitamin B3 Niacin	Involved in the breakdown of carbohydrates and fats; needed in the formation of red blood cells and synthesis of hormones; supports healthy functioning of the nervous and digestive systems; helps maintain healthy skin.	*Females:* 15 mg–50 mg *Males:* 19 mg–50 mg No known toxicity though sometimes dosages over 50 mg can cause tingling and flushing	Fatigue, irritability, insomnia, indigestion, blood sugar fluctuations, skin eruptions. Severe Niacin deficiency causes pellagra.	Liver, organ meats, yeast, dried beans and peas, wheat germ, avocados, figs, dates, and prunes
Vitamin B5 Pantothenic Acid	Involved in the breakdown and use of carbohydrates and fats; involved in adrenal function to counter stress and enhance metabolism; helps the body use other vitamins; supports sinuses.	*Females:* 7 mg–50 mg *Males:* 7 mg–50 mg No known toxicity	None known for vitamin B5 alone, but deficiency of any B vitamin usually means deficiency of others.	Organ meats; Brewer's yeast, egg yolk, fish, chicken, whole grain cereals, sweet potatoes, green beans.

(continued)

214

Table 17–1. *(continued)*

Vitamins	Function	Recommended Daily Intake	Signs of Deficiency	Food Sources
Water Soluble Vitamins (cont.)				
Vitamin B6 (Pyridoxine)	Involved in amino acid metabolism and the breakdown of proteins, carbohydrates and fats; involved in healthy functioning of the nervous and digestive systems; aids fluid balance regulation; involved in the production of red blood cells and antibodies; helps maintain healthy skin.	*Females:* 1.6 mg–15 mg *Males:* 2.0 mg–15 mg *Toxicity:* 2,000 mg	Muscle weakness, nervousness, premenstrual tension, irritability, depression.	Organ meats, wheat germ, fish, poultry, soybeans, bananas, prunes, potatoes
Vitamin B12 (Cobalamin)	Necessary for healthy functioning of the nervous system; involved in production of red blood cells; helps the body use folic acid; influences energy level. May protect against heart disease and nerve damage.	*Females:* 2.0 μcg–20 μcg *Males:* 2.0 μcg–20 μcg No known toxicity	Soreness or weakness of the arms and legs, loss of coordination, irritability, megaloblastic anemia, pernicious anemia	Liver, trout, mackerel, oysters, poultry, fish, yams, egg yolks, yogurt
Biotin	Involved in metabolism of fatty acids; involved in maintaining health of skin, hair, sweat glands, nerves, and bone narrow.	*Females:* 2.05 μcg–20 μcg *Males:* 3.0 μcg–20 μcg No known toxicity	Fatigue, nausea, loss of appetite, muscle cramps, high cholesterol	Egg yolks, brewer's yeast, unpolished rice, nuts, and milk.

(continued)

Table 17-1. *(continued)*

Vitamins	Function	Recommended Daily Intake	Signs of Deficiency	Food Sources
Water Soluble Vitamins (cont.)				
Folic Acid	*Known:* Aids in the production of red blood cells; used in the formation of nucleic acid for RNA and DNA; essential for cell division; helps protect against cervical dysplasia *Possible:* May reduce heart disease by lowering homocysteine. May reduce risk of neural tube birth defects	*Females:* 400–1000 μcg; especially important in pregnancy *Males:* 200 mg–400 μcg No known toxicity, but excess folic acid intake can mask symptoms of B12 deficiency.	Anemia, digestive problems, poor memory, fatigue	Spinach, kale, beet greens, chard, asparagus, broccoli; corn, lima beans, oranges, cantaloupe, liver, kidney.
Vitamin C	*Known:* Active in the formation and maintenance of collagen for skin, ligaments, cartilage, capillary linings, bones, and teeth. Helps maintain normal enzyme function; involved in production of neurotransmitters and adrenal gland hormones; *Possible:* may strengthen the immune system and support wound healing; may reduce risk of cancer and heart disease and protect against macular degeneration.	*Females:* 60–1000 mg *Males:* 260–1000 mg No known toxicity, but speculation that very high intake of vitamin C may cause kidney stones.	Slow wound healing, poor resistance to infection, bleeding gums, easy bruising and petechiae (tiny hemorrhages) in the skin.	Lemons, grapefruits, oranges, red/green peppers, cauliflower, kale, asparagus, brussel sprouts, tomatoes, strawberries, papayas, cantaloupe, kiwis. Highest in fresh, uncooked food.

(continued)

Table 17–1. *(continued)*

Mineral	Function	Recommended Daily Intake	Signs of Deficiency	Food Sources
Bulk Minerals				
Calcium	Plays a role in development and maintenance of bone and teeth; needed for muscular contraction and regulating the heartbeat; important in nerve transmission, and proper functioning of cell membranes; prevents osteoporosis.	*Females:* 800–1200 mg *Males:* 800–1,000 mg No known toxicity, although possible that prolonged high amounts of calcium can lead to hypercalcemia (high blood calcium levels) and soft tissue calcification.	Easy bone fractures, muscle cramps, irritability, insomnia, brittle nails	Yogurt, milk and dairy products, collards, turnip greens, broccoli, kale, tempeh, tofu
Magnesium	Functions to relax skeletal muscles; involved in blood sugar metabolism and energy maintenance; assists intra cellular exchange of nutrients; involved in structuring of basic genetic material (DNA and RNA).	*Females:* 300 mg *Males:* 300 mg No known toxicity, although possible symptoms of magnesium toxicity can occur with low calcium intake.	Fatigue, insomnia, muscle tension, irritability, muscle twitching. Dietary inadequacy considered unlikely	Soybeans, whole grains, shellfish, salmon, liver, almonds, cashews, molasses, bananas, potatoes, milk, green vegetables, honey.
Phosphorus	Involved in bone and tooth formation, cell growth and repair; involved in breakdown of carbohydrates and fats for energy; supports nerve conduction, muscle contraction and the body's use of vitamins.	*Females:* 850-1200 mg *Males:* 850-1000 mg No known toxicity, though high intake of phosphorus can interfere with calcium absorption. The ratio of phosphorus to calcium should be 1:1.	Weight loss, muscle cramps, dizziness, stiff joints, bone pains. Dietary inadequacy unlikely to occur if protein and calcium intake is adequate	Fish, poultry, eggs, whole grains, yellow cheese, sodas
Potassium	Involved in healthy, steady functioning of the nervous system; helps generate muscle contraction and regulates the heartbeat. With sodium, regulates the water balance and acid-base balance of the blood and tissues.	*Females:* 2000 mg *Males:* 2000 mg No known toxicity, though elevated potassium levels (hyperkalemia) can occur with some medical conditions, ie, decreased renal function.	Muscle fatigue, general fatigue, swelling in extremities, irregular heartbeat, hypertension. Dietary inadequacy considered unlikely.	Dried apricots, yams, bananas, citrus fruit, lima beans, potatoes, avocados, broccoli, wheat germ, milk
Sodium	Helps maintain normal fluid levels in the body; involved in healthy muscle functioning. Supports hydrochloric acid production in the stomach. With potassium, regulates the fluid balance in the body and acid-base balance of the blood and tissues.	*Females:* 2000-5000 mg *Males:* 2000-5000 mg *Toxicity:* high sodium diets have been linked to hypertension.	Fainting, intolerance to heat, muscle cramps, swelling in extremities, confusion. Dietary inadequacy considered unlikely.	Most foods and water, especially salt, salted foods, soy sauce, cheese, chips, seafood

(continued)

Table 17–1. *(continued)*

Mineral	Function	Recommended Daily Intake	Signs of Deficiency	Food Sources
Trace Elements				
Chromium	*Known:* Enhances effect of insulin in the body; involved in maintaining blood sugar level and in healthy functioning of the circulatory system. *Possible:* in conjunction with exercise may promote acquisition of lean muscle.	*Females:* 50 mcg–400 mcg *Males:* 50 mcg–500 mcg No known Toxicity	Blood sugar fluctuations, abnormal cholesterol metabolism, fatigue	Brewer's yeast, liver, beef, oysters, whole wheat, rye, black pepper, molasses, beer.
Cobalt	Involved in formation and healthy functioning of red blood cells.	Cobalt is an essential trace element, though no specific RDA is established.	Pernicious anemia, weakness, nausea. Deficiency usually not a problem if B12 intake is adequate.	Organ meats, oysters, milk, sea vegetables, spinach, cabbage.
Copper	Plays a role in formation of bone, hemoglobin, and red blood cells. Involved in healing processes, energy production, hair and skin color, and taste sensitivity. Works with vitamin C to form collagen.	*Females:* 1.5 mg-3.0 mg *Males:* 1.5 mg-3.0 mg No known toxicity, though high copper levels may cause fatigue, and muscle and joint pain.	Anemia, inflammation, paleness, skin eruptions.	Shellfish, liver, poultry, cherries, nuts, cocoa gelatin, whole grains, eggs; legumes, peas, avocados.
Iron	Involved in the production of hemoglobin and oxygenation of red blood cells; helps immune system and energy production.	*Females:* 18 mg *Males:* 10 mg *Toxicity:* 75 mg	Fatigue, anemia, lack of stamina, headaches, decreased appetite.	Meat; liver, blackstrap molasses, eggs, fish, spinach, asparagus, prunes, raisins, sea vegetables. Enriched breads and cereals
Selenium	*Known:* Helps protect cell membranes and intracellular structures from lipid peroxidation; supports pancreatic functioning *Possible:* May be involved in increasing resistance to cancer; Works as an antioxidant with vitamin E to neutralize free radicals and produce antibodies.	*Females:* 55mcg-200 mcg *Males:* 70mcg-200 mcg *Toxicity:* may occur in amounts greater than 1 mg	Dry flaky scalp, skin problem.	Whole grains, soybeans, tuna, seafood, Brazil nuts, brown rice, pineapples, some drinking water
Silicon	Involved in bone formation; supports firmness and strength in tissues of the skin, blood vessels, tendons, and eyes.	Silicon is an essential trace element, though no specific RDA is established.	Reduced stamina, connective tissue disorders, muscle cramps, insomnia.	Foods high in fiber such as apples, wheat, oat, and rice hulls, lettuce, cucumbers.

(continued)

Table 17–1. *(continued)*

Mineral	Function	Recommended Daily Intake	Signs of Deficiency	Food Sources
Trace Elements (cont.)				
Zinc	Important in prostate gland function and growth of the reproductive organs; promotes burn and wound healing; supports the immune system involved in carbohydrate and protein digestion.	Females: 12mg–30 mg Males: 15mg–30 mg Toxicity: amounts over 150 mg may interfere with assimilation of other minerals	Fatigue, white spots on fingernails, reduced sense of smell or taste, menstrual irregularities, slow wound healing.	Oysters, Brewer's yeast, liver, seafood, wheat germ, bran, oatmeal, nuts, peas, carrots, spinach, sunflower seeds.
Iodine	Important in fat metabolism; supports healthy thyroid function; prevents goiter.	*Females:* 150 mcg *Males:* 150 mcg No known toxicity although amounts over 700 mcg may reduce thyroid function	Goiter, hypothyroidism, slower metabolism, fatigue.	Iodized salt, seaweed, ocean fish, kelp.

References

1. Beasley J, Swift J. The Kellogg Report: The impact of nutrition, environment and lifestyle on the health of Americans. Institute of Health Policy and Practice. Bard College Center, Annandale-on-Hudson, 1989.

2. National Research Council. *Diet and Health; Implication for Reducing Chronic Disease Risk.* Washington DC: National Academy Press; 1989,

3. Shils M, Olson, B, Shike M, eds. *Modern Nutrition in Health and Disease.* 4th ed. Philadelphia, Pa: Lea and Febiger; 1994.

4. Sataloff, RT. Introduction. *Professional Voice: The Science and Art of Clinical Care*, New York, NY: Raven Press; 1991:1–5.

5. Yaspelkis B. Carbohydrates spare muscle glycogen during variable-intensity exercise. *J Appl Physiol.* 1993;75(4):1477–1485.

6. Johnson H. The requirements for fluid replacement during heavy sweating and benefits of carbohydrates and minerals. Presented at the American Chemical Society National Meeting; April, 1993.

7. Haas E. Special diets and supplement programs: executives and travel. *Staying Healthy with Nutrition*, Berkeley Calif: Celestial Arts; 1992:769–775.

8. Haas E. The building blocks of nutrition. *Staying Healthy with Nutrition.* Berkeley Calif: Celestial Arts; 1992:13.

9. *National Academy of Sciences Recommended Dietary Allowances* 10th ed. Washington, DC: National Academy Press; 1989.

10. Koop CE. *The Surgeon General's Report on Nutrition and Health.* Washington, DC: National Academy Press; 1988.

11. *Health and Nutrition Examination Survey.* Washington, DC: National Center for Health Statistics. US Public Health Service; 1982. Department of Health, Education and Welfare publication. 79-1697.

12. *National Health Survey. Series II.* Washington, DC: National Center for Health Statistics; 1984. US Dept of Health and Human Services, 1984. publication 231.

13. *Ten State Nutritional Survey.* Rockville MD; 1972.US Dept of Health Education and Welfare publication 72–8130.

14. Burr M. Effects of changes in fish, fat and fiber intakes on death and myocardial reinfarctions: diet and rein-farction trial (DART). *Lancet.* 1989;2:757–761.

15. *Eating Right Pyramid.* US Dept. of Agriculture, 1992; Hyattsville, Md: US Dept of Agriculture publication 253

16. Dietary guidelines and the results of food consumption surveys. United States Dept of Agriculture Human Nutrition Information Service. US Dept. of Agriculture publication 342 Hyattsville MD, 1993, USDA.

17. Waslien C. Micronutrients and antioxidants in processed foods—analysis of data from 1987 food additives survey. *Nutr Today*, 1990;23(2):36–42.

18. Karmas E, Harris R, eds. *Nutritional Evaluation of food Processing.* 3rd ed. New York NY: Van Nostrand Reinhold; 1988.

19. *Provisional Table on Percent Retention of Nutrients in Food Preparation.* Hyattsville MD: US Dept of Agriculture Human Nutrition Information Service. US Dept of Agriculture publication 186;1991.

20. Carlson B. Loss of vitamin C in vegetables during the food service cycle *J Am Dietetic Assoc.* 1988; 88(4)65–67.

21. Dietz J. Effects of processing upon vitamins and proteins in foods. *Nutr Today.* 1989;16(1)6–14.

22. Patterson B. Fruit and vegetables in the American diet: data for the NHANES II survey. *Am J Public Health.* 1990;80 (5):1443–1449.

23. Watt B, Merrill A. *Composition of Foods, Agriculture Handbook No. 8.* Washington DC: Agricultural Research Service; US Dept of Agriculture; 1975.

24. *Foods Nutrition Encyclopedia.* Clovis, Calif: Pegus Press, 1983;2: 2232–2269.

25. Shrouder H. The insidious disappearance of vital trace minerals in the American diet. *Health News Res.* 1993;3(1)12–16.

26. National Research Council. *How Should the Recommended Daily Allowances be Revised?* Washington, DC: National Academy Press; 1994.

27. *Dynamic Health and Nutrition Infobase.* Redwood Calif: Intelligent Health Inc. (209) 299–3060.

28. Cutler R. Antioxidants and aging. *Am J Clin Nut* 1991;53(suppl 1):373S–379S.

29. Blumberg J. Dietary antioxidants and aging. *Contemp Nutr.* 1992;17(3):1–7.

30. Goldfarb A. Antioxidants: role of supplementation to prevent exercise-induced oxidative stress. *Med Sci Sports Exer .* 1993;25(2):232–236.

31. Singh V. A current perspective on nutrition and exercise. *J Nutr.* 1992;122(3):760–765.

32. Dragsted L, Strube M, Larsoen J. Cancer-protective factors in fruits and vegetables: biochemical and biological background. *Pharmacal Toxicol.* 1993;72(suppl 1): 116–135.

33. Hennekens C. Antioxidant vitamins and cancer. *Am J Medicine.* 1994;97(3):22S–28S.

34. Comstock G. Serum retinol, beta-carotene, vitamin E, and selenium as related to subsequent cancer of specific sites. *Am J Epidemiol* 1992;135(2):115–123.

35. Potischman N, Hoover R, Brinton L, et al. The relations between cervical cancer and serological markers of nutritional status. *Nut Cancer.* 1994;21(3):193–201.

36. Flora S. Antioxidant activity and other mechanisms of thiols involved in chemoprevention of mutation and cancer. *Am J Med.* 1991;91(suppl 3C):9C–13C.

37. Weisburger JH. Nutritional approach to cancer prevention with emphasis on vitamins, antioxidants, and carotenoids. *Am J Clin Nutr.* 1991;53(suppl 1):226S–237S.

38. Ziegler RG. Vegetables, fruits, and carotenoids and the risk of cancer. *Am J Clin Nutr.* 1991;53(suppl 1):251S–259S.

39. lock G.Vitamin C and cancer prevention: the epidemiologic evidence. *Am J Clin Nutr.* 1991;53(suppl 1): 270S–283S.

40. Knekt P, Aromaa A, Maatela J, et al. Vitamin E and cancer prevention. *Am J Clin Nutr.* 1991;53(suppl 1): 283S–286S.

41. Prasad K. Vitamin E and cancer prevention: recent advances and future potentials. *J Am College Nutr.* 1992;11(5):487–500.

42. Schorah CJ, Sobala G, Sanderson M, Collis N, Primrose J. Gastric juice ascorbic acid: effects on disease and implications for gastric carcinogenesis. *Am J Clin Nutr.* 1991;53(suppl 1):283S–286S.

43. Byers T, Perry N. Dietary carotenes, vitamin A and vitamin E as protective antioxidants in human cancers. *Ann Rev Nutr.* 1992;12:139-159.

44. Garewal H. Potential role of beta-carotene in prevention of oral cancer. *Am J Clin Nutr.* 1991;53(suppl 1):294S–297S.

45. Gridley G. Vitamin supplement use and reduced risk of oral and pharyngeal cancer. *Am J Epidemiol.* 1992;135(10): 1083–1092

46. Garewal H. Emerging role of beta-carotene and antioxidant nutrients in prevention of oral cancer. *Arch Otolaryngol Head Neck Surg.* 1995;121(2):115–121.

47. Stich H, Matthew B, Sankaranarayanaan R, and Krishnan Nair M. Remission of precancerous lesions in the oral cavity of tobacco chewers and maintenance of the protective effect of beta-carotene or vitamin A. *Am J Clin Nutr.* 1991;53(suppl 1):2298S–2304S.

48. Gaziano JM. Dietary antioxidants and cardiovascular disease. *Ann NY Acad Sci.* 1992;669:249–254.

49. Selhub J, Jacques P, Bostom A, et al. Association between plasma homocysteine concentrations and extracranial carotid artery stenosis. *N Engl J Med.* 1995; 332:286–291.

50. Harris W. The prevention of atherosclerosis with antioxidants. *Clin Cardiol.* 1992:15(4)636–640.

51. Luc G, Fruchart J. Oxidation of lipoproteins and atherosclerosis. *Am J Clin Nutr.* 1991;53(suppl 1):206S– 209S.

52. Hodis H, Mack W, LaBree L, et al. Serial coronary angiographic evidence that antioxidant vitamin intake reduces progression of coronary artery atherosclerosis. *JAMA.* 1995;273(23)1849–1854.

53. Jill I, Grundy S. Influence of antioxidant vitamins of LDL oxidation. *Ann NY Acad Sci.* 1993;721:237.

54. Waeg G. Role of vitamin E in preventing the oxidation of low-density lipoprotein. *Am J Clin Nutr.* 1991;53 (suppl 1):189–93S.

55. Prasad K. Oxygen free radicals and hypercholesterolemic atherosclerosis: effect of vitamin E. *Am Heart J.* 1993;125:958.

56. Rimm E. Vitamin E consumption and the risk of coronary heart disease in men. *N Engl J Med.* 1993;328(20): 1450-1456.

57. Stampfer M, Hennekens C, Manson J, et al. Vitamin E consumption and the risk of coronary disease in women. *N Engl J Med.* 1993;328(20):1444–1449.

58. Steinberg D. Antioxidants in the prevention of human atherosclerosis. Summary of the Proceedings of National Heart, Lung, and Blood Institute Workshop; Bethesda, Md; Sept, 1991.

59. Werler M. Periconceptual folic acid exposure and risk of occurent neural-tube defects. *J Am Med Assoc.* 1993;269(10):1257–1261.

60. Varma S. Scientific basis for medical therapy of cataracts by antioxidants. *Am J Clin Nutr.* 1991;53(suppl 1):335S–345S.

61. Robertson J, Donner A, Trevithick J. A possible role for vitamins C and E in cataract prevention. *Am J Clin Nutr.* 1991;53(suppl 1):346S–351S.

62. Jacques P, Chylack L, Jr. Epidemiological evidence of a role for the antioxidant vitamins and carotenoids in cataract prevention. *Am J Clin Nutr.* 1991;53(suppl 1):352S–355S.

63. Schmidt K. Antioxidant vitamins and beta-carotene: effects on immunocompetence. *Am J Clin Nutr.* 1991;53(suppl 1):383S–385S.

64. Chandra R. Effect of vitamin and trace mineral supplementation on immune responses and infection in elderly subjects. *Lancet.* 1993;341(130):306–307.

65. Sohal R. The free radical hypothesis of aging: an appraisal of the current status. *Aging Clin Exp Res.* 1993;5(1):3–17.

66. Scandalios J., Molecular biology of free radical scavenging systems. *Free Rad Biol Med.* 1993;14;227–335.

67. Halliwell B, Gutteridge J. *Free Radicals in Biology and Medicine.* Oxford: Clarendon Press; 1985.

68. Sies H. Oxidative stress: from basic research to clinical application. *Am J Med.* 1991;91(suppl 3C):3–31.

69. Jenkins R. Oxidant stress, aging, and exercise. *Med Science Sports Exer.* 1993;25(2):210–215.

70. Alessio H. Exercise-induced oxidative stress.*Med Science Sports Exer.* 1993;25(2):218–224.

71. Halliwell B. Reactive oxygen species in living systems: source, biochemistry, and role in human disease. *Am J Med.* 1991;91(Suppl 3C):9C–13C.

72. Cacciuttolo M. Hyperoxia induces DNA damage in mammalian cells. *Free Radical Biol Med.* 1993;14:267–276.

73. Cochrane C. Cellular injury by oxidants. *Am J Med.* 1991;91(suppl 3C):3C–23C.

74. McCord J. Human disease, free radicals and the oxidant/antioxidant balance. *Clin Biochem.* 1993;26(5): 351–358.

75. Crystal RG.Oxidants and respiratory tract epithelial injury: pathogenesis and strategies for therapeutic intervention. *Am J Med.* 1991;91(suppl 3C):3C–39C.

76. Ferrari R. Oxygen free radicals and myocardial damage: protective role of thiol-containing agents. *Am J Med.* 1991;91(suppl 3C):9C–13C.

77. Flaherty J. Myocardial injury mediated by oxygen free radicals. *Am J Med.* 1991;91(suppl 3C): 19C–23C.

78. Ferrari R, Ceconi C, Curello S, et al. Role of oxygen free radicals in ischemic and reperfused myocardium. *Am J Clin Nutr.* 1991;53(suppl 1):189S-193S.

79. Merry P, Grootveld M, Lunec J, Blake D. Oxidative damage to lipids within the inflamed human joint provides evidence of radical-mediated hypoxic reperfusion injury. *Am J Clin Nutr.* 1991;53(suppl 1): 362S–369S.

80. Hirsch E. Does oxidative stress participate in nerve cell death in Parkinson's disease? *Eur Neurol.* 1993;33(suppl 1):52–59.

81. Adams J. Oxygen free radicals and Parkinson's disease. *Free Rad Biol Med.* 1991;10(1):161–169.

82. Ames B, Shigenaga M, Hagen T. Oxidants, antioxidants and the degenerative diseases of aging. *Proc Nat Acad Sci.* 1993;90:7915–7922.

83. Krinsky N. Mechanism of action of biological antioxidants. *Proc Soc Exper Biol Med.* 1992;200:248.

84. Martins E. Role of antioxidants in protecting cellular DNA from damage by oxidative stress. *Mutat Res.* 1991;250:95–101.

85. Diplock AT. Antioxidant nutrients and disease prevention: an overview. *Am J Clin Nutr.* 1991;53(suppl 1):189S–193S.

86. Sies H. Antioxidant functions of vitamins—vitamins E and C, beta-carotene, and other carotenoids. *Ann NY Acad Sci.* 1992;669:7–20.

87. Blumberg J. Changing nutrient requirements in older adults. *Nutr Today.* 1992;27(5):15.

89. Pantox Antioxidant Profile (PxP). Pantox Laboratories. (617) 683-0004. Boston, Mass.

90. Matthews K. Nutrition of cells in culture In: Shils M, Olson B, Shike M, eds. *Modern Nutrition in Health and Disease.* 4th ed. Philadelphia, Pa: Lea and Febiger; 1994.

91. Buck L. A functional analytical technique for monitoring nutrient status and repletion. *Am Clin Lab.* 1993;12(6):8–10.

92. Essential metabolics analysis.*Technical Bulletin.* SpectraCell Laboratories, Inc. Houston, Tex. (800) 227–5227.

93. Spectrox: A total antioxidant function test. *Technical Bulletin.* SpectraCell Laboratories, Inc. Houston, Tex. (800) 227–5227.

94. Packer L. Interactions among antioxidants in health and disease. *Proc Soc Exper Biol Med.* 1992;200–:271.

95. Trio of vitamins are recruited in the fight against heart disease. *Environ Nutr. Sept.* 1992;15:9.

96. Palozza P. Communication: beta carotene and alpha tocopherol are synergistic antioxidants *Arch Biochem Biophys.* 1992;297(11):184–187.

97. Hunter B. Glutathione: an unheralded antioxidant. *Nutr Res.* 76(8):8–10.

98. Erdman J. Factors affecting the bioavailability of vitamin A, carotenoids, and vitamin E. *Food Technol.* 1988;14(3):214–221.

99. US Patent # 4,822,816. Inter-Cal Corp, 4-18-89.

100. King G. Rate of excretion of vitamin C in human urine. *Age .*1994;17(1):1–6.

101. *The Vitamin E Fact Book.* San Francisco, Calif. Vitamin E Research and Information Service; 1984.

102. Neve J. Clinical implication of trace elements in endocrinology. *Biol Trace Element Res.* 1992;32(2);173–185.

103. Ashmead H. *Conversations on Chelation and Mineral Nutrition.* New Canaan, Conn: Keats Publishing; 1989.

104. Informed Nutrition Services, Provo, Utah. 1-800-497-1076.

105. Hegenauer J. U.S. RDA vs. RDI: the alphabet soup of nutrition labeling. *Nutrition and the MD.* 1993;19(1)3–5.

106. Howe G. Dietary intake of fiber and decreased risk of cancers of the colon and rectum: evidence from analysis of 13 controlled studies. *J Nat Cancer Inst.* 1992; 84(24):1887–1896.

107. Winter R. *Medicines in Foods: Neutraceuticals That Help Prevent and Treat Physical and Emotional Illnesses.* New York, NY: Random House; 1995 .

108. Rennard S. Chicken soup passes a scientific examination. Proceedings of the International Conference of the American Lung Association; May, 1994, Atlanta Ga.

109. Korets R. The chicken in the history and in the soup. *Allergy Proceedings.* 1993;13(2):105–112.

110. Krichevsky D. Garlic and cardiovascular disease. *Nutrition and the MD.* 1995;21(2)1–5.

111. Warshafsky S. Effect of garlic on total serum cholesterol: a meta-analysis. *Ann Int Med.* 1993;119(7):599–605.

112. McMahon F. Can garlic lower blood pressure: a pilot study. *Pharmacotherapy.* 1993;13(4);406–407.

113. Barnes S. The isoflavone Genistein: a good reason for eating soy. Presented at the 20th American Cancer Society National Meeting; August, 1994; Washington DC.

114. Messina M. The role of soy products in reducing risk of cancer. *J Nat Can Inst.* 1991; 83(8) 541–546.

115. Barnes S. Soybeans inhibit mammary tumors in models of breast cancer. in Pariza M, ed. *Mutagens and Carcinogens in the Diet.* New York, NY: Wiley-Liss; 1990.

116. Pierson H. Food phytochemical pharmacology—the basis for designer food development. *Regulatory Affairs.* 1993;5(1)219–222.

117. Chodzko-Zajko W, Ringel R. Physiological aspects of aging. *J Voice.* 1987;1(1):18–26.

118. Kahane J. Connective tissue changes in the larynx and their effects on voice. *J Voice.* 1987;1(1):27–30.

18

Medications: Effects and Side Effects in Professional Voice Users

Robert Thayer Sataloff, Mary Hawkshaw, and Deborah Caputo Rosen

Medications are used to treat many problems commonly encountered in voice professionals. Some are illnesses located in the head and neck, others occur elsewhere in the body. However, virtually all medications have some potential effect on the voice as discussed in the first edition of this book and other literature.[1,2] In many cases, the effects are minor and not clinically significant. However, all physicians and others caring for professional voice users should be familiar with drug-induced phenomena that may affect voice function.

In addition to the recognized effects and side effects of medications, it is important also to consider biological variability when trying to predict or recognize vocal consequences of pharmacologic agents. The effects of medication are influenced by sex, age, body size, metabolic status, individual biological response proclivities, and concurrent use of other medications or recreational drugs. "Recommended doses" are the amounts of drug generally required to achieve the desired balance between effect and side effect. However, they are merely guidelines based on average responses in test populations. Optimizing the relationship between desired effect and undesirable side effect requires individualization, especially in professional voice users for whom "minor" side-effects may be disabling.

Antihistamines

Antihistamines may be used to treat allergies. However, virtually all antihistamines can exert a drying effect on upper respiratory tract secretions, although severity varies widely from drug to drug, and from person to person. In addition, antihistamines are often combined with sympathomimetic or parasympatholytic agents, which further reduce and thicken mucosal secretions and may reduce lubrication to the point of producing a dry cough. This may be more harmful to phonation than the allergic condition itself. Normal mucosal secretions and free movement of the vibratory margin of the vocal folds are extremely important. If vocal tract lubrication is impaired by dehydration, or by shifting the normal balance of serous and mucinous secretions, alterations in phonation occur. When professional voice users develop thick, viscous vocal fold secretions during performance, results can be disastrous.

Laryngologists frequently discover that a patient has self-medicated with an over-the-counter (OTC) antihistamine preparation. The majority of antihistamine agents are acetylcholine antagonists, and this parasympatholytic activity probably accounts for the increased viscosity of secretions. Interestingly, antihistamines used to treat allergies do not act to block the stimulant effects of histamine on gastric acid secretions, but they do affect salivary glands and mucous-secreting membranes of the respiratory tract. They may also have sedative effects that impair sensorium and disturb performance. They are different from the effects achieved by antihistamines used to treat other conditions such as reflux (cimetidine, ranitidine, and other H_2 blockers). Mild, newer antihistamines such as loratadine (Claritin) produce less drowsiness and often less dryness; but in many people they are also less effective than drugs with more disturbing side effects. Mild antihistamines in small doses may be helpful for performers with intermittent allergic symptoms, but the medications should be tried between performances, not immediately prior to professional engagements. When medication is needed to treat an acute allergic response shortly before performance, oral or injected cortico-steroids usually accomplish the desired result without causing significant side effects.

The most commonly encountered antihistamines are those belonging to the alkylamine or chlorpheniramine family. Because they have been deregulated by the FDA, these agents are being used with increasing frequency. Diphenhydramine is also present in some OTC sleep aids. Some of these aids also include scopolamine (which has a significant drying effect), presumably for its sedative effect. Promethazine is contained in several antitussive mixtures and can dry glottic secretions. Meclizine, an antihistamine used for dizziness and motion sickness, is also encountered commonly. All antihistamines provide some de-gree of relief from motion sickness, and to a greater or lesser degree, all cause drying.

Mucolytic Agents

Normal respiratory lubricant viscosity and vocal fold surface tension are essential to normal phonation. Dehydration and/or thickening of secretions may be caused by medications such as antihistamines, generalized dehydration, or other factors. Dehydration may occur as the result of athletic or recreational activities or environmental factors such as the dry air on airplanes and exposure to the high altitudes of certain cities. It must be remembered that the viscosity of respiratory secretions is directly related to available body water, assuming the absence of metabolic or pharmacologic interference. No medications, including mucolytic agents, are substitutes for adequate hydration. However, expectorants or mucolytics may be helpful in counteracting the effects of drugs like antihistamines and in ameliorating the mucosal consequences of dehydration quickly. Entex is a useful expectorant and vasoconstrictor that increases and thins mucosal secretions. Guaifenesin also thins and increases secretions. Humibid is currently among the most convenient preparations available. These drugs are relatively harmless and may be helpful in singers who complain of thick secretions, frequent throat clearing, or postnasal drip. Awareness of postnasal drip is often caused by secretions that are too thick rather than too plentiful.

Corticosteroids

Corticosteroids are potent anti-inflammatory agents and may be helpful in managing acute inflammatory laryngitis. Although many laryngologists recommend using steroids in low doses (methylprednisolone, 10 mg), the author (R.T.S.) has found higher doses for short periods of time more effective. Depending on the indication, dosage may be prednisolone (60 mg) or dexamethasone (6 mg) intramuscularly once and a similar starting dose orally tapered over 3 to 6 days. Regimens such as a dexamethasone or methylprednisolone (Decadron Dosepak or Medrol Dosepak) may also be used. Physicians should be familiar with the dose relationship among steroids (Table 19–1). Adrenocorticotropic hormone may also be used to increase endogenous cortisone output, decreasing inflammation and mobilizing water from an edematous larynx,[3] although the author (R.T.S.) has found traditional steroid therapy entirely satisfactory. Care must be taken not to prescribe steroids excessively. They should be used only when there is a pressing professional commitment that is being hampered by vocal fold inflammation. If there is any question that the inflammation may be of infectious origin, antibiotic coverage is recommended.

Corticosteroids may have adverse effects. Although they are not generally seen after the short-term steroid use appropriate for acute voice problems, they may occur in any patient. The more common corticosteroid side effects include gastric irritation with possible ulceration and hemorrhage, insomnia, mild mucosal drying, blurred vision, mood change (euphoria, occasionally psychosis), and irritability. Long-term effects such as muscle wasting and fat redistribution are generally not encountered after appropriate short-term use of steroids in professional vocalists. Another potential problem peculiar to professional voice users is steroid abuse. Because side effects are uncommon and steroids work extremely well, there is a tendency (especially among singers) to overuse or abuse them. This practice must be avoided.

Diuretics and Other Medications for Edema

In the premenstrual period, decreased estrogen and progesterone levels are associated with altered pituitary activity. An increase in circulating antidiuretic hormone results in fluid retention in Reinke's space as well as in other tissues. The fluid retained in the vocal fold during inflammation and hormonal fluid shifts is bound, not free, water.[4] Diuretics do not remobilize this fluid effectively and dehydrate the singer, resulting in decreased lubrication and thickened secretions and persistently edematous vocal folds.

Diuretics should not be used for vocal fold symptoms related to menses. If they must be used for other

Table 18–1. Steroid Equivalency.

Adrenocorticosteroids	Common Trade Name	Glucocorticoid (Anti-inflammatory Potency) Equivalent Dose (mg)	Mineralocorticoid (Sodium Retention) Relative Potency
Betamethasone	Celestone (Schering)	0.06	0
Cortisone	Cortone (M-S-D)	25	0.8
Dexamethasone	Decadron (M-S-D) Deronil (Schering) Dexameth (Major) Gammacorten (CIBA) Hexadrol (Organon)	0.75	0
Fludrocortisone	Florinef (Squibb)	0.1	100
Fluprednisolone	Alphadrol (Upjohn)	2	0
Hydrocortisone	Cort-Dome (Dome) Cortef (Upjohn) Cortenema (Rowell) Cortril (Pfizer) Hydrocortone (M-S-D)	20	1
Methylprednisone	Depo-Medrol (Upjohn) Medrol (Upjohn) Solu-Medrol (Upjohn)	4	4
Paramethasone	Haldrone (Lilly) Stemex (Syntex)	2	0
Prednisolone	Delta-Cortef (Upjohn) Hydeltra T.B.A. (M-S-D) Hydeltrasol (M-S-D) Meticortelone (Schering) Nisolone (Ascher) Sterane (Pfizer)	5	0.8
Prednisone	Delta Dome (Dome) Deltasone (Upjohn) Deltra (M-S-D) Meticorten (Schering) Paracort (Parke-Davis) Servisone (Lederle)	5	0.8
Triamcinolone	Aristocort (Lederle) Aristospan (Lederle) Kenacort (Squibb) Kenalog (Squibb)	4	0

Note: M—S—D, Merck, Sharp & Dohme.

purposes, the voice should be monitored closely. Steroids may be efficacious and can be used judiciously under crucial performance circumstances. However, they should certainly not be used habitually for monthly dysphonia premenstrualis.

Physical trauma is also a common cause of vocal fold mucosal edema. This condition is seen most commonly as a consequence of voice misuse or abuse such as athletic event or speaking too loudly in a bar. Highly trained voice users rarely have vocal fold edema as a result of their occupations (ie, the operatic singer),

but even these persons sometimes experience edema as a result of direct trauma to the laryngeal mucosa from inappropriately loud singing or yelling. Such problems are encountered much more commonly in performers without extensive voice training, including many pop and rock singers, and young students whose training may not be sufficient for the tasks assigned to school musical productions. Specific agents that provoke edema of the vocal folds include all of the respiratory allergens and other agents related to the endocrine system, primarily the estrogens.

In response to a variety of stimuli, water leaves the circulatory system and enters the submucosal spaces of the vocal tract, including areas in the vocal folds and in the air passages themselves. Under many circumstances, edema of the vocal folds will be caused by protein-bound water.[5] As such, it will not be ameliorated by diuretic agents commonly prescribed for tissue edema.

Systemic and topical decongestants have also been used to treat edema in the respiratory tract. Their primary action involves reduction in the diameter and volume of vascular structures in the submucosal area, but they may also produce "rebound" phenomena. These decongestants include epinephrine used as an inhalant and pseudoephedrine. Effects of sprays are discussed below.

Sprays, Mists and Inhalants

Diphenhydramine hydrochloride (Benadryl), 0.5% in distilled water, delivered to the larynx as a mist may be helpful for its vasoconstrictive properties, but it is also dangerous because of its analgesic effect and is not recommended by this author (R.T.S.). However, Punt advocated this mixture and several modifications of it.[6] Other topical vasoconstrictors that do not contain analgesics may be beneficial in selected cases. Oxymetazoline hydrochloride (Afrin) applied by a large particle mist to the larynx is particularly helpful in treating severe edema immediately prior to performance, but it should be used only under emergent, extreme circumstances. Five percent propylene glycol in a physiologically balanced salt solution may be delivered by large particle mist and can provide helpful lubrication, particularly in cases of laryngitis sicca after air travel or as associated with dry climates. Such treatment is harmless and may also provide a beneficial placebo effect. Water, saline, or other balanced fluid delivered via a vaporizer or steam generator is frequently effective and sufficient. This therapy should be augmented by oral hydration, which is the mainstay of treatment for dehydration. Singers can monitor their state of hydration by observing their urine color as noted previously by Dr Van Lawrence, who popularized the extremely useful instruction: "pee pale."

Nasal medications such as Beconase, Rhinocort, and Nasacort do not seem to harm the voice. However, most oral inhalers are not recommended for use in professional voice users. Many people develop contact inflammation from sensitivity to the medications or propellants used in oral inhalers; and propellants may also cause mucosal drying. Steroid inhalers used orally for prolonged periods may result in candida laryngitis. In addition, dysphonia occurs in up to 50% of patients using steroid inhalers, related to the aerosolized steroid itself and not to the Freon propellant.[7] Prolonged steroid use, as is common in asthmatics, also may be capable of causing wasting of the vocalis muscle.

Antibiotics

In professional voice users, when antibiotics are used, high doses to achieve therapeutic blood levels rapidly are recommended, especially if important performances are imminent. When patients have no pressing engagements, antibiotic use should be based on cultures whenever appropriate (eg, throat infections), as is the case with patients who are not voice professionals. However, in the common situation in which a performance must proceed and when there is clinical evidence of bacterial infection, antibiotics should be instituted after cultures are taken, without waiting for the results. The potential damage of delayed treatment in an active performer is greater than the potential harm of antibiotic use of an unproven organism.

When there is little time between initial treatment and performance, starting treatment with an intramuscular injection may be helpful. Selecting oral antibiotics that are absorbed rapidly and achieve optimal blood levels fast may also be helpful.

Antiviral Agents

A limited number of antiviral agents are commercially available. Acyclovir is used specifically for herpes and may be appropriate in patients with herpetic recurrent superior laryngeal nerve paresis or paralysis. Amantadine appears useful against influenza.[8-11] It may also have some beneficial effects against other viruses. If a performer must work in an area in which there is a flu epidemic, it may be reasonable to use this drug. However, agitation, tachycardia, and extreme xerostomia and xerophonia may occur. When those side effects are present, they are generally severe enough to require cancellation of a performance.

Antitussive Medications

Cough suppressant mixtures often include agents that have a secondary drying effect on vocal tract secretions,[12] especially those preparations containing codeine.[13] Antihistamines are also common ingredients in antitussives. Dextromethoraphan has pharmacologic effects similar to those of codeine and is encountered in a variety of OTC preparations. Generally, preparations that contain dextromethoraphan and a wetting agent such as guaifenesin work well for voice professionals.

Antihypertensive Agents

Almost all of the current antihypertensive agents have some degree of parasympathomimetic effect and thus dry mucous membranes of the upper respiratory tract. They commonly are used in combination with diuretic agents that also promote dehydration. In some circumstances, the laryngologist may find this drying effect substantial enough to merit recommending that the patient's internist prescribe another antihypertensive agent. The authors have frequently noted dryness with reserpines and agents of the methyldopa group.[14]

Gastroenterologic Medications

Pharmacologic treatment of gastroesophageal reflux currently includes neutralization of gastric acid with antacids, inhibition of acid secretion with a histamine H_2 receptor antagonist, and blocking the gastric proton pump (H+/K+ATPase) with antagonists such as omeprazole. In some people, antacids cause constipation, diarrhea, or bloating that may impair performance. Occasionally, they also have a drying effect. However, it is usually possible to find an antacid tolerated by any individual. It is also possible to select antacids that do not contain chemicals (such as aluminum) that some people wish to avoid (Tables 18–2 and 18–3). H_2 blockers have revolutionized the treatment of gastric ulcers and have proved very useful in laryngology for the treatment of gastric acid reflux laryngitis. Although drying of the laryngeal mucosa is

Table 18–2. Contents of Liquid Antacids (in mg/tsp).

	Aluminum Hydroxide	Magnesium Hydroxide	Calcium Carbonate	Magnesium Carbonate	Magaldrate	Simethicone	Sodium
Alternagel	600						<2.5
Aludrox	307	103					
Amphogel	320						
Camalox	225	200	250				
Delcid	600	665					<15
Di-Gel	200	200				20	
Gaviscon (mg/tbsp)	95			412			
Gelusil	200	200				25	
Gelusil II	400	400				30	
Kolantyl	150	150					
Maalox	225	200					
Maalox Plus	225	200					
Mag-Ox		400				25	
Mylanta	200	200				20	
Mylanta II	400	400				40	
Riopan					540		0.1
Riopan Plus					540	20	0.1
Riopan Plus E-S					1,080	30	0.3
Uro-Mag		140					

Table 18–3. Contents of Antacids: Tablets-Chewables-Gums (in mg).

	Aluminum Hydroxide	Magnesium Hydroxide	Calcium Carbonate	Simethicone	Dihydroxy-Aluminum Na Carbonate	Magnesium Carbonate
Alka-Mints			850			
Algicon	360					320
Alu-cap			194			
Alu-tab			585			
Bisodol		178				
Calcitrel		120	585			
Chooz		500				
Remegel	Mg carbonate codried gel 476.4					
Rolaids (cherry)			550		334	
Rolaids (plain)		64	317			
Tempo	133	81	414	20		
Titralac			420			
Tums			500			
Tums E-X			750			

not a major side effect of the H_2 blockers, it does occur and must be considered. Occasionally, drying effects of H_2 blockers can be severe enough to cause not only dry mouth and impair voice, but also dry and irritated eyes. This condition makes it difficult to read scores and causes excessive blinking especially under spotlights, which can be misinterpreted by an audience as nervousness. H_2 receptor antagonists inhibit the stimulation of acid secretion and are generally effective in reducing acid output from gastric parietal cells, although they have little effect on the basal rate of acid production. Gastric proton pump (H+/K+ATPase) inhibitors use an alternative approach that is generally highly effective in suppressing acid. Medications such as omeprazole inhibit the H+/K+ATPase system, which is virtually unique to the gastric parietal cell. In most patients, 20–40 mg a day provides excellent control of acidity, but it must be remembered that some patients are resistant to omeprazole.[15] H+/K+ATPase competitive inhibitors such as omeprazole cause inactivation of the enzyme, suppressing both basal and stimulated acid secretion for prolonged periods of time in most patients. Omeprazole does not adversely affect the lower esophageal sphincter or esophageal motility, but it does slow the linear emptying rate of solids from the stomach.[16] Although its incidence of other side effects is low, they include diarrhea, abdominal pain, and nausea. Liver enzymes may also be ele-

vated. This is also true of most H_2 blockers. Dry mouth, esophageal candidiasis, muscle cramps, depression, tremors, dizziness, fatigue, constipation, diarrhea, and other complications of omeprazole have also been reported, but most of them are relatively rare. Similar effects and side effects are seen with other proton pump inhibitors such as lansoprazole.

Hyperkinetic agents improve motility and help reflux by speeding gastric emptying. For several years, metoclopramide (Reglan) was the only such agent available. Because of troublesome side effects, particularly neurological abnormalities in approximately 10% of patients, the drug was never used extensively in professional singers; and it has now been largely replaced by newer agents. At present, the most commonly used is cisapride (Propulsid). Cisapride increases lower esophageal sphincter and lower esophageal peristalsis and significantly accelerates gastric emptying of liquids and solids. The most common side effects are headache, abdominal pain, nausea, diarrhea, constipation, dizziness, pharyngitis, depression, dehydration, and rhinitis. Dry mouth, tremor, and somnolence have been reported in less than 1% of patients; and numerous other adverse reactions are seen uncommonly. Other gastric medications include phenobarbital, prochlorperazine, isopropamide, and propantheline bromide. Members of the belladonna alkaloid group including scopolamine and atropine are widely used and prescribed for their antispasmodic effects. All of these agents have significant drying effects on sections in the vocal tract.

Vitamin C

Not infrequently the laryngologist may encounter a patient who consumes large amounts of vitamin C (ascorbic acid) in an effort to maintain health or to prevent the occurrence of a common cold. In some patients, a drying effect similar to that of a mild antihistamine occurs when vitamin C is taken in large doses.[15] Additionally, a patient with less than optimal renal function may produce acid urine and possibly form renal calculi.

Sleeping Pills

In general, sleeping pills should not be necessary for healthy people. Occasionally, the stresses of a tour and the aggravations of travel, along with frequent changes in time zone, can disturb sleeping patterns. Sleeping pills should be used with great caution. However, especially when going on tour for the first few times, a small supply of mild sleeping medication is appropriate. These should be prescribed only with instruction regarding rebound insomnia and the risk of habituation and physical dependence. Performers should avoid using diphenhydramine (Benadryl), an antihistamine frequently also used as a sleeping medication. It is a safe drug and works well, but it produces excessive drying, which may impair singing.

Analgesics

Aspirin and other analgesics frequently have been prescribed for relief of minor throat and laryngeal irritations. The platelet dysfunction caused by aspirin predisposes one to hemorrhage, especially in vocal folds traumatized by excessive voice use in the face of vocal dysfunction. Mucosal hemorrhage can be devastating to a professional voice user, and aspirin products should be avoided altogether in singers. Acetaminophen is the best substitute, as even the most common nonsteroidal anti-inflammatory drugs such as ibuprofen may interefere with the clotting mechanism. Caruso used a spray of ether and iodoform on his vocal folds when he had to sing with laryngitis. Nevertheless, the use of analgesics is extremely dangerous and should be avoided. Pain has an important protective physiologic function. Masking it risks incur-

ring significant vocal damage, which may be unrecognized until after the analgesic or anesthetic wears off. If a singer requires analgesics or topical anesthetics to alleviate laryngeal discomfort, the laryngitis is severe enough to warrant canceling a performance. If the analgesic is for headache or some other discomfort not intimately associated with voice production, symptomatic treatment should be discouraged until singing commitments have been completed.

There is no place for the use of narcotic analgesics shortly before performance, if the medications are being used for laryngeal discomfort. Even when the pain is outside the head and neck, narcotic medications may cause sufficient change and sensorium to impair performance, and risk vocal fold injury through unconscious technical abuse. Occasional exceptions can be made. For example, if a low dose of codeine early on a performance day is sufficient to control moderate menstrual cramping, its use is certainly not unreasonable. However, if menstrual cramps are so severe that high doses of codeine (in the 60 mg range) are required within a few hours of performance, cancellation may be more appropriate.

Hormones

Hormone medications may cause changes in voice quality due to alterations in fluid content, or to structural changes. Structural alterations in laryngeal architecture seldom occur as the result of pharmacologic influences, but androgens are an exception. They may produce permanent lowering of fundamental frequencies especially in females, and coarsening of the voice.[18–23] Androgenic agents are frequently used in the treatment of endometriosis, and as part of chemotherapy regimens for some breast cancers, and to treat postmenopausal sexual dysfunction. Professional voice users should be informed of potential voice changes before these medications are employed, and their use should be avoided whenever possible.

Birth control pills with relatively high progesterone content are most likely to produce androgenlike changes in the voice.[24–31] Most oral contraceptives marketed in the United States during the last several years have had an appropriate estrogen-progesterone balance, and voice changes are seen in only about 5% of women who use birth control pills (C Carroll, M.D., and H von Leden, personal communication, September, 1992). These changes generally are temporary, abating when oral contraceptive use is discontinued. Estrogen replacement is helpful in forestalling the typical voice changes that follow menopause. Sequential hormone replacement is the most physiologic regimen. Unless medical contraindications are present, professional voice users should be offered hormone replacement under appropriate medical supervision at the time of menopause.

Other endocrine medications may also affect the voice, often beneficially. Thyroid replacement may restore vocal efficiency and "ring" lost with even a mild degree of hypothyroidism. Agents used to treat maladies in any part of the diencephalic pituitary axis should be presumed to have laryngeal effects, and warrant close monitoring of voice function.

Bronchoactive Medications

Phonatory function depends on the availability of a powerfully supported airstream passing between the vocal folds. Impairment of pulmonary function can cause severe problems for professional voice users. Pulmonary function is affected deleteriously by bronchoconstricting agents. Bronchodilators are often helpful, especially for patients with reactive airway disease, although inhaled bronchodilators may produce laryngitis, as discussed above in the section on other inhalers. Clinically, inhaled cromolyn sodium appears to cause fewer problems than most of the other agents commonly used in the treatment of asthma. The most commonly used bronchodilator is epinephrine and its related compounds, including xanthines (aminophylline is an example). In professional voice users, the author (R.T.S.) favors control primarily with oral medications, minimizing inhaler use, as discussed in chapter 30. They can be used to counteract the bronchoconstrictive effects of such environmental factors as house dust, pollen, other allergenic agents, and common air pollutants produced by our increasingly industrialized society. Active bronchoconstriction occurs in allergic reactions and in asthma. These conditions may already hamper or prevent vocal performance unless recognized and treated properly.

Beta-Blockers

Propranolol and other beta-blockers have been described in the literature as useful for stage fright. Although British investigators[32] found that instrumental musicians given this potent beta-blocker did, in fact, exhibit less anxiety during performance, a unanimous response in voice professionals was not seen.

A subsequent study appears to indicate that propranolol, given for preperformance anxiety, lessened anxiety and also produced an increase in salivation.[33] This investigation was conducted by measuring the

weight increase in saliva-saturated dental rolls of cotton placed in the mouth during performance. This indicated that the problem of upper respiratory tract secretion dryness had been avoided and that some of the parasympathomimetic effects of performance anxiety had been negated.

The laryngologic community generally agrees that these drugs should not be used for singers. They are potentially dangerous, affecting heart rate, blood pressure, and provoking asthma attacks in susceptible patients. In addition, when given in doses sufficient to ameliorate stage fright, they produce a lackluster performance.[14] As discussed previously, any professional voice user who requires an ingested substance to perform the daily activities of his or her chosen profession is revealing a significant problem and should be referred for appropriate counseling and treatment of the cause of the problem, not merely medicated.

Neurologic Medications

Professional users of the voice may be diagnosed with neurologic disease entities either in the course of the evaluation of their voice complaint or as a co-existing illness. A number of highly potent medications are available for use in a medical treatment regimen. The side effects of the medication or the course of the illness itself may ultimately force the end of a performance carreer, or at the very least require significant modifications. Some of the most common illnesses and the usual medications prescribed are discussed.

Parkinson's disease may be treated by anticholinergic agents, L-dopa (and L-dopa in combination with other agents), dopamine receptor agonists, amantidine hydrochloride, and MAO (monamine oxidase) inhibitors. Side effects are related to the drug's mechanisms of action in the central nervous system and peripheral target organs.[35] Anticholinergic side effects include blurred vision, dryness, impaired urination, constipation, nervousness, dizziness, drowsiness, and confusion; memory loss, and headache, hallucination and delusions.[35] Side-effects most commonly associated with L-dopa are: GI disturbance, orthostatic hypotension, syncope, oral dryness, blurred vision and cardiac arrthymias. Dyskinesias, nightmares, confusion, agitation, psychosis, depression, increased libido and end-of-dose akinesia are reported.[35] L-dopa is sometimes given as in a drug combination to decrease peripheral systemic side effects.[35]

Amantadine has side effects similar to the anticholinergics. Dopamine receptor agonists produce GI disturbance, postural hypotension, and fatigue as well as skin rash, headache, involuntary movements, depression and sometimes confusion or hallucinations.[35] The side effects of monamine oxidase inhibitors are described in detail in the section on psychoactive drugs. Parkinsonian syndromes, not secondary to Parkinson's disease, may also be a focus of treatment with these drugs.

Myasthenia gravis is an autoimmune disease in which there are blood antibodies which impair synaptic transmission at the neuromuscular junction by disturbance of the neurotransmitter acetylcholine.[35] Drugs are used to treat myasthenia by enhancing the action of aceytlcholine (by inhibiting acetylcholinesterase) or by immune suppression. Acetylcholinesterase inhibitors most commonly cause side effects of excessive salivation or GI disturbances. Skin, rash, nervousness, confusion, or weakness are also reported.[35] Corticosteroid side effects have been previously described. Other immunosuppressants may also be used in patients with an inability to tolerate corticosteroids, but these side effects are potentially extremely serious.

Multiple sclerosis involves the progressive loss of myelin in white matter adjacent to the ventricles, optic nerves, brainstem, cerebellum, and spinal cord.[35] Drug therapy aims at reducing the frequency of exacerbations and/or reducing the degree of myelin loss during an attack. These medications include immunosuppressants such as corticosteroids, adrenocorticotrophic hormone, azothioprine, and cyclophosphamide, which have been previously described. Beta-interferon side effects include local inflammation and flulike syndrome.[35] Medications are also used to treat associated symptoms such as spasticity, cerebellar dysfunction, and depression.[35]

Psychoactive Medications

All psychoactive agents have effects that can interfere with vocal tract physiology. Treatment requires frequent, open collaboration between the laryngologist and the psychiatrist specializing in psychopharmacology. The patient and physicians need to carefully weigh the benefits and side effects of available medications. Patients must be informed of the relative probability of experiencing any known side effect. This is especially critical to the professional voice user and will play an important role in developing a treatment plan where there is no imminent serious psychiatric risk.

Antidepressant medications include compounds from several different classes. Tricyclic and tetracyclic antidepressants (TCAs) block the reuptake of norepinephrine and serotonin and have secondary effects on presynaptic and postsynaptic receptors. H_1 and H_2 receptor blockade has also been demonstrated.[34] These drugs include: imipramine hydrochloride (Tofranil), trimipramine maleate (Surmontil), amitriptyline (Elavil), doxepine hydrochloride (Sinequan), desipramine (Norpramin), protriptyline (Vivactil), and nortriptyline hydrochloride (Pamelor).[35]

Schatzberg and Cole summarize the side effects of TCAs as *anticholinergic* (dry mouth and nasal mucosa, constipation, urinary hesitancy, gastroesophageal reflux); *autonomic* (orthostatic hypotension, palpitations, increased cardiac conduction intervals, diaphoresis, hypertension, tremor); *allergic* (skin rashes); *CNS* (stimulation, sedation, delirium, twitching, nausea, speech delay, seizures, extrapyramidal symptoms); *other* (weight gain, impotence). These may be dose-related and agent-specific.[34]

Monamine oxidase inhibitors (MAOIs) are useful in depression that is refractory to tricyclics. The mode of action involves inhibiting monoamine oxidase in various organs, especially MAO-A for which norepinephrine and serotonin are primary substrates. The full restoration of enzyme activity may require 2 weeks after the drug is discontinued. The most commonly prescribed MAOIs are phenelzine (Nardil), tranylcypromine (Parnate), and isocarboxazid (Marplan).

The side effects of MAOIs may be extremely serious and troublesome. The one most commonly reported is dizziness secondary to orthostatic hypotension. When taking MAOIs, hypertensive crisis with violent headache and potential cerebrovascular accident or hyperpyrexic crisis with monoclonus and coma may be produced by ingesting foods rich in tyramine and many medications. These include Demerol, epinephrine, local anesthetics containing sympathomimetics, decongestants, surgical anesthetics, and nasal sprays. Patients for whom these medications are prescribed must be carefully instructed and ordinarily sign informed consent indicating that they understand the potential drug and food interactions. They must carefully monitor their diets. Other side effects include sexual dysfunction, sedation, insomnia, overstimulation, myositislike reactions, myoclonic twitches, and a small incidence of dry mouth, constipation, and urinary hesitancy.[34-37]

A few antidepressants have been developed with different chemical structures and side effect profiles. Trazodone (Desyrel) is a pharmacologically complex agent that blocks 5-HT receptors and inhibits 5-HT reuptake. It is not as potent a reuptake inhibitor as fluoxetine, sertraline, or paroxetine.[38] It has proven helpful in depression associated with initial insomnia. The side effects are particularly noteworthy: sedation, acute dizziness with fainting (especially when taken on an empty stomach), gastrointestinal disturbance, blurred vision, dry mouth, extrapyramidal symptoms, arrhythmias, leukopenia, and priapism.[34,35]

Bupropion (Wellbutrin) was released in 1989. Its biochemical mode of action is not well understood. It is neither an uptake inhibitor nor an MAOI. Its probable mode of action is on the dopamine mechanism. The most commonly reported complaint is nausea. However, a potential risk of seizures exists, and the drug is not recommended in patients with a history of seizure, head trauma, or anorexia/bulimia.[34,36]

A smaller group of antidepressant drugs that selectively inhibit the reuptake of serotonin are most likely to be selected as first pharmacologic agents. These include fluoxetine (Prozac), sertraline (Zoloft), and paroxetine (Paxil). They appear to be effective in typical episodic depression and for some chronic refractory presentations.[3] Major side effects are significant degrees of nausea, sweating, headache, mouth dryness, tremor, nervousness, dizziness, insomnia, somnolence, constipation, and sexual dysfunction, although the relative incidence of these varies from agent to agent. Venlafaxine hydrochloride (Effexor) is a reuptake inhibitor of serotonin, norepinephrine, and, weakly, dopamine. Its major side effect is sustained hypertension which is partially dose-dependent.[38] There are drug interactions with concomitant administration of tryptophan, MAOIs, warfarin, cimetidine, phenobarbital, and phenytoin.[39]

"Mood stabilizing" drugs are those that are effective in manic episodes and prevent manic and depressive recurrences in patients with bipolar disorder. These include lithium salts and several anticonvulsants. Lithium is available in multiple formulations and prescribing is guided by both symptom index and blood levels. Lithium side effects are apparent in diverse organ systems. The most commonly noted is fine tremor, especially noticeable in the fingers. With toxic lithium levels, gross tremulousness, ataxia, dysarthria, and confusion or delirium may develop. Some patients describe slowed mentation, measurable memory deficit, and impaired creativity. Chronic nausea and diarrhea are usually related to GI tract mucosal irritation, but may be signs of toxicity. Some patients gain weight progressively and may demonstrate edema or increased appetite. Lithium therapy affects thyroid function. In some cases it is transitory, but there may be goiter, with normal T_3 and T_4, but elevated TSH. Other undesirable effects of carbamazepine include serious adverse consequences such as severe dermatitis, stomatis, lymphadenopathy, renal damage, depression and agitation, diplopia, peripheral neuritis, and potential thrombophlebitis. Latent psychosis and systemic lupus erythematosus

have been reported to be activated by use of this drug. More minor complications include headache, dizziness or vertigo, drowsiness, ataxia, visual blurring, tinnitus, appetite and gastrointestinal disturbances, edema, changes in skin pigmentation, alopecia, and aching discomfort in the muscles and joints.[34,35]

Polyuria and secondary polydipsia are complications of lithium and may progress to diabetes inipidus. In most cases, discontinuing the medication reverses the renal effects. Prescribed thiazide diuretics can double the lithium level and lead to sudden lithium toxicity. Nonsteroidal anti-inflammatory drugs decrease lithium excretion. Cardiovascular effects include the rare induction of "sick sinus syndrome." Aggravation of psoriasis, allergic skin rashes, and reversible alopecia are associated with lithium therapy, as are teratogenic effects.[34]

Three anticonvulsant compounds appear to act preferentially on the temporal lobe and the limbic system. Carbamazepine (Tegretol) carries a risk of agranulocytosis or aplastic anemia, and it is monitored by complete blood cell count and symptoms of bone marrow supression. Care must be taken to avoid the numerous drug interactions that accelerate the metabolism of some drugs or raise carbamazepine levels.[34]

Valproic acid (Depakote, Depakene) is especially useful where there is a "rapid cycling" pattern. The major side effect is a risk of hepatocellular toxicity. Thrombocytopenia and platelet dysfunction have been reported. Sedation is common and tremor, ataxia, weight gain, alopecia, and fetal neural tube defects are all side effects that patients must comprehend.[34]

Anxiolytics are the most commonly prescribed psychotropic drugs, usually by nonpsychiatric specialists for somatic disorders. It behooves the laryngologist to probe for a history of past or current drug therapy in markedly anxious or somatically focused patients with vocal complaints. Commonly prescribed benzodiazepines include alprazolam (Xanax), chlordiazepoxide hydrochloride (Librium), clorazepate dipotassium (Tranxene), diazepam (Valium), lorazepam (Ativan), oxazepam (Serax), and clonazepam (Klonopin). Benzodiazepines produce effective relief of anxiety but have a high addictive potential, which includes physical symptoms of withdrawal, including potential seizures, if the drug is stopped abruptly. The most common benzodiazepine side effect is dose-related sedation, followed by dizziness, weakness, ataxia, decreased motor performance, and mild hypotension.[34] Clonazepam (Klonopin) is a benzodiazepine and may also produce malcoordination as well as disinhibition, agitation, or asituational anger.[34,35] Alterations of sensory input, either by CNS stimulants (cocaine, amphetamines, and OTC vasoconstrictors) or depressants, are potentially dangerous in a voice professional. An idiosyncratic response to a vasoconstrictor such as a pseudoephedrine, or an overdose of such an OTC medication, may manifest itself as acute central nervous system stimulation. Added to the "adrenaline high" of performance in the actor or musical performer, the combination of effects may very well be deleterious. The patient who is unaware of these effects should be apprised of them promptly by the laryngologist.[1,37,40]

Phenobarbital and meprobamate are no longer commonly used as anxiolytics in the United States. Clomipramine (Anafranil) is useful in the anxiety evident in obsessive-compulsive disorder. The side effects are similar to tricyclic antidepressants: dry mouth, hypotension, constipation, tachycardia, sweating, tremor, and anorgasmia. Prozac has also proven effective for some patients with obsessive-compulsive disorders, and appears better tolerated.[34]

Hydroxyzine, an antihistamine, is occasionally prescribed for mild anxiety and/or pruritus. It does not produce physical dependence, but does potentiate the CNS effects of alcohol, narcotics, CNS depressants, and tricyclic antidepressants. Side effects include notable mucous membrane dryness and drowsiness. Buspirone (Buspar) is not sedating at its usual dosage levels and it has little addictive potential. Side effects include mild degrees of headache, nausea, and dizziness. However, it is poorly tolerated in patients accustomed to the more immediate relief of benzodiazepines.[34]

Various antipsychotic drugs have a mode of action that involves dopamine antagonism, probably in the mesolimbic or mesocortical areas. They also have endocrine effects through dopamine receptors in the hypothalamic-pituitary axis.[34] The antipsychotic agents most commonly ordered currently include haloperidol (Haldol, in various preparations), chlorpromazine hydrochloride (Thorazine), chlorpromazine hydrochloride (Sparine), fluphenazine hydrochloride (Prolixin), thioridazine (Mellaril), perphenazine (Trilafon), trifluoperazine hydrochloride (Stelazine), prochlorperazine (Compazine), molindone (Moban), loxapine hydrochloride (Loxitane), and clozapine (Clozaril). These potent agents have very significant side effects. Clozaril is used primarily in patients who are refractory to other neuroleptics and requires very close monitoring for bone marrow supression. Sedation, accompanied by fatigue during early dosing, and akinesia with chronic administration are frequently described. Anticholinergic effects include postural hypotension, dry mouth, nasal congestion, and constipation. The endocrine system is also affected, with a direct increase in blood prolactin levels. Breast enlargement and galactorrhea are seen in males and females and correlate with impotence and amenorrhea. Weight gain is often excessive and frequently leads to noncompliance. Skin complications such as rash, retinal pigmentation, and photosensitivity occur. Rare but serious complications include agranulocytosis, allergic obstructive hepatitis, seizures, and sudden death secondary to ventricular fibrillation.[34,37]

Approximately 14% of patients receiving long-term (greater than 7 years) treatment with antipsychotic agents will develop tardive dyskinesia ranging from minimal tongue restlessness to incapacitating, disfiguring choreiform and/or athetoid movements, especially of the head, neck, and hands. Unfortunately, there is no cure for the condition once it develops, nor are there accurate predictors for which patients will be affected.[34,37] One 1992 study suggested that therapy with vitamin E might modulate the symptoms of tardive dyskinesia.[41]

The mode of action in neurologic side effects of the neuroleptics is primarily a cholinergic-dopaminergic blockade. Dystonia usually involves tonic spasm of the tongue, jaw, and neck, but may range from mild tongue stiffness to opisthotonos.[34] Pseudo-Parkinsonism may occur very early in treatment. Drug-induced Parkinsonism occurs in 90% of cases within the first 72 days of treatment with a peak onset of 5–30 days.[35] It is evidenced by muscle stiffness, cogwheel rigidity, stooped posture, masklike facies with loss of salivary control, dysarthria, and dysphagia. Pill-rolling tremor is rare. Akathisia, an inner-driven muscular restlessness with rhythmic leg jiggling, hand-wringing, and pacing, is extremely unpleasant. Multiple drug regimens are employed to diminish these symptoms.[34,37] A drug that selectively blocks dopamine receptors without blocking receptors in the basal ganglia is risperidone (Risperdal).

Neuroleptic malignant syndrome is a potentially fatal complication of these drugs. Patients will manifest hyperthermia, severe extrapyramidal signs, and autonomic hyperarousal. Neuroleptics also affect temperature regulation generally and can predispose to heatstroke.[34,37]

Ongoing psychiatric treatment of patients with voice disorders mandates a careful evaluation of current and prior psychoactive drug therapy. In addition, numerous psychoactive substances are used in the medical management of neurologic conditions such as Tourette's syndrome (haloperidol [Haldol], pimozide [Orac], and clonidine [Catapres]); chronic pain syndromes (carbamazepine, clonazepam), and vertigo (diazepam).

It is essential for laryngologists caring for professional singers to be familiar with these agents and alert for drug side effects and interactions. The numerous potential side effects of psychoactive medications highlight the importance of obtaining a good, comprehensive history. Some patients are reluctant to volunteer psychiatric information, especially to an ear, nose, and throat doctor for whom the relationship may not be obvious to the patient. It is critical to take the time to get the rapport and patient confidence to permit acquisition of a complete, accurate history of psychological dysfunction and treatment. It is appropriate (with the patient's consent) to consult with the prescribing physician directly to advocate the use of the psychoactive drug least likely to produce adverse effects on the voice while adequately controlling the psychiatric illness.[1,35]

Summary

Virtually everyone takes medications at one time or another. Nearly all medicines have potential effects on the voice. Voice professionals should be aware of the principal side effects of common medications such as analgesics, antihistamines, antidepressants, corticosteroids, antibiotics, antihypertensives, and diuretics. They must also be sufficiently familiar with the problems and principles of medication actions to knowledgeably inquire about the potential vocal effects of any medications prescribed.

Review Questions

1. Over-the-counter allergy medicines that do not require prescriptions are safe for singers and are not likely to cause side effects such as mucosal drying.
   a. true
   b. false

2. Common side effects of corticosteroids include:
   a. stomach irritation
   b. insomnia
   c. blurred vision
   d. all of the above
   e. none of the above

3. The drying effects of antihistamines can be relieved to some extent by:
   a. diuretics
   b. corticosteroids
   c. mucolytic agents
   d. all of the above
   e. none of the above

4. The most vocally dangerous hormone medication for female singers is:
   a. estrogen
   b. androgen
   c. progestin
   d. all of the above
   e. none of the above

5. Beta blockers are safe and effective for stage fright and may be routinely used.
   a. true
   b. false

References

1. Sataloff RT, Lawrence VL, Hawkshaw M, Rosen DC. Medications and their effects on the voice. In: Benninger, MS, Jacobson BH, Johnson AF, eds. *Vocal Arts Medicine: The Care and Prevention of Professional Voice Disorders.* New York, NY: Thieme Medical Publishers; 1994: 216–225.

2. Lawrence VL. Common medications with laryngeal effects. *ENT J.* 1987;66(8):318–322.

3. Schiff M. Medical management of acute laryngitis. In: Lawrence VL ed. *Transcripts of the Sixth Symposium: Care of the Professional Voice.* New York, NY: The Voice Foundation; 1977;99–102.

4. Schiff M. Comment at the Seventh Symposium: Care of the Professional Voice. New York, NY: The Juilliard School, June 15 and 16, 1978.

5. Sataloff RT. Professional singers: the science and art of clinical care. *Am J Otolaryngol.* 1981;2(3):251–266.

6. Punt NA. Applied laryngology—singers and actors. *Proc R Soc Med.* 1968;61:1152–1156.

7. Toogood JH, Jennings B, Greenway RW, Chuang L. Candidiasis and dysphonia complicating beclomethasone treatment of asthma. *J Allergy Clin Immunol.* 1980;65(2):145–153.

8. Davies WL, Gunert RR, Hoff RF, McGahen JW, et al. Antiviral activity of 1-Amantanamine (Amantadine). *Science.* 1964;144:862–863.

9. McGahen JW, Hoffman CE. Influenza infections of mice. 1. Curative activity of Amantadine HCL. *Proc Soc Exp Biol Med.* 1968;129:678–681.

10. Wingfield WL, Pollock D, Gunert RR. Therapeutic efficacy of Amantadine-HCL and Rumantidine-HCL in naturally occurring influence A2 respiratory illness in many. *N Engl J Med.* 1969;281:579–584.

11. Council on drugs. The Amantadine controversy. *JAMA.* 1967;201:372–373.

12. Martin FG. Drugs and vocal function. *J Voice.* 1988; 2(4):338–344.

13. *Nursing '89 Drug Handbook.* Springhouse, Pa: Springhouse Corporation; 1989:236.

14. Gates GA, Saegert J, Wilson N, Johnson L, Sheperd A, Hearnd EM. Effects of beta-blockade on singing performance. *Ann Otol Rhinol Laryngol.* 1985;94:570–574.

15. Bough ID, Sataloff RT, Castell DO, Hills JR, Gideon RM, Spiegel JR. Gastroesophageal reflux laryngitis resistant to omeprazole therapy. *J Voice*. 1995;9(2):205–211.

16. Rasmussen L, Oster-Jorgensen E, Qvist N, Kraglund K, Hovendal C, Pedersen SA. Short report. A double-blind placebo-controlled trail of omeprazole on characteristics of gastric emptying in healthy subjects. *Aliment Pharmacol Ther*. 1991;5:85–89.

17. Lawrence VL. Medical care for professional voice (panel). In: Lawrence VL, ed. *Transcriptions from the Annual Symposium: Care of the Professional Voice*. New York, NY: The Voice Foundation; 1978;3:17–18.

18. Damste PH. Virilization of the voice due to anabolic steroids. *Folia Phoniat*. 1968;16:10–18.

19. Damste PH. Voice changes in adult women caused by virilizing agents. *J Speech Hear Dis*. 1967;32:126–132.

20. Saez S, Françoise S. Recepteurs dandrogenes: mise en évidence dans la fraction cytosolique de muqueuse normale et d'epitheliomas pharyngolarynges humains. *CR Acad Sci* (Paris). 1975;280:935–938.

21. Vuorenkoski V, Lenko HL, Tjernlund P, Vuorenkoski L, Perheentupa J. Fundamental voice frequency during normal and abnormal growth, and after androgen treatment. *Arch Dis Child*. 1978;53:201–209.

22. Arndt HJ. Stimmstörungen nach Behandlung mit androgenen und anabolen Hormonen. *Munch Med Wochenschr*. 1974;116:1715–1720.

23. Bourdial J. Les troubles de la voix provoques par la therapeutique hormonale androgene. *Ann Otolaryngol* (Paris). 1970;87:725–734.

24. Dordain M. Étude statistique de l'influence des contraceptifs hormonaux sur la voix. *Folia Phoniat*. 1972;24:86–96.

25. Pahn V, Goretzlehner G. Stimmstörungen durch hormonale Kontrazeptiva. *Zentralb Gynakol*. 1978;100:341–346.

26. Schiff M. The "pill" in otolaryngology. *Trans Am Acad Ophthalmol Otolaryngol*. Jan–Feb 1968;72:76–84.

27. Brodnitz F. Medical care preventive therapy (panel). In Lawrence V, ed. *Transcripts of the Seventh Annual Symposium: Care of the Professional Voice*. New York, NY: The Voice Foundation; 1978;3:86.

28. Bausch J. Effects and side-effects of hormonal contraceptives in the region of the nose, throat and ear. [In German]. *HNO*. 1983;31(12):409–414.

29. Could contraceptives with progestation effect cause voice change? [In Dutch]. *Ned Tijdschr Geneeskd*. 1975; 119(44):1726–1727.

30. Krahulec I, Urbanova O, Simko S. Voice changes during hormonal contraception. [In Czech]. *Cesk Otolaryngol*. 1977;26(4):234–237.

31. Wendler J. Cyclicly dependent variations in efficiency of the voice and its influencing by ovulation inhibitors. [In German]. *Folia Phoniatr* (Basel).1972;24(4):259–277.

32. James IM. The effects of oxprenolol on stage fright in musicians. *Lancet*. 1977;2:952–954.

33. Brantigan CD. The effect of beta blockage and beta stimulation on stage fright. *Am J Med*. 1982;72(1):88–94.

34. Vogel D, Carter J. *The effects of drugs on communication disorders*. Clinical competence series. San Diego, Calif.: Singular Publishing Group, Inc; 1995:29–135.

35. Schatzberg A, Cole J. *Manual of Clinical Psychopharmacology*. 2nd ed. Washington, DC: APAPress; 1991:40, 50, 55, 58, 66, 68, 69, 72, 73–77, 110–125, 158–165, 169–177, 185–227, 313–348.

36. Cole, J, Bodkin J. Antidepressant drug side-effects. *J Clin Psychiatry*. 1990(suppl 1);51:21–26.

37. Janitec P, Davis J, Prescorn F, Ab S. *Principles and Practice of Psychopharmacology*. Baltimore, MD: Williams & Wilkins; 1993: 164–184, 230–289, 433–439.

38. Wyeth Laboratories. Physician prescribing package insert information. Philadelphia, PA: Wyeth Laboratories; 1983, for Effexor.

39. *Physicians' Desk Reference*. Oradell, NJ: Medical Economics Data; 1994:2000–2003, 2267–2270.

40. Carpenter B. Psychological aspects of vocal fold surgery. In: Gould WJ, Sataloff RT, Spiegel JR, eds. *Voice Surgery*. St. Louis, MO: Mosby; 1993:339–343.

41. Egan M, Hyde T, Alvers A, Alexander M, Reeve A, Blom A, Saenz R, Wyatt R. Treatment of tardive dyskinesia with vitamin E. *Amer J Psychiatr*. 1983;149(6):773–777.

19

Medications for Traveling Performers

Robert Thayer Sataloff

No physician likes treating patients without examining them. We like even less giving nonmedical personnel a collection of medications to take at their own discretion. However, we are frequently called on to care for actors and singers who must travel in foreign countries for prolonged periods of time. Many of these patients have been under our care for years and are good judges of their health under most circumstances. In some instances, their health can be best served by providing them with a supply of medications and instructions on how to use them. This chapter constitutes not only suggestions on what medications to include, but also suggestions to the performer on how and when they should be used. As a convenience, a copy of this chapter may be given to a performer as a written guideline to safe use of medications in the travel kit (unless the performer has a copy of the book, of course).

Rationale and Warning for Performers

"Don't take medicine without consulting your doctor." That is standard, safe, sage advice. Whenever possible, it should be followed. Even the most experienced performer cannot accurately diagnose his own maladies consistently. Moreover, the wrong medication, or even the right medication taken the wrong way, can make an illness worse. However, having been a singer a lot longer than I have been a laryngologist, I must confess that I have never traveled anywhere without a "First Aid Kit" stocked with medications for every contingency. Many of my regular singer and actor patients are quite knowledgeable about their own health and recurrent maladies. Many of them, too, travel with a "bag of goodies," especially when they are touring outside the United States. In many foreign countries, it is particularly difficult to find

a physician with whom a singer can communicate and in whom he has confidence. It is also sometimes difficult to know the contents of various European medications. This can be dangerous, especially if a performer has a known medication allergy. For this reason, and with all admonitions and warnings, this chapter provides a list of medications reasonable for a First Aid Kit and guidelines for their administration, but it must be emphasized that self-medication is fraught with hazards and should be avoided whenever a doctor is available. The price of the visit is less than the consequences of a medication error. Moreover, should a singer fail to respond favorably to any of these medications, or should he suffer a reaction, it is essential to obtain medical care promptly, no matter how inconvenient.

Ground Rules

If carried at all, medications for a performer's First Aid Kit should be obtained through the performer's physician and with his approval. In addition to this chapter, consultation with one's personal physician will help guide the performer on appropriate conservatism in using the drugs, in their proper applications, and in avoiding allergic reactions. The singer or actor should be certain before each trip that all medications are fresh and their dates for safe use have not expired. Expiration dates are printed on the sides of the bottles. Medications should also be kept in the properly labeled bottles in which they are purchased. They should not be shared with friends and colleagues. Another person's medical condition and potential allergies may be much more complicated than either person knows. No professional voice user who is not a physician should assume the responsibility and liability for providing unlicensed medical or pharmaceutical help. What may seem like a simple act of friendship may be neither simple nor friendly. When a performer uses any of the medications in his First Aid Kit, he should keep a written record of what he used, when, and why. This information should be communicated to his physician to be kept as part of his permanent medical chart. This will also provide feedback for the singer on the appropriateness of his medicine use. At this time, the performer may also request a new prescription to replace the medication if another trip is planned in the near future. Medications should be packaged in a secure, padded, water-resistant container. If there is a lot of extra space in some of the bottles, this may be filled with clean cotton, so that the medications are not jostled or broken in travel.

Individual Customary Medications

A performer should bring an ample extra supply of any prescription medications used regularly such as thyroid pills, oral contraceptives, blood pressure medication, and heart medication. Even for a long trip, an extra month's supply is usually sufficient If regular medications are lost, a month usually provides enough time to contact home and send for a new supply. The performer should check with his physician or pharmacist to be certain that his regular medications do not have adverse cross-reactions with any of the other medications in the First Aid Kit.

Analgesics

Aspirin is contraindicated in professional voice users because of its tendency to cause bleeding, particularly vocal fold hemorrhage. Many analgesics (pain medicines) and cold medications contain aspirin. Read the labels! Bring Tylenol (McNeil Consumer Products) or a similar medication that does not contain aspirin. This can be used for minor pain such as headache, back pain after long plane flights, or menstrual cramps. If there is sufficient throat pain associated with laryngitis to require medications in order to sing, the condition is probably too severe to allow safe performance. In any case, self-medicating for a laryngeal ailment without having the vocal folds visualized is extremely hazardous and should be avoided.

Antacids

Gastric reflux laryngitis is common among performers. This condition is aggravated by stress and eating late at night, both of which are common while travel-

ing. Reflux may be aggravated in foreign countries by consumption of certain unfamiliar foods. While on tour, even people who do not regularly have problems with reflux may experience heartburn, a hoarse and low voice in the morning, bad breath in the morning, and prolonged warm-up time. A supply of liquid antacid or the newer chewable tablets designed to combat reflux [Algicon (Rorer) or Gaviscon (Marion), for example] may be helpful. Stronger medications such as Prilosec (Astra/Merck) and Prevecid (TAP Pharmaceutical) may be included if the performer has had to use them in the past for significant reflux problems. Medication for reflux should always be supplemented by avoidance of eating for 3 to 4 hr before going to sleep and by elevation of the head of the bed.

Antibiotics

Antibiotics are among the most overused medications. Singers and actors must avoid the tendency to use them for every little cold or sore throat. They may produce adverse reactions, predispose to more severe infections, possibly impair the body's ability to fight off infections on its own, or produce other undesirable side effects. Performers should be extremely wary of packing any medication they have not used before, especially antibiotics that commonly produce allergic reactions. If a performer has had good experience taking a specific antibiotic on several occasions, it is reasonable to have one or two 10-day courses of the medication on hand during lengthy trips. Ampicillin, erythromycin, and tetracycline are relatively good broad-spectrum antibiotics that may be considered for inclusion in the First Aid Kit. Tetracyclines are inactivated by milk products and antacids. Consequently, they are not a good choice for anyone with reflux problems.

Antibiotics have no effect on viral infections, only on bacterial illnesses. If bacterial infection is suspected, it is best to consult a physician for examination and possibly for a culture. When this is not possible, antibiotic use is reasonable for severe sore throat, especially associated with white spots on the tonsils or a cough productive of yellow or green sputum, or for urinary tract infection with burning and frequency. A physician should be consulted as soon as possible. Once antibiotics are started, the 10-day course should be completed to avoid development of resistant organisms. In addition to allergic reactions, antibiotics may also cause nausea, diarrhea, abdominal cramping (which may interfere with singing or speaking), photophobia (hypersensitivity to sunlight), vaginitis, and other problems.

Antiviral Agents

A few antiviral agents are now available. However, they generally are not as effective as antibiotics, and they may produce side effects. For example, amantadine is useful against influenza A. If a performer has to work in a city in which there is a flu outbreak, it may be reasonable to use this drug. However, it can produce profound side effects including extremely dry mouth, agitation, and rapid heart beat; these side effects may be severe enough to require cancellation of a performance. We do not generally include this drug among travel medications.

If a performer is prone to recurrent infections with herpes, it is reasonable to bring a supply of Acyclovir. If repeated herpetic infections that typically involve the superior laryngeal nerves occur, appropriate courses of high doses of steroids should be included in the first aid kit.

Vaginal Medications

One of the most common complications of antibiotic use is vaginal candidiasis, or yeast infection. This is caused by overgrowth of yeasts that are normally present in the vagina but live in balance with other normal flora including bacteria that are killed by the antibiotics. When the bacteria are absent, the yeast grows unchecked. Especially in women who are prone to develop yeast infections, a supply of Monistat (Ortho Pharmaceutical) is prudent. It may be started for vaginal itching or cheesy discharge that occurs during antibiotic use. Early consultation with a physician is advisable to be sure that this is really the only problem. If vaginal symptoms develop independent of antibiotic use, a gynecologist should be consulted before any medication is started.

Nose Sprays

Decongestant nose sprays should generally be avoided and should rarely be used for more than 3 to 5 days. When necessary, Afrin (Schering) is a good choice. It can be used in the morning and at night, or only at night. Prolonged use causes dependence and rebound congestion when the spray is stopped. Nose spray may be appropriate for an infection or allergy that causes enough congestion to block nasal breathing, especially shortly before performance. Breathing through the nose warms, filters, and humidifies air and saves a great deal of wear and tear on the larynx. It is a good idea to carry nasal spray and a decongestant with one's carry-on items on an airplane. On a poorly pres-surized flight, the use of an oral decongestant and nasal spray 1 hour before landing helps prevent ear problems. However, decongestants may have side effects, including excessive drying of laryngeal mucosa, and should only be used in performers who have used the medication previously without difficulty.

Antihistamines and Decongestants

The use of antihistamines and decongestants in singers is very tricky, because the side effects are often worse than the problem they are supposed to treat. In a singer with true allergies, formal allergy evaluation and desensitization are often helpful. If the problems are minimal, through trial and error, performers can often find a mild antihistamine that controls the allergic symptoms adequately without producing too much dryness. If antihistamines are to be included, the performer should try them under a physician's supervision prior to traveling to choose the optimal medication. Decongestants without antihistamines (such as Sudafed [Burroughs Wellcome] have less drying effect but often produce a slight tremor (which may be heard in the voice), hyperirritability, and insomnia. They should also not be ingested for the first time shortly before a concert. However, they may be useful in some people to relieve the nasal congestion associated with a cold or mild allergy.

Mucolytic Agents

The drying effects of antihistamines may be partially counteracted by medications that increase or thin upper respiratory secretions. Such medications also help with the dryness from overuse of the voice and undesirable atmospheric conditions. However, they are no substitute for adequate hydration. The singer must be certain to drink enough liquid to keep his urine color extremely light and not try to compensate with medicines for insufficient fluid intake. This is the best way to be certain of adequate hydration. Mucolytic agents are also useful to treat "postnasal drip," a condition caused by secretions that are too thick, rather than too copious. Mucolytic medicines thin the secretions and make them easier to handle. The most common medications in this category are Entex (Norwich Eaton), Robitussin (Robbins), and Humibid (Adams).

Steroids

Avoid overusing steroids! They are commonly abused by singers and actors and should be taken only for very specific indications, usually with a physician's guidance. They may be helpful in cases of acute inflammatory laryngitis associated with recent travel, smoke exposure, and oversinging. In this setting, they should be combined with hydration, relative voice rest, and sometimes other therapy. They are particularly helpful in combating acute allergic reactions to allergens in a new locale, medications, foods, or insect bites. I recommend including them in the First Aid Kit, especially for the latter indications. For example, if a performer develops acute nasal congestion, sneezing, and tearing and itching of the eyes immediately before a concert in a new city, steroids may be appropriate. They may also be helpful for a person who breaks out in hives after eating shellfish, for example. In either case, medical consultation is particularly important and should be obtained as soon as possible. Self-medication with steroids is strictly a last resort. A Medrol Dosepak (Upjohn) or Decadron dose pack (Merck, Sharp & Dohme) should suffice. An entire course of these drugs need not be taken as indicated on the dose pack. For inflammatory laryngitis, for example, two or three pills may be suffcient, rather than the six-pill first-day regimen suggested on the package. Each performer should seek advice from the doctor who prescribes the drug and should be particularly cautious about using these medications for the first time unsupervised. In some people, they aggravate stomach problems, and they also may cause hyperirritability and insomnia in larger doses. Antacids should generally be taken while steroids are being used. Prolonged use of steroids is almost never indicated, except for serious diseases, and should never be undertaken without close medical supervision.

Anti-dizziness Medications

Singers and actors who get seasick and perform on cruises have a special problem. Antivert (Roerig) and Dramamine (Searle Pharmaceutical), medicines for dizziness and motion sickness, are actually antihistamines that cause drying, as do scopolamine patches. Before leaving on a cruise, the performer should try wearing a patch and/or taking a dose or two of Antivert (Roerig) to assess the side effects. In most of my patients, the patch has worked well. However, some people have excessive drying, as well as dilatation of the pupils with blurring of vision, and cannot tolerate the medication. It is best to find this out in advance.

Anti-diarrheal Medications

Performers touring in certain parts of the world are likely to encounter traveler's diarrhea. This can often be avoided by taking Vibramycin (Pfizer) or Pepto Bis-

mol (Procter & Gamble) prophylactically. The performer should consult his physician before leaving. Lomotil (Searle Pharmaceutical) should be included in the First Aid Kit in case severe diarrhea develops. However, this medication contains a small amount of atropine, which has a drying effect. Although it is usually tolerated well by most singers, it should be taken with caution. It also should not be taken more often than one pill every 4 to 6 hours. In higher doses, mucosal drying becomes a significant problem. Most other antidiarrheal medications also have potential side effects.

Ear Drops

"Swimmer's ear" is a common problem during travel, particularly in tropical climates. It usually follows exposure to water, especially if cotton swabs are used to dry the ears. Manipulation of the ears should be avoided. The old adage is a good one: "Put nothing smaller than your elbow in your ear." Otitis externa is characterized by pain and swelling of the ear canal. It is treated with ear drops such as Colymycin (Parke-Davis), Cortisporin (Burroughs Wellcome), Vasocidin (Iolab Pharmaceuticals), or Domeboro (Miles Pharmaceuticals). It is important to distinguish otitis externa from middle ear infection, which is usually associated with a cold. It is absolutely necessary to have the ear examined by a physician as quickly as possible after ear symptoms develop. However, in the healthy performer who develops ear pain, redness, and obvious swelling following water exposure, it is reasonable to start treatment with ear drops if a doctor is not immediately available. Nevertheless, a physician should definitely examine the ear as soon as possible. Allowing progression of this condition is not only potentially serious and painful, but it may also be associated with swelling in the face and jaw joint, which makes it difficult to open the mouth. This painful temporomandibular joint restriction can interfere with singing performance.

Sleeping Pills

In general, sleeping pills should not be necessary for healthy people. However, occasionally, the stresses of a tour and the aggravations of travel, along with frequent changes in time zone, can disturb sleep patterns. Sleeping pills should be used with great caution. However, especially when going on tour for the first few times, a small supply of mild sleeping medication is not a bad idea. Performers should avoid using Benadryl® (Parke-Davis), an antihistamine frequently also used as a sleeping medication. It is a safe drug and works well, but it produces excessive drying, which may hinder singing.

Topical Medications

Topical medications such as antibiotic ointments, topical steroid creams, and over-the-counter medications used for insect bites may be appropriate, especially when traveling in areas where scratches or insect bites are likely. In people who are prone to get recurrent cold sores, Acyclovir® cream may also be included.

Nonmedicinal Items

Band-Aids (Johnson & Johnson), alcohol swabs, disinfectant, antibiotic ointment for superficial cuts, cotton and sterile gauze pads, and adhesive tape also come in handy.

Medications Intentionally Excluded

Diuretics are often prescribed by gynecologists to help alleviate premenstrual fluid bloating. Unfortunately, they diurese free body water, such as that needed for mucosal lubrication, but not protein-bound water, such as that in the vocal folds. Consequently, they produce a dry singer or actor with persistently boggy vocal folds, making matters worse.

Narcotics are strong pain killers. They should only be used under a physician's direct supervision. Moreover, they dull sensorium and interfere with good singing, making performance dangerous.

Valium (Roche), Inderal (Ayerst), and other medications for preperformance anxiety should generally be avoided. They are unnecessary in the healthy, well-trained performer, and they have side effects that can be dangerous not only to the voice, but also to the cardiopulmonary system.

Summary

Performers frequently have to travel for long periods of time, often outside their native countries. In such circumstances, it is reasonable for them to bring a collection of medications for use in the event of an illness. These medications should be prescribed by a physician. They must be current (not expired), and the performer must understand clearly the indications for use and the potential side effects. Such medications are no substitute for medical examination and care, but they may be conservatively used under selected circumstances and are a reasonable and practical precaution for well-informed performers.

Review Questions

1. It is not necessary to carry analgesics because aspirin products are readily available and can be obtained and safely used by singers and actors throughout the world
   a. true
   b. false

2. If a singer has an ample supply of antibiotics and a fellow performer becomes sick in a foreign country, it is reasonable for the singer to provide antibiotics to his or her friend.
   a. true
   b. false

3. Diuretics are helpful in singers for premenstrual fluid retention (bloating) of the vocal folds.
   a. true
   b. false

4. Mucosal drying may be produced by:
   a. antihistamines
   b. antidizziness medication
   c. antidiarrheal medication
   d. all of the above
   e. none of the above

5. In a singer with an acute allergic reaction to roses 2 hours before a performance, the most appropriate treatment is:
   a. antibiotics
   b. antihistamines
   c. corticosteriods
   d. all of the above
   e. none of the above

20

Psychological Aspects of Voice Disorders

Deborah Caputo Rosen and Robert Thayer Sataloff

Patients seeking medical care for voice disorders come from the general population. Consequently, a normal distribution of comorbid psychopathology can be expected in a laryngology practice. Psychological factors can be causally related to a voice disorder and/or consequences of vocal dysfunction. In practice, they are usually interwoven. The first task of the otolaryngologist treating any patient with a voice complaint is to establish an accurate diagnosis and its etiology. Only as a result of a thorough, comprehensive history and physical examination (including state-of-the-art technology) can the organic and psychological components of the voice complaint be elucidated. All treatment planning and subsequent intervention depend on this process. However, even minor voice injuries or health problems can be disturbing for many patients and devastating to some professional voice users. In some cases, they even trigger responses that delay the return of normal voice. Such stress, and fear of the evaluation procedures themselves, often heighten the problem and may cloud diagnostic assessment. Some voice disorders are predominantly psychogenic, and psychological assessment may be required to complete a thorough evaluation.

The essential role of the voice in communication of the "self" creates special potential for psychological impact. Severe psychological consequences of voice dysfunction are especially common in individuals in whom the voice is pathologically perceived to be the self, such as professional voice users. However, the sensitive clinician will recognize varying degrees of similar reaction among most voice patients who are confronted with voice change or loss.

Our work with professional voice users has provided insight into the special intensification of psychological distress they experience in association with lapses in vocal health. This has proven helpful in treating all patients with voice disorders, and has permitted recognition of psychological problems that may delay recovery following vocal injury or surgery.

In all human beings, self-esteem comprises not only who we believe we are, but also what we have chosen to do as our life's work. A psychological "double-exposure" exists for performers who experience difficulty separating the two elements. The voice is in, is therefore of, indeed *is* the self. Aronson's extensive review of the literature provides an opportunity to examine research that supports the maxim that the "voice is the mirror of the personality"—both normal and abnormal. Parameters such as voice quality, pitch, loudness, stress pattern, rate, pauses, articulation, vocabulary, syntax, and content are described as they reflect life stressors, psychopathology, and discrete emotions.[1] Sundberg describes Fonagy's research on the effects of various states of emotion on phonation. These studies revealed specific alterations in articulatory and laryngeal structures and in respiratory muscular activity patterns related to 10 different emotional states.[2] Vogel and Carter include descriptive summaries of the features, symptoms, and signs of communication impairment in their text on neurologic and psychiatric disorders.[3] The mind and body are inextricably linked. Thoughts and feelings generate neurochemical transmissions that affect all organ systems. Therefore, not only can disturbances of physical function have profound emotional effects, disturbances of emotion can have profound bodily and artistic effects.

Professional Voice Users: A Special Case

It is useful to understand in greater depth the problems experienced by professional voice users who suffer vocal injuries. Most of our observations in this population occur among singers and actors. However, it must be remembered that, although they are the most obvious and demanding professional voice users, many other professionals are classified as professional voice users. These include politicians, attorneys, clergy, teachers, salespeople, broadcasters, shop foremen (who speak over noise), football quarterbacks, secretaries, telephone operators, and others. Although we are likely to expect profound emotional reactions to voice problems among singers and actors, many other patients may also demonstrate similar reactions. If we do not recognize these reactions as such, they may be misinterpreted as anger, malingering, or other difficult patient behavior. Some patients are unconsciously afraid that their voices are lost forever and are psychologically unable to make a full effort at vocal recovery after injury or surgery. This blocking of the frightening possibilities by rationalization ("I haven't made a maximum attempt so I don't know yet if my voice will be satisfactory.") can result in prolonged or incomplete recovery after technically flawless surgery. It is incumbent upon the laryngologist and other members of the voice team to understand the psychological consequences of voice disturbance and to recognize them not only in extreme cases, but even in their more subtle manifestations.

Typical successful professional voice users (especially actors, singers, and politicians) may fall into a personality subtype that is ambitious, driven, perfectionistic, and tightly controlled. Externally, they present themselves as confident, competitive, and self-assured. Internally, self-esteem, the product of personality development, is often far more fragile. Children and adolescents do the best they can to survive and integrate their life experiences. All psychological defense mechanisms are means to that end. Most of these defenses are not under conscious control. They are a habitual element of the fabric of one's response to life, especially in stressful or psychologically threatening situations.

It is the task of personality theorists to explain this process, the genesis of the self. There are numerous coherent personality theories, all substantially interrelated. The framework of Karen Horney (1885–1952) is particularly useful in attempting to understand the creative personality and its vulnerabilities. In simplification, she formulated a "holistic notion of the personality as an individual unit functioning within a social framework and continually interacting with its environment." In Horney's model, there are three selves. The *actual self* is the sum-total of the individual's experience; the *real self* is responsible for harmonious integration; and the *idealized self* sets up unrealistically high expectations which, in the face of disappointment, result in self-hatred and self-alienation.[4] We have chosen Horney's theory as a working model in evolving therapeutic approaches to the special patient population of professional voice users. They are the laryngologist's most demanding consumers of voice care and cling to their physician's explanations with dependency.[5]

It may be useful, for theoretical clarity, to divide the experience of vocal injury into several phases. In practice, however, these often overlap or recur and the emotional responses are not entirely linear.

1. *The phase of problem recognition*: The patient feels that something is wrong, but may not be able to clearly define the problem, especially if the onset has been gradual or masked by a coexisting illness. Usually, personal "first-aid" measures will be tried, and when they fail, the performer will manifest some level of panic. This is often followed by feelings of guilt when the distress is turned inward against the self, or rage or blame when externalized.

2. *The phase of diagnosis:* This may be a protracted period if an injured performer does not have immediate access to a laryngologist experienced in the assessment of vocal injury. He or she may have already consulted with voice teachers, family physicians, allergists, nutritionists, peers, or otolaryngologists and speech-language pathologists without specialized training in caring for professional voice users. There may have been several, possibly contradictory, diagnoses and treatment protocols. The vocal dysfunction persists, and the patient grows more fearful and discouraged. If attempts to perform are continued, they may exacerbate the injury and/or produce embarrassing performances. The fear is of the unknown, but it is intuitively perceived as significant.

3. *Phase of treatment:* Acute/Rehabilitative: Now, fear of the unknown becomes fear of the known, and of its outcome. The performer, now in the sick role, initially feels overwhelmed and powerless. There is frequently a strong component of blame that may be turned inward. "Why me, why now?" is the operant, recurrent thought. Vocal rehabilitation is an exquisitely slow, carefully monitored, frustrating process, and many patients become fearful and impatient. Some will meet the criteria for major depression, which will be discussed in additional detail, as will the impact of vocal fold surgery.

4. *Phase of acceptance:* When the acute and rehabilitative treatment protocol is complete, the final prognosis is clearer. When there are significant lasting changes in the voice, the patient will experience mourning. Even when there is full return of vocal function, a sense of vulnerability lingers. These individuals are likely to adhere strictly, even ritualistically, to preventive vocal hygiene habits and may be anxious enough to become hypochondriacal.[6]

Psychogenic Voice Disorders

Voice disorders are divided into organic and nonorganic etiologies. Various terms have been used interchangeably (but imprecisely) to label observable vocal dysfunction in the presence of emotional factors that cause or perpetuate the symptoms. Aronson argues convincingly for the term *psychogenic*, which is "broadly synonymous with functional, but has the advantage of stating positively, based on an exploration of its causes, that the voice disorder is a manifestation of one or more types of psychological disequilibrium, such as anxiety, depression, conversion reaction, or personality disorder, that interfere with normal volitional control over phonation."[1]

Psychogenic disorders include a variety of discrete presentations. There is disagreement over classification among speech pathologists, with some excluding musculoskeletal tension disorders from this heading. Aronson, and Butcher et al conclude that the hypercontraction of extrinsic and intrinsic laryngeal muscles, in response to emotional stress, is the common denominator behind the dysphonia or aphonia in these disorders. In addition, the extent of pathology visible on laryngeal examination is inconsistent with the severity of the abnormal voice. They cite four categories:

1. *Musculoskeletal tension disorders:* including vocal abuse, vocal nodules, contact ulcers, and ventricular dysphonia.
2. *Conversion voice disorders:* including conversion muteness and aphonia, conversion dysphonia, and psychogenic adductor "spasmodic dysphonia."
3. *Mutational falsetto* (puberphonia).
4. *Childlike speech* in adults.[1,7]

Psychogenic dysphonia often presents as total inability to speak, whispered speech, extremely strained or strangled speech, interrupted speech rhythm, or speech in an abnormal register (such as falsetto in a male). Usually, involuntary vocalizations during laughing and coughing are normal. The vocal folds are often difficult to examine because of supraglottic hyperfunction. There may be apparent bowing of both vocal folds consistent with severe muscular tension dysphonia creating anterior-posterior "squeeze" during phonation. Long-standing attempts to produce voice in the presence of this pattern may even result in traumatic lesions associated with vocal abuse patterns, such as vocal fold nodules. Normal abduction and adduction of the vocal folds may be visualized during flexible fiberoptic laryngoscopy by instructing the patient to perform maneuvers that decrease supraglottic load, such as whistling or sniffing. In addition, the singing voice is often more easily produced than the speaking voice in these patients. Tongue extension by the laryngologist during the rigid telescopic portion of the examination will often result in clear voice. The severe muscular tension dysphonia associated with psychogenic dysphonia can often be eliminated by behavioral interventions by the speech-language pathologist, sometimes in one session. In many instances moments of successful voice have been restored during stroboscopic examination.

Electromyography may be helpful in confirming the diagnosis by revealed simultaneous firing of abductors and adductors. Psychogenic dysphonia has been frequently misdiagnosed as spasmodic dysphonia, partially explaining the excellent "spasmodic dysphonia" cure rates in some series.

Psychogenic voice disorders are not merely the *absence* of observable neurolaryngeal abnormalities. This psychiatric diagnosis cannot be made with accuracy without the presence of a psychodynamic formulation based on "understanding of the personality, motivations, conflicts, and primary as well as secondary gain" associated with the symptoms.[8]

Conversion disorders are a special classification of psychogenic symptomatology and reflect loss of voluntary control over striated muscle or the sensory systems as a reflection of stress or psychological conflict. They may occur in any organ system, but the target organ is often symbolically related to the specifics of the unconsciously perceived threat. The term was first used by Freud to describe a defense mechanism that rendered an intolerable wish or drive innocuous by translating its energy into a physical symptom. The presence of an ego-syntonic physical illness offers *primary gain*: relief from the anxiety, depression, or rage by maintaining the emotional conflict in the unconscious. *Secondary gain* often occurs by virtue of the sick role.

Classic descriptions of findings in these patients include indifference to the symptoms, chronic stress, suppressed anger, immaturity and dependency, moderate depression, and poor sex role identification.[9,10] Conversion voice disorders also reflect a breakdown in communication with someone of emotional significance in the patient's life; wanting but blocking the verbal expression of anger, fear, or remorse, and significant feelings of shame.[1]

Confirmed neurological disease and psychogenic voice disorders do coexist and are known as somatic compliance.[11,12] Of course, potential organic causes of psychiatric disorders must always be thoroughly ruled out. Insidious onset of depression, personality changes, anxiety, or presumed conversion symptoms may be the first presentation of CNS disease.[13]

General Psychopathologic Presentations

Otolaryngologists and all other healthcare providers involved with patients with voice disorders should recognize significant comorbid psychopathology. Patterns of voice use may provide clues to the presence of psychopathology, although voice disturbance is certainly not the principal feature of major psychiatric illness. Nevertheless, failure to recognize serious psychopathology in voice patients may result not only in errors in voice diagnosis and failures of therapy, but more importantly in serious injury to the patient, sometimes even death.

Although a full depressive syndrome, including melancholia, can occur as a result of loss, it fulfills the criteria for a major depressive episode when the individual becomes preoccupied with feelings of worthlessness and guilt, demonstrates marked psychomotor retardation, and becomes impaired in both social and occupational functioning.[14] Careful listening during the taking of a history will reveal flat affect, including slowed rate of speech, decreased length of utterance, lengthy pauses, decreased pitch variability, monoloudness, and frequent use of vocal fry.[3,15] William Styron described his speech during his depressive illness as "slowed to the vocal equivalent of a shuffle."[16]

Major depression may be part of the patient's past medical history, may be a comorbid illness or may be a result of the presenting problem. The essential feature is a prominent, persistent dysphoric mood characterized by a loss of pleasure in nearly all activities. Appetite and sleep are disturbed and there may be marked weight gain or loss, hypersomnia, or one of three insomnia patterns. Psychomotor agitation or retardation may be present. Patients may demonstrate distractibility, memory disturbances, and difficulty concentrating. Feelings of worthlessness, helplessness, and hopelessness are a classic triad. Suicidal ideation, with or without plan, and/or concomitant psychotic features may necessitate emergency intervention.

Major affect disorders are classified as *unipolar* or *bipolar*. In bipolar disorder, the patient will also experience periods of mania: a recurrent elated state first occurring in young adulthood. (First manic episodes in patients over 50 should alert the clinician for medical or CNS illness, or to the effects of drugs.) The presentation of the illness includes the following major characteristics on a continuum of severity: elevated mood, irritability/hostility, distractibility, inflated self-concept, grandiosity, physical and sexual overactivity, flight of ideas, decreased need for sleep, social intrusiveness, buying sprees, and inappropriate collections of possessions. Manic patients demonstrate impaired social and familial behavior patterns. They are manipulative, alienate family members, and tend to have a very high divorce rate.[14,17] Vocal presentation will manifest flight of ideas (content), rapid-paced, pressured speech, and often increased pitch and volume. There may be dysfluency related to the rate of speech, breathlessness, and difficulty in interrupting the language stream. Three major theories, based on neuroanatomy, neuroendocrinology, and neuropharmacology are the most currently promulgated explanations for these disease states, but they are beyond the scope of this chapter.[18,19]

Treatment of affective disorders includes psychotherapy. Diagnosis and short-term treatment of reactive depressive states may be performed by the psychologist on the voice team, utilizing individual or group therapy modalities. Longer term treatment necessitates a referral to a community-based psychotherapist, ideally one whose skills, training, and understanding of the medical and artistic components of the illness are well known to the referring laryngologist. The use of psychopharmacologic agents is a risk/benefit decision. When the patient's symptom severity meets the criteria for major affective disorder, the physiologic effects of the disease, as well as the potential for self-destructive behavior, must be carefully considered.

Anxiety is an expected response in reaction to any medical diagnosis and the required treatment. However, anxiety disorders are seen with increasing incidence. Vocal presentations of anxiety vary with the continuum of psychiatric symptoms, ranging from depression to agitation and including impairment of concentration. Psychotherapy, including desensitization, cognitive/behavioral techniques, stress management, hypnosis, and insight-oriented approaches are helpful. Patients must learn to tolerate their distress and identify factors that precipitate or intensify their symptoms (see Stress Management). Medication may be used to treat underlying depression and decrease the frequency of episodes. However, it leaves the underlying conflict unresolved and negatively affects artistic quality.[7,20] Some medical conditions are commonly associated with the presenting symptom of anxiety. These include central nervous system (CNS) disease, Cushing's syndrome, hyperthyroidism, hypoglycemia, the consequences of minor head trauma, premenstrual syndrome, and cardiac disease such as mitral valve prolapse and various arrhythmias. Medications prescribed for other conditions may have anxiety as a side effect. These include such drugs as amphetamines, corticosteroids, caffeine, decongestants, cocaine, and the asthma armamentarium.[3]

Although psychotic behavior may be observed with major affective disorders, organic CNS disease or drug toxicity, schizophrenia occurs in only 1–2% of the general population.[21] Its onset is most prominent in mid to late adolescence through the late 20s. Incidence is approximately equal for males and females and schizophrenia has been described in all cultures and socioeconomic classes. This is a group of mental disorders in which massive disruptions in cognition or perception, such as delusions, hallucinations, or thought disorders are present. The fundamental causes of schizophrenia are unknown but the disease involves excessive amounts of neurotransmitters, chiefly dopamine. Genetic predisposition is present. Somatic delusions may present as voice complaints. However, flattening or inappropriateness of affect, a diagnostic characteristic of schizophrenia, will produce voice changes similar to those described for depression and mania. Where hallucinatory material creates fear, characteristics of anxiety and agitation will be audible. Perseveration, repetition, and neologisms may be present. The signs and symptoms also include clear indications of deterioration in social or occupational functioning, personal hygiene, changes in behavior and movement, an altered sense of self, and the presence of blunted or inappropriate affect.[3,14] The disease is chronic and control requires consistent use of antipsychotic medications for symptom management. Social support in regulating activities of daily living is crucial in maintaining emotional control. Family counseling and support groups offer the opportunity to share experiences and resources in the care of individuals with this difficult disease.

Psychoactive Medications

Psychoactive medications are discussed in chapter 18.

Eating Disorders and Substance Abuse

The rapport of the laryngologist and voice team may also allow patients to reveal other self-defeating disorders. Among the most common in arts-medicine are body dysmorphic (eating) disorders and substance abuse problems. Comprehensive discussion of these subjects is beyond the scope of this chapter but it is important for the laryngologist to recognize such conditions not only because of their effects on the voice, but also because of their potentially serious general medical and psychiatric implications. In addition to posterior laryngitis and pharyngitis, laryngeal findings associated with bulimia include subepithelial vocal fold hemorrhages, superficial telangiectasia of the vocal fold mucosa, and vocal fold scarring.[20] *Bulimia* is a disorder associated with self-induced vomiting following episodes of binge eating. It may occur sporadically, or it may be a chronic problem. Vomiting produces signs and symptoms similar to severe chronic reflux as well as thinning of tooth enamel. Bulimia nervosa can be a serious disorder and maybe associated with anorexia nervosa. Bulimia may be more prevalent than is commonly realized. It has been estimated to occur in as many as 2% to 4% of female adolescents and female young adults. Laryngologists must be attentive to the potential for anorexia and exercise addiction in the maintenance of a desirable body appearance in performers. Alcohol, benzodiazepines, stimulants, cocaine, and narcotics are notoriously readily available in the performing community and on the streets. Patients who demonstrate signs and symptoms, or who admit that these areas of their lives are out of control have taken the first step to regaining control, and this should be acknowledged while efficiently arranging treatment for them. The window of opportunity is often remarkably narrow. The physician should establish close ties to excellent treatment facilities where specialized clinicians can offer confidential outpatient management, with inpatient care available when required for safety.

Neurogenic Dysphonia

Patients with neurologic disease are likely to experience psychiatric symptoms, especially depression and anxiety. These disorders cause physiologic changes that may exacerbate or mask the underlying neurologic presentation. Metcalfe and colleagues cite the incidence of severe depression and/or anxiety in neurologic patients at one third.[22] Site of lesion affects the incidence, with lesions of the left cerebral hemisphere, basal ganglia, limbic system, thalamus, and anterior frontal lobe more likely to produce depression and anxiety.[23] These same structures are important in voice, speech, and language production, so, depression and anxiety logically coexist with voice and language disorders resulting from CNS pathology.[23,24] Dystonias and stuttering are also associated with both neurologic and psychogenic etiologies, and must be carefully distinguished by the laryngologist before instituting interdisciplinary treatment.[25]

Stress Management

Stress pervades virtually all professions in today's fast-moving society. Whether one is a singer preparing for a series of concerts, a teacher preparing for presentation of lectures, a lawyer anticipating a major trial, a businessperson negotiating an important contract, or a member of any other goal-oriented profession, each of us must deal with a myriad of demands on our time and talents. In 1971, Brodnitz reported on 2286 cases of all forms of voice disorders and classified 80% of the disorders as attributable to voice abuse or psychogenic factors resulting in vocal dysfunction.[26] However, regardless of the incidence, it is clear that stress-related problems are important and common in professional voice users. Stress may be physical or psychological, and it often involves a combination of both. Either may interfere with performance. Stress represents a special problem for singers, because its physiologic manifestations may interfere with the delicate mechanisms of voice production.

Stress is recognized as a factor in illness and disease and is probably implicated in almost every type of human problem. It is estimated that 50%–70% of all physicians visits involve complaints of stress-related illness.[27] *Stress* is a psychological experience that has physiologic consequences. A brief review of some terminology may be useful. Stress is a global term that is used broadly. However, one definition is emotional, cognitive, and physiological reactions to psychological demands and challenges. The term *stress level* reflects the degree of stress experienced. Stress is not an all-or-none phenomenon. The psychological effects of stress range from mild to severely incapacitating. The term *stress-response* refers to the physiological reaction of an organism to stress. A *stressor* is an external stimulus or internal thought, perception, image, or emotion that creates stress.[28] Two other concepts are important in a contemporary discussion of stress: *coping* and *adaptation*. Lazarus has defined coping as "the process of managing demands (external or internal) that are appraised as taxing or exceeding the resources of the person."[29] In the early 1930s, Hans Selye, an endocrinologist, discovered a generalized response to stressors in the animals under study. He described their responses using the term *General Adaptation Syndrome*. Selye (cited in Green and Snellenberger)[28] postulated that the physiology of the test animals was trying to adapt to the challenges of noxious stimuli. The process of adaptation to chronic and severe stressors was harmful in the long run. There were three phases to the observed response: *alarm*, *adaption*, and *exhaustion*. These phases were named for physiologic responses described by a sequence of events. The alarm phase is the characteristic fight or flight response. If the stressor continued the animal appeared to adapt. In the adaptation phase, the physiologic responses were less extreme but the animal eventually became more exhausted. In the exhaustion phase, the animal's adaptation energy was spent, physical symptoms occurred, and some animals went on to die.[30]

Stress responses occur in part through the autonomic nervous system. A stressor triggers particular brain centers which in turn affect target organs through nerve connections. The brain has two primary pathways for the stress response, neuronal and hormonal, and these pathways overlap. The body initiates a stress response through one of three pathways: through sympathetic nervous system efferents which terminate on target organs such as the heart and blood vessels; via the release of epinephrine and norepinephrine from the adrenal medulla; and through the release of various other catecholamines.[28] A full description of the various processes involved is beyond the scope of this chapter. However, stress has numerous physical consequences. Through the autonomic nervous system, it may alter oral and vocal fold secretions, heart rate, and gastric acid production. Under acute, anxiety-producing circumstances, such changes are to be expected. When frightened, a normal person's palms become cold and sweaty, the mouth becomes dry, heart rate increases, his or her pupils change size, and stomach acid secretions may increase. These phenomena are objective signs that may be observed by a physician, and their symptoms may be recognized by the performer as dry mouth and voice fatigue, heart palpitations and "heartburn." More severe, prolonged stress is also commonly associated with increased muscle tension throughout the body (but particularly in the head and neck), headaches, decreased ability to concentrate, and insomnia. Chronic fatigue is also a common symptom. These physiological alterations may lead not only to altered vocal quality, but also to physical pathology. Increased gastric acid secretion is associated with ulcers, as well as reflux laryngitis and arytenoid irritation. Other gastrointestinal manifestations, such as colitis and irritable bowel syndrome, and dysphagia are also described. Chronic stress and tension may cause numerous pain syndromes although headaches, particularly migraines in vulnerable individuals, are most common. Stress is also associated with more serious physical problems such as myocardial infarction (heart attack), asthma, and the depression of the immune system.[20,28,30] Thus, the constant pressure under which many performers live may be more than a modest inconvenience. Stress factors should be recognized, and appropriate modifications should be made to ameliorate them.

Stressors may be physical or psychological, and often involve a combination of both. Either may interfere with performance. There are several situations in which physical stress is common and important. Generalized fatigue is seen frequently in hard-working singers, especially in the frantic few weeks preceding major performances. In order to maintain normal mucosal secretions, a strong immune system to fight infection, and the ability of muscles to recover from heavy use, rest, proper nutrition and hydration are required. When the body is stressed through deprivation of these essentials, illness (such as upper respiratory infection), voice fatigue, hoarseness, and other vocal dysfunctions may supervene.

Lack of physical conditioning undermines the power source of the voice. A person who becomes short of breath while climbing a flight of stairs hardly has the abdominal and respiratory endurance needed to sustain him or her optimally through the rigors of performance. The stress of attempting performance under such circumstances often results in voice dysfunction. This deficiency probably shortens a singer's career.

Oversinging is another common physical stress. As with running, swimming, or any other athletic activity that depends upon sustained, coordinated muscle activity, singing requires conditioning to build up strength and endurance. Rest periods are also essential for muscle recovery. Singers who are accustomed to singing for 1 or 2 hours a day stress their physical voice-producing mechanism severely when they suddenly begin rehearsing for 14 hours daily immediately prior to performance.

Medical treatment of stress depends on the specific circumstances. When the diagnosis is appropriate but poorly controlled anxiety, the singer can usually be helped by assurance that his or her voice complaint is related to anxiety and not to any physical problem. Under ordinary circumstances, once the singer's mind is put to rest regarding the questions of nodules, vocal fold injury, or other serious problems, his or her training usually allows compensation for vocal manifestations of anxiety, especially when the vocal complaint is minor. Slight alterations in quality or increased vocal fatigue are seen most frequently. These are often associated with lack of sleep, oversinging, and dehy-

dration associated with the stress-producing commitment. The singer or actor should be advised to modify these and to consult his or her voice teacher. The voice teacher should ensure that good vocal technique is being used under performance and rehearsal circumstances. Frequently, young singers are not trained sufficiently in how and when to "mark." For example, many singers whistle to rest their voices, not realizing that active vocalization and potentially fatiguing vocal fold contact occur when whistling. Technical proficiency and a plan for voice conservation during rehearsals and performances is essential under these circumstances. A manageable stressful situation may become unmanageable if real physical vocal problems develop.

Several additional modalities may be helpful in selected circumstances. Relative voice rest (using the voice only when necessary) may be important not only to voice conservation but also to psychological relaxation. Under stressful circumstances, a singer needs as much peace and quiet as possible, not hectic socializing, parties with heavy voice use in noisy environments, and press appearances. The importance of adequate sleep and fluid intake cannot be overemphasized. Local therapy such as steam inhalation and neck muscle massage may be helpful in some people and certainly does no harm. The doctor may be very helpful in alleviating the singer's exogenous stress by conveying "doctor's orders" directly to theater management. This will save the singer the discomfort of having to personally confront an authority and violate his or her "show must go on" ethic. A short phone call by the physician can be highly therapeutic. Singers should not hesitate to ask the doctor to make such a call if she or he does not offer.

When stress is chronic and incapacitating, more comprehensive measures are required. If psychological stress manifestations become so severe as to impair performance or necessitate the use of drugs to allow performance, psychotherapy is indicated. The goal of psychotherapeutic approaches to stress-management include: (1) changing external and internal stressors; (2) changing effective and cognitive reactions to stressors; (3) changing physiological reactions to stress; and (4) changing stress behaviors. A psychoeducational model is customarily used. Initially, the psychotherapist will assist the patient in identifying and evaluating stressor characteristics. A variety of assessment tools are available for this purpose. Interventions designed to increase a sense of efficacy and personal control are designed. Perceived control over the stressor directly affects stress level and it changes one's experience of the stressor. Laboratory and human research has determined a sense of control to be one of the most potent elements in the modulation of stress responses. Concrete exercises that impose time management are taught and practiced. Patients are urged to identify and expand their network of support as well. Psychological intervention requires evaluation of the patient's cognitive model. Cognitive restructuring exercises as well as classical behavioral conditioning responses are useful, practical tools that patients easily learn and utilize effectively with practice. Cognitive skills include the use of monitored perception, thought, and internal dialogue to regulate emotional and physiologic responses. A variety of relaxation techniques are available and are ordinarily taught in the course of stress-management treatment. These include progressive relaxation, hypnosis, autogenic training, and imagery and biofeedback training. Underlying all these approaches is the premise that making conscious normally unconscious processes leads to control and self-efficacy.

As with all medical conditions, the best treatment for stress in singers is prevention. Awareness of the conditions that lead to stress and its potential adverse effect on voice production often allows the singer to anticipate and avoid these problems. Stress is inevitable in performance and in life. Performers must learn to recognize it, compensate for it when necessary, and incorporate it into their singing as emotion and excitement—the "edge." Stress should be controlled, not pharmacologically eliminated. Used well, stress should be just one more tool of the singer's trade.

Performance Anxiety

Psychological stress is intrinsic to vocal performance. For most people, sharing emotions is stressful even in the privacy of home, let alone under spotlights in front of a room full of people. Under ordinary circumstances, during training, a singer or actor learns to recognize his or her customary anxiety about performing, to accept it as part of his or her instrument, and to compensate for it. When psychological pressures become severe enough to impair or prohibit performance, careful treatment is required. Such occurrences usually are temporary and happen because of a particular situation such as short notice for a critically important performance, a recent family death, etc. Chronic disabling psychological stress in the face of performance is a more serious problem. In its most extreme forms, performance anxiety actually disrupts the skills of performers; in its milder form it lessens the enjoyment of appearing in public.[31]

Virtually all performers have experienced at least some symptoms of hyperarousal during their performance history and all fear their reemergence. Some fortunate people seem to bypass this type of trauma, exhibiting only mild symptoms of nervousness ahead of performance, which disappear the moment they walk on stage. In these individuals, personal physiology works consistently for instead of against them. The human nervous system functions exquisitely for the great majority of our needs, but in performance anxiety it begins to works against the performer in those very circumstances when he or she wants most to do well. Human autonomic arousal continues to be under the sway of primal survival mechanisms, which are the basic lines of defense against physical danger: they prepare the individual to fight or flee in response to the perception of threat. They are essential to our survival in situations of physical danger.[35] However, the dangers that threaten performers are not physical in nature, but the human nervous system cannot differentiate between physical and psychological dangers, producing physiologic responses that are the same. When the physical symptoms associated with extreme arousal are enumerated, it is easy to understand why they can be major impediments to skilled performance and may even be disabling. They include rapid heart rate, dry mouth, sweating palms, palpitations, tremor, high blood pressure, restricted breathing, frequency of urination, and impaired memory.[31]

This process is cognitive, and Beck and Emory describe the development of cognitive sets using an analogy to photography. The individual scans the relevant environment and then determines which aspect, if any, on which to focus. Cognitive processing reduces the number of dimensions in a situation, sacrifices a great deal of information, and induces distortion into the picture. Certain aspects of the situation are highlighted at the expense of others, the relative magnitudes and prominence of various features are distorted, and there is loss of perspective. In addition, they describe blurring and loss of important detail. These are the decisive influences on what the individual sees. They describe how the cognitive set influences the picture that is perceived. The existing cognitive sets determine which aspects of the scene will be highlighted, which glossed over, and which excluded. The individual's first impressions of an event provide information that either reinforces or modifies the pre-existing cognitive set. The initial impression is critical because it determines whether the situation directly affects the patient's vital interests. It also sets the course of subsequent steps in conceptualization and the total response to a situation.[32] According to the cognitive model, at the same time the individual is evaluating the nature of the threat, he or she is also assessing internal resources for dealing with it and their availability and effectiveness in deflecting potential damage. The balance between potential danger and available coping responses determines the nature and intensity of the patient's stress response. Two major behavioral systems are activated, either separately or together, in response to the threat. Those mediated by the sympathetic branch of the autonomic nervous system, "the fight or flight response," and those related to the parasympathetic branch, "the freeze or faint," response.[32]

A major feature of performance anxiety is that, prior to entering the situation, the fear appears plausible. A complex web of factors in this situation may aggravate the patient's fears. These may include the relative status of the performer and the evaluator, the performer's skill, his or her confidence in the ability to perform adequately in a given "threatening situation," and the appraisal of the degree of threat (including the severity of potential damage to one's career and self-esteem). The individual's threshold of automatic defenses that undermine performance and the rigidity of the rules relevant to the performance in question are also factored into the intensity of the response. Unfortunately, the experience of fear increases the likelihood of the undesirable consequences. A vicious cycle is created in which the anticipation of an absolute, extreme, irreversible outcome makes the performer more fearful of the effects and inhibited when entering the situation.[32] Negative evaluation by judges or audiences is the common psychic threat. The individual suffering from performance anxiety believes that he or she is being scrutinized and judged. Components under observation include fluency, artistry, self-assurance, and technique.

Although most fears tend to decline with continued exposure and expertise, Caine notes that even highly skilled performers do not always experience lessening of performance anxiety over time.[31] Indeed, she describes a dilemma for the expert performer in which a potentially humiliating and frightening mistake is less and less tolerable. A behavioral feedback loop becomes established. The act of performance becomes the stimulus perceived as a threat. In situations of danger, the individual's physiology primes him or her to become more alert and sensitive to all potential threats in the surrounding environment. Anticipating mistakes increases arousal, which further enhances access to memories of mistakes and feelings of humiliation, which activates more fears and more arousal. This process is linked by catastrophic thoughts, physiologic manifestations of anxiety, and imagery. Unfortunately, this process is often initiated very early in a young performer's training.

A variety of psychotherapeutic treatment approaches to performance anxiety have been described in the literature. The most effective of these are cognitive and behavioral strategies, which assist performers in modulating levels of arousal to more optimal levels. Cognitive therapy addresses the essential mechanism sustaining performance anxiety: the cognitive set a performer brings to the performance situation. The autonomic nervous system is merely responding to the threat as it is perceived, and the intensity of the response correlates to the degree of threat generated by the sufferer's catastrophic expectations and negative self-talk. Cognitive restructuring techniques are extremely effective in producing the necessary adjustments. Monitoring internal self-dialogue comprises the first step in recognizing the dimension of the problem. These excessively self-critical attitudes enhance the probability of mistakes. Homework exercises designed to monitor critical thoughts are assigned. In the second step of cognitive treatment, adaptive, realistic self-statements are substituted. Behaviorally based treatment approaches such as thought-stopping, paired relaxation responses, and "prescribing the symptom" are also utilized. Hypnosis is efficacious, providing relaxation techniques and introducing positive, satisfying, and joyful imagery.

Brief psychotherapeutic approaches produce effective outcomes, but some proponents of the psychodynamic approach argue that the underlying conflicts will resurface in some form of symptom substitution. This author's (DCR) clinical approach includes an exploration for secondary gain offered by disabling performance anxiety. The performer's unconscious fear must be addressed for these treatments to remain effective and to avoid eventual symptom substitution. Patients are asked "What does this symptom accomplish for you?" The question may sound unsympathetic, and the patient may need to search deeply for the answer. This search requires significant courage. If the patient makes effective use of the treatment strategies, what might be expected of him or her? Where might success lead? Is he or she ready to go on to the next phase in a performance career, or does it remain safer to be immobilized? Which problem is honestly more terrifying: the symptom of performance anxiety or the possibility of success? What would be the consequences of resolving the immobilizing performance anxiety? The patient is asked to imagine a life in which the problem is no longer present. This exploration is often conducted using the relaxation and enhanced perception available in hypnosis. Most of these questions are painful to answer. For some performers, success beckons with one hand and signals caution with the other. Eloise Ristad describes this with extraordinarily pragmatic wisdom: "The part of us that holds back knows that change involves challenges—losses as well as gains. Change always means dying a little; leaving behind something old and tattered and no longer useful to us even though comfortably familiar."[33(p155)] A successful psychotherapeutic response to disabling performance anxiety requires a thorough explanation of the personal meaning of the symptom to the patient as well as an extensive and exciting repertoire of strategies for effecting personal change.

The Surgical Experience

When vocal fold surgery is indicated, many individuals will demonstrate hospital-related phobias or self-destructive responses to pain. Adamson et al describe the importance of understanding how the patient's occupational identity will be affected by surgical intervention.[34] Vocal fold surgery impacts on the major mode of communication that all human beings utilize; the impact is extraordinarily anxiety-producing in professional voice users. Even temporary periods of absolute voice restriction may induce feelings of insecurity, helplessness, and dissociation from the verbal world. Carpenter details the value of an early therapy session to focus on the fears, fantasies, misconceptions, and regression that frequently accompany a decision to undergo surgery.[35]

A proper surgical discussion highlights vocal fold surgery as *elective*. The patient chooses surgery as the only remaining means to regaining the previously "normal" voice, or to a different but desirable voice. Responsible care includes a thorough preoperative and written discussion of the limits and complications of surgery, with recognition by the surgeon that anxiety affects both understanding and retention of information about undesirable outcomes. Personality psychopathology or unrealistic expectations of the impact of surgery on their lives are elements for which surgical candidates can be screened.[34,36,37] Recognizing such problems preoperatively allows preoperative counselling, and obviates many postoperative difficulties.

Although a thorough discussion is outside the scope of this chapter, surgically treated voice patients include those undergoing laryngectomy, with or without a voice prosthesis. The laryngectomized individual must make major psychological and social adjustments. These include not only adjustments related to a diagnosis of cancer, but also to a sudden disability: loss of voice. With the improvement in prognosis, research has begun to focus on the individual's quality of life after the laryngectomy. There is wide variability in the quality of preoperative and postoperative psychological support reported by patients during each phase of

care. Providing this support is a crucial role for the voice team's psychologist.[38-40]

Reactive Responses

Reaction to illness is the major source of psychiatric disturbance in patients with significant voice dysfunction. Loss of communicative function is an experience of alienation that threatens human self-definition and independence. Catastrophic fears of loss of productivity, economic and social status, and, in professional voice users, creative artistry, contribute to rising anxiety. Anxiety is known to worsen existing communication disorders, and the disturbances in memory, concentration, and synaptic transmission secondary to depression may intensify other voice symptoms and interfere with rehabilitation.

Families of patients are affected as well. They are often confused about the diagnosis and poorly prepared to support the patient's coping responses. The resulting stress may negatively influence family dynamics and intensify the patient's depressive illness.[41] As the voice-injured patient experiences the process of grieving, the psychologist may assume a more prominent role in his or her care. Essentially, the voice-injured patient goes through a grieving process similar to patients who mourn other losses such as the death of a loved one. In some cases, especially among voice professionals, the patients actually mourn the loss of their self as they perceive it. The psychologist is responsible for facilitating the tasks of mourning and monitoring the individual's formal mental status for clinically significant changes. There are a number of models for tracking this process. The most easily understood is that of Worden, as adapted by the author (DCR).[42] Initially, the task is to *accept the reality of the loss*. The need for and distress of this is vestigial during the phase of diagnosis, is held consciously in abeyance during the acute and rehabilitative phases of treatment, but is reinforced with accumulating data measuring vocal function. As the reality becomes undeniable, the mourner must be helped to express the full range of grieving affect. The rate of accomplishing this is variable and individual. Generally, it will occur in the style with which the person usually copes with crisis and may be florid or tightly constricted. *All* responses must be invited and normalized. The psychologist facilitates the process and stays particularly attuned to unacceptable, split-off responses or the failure to move through any particular response.

As attempts to deny the loss take place and fail, the mourner gradually encounters the next task: *beginning to live and cope in a world in which the lost object is absent.* This is the psychoanalytic process of *decathexsis*, requiring the withdrawal of life energies from the other and the reinvesting of them in the self. For some professional voice users, this may be a temporary state as they make adjustments required by their rehabilitation demands. In other cases, the need for change will be lasting; change in fach, change in repertoire, need for amplification, altered performance schedule or, occasionally, change in career.

As the patient so injured seeks to heal his or her life, another task looms. Known as *recathexis*, it involves *reinvesting life energies in other relationships, interests, talents, and life goals.* The individual is assisted in redefining and revaluing the self as apart from the voice. The voice is then seen as the *product* of the self, rather than as equivalent to the self. For many performers this is painfully difficult.[6,42]

Role of the Psychological Professional

Both psychology and psychiatry specialize in attending to emotional needs and problems. Psychiatrists, as physicians, focus on the neurological and biological causes and treatment of psychopathology. Psychologists have advanced graduate training in psychological function and therapy. They concern themselves with cognitive processes such as thinking, behavior, and memory; the experiencing and expression of emotions; significant inner conflicts, characteristic modes of defense in coping with stress; and personality style and perception of self and others, including their expression in interpersonal behavior. In the authors' practice, clinical psychologists serve as members of the voice team. They work directly with some patients and offer consultation to the physician and other professionals.

Assessment of patients is done throughout the physician's history taking and physical examinations, as well as in a formal psychiatric interview when appropriate. Personality assessment, screening for or evaluating known psychopathology, and assessing potential surgical candidates is performed. Occasionally, psychometric instruments are added to the diagnostic interview. Confidentiality of content is extended to the treatment team to maximize interdisciplinary care. Because of their special interest in voicing parameters, the voice team psychologists are especially attuned to the therapeutic use of their own voices for intensifying rapport and pacing/leading the patient's emotional state during interventions.[43-47]

Psychotherapeutic treatment is offered on a short-term, diagnosis-related basis. Treatment is designed to identify and alleviate emotional distress and to increase the individual's resources for adaptive functioning. Individual psychotherapeutic approaches include brief insight-oriented therapies, cognitive/behavioral techniques, gestalt interventions, stress-management skill building, and clinical hypnosis.

After any indicated acute intervention is provided, and in patients whose coping repertoire is clearly adequate to the stressors, a psychoeducational model is used. The therapy session focuses on a prospective discussion of personal, inherent life stressors and predictable illnesses. Stress management skills are taught and audiotapes provided. These offer portable skills, and supplemental sessions may be scheduled by mutual decision during appointments at the center for medical examinations and speech or singing voice therapy. A group therapy model, facilitated by the psychologist, has also been used to provide a forum for discussion of patient responses during the various phases of treatment. Participants benefit from the perspective and progress of other patients, the opportunity to decrease their experience of isolation, and the sharing of resources.

Long-term psychodynamic psychotherapy, chronic psychiatric conditions, and patients requiring psychopharmacologic management are referred to consultant psychologists and psychiatrists with special interest and insight in voice-related psychological problems. The voice team's psychologists also serve in a liaison role when patients already in treatment come to the practice for voice care. In addition, the psychologist participates in professional education activities in the medical practice. These include writing, lecturing, and serving as a preceptor for visiting professionals. Specially trained psychologists have proven to be an invaluable addition to the voice team, and close collaboration with team members has proven to be valuable and stimulating for psychologists interested in the care of professional voice users.

Summary

Psychological problems are common among voice professionals who develop voice problems. In addition, psychological problems seen in the general population also occur in voice professionals. Such conditions and their treatment may affect performance. Teachers, therapists, and performers should be familiar with the complex psychological concomitants to voice performance. Teachers and voice therapists commonly and appropriately provide psychological support for students and patients. However, it is critical for teachers and health care providers to recognize the limits of their training and the circumstances under which referral to a psychological professional is required.

Review Questions

1. Singers may have particularly strong psychological reactions to organic voice disorders because of difficulties separating who they are from what they do.
   a. true
   b. false

2. Defined psychological phases of vocal injury include all of the following except:
   a. problem recognition
   b. diagnosis
   c. rejection
   d. treatment
   e. acceptance

3. The classification of psychogenic voice disorders includes each of the following except:
   a. musculoskeletal tension disorders
   b. thyrogenic dysphonia
   c. conversion voice disorders
   d. mutational falsetto
   e. childlike speech in adults

4. Loss of voluntary control over striated muscle or sensory systems due to stress or psychological conflict is known as:
   a. musculoskeletal tension disorders
   b. thyrogenic dysphonia
   c. conversion voice disorders
   d. mutational falsetto
   e. childlike speech in adults

5. Following vocal injury, the task of reinvesting life energies in other relationships, interests, talents and life goals, is known as:
   a. recathexis
   b. conversion
   c. decathexis
   d. all of the above
   e. none of the above

References

1. Aronson A. *Clinical Voice Disorders*. 3rd ed. New York, NY: Thieme Medical Publishers; 1990: 117-145.
2. Sundberg J. *The Science of the Singing Voice*. DeKalb, IL: Northern Illinois University Press; 1985:146-156.
3. Vogel D, Carter J. *The effects of Drugs on Communication Disorders*. San Diego, Calif: Singular Publishing Group; 1995:31-143.
4. Horney K. Cited by: Meissner W. Theories of personality. In: Nicholi A. ed. *The New Harvard Guide to Psychiatry*. Cambridge, Mass: Harvard University Press; 1988: 177-199.
5. Ray CJ, Fitzgibbon G. The socially mediated reduction of stress in surgical patients. In: Oborne DJ, Grunberg M, Eisner JR, eds. *Research and Psychology in Medicine*. Oxford: Pergamon Press; 1979;2:521-527.
6. Rosen DC, Sataloff RT, Evans H, Hawkshaw M. Self-esteem in singers: Singing healthy, singing hurt. *NATS J*. 1993;49:32-35.
7. Butcher P, Elias A, Raven R. *Psychogenic Voice Disorders and Cognitive-Behavior Therapy*. San Diego, Calif: Singular Publishing Group; 1993:3-22.
8. Osterwold P, Avery M. Psychiatric problems of performing artists. In: Sataloff RT, Brandfonbrenner A, Lederman R, eds. *Textbook of Performing Arts Medicine*. New York, NY: Raven Press; 1991:319-335.
9. Nemiah J. Psychoneurotic disorders. In: Nicholi A, ed. *The New Harvard Guide to Psychiatry*. Cambridge, Mass: Harvard University Press; 1988:234-258.
10. Ziegler FS, Imboden JB. Contemporary conversion reactions: II conceptual model. *Arch Gen Psychiatry*. 1962;6:279-287.
11. Sapir S, Aronson A. Coexisting psychogenic and neurogenic dysphonia: a source of diagnostic confusion. *Br J Disord Commun*. 1987;22:73-80.
12. Hartman D, Daily W, Morin K. A case of superior laryngeal nerve paresis and psychogenic dysphonia. *J Speech Hear Disord*. 1989;54:526-529.
13. Cummings J, Benson D, Houlihan J, Gosenfield L. Mutism: loss of neocortical and limbic vocalization. *J Nerv Ment Dis*. 1983;171:255-259.
14. American Psychiatric Association. *Diagnostic and Statistical Manual of Mental Disorders* III-R. Washington, DC: American Psychiatric Association; 1987:206-210.
15. Rubin J, Sataloff RT, Korovin G and Gould WJ. *The Diagnosis and Treatment of Voice Disorders*. New York, NY: Igaku-Shoin Medical Publishers Inc; 1995.
16. Styron W. *Darkness Visible: A Memoir of Madness*. New York, NY: Random House; 1990:85.
17. Klerman G. Depression and related disorders of mood. In: Nicholi A ed. *The New Harvard Guide to Psychiatry*. Cambridge, Mass: Harvard University Press; 1988: 309-336.
18. Weissman M. The psychological treatment of depression: evidence for the efficacy of psychotherapy alone, in comparison with and in combination with pharmacotherapy. *Arch Gen Psych*. 1979;38:1261-1269.
19. Ross E, Rush A. Diagnosis and neuroanatomical correlates of depression in brain-damaged patients: implications for a neurology of depression. *Arch Gen Psych*. 1981;38:1344-1354.
20. Sataloff RT. Stress, anxiety and psychogenic dysphonia. In: *Professional Voice: The Science and Art of Clinical Care*. New York. NY: Raven Press; 1991:195-200.
21. Tsuang M, Faraone S, Day M. Schizophrenic disorders. In: Nicholi A, ed. *The New Harvard Guide to Psychiatry*.

Cambridge, Mass: Harvard University Press; 1988: 259-295.

22. Metcalfe R, Firth D, Pollack S, Creed F. Psychiatric morbidity and illness behavior in female neurological inpatients. *J Neurol Neurosurg Psych*. 1988;51:1387-1390.

23. Gianotti G. Emotional behavior and hemispheric side of lesion. *Cortex*. 1972;8:41-55.

24. Alexander M, Loverne S. Aphasia after left hemispheric intracranial hemorrhage. *Neurology*. 1980;30:1193-1202.

25. Mahr G, Leith W. Psychogenic stuttering of adult onset. *J Speech and Hearing Research*. 1992;35:283-286.

26. Brodnitz F. Hormones and the human voice. *Bull NY Acad Med*. 1971;47:183-191.

27. Everly GS. *A Clinical Guide to the Treatment of the Human Stress Response*. New York, NY: Plenum Press;1989: 40-43.

28. Green J, Snellenberger R. *The Dynamics of Health and Wellness. A Biopsychosocial Approach*. Fort Worth, Tex: Holt, Reinhardt, Winston Inc; 1991:61-64,92,98, 101-136.

29. Lazarus RS, Folkman S. Stress Appraisal and Coping. New York, NY: Springer-Verlag Publications; 1984:283.

30. Stroudmire A, (ed). *Psychological Factors Affecting Medication Conditions*. Washington, DC: American Psychiatric Press, Inc; 1995:187-192.

31. Caine JB. Understanding and treating performance anxiety from a cognitive-behavior therapy perspective. *NATS J*. 1991:27-51.

32. Beck A, Emery G. *Anxiety Disorders and Phobias: A Cognitive Perspective*. New York, NY: Basic Books Inc; 1985: 38-50,151.

33. Ristad E. *A Soprano on Her Head: Right Side Up Reflections on Life and Other Performances*. Moah, Utah: Real People Press; 1982:154,155.

34. Adamson JD, Hersuberg D, Shane F. The psychic significance of parts of the body in surgery. In: Howells JG, ed.

Modern Perspectives in the Psychiatric Aspects of Surgery. New York, NY: Brunner Mazel; 1976:20-45.

35. Carpenter B. Psychological aspects of vocal fold surgery. In: Gould WJ, Sataloff RT, Spiegel JR, eds. *Voice Surgery*. St. Louis, Mo: CV Mosby; 1993:389-343.

36. MacGregor FC. Patient dissatisfaction with results of technically satisfactory surgery. *Aesthetic Plast Surg*. 1981;5:27-32.

37. Shontz F. Body image and physical disability. In: Cash T, Pruzinsky T eds. *Body Images: Development, Deviance and Change*. New York, NY: The Guilford Press; 1990: 149-169.

38. Berkowitz J, Lucente F. Counselling before laryngectomy. *Laryngoscope*. 1985;95:1332-1336.

39. Gardner W. Adjustment problems of laryngectomized women. *Arch Otolaryngol*. 1966;83:57-68.

40. Stam H, Koopmans J, Mathieson C. The psychological impact of a laryngectomy: a comprehensive assessment. *J Psychosoc Oncol*. 1991;9:37-58.

41. Zraick R, Boone D. Spouse attitudes toward a person with aphasia. *J Speech Hear Res*. 1991;34:123-128.

42. Worden W. *Grief Counselling and Grief Therapy*. New York, NY: Springer-Verlag Publications; 1982:7-18.

43. Bady SL. The voice as curative factor in psychotherapy. *Psycho Rev*. 1985;72:479-490.

44. Crasilneck HB, Hall J. Clinical Hypnosis: *Principles and Applications*. 2nd ed. Orlando, Fla: Grune and Stratton; 1985:60-61.

45. Watkins J:. *Hypnotherapeutic Techniques*. New York, NY: Irvington Publishers; 1987:114.

46. Lankton S. *Practical Magic: A Translation of Neuro-Linguistic Programming into Clinical Psycho-Therapy*. Cupertino, Calif: Meta Publications; 1980:174.

47. King M, Novick L, Citrenbaum C. *Irresistible Communication*. Philadelphia, Pa: WB Saunders; 1983:21,22, 115-127.

21

Introduction to Treating Voice Abuse

Robert Thayer Sataloff

Abnormalities Associated with Voice Dysfunction

As discussed in chapter 6, a great number of physical and psychological problems may be responsible for voice dysfunction. These include derangements in virtually any body system. Most of the organic, psychological, and technical problems that may be related to voice complaints are discussed in detail in other chapters. It is important for the physician to identify and sort out dysfunction in each category (organic, psychological, and technical); abnormalities in all three categories are frequently present simultaneously. For example, if the initial problem is an abnormality on the vocal fold, fear and psychological stress are normal reactions, and the performer frequently changes his or her technique (often unconsciously) in an effort to compensate for vocal impairment. Alternatively, technical dysfunction (such as hyperfunctional voice abuse or muscular tension dysphonia) may have been the initiating factor. This may have produced vocal fold pathology (such as nodules) and subsequent psychological reaction. In contrast, extreme, poorly compensated anxiety may have been the original culprit and caused laryngeal and technical problems. For each scenario, the treatment approach is different, and all appropriate members of the voice care team must understand the pathogenesis in order to design a treatment program that addresses not only immediate performance crises, but, long-term solutions to the principal problem. It is usually best to address all existing problems through a team approach. The team should include consultants in various specialties with special interest in and knowledge of professional voice users. Because of the frequency and importance of voice abuse problems, the otolaryngologist must acquire extra training in technical aspects of voice pro-duction for speech and singing and should work closely with a speech-language pathologist and singing voice specialist.

Voice Abuse

Vocal complaints are often due to abusive speaking or singing habits, especially hyperfunctional techniques. These problems and therapeutic approaches to them are discussed in detail later in this book. Laryngologists must be familiar with the specific techniques used by speech-language pathologists and singing teachers to diagnose and modify vocal abuses.

Physicians must be careful not to exceed the limits of their expertise or responsibility in applying this knowledge in the office. However, if the physician is trained in singing and notices a minor technical error such as isolated excess muscle tension in the tongue, this may be pointed out. Nevertheless, the singer should be referred back to his or her voice teacher or to a competent singing-voice specialist for management of these problems. Abdominal muscle problems should be noted and should also be referred back to the vocal teacher. Of course, any medical cause must be corrected.

Most of the important historical aspects and many treatment suggestions regarding voice abuse in speaking and singing are covered in chapters 6, 23, and 27, although these chapters concentrate on the responsibilities of the team members other than the laryngologists.

When voice abuse is due to extracurricular activities such as conducting, screaming during athletic events, or shouting at children, the physician should advise the patient about measures to protect the speaking voice and, consequently, the singing voice. However, if it is a matter of strain in the singing or speaking voice under ordinary circumstances, treatment should be deferred to a voice teacher or speech-language pathologist. In many instances, training the speaking voice will benefit the singer greatly, and physicians should not hesitate to recommend such training. Similarly, most singers benefit from formal training of the speaking voice. Surprisingly, most singers have not had such training, and they often speak much more abusively than they sing. The specially trained speech-language pathologist can be of great value to these singers, and usually only a few sessions are required. Subsequently, work with an acting voice trainer is often invaluable.

Speech-Language Pathologists

An excellent speech-language pathologist is an invaluable asset in caring for professional voice users. However, laryngologists should recognize that, like physicians, speech-language pathologists have varied backgrounds and experience in treatment of voice disorders. In fact, most speech-language pathology programs teach relatively little about caring for professional speakers and nothing about professional singers. Moreover, there are few speech-language pathologists in the United States with vast experience in this specialized area. Speech-language pathologists often subspecialize. One who expertly treats patients who have had strokes, stutter, have undergone laryngectomy, or have swallowing disorders will not necessarily know how to manage professional voice users optimally. The laryngologist must learn the strengths and weaknesses of the speech-language pathologist with whom he or she works. After identifying a speech-language pathologist who is interested in treating professional voice users, the laryngologist and speech-language pathologist should work together closely in developing the necessary expertise. Assistance may be found through laryngologists who treat large numbers of singers or educational programs such as the Voice Foundation's annual Symposium on Care of the Professional Voice. In general, therapy should be directed toward relaxation techniques, breath control, and abdominal support.

Speech-language pathology may be helpful, even when a singer has no obvious problem in his or her speaking voice but has significant technical problems singing. Once a person has been singing for several years, it is often very difficult for a singing teacher to convince him or her to correct certain technical errors. Singers are much less protective of their speaking voices. Therefore, a speech-language pathologist may be able rapidly to teach proper support, relaxation, and voice placement in speaking. Once mastered, these techniques can be carried over fairly easily into singing through cooperation between the speech-language pathologist and voice teacher. This "back door" approach has proved extremely useful in the author's experience. For the actor, it is often helpful to coordinate speech-language pathology sessions with acting lessons, especially with the training of the speaking voice provided by the actor's voice teacher or coach. Information provided by the speech-language pathologist, acting teacher, and singing teacher should be symbiotic and should not conflict. If there are major discrepancies, bad training from one of the team members *should* be suspected, and changes should be made.

Singing Teachers

In selected cases, singing lessons may also be extremely helpful for nonsingers with voice problems. The techniques used to develop abdominothoracic strength, breath control, laryngeal and neck muscle strength, and relaxation are very similar to those used in speech therapy. Singing lessons often expedite therapy and appear to improve the result in some patients.

Laryngologists who frequently care for singers often are asked to recommend a voice teacher. This may put the laryngologist in an uncomfortable position, particularly if the singer is already studying with someone in the community. Most physicians do not have sufficient expertise to criticize a voice teacher, and we must be extremely cautious about recommending that a singer change teachers. However, there is no certifying agency that standardizes or assures the quality of a singing teacher. Although one may be slightly more confident of a teacher associated with a major conservatory or music school or one who is a member of the National Association of Teachers of Singing, neither of these credentials assures excellence, and many expert teachers hold neither position. However, with experience, a laryngologist ordinarily develops valid impressions.

The physician should record the name of the voice teacher of each of his or her patients and should observe whether the same kinds of voice abuse problems occur with disproportionate frequency in the pupils of any given teacher. He or she should also observe whose pupils usually have few technical problems and are seen only for organic disease such as colds. Technical problems can cause organic pathology such as nodules. So, any teacher who has a high incidence of nodules among his or her students should be viewed with careful concern. The physician should be particularly wary of teachers who are reluctant to allow their students to consult a doctor. The best voice teachers usually have a very low threshold for referral to a laryngologist if they hear anything disturbing in a student's voice. It is proper for the laryngologist to write a letter to the voice teacher (with the patient's permission) describing his findings and recommendations as he would to a physician, speech-language pathologist, or any other referring professional. A laryngologist seriously interested in caring for singers should take the trouble to talk with and meet local singing teachers. Taking a lesson or two with each teacher provides enormous insight as well. Taking voice lessons regularly is even more helpful. In practice, the laryngologist will usually identify a few teachers in whom he or she has particular confidence, especially for patients with voice disorders. He or she should not hesitate to refer singers to these colleagues, especially those singers who are not already in training.

Pop singers may be particularly resistant to the suggestion of voice lessons. Yet, they are in great need of training. It should be pointed out that a good voice teacher can teach a pop singer how to protect and expand his or her voice without changing its quality or making it sound "trained" or "operatic." The author finds it helpful to point out that singing, like other athletic activities, requires exercise, warm-up, and coaching for anyone planning to enter the "big league" and stay there. Just as no major league baseball pitcher would go without a pitching coach and warm-up time in the bullpen, no singer should try to build a career without a singing teacher and appropriate strength and agility exercises. This approach has proved palatable and effective.

Physicians should also be aware of the difference between a voice teacher and a voice coach. A voice teacher trains a singer in singing technique and is essential. A voice coach is responsible for teaching songs, language, diction, style, operatic roles, and so on, but is not responsible for exercises and basic technical development of the voice. More specific details of evaluation and treatment are included in chapters 24, 25, and 27.

Voice Trainers

Drama voice trainers and coaches are the newest professionals on the voice care team. Ordinarily, they work in theaters, being responsible for training, polishing, and preserving the voices of actors. Like singing teachers, they may work with naive students, or world-renowned thespians. Also like singing teachers, they have no formal licensing or certification body.

However, they do have a national organization called the *Voice and Speech Trainers Association* (VASTA). Membership in this organization is at least encouraging evidence of serious study and exposure, although it certainly does not assure expertise. In recent years, a few distinguished voice coaches such as Bonnie Raphael, Lucille Rubin, and Sharon Freed have acquired experience working with patients with vocal fold injury, referred to them by laryngologists such as Dr. Wilbur James Gould and myself. To the best of our knowledge, the addition of Sharon Freed to our team in 1994 marked the first time a voice trainer was employed in a medical office for the purpose of collaborating with speech-language pathologists and singing voice specialists in the rehabilitation of injured voices. Our initial experience has left us convinced that this is an extremely valuable addition to the voice team, and is long overdue. Unfortunately, as with singing teachers, obtaining training in pathologic voice care is extremely difficult for voice trainers, as discussed in a subsequent chapter. We are currently working on solutions to this problem.

Voice Maintenance

Prevention of vocal dysfunction should be the goal of all professionals involved in the care of vocalists. Good vocal health habits should be encouraged in childhood. Screaming, particularly outdoors during athletic events, should be discouraged. Promising young singers who join choirs should be educated to compensate for the Lombard effect. The youngster interested in singing or acting should receive enough training to avoid voice abuse and should receive enthusiastic support for singing works suitable for his or her age and voice. Singing advanced pieces and playing Metropolitan Opera stars should be actively discouraged. Training should be continued during or after puberty, and the voice should be allowed to develop naturally without pressure to perform operatic roles prematurely. Excellent regular training and practice are essential, and avoidance of irritants, particularly smoke, should be stressed early. Educating the singer with regard to hormonal and anatomic alterations that may influence the voice allows him or her to recognize and analyze vocal dysfunction and to compensate for it intelligently when it occurs. Cooperation among the laryngologist, speech-language pathologist, acting teacher, and singing teacher provides an optimal environment for cultivation and protection of the vocal artist.

Summary

Voice abuse is common. It may involve speaking, singing, or both. Abusive techniques, especially those that involve hyperfunction, are potentially dangerous and can lead to vocal injuries. Resulting problems include nodules, cysts, hemorrhages, and other organic changes that may permanently injure the vocal folds. Treatment involves neuromuscular reeducation. The therapeutic process of teaching correct voice use is best accomplished by a team, including a laryngologist, speech-language pathologist, singing voice specialist, acting-voice specialist, and others.

Review Questions

1. A singer who develops nodules is best managed by an expert singing teacher and does not usually require a speech-language pathologist.
   a. true
   b. false

2. Pop singers have limited vocal demands and do not require formal voice lessons.
   a. true
   b. false

3. Singing teachers are important for the rehabilitation of singers, but are not generally necessary or helpful for nonsingers.
   a. true
   b. false

4. A voice coach is responsible for teaching singing technique.
   a. true
   b. false

5. Care of professional vocalists is a routine part of medical training, and any board-certified otolaryngologist is likely to have the expertise necessary to care for professional singers.
   a. true
   b. false

22

Speech-Language Pathology and the Professional Voice User: An Overview

Carol N. Wilder

The practice of speech-language pathology means the application of principles, methods, and procedures for measurement, testing, identification, prediction, counseling, or instruction related to development and disorders of speech, voice, and language. It may be used for identifying, preventing, managing, habilitating or rehabilitating, ameliorating, or modifying such disorders in individuals or groups of individuals.[1] Although speech-language pathologists work with individuals with voice disorders, we do not diagnose or treat laryngeal disease or other physiological disorders, as does the laryngologist. Rather, speech-language pathologists are concerned with understanding, analyzing, and modifying vocal function, that is, with changing vocal behaviors. If the voice is within normal limits perceptually, and if it is being produced in a reasonably efficient, nonabusive manner, the speech-language pathologist does not seek to provide the special training that will develop the range, power, control, stamina, and esthetic quality of voice that are required for artistic expression, as does the singing or acting teacher. We are concerned primarily with the voice that presents a current problem or signs of a potential problem in one or more physical, perceptual, or behavioral dimensions. What happens when such a problem occurs in a professional voice user?

For the purposes of this chapter, the term professional voice user will be arbitrarily limited to individuals who use the voice extensively for some form of artistic expression, in other words, to performers. The definition includes professional singers and actors (eg, those who earn their living by performing), those seeking to become professional singers or actors, and those for whom skilled amateur performance is a major, personally important activity. Excluded for the purposes of this chapter are those individuals who indeed rely heavily on their speaking voices in their professional activities, but who do not use their voices for artistic purposes (eg, the classroom teacher, the trial lawyer, the clergyman, etc.).

Having said what speech-language pathologists do *not* do, let me give the briefest possible summary of what we *do* do. First, we analyze, systematically and sensitively, the presenting vocal behaviors, both perceptually and with such objective measures as are clinically appropriate. Second, we analyze vocational, educational, and psychosocial factors that may interact with vocal behaviors to precipitate, maintain, or exacerbate the voice problem. Finally, we design and implement an individualized program for modifying vocal behaviors and, insofar as is possible, any contributing factors. I stress the terms systematically and sensitively, because both need to be equally emphasized when we work with voice disorders. This is both a science and an art.

With this summary in mind, let us consider two questions: (1) When compared with voice disorders in a nonperformer, will the speech-language pathologist find that there is anything significantly different about evaluating and remediating voice problems in the performer? (2) Is any special knowledge needed in order to do so? The answer to both these questions is affirmative, because of the complexity of vocational, environmental, and psychosocial factors that are unique to this population. These factors are so complex and interactive and beyond the scope of any single chapter, or even book. Nevertheless, I should like to highlight just a few of them that can be expected to have an impact on the activities of the speech-language pathologist.

The obvious factor that is special to this population is the way the voice is used. On the one hand, the range of vocal activities extends beyond the functional parameters we are used to dealing with in the nonprofessional voice patient, with respect to such things as pitch range, loudness extreme, control, and endurance. On the other hand, voice problems in the professional may be signaled by decrements in quality, sensation, or control, which are much more subtle than those we are used to working with. We cannot just sit back and be dazzled by the vocal displays in the cadenza or soliloquy, or be puzzled by the performer's intense concern about what might seem (in the nonprofessional) like a clinically insignificant change in voice control. It is our task to attempt to understand the physical processes that underlie both and to determine whether they relate to the presenting disorder. We must develop reasonable hypotheses about what is going on with respect to chest wall and laryngeal and supralaryngeal behaviors as they relate to lung volumes, pressure differentials, and the like, keeping firmly in mind the relationship of these hypotheses to our clinical purposes. Having made the hypotheses, we must test them. For these reasons, speech-language pathologists who want to work with the voice problems of the performer will find it useful to expand their knowledge of voice and speech science beyond the level that suffices for work with the nonperformer and to make a determined effort to keep abreast of the rapidly accumulating research on voice production.

To achieve a better understanding of the demands on the vocal mechanism of the performer, it is also useful to know something about music, if you are working with singers, or about the theater, if you are working with actors. One should develop an appreciation of the styles and vocal characteristics called for by different schools of performance or vocal training, or by specific composers and dramatists, because they may each call for very different kinds of vocal behaviors. Not only does this help us better understand the physical demands that may have contributed to the disorder, but it also helps us appreciate what kinds of vocal activities comprise the patient's hoped-for goals of therapy, to determine stepwise approximations toward the goals, and to better estimate whether these hoped-for goals are realistic.

The goals of therapy are another feature that distinguishes our work with the performer from our work with the nonperformer. With performers, there are no degrees of freedom with respect to the desired outcome, whereas, with our other voice patients, there is much more latitude in the range of vocal behaviors that constitute an acceptable outcome.

For better understanding of and more effective communication with both the patient and the voice teacher or coach (with whom we want to cooperate closely), speech-language pathologists should also try to become familiar with some of the technical rudiments of these disciplines and with their terms of imagery and their technical vocabulary. For example, if a singer mentions problems with *tessitura* or *leggiero* passages, or with vibrato, it is helpful if the speech-language pathologist can appreciate the physical implications of these terms, which are not a part of our general professional lexicon. If an actor complains about being upstaged, the speech-language pathologist should be aware that the term is not a cliché, but that it describes a specific physical situation that could be contributing to vocal stress.

Speech-language pathologists are always concerned about environmental contributors to voice disorders. However, there are a number of special environmental factors in the performer's world with which many speech-language pathologists (or any other nonperformers, for that matter) may be unfamiliar. To get a better appreciation about conditions that may affect performers' vocal behaviors, it is a good idea for the speech-language pathologist to visit a variety of performance environments (not just theaters and concert halls, but studios, rehearsal halls, and practice rooms) to experience first-hand the dust, fumes, temperature differentials, and ambient noise levels, as well as the general "feel" of the acoustic environment. The conditions are often far from ideal from the standpoint of what is good for the voice. See if you can arrange to visit when you can have the place to yourself as well. Go ahead and sing a song or recite a speech; the insights you get from those few moments may be better than those you get from hours of watching someone else do it.

When trying to delineate all the factors that may contribute to the voice problem, such things as stage direction, set design, and costume design should also be considered. Even an otherwise excellent vocal technique may be put under stress when the performer is in a situation that is physically awkward, uncomfortable, or even precarious. This is not at all uncommon. When some directors or designers are in hot pursuit of a particular artistic vision, concern about vocal stress is not exactly at the top of their priority list. A few years ago, I saw a Royal Shakespeare Company production in which a leading actor was required to deliver a long speech while hanging by his knees, upside down, from the top of a tall ladder. Fortunately, both his knees and his aplomb were equal to the task; but, not surprisingly, one heard signs of vocal tension that were never apparent when he was right-side up. In a memory that remains vivid after many years, I recall the awkwardness and discomfort I felt singing while wearing a costume that included a heavy pointed hat 3 feet long. It was the designer's idea of a medieval effect. I remember complaining that I had to tighten all the muscles of my neck in order to balance the hat to keep it from falling off. Looking back on it from my present perspective as a speech-language pathologist, it seems reasonable to assume that this feeling of tension reflected a degree of strap muscle tension that might well have contributed to vocal stress.

The voice may also be stressed if the performer gets so "carried away" by the emotional sweep of the performance that vocal techniques go by the boards, as it were. Muscles tighten; postures change subtly. These behaviors may not occur in any other vocal situation, making it useful for the speech-language pathologist to observe the patient in an actual performance situation whenever possible.

The essential point is that the performance environment is liberally endowed with "vocal ill-health potential." Some potential stressors are less obvious than others; some the performer may not be aware of and hence may not volunteer when you are taking a case history. If the speech-language pathologist is to understand what areas need to be explored as factors potentially contributing to the voice disorder, he or she must become familiar with the full range of vocal stressors that may be found in the performance environment.

Now, back to that pointed hat. It might be asked why I simply did not refuse to wear it. It is in the answer to that question that the speech-language pathologist begins to encounter the unique psychosocial pressures experienced by vocal professionals, pressures that, indeed, make working with professionals different from working with other voice patients, pressures that may contribute to the development and maintenance of a voice disorder, pressures that can negatively influence the course of therapy if they are not taken into account by the speech-language pathologist.

A major and continuing source of pressure is the intense competition in the performing environment, the extent of which is sometimes difficult to appreciate unless you have experienced it. I did not refuse to wear the hat, because I was just beginning to develop as a performer and I did not want to make waves. I knew full well that many competent replacements were waiting in the wings, any one of whom would have been only too happy to have a chance to sing the role—hat and all. Star level performers may be able to insist on certain performance conditions, but the great majority of performers cannot afford this luxury. Moreover, there is ample evidence in revealing remarks, publicized feuds, and sensitivity over prerogatives that even superstars are not immune to the pressures of competition. Having got to the top, there is pressure to stay there. The reality of this pressure must be acknowledged by the speech-language pathologist. There are times when a performer simply cannot follow your suggestions; cannot cancel a performance, audition, or competition; or cannot follow a therapeutic regimen that would change performance frequency, conditions, or style. It is up to us to understand and to adapt our therapeutic programs to this reality.

Another source of pressure is that the professional voice user is constantly on the line, with his or her performance judged not only by the audience, but by critics, conductors, managers, directors, producers, agents, teachers, and coaches. Most of us are not subject to such constant external scrutiny of our endeavors. The professional voice user lives with the realization that, if he or she makes even a minor goof during a performance, it will very likely be noticed, perhaps even pounced on. As if this were not a sufficient source of pressure, the standards of judgment to which the voice professional is held are frequently subjective, variable, and situation-bound. For example, two critics turn in such disparate reviews that you wonder if they went to the same concert, or contest judges disagree on a winner. After an audition, the performer may never find out *why* he or she did not get the contract or the part. Yet all these subjective, variable, and situation-bound judgments play major roles in determining the performer's career opportunities. No wonder there is performance anxiety; no wonder there are displays of insecurity or bravado. Clearly, this constellation of psychosocial pressures is also shared by instrumental musicians. However, the effect on vocal professionals may be even more profound because, for them, the instrument itself, the vocal mechanism, is known to be sensitive not only to stress-related muscle tension, but also to stress-related responses to the autonomic nervous system.

If there are all these pressures, if the rules of the game are so difficult, why is there so much competition? Why are so many people out there doing everything they can to become professional users of the voice? What possesses them? I am not sure there is any better answer to these questions than to say that they do, in fact, seem to be possessed (in some cases almost obsessed) by some sort of drive toward artistic vocal expression; and that brings me to the final area I would like to highlight that distinguishes our practice with this population.

If one is possessed by a drive toward artistic vocal expression, how devastating it is to develop any sort of a problem in the vocal mechanism, which is the foundation of one's endeavors? How frustrating it is if the problem develops at a pivotal or critical point in career development. How threatening for the established performer whose financial well-being rests on the condition of his or her vocal mechanism. As a consequence, speech-language pathologists who regularly work with professional voice users find that the response to the voice disorder is usually different from what we find with other types of voice patients—different not only in degree, but in kind. This response is a major consideration that must be factored into the management program. An experienced speech-language pathologist who has only relatively recently begun to work with the professional voice said to me that he had not entirely anticipated the intensity of the emotional reactions he has encountered with his professional voice patients. He described how one young woman's responses had ranged from shock at learning that she had a mass lesion of the vocal folds, to hope that it might be resolved through therapy, to tearful despair when she learned that, although the lesion was much smaller, it had not completely disappeared. This speech-language pathologist said that he had found the counseling of professional voice users to be a very heavy issue. Indeed, the ongoing education and counseling that are a part of our program with any voice patient must be handled with special thoroughness and exquisite sensitivity in the professional voice user.

These general highlights are intended for speech-language pathologists who have not yet had much clinical contact with professional voice users. Details of practice are discussed in chapter 23. An active effort to become further acquainted with special vocational, environmental, and psychosocial factors performers experience will help you to incorporate them—systematically and sensitively—into your evaluation and therapeutic procedures. Working with professional voice users is stimulating and enjoyable. Moreover, speech-language pathologists are not alone in their need to explore areas that were not included in their professional training curriculum. Currently, no single discipline adequately addresses the totality of skills needed in the care of the professional voice in its training program. Therefore, all of us with a special interest in this area can profit from learning from each other in a spirit that maximizes cooperative efforts and optimizes patient care.

Summary

Speech-language pathologists analyze and modify vocal behaviors. In general, speech- language pathologists are trained to restore "normalcy" to the voice. They do not routinely seek to provide special training that will develop the range, power, control, stamina, and aesthetic qualities of voice that are required for artistic expression. In order to effectively work with such voice professionals, speech-language pathologists must acquire special knowledge and skills. They need to become acquainted with the unique demands and hazards of high-level voice performance, master techniques for recognizing and measuring subtle impairments, and utilize techniques for restoring *optimal* voice performance.

Review Questions

1. The speaking problems of voice professionals (such as singers and actors) are similar to those in the general population, and can be routinely well managed by any certified speech-language pathologist.

   a. true
   b. false

2. The speech-language pathologist working with professional singers and actors requires special training beyond that available in most graduate programs.

   a. true
   b. false

3. The goals of therapy are the same in performers and nonperformers.

   a. true
   b. false

4. In order to work with voice professionals, speech-language pathologists need to understand:

   a. vocal performance demands
   b. the performance environment
   c. costume and makeup requirements
   d. all of the above
   e. none of the above

5. A specially trained speech-language pathologist possesses the totality of skills needed to care for professional voice disorders.

   a. true
   b. false

Reference

1. California Speech Pathologists and Audiologists Licensure Act, Chapter 5.3, Division 2 of the Business and Professions Code, as cited in Flower R. Delivery of speech-language pathology and audiology services. Baltimore, Md: Williams & Wilkins; 1984:6.

23

Voice Therapy

Rhonda K. Rulnick, Reinhardt J. Heuer, Kathe S. Perez, Kate A. Emerich, and Robert Thayer Sataloff

Professional voice users who need voice therapy require special diagnostic and intervention strategies. Each of these individuals has a vested interest in preserving and protecting the voice. They differ from the general voice population because of the unusual demands placed on their voices, especially singers, teachers, and actors. These demands are greater in both quantity and quality. In addition, they differ in many instances by requesting therapy for voices that might generally be regarded as "normal." However, since they may be required to perform in the super-normal range of voice production, speech-language pathologists must learn to recognize and help restore optimal not merely normal voice.

The focus of this chapter is on the unique requirements of the behavioral treatment of professional speakers whose careers have been disrupted by voice rest, surgery, or diminished vocal power associated with a disordered or diseased larynx. The following are eight prerequisites for speech-language pathologists when dealing with voice-disordered professional speakers. They are in no special order, but all are equally important in the success of treating these special patients.

1. The clinician needs to be super-sensitive to super-speaking. The goal in treating professional speakers is not just adequate speech and voice but excellent speech and voice. The patient may complain of problems that may seem insignificant to a clinician who does not have this supersensitivity, and that clinician may lose the respect and cooperation of the patient for minimizing such subtleties. Correction of minor technical faults is required to enable a patient who has already experienced voice difficulties to compete again in the professional arena.

2. The clinician needs to be skilled in counseling and in critiquing, in a positive manner, professional speakers who may perceive their current abilities as excellent. Professional speakers who have suffered vocal injury are traumatized psychologically as well as physically. Most professional speakers believe they are proficient voice users. It may be difficult for them to admit that they have technical problems. Tactful handling, including gentle objective proof of the vocal faults related to the voice disorder, is necessary if the clinician wishes to gain the patient's confidence and cooperation. The patient may be unable to modify his or her vocal behavior easily, until emotional reactions to the voice disorder and its effects on the professional speaker's career have been discussed and resolved.

3. The clinician needs to concentrate on enhancing the professional speaker's vocal repertoire rather than teach new skills. Rarely are appropriate behaviors missing from the professional speaker's repertoire; rather, faulty techniques have become preferred, either because of inappropriate training, or because of the professional speaker's frantic struggle to *sound normal* in the presence of laryngeal change. Such an approach saves the patient from guilt and embarrassment about his or her skills and abilities. It also provides the patient with confidence that he or she still retains the ability to perform.

4. The clinician needs to focus on rebalancing the three-part system (respiration/phonation/resonance) rather than isolated skill drills. The clinician needs to remember that in treating voice-disordered individuals, changes in one function will produce subtle, or not so subtle, changes in the rest of the system. The patient needs to learn to hear and feel the results of each modification in all aspects of

the speaking mechanism. We believe in a holistic approach to the treatment of voice disorders.

5. The clinician needs to explicitly describe the need, purpose, and function of each therapeutic activity. The complaint we hear most often from professional speakers who have had previous therapy is that they did what was asked of them, but had no idea why they were doing it. Obviously, on occasion, the patient's memory may be faulty, but we need to continually remember that, although the rationales for our therapeutic tasks are obvious to us, they may not be so obvious to our patients. Professional voice users are bright, creative individuals who deserve to be informed of what we are attempting to achieve and why.

6. The clinician needs to emphasize carryover into every day speech and professional activities rather than to assign practice periods only. Especially singers, but also trained speakers tend to believe that dutifully practicing exercises will automatically make their voices better. They need to be reminded that the exercises are only practice for what they should be doing all the time. Patients will often ask, "I practiced the exercises regularly, why isn't my voice better?" unless they have been indoctrinated into the philosophy that the exercises are skill builders and reminders of what the professional speaker should be attempting to do whenever speaking.

7. The clinician needs to be prepared for rapid changes and have appropriate materials ready and available. Professional speakers are skilled at modifying vocal behaviors. Once a concept is grasped and a skill developed, that behavior must be generalized immediately into usage. A patient's progress should not be impeded because the clinician is not prepared to shift to a new and more difficult level. Voice therapy with professional speakers should not take a long time. If it does, either something is wrong, or the patient has not resolved his or her anxiety about the vocal disorder or his or her speaking abilities.

8. The clinician may need to help the patient establish a good voice in spite of, or in the presence of, vocal pathology if approved by the otolaryngologist. The psychological, monetary, or career needs of a professional voice-disordered person may require the development of safe voice/speech skills prior to the completion of medical/surgical treatment. Often by focusing on compensation by the respiratory and resonatory systems and reducing the patient's effortful use of the larynx (voice = larynx for many professional speakers), adequate, nondamaging voice can be achieved to allow the professional to continue performing during the treatment and healing process.

In this chapter, we will often refer to the singer. The singer's need for flawless vocal technique is paramount, and singers are particularly capable of detailed vocal self-analysis and critical assessment of therapy. The vocal mechanism of the professional speaker needs the same specialized care and training as the voice of the singer. Our approach to evaluating and treating singers is applicable to all professional voice users.

Classically trained singers are aware of the deleterious consequences of poor singing technique on the delicate tissues of the vocal folds. Even though they are usually conscientious in caring for their voices during singing, they often give little thought to how they use the same anatomy in speech, even though they may spend more time speaking than singing. Appropriate speaking technique is just as important for singers as for other professional voice users. They have much to gain from voice therapy. The elimination of vocal abuse during speaking can have a dramatic and positive effect on the singing voice. The process of acquiring good speaking technique often facilitates better singing, as well.

Many voice professionals, in particular teachers, have never received formal speech training. Hence, it is not surprising that vocal dysfunction occurs. This chapter outlines our approach to preventing voice problems and to treating injured voices. The approach is primarily behavioral. Voice problems are not solely mechanical in nature. Voices have people behind them, and therefore a myriad of personalities, stresses, and other mitigating circumstances that can drastically affect one's voice, the therapy program devised, and the patient's ability to benefit from our approach. When the need arises, we solicit the assistance of other professionals (team members) so that each patient may be treated holistically.

We address the unique considerations of the voice professional as a team. The primary interdisciplinary team consists of:

- the *laryngologist*, whose primary responsibility is diagnosing and restoring the structure of the larynx through medical/surgical means
- the *speech-language pathologist*, whose responsibility is evaluating and treating specific abusive/misusive behaviors of the speaking voice
- the *singing-voice specialist/vocal teacher*, whose province is singing technique and voice production during singing
- the *stress manager/speaking coach* whose expertise lies in overall body response to the speaking act.
- the *acting-voice specialist* who works with high performance, projected speech, and related communication skills

Additional adjunct team members include:

- *voice researcher* or voice scientist
- *singing coach* (involved primarily with repertoire and style)

- *psychologist, hypnotherapist,* and *physicians* in different specialties (especially pulmonology, allergy, and neurology).

It is important for all team members to understand the principles and approach employed in voice therapy, and for the voice therapist to understand the expertise of each of the other members of the team.

Ideally the members of the primary team should be housed in the same facility to provide for direct and immediate interaction for the benefit of the professional voice user.

Evaluation

When working with singers and other voice professionals, our expectations of *normal* must be heightened, and stricter criteria must be used to assess these patients. State-of-the-art equipment and advanced techniques in voice analysis are routinely incorporated into the voice evaluation and are described in chapter 8. This provides extremely valuable baseline information and documentation that help to quantify and qualify the patient's voice problem. These instruments are important, but clearly our best clinical tools remain our own eyes and ears. With a few exceptions, this is especially true in recognizing degrees of supernormal function. Most of the commonly used instrumentation is better at distinguishing *abnormal* from *normal* than at identifying differences between "excellent" and "great" voices. The voice therapist may acquire the necessary skills to make these distinctions by learning to use adjunct instrumentation; by studying singing, acting, and public speaking; by observing as many singing and acting teachers as possible so as to refine their listening skills; and through experience working with a team, exchanging judgments after listening to the singing and speaking voice.

The voice evaluation is divided into five parts: case history, objective evaluation, subjective evaluation, trial therapy, and impressions/recommendations. This chapter includes a brief overview of our evaluation procedures.

Case History

A careful case history involves a description of the circumstances leading to the development and maintenance of the present vocal problem. In a medical setting, where the patient is seen by all team members during the initial visit, the laryngologist and speech-language pathologist cooperate in gathering the background information. The information required is discussed in chapter 6, Patient History. Additional history obtained by the speech-language pathologist is specific in exploring how vocal abuses and vocal misuse affect the patient's voice on a daily basis. The focus is on the nature of the disorder, activities in daily professional or social life that may cause or aggravate vocal problems, voice patterns of other family members that may reinforce undesirable vocal behavior, daily vocal usage patterns, and details of previous voice therapy. For patients who have had previous voice therapy, asking the patient to demonstrate techniques and exercises used may provide valuable insight that can affect the current therapy plan. A complete inventory is made of vocal abuse factors that may have contributed to the present voice problems, with special attention paid to smoking, passive smoking, caffeine consumption, alcohol consumption, poor rest and sleep patterns, environmental factors (dryness, chemicals), excessive talking, yelling, loud talking, throat clearing, coughing, whispering, poor hydration, and stress and tension.

Singers are asked additional questions regarding the type of music they sing (rock, popular, classical, show/night club, gospel, jazz/blues), the extent of their training, their present singing difficulties, and their professional career goals. This case history information is obtained in cooperation with the singing specialist. All singers also complete a written questionnaire (appendix IIa) and teachers are requested to complete a vocal abuse checklist (appendix III). In addition to inquiries regarding duration of training, the patient's current goals with his or her singing teacher are explored in detail.

Although this section on history is covered only briefly in this chapter (because relevant areas of inquiry are discussed elsewhere in this book), it should be emphasized that a thorough history is of paramount importance. The speech-language pathologist must do more than merely ask the usual questions and add special questions relevant to performers and their specialized settings. The voice therapist must also pay attention not merely to the content of the history, but also to the voice used by the patient in reporting it. In addition, the clinician should explore in greater detail any discrepancies between the history given to the otolaryngologist and that given to the speech-language pathologist. Occasionally, patients will reveal information to one team member that they are reluctant to reveal to another. Questions to which answers change from one team member to another are often closely related to the patient's underlying problem and deserve delicate but diligent scrutiny.

Objective Evaluation

Data collection and its subsequent analysis furnish a detailed objective description of the voice. An audio recording is obtained using a high-quality analog tape recorder or a DAT recorder. As much vocal analysis as possible is done on line or with digitized samples. The protocol for the objective voice tasks is provided in appendix IV, and details of the voice laboratory and therapeutic uses of laboratory equipment are discussed in chapter 8. Briefly, a sample of sustained spoken and sung vowels, conversational speaking, and reading (see appendix V) is analyzed. The acoustic voicing parameters that are measured include: speaking fundamental frequency (for conversation and reading), multiple estimates of pitch and intensity, perturbation, harmonics/noise ratios, percent voicing (for a reading sample), and physiological and musical frequency range. Aerodynamic measures include maximum exhalation or phonation times for /ʌ/, /i/, /u/, and /s/, and /z/, s/z ratio, mean flow rates, and inverse filtered estimates of minimal and AC glottal flow. Respiration is measured by pulmonary function testing. Pulmonary function testing of all voice patients has proven beneficial in identifying singing-related respiratory dysfunction (ie, exercise-induced asthma). Measures are compared to normative data and judgments regarding the patient's phonatory ability are made. Aerodynamic measures are particularly useful in determining how the patient is using respiratory/vocal control in producing vocalization. Further information about the clinical usefulness of instrumentation is discussed in chapter 8.

Subjective Evaluation

Respiration

Many vocal problems are the result of improper breathing technique. When evaluating respiration, the volume of air is important, but more important is the manner in which the patient takes in the air (inhalation), and how the air is used to produce the voice (exhalation).

Abdominal/diaphragmatic breath control and support are desirable and the most efficient manner of providing the power source for the voice. The patient's respiration is observed in conversational speech and in reading. The following observations are made:

1. The pattern of breath support:
   - ☐ Abdominal/diaphragmatic
   - ☐ Upper thoracic
   - ☐ Clavicular
   - ☐ Combined or Mixed (thoracic and abdominal)

2. Improper body posture or head/neck alignment that may affect respiration adversely
3. Phrasing—Are the phrases too long or too short? Are pauses taken at appropriate places during on-going speech?
4. Audible inspiration, forced exhalation or, labored breathing

Phonation

Phonation refers to the production of sound at the level of the vocal folds. Judgments about the voice quality (hoarseness, breathiness), loudness (appropriate, too loud, too soft), and pitch are made during conversational speech and reading (appendix V). The following characteristics are particularly important:

☐ Hoarseness	☐ Diplophonia
☐ Breathiness	☐ Phonation breaks
☐ Glottal fry	☐ Harsh glottal attacks

Harsh glottal attacks are counted during a standard reading passage (see appendix Vj) and a percentage is calculated.

Measures of respiratory and phonatory efficiency are obtained using measurements of maximum exhalation or phonation for the following sounds:

/ʌ/___ /i/___ /u/___ /s/___ /z/___

An s/z ratio[1] is obtained, which provides a quick comparison of the patient's ability to control airflow for these two speech sounds (voiceless and voiced). Although an s/z ratio is not necessarily a reliable assessment of phonatory ability or an indicator of laryngeal pathology, it provides useful information about the patient's ability to control exhalation in the presence or absence of voicing. That is, it is an indicator of laryngeal efficiency.

General observations are made regarding the patient's habitual speaking pitch. It is important to note whether the patient speaks too high (falsetto) or too low (glottal fry). The concept of *optimal pitch* is controversial, as *optimal* may not exist. More accurately there is an *optimal* manner of laryngeal function that yields an appropriate pitch level. Generally, an inappropriate pitch level can be the effect of a mass lesion, which may lower the pitch, or be symptomatic of muscular tension, which may raise the pitch. However, muscular tension dysphonia may also be present in association with low pitch, especially in a patient who forces his or her voice down near the lower end of the physiological frequency range.

Resonance

Resonance refers to the concentration of specific acoustic frequencies or harmonics within the cavities of the vocal tract (oral cavity, oropharynx, nasopharynx, hypopharynx), as described in chapter 4. Clinically, certain resonant patterns have been labeled as being associated with specific anatomic areas. The terminology is useful, even if not completely accurate. Excessive pharyngeal or "throaty" resonance is a common characteristic and can be associated with physical discomfort in speaking. Oral resonance is desirable and is affected by the size and shape of the oral cavity. Many patients exhibit mandibular restriction while speaking, which dimin-ishes the effectiveness of the oral cavity as a resonator. The presence of hypernasal or hyponasal speech is carefully assessed to rule out velopharyngeal incompetence. Functional or regional resonance deviations can be assessed using selected reading passages.

Tongue retraction occurs when the anterior portion of the tongue is pulled back from the lower incisors. The result is tongue muscle tension and a change in vocal tract shape that affects the resonance of the voice. Tongue position is observed during sustained production of /ʌ/. Posterior tongue tension often cannot be directly observed without instruments during speech and may be present even if the anterior tongue is relaxed. Posterior tongue tension is often responsible for a pharyngeal resonance quality.

Articulation

A judgment is made regarding the patient's general ability to precisely produce the sounds of the English language. If English is not the patient's native language, comparisons are made between speech in English and the mother tongue if the person is actively communicating in English. The ability of the articulators (tongue, lips, teeth, jaw, and velum) to function in a smooth and connected manner is determined. Although articulation disorders are rare in this population, occasionally a lisp has been identified. Particular attention is paid to any "hyperfunctional" articulation or tension sites in the articulators themselves. While tongue tension is common, it is addressed as a resonance imbalance and not an articulation problem.

Prosody

The prosodic features of speech (rhythm, fluency, timing, rate, pauses, and intonation or inflection patterns) are assessed very generally. These features often subtly affect the voice. The patient who demonstrates excessive laryngeal and strap muscle tension will often demonstrate faulty flow and blending of words in connected speech. A voice/speech pattern that lacks the normal prosodic features may be perceived as monotonous. Further, a voice that lacks vocal variety may indicate that a patient is not gaining maximum flexibility from the voice, either physically or artistically.

Sites of Muscular Tension

Poor respiratory control and support can lead to muscle tension in specific muscle groups. While this tension is observed in association with poor breath control, it can be created for a variety of reasons. We observe these tension sites as we examine the levels of speech production, and have found a checklist helpful.

☐ Tongue	☐ Anterior or posterior neck
☐ Laryngeal rise or fall	☐ Shoulders
☐ Jaw or masseter muscle	☐ Upper chest wall

Oral/Facial

A screening of the oral/facial mechanism should be included to rule out any abnormalities in the structure, symmetry, strength, range of motion, or coordination that might impact on normal vocal function. This includes neurological problems.

Singing

The speech-language pathologist (unless specifically trained) is not qualified to evaluate the singer's technique in detail. However, observations are made that are extremely useful in determining the constancy of technique from one modality (singing) to another (speech). A checklist for observing the singer's technical misuses includes:

☐ Sites of tension: face, neck, tongue, jaw, shoulders, forehead	☐ Poor breath support
☐ Tongue retraction	☐ Hoarseness following singing
☐ Tone focus	☐ Difficulties through the passagio

☐ Vocal placement   ☐ Loss of upper/lower range

Trial Therapy

Various facilitating techniques are introduced on a trial basis during the evaluation. This gives the examiner an opportunity to observe how these changes affect vocal quality and whether the patient can feel and hear differences in vocal production. Further, it enables the examiner to make inferences about the patient's learning ability and prognosis for remediation through therapy.

Impression and Recommendations

The voice evaluation, in addition to establishing baseline measures, affords the speech-language pathologist the opportunity to observe the patient and to formulate an impression of the factors that may have contributed to the voice problem. Techniques to facilitate improved vocal production were introduced during the *trial therapy* portion of the evaluation. The speech-language pathologist assesses which modifications resulted in an immediate change in vocal quality or ease of production, and a starting point for therapy is established.

The interpretation of what was observed is discussed with the patient. Providing a thorough explanation of which factors have been most contributory to the voice problem is essential. The goals of therapy are enumerated along with the procedures and their rationales. There is no clear delineation between where evaluation ends and therapy begins. Evaluation occurs throughout the therapy process as the speech-language pathologist continually monitors the efficacy of treatment.

At the conclusion of the evaluation, recommendations are made regarding whether voice therapy is indicated. Goals are defined. Often other referrals are made, such as specialized singing instruction. Occasionally other testing is needed (ie, articulation or motor speech). The recommendations, including the anticipated length of time (in weeks or months), approximate number of sessions, and how often the sessions are to be scheduled (weekly, biweekly, monthly) are reviewed. The patient is informed of the need for home practice and active participation, so that the goals can be met.

Therapy

Owing to the inordinate length of this chapter, therapy will be limited to that appropriate for professional speakers/singers with behavioral voice problems, whether or not structural changes such as vocal nodules, cysts, or inflammation have developed. Therapy for organic problems such as vocal fold paralysis, central neurogenic dysphonias, cancer, or congenital problems will not be discussed.

Initially, the goals of therapy must be set. Goals may include establishing an excellent speaking voice of professional quality; developing a temporarily breathy or soft speaking voice to allow healing after vocal surgery or to allow nodules to be reduced; or establishing an easy, efficient speaking voice that does not fatigue or cause strain, which is then better preserved for singing or formal speaking situations. Ideally the goal is to produce an excellent speaker; realistically, the goal may be to develop a more efficient, less abusive speaker.

Level-One Therapy

Therapy for behavioral voice problems can be organized into several levels although this classificiation is not intended to imply that they must be stratified or done sequentially. In this chapter *Level-One Therapy* refers to an educational level, utilizing instruction, discussion, and modeling as its primary therapeutic tools. The patient and therapist talk about various vocal misuse or abuse patterns, make decisions about which can be deleted from the patients usual life-style and which must be retained to allow the patient to feel like him- or herself. Often singers, especially older ones, may object to modifying their breathing, voicing, or resonance patterns because such patterns have been effective in a long and successful career. Attempts to begin learning and practicing a new method are met with resistance, whereas discussion of what can or cannot be changed may be a gentler way to convince the more resistant patient that other changes may also be appropriate. Often modeling, without overt suggestions for change, may modify the patients' behavior sufficiently to improve the speaking voice. The clinician continues to model easy, relaxed voicing. Frequently the patient begins to use the same type of voice within the context of the session and begins to carry over this behavior outside the session. This level of intervention is frequently effective and may be all that is needed for professional singers who are attuned to their bodies and in touch with the need to modify their life-style in order to maintain vocal health.

Voice professionals, singers and nonsingers, come to speech-language pathologists with varying degrees of knowledge about the factors that are responsible for their current problems. Positive alternatives to their vocally abusive behaviors are developed through a vocal hygiene program. A discussion of vocal hygiene is important at Level-One Therapy.

1. Throat Clearing
   In some cases, excessive mucus is a problem (associated with gastric reflux, post-nasal drip, and allergies). More often, patients clear their throats out of habit, rather than need. This behavior, because it is traumatic to the vocal folds, should be eliminated. The following alternatives are useful:
   a. Dry swallow: Swallowing closes the vocal folds and can help rid them of mucus. The action of swallowing (in the post-abduction phase) can also relax the larynx, helping to alleviate the perceived need to clear the throat.
   b. Take small sips of water.
   c. Use a "silent cough." This is achieved by using abdominal support to push air through the folds (as if producing an /h/ sound). The strong airflow blows mucus off the vocal folds.
   d. Pant lightly, then swallow.
   e. Hum lightly.
   f. Laugh gently or giggle lightly, then swallow.
   g. Talk through the mucus. The natural vibration of the vocal folds may rid the vocal folds of secretions.
   h. For singers, vocalize lightly on five note scales in a comfortable range on /ɑ/, or slide up an octave softly on /ɑ/, and crescendo (get louder).
2. Whispering
   Many patients, especially singers, are aware that whispering should be avoided. During whispering in many instances, the anterior two thirds of the vocal folds approximate. Forced or loud whispering appears most harmful. The adverse effects of whispering have not been fully documented, but ample clinical experience supports the proscription. Although extremely soft whispering without vocal contact may be safe, few patients maintain this technique, and most resort to using forced whispering to be heard without even realizing it. Therefore, patients are cautioned that all whispering should be avoided. However, actors may need to make use of this type of vocal production in their work. In this case, specialized training is indicated.
3. Grunting/Noisy Vocalization
   Grunting when lifting or exercising creates forceful, traumatic adduction of the folds. Instead:
   a. Exhale slowly on the exertion phase of any exercise (preferred method), or
   b. Adduct the vocal folds gently, prior to initiating each exercise event (such as a sit-up or weight lift) and release (abduct) after each event.

4. Yelling/Screaming or Loud Talking
   Many performers and singers have gregarious, outgoing personalities. They commonly yell or scream as an expression of anger, frustration, elation, or joy. We advise them to save their voice for the performance and instead:
   a. Use a whistle or bell.
   b. Educate friends and family members about the harmful effects of yelling or screaming.
   c. Engage the help of others for monitoring.
   d. Use facial and other physical gestures to express emotions.
   e. Use hissing as another nonvoiced outlet to express anger or frustration.
   f. Know the limits of your vocal abilities. Be aware of how much loud talking can be tolerated before fatigue is experienced.
   g. Cultivate the dramatic power of soft, articulated speech, which is often more effective than yelling.
5. Noisy Environments
   Certain environments are inherently noisy (cars, airplanes, restaurants, social gatherings, night clubs). Special care should be taken not to speak over the noise level for long periods of time. Alternatives include:
   a. Face the listener.
   b. Gently over articulate rather than increase loudness.
   c. Speak at a rate to avoid the need for repetition.
   d. Speak at normal pitch. There is a tendency to raise pitch and loudness in background noise. The normal, lower pitch often cuts through the ambient noise, decreasing the need to speak more loudly.
6. Excessive Talking
   Gregarious patients find this a difficult habit to break. Modification can be facilitated using the following:
   a. Schedule vocal naps. Observe 20 minutes of silence, 2–3 times a day. Wear an alarm watch as a reminder. In addition, inexpensive digital watches are available with time-elapsed functions that beep every 10 minutes or every hour. This signal can be used early in retraining as a reminder to check vocal behavior.
   b. Limit the amount of time on the telephone.
   c. Limit interrupting others in conversation. Be a good listener.
7. Caffeine Consumption
   Excessive caffeine intake has a diuretic effect and depletes the vocal fold tissues of needed hydration. The patient should:

a. Avoid caffeinated beverages (coffee, soda, tea) especially before heavy voice use, dress rehearsals, performances, lectures, trials, sermons, or teaching

b. Switch to decaffeinated beverages (water is the best substitute).

c. Drink a glass of water for every cup of coffee or soda, and follow the recommendations below for systemic dryness.

8. Systemic Dryness

Good systemic hydration is necessary for all patients. They are instructed to:

a. "Sing wet—pee pale" (in the words of Dr Van Lawrence). We have adapted this to: "Speak wet—pee pale."

b. Drink water every time they eat.

c. Keep water at hand at all times.

d. If a patient absolutely cannot tolerate water, try bottled spring water or tap water with a mild citrus twist.

9. Environmental Dryness

Environmental factors can create a drying effect on the vocal mechanism. If the patient is singing or performing in geographical regions where relative humidity is low, special attention to improving environmental hydration is needed. The best way to humidify room air is controversial at present. There is no convincing evidence for or against the use of hot or cold steam, or ultrasonic mist. Research is needed to determine which is best. The relative humidity on airplanes is initially about 5%, as discussed in chapter 6, Patient History, and special precautions must be taken.

a. Super-hydrate prior to and during air travel.

b. Use a humidifier and travel with it if possible.

c. Minimize talking on the airplane.

d. Provide a moist environment in hotel rooms by running the hot water in the shower.

10. Inadequate Rest and Sleep Patterns

General body fatigue is reflected in the voice. Optimal vocal efficiency may not be achieved when the performer or speaker is tired.

a. Get more rest and sleep prior to heavy voice use.

b. Be particularly careful when traveling (jet lag).

c. Allow time for a short nap before important speaking commitments whenever possible.

Additional vocal abuse and misuse problems typically exhibited by teachers and singers are enumerated in appendixes IIa and IId.

Level-Two Therapy

Level-Two Therapy involves the careful modification of inappropriate breathing, voicing, or resonance behaviors that do not resolve through Level-One discussions. The primary therapeutic tools are those of behavior modification, including drills, practice material, and small step changes in current behavior to extinguish inappropriate behavior and reinforce more natural and correct behaviors. During the evaluation and trial therapy, the clinician has had the opportunity to determine if a client needs to begin at Level One or Level Two. It is our experience that school teachers, lawyers, and other professional speakers who have not had singing training, often need to begin at Level Two.

Breath Control and Support

We are born with an innate ability to breathe healthfully and appropriately for the production of normal speech. Watch a newborn during quiet (tidal) breathing. The abdomen expands during inhalation. During vocalizations such as screaming or crying (exhalation), the abdominal muscles contract. Most adults have lost this natural habit of effortless breathing.

In the initial stages of therapy, difficulty arises when attention is called to breathing. Observe what happens when a patient is asked to take a nice deep breath. The abdomen is sucked in, the chest and shoulders rise, and the breath is held with the vocal folds tightly adducted. This is not the desired behavior.

There are certain maladaptive behaviors that are automatically exhibited in response to certain words (eg, "breathe," "inhale," and "exhale"). Using appropriate vocabulary early in therapy facilitates the training of correct speech breathing. *Abdominal breathing* is referred to as *abdominal support*. The terms *expansion*, or *softening the belly*, are used for the inhalation phase, and *pulling* in is used cautiously (to avoid tension) for the exhalation phase.

When explaining abdominal/diaphragmatic breathing, a description of the process is as follows.[2]

In deep inspiration, the diaphragm contracts and moves downward, displacing the underlying stomach and liver downwards. In order for the diaphragm to drop, room must be made for the stomach and liver in the abdominal cavity. This is accomplished by a relaxation of the front of the abdomen. This flattening of the diaphragm thus causes a protrusion of the belly with the relaxation of the abdominal muscles. During expiration, the diaphragm relaxes and the abdomen contracts, exerting upward pressure on the abdominal organs, thus squeezing air out of the lungs.

Experience has shown that it is easier to teach a patient to pull-in the abdominal muscles than to expand or soften the belly. Therefore, we begin the process of training appropriate speech breathing from the exhalation phase. The patient uses his or her expiratory reserve volume to begin speaking.[3] When the air is expelled, it triggers a spontaneous inhalation, a concomitant softening of the belly.

We provide an appropriate rhythm for this abdominal motion, which will be used extensively in later sessions. We explain that the rhythm is similar to a 3/4 time signature or slow waltz (58 or 62 bpm on a metronome). We count out the pace "1-2-3" as the patient pulls in the abdominal muscles, and "1-2-3" as they expand.

A discussion of the differences between support for speaking and support for singing is provided. Classically trained singers especially need the experience of adjusting the inspiratory phase of breathing. The respiratory needs for conversational speaking are considerably less than for singing. Although the basic principles are the same in both voice modes, by taking the focus off *breathing* and providing experience in the abdominal *pump* using the 3/4 rhythm, the singer learns how to feel appropriate speaking support and avoids exerting so much muscular tension that his or her support efforts become counterproductive.

The beginning steps in establishing breath control are incorporated into the warm-up and cool-down routines discussed in a later section. For convenience, a step-by-step approach is presented. However, it must be emphasized that, although this outlines our customary therapeutic direction, it is not a "cookbook" of techniques that can be applied indiscriminately without considerable clinical judgment and modification. This caveat applies not only to teaching breath control and support, but to all of the other topics covered in this chapter.

Step 1

We begin by introducing the concept of appropriate speech breathing for non-speech tasks and isolated speech sounds.

Exercise 1: The patient is asked to pull in his or her abdominal muscles while blowing, as if blowing out a candle. Once the air has been fully expelled, the abdominal muscles expand naturally and the patient inhales spontaneously. This is repeated several times until it can be accomplished easily. During the process, the patient learns to sense and use abdominal and back muscles efficiently to support phonation.

Exercise 2: An alternative initial approach breaks down the abdominal breathing into muscular and res-

piratory components. The patient is asked to pull in his or her abdominal muscles and then to expand the abdomen as described above. However, an abdominal pump, with special attention to rhythm, is introduced. It is the rhythmic pattern and visual cuing that provide the patient with the appropriate mechanics of abdominal breath control and support. Once the rhythm of the pump is established, breath is added. The patient is instructed not to concentrate on inhaling, but instead to focus on blowing out. Once he or she is comfortable with the pump and blowing out, his or her attention is focused on the smooth and easy exchange of air. We describe this as a "cycle of breathing" and encourage the patient to feel breathing as a continuous action and motion. It is important to establish early in therapy that the breath should neither be held nor restricted. Breathing techniques established through either initial approach are gradually shaped into usual speech support through a series of steps.

Step 2

Quiet Breathing. The patient is asked to pay attention to his or her quiet or tidal breathing.

Exercise 1: The patient is asked to begin the exercise with active breathing for the "candle blowing" task using good abdominal support. The clinician provides the visual prompt to slow the breath, and the patient gradually changes the candle blowing to quiet breathing. He or she is asked to practice this exercise 10 times each day until a natural carryover of abdominal breathing for all quiet (nonspeech) breathing is established. The patient is also reminded to practice breath support while working on all other aspects of voice such as easy onset, decreased volume, or relaxation. Breathing exercises should be done in a sitting or standing position, the way most speaking is done. On occasion a patient may require early practice in more facilitating positions. Have the patient stand, bend at the waist and extend his or her arms to the arms of an armchair, positioning the feet in such a fashion that the patient's back is parallel with the floor. In this position the patient cannot lift his or her chest or shoulders and gravity assists the patient in being able to feel belly softening/expansion during inhalation exercises, and belly contraction during speech production.

Step 3

The transition from nonspeech tasks to speech tasks is accomplished systematically.

Exercise 1: The patient is asked to gradually pull in and to count from 1 to 50, with five numbers to a support group (eg, "1-2-3-4-5," expand, "6-7-8-9-10," expand).

Exercise 2: The patient is asked to count again from 1 to 50, this time varying the breath support group. For example, the patient may choose to inhale after the fifth number or whatever feels comfortable. The goal of this exercise is to achieve a flow and rhythm of the breath for simple ongoing speech tasks.

Step 4

Phrasing is an important component of using appropriate breath control and support in ongoing speech.

Exercise 1: The patient is provided with a list of phrases from which to read (appendix V). The phrases vary from 3 to 12 syllables per phrase. Onset and maintenance of breath control and support are monitored closely. The concepts of rhythm and of pacing the breath are of paramount importance. Imagery is helpful in establishing a relaxed, easy speech-breathing rhythm.

Exercise 2: The patient is provided with longer sentences that he or she is asked to phrase appropriately. At this time, the patient begins to exercise spontaneity and freedom of where to plan the breath. If need be, visual cues can be provided such as breath marks identified on the written page.

Exercise 3: Paragraphs are introduced. Phrases may be marked, or the patient may be asked to read the paragraph "cold," while it is audiotaped. This allows the patient and clinician to critique the paragraph together, then mark phrases and repeat the reading. Additional markings may include cues for easy onset of troublesome words and for attention to oral resonance or any other aspect that has been trained.

Exercise 4: The patient is provided with additional unmarked paragraphs for practice in breath control and support and phrasing.

Step 5

The transition from structured tasks to conversation is highly individualized. Some patients require very few techniques or strategies, whereas others need very organized exercises.

Exercise 1: Initially, the patient is asked to describe three things he or she will do during the rest of the day. Cues and prompts are provided as needed.

Exercise 2: Additional practice is gained by asking the patient to discuss specific topics, and to read aloud on a daily basis from a newspaper or magazine. It may be helpful for the patient to tape-record these practice

sessions at home for review with the voice therapist in a subsequent therapy session.

Reducing Harsh Glottal Attacks

The term *harsh* or *hard glottal attacks* refers to the forceful or abrupt approximation of the vocal folds on words that begin with vowels. The acoustic result is a sudden, sharp, or explosive sound often called a *glottal click* or *glottal stroke*. The onset of voicing or phonation for vowels should be initiated gradually and easily. The key to easing harsh glottal attacks lies in the timing of the airflow with phonation.

Easy Onset Exercise 1: Negative Practice

The clinician demonstrates contrasts for the patient, using an abrupt initiation of the vowel sound in single words. These same words are then produced with an easy onset. Discrimination of easy versus hard onset can be provided for home practice. This is especially useful for adolescents or children. This negative practice is limited to only a few trials. After the clinician demonstrates, the patient is asked to say a word hard, then say it easy. Instructions to produce the word easily may include initiating the word with an /h/ sound, or feeling the air first.

Easy Onset Exercise 2: Minimal Pairs

A list of minimal-paired words (hate/ate, high/I, etc.) is provided. The patient is directed to feel the openness of the glottis on the /h/ and the closure on the vowel-initiated cognate.

Easy Onset Exercise 3: Single Words

Air naturally precedes vocal fold adduction when producing h-initiated words; therefore, easy vowel initiation can be shaped from such words. The word list (appendix V) is used as stimulus material in a variety of ways. One alternative is asking the patient to produce a light /h/ sound before each word. It is discussed that using the /h/ to slide into the word helps to initiate an easy onset. In some cases, the patient is asked to produce a breathy quality to ensure an easy onset. It is also useful to encourage a slide into the word with a slight elongation of the initial vowel.

A second method is to focus on the relationships between the initiation of exhalation and sound. Instruct the patient to "know what you are going to say before you take in air to say it." Begin by simply breathing in and breathing out in a regular cycle. Then try vowel-initiated words, making sure the patient is into the exhalation phase before attempting voicing. Cues of "Don't stop at the end of exhalation" and "Begin to voice just after you have begun to breath out" are helpful.

Easy Onset Exercise 4: Long vs. Short Vowels

It is helpful to begin with single words initiated with the long vowels in English (eg, *eat, ice*) (appendix V). The practice material is structured such that words beginning with the same vowel shape are rehearsed in a string (eg, *are, art, arm*). Minimizing the changes in oral cavity shape helps the patient focus his or her attention on the details of appropriate breathing, which assists in decreasing laryngeal tension. The task hierarchy proceeds from single words containing the long vowels to words beginning with short vowels (eg, *ill, it, is*). Once easy onset is established, a hierarchical approach is employed, moving from vowel-initiated words to vowel-initiated phrases to monitored reading to conversational speech.

Easy Onset Exercise 5: Delay Approach

Timing the onset of breath support is the key to a soft onset for words that begin with vowels. Singers are asked to imagine a score of music that begins with an eighth-note rest. Visual cuing is provided to help with the slow onset time. The patient is asked to posture his or her mouth for the word that will be produced, but delay the onset of phonation until the air, which is achieved with good abdominal/diaphragmatic support, has reached the level of the vocal folds. Additional suggestions include "breathe space between the vocal folds," "imagine that you are exhaling on the sound /h/" (an audible /h/ should not be produced for this exercise), "wait for the air to reach the folds, then produce the word" (eg, *are*).

Easy Onset Exercise 6: Downward Slide

Using a downward slide on the vowel sound that begins the word is another technique to reduce harsh glottal attacks. The patient is asked to expand the abdomen (to ensure a good supply of air), then slide down from a high pitch to a lower pitch on the vowel sound. Modeling is provided. It is important that the patient not think of this as singing.

Easy Onset Exercise 7: Key Word Approach

A key word carryover approach is used, with "I," "and," and other frequently occurring words in Eng-

lish. The patient may generate a list of vowel-initiated words (names of family members and friends) and practice using any of the other techniques described in this section.

Easy Onset Exercise 8: Blending

The above techniques pertain to vowel-initiated words that begin a breath group (words which are said on one breath). For vowel-initiated words that do not begin a breath group, a "linking" technique is used. Vowel-initiated words are linked to the word that precedes them. Connecting vowel-initiated words in on-going speech is generally an easy task for singers. They are reminded that the same connected (legato) line and rules of phrasing in song apply to speech as well. A short list (appendix V) of two-word combinations is used in which the first word is linked or blended to the second word.

Easy Onset Exercise 9: Conversation or Monologue

Conversation or a monologue is elicited. The patient's attention is directed to blending words and easing the onset of vowel-initial words as he or she begins a breath group. This should be tape recorded and reviewed with the patient.

Oral Resonance

The distinction between *oral resonance* and *tone focus* is subtle. Speech-language pathologists use concepts of oral resonance as they are reported in therapy texts for the profession. Vocabulary such as *vocal placement* or *tone focus* is borrowed from the singing literature. There are numerous techniques to improve the resonance quality of the voice. We use exercises to increase oral cavity space. These include palatal, pharyngeal, and tongue exercises. The goal is to increase the oral cavity space anteriorly and posteriorly. We generally begin with awareness exercises that are especially important for the nonsinger or others who have not had any formal voice or speech training. Many speakers tend to keep the jaw closed and open it only when necessary on low vowels. A more appropriate resonance pattern is to keep the jaw relaxed and open, and to only close when necessary on such sounds as /s/, /z/, /tʃ/, /dʒ/, /ʃ/ and /ʒ/. This necessitates increased activity of the anterior part of the tongue, in disassociation with jaw movements and may require additional practice, particularly with individuals with myofacial imbalance syndrome.

Jaw and facial tension are commonly observed in hyperfunctional voice users. Tension is often expressed as a "clenched teeth" posture, with little excursion of the jaw while speaking. By maintaining the jaw in a relatively fixed position, the tongue, pharynx, and other structures are forced to work harder to make the necessary adjustment for vowel differentiation. Further, the diminished space within the oral cavity compromises its effectiveness as a resonator.

In discussing the concept of jaw relaxation, it is preferable to use words such as "creating space" rather then "opening the mouth." "Opening" can be accomplished rather easily, but not necessarily in a relaxed position. Instructing the patient to feel space between the back teeth seems to achieve openness without tension.

Oral Resonance Exercise 1: Palatal Awareness

This exercise is useful for patients with functional or regional nasality and is often used to shape resonance for nonsingers. The patient is asked to stand and suggestions regarding appropriate head and neck position are provided. The patient is asked to sustain an /N/ using good abdominal/diaphragmatic breath support. Cues are provided to facilitate self-monitoring and to direct the patient's attention to the soft palate. Visual monitoring (using a hand mirror) is especially useful. The /N/ is repeated at least 10 times. While continuing to use the mirror, the patient is asked to change the sustained /N/ to /A/, and is guided to observe the movement of the soft palate and the tongue. The mirror is taken away, and the patient is asked to feel this action. The /N/ to /A/ is repeated 10 times while sustaining one tone. Changing the tone by using an upward or downward slide is an option. However, this should be incorporated only after the patient has acquired good soft palate movement.

Oral Resonance Exercise 2: Pharyngeal "Surprise"

This uses imagery to create an open pharynx and high soft palate position. The patient is asked to imagine walking into a freezer and being surprised by the coldness. A gentle gasp is produced. We take care to instruct that the gasp be produced softly, without tension. This is incorporated into the cycle of breathing for the inspiratory phase. The candle blowing maneuver or any isolated speech sound may be used. As the patient exhales (which we sometimes continue to use as the first step in the breathing cycle) the patient is asked to express the surprise upon inhaling. The patient is asked to observe the feeling of cold air as it touches the pharynx ("back of the throat") and soft palate. We ask the patient to imagine that the cold air lifts the palate.

Oral Resonance Exercise 3: Tongue Protrusion

Hyperextending the position of the tongue for a simple task such as counting or reading short phrases is an extremely useful technique for finding immediate relief to tongue tension. This technique is often used when the patient feels vocally fatigued or in physical discomfort from speaking. The patient is asked to protrude the tongue so that it rests lightly on the lower lip (but not beyond the lip). Instructions are provided to ensure good speech breathing. The patient repeats one number per breath up to the number 10, then repeat the sequence. This sequence (counting from 1 to 10) is repeated three times to ensure that the posterior tongue muscles have stretched and relaxed. Essentially, the posterior tongue fatigues during this exercise, making hyperfunction more difficult, while it increases patient awareness. When the tongue is placed back in the mouth, it is easier to maintain a comfortable, more forward tongue placement, and the tone quality produced is often strikingly free and clear.

Additional tongue protrusion exercises may be useful in some cases. After the sequence of counting from 1 to 10 is completed, the patient may be asked to count in groups of three (eg, 1-2-3) and to breathe after every third number. When using short phrases for this task, the patient is instructed to repeat the phrase three times, and to attempt to produce clearly identifiable words, using appropriate articulation especially of difficult consonants (/t/, /d/, /p/, /b/, etc).

Oral Resonance Exercise 4: Natural Open Vowels

Certain vowels and diphthongs have an inherent "openness" to them (eg, /A/, /Ai/, /˘/, /Au/) and naturally facilitate more vertical space within the oral cavity. The patient is provided with a practice list of words containing these vowels (appendix V). These words are used as targets in phrases to enable the patient to experience this openness in connected speech. The patient is then asked to identify such words in longer phrases, paragraphs, and conversational speech.

Oral Resonance Exercise 5: Lowered Posterior Tongue

Increase the posterior dimension of the mouth space. Back vowel sounds such as /u/, /o/, and /O/ are used in conjunction with a downward slide to increase posterior oral dimension. The series of slides is practiced in consonant-vowel-consonant combinations. It is easier for a nonsinger to begin with a continuous consonant sound such as /S/, /s/, /m/, and /l/. The combinations of sounds include /ʃu-t/; /s-u-t/, and the like. A series of downward slides is used. The pharyngeal surprise can be incorporated into this exercise to maximize the space in the pharynx.

Tone Focus/Vocal Placement in Speech

Incorrect vocal placement or tone focus is a common speaking error. The tendency to overuse the muscles of the pharynx and posterior tongue creates a distinct resonance quality. The terms used to describe this quality include: "throaty," "muffled," "swallowing the words," "heavy," "guttural," and "pressed." This excessive muscular tension can lead to physical discomfort and vocal fatigue.

The concept of "vocal placement" is a distinct entity and not synonymous with "pitch," even though changes in placement may concomitantly affect pitch. We usually avoid the use of the word pitch in therapeutic directions as it carries with it certain preconceived ideas that can interfere with desirable behavioral change.

Vocal placement can be conceptualized as occurring along two axes: up/down and front/back. Therapy begins with a discussion of this "two-axis theory," the difference between pitch and placement, and a heightening of awareness of articulatory placement within the oral cavity. We begin with consonants because they are easier to conceptualize, having a definite point of contact or placement. Any sound articulated on the alveolar ridge or anterior to that point is considered a "front" sound, including /t/, /d/, /n/, /l/, /s/, /z/, /ʃ/, /tʃ/, /ʤ/, /ʧ/ (voiced and voiceless), /f/, /v/, /p/, /b/, and /m/. "Middle" sounds include /r/ and /j/. Back sounds are represented by /k/ and /g/. Once frontal consonant placement is established, an attempt is made to create the image of vowels being carried forward with the consonants. A tape recorder is useful so that the patient can hear, as well as feel, the difference in production.

Vocal Placement Exercise

We begin by having the patient contrast naturally front words (eg, *neat*) with naturally back words (eg, *clock*) to heighten the patient's awareness. A list of the front-placed words is provided to reinforce the feeling of the voice buzzing in the front of the mouth (appendix V). The patient then produces these words, following them with a phrase ending in that target word. If good placement is achieved at the beginning and the end of the utterance, it can hopefully be maintained in between (eg, *neat—please be neat*). The patient is then instructed to repeat and read sentences and short paragraphs, concentrating on the placement of the articulators and the focus of the voice. Conversational speech and short monologues are practiced in order to make more spontaneous use of this technique.

Glottal Fry

Glottal fry (also called *pulse register*) occurs in the voice in the lowest frequency (24 Hz to 44 Hz). The tone that is produced in this range is perceived as rough or gravelly. Glottal fry often occurs in association with inadequate breath support and/or pharyngeal vocal placement. Techniques to improve breath support, enhance appropriate vocal placement, negative practice, and attention to auditory feedback are particularly useful in eliminating this tonal quality.

Loudness vs. Projection

The difference between *loudness* and *projection* is reviewed with each patient. We discuss the idea of frivolous loudness, which is most loud talking, yelling, or screaming. Projection is defined as maximizing listener intelligibility with minimal speaker effort. Projection techniques are preferable to loud talking or yelling. While adjustments in breath support provide the foundation, making changes in the production of speech can enhance the perception of increased loudness. We suggest gentle overarticulation, which helps to maximize the production of words. These projection exercises are intended for conversational settings in the presence of loud background noise, for the telephone, for classroom teaching, and for some public-speaking situations. They are not intended for the stage. Many years of training are required for stage projection. The patient's skills are developed using a hierarchy that begins with breath support tasks.

Projection Exercise 1: Single Words

Word lists (see appendix V) are presented which contain tongue-tip and other frontal consonant sounds, and we introduce a game of "baseball." *Game rules:* The therapist "pitches" (by swinging an arm toward the patient) a word. A small arm swing indicates that the word is to be spoken at a comfortable loudness. Very gradually, the therapist increases the excursion of the arm swing, which is the patient's cue to use more breath support (by pulling in the abdominal muscles with more energy). The result is a naturally louder production of the word. It usually takes 10 trials for the patient to reach maximum loudness for a given word. Tactile-kinesthetic monitoring of the strap muscles and posterior tongue ensures relaxation of these muscles.

Projection Exercise 2: Using Speech Sounds in Phrasing

Often the perception of loudness is related to the clarity of the tone, word, or phrase. We use diction exercises to enhance the speaker's understandability and refer back to our lists of words and phrases. The patient is instructed to produce ending consonants sounds precisely. Care is taken to insure that hyperfunctional overarticulation does not result.

Projection Exercise 3: Combination

After the patient has had experience with the baseball game and improving diction for selected phrases, two exercises are combined: The therapist pitches specific phrases to the patient. The phrases are usually kept short (three, four, five, or six syllables per phrase) for this exercise. Again, the patient is instructed to use breath support more efficiently and not to focus on merely getting louder.

Projection Exercise 4: Prosody

Prosody exercises also enhance loudness and projection in longer phrases. Patients are asked to decide which word or words carry the meaning of a phrase and are then asked to accent that word by raising the intonation slightly and adding more breath support. If the selected word begins with a vowel, care is taken to ensure an easy onset.

Oral Resonance Exercise 4 is also useful in enhancing vocal projection.

Prosody

Major prosodic disturbances are not commonly observed in the professional voice population. However, a loss of vocal variety may occur during therapy as other aspects of speech/voice production are changed. In some cases prosody exercises may be necessary.

Prosody Exercise 1: Polysyllabic words

Polysyllabic words are used and the patient is instructed to exaggerate an upward inflection on the accented syllable (eg, *ed-u-ca-tion-al*). (Not only *educational* but *beautifully*.) The patient is taken through a hierarchy of tasks to establish this technique. The

patient's conversational speech is taped. On playback, the patient and clinician mutually critique the patient's success in implementing this strategy. Improper responses are repeated in corrected form.

Prosody Exercise 2: Homographs

A list of words that differ in meaning depending on how they are accented is provided (*content-content*). A slightly exaggerated rising intonation for the accented syllable is demonstrated. These words are produced in a string of pairs. The patient's attention is oriented directly to the intonation variation (appendix V).

Prosody Exercise 3: Phrases

The patient is asked to use polysyllabic words in self-generated phrases while still using the exaggerated intonation.

Prosody Exercise 4: Reading

The patient is asked to identify the polysyllabic words in a reading paragraph. These words are used as the basis for the exaggerated intonation as the patient reads.

Prosody Exercise 5: Conversation

The patient's conversational speech is audiotaped. On playback, the therapist and patient mutually critique the patient's use of this exaggerated technique. Error responses are repeated in the correct form.

Pitch

Specific methods for changing pitch will not be addressed in this chapter. Inappropriate pitch is rarely the cause of a patient's vocal dysfunction. Rather, inappropriate vocal usage may cause deviant pitch. When proper breath support and vocal placement are established, appropriate pitch usually follows.

Bridging Exercises

Bridging exercises are used with all patients (singers and nonsingers) who receive joint specialized singing instruction. These exercises are designed to bridge the gap (when one exists) between singing and speaking technique. The patient is provided with experience in maintaining appropriate tonal balance with breath control and support when the task changes from singing to speaking exercises. These techniques are especially useful for experienced singers who have not applied their trained vocal production and technique to speaking. They are also valuable for nonsingers who have worked successfully with the singing-voice specialist.

Bridging Exercise 1: Descending Slide on /m/

The patient is instructed to start in a high falsetto range and very slowly slide down on the /m/ sound. Care is taken to ensure good abdominal support, appropriate head/neck position, and appropriate tongue placement. This same slide is repeated five times and the starting pitch is slightly lowered each time.

Bridging Exercise 2: Descending slide for /m/ and /ɑ/.

The patient is asked to slide down on the /m/. About halfway down the slide the patient is instructed to open his or her mouth. The resulting sound is an /ʌ/. The important aspect of this exercise is the careful transition from the /m/ to the /ʌ/. The patient is directed to feel the slow, gradual change to the /ʌ/.

Bridging Exercise 3: Sustained /m/ to Counting

The patient is asked to sustain an /m/ at a comfortable pitch and loudness. Cues are provided to help the patient focus on the sensory aspects that had been previously trained (eg, open/relaxed pharynx, relaxed tongue position). The patient is asked to change from the /m/ to counting. The /m/ serves to bridge from a tone that sounds like light humming to speech.

Bridging Exercise 4: Lip Trills

The singing-voice specialist and the speech-language pathologist incorporate the use of lip trills. For singers, this is often a familiar task, but nonsingers require careful instruction. Tactile monitoring of the strap muscles is needed to ensure that tension is not created as this task is learned. We begin with a silent lip trill that sounds much like the neigh of a horse, sometimes referred to as a "flub." Visual prompts are provided, which help pace the timing the breath. After several trials with the flub, voicing is added. It is helpful to have the patient initiate the flub first, then add phonation. Lip trills are used on ascending and descending slides. It is important for the patient to produce a tone that is smooth and free of tension.

Bridging Exercise 5: /ɴ/ to /ɑ/

Palatal awareness exercises are routinely incorporated into voice training. When used as a bridging exercise,

the /ɴ/ — /ʌ/ is used during the production of ascending and descending slides.

Bridging Exercise 6: Ascending-Descending Slide on /m/

The patient is asked to slowly slide up, then down in pitch on one breath for /m/. Modeling is provided so that the higher pitch is not too high. Occasionally, a replenishing breath needs to be taken before the descending slide.

Bridging Exercise 7: Siren

The circular sound an emergency vehicle makes is used with isolated sounds such as /m/, /l/, /v/, and lip trills. The number of repetitions per breath depends on the patient's speech-breathing ability. This is also an excellent warm-up exercise for the morning.

Recitative

Classical singers are generally trained in *recitative*, a cross between singing and speaking that occurs between arias in opera and oratorio. Singers who have mastered recitative can carryover good vocal technique by gradually dropping pitch specificity during recitative passages, letting them gradually convert to spoken dialogue. Similarly, singers may read passages as recitative on improvised notes, learning how to apply their musically trained breathing, support, and placement techniques to conversational speech. For singers who do not have an operatic background, patter songs (eg, Gilbert and Sullivan) and rap are of similar value as bridging exercises.

Level-Three Therapy

Level-Three Therapy involves the management of emotional stress. Some professional voice users react strongly to voice change. Voice therapy is designed to help the patient feel better and sound better. Most patients come to therapy with somatic complaints such as pain, tension, and vocal fatigue. Therefore, it is important that they begin to find relief quickly. This helps to elicit their cooperation and motivation early in the training process.

In addition, management of the stresses of everyday living, performing, or teaching is essential in the overall management of the injured speaker or singer. Many voice patients experience tremendous stress and tension in their daily lives. Decisions as to whether these stresses may be managed by the speech-language pathologist or are deep seated enough to require the expertise of the psychological professional need to be made during the initial evaluation session and reevaluated as therapy progresses. Often the tension associated with deep-seated stress interferes with the patient's ability to respond to Level Two or Level-One therapeutic techniques, and it should be addressed first.

Simple stress management techniques can be applied by the speech-language pathologist. More deep-seated stress and reaction to emotions or environmental influences will require the special skills of a psychologist or psychiatrist.

Relaxation

Many voice therapy programs incorporate relaxation techniques. While this is useful for stress management, progressive or deep relaxation is not necessarily an integral part of voice therapy for all patients. We use relaxation techniques to reduce muscular tension and to energize those muscle systems used in voice production. We routinely use range of motion, muscle stretch, and physical energizing tasks. There are many popular techniques used to facilitate relaxation. Jacobson's Progressive Relaxation[4] allows the patient to contrast muscular tension with relaxation. We have found it useful with muscular tension dysphonia and for some hyperfunctional voice users. However, carryover of this relaxed state to voice production is often difficult to achieve, and we find additional techniques desirable for most patients.

The yawn-sigh technique has traditionally been a part of voice therapy and speech training.[3] Although it benefits some patients, it is not a technique that should be used indiscriminately. The initial inspiratory phase of a yawn creates a high soft palate position, a lowered vertical laryngeal position, and an open pharynx. However, once the yawn reflex is triggered, the same structures and muscles become tense. Phonating with this degree of tension is not desirable. The natural yawn may have some benefit in voice retraining, but the artificial yawn used as a therapy technique has many potential pitfalls. The yawn-sigh technique may be appropriate for:

1. Improving the patient's sensory awareness of the soft palate, muscles of the pharynx, and tongue.
2. Creating an open, relaxed pharynx.
3. Establishing a high soft palate position, useful for oral resonance improvement.

For relieving specific sites of muscular tension: Excessive muscular tension is observed in association with almost all voice problems. Developing tactile awareness of the muscle movements of voice and speech production is a supplemental goal of voice therapy and is facilitated through the muscle stretch exercises. Even if minimal muscular tension is observed, range of motion and self-massage exercises are often helpful. Patients with a history of head/neck injuries or cervical arthritis are not candidates for these exercises.

Range of Motion

We recommend these exercises only for patients who do not have a history of head or neck injuries, back pain, spinal cord problems, or cervical arthritis. This exercise is designed to provide a complete stretch to isolated muscles of the neck. The instructions are routinely put on an audiotape, which allows for correct home practice. Specific instructions are provided to the patient to stretch the trapezius muscle and the anterior and lateral strap muscles. The following outline is provided:

1. *Head Forward and Backward:* The head comes forward and is held in that position for a count of 10. Slowly the patient rotates the head from side to side as if watching a ball roll back and forth in his lap. The patient is then asked to tip the head backward while gently opening the mouth, look at the ceiling, and hold that position for a count of 5. These steps are usually repeated twice, but more repetitions may be indicated for some patients.
2. *Head Side-to-Side:* The head rocks toward the right shoulder, as if the patient were trying to touch the right shoulder with the right ear. Instructions are provided to ensure that only the head moves and not the entire torso. While leaning toward the right, the head rocks forward and backward in one sweeping nod (as if nodding "yes"). The patient is asked focus on the muscles on the left side of the neck as they stretch and elongate. The instructions are repeated with the head leaning to the left.
3. *Looking Over Each Shoulder:* The patient is reinstructed regarding appropriate head and shoulder alignment. The patient is then asked to look over the right shoulder as if something were behind him. This position is held for a count of 10, and the patient is instructed to feel the stretch of the sternocleidomastoid muscle. The same instructions are repeated for the left side.
4. *Shoulder Rolls:* The shoulders are rolled forward and backward, in isolation, and then together. Specific instructions are provided to help the patient attend to the muscles he or she is stretching.

5. *Shoulder Shrugs:* The patient is asked to raise the shoulders, hold for a count of three, and then allow the shoulders to drop. Attention is directed to the contrast between tension and relaxation. As the shoulders drop, the patient is asked to feel the tension leave the shoulders through the fingertips.

6. *Jaw Relaxation:* The patient is asked to let the jaw drop open or down to create space between the back teeth. The clinician observes that the jaw is comfortably open and gently hyperextended or "unhinged." This position is held for 3 seconds, then the jaw is closed. These steps are repeated five times.

7. *Tongue Stretch:* Posterior tongue tension is usually observed in association with pharyngeal or "throaty" resonance. The patient is asked to rest the tongue lightly against the bottom teeth or inside the lower lip. The patient is prompted to hyperextend the base of the tongue. This is repeated at least 10 times; 30 times is preferred. This repetition tires the posterior portion of the tongue and often has an immediate effect of producing a clearer resonant quality. Another approach consists of rapid repetitions of the same stretch. The patient is provided with the identical prompts, but using a double-time pace. The clinician counts the rhythm (eg, "one-two; one-two; one-two") to help the patient maintain this pace.

8. *Tongue Tension in Speech:* Ongoing observations of the patient's performance and reaction to the suggestions provided by the clinician is very important. During the warm-up/cool-down routine, watch the neck just under the chin for signs of tongue movement. Posterior tongue tension is especially obvious during production of /s/. To insure good tactile monitoring, the patient is instructed to observe the difference in the tongue for /s/, then /ʃ/. If need be, a sloppy /s/ production will minimize tongue tension. Using a staccato rhythm challenges the patient and should be employed after success is achieved for the prolonged /s/.

9. *Strap Muscle Hyperfunction:* The use of voiced/voiceless cognate pairs (eg, f/v, s/z, ʃ/ʒ, T/D) facilitates relaxed/easy voicing. In making the transition from voiceless to voiced speech sounds, we often see the vertical laryngeal position shift upward, which squeezes the strap muscles and muscles of the pharynx. The result is a tight or pressed resonant quality. Occasionally, a downward shift of the larynx is observed. The patient is instructed to monitor neck tension (tactile-kinesthetic monitoring) and observe the transition from the voiceless sound to the voiced sound. The patient learns how to add voicing without the tension.

10. *Chewing:* A modified "chewing approach" is used to promote mobility and stretch of the muscles of the face, lips, jaw, and tongue.[5] The patient is instructed to chew slowly, with his mouth open, and to make smacking noises "like a cow on a lazy summer afternoon." The patient is encouraged to use all the muscles of the lips, tongue, face, and jaw. When phonation is superimposed on the relaxed muscular complex the result should be a clearer sound with more oral resonance.

This technique should not be applied indiscriminately. The chewing exercise is not a relaxing activity for all patients. Some patients are uncomfortable with the crudeness of chewing in such a socially unacceptable manner and therefore cannot relax with it. Chewing exercises may also be contraindicated for patients with temporomandibular joint syndrome.

Self-Massage

The face, temporal muscles, posterior neck, shoulders, and occasionally the anterior strap muscles are massaged by the patient.

1. *Facial massage:* The masseter muscle is identified. The patient is asked to press in firmly with the fingertips under the zygoma bones, and to hold the pressure for a count of 10. The patient is always reminded to continue to breathe at this point. Holding the breath can reinforce muscle tension. The fingertips are then released, and the patient is asked to go to the same spot and massage this muscle using a firm, slow circular motion. These same instructions are repeated on the jaw line, where the masseter muscle finishes its course. Massaging the temporal muscles (on both sides of the forehead) is extremely beneficial for relieving jaw tension. The same instructions of pressing, then massaging are provided.

2. *Posterior Neck and Shoulder Massage:* Excessive posterior neck muscle tension is often created by inappropriate head/neck alignment. To massage the right side, the patient is asked to take the left hand, cross over to the right side, and press in on the trapezius muscle. The press is held for a count of 10, and is then released. The patient is instructed to keep breathing. Next, the instruction is given to go back to the same spot, press in firmly, then let the hand slide forward and down. These steps are repeated for two other places in the posterior neck and then two places on the shoulders. Both sides are massaged equally. The right hand is used to massage to left posterior neck and shoulder.

Body Posture and Head/Neck Alignment

Appropriate head and neck alignment and body posture are essential to developing efficient vocal production. Excessive anterior strap muscle and posterior neck tension is created when the head is tilted backward or the chin is jutted forward. Suggestions and prompts are provided in conjunction with the other therapy techniques including generalized overall body relaxation techniques.

The following exercises have been helpful for refocusing the patients' general overall stress reaction. The exercises can be practiced routinely each day or used in times of high stress. Each of these exercises can be put on an audiotape for playback at a later time. Many of our patients find it helpful to hear the therapist's voice guide them through the relaxation protocol.

Two Minute Spot Check: This short exercise is practical and easy. It is also extremely useful in reinforcing self-monitoring skills, and facilitating the carryover phase of therapy. We tell the patient to:

1. Interrupt your thoughts—switch your thoughts to your breathing. Begin with the candle blowing, taking time to inhale and exhale fully. Take several cleansing breaths (quicker fuller breaths), which requires a more active exchange of air.
2. Scan your body for specific sites of tension (forehead, jaw, shoulders, neck, or tongue). Attempt to loosen this area (move gently, use the range of motion exercises, or self-massage).
3. Take two more cleansing breaths, then return to easy candle blowing, and return to your activity.

Range of Motion for Stress Management: This is similar to the range of motion provided as a daily warm-up exercise. For this purpose, more time is taken and more breathing is incorporated. On an audiotape, the patient is provided with instructions beginning with: "Find yourself sitting in a comfortable chair. Let your head come forward as if you wanted to place your chin on your chest. Let it remain there for a moment. The muscle you are now stretching is called your trapezius. Can you imagine the point where it begins at the base of your skull, and feel where it ends in the middle of your back?" The patient is led on tape through a brief muscle relaxation program that helps dissipate stress.

The Quieting Response: This takes less than one minute to complete. It can be done in the midst of chaos, panic, or stage fright.

1. Pant quickly using a forced expiration, gradually slow down your breathing, turn it into the candle blowing, then gradually return to quiet breathing.

2. Smile outwardly and inwardly. Suggest to yourself (silently or aloud) that you will be accepted and successful in what you are about to do. Imagine a positive outcome. Picture yourself being in a relaxed controlled state 5 minutes from now. Enjoy the feeling of accomplishment.
3. Resume your activity.

A Short Meditation: The patient is provided with a tape of this relaxation exercise which lasts 5–10 minutes. The therapist guides the patient through each step, then finishes with the guided imagery. The patient is instructed to:

1. Spot check the body for muscular tension. Release specific areas of tension with the stretch and/or range of motion exercises. Focus on a warm, glowing feeling sweeping throughout your body.
2. Warm your hands by rubbing them together vigorously. Visualize the sun's warmth on your hands. Place them gently on your face and sweep downward and outward.
3. Focus now on your thoughts. Imagine a panel of switches. As your turn off each switch (one by one) your breathing slows and becomes very regular.
4. In your mind, travel to a place that's warm and safe, and brings a smile to your face—the seashore, the country, your home, a good friend. Stay with this pleasant feeling.

Guided Imagery: Guided imagery works best once the patient is in a quiet and calm state with very slow, regular breathing. The patient is led through individualized images. For example:

Imagine yourself lying on a carpet of soft grass in a shaded forest. It is a warm, pleasant day. The sky is a bright clear blue. Sun rays filter through the leaves of the forest canopy above. The tree branches seem to embrace and protect this spot where you lie. A gentle breeze sings through the green grass and tickles the skin of your face. Imagine that there is a clearing in the branches and a shaft of yellow light is descending on you. Feel the warmth. Feel the warmth seeping onto your forehead, your cheek bones, your mouth, your chin. Feel the warmth flowing down your neck and into your chest. Take a deep breath . . . Smell the fragrant air . . . Hold the breath . . . Then, slowly let it go as you feel the tightness flow from your chest on down your arms, and out your finger tips. Let the sun's rays warm your chest, your abdomen. Take a deep breath . . . Hold the warmth in your torso, then slowly let it drift slowly down your legs, and out your toes. You may stay in this moment and enjoy this perfect summer day and a feeling of deep contentment.

The patient is cued that the clinician will stop talking for a moment so he or she can enjoy the feeling. The patient is cued that he or she is brought back to that moment in time by counting from 1 to 10. Once the patient is accustomed to this technique, it can be used essentially as a form of self-hypnosis in times of stress (such as immediately before a performance).

Warm-up and Cool-down Exercises: The warm-up and cool-down routine is important in training the voice. Singers appreciate the need to exercise the voice before singing. Speaking exercises provide the patient with the equivalent of vocalises (singing scales) for the speaking voice. Consistent practice each morning prepares the vocal folds and muscles of the vocal mechanism for the demands of the day. The evening cool-down regimen is similar to the athlete stretching and cooling down after running. An outline of the daily practice exercises (appendix V) is provided on each visit. The routine includes a muscular stretch and range of motion exercises, which are useful for relaxation, but are specifically used to heighten the patient's tactile feedback system. The patient is then asked to vocalize (singing scales), which have been provided by the singing specialist and provide "aerobic" conditioning. If the patient does not received concurrent singing instruction, this step is omitted. The speech-language pathologist does not provide instruction in this area. The final step in the daily routine is the speaking exercises. These usually include a variety of nonspeech tasks, voiceless speech, and voiced speech sounds, and bridging exercises. The therapist reviews each exercise and provides new tasks as the need arises. Any of the techniques described in this chapter may be suitable as a warm-up or cool-down exercise.

Level-Four Therapy

Preparation for Referral to Mental Health Specialists

Occasionally a professional speaker will demonstrate stress and emotional reactions that are not directly related to performance and are pervasive in his or her personality and reaction to the world. These patients are often unable to respond to the educational processes at Level One, are intermittently and inconsistently successful in changing vocal behaviors at Level Two, and are unable to carryover stress management techniques beyond the actual performance of the relaxation exercises.

The therapy process can be disrupted by the patient's need to talk about unrelated problems and incidents. Often patients with mental health problems may be able to admit to a voice disorder but are unable to acknowledge emotional issues that may be interfer-

ing with their ability to cope with their relationships or environment. Making a referral to a mental health professional may not be sufficient when the patient denies the need for such a referral.

Referral Technique 1

The patient may need to experience the supportive, noncritical one-on-one therapeutic relationship. The process of participating in a caring therapeutic environment may be sufficient to improve the patient's likelihood of following through on a referral to a mental health specialist. Deferring the referral until the patient has been in voice therapy for a period of time may be helpful in achieving compliance with such a referral.

Referral Technique 2

If the therapeutic process continues to be interrupted by the patient, stop and listen sympathetically to the problems the patient wishes to discuss. If the patient has developed trust in you, he or she may begin to vent emotional stress related to verbal and physical abuse, feelings of entrapment, signs of depression, or other pervasive emotional problems. Vocalize your concerns about such problems and admit that you are not trained sufficiently to deal with or provide advice about such matters. Provide an immediate referral source to someone who may be better able to help with such problems and difficulties.

Where to Begin

Organizing therapy strategies into levels may assist the speech-language pathologist in determining, on the basis of the initial evaluation, where to begin with therapy and, if therapy is unsuccessful, what to try next. The ideal and easy patient with the best prognosis is the patient who with Level-One educational techniques and information is able to say "Oh, I can do that" and proceeds to modify both life-style and vocal behavior. Often patients are unable to alter their speaking or singing requirements and are not trained well enough to be aware of what they are doing physically when speaking or singing. For these patients, Level-Two strategies and direct behavioral change of vocalization is required and may be most effective. Others may present with stress and tension levels so high that they are unable to respond to direct behavioral change and require the use of Level-Three techniques to condition patients to a level of relaxation that will permit them to respond to Level-Two vocal exercises and Level-One education. Finally, there are patients whose mental energy is so absorbed in day-to-day coping that they must deal with these mental problems before they can focus on the vocal problems manifested from their emotional problems. Patients who are unsuccessful with activities on one level may need activities found at a higher level.

Carryover Strategies

All the therapy techniques and exercises we have to offer are essentially worthless if the patient does not use them in his or her daily life. *Carryover* is the term used to describe the process of extending the use of new skills outside the speech-language pathologist's office. Traditionally, carryover occurs toward the end of therapy and is accomplished by gradually changing the contexts in which desired behaviors are emitted. This is accomplished by changing the physical environment (eg, moving from the therapy office to the waiting room and beyond) and expanding the social contexts in which the new behaviors are to be demonstrated (eg, bringing significant others into the therapy office). However, we believe that carryover should begin in the early stages of therapy. Consistent practice on the patient's part may be the best way to facilitate this.

Beyond the carryover that occurs spontaneously with practice, there are other ways to encourage the use of newly learned behaviors in the patient's daily conversation. A key word/key phrase approach has been used successfully in facilitating the transfer of new skills. Patients tend to use certain words or phrases frequently in the course of their daily interactions and they are encouraged to employ specific strategies on those specific words or phrases. For example, when working toward the elimination of hard glottal attacks, ascertain the names of important people in the patient's environment that may be vowel-initiated. *I* and *and* are very frequently occurring words in the English language and are good key words for most patients.

Utilize environmental cues to signal the use of certain desired behaviors. For example, when trying to facilitate the carryover of breath support, the patient is instructed to "support" every time he or she answers the telephone. The telephone receiver becomes an external reminder of what the individual should be doing.

Choose particular time periods or situations when the patient is to consciously use a particular technique. "Every lunch hour, while conversing with your colleagues, make an effort to use your frontal consonant focus;" or "At every red light, check to see that you have space between your back teeth."

Carryover Exercise 1: Greetings as Reminders

The patient is instructed to use all greetings and departures (hello, goodbye, etc) as reminders to use appropriate support. These greeting words should be practiced in the office, and then serve to trigger the patient's awareness of speaking technique in person and during telephone conversations.

Carryover Exercise 2: Telephone Strategies

Most professional voice users report some degree of vocal fatigue if extended telephone use is required. We routinely provide details in how to "survive" with the telephone. These suggestions include:

1. Observe appropriate head and neck position.
2. Slow speaking rate.
3. Make more effective use of pauses by stopping before or after important content words.
4. Hold each pause slightly longer than usual. This helps to give your listener more processing time.
5. Use projection techniques to get volume with ease.
6. Use projection techniques to maximize diction.
7. Switch which hand you typically use to hold the receiver. This adds a novelty to the situations and helps to focus on the voice.

Carryover Exercise 3: People and Places/Situations

The patient is asked to identify three situations and persons with whom he or she will practice the speaking techniques. The three people consist of a personal relationship (spouse, child, parent); a social acquaintance (work colleague, neighbor); and a stranger (grocery clerk, bank teller). A hierarchy is developed depending on the patient's feelings of comfort in each of these situations. Some patients report that it is easier to practice with a stranger. Others report that the techniques work best at work. This carryover strategy is highly individualized. The patient makes these active choices and the therapist helps guide his or her perceptions and practice.

Carryover Exercise 4: Reminders

The patient is asked to describe his or her activities during the course of a typical day from the time the alarm clock rings until it is reset at night. A few events are selected as reminders to check vocal technique. These may include activities such as walking through the office door, taking a coffee break, coming through the door at home, and so on. The effectiveness of each of these activities as a vocal "reminder" is checked during subsequent therapy sessions.

Carryover Exercise 5: Communicative Stress

Since the general approach is geared toward relaxation, specific practice in dealing with pressured situations is beneficial. The clinician will provide a series of rapid questions. These questions vary in the complexity of answers they require. A sample of questions includes:

1. What's your birthday?
2. What's your spouse's birthday?
3. What's your telephone number?
4. Why do we use napkins?
5. Why do we have traffic lights?
6. Why do we have income tax?
7. How do you make a bed?
8. Describe how to make your favorite meal.
9. What if a child was left unattended?

The clinician helps the patient identify vocal stress that develops in response to these questions, and instructions are given for identifying and ameliorating vocally abusive behavior in daily situations.

Carryover Exercise 6: Habituation and Maintenance

The patient is instructed to read aloud at least 3–4 times weekly.

Carryover Exercise 7: Professional Feedback

The patient is instructed to converse with the voice therapist or a similarly skilled listener periodically (timing depends upon the stage of therapy). While this is not exactly an exercise, the importance of skilled feedback cannot be underestimated.

Concurrent Specialized Singing Lessons

Most patients (singers and nonsingers) are routinely evaluated by the singing voice specialist. Singing provides the nonsinger with exercises and training that greatly enhance the speaking voice. Professional voice users find that the demands of speaking seem less when they have had the "aerobic" workout that singing provides, and the symbiotic techniques of the singing teacher enhance the teaching of breathing, support, placement and other speaking techniques.

Interrelation of Voice Functions

Although a number of common vocal misuses have been identified and their remediation discussed individually, deviant vocal behaviors do not occur in isolation. Therapy for one behavior may obviate the need for specific, intensive work on another. For example, patients who speak too rapidly usually exhibit jaw tension. The reason for the association between the two is that in order to speak at a rapid rate, the speaker cannot afford the time needed for the mandible to make the necessary excursion consistent with jaw relaxation. Breath support and vocal placement are similarly related. When a patient successfully achieves good abdominal breath support, the voice is naturally carried to a more frontal placement, on the well-sustained airflow. The importance of these examples is to emphasize the dynamic nature of vocal production.

Value of Instrumentation in Voice Therapy

Use of instrumentation for voice therapy will not be discussed in detail in this chapter. However, under special conditions voice therapy techniques in combination with instrumentation such as the Kay CSL programs, Visi-pitch, Sona-Graph, Laryngograph, PM-Pitch Analyzer, flexible fiberoptic scope, or rigid endoscope can be helpful. For example, the laryngograph in combination with the Sona-Graph has served as useful biofeedback for such disorders as spasmodic dysphonia or muscle tension dysphonia. After brief training and orientation, the patient can visually monitor correct versus incorrect productions for specific tasks. The PM-Pitch Analyzer has a built-in program designed for use in direct therapy. Since it can interpret longer speech samples, it is ideal for monitoring speaking misuses such as harsh glottal attacks in ongoing speech.

Summary

Professional voice users who need voice therapy require special diagnostic and intervention strategies. The clinician must be familiar with the requirements of "superspeaking" and have a detailed knowledge of performance environments and requirements. The clinician also needs to have a structured technique for evaluating voice, taking into account the extremely demanding definition of "normalcy" required by voice professionals. The speech-language pathologist should also use a progressive therapy program incorporating a variety of individualized exercises in order to optimize speaking technique. The techniques used should be symbiotic with those employed by singing-voice specialists and acting-voice specialists.

Review Questions

1. For professional speakers with voice problems, it is usually necessary for the clinician to concentrate on teaching new skills.
   a. true
   b. false

2. The diagnosis of vocal nodules should be established by:
   a. the speech-language pathologist
   b. the laryngologist
   c. the singing-voice specialist
   d. the acting-voice specialist
   e. the psychologist

3. Level I therapy includes all of the following except:
   a. a review of alternatives to throat clearing
   b. strategies to avoid yelling
   c. exercises to reduce harsh glottal attack
   d. a review of the effects of caffeine
   e. discussion of rest and fatigue

4. Glottal fry is also called:
   a. modal register
   b. pulse register
   c. falsetto register
   d. head register
   e. chest register

5. Once vocal skills are mastered in the speech-language pathologist's office, patients routinely and

automatically apply them to everyday situations such as telephone conversations.
   a. true
   b. false

References

1. Eckel FC, Boone DR. The s/z ratio as indication of laryngeal pathology. *J Speech Hear Dis*. 1981;46:147.
2. Aronson A. *Clinical Voice Disorders: An Interdisciplinary Approach*. New York, NY:Thieme, Medical Publishers, Inc; 1985.
3. Boone D. *The Voice and Voice Therapy*. Englewood Cliffs, NJ: Prentice-Hall; 1983.
4. Jacobson E. *You Must Relax*. New York, NY: McGraw-Hill Books; 1957.
5. Froeschels E. Chewing method as therapy. *Arch Otolaryngol*. 1952;56:427-434.

Suggested Reading List

1. Andrews M. *Manual of Voice Treatment*. San Diego, Calif: Singular Publishing Group, Inc; 1995.
2. Keith RL, Thomas JE. *Speech Practice Manual for Dysarthria, Apraxia, and Other Disorders of Articulation: Compare and Contrast*. Toronto: BC Decker Inc; 1989.
3. Linklater K. *Freeing the Natural Voice*. New York, NY: Drama Book Publishers; 1976.
4. Richards KB, Fallow MO. *Workbook for the Verbally Apraxic Adult: Reproducibles for Therapy and Home Practice*. Tucson, Ariz: Communication Skill Builders; 1987.
5. Smith MC. *The Phonemic Speech Workbook for Dysarthria Therapy*. Tucson, Ariz: Communication Skill Builders; 1986.
6. Colton R, Casper J. *Understanding Voice Problems*. Baltimore, Md: Williams & Wilkins; 1990.
7. Boone DR, McFarlane SC. *The Voice and Voice Therapy*. 4th ed. Englewood Cliffs, NJ: Prentice-Hall; 1988.
8. Stemple JC. *Clinical Voice Pathology: Theory and Management*. Columbus, Oh: Charles E. Merrill Publishing Co; 1984.
9. Aronson A. *Clinical Voice Disorders*. New York, NY: Thieme, Inc; 1985.

24

Increasing Vocal Effectiveness

Bonnie N. Raphael and Robert Thayer Sataloff

Preparation for Oral Presentations

Physicians, speech-language pathologists, teachers, students, executives, and people in most walks of life are called on at some time or another to speak in public. Few people are naturally skilled, organized, comfortable public speakers. Most people are somewhat uncomfortable about speaking in public, some are petrified, and nearly all make less than optimal use of their vocal and dramatic skills without some instruction and preparation. Although this book is not intended as a text to teach singing, conversational speech, or public speaking, we have selected this subject for our "example" chapter, because it is a common concern for most of our readers.

Not all considerations for voice preservation are "vocal." Many vocal stresses are controlled by eliminating psychological stress, understanding room acoustics, organizing material to be presented, and other similar preparations. This chapter describes our basic initial approach to training someone such as a physician to present a paper or lecture. It includes a few vocal exercises, although they are rudimentary and no substitute for formal training with a speech-language pathologist, a singing or speech teacher, or an acting coach. It also includes descriptions of physical warmup exercises used by many actors. Such exercises are frequently regarded as superfluous by the physician, but professional performers have found them extremely helpful. Use of appropriate preparation helps make a speaker appear relaxed, effective, and well-focused. Such preparation is also invaluable for controlling preperformance anxiety. Most outstanding speakers do, in fact, work hard at making their presentations appear natural and unrehearsed.

All too often, talented and intelligent speakers will spend considerable time in preparing the content of upcoming presentations but will spend virtually no time preparing themselves for the most effective spoken presentation of their research or position papers. Content that is interesting, valuable to the listeners, and important to the profession is too often lost or short-changed because of ineffective presentation. Far too many speakers present what they have to say in a way that makes it either too difficult to grasp or too dull to have a favorable impact on a listening audience. This chapter outlines a methodical procedure through which oral presentations can be more effectively prepared. Various texts are available to supplement the material presented in this chapter.[1–4]

Preparation of Written Materials

Ideally, the research should be completed and all materials to be presented should be available to the speaker no later than 1 month before the date of the presentation. This allows the speaker sufficient time to get the presentation into a form best suited to communicate the chief features of the research. Approximately 1 month before presentation, the speaker should write out as many drafts of the presentation as are necessary, until it expresses orally what he or she wishes to say in the clearest and most effective manner possible. Rather than simply reading from the same text submitted for publication, the speaker would do better to substitute words that are easier on the tongue and to use grammatical structure that is easier on the listener's ear. Sentences should be shorter and more concise for listeners than they might be for readers. The speaker should check the effectiveness of the presentation by reading the speech aloud a number of times, making certain that it fits easily into the time allotment assigned and it is stylistically suited to the particular audience to be addressed. Effective speakers will prepare two drafts of a given presentation at this stage: one to meet the needs of the oral presentation and another that meets the needs of publication.

If the speaker is more experienced or more comfortable working in a somewhat but not totally structured manner, then he or she may decide to work from note cards or a simple outline of the presentation. Less experienced presenters or those dealing with a large amount of information that needs to be precisely stated may prefer to work from a written text of the speech. Even this written text, however, can be prepared in such a way that it does not intrude between the speaker and the audience.

One way in which the written presentation can be moved toward effective oral performance is via a structural rewriting of the speech. In a structural rewriting, the way in which the speech appears on the page to the reader's eye is the way he or she wishes to express it aloud. Use of a structurally rewritten text is particularly important to presenters for whom English is not their native language and to presenters inexperienced in formal speaking before large audiences. A structural version of a speech makes phrasing and pausing at appropriate intervals far easier for the speaker, because it replaces arbitrary paragraph form with functional form. In order to better understand how this works, read aloud both versions of the Gettysburg Address which follow. Most readers will find that, with virtually no preparation, the second rendering of the same written material is far easier to deliver than the first, because the eye guides effective phrasing and pausing choices.

The Gettysburg Address
by: Abraham Lincoln

Fourscore and seven years ago our fathers brought forth on this continent a new nation, conceived in Liberty and dedicated to the proposition that all men are created equal.

Now we are engaged in a great civil war, testing whether that nation, or any nation so conceived and so dedicated, can long endure. We are met on a great battlefield of that war. We have come to dedicate a portion of that field, as a final resting-place for those who here gave their lives that this nation might live. It is altogether fitting and proper that we should do this.

But, in a larger sense, we cannot dedicate—we cannot consecrate—we cannot hallow this ground. The brave men, living and dead, who struggled here, have consecrated it far above our poor power to add or detract. The world will little note nor long remember what we say here, but it can never forget what they did

here. It is for us, the living, rather, to be dedicated here to the unfinished work which they who fought here have thus far so nobly advanced. It is rather for us to be here dedicated to the great task remaining before us—that from these honored dead we take increased devotion to that cause for which they gave the last full measure of devotion—that we here highly resolve that these dead shall not have died in vain—that this nation, under God, shall have a new birth of freedom—and that government of the people, by the people, for the people, shall not perish from the earth.

The Gettysburg Address
by: Abraham Lincoln
(structurally rendered)

Fourscore and seven years ago
  our fathers brought forth on this continent
  a new nation,
      conceived in Liberty and dedicated to the proposition
      that all men are created equal.
Now we are engaged in a great civil war,
  testing whether that nation,
  or any nation so conceived and so dedicated,
  can long endure.
We are met on a great battlefield of that war.
  We have come to dedicate a portion of that field as a
      final resting-place
      for those who here gave their lives that this nation
might live.
  It is altogether fitting and proper that we should do this.
But, in a larger sense,
  we cannot dedicate—we cannot consecrate—we cannot hallow this ground.
The brave men, living and dead, who struggled here,
  have consecrated it far above our poor power to add
      or detract.
The world will little note nor long remember what we
  say here,
  but it can never forget what they did here.
It is for us, the living, rather,
  to be dedicated here to the unfinished work
      which they who fought here have thus far so nobly
      advanced.
It is rather for us to be here dedicated to the great task
  remaining before us—
  that from these honored dead
  we take increased devotion to that cause
      for which they gave the last full measure of devotion—
that we here highly resolve
  that these dead shall not have died in vain—
  that this nation, under God, shall have a new birth of
      freedom—

and that government of the people, by the people,
for the people,
shall not perish from the earth.

Just through this simple experiment the reader should be able to see the benefits of creating and rehearsing with a structured rendition of the presentation. The Gettysburg Address was, in fact, written as a speech rather than as an essay. Presenters who are both rewriting materials for oral presentation and restructuring their texts for more effective reading will find this technique of even greater value when dealing with materials that are more technical and less poetically phrased than this memorable address.

After creating the structural rendition of the presentation, the presenter can then spend the next week or so continuing the preparation process in one of two ways:

1. The speech can be read aloud about twice a day from the structural script until the phrasing and pausing seem very natural and comfortable to the presenter; or
2. The presenter can tape record the speech after just a few readings through of the structural script. This way, if rehearsal time is severely limited but commuting time to work or meetings is not, the tape can be played in a car, train, or airplane until it is virtually memorized as a result of the repeated listening.

If the presenter wishes to work from a written text of the speech but, because of excessive length, the structural version of it seems to involve too many pages, then it can be retyped into manuscript form, but with the following modifications:

1. The text should be double or triple spaced between lines.
2. The text should not extend lower than two inches from the bottom of any page, so that, if the podium has a "lip" to it, no lines are lost from view.
3. No sentence should begin on the bottom of one page and conclude on the top of the next page.
4. The speaker may choose to have the text of the speech photocopied in a way that the type is enlarged or darkened in the duplication process and, therefore, easier to read.
5. The text should be enclosed in some kind of cover or loose-leaf binder with the pages consecutively numbered, so that it is easier to handle and keep under control, in the days preceding delivery of the paper and while traveling to the performance site. However, the pages should be loose rather than bound or stapled during the presentation.

This allows the speaker to slide them aside quietly during the talk.

If the speaker prefers to work from an outline or a series of note cards, then these can be prepared in a similar manner.

Audiovisual Materials

The decision as to whether to use audiovisual aids and the specific aids selected depend on the speaker's style and subject. An exhaustive review of audiovisual devices to assist presentations is beyond the scope of this chapter. However, a few principles and suggestions warrant inclusion. Visual aids are used much more commonly than audio aids. The two most common types of visual aids are handouts and slides.

Handouts

Handouts vary from a brief outline of the material presented to a word-for-word transcription of the talk. They may include a bibliography of sources that amplify the material presented. All handouts should have a definite purpose. That purpose will determine the time of distribution, the length of the handout, and the size of the print. In general, if the speaker intends to refer to the handouts during the presentation, they should be prepared in large, bold type that can be read in dim light. Pages should be numbered, and each item should be marked for easy reference. Naturally, under these circumstances, handouts should be distributed prior to the presentation. It is often helpful to have figures in the handouts duplicated on slides for the speaker's use.

If the handouts will not be referred to, they will only distract the listener's attention away from the presentation. Under such circumstances, the handouts should be distributed after the presentation. This is also advisable when the handouts duplicate the speech. If handouts are distributed in advance by the host of a conference and a speaker wishes to prevent them from distracting his audience, the speaker should direct the room lights to be turned all the way down, so that the audience cannot see the handouts. This nullifies their potentially distracting effect and encourages the audience to focus its attention on the speaker. It is often helpful to supplement brief outlines with suggested readings. All handouts should include the speaker's name and address, so that listeners can write for additional advice, information, or to invite the speaker for future presentations.

Slides

Slide projectors are available in most lecture halls, and slides can be easily stored, transported, and seen when properly prepared. A well-organized slide lecture highlights important concepts for the audience, serves as an outline for the speaker, and projects figures important to the talk. Each slide projected should have a specific purpose. In general, a speaker can rarely use effectively more than approximately one slide per minute.

Slides should be prepared in bold type and are usually unreadable if they exceed six lines. Limiting each slide to four or five lines is recommended. As a rule of thumb, it should be possible for the speaker to read each slide held toward a room light at arm's length. If this is not possible, the slide will generally not project well in a large hall. In addition to being easy to read, slides generally should be easy to look at. Diazos, the standard white-on-blue slides, can be made inexpensively and are much easier on the eye than is typed print on a white background. Computer-generated slides are also relatively easy and inexpensive if the speaker has access to the necessary hardware and software. Slides should always be numbered, so that, if a slide tray is spilled at the last moment, the lecture can be reorganized. It is also advisable for the speaker to put his or her name on each slide, especially when the speaker does not use his or her own carousel. Whenever possible, the speaker should bring the slides already inserted in the carousel and checked in advance for order and position. In this case, the speaker's name should appear on the outside of the carousel. It is important to inquire in advance as to whether a standard carousel projector is available and whether front projection or rear projection will be used. In rear projection, the slides must be turned around from their usual position. When one is traveling, slides should always be carried with the speaker, not checked through airplane, ship, or train luggage. This is true for any important visual or auditory aid.

In some cases, dual projection (use of two projectors at the same time) may be desirable. When needed, both sets of slides should be numbered, so that the projectors can be easily coordinated (for example, slide IA in one projector, lB in the second projector). If slides will be shown on only one projector during the middle of the talk, it is advisable to match them with blank slides in the second projector. Keeping the same number of slides in both projectors decreases the risk of losing synchronization between the two projectors.

Transparencies

In general, transparencies are not as good as slides. They may work fairly well in a small classroom, but in large halls they are difficult to see and frequently look as if they have been made just moments before the lecture. If a speaker wishes to use transparencies to draw a figure and show the development of a concept or design, this can be done equally well (usually better) by a sequence of prepared slides. Transparencies are not significantly easier to make or cheaper than well-prepared slides, and their use should be discouraged.

Videotape

Videotape has become extremely popular and is a fine teaching tool. To be effective in a public presentation, it must be well-made, neatly edited, and self-sufficient. It is undesirable for the speaker to have to talk over the video in order for its message to be understood. In addition, there must be enough high-quality monitors in the auditorium to allow easy viewing by everyone in the audience. If the subject of the videotape is highly detailed, as may occur with microsurgery or histologic slides, numerous high-quality monitors often provide better resolution than projection video, and front projection usually provides better resolution than rear projection. It is important to be certain that the speaker's video format is compatible with the auditorium's equipment. This is a special concern if the speaker is presenting in a foreign country.

Film

With the advent of videotape, 16 mm sound movie projection has become less popular. However, this medium still provides excellent audio and video reproduction, and it may be preferable in some cases. Movie projection is especially useful if the speaker is required to use one central screen in a large room.

Pointers

Pointers are designed to direct the attention of the audience to specific items on the visual aids. If a mechanical pointer is being used, it is imperative to be sure that it is long enough to reach the top of the projected images and that the microphone and slide controls are long enough to allow the speaker to get close enough to the screen to point. When using electrically lit pointers, the arrow should be focused in advance of the presentations; and the speaker should make sure that the pointer is bright enough to be seen from the back of the room. Laser pointers are now used most commonly. They, too, should be checked for visibility. In any case, pointers should be used only for their intended purpose. The speaker must avoid the tendency to tap mechanical pointers, or flash electric or laser pointers randomly. These gestures are distracting, and diminish the effect of the pointers when they are used appropriately at other times during the lecture.

Audiotapes

Talks are often enhanced by the playing of audiotapes, but effective audio reproduction requires as much thought, planning, and equipment as videotape or film. Generally, playing an audio sample from a pocket cassette recorder through a podium microphone is ineffective. Such demonstrations are usually difficult to hear or understand, the sound is distorted, and they appear improvised. If audio samples are important to a talk, arrangements should be made in advance for high-quality audio playback equipment. The tapes should be cued for the sound engineer, and short leaders of known time duration should be placed between audio samples. If it will be necessary to turn tapes on and off several times during the presentation, it is helpful to put an audio signal (such as beep) at the end of each sample, so that the sound engineer will know when to turn the tape off. The next sample should come approximately 10 sec after the beep, allowing adequate time for the sound engineer to react and turn the tape recorder off, and for the tape recorder to be turned on and resume steady speed before the next example is heard. Either cassettes or reel-to-reel tapes may be used, but reel tapes can be repaired and played again more easily if they are damaged during a presentation. It is advisable to bring a backup copy and to bring both formats if equipment arrangements have not been confirmed.

Warm-up and Preparatory Exercises

Approximately 1 month before the presentation, effective presenters will begin an exercise regimen to get the voice primed for performance. A simple but demanding physical/vocal warm-up done on a regular basis (every day for at least 3 weeks before performance) will get body alignment, breathing, and voice in condition to present research and opinion in the manner they deserve. Use of such a warm-up can make the difference between a bland, forgettable rendering of a presentation and a dynamic delivery of the materials in a way that will more than do them justice.

The following series of exercises is divided into four parts. It is important that they are done regularly. Doing them all with attention to the sensations experienced as they are done will produce the most noticeable results. These exercises are very helpful if done correctly, but they may be difficult to master from written descriptions alone. Speakers interested in per-

fecting these skills will benefit from a few sessions with a performance coach or from a public speaking workshop such as those offered by Executive Performance in Training Centers.[5] If pressed for time, the presenter should select and do at least one exercise in each of the four categories. As they are done, it is important to make them enjoyable rather than hard work.

I. General Relaxation and Energizing

The first category of exercises can serve to relax a speaker on days he or she is feeling tight or tense and to energize a speaker on days he or she is feeling weary or spent. If the speaker will take a moment to scan the body to ascertain physical and psychological state, then he or she will know best which exercises need to be emphasized and how much time to spend with each.

A. Full-body yawns, physically stretching out in all directions. Loosen belt and/or tie if necessary to give the stretches full excursion. Yawns should be genuine and not mere tokens.

B. Gentle shaking in many different areas of the body in order to loosen tension or to energize: hands, arms, shoulders, legs, small of the back, and so on. (Some individuals prefer energetic dancing to music, jumping rope, yoga, or stair climbing.)

II. Breathing and Alignment

If there are any back problems that restrict flexibility or make certain movements uncomfortable, the exercises below can and should be modified accordingly.

A. Extended breathing out and then softening the belly to initiate effortless inhalation without any shoulder involvement. Allow the air out again easily and completely but without postural collapse. This can be done on just breath or with full sound (haaaaaaaaahhhhhhh). Repeat slowly and enjoyably a half-dozen times and notice the calming and energizing effect.

B. Place the palms of the hands on the rib cage (without tensing the shoulders in order to do so) to encourage rib flexibility during inhalation and exhalation. During inhalation, allow the ribs to move out in the direction of the palms of the hands. During exhalation, use the palms of the hands to encourage the ribs to move back in, but without any postural collapse in the spine. Repeat slowly four to five times, then drop the arms and shoulders heavily at the sides and enjoy the free movement of the rib cage when not inhibited by the pressure of the hands.

C. Slowly roll down through the spine, leading with the head and relaxing over with knees slightly bent, going only as far down as is comfortable. Slowly and comfortably "rebuild" the spinal column, initiating the upward movement by pressing the soles of the feet into the floor and releasing the legs out of the hip joints, making sure that the head is the last thing to be added to the upright spinal column. Repeat three to four times until the body fully appreciates the connection between the feet and the head and moves as one connected and coordinated unit with no sharp division. Use full breaths to help maintain the sensation of internal space.

III. Top Quarter of the Body

A. Intertwine the fingers of both hands and place them on the back of the skull. Without tensing the shoulders or holding the breath, pull forward with the elbows and back with the head steadily for about 20 to 30 seconds. Release the isometric pull and enjoy the freedom that results in the cervical area of the spine.

B. With hands on shoulders, allow elbows to touch in front and to approach each other in back. Repeat until the muscles facilitating this activity fatigue just a bit. With hands on shoulders, "flap your wings" slowly until the muscles involved fatigue slightly. With hands on shoulders, allow elbows to make large, full circles first forward and then backward until muscles fatigue. Lift and drop shoulders easily until muscles fatigue somewhat. Notice any changes that may occur in your ability to breathe freely.

C. Stand tall through the spine with shoulders relaxed and spread. Reach your right hand across the chest to your left shoulder and firmly massage the band of muscles that extends from the shoulder to the base of the neck. If any knots are present, gently knead them and coax the tension to melt away, helping with free and easy breathing throughout. Repeat this activity on the other side.

D. With your face continuing to remain forward instead of facing either shoulder, use a slow, even count of 16 to complete one full head roll to the right, enjoying an easy relaxing stretch in each direction through which the head passes as it makes a single rotation. Reverse, making a full, slow rotation to the left. This can be repeated a few times, keeping the rolls slow and easy and the breath moving throughout.

E. With the heels of the hands, use even, steady pressure right in front of the ears as you make big circles releasing and relaxing the jaw on both sides. If the urge to yawn occurs, so much the better. Allow the hands to slide down the jaw on both sides, toward the chin, easing the jaw down as they do so. Yawn again to feel the deep relaxation. Use the thumbs on either side of the face, in the vicinity of the molars, to locate and firmly press into the masseter muscles. Continue the pressure while breathing deeply for about 30 sec

before releasing the thumbs and enjoying the freedom and release in the jaw itself. (This exercise can be repeated anytime during the day when the jaw is feeling held and tight.)

F. Move the tongue around in the mouth to loosen it up. Use it to count the teeth, or stick it out in the direction of the nose, the right ear, the chin, and the left ear. With a loose, relaxed jaw, move just the tongue from top lip to bottom lip to top lip to bottom lip as you say or sing, la-la-la-la-la-la-lala-la-laaaahhhh.

G. Move the different parts of the face around slowly and quickly. Stand in front of a mirror, if necessary, to make sure that movement is actually taking place: eyebrows, eyes, bridge of nose, nostrils, cheeks, lips. See whether you can appear very surprised, very happy, very angry. Repeat these manipulations easily, without holding the breath until, the muscles being used are a bit fatigued.

IV. Voice and Speech

A. Drop the jaw, take a breath, and release a long sigh, which starts high and finishes low in the pitch range (haaaaaahhhh). Repeat three to four times, each time starting just a bit higher in pitch and finishing a bit lower without allowing the voice to either screech or growl. Explore the full extent of available range.

B. Use the fingers to rub and stimulate the face gently. Unfurrow the brow and relax the jaw. With the hands gently covering the cheeks and eyes and the lips gently touching, hum directly into the palms of the hands, feeling and enjoying the vibrations produced by the voice. Allow the pitches to move up and down while continuing to rub the face and hum. Then drop the hands and feel the vibrations in the bones of the face and skull instead of in the palms of the hands as the humming continues.

C. With the jaw relaxed (mouth open) and the tip of the tongue gently tucked behind the bottom front teeth, raise and lower the back of the tongue in order to move easily from "ng" (as in sing) to "aaaahhhhh," keeping the sound forward. This combination can be either spoken or sung, but primary vibration of sound should ideally move from the nose to the mouth as the sounds alternate. Repeat enough times to make this comfortable.

D. Use full and steady breath from the midsection as you call out easily on full voice: "Hey, Joe! O.K.! Hello! How are you?"

E. Use a combination of different tongue twisters to help train the articulators to move more efficiently: red leather, yellow leather, blue leather; nuclear regulatory commission; blue-backed blackbird; delectable delicacy, and so on. (A number of bookstores carry collections of enjoyable tongue twisters. Some children's books [e.g., the Dr. Seuss series] are quite useful in this regard as well.)

The more often these exercises are done attentively, the easier they become. They are representative of a far greater range of warm-up and developmental exercises available to the presenter who wishes to build the voice into an effective and expressive communication tool.

Final Rehearsal and Preparation

Approximately 2 weeks before performance, the opening sentence, the closing sentence, and any key ideas or quotations that would benefit from direct eye contact with the audience should be memorized.

The speech should be rehearsed at least once a day, until the presenter is very familiar and comfortable with its contents, its structure, and any accompanying visual materials to be included.

If possible in the final week of preparation, the presentation should be rehearsed with a podium, at a microphone, and/or to a camera. The more the presenter can simulate the actual conditions under which the speech will be delivered, the fewer surprises will occur when the speech actually takes place. If someone can videotape a performance of the presentation, the presenter can use it to make any necessary corrections or adjustments in either content or style.

About 1 week before the presentation, the speaker should add two important exercises to the warm-up regimen:

1. *Visualization.* Sit or lie down, do some deep breathing to relax your muscles, and focus your concentration; then imagine you are watching yourself giving the presentation perfectly—without a hitch from beginning to end. Include details, colors, emotions throughout; take your time. Get into the habit of envisioning it perfectly done so that the actual performance is a simple, direct repetition of a task already mastered.

2. *Directing Energy.* People who suffer "stage fright" often describe a sensation of self-consciousness. All those eyes focused right on the speaker can be intimidating if the presenter does not know how to direct that energy. As the speaker continues to practice the presentation, he or she should imagine the audience as a large slice of pie, which can be divided into six different sections. No matter how large an audience may be, it may help the speaker to remember that each person seated in that audience is only one human being. Instead of speaking to an undefined mass of faces, the speaker can think of presenting to a series of individuals seated in different locations throughout the audience. Figures 24–1 and 24–2 indicate possible "traffic

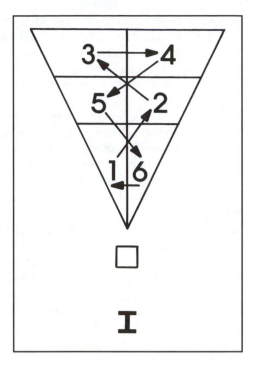

Fig 24–1. Practiced, planned patterns of eye contact help assure that members of the audience will feel as if they are being spoken to personally. This figure contains one suggested eye-contact pattern that is particularly well suited to relatively narrow and/or deep auditoriums.

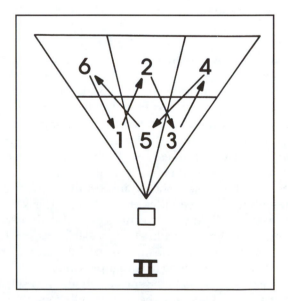

Fig 24–2. This alternate pattern of eye contact may be better suited in a shallow and/or wide auditorium than that illustrated in Fig 24–1.

patterns" for eye contact. If the speaker allows his or her gaze to linger with a specific individual for the length of a sentence or two and then to travel from section one to section two and so forth during transitions, then these individuals feel themselves an important part of the event rather than merely present. Any speaker who learns to make genuine rather than token eye contact with specific individuals in each section of the audience invites participation and interest in the presentation; he or she succeeds in making those present actual participants in the event. An act of communication demands not only a sender but an implied or actual recipient of the message.

Furthermore, stage fright and self-consciousness can be dramatically lessened if and when the speaker shifts attention away from the self and to the members of the audience. If the speaker gives full attention to the receivers (Are they paying attention? Are they understanding what I am saying? Do they need me to repeat that statement or to slow down a bit? Am I loud enough for the people in the back?), the focus of attention shifts from the self to them, and the task of communicating is that much more enjoyable.

During this final stage of rehearsal, a room of decent size should be used, in which should be placed three or four individual listeners, each sitting in a different section. After the presentation, the speaker can check with each listener to make sure he or she felt as though all present were being talked to rather than at. In the absence of cooperative helpers, the speaker can place specific objects in different locations in the room (a trash bin, a coffee mug on a seat, a sweater over another chair, etc.) and make sure really to see each object in turn.

Reading the Room

It is extremely helpful for any speaker to assess the room or hall prior to speaking. While this may not be quite so critical for the physician presenting research results through a microphone as it is for a singer presenting an unamplified recital, the comfort gained from the mistakes avoided is comparable. Whenever possible, the speaker should inspect the room before presenting: during a coffee break or lunch break or on a previous day. Any inconvenience is worth the effort. If this inspection is absolutely impossible, the speaker may gain some of the necessary information by observing and listening to earlier presenters.

In assessing a room, the speaker should investigate acoustics (Can speakers be heard well from all portions of the room?), type of microphones available, room temperature, availability of water, lighting on

the podium, availability of a pointer, placement of projector controls, number and position of stairs leading to the stage, location of the nearest bathroom for possible use shortly before presentation, presence and quality of projectors, type of projection (front versus rear screen), location and operation of lighting controls, and presence or absence of a stage manager and projectionist. Familiarizing oneself with these matters can prevent numerous embarrassing moments. If the presentation is long and there is no water available, the speaker can place a glass of water under the podium before the audience arrives. If a fixed microphone is used, the speaker must be prepared to maintain a reasonably constant mouth-to-microphone distance and direction. With fixed microphones (such as those attached to a podium), the microphone needs to be adjusted immediately prior to the speech. It should be approximately at chin level (no higher) and should be no more than four to six inches away from the speaker's face. Whenever possible, it should be tested prior to the arrival of the audience.

If a lavaliere microphone is used, the speaker must remember not to brush the microphone cord by putting his or her hands into pockets and not to brush papers across the microphone. If a wireless microphone is used, the speaker should be certain to turn it off at the end of the presentation. There are many stories, humorous to everyone except the speaker, of presenters who have left microphones on during bathroom breaks or exceedingly frank conversations about previous speakers or hosts of the event. Many high-quality wireless microphones work well even through walls!

If a stage manager or projectionist is provided, the speaker should introduce him- or herself ahead of time. These colleagues can greatly facilitate the smooth flow of the performance. They are used to being ignored by most speakers. However, they generally appreciate and deserve a little recognition. Taking a few moments prior to presentation to discuss one's needs or at least shake hands is worthwhile.

Occasionally, disasters occur. Some of them can be anticipated. For example, the author (RTS) depends heavily on slides for many presentations. Consequently, he generally travels with a carousel replacement bulb and pointer; sometimes with a remote slide changer; and with a projector when speaking in a nonacademic building where audiovisual arrangements are questionable. However, any speaker should be prepared, in the event of major problems, to proceed with no amplification or visual aids at all.

Room temperature can also be a potent detriment to good delivery. If the air conditioning is turned up so high that the speaker is shivering, the audience will perceive this as nervousness. Identifying this problem in advance allows the speaker to dress appropriately and/or have the room temperature adjusted. At the opposite extreme, a room that is too hot or stuffy can make the audience uncomfortable enough to lessen the effectiveness of even the best speaker; adequate ventilation may make all the difference to his/her success.

Delivering the Speech

On the day of the performance, the speaker should make sure he or she is rested and physically comfortable. Shoes should be comfortable, breathing should not be restricted by either belt or collar, and even new clothing should have been tested in advance to ensure that the speaker will be com-fortable performing whatever range of movement is called for during the presentation. Time should be allowed for a concentrated, uninterrupted warm-up and a visualization of the presentation perfectly performed. The speaker should make sure not to overeat before speaking and should drink enough water to maintain a good level of hydration without unduly taxing the kidneys and bladder in the process.

If there are a series of speakers in one program and/or the introduction is lengthy, there are some "hidden" warm-up activities that can be done in the interim: easy, gentle head and neck movement; small sips of water; moving the tongue easily around the mouth; releasing the jaw with lips closed; deep, easy breathing through the nose into the midsection of the body; finding supportive friends in the audience.

Finally, there is a "trick" that a number of successful speakers use to increase their degree of comfort during a presentation. They think of someone who loves their work, who thinks they can do no wrong; who is an ardent fan; and, in their imaginations, they bring this friend right into the audience they are about to address. It can be a young son, a grandmother who is no longer alive, or even a family dog. The speaker can just place this admirer in the audience and allow unqualified approval to inspire a confidence and ease that might otherwise be elusive.

During the presentation, the body should be fully erect but loose and easy rather than tight and held. Remembering to breathe easily and fully will be of great assistance in this regard. The speaker's feet should be slightly apart (one may be a few inches in front of the other), the weight should be forward over the metatarsal heads, the knees should be unlocked, and the speaker should be well balanced. This is an athletic "ready" stance, not far different from that seen in a shortstop or other athlete prepared to perform. It is also approximately the same position used in recital by classical singers.

The podium should not be used as a weight-bearing surface but rather as a script holder. A few gestures, all of which are directly related to the content of the material, are all that is needed. Constant shifting of weight from one leg to another and arbitrarily waving one's arms needlessly in the air simply serve to communicate the speaker's general discomfort and lack of real communication skills to the audience members. If the speaker makes genuine eye contact with specific people in different locations in the audience at the beginning of the speech, at key times during the speech, and again at the end, then there is a real sense of significant communication taking place.

Instead of simply twisting the head at the neck, if the speaker can face different sections of the audience at different times during the speech with the whole body (keeping the microphone between him- or herself and the audience at all times), then a sense of real commitment to what one is saying is effectively and easily transmitted, and the head and trunk of the body are both in a better position to produce free breathing and a well-produced vocal sound. If the voice has been well prepared and exercised enough to respond easily and fully—in terms of pitch, loudness, rhythm, pause, quality—to the content of the speech, then what is being said by the speaker is wonderfully augmented by how the content is being transmitted. Finally, if the speaker can avoid any sense of collapse or visible relief when the speech is over— if, instead, he or she can make the final point, reestablish real eye contact with specific individuals, and then accept and acknowledge applause and reaction—then the delivery will be at least as remarkable as the content itself. Such techniques not only maximize a speaker's communicative impact but also help to minimize both the physical and the psychological stresses related to public speaking. Learning to present comfortably and effectively in person can make sharing one's research and opinions both healthy and enjoyable.

Summary

Most professional voice users, educators, executives, and many others from all walks of life are required to give oral presentations from time to time. Most people benefit from acquisition of specific skills and training. Preparation of written materials, use of audiovisual aids, performance preparation, and vocal preparation must all be considered.

Review Questions

1. Ideally, materials for a major oral presentation should be available to the speaker no later than:
   a. 24 hours before the presentation
   b. 1 week before the presentation
   c. 2 weeks before the presentation
   d. 1 month before the presentation

2. Channel relaxation and energizing exercises include each of the following except:
   a. full body yawns
   b. gentle shaking
   c. shoulder rolls
   d. all of the above
   e. none of the above

3. Which of the following are helpful in preparing for an oral presentation?
   a. memorizing the first and last paragraph
   b. tape recording the speech for repeated play in the weeks prior to delivery
   c. assessing the room in which the speech will be delivered
   d. all of the above
   e. none of the above

4. For speakers who are not comfortable making eye contact with individuals in the audience, practiced, planned patterns of audience eye contact should be utilized.
   a. true
   b. false

5. If a speech is to be read rather than memorized or delivered "off the cuff," structurally rewriting the text often enhances delivery.
   a. true
   b. false

References

1. Eisenson J. *Voice and Diction: A Program for Improvement.* 5th ed. New York: Macmillan; 1985.
2. Fisher HB. *Improving Voice and Articulation.* 2nd ed. Boston: Houghton Mifflin, 1975.
3. Machlin E. *Speech for the Stage.* New York: Theatre Arts Books; 1966.
4. Wilder L. *Professionally Speaking.* New York: Simon & Schuster; 1986.
5. Executive Performance In Training Center (EPIC), 1721 Pine Street, Philadelphia, PA, 19103, (215) 735-3742.

25

The Singing Teacher in the Age of Voice Science

Richard Miller

What should a responsible voice teacher be teaching in a scientific age? Perhaps we should recall William Faulkner's opinion that the past is all that anyone living in whatever age actually has. What a responsible voice teacher does in this scientific age is not really different from what responsible voice teachers have been doing over several centuries, most of which have been replete with people who considered themselves enlightened and "scientific." Still, in light of recent expansion in knowledge and technology, it seems particularly important in the 1990s for singing teachers to be cognizant of developments in related fields and their potential to enhance teaching.

There is a prevalent opinion that, in past centuries, singers had little interest in science. That viewpoint is not supported by historical review. Consider, for example, the following description of respiration in singing:

The ribs raise outwardly, and ... the diaphragm ... descends and compresses the abdomen .... For good expiration ... air must be made to leave with more or less force, with more or less volume, according to the character of the song.l

Those words were written not by Bouhuys in the 1970s, nor by Hixon in the 1980s, but by Jean-Baptiste Berard in 1755. Similarly, current interests in the study of vowel tracking were preceded by generations of interest in acoustic adjustments, as expressed by Mancini in 1774.[2]

If the harmony of ... the mouth and "fauces" is perfect, then the voice will be clear and harmonious. But if these organs act discordantly, the voice will be defective, and consequently the singing spoiled.

Manual Garcia, inventor of the laryngeal mirror and a renowned singing teacher, clearly appreciated the practical importance of scientific knowledge about the voice. His comments of 1847 could easily have been written today[3]:

The capacity of the vocal cords to vibrate, the dimensions of the larynx, the thorax, the lungs, the pharyngeal, buccal and nasal cavities, the disposition of these cavities to resonate, constitute the absolute power of the voice of an individual .... The singer, in order to dominate the material difficulties of his art, must have a thorough knowledge of the mechanism of all these pieces to the point of isolating or combining their action according to the need.

A case could be made that teachers of singing have always wanted to know how the instrument functions. Certainly, both the great Lampertis made use of then-current scientific information. In the 20th century, such noted voice teachers as Marchesi, Shakespeare, Bachner, Herman Klein, Bartholomew, Mills, Curtis, Plunkett Greene, Witherspoon, Frank Miller, Clippinger, Martienssen-Lohman, Stanley, Westerman, Coffin, Appelman, and Vennard (the list could be greatly expanded) have called on factual information in support of pedagogical tenets. Rather than being new, interest in the available factual information characterizes the mainstream of historical vocal pedagogy.

We should not fool ourselves, however, into believing that what generally takes place today in vocal studios is based on intimate acquaintance with the current literature of science. Most teachers of singing give a nod of approval to the helpful scientist, and exhibit tolerance and indulgence toward those who want to play with machines, but, deep down in our hearts, we "know" that singing and teaching are matters of "instinct" and "artistry," and that there is no real possibility of improving on what Madame X handed down to Maestro Y, who in turn gave it unadulterated to my teacher.

Comparative vocal pedagogy reveals an immense stratified structure of both fact and nonsense. There exist systems of vocal technique built on assumptions without foundation in fact. Several brief illustrations will suffice: a world-renowned premier tenor recently explained during a master class that the vowel /i/ was the only vowel narrow enough to enter the frontal sinuses, while a rival tenor who occupies the very pinnacle of the heap informed his master class participants (while demonstrating slight laryngeal descent on inspiration) that, for the "open throat," the epiglottis must be held low at all times. A third noted artist advised "squeezing the uvula with the tonsils." Results from students trying to apply such advice were just short of disastrous.

What should today's voice teacher be doing in the studio? In any age, the main duties of a teacher of singing, with regard to technique, have always been chiefly to (a) analyze vocal problems and (b) design proper solutions for them. It is a pleasure to have students who exhibit few vocal problems, but teaching such pupils is not really teaching voice so much as it is sophisticated coaching and performance preparation. The teacher who helps the less natural singer establish a solid technical basis is a real voice teacher. The potential of the student must be discovered and technical means offered for rectifying problems impeding fine performance. How can this be done?

One choice is to try to pass on to the student what the teacher has learned about his or her own instrument. However, no teacher of singing has personally experienced all the possible forms of uncoordinated function that are exhibited daily in every active studio. In attempting to communicate impressions, instincts, and sensations through impressionistic, instinctive, and descriptive language, the teacher may not communicate the concrete information that the student requires.

Another choice is to teach by modeling—by imitation. If a teacher can demonstrate a beautifully free vocal sound, one may gain some insight into how it is produced. If the teacher has been a great singer, an astute student may glean certain subtle aspects of style and even a little technique. If the teacher is an over-the-hill opera diva, one may also pick up some tendencies it might be better not to have picked up. If a teacher has never mastered his or her own instrument sufficiently to be professionally useful, the student may be in real trouble when he or she models the master's voice!

It is important for the teacher to have a basic knowledge of bodily function and vocal acoustics and to be able to explain what students are doing wrong and why, in whatever language is necessary to reach any individual student. The *main* prerequisite for teaching singing today is none of the following: a fabulous ear, excellent musicianship, highly refined taste, a bubbling personality, goodwill, or a successful singing career, although *all* of these factors are helpful. The main prerequisite is to know what is malfunctioning in a singing voice and how to correct it. It is foolhardy to think one can reach a wise and consistently accurate assessment and resolution if one does not know something about how the vocal machine operates.

How much scientific information does the voice teacher need? As much as he or she can get. There is a growing, credible body of information to help the voice teacher understand what is really happening to a singer's voice, what various exercises can and should be done, and the real intent of the images used traditionally in voice teaching. In addition, learning such information increases the teacher's vocabulary, providing new language for those students in whom traditional constructs have not worked. There exists a fair battery of helpful scientific instrumentation that provides some exact information on singing. It includes a number of electronic devices. The spectrum analyzer tells us much about what singers describe as "resonance." The fiberscope and the electroglottograph also provide new possibilities.[4] (Studio uses of instrumentation are discussed in greater detail in chapters 8 and 28.)

Unfortunately, many of the physiological explanations put forth in the voice studio are still surprising to all but those of us who are singers, and most "acoustic" explanations are pure fantasy. Yet, as soon as a teacher of singing requests alteration in vocal sound, he or she is dealing in physiology and acoustics. However, unlike the car mechanic, the voice teacher is not dealing simply with a mechanically complex instrument. Knowing how the voice functions has never yet produced a great teacher of singing. A fine teacher combines mechanistic information with the psychological and the aesthetic.

Once having chosen to pursue such a complex profession and accept the enormous responsibility (and liability) for a student's vocal health and longevity, to rely entirely on imagery is to saddle oneself with a serious handicap. For example, when the relative amplitudes of overtones in the voice do not produce the particular goal the teacher has in mind, how much helpful information is conveyed by requesting, "Put more space around the tone"? Although a teacher has a distinct tonal concept in mind, the student putting "space around the tone" may make alterations to the acoustic tract, to the laryngeal position, and in airflow rate that have no relationship to a teacher's tonal aesthetic. Trying to "sing on the breath," "spin the tone," "place the tone in the forehead," "send it up and over," and so on, will, without doubt, have immediate influence on resulting timbre. By hit and miss, the teacher and student may finally get what the teacher wants. Persons using divining rods have also been known to locate underlying groundwater.

Today's singing teacher has access to a greater body of solid information and rational tools than ever before. We owe it to our students to be able to take advantage not only of everything that was known 200 years ago, but also of everything that is known today.

The advice of Bartholomew,[5] a pioneer in the study of the acoustics of the singing voice, still is appropriate:

Imagery should be used merely to suggest indirectly through its psychological effects a certain muscular setting which is awkward for the beginner. The teacher, though using it, should bear in mind at all times the true facts, because when imagery becomes so vivid that it is transferred into the physical field and used to explain physiologic and acoustic phenomenon, it becomes extremely dubious, unreliable, and even false. It is this misuse which is largely responsible for the bitter controversies over vocal methods, as well as for their often comical explanations. Furthermore, since imagery is largely individual and thus variable, when it is trusted as a physical explanation, the so- called "True Method" becomes as variable as the individual temperament, instead of as stable as Truth is usually expected to be.

It is the responsibility of the singing teacher in a scientific age to interpret and expand vocal traditions through the means of current analysis so that the viable aspects of tradition can be communicated in a systematic way. The advantage of teaching singing in the era of the voice scientist is that today's teacher has the means of sorting through what is offered, both historically and currently, at the vocal pedagogy smorgasbord, and of choosing rationally what is most nutritious, while discarding the garbage, of which there is plenty.

How can emerging information for use in the studio be expanded? Singers of stature should be willing to cooperate in noninvasive investigations of the singing voice. To make such information useful, various schools and techniques of singing should tee identified in research reports. Participants should not all be indiscriminately lumped together as "professional singers," nor should students, even at graduate level, be designated professional opera singers in published reports. The subtle individual properties that set one voice apart from another should not be averaged out.

For scientific research to be valid and have practical value in the studio, teachers of singing must be involved, knowledgeable, and interested. Our input, in areas of expertise best understood by voice teachers, is essential.

Unless it is recognized that a number of separate techniques of singing exist, conclusions reached in studies about singers need to be read cautiously. There is little doubt, for example, that if five baritones studying with Dr. X have been taught to modify the vowel /ʌ/ to the vowel /o/ at the pitch B_3, spectral analysis will reveal changes in the region of vowel definition at that point. It cannot, therefore, be concluded that professional baritones modify /ʌ/ to /o/ at the pitch B_3, but only that baritones involved in the study who have been taught that particular method have learned their lesson well. Singing teachers must learn to read studies critically, so that the lessons they learn are the correct ones. They must also learn enough to know what kind of studies to seek out. For example, although perceptual studies are necessary, singing teachers really want to know more about how the vocal instrument produces the timbres singing voices are capable of making. They already hear those timbres. They need practical information on the mechanisms so it can be applied in the studio.

Much of what goes on in the vocal studio today is extraneous activity, or even counterproductive. This is true in the teaching of all athletic skills (of which singing is one). For example, in discussing sports biomechanics in 1984, Abraham[6] reported:

Analysis of high-speed films of elite performers has led to many interesting observations. Baseball pitchers, for instance, have been apparently wasting much time in the past strengthening their wrist flexor muscles to improve speed of their pitches. Research at the University of Arizona has revealed that the wrist "snap," which does contribute heavily to the speed of the pitched ball, is actually caused by the sudden deceleration of the forearm and occurs so fast that the wrist flexor muscles cannot even keep up, much less contribute to the motion.

Many exercises thought to strengthen or relax the musculature of singing may have no more relationship to actual function than do those for the major league pitcher mentioned above. Learning to "relax," or to "energize," or to "strengthen" certain muscles of the face, neck, and torso may have little to do with singing, yet some vocal instruction is largely directed to such activities.

A main goal of teaching in this and any age should be to do no harm. Every aspect of vocal technique must be in agreement with what is known about healthy vocal function. Any teacher assuming responsibility for a student's artistic and vocal health is obligated to educate him- or herself in the wisdom of a wide community of experts. There is no such thing as a unique vocal method or a unique teacher of singing. It is not necessary for each student and each teacher to rediscover the art of singing alone. There is a body of information that ought to be drawn on by anyone who claims to teach anything to anybody. No one can know it all, but we must be willing to modify what we do know as information expands. Demythologizing the language of vocal pedagogy is part of that process. Consultation with experts in related disciplines, through reading and offering our professional services to help discover new information, is another. Above all, as teachers of singing in a scientific age, we must ask ourselves how much we really know about the subject matter we deal with. Do we have facts, or do we rely on anecdotal opinions? Do we know the literature of our own field, as well as that of related fields?

Singing today is not a dying art. It is very much alive and growing. At this moment, it occupies an advantageous position where the traditions of the past and the information of the present can be combined in an exciting way. The responsibility, excitement, and reward of our profession lie in rising to the challenges of new opportunities to make the present and future of voice teaching even greater than the past.

Summary

For centuries, there have been singing teachers who consider themselves enlightened and "scientific." Because of recent dramatic scientific advances, it is especially important for singing teachers to be cognizant of developments in related fields, and their potential to enhance teaching. A growing body of credible information is available to help voice teachers understand what is really happening to a singer's voice, what various exercises can and should be done, and the real intent of the images traditionally used in voice teaching. It is the responsibility of the voice teacher in a scientific age to interpret and expand the vocal traditions through the means of current analysis so that the viable aspects of tradition can be communicated in a systematic way.

Review Questions

1. In past centuries, singers and teachers relied upon tradition and had little interest in science.
   a. true
   b. false

2. A singing teacher should have a:
   a. basic knowledge of bodily functions and vocal acoustics
   b. familiarity with traditional imagery of the voice studio
   c. scientific understanding of the intent of the imagery
   d. all of the above
   e. none of the above

3. Too much scientific information damages voice training and should be avoided by singing teachers.
   a. true
   b. false

4. Most physiologic explanations traditionally put forth in the voice studio are accurately and scientifically based.
   a. true
   b. false

5. Singing teachers and their students benefit from collaboration from voice scientists and health professionals.
   a. true
   b. false

References

1. Berard JB, Murray S, trans-ed. *L'Art du chant.* Milwaukee: Pro Music Press; 1969.
2. Mancini G, Foreman R, trans. *Practical reflections on figured singing.* Champaign: Pro Music Press, 1967.
3. Garcia M. *A complete treatise on the art of singing, part one.* New York: Da Capo Press; 1983.
4. Titze I. Instrumentation for voice research. *NATS Bull.* 1983;38(5):29.
5. Bartholomew WT. *The role of imagery in voice teaching.* Proceedings of the Music Teachers National Association, 1935.
6. Abraham L. Sports biomechanics: application of high tech to Olympic engineering. *Tex Prof Engineer.* 1984; July–August:16–19.

26

Historical Overview of Vocal Pedagogy

Richard Miller

The vocal instrument does not need to be constructed; it is available for immediate use. Lodged in a physical machine, it receives its impetus from mental and spiritual parameters of human personality. Its adaptability in channeling communication is the foundation on which human civilizations are built.

The capacity to communicate through vocal sound inevitably led to the voice of singing. Singing predates all other forms of music performance. In every primitive society, a few individuals were more attuned to the inherent emotive power of voicing than were others. They are the ancestors of the solo singer. As the potentials of the singing voice became increasingly evident, techniques for the realization of enhanced vocal skills were developed and passed on.

People of all ages and cultures have crafted indigenous styles of singing. Witness the Greek tragedian searching beyond the boundaries of normal speech for the best method by which to become audible in the amphitheater (however grateful its architectural acoustic); the citharoedus accompanying himself on the lyre or cithara in public Olympic competition; David singing and playing his harp privately before distressed King Saul; the cantor leading vigorously sung ancient liturgies—the synagogue *hazan*, the mosque *muezzin*; the ascetic monk intoning initial phrases of subdued Gregorian chant; the occult shaman inciting emotive responses in his listeners; the operatic soprano and tenor bringing down the house with ringing high Cs.

In early records of secular song, the late Medieval Goliards (students who protested the moral strictures of the universities), the early Renaissance trouvères and troubadours, the Minnesingers, and the Meis-

tersingers exemplify solo balladeering. Almost no evidence exists as to how these singers executed technical aspects of their art. References to breath management, laryngeal action, and resonation (the three components of the tripartite vocal instrument) are so minimal as to be of little use in determining how vocal color was achieved. Internal evidence from existing musical fragments suggests that vocal demands seldom exceeded those of speech.

Treatises written before the 19th century restrict themselves largely to matters of style. To the 16th century and the 17th century writer, codification of performance rules was of primary concern. Even in the 18th century, technical aspects of the singing voice were only tangentially treated. Indeed, there is peril in applying information from those centuries to vocal literature general performance, because much of what was written about performance practice could not pertain to the singing voice. Given the structure of the vocal instrument, it is clear that a singer was never expected to match the sounds of the mechanically constructed instruments with which he performed.

Current assessments of the character of pre-19th century vocalism are largely speculative, based on personal tonal preferences that enjoy minimal scholarly documentation. Beyond general aesthetic guidelines, both pedagogic and critical period literatures reveal little as to how vocal qualities were produced. Especially regarding late vocal Baroque literature, current "historically authentic performance" most probably remains wide of the mark.

A 15th century voice-pedagogy note comes from Franchinus Gaffurius in the *Practica musicae* of 1496[1]:

Singers should not produce musical tones with a voice gaping wide in a distorted fashion or with an absurdly powerful bellowing, especially when singing at the divine mysteries; moreover they should avoid tones having a wide and ringing vibrato, since these tones do not maintain a true pitch and because their continuous wobble cannot form a balanced concord with other voices.

Clearly, for Gaffurius a wide vibrato and a bellowing voice were as common and as undesirable in his day as are broad vocal oscillations and shouting in present-day singing. He did not suggest that the singing voice should avoid natural vibrancy but that an uncontrollable vibrato was not acceptable. Graffurius offered no instruction as to how these technical errors were to be avoided.

At Venice in 1592, in his *Prattica di musica utile et necessaria si al conpositore per comporre i canti suoi regolatamente, si anco al cantore,* Ludovico Zacconi recommended continuous use of vibrato, which he termed *tremoloy*[2]:

> This tremolo should be slight and pleasing; for if it is exaggerated and forced, it tires and annoys; its nature is such that, if used at all, *it should always be used,* [italics added] since use converts it into habit. . . . it facilitates the undertaking of *passaggi* [ornamentation]; this movement . . . should not be undertaken if it cannot be done with just rapidity, vigorously and vehemently.

Bénigne de Bacilly (c. 1625–1690) in *Remarques curieuses sur l'art de bien chanter* (Paris, 1668) made a distinction between *cadence* and *tremblement.* A. B. Caswell[3] translates Bacilly's *cadence* as "vibrato," a phenomenon not to be equated with the rapid oscillatory *tremblement.* Bacilly indicated that the singer's *cadence* is a "gift of nature" that sometimes becomes too slow or too fast. The *tremblement* may produce an undesirable *voix chevrotante* (bleating or wobbling). Slow and rapid oscillations are used only as ornaments. Clearly, there was no intention of outlawing natural vibrato. For Bacilly a pretty voice "is very pleasing to the ear because of its clearness and sweetness and above all because of the nice *cadence* [here, *vibrato*] which usually accompanies it. [11]

Other treatises from the late Renaissance make frequent reference to unwanted nasality and to the common fault of singing out of tune. They insist on beauty and consistency of timbre but remain mostly silent as to how desirable vocal quality can be managed. A chief reason for lack of attention in early treatises to the training of the singing voice is that extensive individual solo artistic expression did not emerge until the close of the 16th century. Prior to the "invention of opera" by the Florentine camerata in the last years of the 16th century and the early decades of the 17th century, although replete with complex technical and musicianly demands that required high-level performance, vocal literature had largely been directed to ensemble, not soloistic concerns. It is clear that early singers were highly trained and capable of executing pyrotechnical passages for individual voices, but singing was still adjunctive to social or religious functions, taking place in monastery, chapel, cathedral, salon, or parlor. In the 17th century the individual solo singer became a public performer in his own right, exhibiting remarkable ascendancy by mid-century.

Passing references to vocal technique prior to 1600 are of limited practical value to current performers of the vocal music from those eras. Further, aesthetic tastes are by no means stable from decade to decade, let alone century to century. To achieve "authenticity" by imitating each assumed aesthetic stratum of the past, the professional singer would need to develop technical maneuvers deleterious to vocal health. It is tempting to react to the layers of stylistic information available by nostalgically looking back to some period of lost vocal perfection. It is incumbent upon today's lyric artist to distinguish among vocal styles appropriate to diverse literatures, but Herbert Witherspoon's remark[4] may provide a needed counterbalance:

> There have always been few good singers and fewer great ones so a tirade about present-day conditions in comparison with the glorious past is of no use. . . . Perhaps if we heard the singers of a century or two ago we should not care for them. . . . Our task is with today, not yesterday.

However, to understand the several current strands of today's vocal pedagogy, a knowledge of their roots is essential.

Technical prowess is essential for all solo vocal performance that goes beyond speech or folksong idioms. In order to discover and disseminate technical principles for extended tasks, the discipline of vocal pedagogy arose. Vocal pedagogy of 17th century was mostly directed to the male voice, not to the castrato and female instruments as is sometimes falsely assumed. During the 18th century, a number of treatises concerned the castrati, whose techniques, as documented by such researchers as Duey,[5] Heriot,[6] and Pleasants,[7] were clearly of the highest order. However, it is easy to overlook the fact that public esteem for the female soprano at times rivaled that afforded the castrati. During the first half of the 18th century the low female voice also gradually gained acceptance as a viable vocal instrument for the stage. Male and female larynges are affected differently by puberty. (The effects of puberty were largely avoided with the castrato.) But techniques of breath-management and articulation apply to every gender and category of singer. It is not the case that 17th- and 18th-century vocal instruction was intended only for the altered male larynx.

It is to 18th-century Italy that one must turn in tracing origins of an international vocal pedagogy capable of matching the tasks found within the vocal literature. Even today, much of the early Italian heritage remains dominant among competing national and regional schools. A brief survey of the pedagogic tenets of the historic Italian School follows.

Francesco Antonio Pistocchi (1659–1726) founded a Bolognese singing school around 1700. In pyrotechnical skill, it rivaled the proficiency of the string playing. He was the teacher of Antonio Bernacchi (c. 1690–1756), who in turn taught two of Handel's favorite castrati, Senesino and Carestini.

Another school of outstanding singers flourished under the tutelage of tenor/composer Nicola Porpora (1686–1768) at Naples, and quickly became international. The ability to sustain (*cantabile*) and to move (*cabaletta*) the voice were the pedagogic aims of the Neapolitan vocal school. (These skills became preeminent in the *cavatina/cabaletta* aria form of the following century.) Among Porpora's many successful pupils were two famous castrati, Caffarelli and Farinelli, and the highly regarded female sopranos Mingotti and Gabrielli.

Jean-Baptiste Bérard (also known as Jean-Antoine Bérard), discussing respiration for singing in his *L'art du chant* of 1755,[8] is in accord with the international Italianate School by advocating an outwardly raised ribcage, diaphragmatic descent, and controlled breath emission as technical essentials.

An early significant written source on solo vocal pedagogy[9] comes from the hand of the castrato Pier Francesco Tosi. His *Opinioni de' cantori antichi e moderni sieno osservazioni sopra il canto figurato* was first published in Bologna in 1723, when Tosi was more than 70 years old. It thereafter (1742) appeared in an English translation by a German emigrant to England, Johann Ernst Galliard, and has long been known in British and North American vocal pedagogy circles as *Observations on the Florid Song*. A German translation with commentary by J. H. Agricola, *Anleitung zur Singkunst*, was issued in 1757. Although largely concerned with the execution of embellishments such as the appoggiatura and the shake, and with the management of roulades and scales, Tosi makes general references to technical matters, but he mostly avoids specific advice. For example, with regard to breath management:

> . . . to manage his respiration . . . [the singer must] always be provided with more breath than is needful; and may avoid undertaking what, for want of it, he can not go through with.

Castrato Tosi designated the vocal registers as *voce di petto* (chest voice) and *voce di testa* (head voice) without precise advice as to how they were to be facilitated. He offered more specific information as to the effects of the articulators on the resonator tract. In keeping with the age-old Italian preference for front vowels over the back vowels in upper range, he maintained that the vowels /i/ and /e/ were less fatiguing than the vowel /a/.

Although singing technique may not have adhered to uniform instructional ideals endorsed by all, common technical threads run throughout early treatises. Despite the commonality of pedagogic viewpoints on breathing and enunciation, one is struck by the frequent complaint from renowned teachers that the rest of the pedagogic world has lost the true art of singing (reminiscent of some of today's pedagogic and critical lamentation). Tosi was not happy with the existing status of the singing art:

> Gentlemen! Masters! Italy hears no more: [1723] such exquisite voices as in times past, *particularly among the women*) [italics added], and to to the shame of the guilty I'll tell the reason. The ignorance of the parents does not allow them to perceive the badness of the voices of their children, as their necessity makes them believe, that to sing and grow rich is the same thing, and to learn music, it is enough to have a pretty face. Can you make anything of her?

Tosi's comments on the role of the performing artist as teacher of singing are as sagacious for our era as for his:

> It may seem to many, that every perfect singer must also be a perfect instructor but it is not so; for his qualifications (though ever so great) are insufficient if he cannot communicate his sentiments with ease, and in a method adapted to the ability of the student.

Giambattista Mancini is another oft-cited 18th-century source on the art of singing,[10] yet his *Pensieri, e riflessioni pratiche sopra il canto figurato* of 1774 is, as its title implies, largely devoted to practical reflections on vocal ornamentation. Mancini (b. 1714, Ascoli; d. 1800, Vienna) had studied singing with Bernacchi and must have have had a good grasp of the accepted singing techniques of the period. Much of his pedagogic comment is directed to the resonator system, with particular attention to the maintenance of natural postures of the buccal cavity, and to the smiling posture as an adjustor of the vocal tract. Berton Coffin was struck by Mancini's awareness of the variation in physiologic structure among singers:[11]

> He acknowledged that all faces differ in structure, and some are better proportioned for singing than are others; nevertheless certain positions [of the mouth] were best for a smooth, pure quality of tone, and certain positions would bring out a suffocated and crude tone (too open) or a nasal tone (too closed). He thought the Italian vowels /(a, e, o, u/ could be sung on each note in the position of a smile with the /o/ and /u/ being slightly rounded. . . . Mancini felt the /i/ vowel was difficult and should be sung in the position of a "composed smile."

Another Mancini pedagogic tenet was that in order to be distinct and executed with the greatest possible velocity, all runs and agility passages should be supported by a robust chest, assisted by graduated breath energy, and with light "fauces" [the passage from the mouth into the pharynx].

W. Crutchfield[12,p293] remarks that Domenico Corri (1746–1825) is "probably the most valuable single theorist as far the provision of practical examples is concerned." Corri's extensive variations and cadenzas on Sarti's *Lungi dal caro bene*[12,p302] is cited as an example of vocal embellishment practices of the period. E. Harris[2] quotes Corri's 1810 comment on performance and style[13]:

> The vocal art affords various characters—the sacred, the serious, the comic, anacreontic, cavatina, bravura, etc., etc.—and though each style requires different gifts and cultivation, yet true intonation, the swelling and dying of the voice, with complete articulation of words, is essential to all.

Corri suggested that the voice should increase in volume as it rises and decrease in volume when descending. However, he does not offer significant advice to a reader searching for clues on how best to accomplish the technical complexities of the vocal literature considered.

Tenor Manuel del Popolo Vincent Garcia Rodriguez (1775–1832) is known as Garci *père* to distinguish him from his son Manuel Patricio Rodriguez Garcia (1805–l906). His vocal technique book *Exercises pour la voix*[14] was published in Paris between 1819 and 1822. It was fully within the pedagogical tradition of the 18th-century Italian school. (An English translation was published in London in 1824.) One of Garcia's teachers was Giovanni Ansoni, a member of the Neapolitan singing school. Having already estab-

lished himself as a premier singer in his native country, Garcia left Spain in 1808 to build an international opera career, performing in Paris, Turin, Rome, and Naples. The role of Count Almaviva (*Il barbiere di Siviglia*, by Rossini) was written for him: it is ample evidence of the capability of Garcia *père* in executing the two major aspects of bel canto technique: sostenuto and velocity. In a brief introduction to the 340 vocalises of his technical system, Garcia *père* presents explicit pedagogic advice:

> The position of the body must be erect, the shoulders thrown back, with the arms crossed behind; this will open the chest and bring out the voice with ease, clear and strong, without distorting the appearance of either face or body.
>
> . . . .[the singer ought] never to commence singing in a hurry, always to take breath slowly and without noise, which would otherwise be unpleasant to those who listen, and injurious to the singer.
>
> . . . .The throat, teeth and lips, must be sufficiently opened so that the voice may meet with no impediment, since the want of a strict attention to either of these three is sufficient to destroy the good quality of the voice and to produce the bad one, of the throat, nose, etc.; besides, proper attention to the mouth will give that perfect and clear pronunciation indispensable to singing, and which unfortunately, few possess.

Early 19th-century Garcia *père* resides solidly in the tradition of the 18th-century Italian School. Among his pupils were his daughters (Viardot and Malibran, perhaps the most celebrated female vocal artists of the era), his son Manuel, and Adolphe Nourrit, the leading French tenor of the first half of the 19th century until the advent of Gilbert Duprez.

A thorough examination of the contribution of his son, Manuel Garcia *fils* (1805-1906), becomes all the more intriguing because much subsequent critical comment implies that the younger Garcia introduced technical directions that withdrew from previous tenets of the Italian School. When accounts of his entire teaching career are taken into consideration, it becomes doubtful that such a break with tradition took place. A case (admittedly controversial) could be made that Garcia the younger used his new knowledge of laryngeal and vocal tract anatomy and physiology to verify and enhance what he had learned from his father.

Manuel Garcia's appearance in New York at age 20 as Figaro in Rossini's *Il barbiere* (with his father as Almaviva, his sister as Rosina, and his mother as Berta) indicates that 10 years of vocal study with his father had produced a precocious baritone voice. (It also makes one question if performance standards were as high as current idealization of past vocal eras may imagine.) Garcia's strenuous performing routine while still so young (sometimes even as substitute in tenor roles for his ill father) may well have contributed to his early vocal deterioration. In any event, he was unable to emulate the performance successes of his father and his siblings, and he turned to teaching. His *Traité complet de l'art du chant*[15] appeared in 1840.

In 1841, Manuel Garcia's *Mémoire sur la voix humaine*[16] was presented to the French Academy. His growing curiosity about physical function was further sparked by anatomical observations made at military hospitals. In 1854 these interests led him to the invention of a primitive laryngoscope. (Note that it was a voice teacher, not a physician, who first saw the vocal folds in action during spoken and sung phonations.)

Garcia devised register terminology with the designations Chest Voice, Falsetto Voice, and Head Voice, based on physiologic information and practical knowledge of then-current performance practice. These registration divisions are confusing to modern-day voice researchers. He discussed laryngeal positioning in detail as well as the *coup de glotte* (the stroke of the glottis). His descriptions later generated a variety of pedagogic assumptions, some of which, if one is to believe reports of his students, went far beyond principles he himself taught. In a summary of his method, undertaken in 1870 and published in 1872,[17] one finds distinct parallels with what his father had proposed, even to the inclusion of similar technical exercises. For example, he advised that the head and neck should remain erect on the torso, that the shoulders ought to be well back without stiffness, that the chest must remain in an expanded position, and that inspiration should occur silently and slowly without sudden diaphragmatic lowering. He recommended the use of a breath-management exercise that had come down by word of mouth from the previous century, Farinelli's Exercise, in which the breath cycle is accomplished through a slow tripartite maneuver consisting of an inspiratory gesture, a subsequent suspension of either inhalation or exhalation, and a concluding expiratory gesture, the three segments being of equal duration. He recommended use of *the attacco del suono* (onset) as a basic exercise for the development of breath-management skill. His "open" and "closed" vocal timbres are in line with the *voce aperta/voce chiusa* (open voice/closed voice) and the *copertura* (cover) terminology of the traditional Italian School. Laryngeal posture should be low and stable. His instruction on the relationship of vowel integrity to vowel modification in ascending pitch is a pillar of today's vocal art.

A thorough analysis of Manuel Garcia's technical principles requires extensive consideration not possible here. Proof of the efficacy of his teaching lies in the large number of outstanding singers of many nationalities who were among his pupils. Further insight into Garcia's pedagogy is to be found in *An Essay on Bel Canto* written by his pupil and close associate Herman Klein.[18] Never in the history of solo singing has one individual so influenced vocal pedagogy as did Manuel Garcia. It is fair to suggest that current international mainstream vocalism and many of its divergent nationalist rivulets can be traced directly to interpretations of Garcia's admonitions. His own assessment of the state of singing (when many thought it at its peak) was that singing had become as much a lost art as that of the manufacture of Mandarin china or the varnish used by the old string-instrument masters.

An interim figure, surfacing in the Italian school between the Garcias and the Lampertis, is the Neapolitan Luigi LaBlache (1794–1858), whose career as outstanding *basso* of the era took him to La Scala, Vienna, Paris, and London. Yet his *Méthode de chant*, published undated in Paris, as was the English edition,[19] came late in life. It offers little precise information as to how the art of singing ought to be taught. Evidence of his successful teaching lies in the number of his pupils who managed professional careers.

A *Treatise on the Art of Singing*[20] by Francesco Lamperti (1813–1892) is undated but is presumed to have appeared after 1860. F. Lamperti's chief contribution to the historic Italian School is his description of the *lutte vocale* (It. *lotta vocale*), the basis for the *appoggio* breath-management that is a fundamental precept of the 19th-century Italian School:

> To sustain a given note the air should be expelled slowly; to attain this end, the respiratory [inspiratory] muscles, by continuing their action, strive to retain the air in the lungs, and oppose their action to that of the expiratory muscles, which is called the *lutte vocale* or vocal struggle. On the retention of this equilibrium depends the just emission of the voice, and by means of it alone can true expression be given to the sound produced.

Although the term *appoggio* appears to have first come into use in the second half of the 19th century, the *lutte vocale* (which is analogous to the *appoggio* technique) already existed in the exercise that Farinelli is reputed to have learned a century earlier from Porpora (see above) in order to acquire his phenomenal breath management.

Francesco Lamperti held to the three-register designation of the 19th century Italian School (allowing for gender differences) and he was adamant that whether singing softly or loudly, timbre must be consistent. The *messa di voce* (sung on a single note or phrase beginning at *piano* or *pianissimo* dynamic level, crescendoing to *forte* or *fortissimo*, then returning to the original decibel level) was an important part of his pedagogy. He stressed the need for full, complete-toned production at all dynamic levels.

His son, Giovanni Battista (Giambattista) Lamperti (1839–1910), left an even more enduring mark on international vocal pedagogy: He taught singers who would become identified with the "second golden age" of vocalism, and these students carried on his system well into the first half of the 20th century. Lamperti's advice regarding general posture and events of the breath cycle[21] parallels that of his predecessors: "The shoulders [must] be slightly thrown back to allow the chest due freedom in front." For G.B. Lamperti, breath management was the prime factor in skillful singing. He recognized the unique relationshp of vocal registers to each vocal category and to the individual instrument. Breath renewal should be silently incorporated into the release of the tone at each phrase termination, with subsequent precise onset (attack). Singing *piano* was in all regards the same as singing *forte*, only softer. Above all, good singing necessitated command of the art of legato, which depended on efficient breath-management.[21] Lamperti's opposition to the "relaxed" posture then being advocated by the German school is eminently clear. In contrast to that school's lowered thoracic postures, the singer was to feel broad-shouldered and high-chested, straightened up like a soldier. Despite the reputation of many turn-of-the-century singing artists, Lamperti lamented the general deterioration of the art of singing and of voice teaching:

> There has never been so much enthusiasm for the singing art, nor have there been so many students and teachers as of late years. And it is precisely this period that reveals the deterioration of this divine art and the almost complete disappearance of genuine singers and worse, of good singing teachers.

Could Giambattista Lamperti have had in mind inroads the national schools were making into the historic international Italianate school?

A telling influence in 20th century North America vocal pedagogy is William Earl Brown's *Maxims of G. B. Lamperti*. The book first appeared in print in America in 1931,[22] but the maxims were collected in 1891–1893 when Brown was Lamperti's student and assistant in Dresden. He maintained that the quoted maxims were taken directly from studio notes he made during that period.

> At no time during the song or series of exercises must you relax while replenishing the breath or you [will] lose the feeling of suspension. Only when the song is over may you let go. . . . [Maintain] sustained intensity of initial vibration and continuous release of breath-energy. . . . Tone and breath "balance" solely when harmonic overtones appear in the voice, not by muscular effort and "voice placing."

He said legato was achievable only through the presence of constant vibrancy, a result of the *appoggio*. Lamperti held that loose breath escaping over the vocal folds and not turned into tone was destructive to good function, causing irregular vibration and disruption of breath energy.

> Until you feel the permanency of your vibration you cannot play on your resonances. . . . [E]nergy in regular vibration is constructive. The violence in irregular vibration is destructive.

The influence of the Lamperti maxims has never been surpassed by other pedagogic writing of the 20th century.

In the interest of chronology, the treatises of two other representatives of the Lamperti school, William Shakespeare and Herbert Witherspoon, are considered later. For additional commentary regarding the influence of this school's *appoggio* technique on modern vocal pedagogy, the reader is directed to C. Timberlake's astute remarks on historic pedagogy and performance styles.[23]

The historic Italian School dominated all European professional vocalism; its proponents taught in the major cities of Europe (Garcia in London and Paris, G.B. Lamperti in Munich and Dresden, for example). In the latter half of the 19th century, with the emergence of European nationalism, the conscious development of indigenous regional cultures, and divergences stemming from application of new scientific findings to the art of singing, the reign of Italian vocalism became less encompassing. Whereas opera, the chief performance vehicle for professional singing, had been Italian-centered during the 17th, 18th, and early 19th centuries, in the latter half of the 19th century other performance literatures, such as the *Lied*, the *mélodie*, the orchestrated song, and the oratorio, began to flower, gaining increasing importance toward the close of the century. These literatures continued to burgeon as the 20th century dawned, garnering new impetus in subsequent decades. Even though the Italian model was still preeminent in the international world of professional vocalism, disparate, identifiable tonal aesthetics began to flourish in France, in Germany and Northern Europe, and in England, while

Italy persistently held firm to historic tradition through at least the first third of the 20th century. It is worthy of note that Manuel Garcia is frequently cited in support of the many pedagogic strands that became alternative to the original Italianate model. National digressions resulted from differing emphases in tonal ideals, from emerging vocal literatures, and above all, from an increasing interest in achieving synthesis of word and music, transcending the traditional Italian emphasis on vocalism as the chief aesthetic concern.

The unification of the German political states into a national body, the increasing importance of liturgical choral traditions such as the Germanic/Scandinavian Lutheran and the Anglican, the emergence of the public *Liederabend*, the rise of Romantic German opera, the impact of Wagner, and the shift from royal to public patronage altered the dominant role of the international Italian school, but did not obliterate its influence on national schools. (All pedagogic threads were woven into the North American vocal-pedagogy garment.)

The modern pedagogue may best understand the wide diversity among systems of vocal technique, most of which had their origins in the late 19th century, by gauging the extent to which they break away from the earlier international model and the extent to which they retain its premises. In a number of instances, divergent modern pedagogics continue the late 19th-century search for justification of techniques by applying modern scientific measurement. Some treatises of the latter half of the 19th century were written by teachers with one foot located south of the historic Italian pedagogic alp, the other foot planted north of it. "New" 20th-century pedagogic systems are seldom more than extensions of those diverse formulae.

Julius Stockhausen was born in Paris in July, 1826, and died in Frankfurt-am-Main in September, 1906. Beginning in 1845, Stockhausen undertook theoretic studies at the Paris Conservatoire, but privately studied voice with Manuel Garcia, whom he followed to London in 1849. Despite Stockhausen's future impact on Germanic/Nordic and North American vocal pedagogy, he did not excel chiefly in opera. He was second baritone at the Mannheim theater from 1852–1853. Stockhausen's chief performance successes lay in oratorio and *Lieder* repertories. His public performance of *Die Schöne Müllerin* took place with great success in 1856 at Vienna. Brahms and Stockhausen first collaborated in recital in Hamburg in 1861, performing a program that included Schumann's *Dichterliebe*. Stockhausen's subsequent selection over Brahms as the director of the Hamburg Philharmonische Konzertgesellschaft and of the Singakademie did not interfere with their continued artistic coalition. Stockhausen premiered the baritone role of Brahms's *Ein Deutsches Requiem* in 1868; the rangy, dramatic vocal writing was considered ungrateful to Stockhausen's instrument. The composer's remarkable Magelone cycle was written with Stockhausen in mind. It demands stamina and sensitivity, two facets that the singer seemed able to deliver equally well in the *Lieder* of Schubert, Schumann, and Brahms. After serving as a singing teacher at several institutions, Stockhausen founded his own school of singing in 1880. In 1884, *Gesangsmethode*,[24] translated as *Method of Singing,* appeared.

Stockhausen's publication is a significant step in the history of vocal pedagogy because of its continuing influence on the Germanic/Nordic vocal schools and on a sizable segment of North American pedagogy and because it raises questions as to the accuracy of Stockhausen's interpretation (and that of his disciples) of Manuel Garcia's pedagogic orientation. One of Stockhausen's chief departures from the tenets of the 18th- and 19th-century Italian school lies in his advocacy of a constantly low laryngeal position while singing. Although it remains unclear as to how low Stockhausen's "low larynx " was, he advised a position lower than that of the normal speaking voice. In itself, this admonition is not in conflict with the historic Italian pedagogic tenet that requests the noble posture and silent breath renewal, in which limited laryngeal descent will occur and remain. But most of Stockhausen's followers interpret him as having taught retention of the yawn position, with depressed larynx, as being ideal for sung phonation. His avoidance of a pleasant facial expression, together with his promotion of the lowered jaw, diminished the supraglottic vocal tract flexibility so characteristic of the Italianate school. However, Stockhausen specifically outlawed both nasal and pharyngeal timbres. Inasmuch as it is difficult to envision how distended pharyngeal timbre can be avoided while one consciously induces throat-wall expansion, Stockhausen's comments may invite varying pedagogic interpretations.

Stockhausen requested that the lips be drawn backward on back and mixed vowels, and that for /e/ and /a/ the lips be pursed in forward position. These are withdrawals from the *si canta come si parla* (one sings as one speaks) maxim of the traditinal Italian School. Yet, more in keeping with the Italian pedagogic heritage, Stockhausen recommended the use of closed vowels in ascending pitch patterns, and of open vowels in descending pitch patterns.

Although he did call for full rib expansion in the *respiro pieno* (full breath), another departure from the Italian School was Stockhausen's minimal attention to breath-management. His *passaggio* registration points are located similarly to those of Garcia. He advocated the use of the *messa di voce* so dear to the Lampertis.

The modern pedagogue must conclude that Julius Stockhausen severely adapted traditional Italianate-schooled principles to the performance of the emerging Germanic repertoire in which he excelled and to national tonal preferences. Given his commitment to non-Italianate technical devices, one wonders how well Stockhausen may have managed vocalism and diction in the Italian and French operatic repertoires during his 3-year stint in the Paris Opéra Comique (1856–1859). Stockhausen's pedagogic orientation raises the question as to how far vocal technique can be altered for the performance of different literatures.

Not even a brief overview of historic vocal poedagogy can dispense with at least passing reference to Emma Seiler (c. 1875). Her own experiences as a singer, which she describes as having been in both Italian and German traditions, appear to have been frustrating. She finally associated herself with the eminent physicist/acoustician Hermann Helmholtz, who expressed indebtedness to her in his formulation of acoustic theories of voice production. Some of Seiler's assumptions regarding the function of the laryngeal mechanism are insupportable. In explaining her vocal registration hypotheses, she heavily relied on proprioceptive sensations of mouth, throat, stomach, and sternum. Her treatise[25] is largely important as a prototype of forthcoming Germanic pseudoscientific pedagogic literature that attempts in imaginative ways to apply physiology and acoustics to the singing-voice.

British vocal pedagogy was not immune to Germanic influences. Emil Behnke's *The Mechanism of the Human Voice* published in 1880,[26] and his *Voice, Song and Speech*,[27] in collaboration with Lennox Browne, were highly regarded in turn-of-the-century British pedagogy circles. Yet he was not a follower of Stockhausen, nor were his ideas in line with the Germanic techniques later developed by Armin. Behnke was particularly enamored of the male falsetto.

Enrico Delle Sedie (1822-1907) was a highly successful baritone in Italy, Paris, and London, singing the Verdian roles Di Luna (*Il trovatore*), Renato (*Un ballo in maschera*), and Germond (*La traviata*). Figaro (*Il barbiere di Siviglia*) and Malatesta (*Don Pasquale*) were in his repertoire. In 1876, he published *Arte e fisiologia del canto*, and in 1886, *L'estetico del canto e l'arte melodrammatica*. In 1894 *A Complete Method of Singing*,[28] which included material from his earlier publications, appeared in New York. Drawing on physiologic and acoustic information of the time, Delle Sedie exemplified those singers and teachers who increasingly began to turn to science as a means for verifying tenets of the historic Italian School. His method deals with the resonator tract as a filtering source for laryngeally generated sound. He unites the registration and timbre terminologies of the historic Italian School with emerging acoustic information, especially as regards vowel modification. As such, his writing has had considerable impact on American vocal pedagogy.

An American publication containing accurate drawings of the larynx and confirmable explanations of diaphragmatic function was E. B. Warman's *The Voice: How to Train It and Care for It* (1889). This treatise[29] is a successful effort to undergird the tenets of the Italianate school with scientific information.

A teacher of singing who left no written advice but whose outstanding pupils indicated his impact on vocal pedagogy, is the Neapolitan tenor Giovanni Sbriglia (1832-1916). Sbriglia made his debut at San Carlo in 1853 and his 1860 New York debut at the Academy of Music, where he appeared in *La sonnambula* with Adelina Patti. Both Edward de Reszke and his brother Jean (who underwent change from baritone to tenor), Pol Plançon (who also studied with Duprez), and Lillian Nordica were products of the Sbriglia studio.

Summaries of Sbriglia's teaching have been recorded by his pupils. Assuming these reports to be reliable, it appears that Sbriglia lies within the historic Italian School that extends from Garcia *père* through the Lampertis and into the 20th century. Sbriglia opposed the *Bauchaussenstütze* (outward abdominal-wall thrusting) that became characteristic of the late 19th- and 20th-century Germanic school. According to Byers[30]:

> . . . he believed that all great singers breathed alike—"the same natural way." He did not like what he called 'the new pushing method of singing with the back of the neck sunk in the chest, and the muscularly pushed out diaphragm.

> . . . . The foundation of this teaching is perfect posture. Foremost is a high chest (what nature gives every great singer), held high without tension by developed abdominal and lower back muscles and a straight spine—this will give the uplift for perfect breathing. . . . Your chest literally must be held up by these abdominal and back muscles, supported from below, and your shoulder and neck will be free and loose.

It is easy to assume that Mathilde Marchesi was a proponent of the Italian School. However, Mathilde Marchesi (b. 1821, Frankfurt-am-Main; d. 1913, London) was a German mezzo-soprano who in 1852 married the singer Salvatore Marchesi. Her early training took place in Germany. In 1845, she went to Paris to study with Manuel Garcia for a period of several years. Although she had some success as a public performer, her energies were largely devoted to teaching. Outstanding female singers were numbered among her pupils, among them Eames, Calvé, Garden, and Melba.

Theoretical and Practical Vocal Method[31] and *Ten Singing Lessons*[32] attest to Marchesi's organized approach to vocal pedagogy. Her description of the singing-voice as a three-part instrument consisting of motor, vibrator, and resonator system has a remarkably modern ring. In regards to posture for singing, she is directly in the lineage of Garcia *père*, Manuel Garcia, and both Lampertis, as evidenced by her suggestion that students should position the arms at the back in order to achieve proper chest elevation and to induce low breathing. She taught the *coup de glotte* (probably the balanced *attacco del suono*) which she described as producing firm, complete approximation of the glottis, and which she believed used minimal air to set the vocal folds in vibration. She adhered to the three-register concept of the Italian School. Marchesi modified the Italianate model by suggesting that the jaw drop into low position and remain nearly immobile during singing. Much of her success as a teacher appears to have been a result of her systematic approach, which was summarized in the maxim "First technique, afterwards aesthetics."

Lilli Lehmann's *Meine Gesangskunst* (1902), published in 1914[33] as *How to Sing* (later revisions appeared), has exerted lasting influence on aspiring North American, European, and Asian singers. It is not easy to classify Lehmann (1848–1929) by school because her language, both subjective and specific, borrows from several traditions and appears ultimately to be a search for justification of her personal vocal technique through physiologic and acoustic verification, much of it inaccurate. This combining of the subjective and the objective were expressed as follows:

> Technique is inseparable from art. Only by mastering the technique of his material is the artist in a condition to mold his mental work of art. . . . [M]uscles contract in activity, and in normal inactivity are relaxed. . . . [W]e must strengthen them by continued vocal gymnastics so that they may be able to sustain long-continued exertion; and must keep them elastic and use them so. It includes also the well-controlled activity of diaphragm, chest, neck, and face muscles. . . . Since these things all operate together, one without the others can accomplish nothing; if the least is lacking, singing is quite impossible, or is entirely bad.

One of the most influential pages in vocal pedagogy contains Lehmann's schema for subjective tone-placement sensations that move upward into the bony skull in response to ascending pitch. Lehmann's reputation as a gifted artist who could sing widely diverse roles, together with the longevity of her career, helped establish the importance of her opinions.

A major figure in 20th-century German-language vocal pedagogy literature is Franziska Martienssen-Lohmann, who precisely describes breath-management procedures, registration practices, and timbre designations within the Germanic/Nordic School.[34-36] By taking exception at times to typical Germanic practices of heavy Deckung (covering), excessive *Kopfstimme* (head voice) and the *Tiefstellung* (low positioning) of the larynx, Martienssen-Lohmann appears to move in the direction of the international Italianate school, as do many contemporary Germans.

The teaching of Georg Armin, beginning in the 1930s, left a lasting imprint on the "heroic" segment of the German School and on its North American derivative. His breath-damming *Staumethode*,[37] by which he believed the *Urkaft* (primal strength) of the vocal instrument could be rediscovered,[38] led to several techniques of induced low-trunk breath-management maneuvers, including anal-sphincteral occlusion and the cultivated grunt (extension of the vocal fold closure phase during phonatory cycles, with sudden release of glottal tension at phrase terminations).

Frederick Husler, with his collaborator Yvonne Rodd-Marling, made a 20th-century attempt to recover a presumed primitive vocal Atlantis. Through a series of exercises (including what he considered to be prespeech maneuvers), he meant to reestablish the vocal freedom he believed to have been lost through civilization's harnessing of the vocal instrument to the functions of speech.[39] A large group of teachers follow the Husler Method; they are found mostly in German, British, and Canadian conservatory enclaves.

The great Polish artist Jean de Reszke (1850–1925) stated that he did not wish to establish a method but only to express his personal ideas about the art of singing, yet his influence on the future of singing in France was monumental. Despite some study with Cotogni (a representative of the Lamperti school), de Reszke did not advocate postural attitudes of the Italian school, preferring that the student discover "relaxed" breathing by sitting with collapsed and rounded shoulders and by dropping all muscles of the torso except the diaphragm. According to reports,[40] he advised, "Imagine yourself to be a great church bell, where all the sonority is round the rim." He aimed for local control of the diaphragm and recommended that "the body sit down on the diaphragm." He suggested the use of the sigh, together with hot-air expulsion to be felt on the hand, as means for "relaxing" the glottis, the throat, and the tongue. These admonitions are in line with a number of non-Italianate models that would take root in mid-20th-century North American soil. De Reszke also advocated principles that remain characteristic of current (but by no means all) 20th-century French voice instruction: (1) Raised head posture (singing to the gallery). (2) Placement of the tone in the masque and at the bridge of the nose. (3) Producing "the singers grimace" (*la grimace de la chanteuse*) for high notes. One of his favorite exercises was based on a phrase containing a series of French nasals: *Pendant que l'enfant mange son pain, le chien tremble dans le buisson.*

For years, Paris was the international operatic center of the world. However, with a few notable exceptions, French singers have not enjoyed international careers in the later decades of the 20th century. Many observers, including French singing teachers, tend to view 20th-century French vocalism as being, at least in part, a de Reszke heritage. A return to international pedagogic orientation is increasingly in progress in France.

At the close of the 19th century, the international Italianate pedagogy model was represented by non-Italian pupils of Giovanni Battista Lamperti. Englishman William Shakespeare's end-of-the-century treatises, made available in 1921 versions called *The Art of Singing*[41] and *Plain Words on Singing*, reiterate the *lutte vocale* of the Lamperti School: opposition between the muscles which draw in the breath. Noiseless and imperceptible breathing was the aim; a phrase was never to be terminated by allowing the torso to collapse. Although some aspects of traditional British vocal technique (such as spreading of the upper back) entered into Shakespeare's pedagogy, in general he was in line with the historic international school.

The same is true of Shakespeare's countryman H. Plunket Greene, who at the close of his 1912 book, *Interpretation in Song*,[42] appended two chapters, one devoted to breath management, the second to legato. Both could have been written by either of the Lampertis. Plunket Greene wanted an axial posture "with the chest as high as ever it will go." He detailed techniques for inducing the *appoggio* and delineated factors that contribute to legato singing.

Current British vocal technique seems to be of two minds, one filled with historic Italianate pedagogic ideals, the other aimed at "purity" of timbre based on influences from the treble-voice liturgical tradition—"cathedral tone." However, the one concept tumbles into the other, so that typical British tonal ideals often take on a recognizable insular flavor. (It is hardly possible to mistake British-trained operatic tenors, sopranos, or mezzo-sopranos for Italian-trained singers.)

At the beginning of the 20th century, the E. G. White Society proposed the theory of Sinus Tone Production.[43] Despite a lack of scientific verification for its basic tenet, the society still claims more than 200 active members, most of them English and North American. It is closely allied with British notions of "tonal purity."

More recently, E. Herbert-Caesari attempted in several volumes[44–46] to fuse the mystical with the mechanical. His books remain influential in British vocal pedagogy.

In 1935 Herbert Witherspoon became director of the Metropolitan Opera Company, where he had already sung for eight seasons. He was a key figure in the performance world and in academia and was one of the founders of the oldest voice-teacher organizations in the world: the American Academy of Teachers of Singing and the Chicago Singing Teachers Guild. As mentioned earlier, Witherspoon is a direct descendant of the historic international Italian School. His 1925 *Singing*[4] remains a classic of modern vocal pedagogy. He studied with G. B. Lamperti and continued that tradition. Witherspoon's unique contribution originated in his conviction (1) that the singing voice primarily is a physical instrument that obeys the laws of efficient physical function, and (2) that the singing voice is an acoustic instrument that must be produced naturally in accordance with the laws of vocal acoustics. His dictum that we do not perform any physical act through relaxation, but with correct tension and action, places him in direct opposition to Germanic/Nordic techniques of the lowered, relaxed torso. His "lifts of the breath," meaning breath-energy increase at registration pivotal points, correspond to the passaggi registration demarcations of the Lamperti school. His treatment of vocal tract filtering is in complete accord with that school. A typical passage reads:

> . . . as pitch ascends . . . the tongue rises coördinately upwards and forwards, changing the shape of the throat and the mouth, the fauces point forward and narrow, or approximate; the uvula rises and finally disappears, the soft palate rises forward, never backward; while the epiglottis, rising up against the back of the lower tongue, seems to have a law of its own regarding quality, clear or veiled.

Not all of his observations precisely corresponded to what modern investigation verifies, yet Witherspoon masterfully combined past international vocalism with then-available scientific and acoustic information; tradition and modern pragmatism found a happy marriage. His pedagogy was based on the language of function, yet Witherspoon stressed that singing deals not simply with mechanics ("muscles and organs cannot be locally controlled") and that it is linguistic and musical interpretation that finally control technique.

In the period immediately before and following WWII, a plethora of writings on vocal technique emerged in Germany. In general, they tend to support low-abdominal breath-management techniques and fixated resonator tracts. Some American pedagogics were not far behind in building on those premises. Pedagogic cultivers of all the national schools flourish on the North American continent, yet the international Italian model is still the predominant exemplar for the professional singer.

The influence of Douglas Stanley, beginning with his 1929 *The Science of Voice*,[47] has been enduring on a small but devoted segment of American voice teaching circles. His viewpoints on register separation and unification have been further expanded by the skillful writing of Cornelius Reid.[48–50]

Among publications that have exerted influence on mid-20th-century vocalism, none has been more forceful than William Vennard's *Singing, the Mechanism and the Technic*.[51] This volume is a reliable source for the study of anatomy, physiology, and acoustics of the vocal instrument. As regards his use of the yawn/sigh device and his stances on "belly breathing," the *passaggi,* vocal registration, and postures of the vocal tract, Vennard indicates partial allegiance to the historic Germanic/Nordic camp. In other respects, he appears to be in tune with international vocalism.

Another important pedagogic strand in recent North American pedagogy comes from the prolific Berton Coffin,[52–54] whose premises unite his knowledge of the phonetic properties of the singing voice with scholarly interest in historic vocalism. Coffin's advocacy of elevated laryngeal and head postures described as "the sword-swallowing position," and his championing of male falsetto as a legitimate extension of the upper voice, ally him with segments of the modern French School, although in most other respects he retains allegiance to the international Italianate school.

A splendid singer himself, Ralph Appelman attempted to unite vocal pedagogy and scientific principles in his ground-breaking volume, *The Science of Vocal Pedagogy*,[55] which is filled with detailed information on physiology and acoustics. It has been difficult for Appelman's admirers to translate his highly systematized pedagogy into accessible lay language.

Even the briefest survey of vocal pedagogy must append a list (by no means definitive) of voice professionals, past and present, who have contributed significant articles or books on the relationships of function, artistic singing, and vocal pedagogy: L. Bachner; R. M. Baken; W. Bartholomew; M. Benninger; M. P. Bonnier; D. Brewer; M. Bunch; V. A. Christy; T. Cleveland; D. Clippinger; R. Colton; A. Cranmer; R. Edwin; J. Estill; V. A. Fields; T. Fillebrown; V. Fuchs; W. J. Gould; J. W. Gregg; T. Hixon; C. H. Holbrook; H. Hol-

lien; R. Husson; J. Klein; J. Large; V. Lawrence; P. Lohmann; R. Luchsinger; M. Mackenzie; M. S. MacKinley; L. Manén; P.M. Marafiotti; W. McIver; B. McClosky; J. McKinney; C. Meano; D. C. Miller; D. G. Miller; F. Miller; R. Miller; G. P. Moore; R. C. Mori; M. Nadoleczny; G. Newton; D. Proctor; A. Rose; R. Rosewal; R. Sataloff; H. K. Schütte; N. Scotto di Carlo ; C. Seashore; R. Sherer; T. Shipp; D. Slater; A. Sonninen; A. Stampa; R. H. Stetson; J. Sundberg; J. Tarneaud; R. Taylor; J. Teachey; I. Titze ; J. B. van Deinse ; W. van den Berg; H. Von Leden ; K. Westerman; H. W. Whitlock ; J. Wilcox; C. Wilder; P. S. Wormhoudt; and B. D. Wyke.

Recent contributors to the literature on vocal pedagogy apply fiberoptic stroboscopy, spectrography, fluoroscopy, and other forms of measurement to the events of voicing. Their intention has not been mostly to invent new ways to sing but to objectively compare traditional, international, national, regional, and idiosyncratic pedagogies in matters of their vocal efficiency and their relationship to vocal aesthetics and to vocal health.

Summary

The history of vocal pedagogy may be traced over a period of centuries. The earliest writings discussed in this chapter date from the 15th century. The Italianate School developed in 18th century, and a subsequently diverse school of pedagogy emerged. A variety of influences have determined the progress of singing pedagogy and the techniques of singing and teaching utilized most widely today.

Review Questions

1. Which school of pedagogy has most strongly influenced international singing pedagogy?
   a. Greek
   b. Italian
   c. Russian
   d. German
   e. French

2. Which of the following individuals was most influential in the development of modern day pedagogy?
   a. Benigné de Bacilly
   b. Piere Francesco Tosi
   c. Burton Coffin
   d. Manuel Garcia
   e. Francesco Lamperti

3. What is the name given to the fundamental breath-management precept of the 19th century Italian

School of Singing, a precept still in wide use today?

a. arpageretora

b. arpeggio

c. appoggia

d. ascension

e. allegro

4. Singing a single note that begins softly, crescendos to a louder volume, and then softens to the original level, is an exercise known as:

a. mezza voce

b. modulation

c. marcato

d. marking

e. messa di voce

5. Who is the singer whose teaching career and vocal pedagogy book, *The Method of Singing*, influenced significantly the German/Nordic vocal schools as well as American pedagogy?

a. Julius Stockhausen

b. Manuel Garcia

c. Giambattista Lamperti

d. Johannes Brahms

e. Giovanni S. Briglia

References

1. Jander O. Singing. In: Sadie S, ed. *The New Grove Dictionary of Music and Musicians*. New York, NY: Grove's Dictionaries of Music; 1980:17.

2. Harris E. The Baroque era voices. In: Brown HM, Sadie S, eds. *Performance Practice: Music After 1600*. New York, NY: WW Norton; 1989.

3. de Bacilly B; Caswell A, trans. 1968. (Originally published as *Remarques curieuses sur l'art de bien chanter*. Paris: 1668.)

4. Witherspoon H. *Singing*. New York, NY: G Schirmer; 1925.

5. Duey P. Bel *Canto in its Golden Age*. New York, NY: King's Crown Press; 1950.

6 Heriot A. *The Castrati in Opera*. New York, NY: Da Capo Press;1964.

7. Pleasants H. *The Great Singers*. New York, NY: Simon and Schuster; 1966.

8. *Bérnard* J-B (J-A). *L'ai-t due Chant*. Paris; 1755.

9. Tosi P-F; Galliard JE, trans. *Observations on the Florid Song*. London; 1742.

10. Mancini G; Buzzi P, trans. *Practical Reflections on the Art of Singing*. Boston, Ma: Oliver Ditson; 1907.

11. Coffin B. Vocal pedagogy classics: practical reflections on figured singing by Giambattista Mancini. In: Miller R. ed. *The NATS Bulletin*. 1981;37(4):47–49.

12. Crutchfield W. The 19th century: voices. In: Brown HM, Sadie S, eds. *Performance Practice: Music after 1600*. New York, NY: WW Norton; 1989.

13. Corri D. *The Singer's* Preceptor. London: 1810.

14. Garcia M.P.V.R. *Exercices pour la voix*. Paris: A Parite; c.1820.

15. Garcia M.P.R. *Trait complet de l'art du chant*. Paris: French Academy of Science, 1840.

16. Garcia M.P.R. *Memoire sur la voix humaine*. Paris: E Suverger; 1841.

17. Garcia, M.P.R. *Garcia's Complete School of Singing*. London: Cramer Beal and Chappell; 1872.

18. Klein H. *An Essay on Bel Canto*. London: Oxford University Press; 1923.

19. Lablache L. *Lablache's Complete of Singing: or, a Rational Analysis of the Principles According to Which the Studies Should be Directed for Developing the Voice and Rendering it Flexible*. Boston, Ma: Oliver Ditson.

20. Lamperti F; Griffith JC, trans. *A Treatise on the Art of Singing*. New York, NY: G Schirmer.

21. Lamperti G-B; Baker T, trans. *The Techniques of Bel Canto*. New York, NY: G. Schirmer; 1905.

22. Brown WE. *Vocal Wisdom: Maxims of Giovanni Battista Lamperti*. New York, NY: Crescendo Press; 1957.

23. Timberlake C. Apropos of appoggio, parts I and II. In: McKinney J, ed. *The NATS Journal*. 1995;52(3,4).

24. Stockhausen J. *Method of Singing*. London: Novello; 1884.

25. Seiler E. *The Voice in Singing*. Philadelphia, Pa: JB Lippincott; 1875.

26. Behne E. *The Mechanism of the Human Voice*. London: J Curwen & Sons; 1880.

27. Browne L, Behnke E. *Voice Song and Speech*. New York, NY: GP Putnam's Sons.

28. Delle Sedie E. *A Complete Method of Singing*. New York: private printing; 1894.

29. Warman EB. *The Voice: How to Train It and Care for It*. Boston, MA: Lee and Shepard; 1889.

30. Byers MC. Sbriglia's Method of Singing. In: *The Etude*. May 1942.

31. Marchesi M. *Theoretical and Practical Vocal Method*. New York, NY: Dover; 1970.

32. Marcesi M. *Ten Singing Lessons*. New York, NY: Harper & Brothers; 1901.

33. Lehmann L. *How to Sing*. New York, NY: Macmillan; 1903.

34. Martienssen-Lohmann F. *Das bewusste Singen*. Leipzig: CF Kahnt; 1923.

35. Martienssen-Lohmann F. *Der Opernsänger*. Mainz: B Schott's Söhne; 1943.

36. Martienssen-Lohmann F. *Der wissende Sänger*. Zurich: Atlantis-Verlag; 1963.

37. Armin G. *Die Technik der Breitspannung: In: Beitrag über die horizontal-vertikalen Spannkräfte beim Aufbau der Stimme nach dem "Stauprinzip."* Berlin: Verlag der Gesellschaft fur Stimmkultur; 1932.

38. Armin G. *Von der Urkraft der Stimme*. Lippstadt: Kistner & Siegel.

39. Husler F. Rodd-Marling Y. Singing: *The Physical Nature of the Vocal Organ*. London: Faber and Faber; 1960.

40. Johnstone-Douglas W. The teaching of Jean de Reszke, In: *Music and Letters*; July, 1925.

41. Shakespeare W. *The Art of Singing*. Bryn Mawr, Pa: Oliv-

42. Greene HP. *Interpretation in Song*. London: Macmillan; 1912.

43. White EG. *Sinus Tone Production*. Boston, Ma: Crescendo; 1970.

44. Herbert-Caesari E. *The Alchemy of Voice*. London: Robert Hale; 1965.

45. Herbert-Caesari E. *The Science and Sensations of Tone*. Boston, Ma: Crescendo; 1968.

46. Herbert-Caesari E. *The Voice of the Mind*. London: Robert Hale; 1969.

47. Stanley D. *The Science of Voice*. New York, NY: Carl Fischer; 1929.

48. Reid C. *Bel Canto Principles and Practices*. New York, NY: Coleman-Ross; 1950.

49. Reid C. *Psyche and Soma*. New York, NY: J Pattelson Music House; 1975.

50. Reid C. *The Free Voice*. New York, NY: Coleman-Ross; 1965.

51. Vennard W. *The Mechanism and the Technic*. 5th ed. New York, NY: Carl Fischer; 1967.

52. Coffin B. *Historical Vocal Pedagogy*. Metuchen: Scarecrow Press; 1989.

53. Coffin B. *Overtones of Bel Canto*. Metuchen: Scarecrow Press; 1982.

54. Coffin B. *The Sounds of Singing: Vocal Technique with Vowel-Pitch Charts*. Metuchen: Scarecrow Press; 1977.

55. Appelman R. *The Science of Vocal Pedagogy*. Bloomington, Ind: Indiana University Press; 1967.

27

The Singing Voice Specialist

Kate A. Emerich, Margaret M. Baroody, Linda M. Carroll, and Robert Thayer Sataloff

How many people have wished "If only I could sing…"? The fact is, virtually everyone can. Anyone who has pitch variation in his or her speaking voice and can tell whether two musical tones are the same or different can be taught to sing. That does not mean that he or she will be the next Luciano Pavarotti, but such a person can usually develop the muscle strength, ear–voice coordination, and confidence to enjoy singing and to be enjoyed by others. However, love of music is not the only reason for learning to sing. The muscles trained in coordination, ear training, and breath control during singing lessons can be extremely helpful in strengthening the speaking voice. A comprehensive voice team incorporates the benefits provided by a singing teacher with those of a speech-language pathologist and acting-voice trainer to optimize and expedite voice improvement.

Singing Lessons: An Overview

Pedagogy

To understand the special considerations for singing voice specialists (SVSs), teachers who specialize in working with injured voices, clinicians must be familiar with singing training under normal circumstances. Within the academic world of voice teachers, the study of the workings of the voice and techniques for training is known as *vocal pedagogy*. There are traditions and schools of thought in vocal pedagogy that date back centuries. They have been reviewed in numerous works by authors such as Richard Miller.[1] Over the years, many approaches have become popular enough to be known as "schools." There are German, French, Italian, and Russian schools, schools that follow the tenets of various famous teachers, and count-

less articles and books on teaching methodology. Many of the ideas and principles of one school of thought conflict with those of others.

Unfortunately, choral pedagogy is another matter. Choral singing has great influence on singers throughout the world, including young singers. Many choral conductors are trained as organists or instrumental conductors and have little or no formal training in singing or vocal pedagogy. Although specific methods for healthy choral singing have been promoted by various far-sighted choir masters, there are few formal training or degree programs in choral pedagogy for the serious choral conductor who wishes to study the methods of producing optimal choral sound with optimal vocal health. Attention is just now being directed to this pervasive problem, as discussed in chapter 61.

Training of Singers

There are basically two types of traditional singing instructors: voice teachers and vocal coaches. The voice teacher works primarily on developing vocal technique through building coordination of musculature in the vocal mechanism. The vocal coach works primarily on repertoire (songs) and interpretation. The SVS is a voice teacher who works with injured voices, as discussed in the following sections. Many singers work with both a voice teacher and a vocal coach. Singers also need to be able to move on stage and feel comfortable with an audience, so some sort of body movement training can be necessary. Singers with a desire to sing opera or musical comedy may take some acting and stage combat training, as well. Aspiring classical singers also require language courses in at least Italian, German, and French. Study of Russian, Spanish, and other languages may also prove useful.

The beginning singer should, first and foremost, learn to omit any abusive vocal behaviors not only in singing, but also in speech. Although many singing teachers work with the speaking voice, most are not formally trained speakers or teachers of speech. Speech-language pathologists are trained and licensed to work with normal and pathological voices. Many, however, have little training or experience working with the refinements of technique required by the professional voice. Speech-language pathologists who have a particular interest in the professional voice should attend symposia, obtain internships, and seek mentors. Fortunately, some speech-language pathologists have a great deal of experience and knowledge in voice, and it is ideal (but still unusual) for a singing teacher to affiliate with such a colleague. At present, it is illegal in most states for anyone but a licensed speech-language pathologist to treat a pathological speaking voice. Pathology, of course, is diagnosed only by a laryngologist. Voice trainers also exist, but there is no licensing or quality control for people who designate themselves in this category. They generally work with the voices of actors or public speakers and can be an invaluable asset to the voice team. There is no set of requirements that must be fulfilled in order for one to call him- or herself a singing teacher. Consequently, it is essential for other professionals to investigate the quality, training, experience, and reputation of singing teachers with whom they anticipate collaborating in patient care. Membership in the National Association of Teachers of Singers (NATS) is an encouraging sign, but the requirements for membership are certainly not rigorous enough to ensure that all members are high quality teachers.

Application of modern scientific insights to improve the training of teachers and singers has been prominent in the last few decades, and was popularized particularly by Vennard.[2] In recent years, increasing interest in interdisciplinary information disseminated through gatherings such as The Voice Foundation Symposia and NATS meetings has resulted in wide availability of undergraduate and graduate training programs in vocal pedagogy.

In this chapter, we make no effort to define good singing teaching or to promulgate any one technique as the *correct way*. In fact, there is great variation in responses from students in the studio, and good singing teachers have a large repertoire of techniques and exercises that allow them to individualize approaches to accomplish the goals of voice training.

In the next few pages, we present a few basic principles that can be used to understand singing teaching in general. Naturally, many details are omitted. However, for the reader who is not a voice teacher, this chapter should provide a basic idea of what a singing teacher does; and for the singing teacher, we have included information on documentation of voice lessons, correspondence with other professionals, and approaches to teaching people with injured voices later in the chapter. These topics frequently are not included in routine training for singing teachers.

In general, singing teaching begins with an assessment of the student. This leads to a determination of the singer's talent and problems, which guides the development of a lesson plan. Specific exercises are chosen to correct problems and improve vocal control and eventually artistry. Training occurs in all areas of the singer's anatomy. Abdominal exercises, pulmonary control, and correct alignment of posture cultivate the power sources of voice. Vocal exercises increase neuromuscular strength and coordination at the laryngeal level, improving not only range, quality, and vibratory symmetry, but also smooth control over changes in subglottal pressure, registers, and other variables. The supraglottic vocal tract is also trained, developing optimal vocal tract position and shape to create the desired harmonics without unnecessary muscle tension and with improved resonance. In general, principles of artistic economy apply. That is, if a good sound can be made without involving a specific muscle group (eg, those muscles that retract the tongue), then using extraneous muscles is generally wrong and deleterious to vocal health and performance. In most cases, voice lessons result in steady, gradual improvement in voice quality, range, efficiency, and endurance. Voice lessons should not end in hoarseness or physical discomfort in the neck or throat (although abdominal and back muscles are often fatigued and ache).

The principles of proper voice production are largely the same in speaking and singing. In fact, many people believe that the singing voice is simply a natural extension of a good speaking voice. In any case, training supplied by a singing teacher and a speech-language pathologist should be compatible and symbiotic. If a singer is receiving contradictory information from these two voice professionals (and is correctly interpreting their instructions), it could be indicative of incorrect training from one of them. Close scrutiny is warranted.

Singing Voice Specialist

As stated previously, singing voice teachers who work primarily with injured or abused voices of singers and nonsingers are known as "singing voice specialists" (SVS). The SVS is an experienced and specially trained voice teacher, usually with a degree in voice performance or pedagogy, who has professional voice performance experience, training in anatomy and physiology, training in the rehabilitation of injured voice users, and other special education. In addition to these basics, the SVS must acquire knowledge of anatomy and physiology of the normal and disordered voice, including neuroanatomy, familiarity with objective voice measurement equipment and assessment, a basic understanding of the principles of laryngology and medications, and a fundamental knowledge of the principles and practices of speech-language pathology. The SVS who works in an arts-medicine setting encounters several differences from routine studio work. The range of potential patients is enormous. Some patients have great potential talent; others may already be world-class professional singers but require special instruction while recovering from an injury. Many are active avocational singers. Still other patients have no interest in singing, but benefit from breath management, relaxation, resonance, and musical training in an effort to improve their speaking voices; singing training for nonsingers should be pursued only in collaboration with traditional voice therapy provided by a certified speech-language pathologist.

The SVS must first be an excellent singing teacher, should have extensive training in the singing voice and, ideally, have personal experience as a professional singer. Being able to relate to performance demands on the basis of personal experience is most helpful. It is also desirable (but not essential) for the SVS to have reasonably good keyboard skills. He or she should be able to play scales with the patient, accompany simple songs, and make individualized practice tapes. It is not essential that the SVS be a highly skilled pianist. However, it is critical that he or she has an exceptional ability to hear minute changes in vocal quality and be an astutely demanding perfectionist.

At present, there are no formal training programs in the United States that teach singing teachers to work with injured voices. In fact, there are few good programs to train interested persons in "how to teach singing" in general. It is illegal in most states for a singing teacher to provide therapy for an injured or pathological voice unless he or she meets licensure requirements, most of which are equivalent to certification by the American Speech-Language-Hearing Association (ASHA). As stated earlier, however, speech-language pathologists generally do not receive training on the care of the professional voice. Very few speech-language pathology training programs provide instruction on care of the professional speaker, and most have no training in the singing voice at all. There is, however, a joint committee of ASHA and NATS that has compiled a list of professionals who have partially or fully met requirements for interdisciplinary training. Information on this joint committee may be obtained by contacting either ASHA or NATS. A few graduate programs have made great strides in combining the knowledge required from both fields, such as the vocology program at the University of Iowa. At present, if an independent voice teacher accepts a student for "voice rehabilitation" without having the student work concurrently with a licensed speech-language pathologist, that teacher may be subject to litigation, even if the student is referred by a laryngologist. A good interdisciplinary team working under one roof not only provides optimal patient care, but also obviates potential legal problems of this sort.

To acquire the necessary knowledge to become a SVS, it is helpful for the interested singing teacher to take advantage of available graduate level courses in speech science, neuroanatomy, neurophysiology, and speech-language pathology. There are also an increasing number of symposia dedicated to the professional voice. These offer additional training by practitioners skilled in the field. The Voice Foundation offers the most extensive annual symposium on care of the professional voice. Information may be obtained by writing to The Voice Foundation, 1721 Pine Street, Philadelphia, Pennsylvania 19103. Important information can also be gleaned from many of the publications listed as suggested readings near the end of this book. In addition, even for experienced voice teachers, a professional internship of some sort is almost imperative. The duration varies with the teacher's experience and need, and it may be broken up into short observation periods. However, a singing teacher interested in becoming active in caring for the injured voice needs to observe laryngologists in the office and operating room, speech-language pathologists specializing in professional voice care, SVSs working with injured voices, and voice laboratory technicians working with instrumentation. Access to such opportunities is limited, but it is available.

The trained SVS aids in the remediation of voice disorders utilizing singing voice exercises specific to the patient's vocal condition. The SVS works with a voice patient when recommended by the otolaryngologist, following strobovideolaryngoscopic examination and objective voice assessment (acoustic, aerodynamic, and other measures). A SVS should never work with a patient without a comprehensive medical examination and diagnosis from an otolaryngologist, because (among other reasons) voice work is contraindicated in some conditions such as recent vocal fold hemorrhage.

A SVS can be useful in the remediation of singers and nonsingers. However, it is *essential* that singers work with the SVS to ensure safe, healthy vocal production and to identify and eliminate potentially dangerous compensatory technical errors that often develop in response to vocal injury or dysfunction. The SVS is not a replacement for the patient's customary voice teacher. Rather, the SVS works with the patient's voice teacher to educate him or her about the patient's voice disorder, includes the voice teacher in the sessions (if approved by the patient), and instructs the patient and teacher regarding appropriate vocal exercises and goals in light of medical limitations established by the laryngologist.

For nonsingers, supplementing traditional voice therapy (by the speech-language pathologist) with singing voice training often facilitates and expedites therapy. There are many differences between singers and typical speakers. For example, conversational speech usually encompasses about a major sixth. Most singers possess a 2-octave range. Interestingly, physiological frequency range is about 3½ octaves in both singers and nonsingers, so most people have more potential than they realize. Pulmonary demands are also much greater during singing than speaking. In speech, we typically use 10% to 25% of vital capacity. The singer frequently uses closer to 65% of vital capacity. In many ways, singing is to speaking as running is to walking. In rehabilitating a patient who has difficulty walking, once a patient has learned to jog and run, walking becomes relatively trivial, since the patient is not working at his physiological limits during this activity. Likewise, once patients have acquired some of the athletic vocal skills employed routinely by singers (including increased frequency range, frequency and intensity variability, prolonged phrasing, breath management and support, etc), the demands of speech seem much less formidable. In many cases, even nonsingers utilize a more relaxed and anteriorly placed voice while performing sung or chant-like exercises. This helps facilitate a more resonant voice quality in the speaking voice, while eliminating pressed phonation.

Assessment

In evaluating a potential student, most singing teachers listen to a song or two, ask the singer to sing a few specific exercises, and discuss the singer's previous training. This process (history, diagnosis, treatment) is the same as that used by physicians and speech-language pathologists. More enlightened singing teachers also discuss matters of vocal health and hygiene in greater detail. Good singing teachers who hear anything abnormal in a voice (hoarseness, breathiness, diplophonia, aphonia) routinely refer the prospective student for a laryngologic evaluation. Although rarely required by music schools, medical assessment and vocal fold visualization of all voice majors prior to matriculation would be beneficial. The SVS's assessment protocol is more involved, not only because the singers have vocal problems, but also because it is necessary that the SVS have extensive knowledge of the experience, habits, and health of the patient. In an arts-medicine setting, the laryngologist has usually examined the patient before the SVS begins the evaluation. Regardless of these circumstances, we find value in a systematic, comprehensive assessment of each patient by the SVS.

The SVS takes his or her own history from the patient, even though he or she may have been present when the laryngologist obtained a similar history. Repetition frequently yields additional information of importance to the voice team. Taking a history also allows the SVS the opportunity to more closely observe the speaking habits of the patient and to establish a comfortable rapport with the patient. The questions asked in the history are the same as those asked by the physician and are summarized in appendix II. If a history form has not been completed for the laryngologist, the SVS asks the patient to complete a similar questionnaire. If a patient history form has already been completed for the physician, the SVS reviews this information and asks additional questions about previous teachers and training, specific techniques used, and other singing experience. The patient is asked to estimate the number of hours that he or she is speaking and singing throughout a typical day and high/low voice use days, if usage varies dramatically. Other questions regarding voice use are asked of the singer-patient, such as:

1. What kind of music do you perform most often?
2. Do you sing in different voice ranges or classifications?
3. Are you playing any instruments while singing?
4. What is the environment like where you are performing?
5. Is there an amplification system? If so, are monitor speakers utilized?
6. Are special costumes and staging involved during singing?
7. How many years of formal singing training have you had?
8. How many teachers have you had?
9. What are your career goals?
10. What is your current career status?
11. Do you have recordings and/or videos of your voice at its best and at its worst?

The singer and nonsinger are asked about vocally abusive habits during speaking, such as:

1. Are you exposed to passive smoke?
2. Do you do any yelling (for or at pets, children, spouses)?
3. Do you do any coughing (in the morning, following meals)?
4. Do you find yourself talking loudly (on the telephone or over ambient noise)?
5. Do you clear your throat frequently?
6. Do you work out with weights? If so, do you breathe on exertion? Do you do aerobics?
7. Do you whisper?

If the patient is a singer, the next portion of the evaluation involves listening to the singer's usual warm-up exercises or warming-up the singer with scales, then listening to a song of the singer's choice. The entire evaluation is tape-recorded, and videotaped, if possible, as are subsequent lessons. Such tapes are good not only for documenting progress, but also for feedback for teaching purposes. In addition to the tape recorder and video camera, basic equipment for a voice studio includes a piano (or keyboard), full length mirror, hand-held mirror, and good lighting. The studio should have reasonably "live" acoustics, with a minimum of sound-treatment materials. It should also be properly heated and humidified, and drinking water should be readily available. The singing evaluation is usually done with the patient standing unless the patient routinely sings in a seated position. The patient is assessed for stance/posture, breath control, support, jaw and oral cavity position, general tension, range and quality of sound. Range should be assessed with a series of scales, beginning comfortably in the patient's lower or middle range. The patient is asked to sing three-note or five-note ascending and descending scales on /ʌ/ or /ma/. The scales should proceed past the upper passaggio (including the falsetto in men) up to the highest musically acceptable note and descend to the lowest musically acceptable note. Voice breaks and other difficulties are noted. The voice should not be strained, and it is the SVS's responsibility to decide when the patient has reached his or her limit. The authors use a form for the SVS to record observations conveniently (Fig 27–1). Specific characteristics are assessed in each area, and a training program is designed to correct any errors observed.

Stance/Posture

The head, neck, and shoulders should be in neutral position. The shoulders should not be elevated, rolled forward, or held back, as these maneuvers introduce unnecessary tension. A singer should stand comfortably straight, but not in a stiffly erect, military fashion. Knees should be slightly bent and flexible, not locked, and weight should be centered over the metatarsal head (balls of the feet), not the heels. The feet should be apart, but not more apparent than the width of the shoulders. Many singers prefer to have one foot slight-

---

TAPE # _____

SUBJECTIVE EVALUATION:
SINGING VOICE

☐ PROFESSIONAL VOICE USER
☐ NONPROFESSIONAL VOICE USER
☐ CLASSICAL SINGER
☐ NON-CLASSICAL SINGER
☐ NONSINGER

NAME: _____

DATE OF EVALUATION: _____

AGE: _____ DATE OF BIRTH: _____

OCCUPATION: _____

SEX: ☐ MALE ☐ FEMALE

YEARS VOICE STUDY: _____

OTOLARYNGOLOGIST: _____

VOICE TEACHERS: _____

MEDICAL DIAGNOSIS: _____

LONGEST TEACHER: _____

SPEECH-LANGUAGE PATHOLOGIST: ____

LAST VOICE LESSION: _____

Fig 27–1. Evaluation form used by singing voice specialists. +, minimal cues; ++, considerable tactile and visual cues required. *(continued)*

CHARACTERISTIC	CORRECTS TECHNIQUE		
	+ CUES	+ + CUES	UNABLE
STANCE/POSTURE:			
FEET POSITION			
WEIGHT FORWARD			
KNEES UNLOCKED			
UPPER TORSO/STERNUM			
SHOULDERS			
STRAP MUSCLES			
LARYNGEAL MOVEMENT			
FOREHEAD TENSION			
HEAD/NECK PROTRUSION			
HEAD/NECK ELEVATION			
BREATH:			
ABDOMINAL/DIAPHRAGMATIC			
THORACIC			
CLAVICULAR			
SHALLOW			
RAPID			
AUDIBLE			
EXCESSIVE ABDOMINAL MOVEMENT			
SUPPORT:			
EFFECTIVE			
DEFICIENT			
INEFFECTIVE			
LATE			
INVERSE PRESSURE			
ORAL CAVITY:			
REDUCED OPENING			
RISORIUS TENSION			
JAW JUTTING			
ANTERIOR JAW TENSION			
POSTERIOR JAW TENSION			
ANTERIOR TONGUE RETRACTION			
ANTERIOR TONGUE CURL			
POSTERIOR TONGUE ELEVATION			
POSTERIOR TONGUE DEPRESSION			

Fig 27–1. *(continued)*

RESONANCE: _____

FOCUS: _____

RANGE: _____ SCALES: _____

QUALITY: _____

PLAN: _____

Fig 27–1. *(continued)*

ly forward. This athletic, well-balanced stance optimizes breathing and support. It behooves the SVS to acquire special knowledge of posture analysis and muscle conditioning. In many cases, it is advisable for the patient to include physical exercises to improve posture and strengthen support muscles. Basic principles of posture analysis and exercise programs can be found in the literature,[3] and consultation with a skilled physiatrist or physical therapist may be valuable in selected cases.

Breathing

The rib cage should be erect, so that the upper thorax appears slightly more full than during comfortable speech, but it should not rise excessively or cause muscle tension in the upper thorax, supraclavicular area, or neck. Most of the active breathing is abdominal, and distension should occur in the front, back, and sides. Breathing should be relatively relaxed, quiet, and nasal breathing is preferable when time between phrases permits. High thoracic breathing patterns, rapid intake, and noisy inspiration frequently indicate tension, which may be carried over into vocalization. Abdominal movement during inspiration and expiration should be efficient. Excessive abdominal activity may occur in singers consciously struggling to optimize breathing and support. Such excessive inflection, contraction, and distension of abdominal muscles undermine the adjustment process between breathing and initiating effective support.

Support

Support is a difficult concept for many singers, and various constructs are used to teach it. The fundamental principle is to generate a vector of force under the airstream, supporting it upward between the vocal folds. Support should be continuous, not static. Some good abdominal and thoracic support may occur

spontaneously in people while singing a rolled /r/, and singing scales on /v/. Good support may also be experienced during the production of /hm/ or the act of blowing out a candle. Muscles in the lower abdomen, upper abdomen, and lower thorax and back are actively involved. Coordinated support should be initiated just before a tone is heard. In many cases, if a teacher advises a student to bring abdominal muscles in and up, the student will also raise his or her shoulder, chest, and neck muscles. Consequently, many teaching constructs have been created in which students are advised to think of their support as going "down and out" (the inverse pressure approach), rather than "inward and upward." This effort may also be an attempt to more precisely balance the flow of air needed for singing. Any teaching imagery can be effective, so long as the student and teacher understand the difference between the language of the imagery and the physical effect they are really trying to achieve. Good support should be present not only when singing high notes, but also in lower ranges. Singers frequently support well going up a scale but relax excessively during descending passages and have virtually no effective support in portions of their mid and lower ranges.

Support may be assessed visually and by palpation. It is often best to evaluate support while testing range, when the singer is not aware that support functions are being scrutinized. Good support is essential. When the power source is not working adequately, many voice users compensate with excess muscle tension in the neck, tongue, and jaw. Such muscular tension dysphonia is inefficient and potentially hazardous to the vocal folds.

Laryngeal Position

For most classical Western singing, the larynx is usually slightly below its neutral vertical position. The larynx should remain relatively stable and should not rise appreciably with ascending pitch or fall with descending pitch. These caveats are not necessarily true in other styles such as pop music (for intermittent special effects), Asian music, and certain other cultural and ethnic styles. In general, note-by-note laryngeal articulation of pitch indicates improper singing technique.

Extrinsic Laryngeal Muscle Tension

All patients are visually evaluated for extrinsic laryngeal muscle tension during voice use. Protrusion of the strap muscles or any of the extrinsic laryngeal musculature may be indicative of muscle tension dysphonia, and such activity is considered indicative of hyperfunctional vocal behavior. Patients exhibiting this kind of behavior will often complain of throat pain lateral to the larynx with prolonged voice use and will present with "throaty" voice production. They commonly also have trouble singing softly, and they may develop a pitch wobble and voice fatigue.

Jaw Position

Jaw position may be assessed while singing /ʌ/. The jaw should be allowed to open to its maximum, relaxed position, but it should not be forced open excessively. Appropriate jaw position is similar to that seen in most people just before the initiation of a yawn. It is generally close to a two-finger span, although no one should be forced to meet this guideline if this degree of opening introduces jaw tension. The corners of the mouth should not be tensed, and the jaw should not quiver or alter position with changes in pitch. The posterior jaw should also be relaxed for all vowels. Decreased oral resonance due to limited mouth opening is often a tell-tale sign of jaw tension. Teeth clenching is characteristic of extreme jaw tension. However, mouth opening may change in relation to pitch.

Tongue Position

Tongue position may also be assessed on /ʌ/. The tip of the tongue should rest in a relaxed posture against the mandibular central incisors or slightly behind. It should not retract, curl anteriorly, or rise posteriorly. The pharynx should generally be visible, not obscured by arching of the posterior aspect of the tongue. The tongue should be noted particularly at the moment when tone is initiated. Sudden tongue tension and retraction upon initiation of tone often indicates delayed or ineffective abdominal support. It is important to assess visually and by listening to the sound of the voice not only the anterior tongue position, but

also the posterior position of the tongue. Most well-trained singers know that the tongue is supposed to be relaxed and should not pull back from the teeth. However, it is possible (especially for the more advanced singer) to maintain the anterior tongue in good position and still introduce excessive posterior tongue tension. This excessive tension results in voice fatigue and sometimes limitation of range. In addition to the criteria noted, tongue position should not change with alterations in pitch, and there should be no tongue activity apparent during routine five-note scales on /ʌ/. The tongue and jaw should be able to function independently.

Face

While singing scales on /ʌ/, virtually no facial muscle activity should be required. Excessive tension in the corners of the mouth, lips, corrugation of the chin, forehead tension, or other extraneous muscle use may indicate hyperfunction and may be associated with insufficient support. The facial expression should be pleasant, but no specific facial muscle gestures should be required to produce an /ʌ/. Eliminating dependence on facial hyperfunction is important not only to optimize technique, but also because the singer and speaker need to be able to use facial muscles independently to show expression and emotion without affecting voice production.

Tone Placement

Singers and nonsingers often present with posterior tone placement in addition to tongue and jaw tension and extrinsic laryngeal muscle tension. A posterior tone will sound heavier and more mature, at least to the singer; and some singers will use this type of placement in an effort to sound older or to achieve a bigger sound. Unfortunately, posterior tone placement is usually indicative of excess muscle tension and improper singing technique. It also impairs the efficiency of the resonator (decreased singer's formant) thereby limiting projection and making the singer work harder to be heard.

Summary

At the completion of the assessment process, observations and findings are reviewed with the student. Fatigue, nervousness, and other variables must be taken into account during the first lesson, but an experienced teacher can usually draw accurate conclusions during the initial evaluation. Specific deficiencies are explained, and plans to remedy them are established.

Specific exercises are selected, and the singing teacher teaches them to the student or patient in the singing studio. A practice schedule is assigned, and arrangements for follow-up and further lessons are made.

To appreciate the special considerations involved in working with injured voices, it is helpful to understand the kind of exercises used routinely in training noninjured voices. Many of these are useful for patients with vocal injuries, as well; but modifications are often necessary. The following section reviews exercises commonly used to train singers.

Exercises for "Routine" Singing Lessons

Singing lessons involve selected exercises to build muscle strength, coordination, and efficiency. Throughout training, a combination of tactile (hands), verbal, visual, and auditory (live and recorded) feedback is used to correct errors and ensure that the singer can tell which techniques and sounds are correct and which are not. The exercises are designed to develop all parts of the vocal mechanism. Like other muscle - building exercises, it is often better to structure such exercises in short sessions to be repeated a few times throughout the day. In beginners, sessions should rarely be more than 20 minutes in length until muscle strength is developed and technique becomes consistent. Exercises to warm-up the voice first thing in the morning and to cool-down the voice following each practice session, rehearsal, performance, and in the evening are especially important. Although the efficacy of vocal warm-up has been understood, the benefits of a vocal cool-down have not been as widely appreciated and followed.

General Body Exercises

The singing teacher must make an assessment of the student's general physical condition. Good aerobic conditioning, abdominal muscle strength, and back muscle development are particularly important. In any student with health problems, or in older students, exercise programs should always be developed in conjunction with medical supervision. Vocal development should include some form of aerobic activity (eg, jogging, fast walking, swimming, aerobic dance, etc), abdominal muscle exercises (eg, sit-ups), and exercises that affect the back and lower abdomen (eg, leg lifts). Only exercises that the singer can perform without inappropriate strain should be chosen. Singers must be instructed to avoid forceful glottic closure and other forms of voice abuse while exercising. Groaning during sit-ups or weight lifting or counting

numbers during aerobic dance can cause vocal injury (in fact, hoarseness and vocal nodules are seen commonly in aerobics instructors). Nevertheless, if a singer cannot run up a couple of flights of stairs without getting excessively winded, pulmonary function should be evaluated.

Breathing

There are many exercises that work well for teaching breath management for singers. In some cases, the teacher simply explains thoracic and abdominal breathing and the desired principles and helps the student experiment with correct and incorrect breathing techniques and postures by pointing out which techniques are correct. In most students, some sort of tactile feedback helps. Placing a student in unusual positions frequently helps him or her sense aspects of breathing technique that are harder to feel in normal positions. Such exercises may be done with the student lying on the floor with a small book under his or her head. Another useful technique is to ask the student to bend from the waist and place his or her hands laterally on the waist, take a full breath and feel rib expansion. The breath is taken slowly, avoiding elevation of the shoulders and maximizing expansion of the lower portion of the rib cage. The student is instructed to exhale slowly and repeats the exercise several times. This exercise is then performed with the student standing one third to one half of the way up, maintaining proper balance. The exercise steps are repeated, trying to maintain the same abdominal and lower back sensations. They are then repeated while standing erect. It should be remembered that these exercises are intended as facilitators. Actually, these positions create modifications in respiratory function that are not appropriate for long-term voice development. These maneuvers are intended to help establish body awareness early in the training process, and students must be cautioned not to practice excessively or vocalize in these unusual postures. Many alternate exercise regimens are also effective. The student may stand with arms perpendicular to the floor, palms upward, elbows slightly bent, shoulders relaxed, and sense upper torso alignment, ease of breath, and efficiency of support. Students are also instructed to practice breathing and to combine relaxed breathing with flexion and relaxation of support musculature periodically during the day, not only during practice sessions, but also while speaking or simply walking from place to place.

Support Exercises

It is important for each student to realize that it is possible to vocalize without hyperfunctional muscle activity. Many students, especially those with previous singing experience, habitually engage superfluous muscle groups in preparation for each sung phrase. For such students, it is often best to start teaching support by eliminating as much extraneous muscle activity as possible by teaching the student simply to breathe in a relaxed fashion, and then add support and sound. For other students with fairly good technique and no significant hyperfunctional abuse, it may be appropriate to proceed directly to discussions of improving support musculature strength and coordination. The latter group of students is easier to teach, and the exercises listed below are examples of the kind of approach used for the former group. Such students may be advised to:

1. Take slow, deep breaths in and out through the mouth, eliminating all muscle tension in the oral cavity, head, and neck. These exercises are done facing a mirror.
2. Take a slow, deep breath, and exhale slowly for as long as possible on "wh," being careful to maintain good posture and not allow the chest to collapse.
3. Take a slow, deep breath, exhale on /s/, /a/, and /ʃ/, being careful to maintain good posture and slow exhalation.
4. Take a slow breath, and initiate a descending sigh on /u/, /o/, and /a/. These vowels are then repeated but initiated with the consonants used in the previous exercise. In particular, /s/ has a tendency to help elicit support. The student is instructed to maintain the same abdominal and lower back sensations during the vowel as initiated during the consonant. The student should not be afraid if this exercise encompasses more than one register. Smooth transition between registers in the long descending sigh should be encouraged.
5. Take a slow breath, and exhale, permitting a gently voiced sigh during the exhalation. The exercise is then repeated, and the singer is asked to sustain the sigh on a descending scale.
6. Take a slow, deep breath, drop the jaw, engage the support musculature as previously explained, and sustain the vowel /a/. Observe the tongue and neck closely. Abdominal support should not create any visible change in the oral cavity, head, or neck.
7. Take a deep breath, initiate support, and sing five-note ascending and descending scales beginning on the note identified during deep sigh exercises. The scales should be done on /a/, and later on /o/ and other vowels (Fig 27–2). Initially, the notes should be connected (legato), and the student should take care to avoid laryngeal rise and fall while changing pitch. For some beginners, even

five notes is too great a range to sing when using improper techniques such as tongue retraction. However, for most students, five-note scales can be performed throughout low and high ranges. Later, when technique is more consistent, more advanced exercises are used.

8. Rolled /r/, /v/, /ʃu/ and lip trills (continuous "br") in descending passages are also good for developing breath management and increasing consciousness of correct skeletal posture (Fig 27–3). The student must be monitored carefully for laryngeal and throat tension. Students who cannot produce a rolled /r/ or lip trills without inappropriate muscle tension should avoid these exercises until later in training.

Technical Exercises

Technical exercises are used to develop agility, increase range, and improve pitch accuracy. Such exercises include (among others):

1. Rapid and slow five-note ascending/descending scales while humming and on various vowels (Fig 27–4). This exercise is good for virtually all students, but should be monitored closely for laryngeal tension as well as throat posterior tongue and jaw tension that often can accompany humming efforts. It may be preceded by a descending five-note slide.
2. Slow sliding scales ascending and descending a major third on /a/ and on /o/ → /a/ (Fig 27–5).

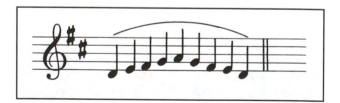

Fig 27–2. Five-note ascending/descending scale.

Fig 27–3. Five-note ascending/descending scale.

Fig 27–4. Repeated ascending/descending scales.

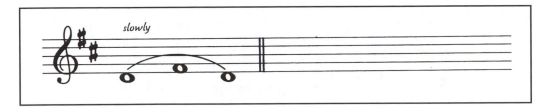

Fig 27–5. Slow ascending/descending slide of major third interval.

3. Arpeggio scales on /ʌ/ and /o/ɪ/ʌ/, slowly, with careful legato connection from note to note (Fig 27–6). This exercise is good for the intermediate singer.

4. Slowly descending five-note scale, beginning on /u/ and changing to /ʌ/ on the last note, with a trill (Fig 27–7). This exercise should be used in the lower part of the voice to increase vocal control and effective use of support in the lower register. The trill should be a true half-step or whole-step trill, not simply excessive vibrato.

5. Lip vowel variation (/ʌ/ to /o/ to /u/ to /o/ to /ʌ/) exercises sung on a sustained tone (Fig 27–8). Tongue vowels may also be approached in this manner. This exercise may be done with tactile cues to keep the sound from "spreading." The vowel variation exercises are good for focusing the voice.

6. A great number of additional exercises are used during the training process. They involve connected and disconnected scales, patterns of scales involving various intervals rather than adjacent notes, exercises at different dynamics, exercises bridging different registers (eg, crescendo/diminuendo singing from falsetto to modal register and back), and many other patterns. Such vocalises may be found in numerous published collections and texts on vocal pedagogy.

Placement, Resonance, and Projection

Detailed discussion of tonal placement, sensations of resonance, and projection is bound to be controversial.

For the purposes of this chapter, suffice it to say that, as respiratory control, muscle strength, and laryngeal coordination improve, various techniques are used to optimize the shape of the vocal tract. The tongue, soft palate, pharynx, jaw, and other regions of the supraglottic vocal tract are trained to generate with minimal effort the desired harmonic spectrum. In particular, the resonators enhance the desirable formant, as discussed in chapter 4. Exercises to accomplish these goals include use of vowels, nasals, consonants, songs, chanting, ear training, and a considerable amount of trial and error with feedback from the teacher. Feedback from instrumentation such as spectrographs may also be helpful in selected cases.

Songs

Building repertoire may begin when the student has mastered several of the vocalises and has developed voice control over a large enough range to permit comfortable singing of the vocal literature. Singers who wish to sing classical repertoire do well to begin with an anthology of early Italian songs and arias and with simple English and American songs. Nonclassical singers should start with standard lyric-legato songs. Rock singers should also begin with ballad like rock songs rather than up-tempo pieces, and use songs that vary between modal and falsetto register, if possible. It is usually easier to begin with new repertoire, rather than trying to relearn old material in a technically correct fashion. Active performers should concentrate on incorporating the new technique into slower songs,

Fig 27–6. Arpeggio scales.

Fig 27–7. Descending scale with trill on last note.

Fig 27–8. Vowel variation exercise.

gradually building the repertoire into an entire set or concert. If the student has been performing actively prior to studying with the teacher, it is especially important for the teacher to attend a performance of the singer. This allows a much deeper understanding of the singer's vocal needs, problems, and progress. Technical aspects of singing are the singer teacher's domain. Many singing teachers also provide training in interpretation, staging, and other artistic aspects of performance, although these matters can be relegated to voice coaches, acting teachers, and other professionals.

Training the Injured Voice

Special Considerations for the Singing Voice Specialist

In designing and individualizing training protocols, SVSs commonly work toward goals different from those familiar to most singing teachers. For example, in many instances, the SVS must be disciplined enough to ignore vocal quality, and to train the patient to practice appropriate techniques regardless of the sound. This is not a natural concept for singers, singing teachers, or even speakers. Ordinarily, a "good" sound is considered paramount, and singers will do whatever they can to sound attractive. This natural tendency may have gotten many of them into medical difficulty in the first place in the form of hyperfunctional muscle compensations. While rehabilitating the singer following disease, injury or surgery, it is essential to develop good technique, healthy muscle use, and to avoid muscle atrophy from prolonged voice rest or abstinence from singing. Neuromuscular rehabilitation can and should begin for many patients long before professional (or even attractive) vocal quality can be achieved. The timing of advancement in vocal training for such patients is determined by the SVS in collaboration with a laryngologist and speech-language pathologist. Early specially designed voice training (as soon as medically safe) is helpful in avoiding reinjury.

One of the most important aspects of training for a SVS is developing the ability to understand medical limitations, goals, prognosis, and expected duration of recovery (often months). Only with a clear understanding of these issues, and with full appreciation of the patient's activities and progress with the speech-language pathologist, can the SVS develop a singing protocol that is medically safe and appropriately helpful to the patient's voice rehabilitation. Training the singing voice with skillfully chosen exercises in the medical setting provides invaluable rehabilitation. Incorrect exercises can easily result in serious permanent vocal injury. Once the SVS has learned when the training process should be guided by tactile versus visual versus auditory feedback, and has mastered the other necessary skills and information, his or her contribution to the medical voice care team is invaluable not only for singers, but also for nonsingers.

Exercises

Singing voice sessions are designed to build muscle strength, coordination, flexibility, and efficiency. They are also designed to eliminate abusive vocal behaviors, promote easy and relaxed phonation, improve abdominal breathing and support, and promote frontal tone placement and resonant voice quality. This should lead to reduction, elimination, or prevention of vocal pathologies, optimal preparation for vocal fold surgery when necessary, and safe vocal production following surgery or injury.

There are no magic sets of vocal exercises. Each patient has his or her own specific needs depending on the pathology, extent of injury, age of injury, and vocal demands. It is important to understand the nature of the patient's vocal pathology, be able to identify probable causes of the pathology, identify compensatory technical behaviors, and understand the physiological and histological effects of the pathology in order to adequately work with an injured voice. Carefully chosen exercises are utilized, addressing each area of deficiency. In general, exercises are designed to develop all parts of the vocal mechanism. Like other muscle-building exercises, it is often better to structure such exercises in short sessions to be repeated a few times throughout the day. In beginners and patients with recent vocal injury, such sessions should rarely be more than 15–20 minutes in length (often less) until muscle strength is developed and technique becomes consistent.

When utilizing singing voice exercises, the patient should take frequent rest periods in order to reestablish appropriate muscle relaxation. Numerous maneuvers can facilitate this relaxation including gentle exhalatory gestures on a quiet, open-throated /hɑ/ or other vowel, stretching and gentle to vigorous movements of the body, massage, or even simply sitting or lying down. The duration of practice periods is strictly dictated by the laryngologist and the individual patient's ability to sing without any inappropriate strain or discomfort. Particularly in cases of resolving vocal fold hemorrhage, vocal fold tear or post-vocal fold surgery, 3–5 minutes of singing 2–4 times a day may prove sufficient. Duration and frequency of practice periods are increased according to the patient's comfort and skill level. It is absolutely critical that the patient be well-informed concerning general vocal hygiene and the need for appropriate stress management and sleep. The need for adequate hydration cannot be overemphasized. The exercises discussed below may be used for injured singers and nonsingers, according to the patient's abilities.

The previous instructions regarding general body exercises, breathing and breath support exercises are applicable for the injured voice. When applying breath support to ascending/descending scales, however, it is often easiest to begin with limited note excursion. A sliding sung scale on a major second may eventually open more comfortably to a major third, then to a major fifth, and so on. Other ascending/descending patterns may also be used. Range in all exercises is strictly determined by the patient's ability to phonate the notes without inappropriate tension. Gentle sliding from note to note as opposed to strict delineation efforts on each note may be less traumatic to the vocal folds. Also, the easy stretching motion of the vocal folds on ascending/descending scales is believed to be effective in helping to regain vocal fold flexibility and in establishing appropriate compensation in the vocal mechanism. Lip and tongue trills may also prove useful on these scales and may be utilized on broader scales such as octaves, ninths, and elevenths, as the voice permits. Sliding sung scales and lip and tongue trills may be used in the rehabilitation of numerous vocal fold injuries including, but not exclusively, vocal fold scarring, vocal fold masses, superior laryngeal nerve paresis, and any resolving disruption of the vocal fold mucosa (Figure 27–9I).

Legato, lightly sung three-note and five-note descending scales are recommended to help regain vocal fold agility. Ascending/descending scales sung in this fashion are also useful. Vowel choice is optional with open vowels such as /ɑ/ and /o/ usually providing the most exposed presentation of the voice. Again, scale excursion and overall range are determined by the patient's ability to maintain reasonable vocal technique (breath support, resonance space and placement) with minimal counter-productive compensatory muscle tension. This exercise is potentially useful in the remediation of most vocal fold injuries. Extreme caution is always recommended during the first sessions following disruption of the vocal fold mucosa (Fig 27–9II).

Exercises involving changes in volume appear to be useful in strengthening the vocal mechanism. They seem particularly effective in cases of superior laryngeal nerve pareses, when the ability of one or both vocal folds to stretch has been compromised. The concept of mezzo-piano to piano to mezzo-piano or piano to mezzo-piano to piano and later, mezzo-forte to piano to mezzo-forte and piano to mezzo-forte to piano may be applied to any number of scale patterns. The patient must be carefully monitored, particularly aurally and visually, to be sure that these alterations in loudness are not accomplished with inappropriate changes in the vocal tract, but rather through subtle breath support adjustments (Fig 27–9III). For patients with superior laryngeal nerve paresis, pitch-stretching exercises are also essential, such as sliding (glissando) passages. These may be combined with volume-variable exercises.

Most singing exercises may be performed on a hum, usually /N/ or /m/. Humming is frequently performed incorrectly so care must be taken to monitor for inappropriate tensions. The /N/ is best utilized with the mid or back portion of the tongue resting lightly against the roof of the mouth and the anterior tip of the tongue relaxed and in contact with the lower front teeth. The lips may be gently closed. The /m/ is most effective when the tongue is relaxed and forward in position but not touching the roof of the mouth, and the lips are resting gently against one another, not tightly pressed. With both hums, no amount of jaw, tongue or throat tension should be allowed. When done correctly, humming can be a particularly effective exercise for establishing better tonal placement and for stabilizing the delicate balance between the breath support system and the larynx. These exercises also help some patients improve kinesthetic recognition of muscle tension. Many patients get improved vocal function and tonal quality by first humming a scale pattern and then immediately repeating the pattern on a vowel sound (Fig 27–9IV).

When working with vocal fold paresis/paralysis patients, especially recurrent laryngeal nerve weakness where adduction and abduction are affected, the goal of more efficient glottic closure may be aided by the use of staccato exercises. Several patterns may prove useful. Vowel choice is optional, but several vowels should be used in the design of any patient's exercise program. Using /p/ or /b/ as an initial consonant can help facilitate the sensation of increased forward tonal placement. /H/ may also be used, but careful monitoring of laryngeal position and tension should be maintained (Fig 27–9V).

When working with the nonsinger, the SVS can offer significant contributions to the speaking voice. First, singing voice exercises may be effective in hastening the patient's adaptation of efficient vocal technique which is needed for correct speech production. Second, singing exercises can also strengthen specific areas of weakness within the vocal system and help establish appropriate compensations for permanent vocal fold injury. When working with the nonsinger, the SVS must choose exercises that allow for smooth carryover of vocal production from singing to speaking.

1. One useful concept is to establish technically well-sung phrases in the general frequency range of the speaking voice and then alternate between singing the phrase and speaking the phrase. Chant-like speaking may be utilized as a bridge between singing and the more normal inflection of the speaking voice. The consonant-vowel construction of the words can provide a useful tool in identifying and maintaining appropriate breath flow and placement of tonal resonance (Fig 27–9VI) during singing and connected speech. Also, note patterns may vary to more closely represent the pitch movement patterns of melodic speech (Fig 27–9VII).

2. Some patients are unable to sing technically well in or near their speaking registers but can produce a better singing voice in their middle or upper singing registers. Obviously, the goal would be to extend the more appropriate method of voice production into the speaking range. A descending scale, starting at the point of optimum vocal production can be moved step-wise downward, finally resting on a note at the upper end of the speaking range. That final note is sustained and gradually moves from singing to speaking voice. This should be done all on one breath, if possible. Each successive scale pattern is one half step lower until the speaking range has been covered. Maintaining steady breath support and the more "open" resonance sensations of the singing voice as the patient moves into speech is the optimum goal. A descending scale on a vowel with the bottom note blended into spoken counting is also helpful (Fig 27–9VIII).

3. The relationship between recitative and speech can be very useful for singers with good speaking voices. Singing teachers frequently teach recitative

by having the student speak the words in rhythm and then add notes in a natural fashion. The connection can be bridged in the opposite direction, as well. Opera and oratorio singers skilled in recitative can start a familiar recitative passage with notes and gradually eliminate specific pitches, slipping into speaking voice. This concept of moving from singing voice smoothly into speaking voice can be utilized with various text passages and may prove useful for nonsingers as well as singers. Such exercises often expedite traditional voice rehabilitation. However, any SVS working with the speaking voice should do so only in conjunction with therapy provided by a speech-language pathologist.

4. Rap music can also work well for nonclassical singers and nonsingers with speaking voice problems. Rap music provides bridging material similar to recitative. When using rap music, the rhythm tract may be gradually faded out during the rap. It is surprising how many singers can sing and rap with appropriate technique, but speak poorly and have trouble grasping traditional speech therapy approaches. Like recitative, rap exercises should be combined with instruction from a speech-language pathologist to facilitate rehabilitation.

We have suggested only a few of the many possible singing voice exercises useful in the treatment of the injured voice. These exercises must not be considered prescriptive. Rather, individual programs must be contoured to the special strengths and weaknesses of each patient. Often, the patient has more than one problem, for instance: reflux, plus bilateral masses; superior laryngeal nerve paresis; reflux and a unilateral cyst; and so forth. The vast majority of patients present with some degree of hyperfunctional voice use. Even the most technically sophisticated classical singer can succumb to the use of counterproductive compensatory muscle tension. Furthermore, no attempt has been made in this chapter to address the extraordinarily complex psychological issues that often accompany voice problems. This infinite combination of variables presents the SVS with many unique challenges. It is important to remember that a singing voice exercise is a means to an end, not an end in itself. The SVS must call upon a refined and educated listening ability, broad practical experience with numerous vocal technical approaches, and a working knowledge of pertinent human anatomy, physiology, and voice disorders to efficiently and effectively impact this important patient population.

Singing Styles

It should be recognized that there are many styles other than classical Western operatic singing. It is essential for laryngologists, singing voice specialists, and all other members of the health care team to avoid biases common to those of us steeped in Western classical tradition. Although the singing techniques and behaviors discussed throughout this book, and in this chapter particularly, represent a healthy, established approach, other singing styles can also be healthy despite significant technical differences. For example, rock, pop, and country western singers may perform two to four 45-minute sets each night, six nights each week for years without vocal problems. These artists do not always use a laryngeal position slightly below neutral, as advocated for operatic singing. Some sing with a raised larynx, others with a neutral or low larynx, and still others vary laryngeal position throughout their pitch ranges. Many use much less respiratory volume than classical singers. However, they also use amplifiers and do not try to project their voices into large halls over orchestras and choirs. Singers in other cultures such as Persian, Turkish, Chinese, African and Tibetan singers use a variety of techniques that initially strike us as abusive. Yodeling, which involves leaps from chest voice to falsetto, also seems potentially hazardous, although it often is accompanied by more breath support than "regular" singing in the same performer. Countertenor singing is a style that utilizes the male falsetto. Incorrect falsetto singing can be extremely abusive; but technically skilled yodelers and countertenors can produce beautiful sounds for decades without vocal problems. Any of these styles may be vocally abusive if performed incorrectly. This is also true of classical operatic singing. However, we must recognize that it is technically possible to perform music in almost any style in a manner that is not only idiomatic, but also vocally safe. The voice team, and especially the laryngologist and singing voice specialist, must be familiar with the special techniques, demands, and problems of the singing style of each individual patient. It is neither helpful nor scientifically justified to dismiss any particular genre (including hard rock) as medically unacceptable. With sufficient understanding, patience, voice team skill and patient compliance, a vocally "right way" can be found to do almost anything.

Frequency of Lessons

Singing lessons should be given every week when possible, and every 10 to 14 days, at least, if weekly

Fig 27-9. Carryover exercise from singing voice to speaking voice.

Fig 27–9. *(continued)*

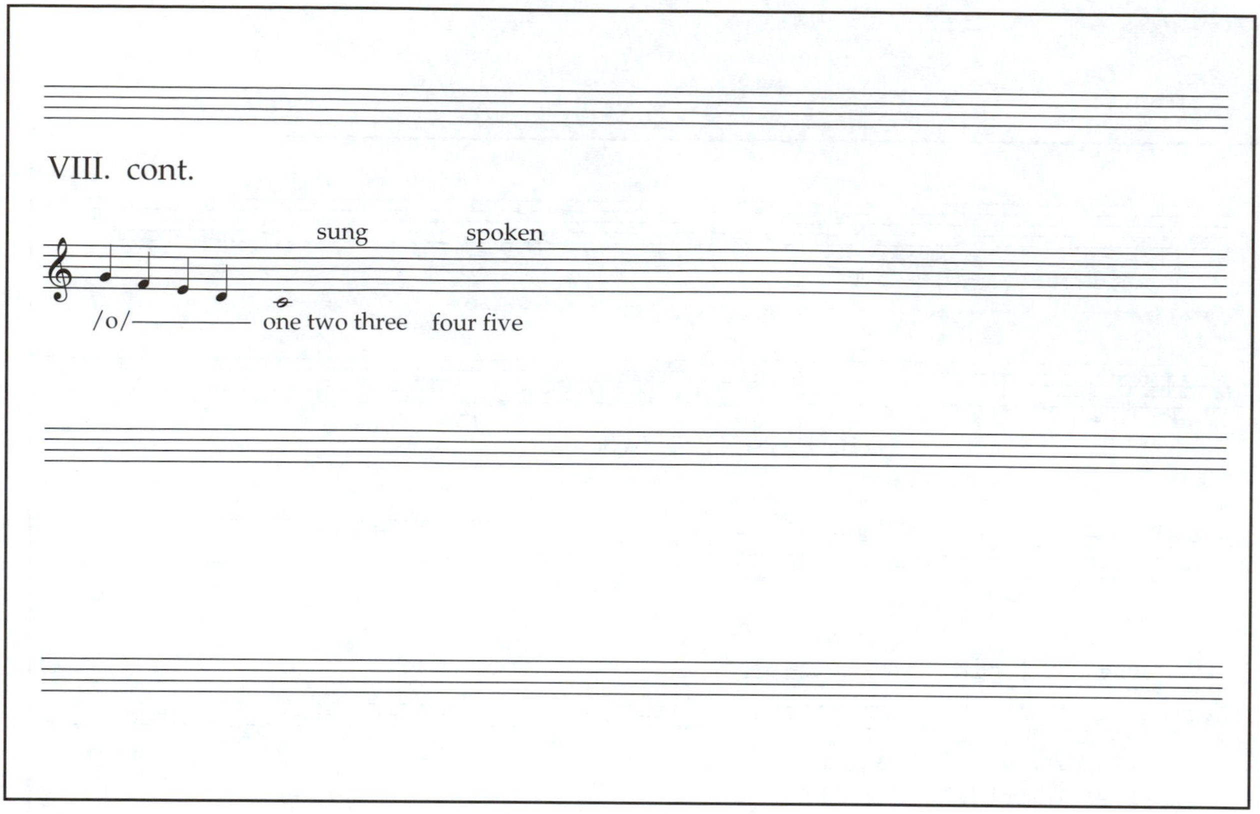

Fig 27–9. *(continued)*

sessions are not possible. Frequent lessons are especially important early in training to be certain that techniques are being implemented correctly in practice sessions between lessons. Often, short lessons, two or three times a week may be most productive at this time. If the patient is working with a SVS and speech-language pathologist, it is particularly helpful if he or she can see both of them on the same day. Ideally, they should be in the same location. The combined team approach is highly effective for singers and speakers, and it is often helpful for the SVS and speech-language pathologist to work together with the patient part of the time. This provides an opportunity to be certain that singing lessons and voice therapy are coordinated and that any potential misconceptions in the patient's mind are resolved.

Reports and Documentation

It is necessary for the SVS to communicate in writing with the laryngologist and speech-language pathologist. An initial report should be sent to the referring professional and should include the behaviors exhibited, exercises used, effectiveness of therapeutic intervention, and treatment plan. If the singer-patient is

from a distant area, this report (along with the reports of the laryngologists, speech-language pathologist, and voice laboratory) will serve as a guideline for the voice teacher in the patient's locality. If the patient intends to continue studying with the SVS, each session is documented on audio (and often video) tape and with progress notes similar to those used by physicians and speech-language pathologists. In our office, these progress notes are kept in the medical chart, along with notes by the other team members. Periodically, summary progress reports are prepared as well. Record keeping is not traditionally a requirement of the singing teacher. However, professional standards have been established in a medical milieu, and SVSs must observe them like any other medical professional. Such documentation may be useful for students without health problems in private studios, as well. A sample initial report is provided in appendix IV.

Summary

Working with injured voices is a complex and challenging process. Nonsingers can benefit from working with a SVS by learning abdominal breathing/support, improved resonance and placement, and an overall relaxed and easy manner of production during singing, and by learning how to carry these techniques over into the speaking voice. Singers benefit from work with a SVS by learning specific exercises to improve vocal function, eliminate abusive vocal behaviors, reduce or eliminate vocal pathologies, maintain muscle tone and coordination during periods when singing is restricted, and, in general, receiving reinforcement in the rules of safe and efficient singing. Singing teachers who acquire special skills in training patients with vocal injuries provide invaluable help in the medical setting. Hopefully, the current demand, along with increasing interest among singing teachers, will result in high quality, interdisciplinary training programs to make it easier for voice teachers to enter this exciting new field.

Review Questions

1. A singing-voice specialist must have:
   a. experience teaching healthy singers
   b. knowledge of vocal anatomy and physiology
   c. familiarity with medical diagnoses and medical treatments
   d. all of the above
   e. none of the above

2. In training a patient with a vocal injury, obtaining a good sound as soon as possible is paramount.
   a. true
   b. false

3. Which exercise is particularly helpful to patients with superior laryngeal nerve paresis?

   a. deep inhalation and controlled exhalation
   b. glissandos
   c. singing Italian ariettas
   d. staccato exercises
   e. recitative

4. Singing exercises may be helpful for the nonsinger with voice dysfunction because:
   a. they may hasten the patient's adaption of efficient vocal technique
   b. they may strengthen specific areas of weakness within the vocal system
   c. they may increase vocal performance ability so their routine speaking needs are no longer at the limits of the individual's performance
   d. all of the above
   e. none of the above

5. Singing-voice specialists must prepare reports and documentation that will become part of a permanent medical record.
   a. true
   b. false

References

1. Miller R. *English, French German and Italian Techniques of Singing: A Study in National Tonal Preferences and How They Relate to Functional Efficiency.* Metuchen, NJ: The Scarecrow Press Inc; 1977.
2. Vennard W. *Singing: The Mechanism and Technique.* New York: Carl Fischer Inc; 1949 (1st ed); 1968 (5th ed).
3. Kendall FP, McCreary EK. *Muscles: Testing and Function.* Baltimore, Md: Williams and Wilkins; 1983:269–320.

28

Use of Instrumentation in the Singing Studio

Robert Thayer Sataloff

Voice Training Applications of Medical Technology

For generations, both medical care and voice teaching have been hampered by the need to rely on subjective assessment of the voice. On those fortunate occasions when the doctor or teacher has a skilled, unbiased ear and excellent auditory memory, subjective assessment may work fairly well. However, the health and safety of patients and students in general are better served by more objective methods of voice assessment. For voice teachers, dependence on the ear alone gives rise to special problems. For example, there is sometimes disagreement as to which vocal productions are good and which are bad; whether a voice is the same, better, or worse after a year or two of training, what exactly is meant by "good" or "bad," and so on. Consequently, it would be valuable for a singing teacher or music department faculty to be able accurately to assess the vocal performance and progress of each student through objective measures of voice function repeated over time. Such technology is no substitute for traditional, excellent voice training. Rather, it provides an extra set of tools for the voice teacher to help identify specific problem areas and to assure steady progress. Physicians have been faced with the same needs in diagnosing voice abnormalities and assessing the results of treatment. Consequently, instrumentation has been developed for medical voice assessment, and much of this instrumentation has potential application in the studio.

Although instrumentation to perform all the tests is not widely available, much of it can be found in large cities with medical schools, especially if there is a laryngologist specializing in voice in the area. All the relevant tests are painless, and occasionally they have the added advantage of detecting an unsuspected and treatable medical problem that may affect vocal training and performance. Even the singing teacher who is not in a position to utilize such technology regularly should be familiar with it, because such analysis may prove extremely revealing and helpful in selected students with special problems that do not respond to a teacher's usual approach.

Without restating information discussed in chapter 8 on each of the six components of objective voice assessment, a few additional comments are worthwhile to shed light on potential teaching applications of medical instrumentation.

Vocal Fold Vibration

For the purposes of vocal training, we include not only true measures of vocal fold vibration, but also visual evaluation of laryngeal posture. The flexible fiberoptic laryngoscope has revolutionized our ability to visualize the larynx. It is small (usually about 3.5 mm in diameter) and passes painlessly through one nostril. Occasionally, a gentle topical anesthetic is placed in the nose, but most people do not find the tube uncomfortable in the nose, even with no anesthetic at all. When connected to a video camera, the flexible fiberoptic laryngoscope allows the student, teacher, and physician to watch the position of the palate, pharynx, tongue base, epiglottis, false and true vocal folds, and other vocal tract structures during speech and singing. At some institutions, such as the Academy of Vocal Arts in Philadelphia, recordings of this sort have been made routinely for many years, prior to each student's matriculation as a freshman. Laryngeal posture, degree of tongue retraction, signs of strain, and other factors can then be compared with future recordings over the course of training. Such recordings are not only instructive for the student and teacher, but they may also provide invaluable feedback in selected cases. For example, occasionally, teachers are faced with a student with extremely "throaty" production, marked tongue retraction, and markedly excessive tension during singing. Most such students can have their techniques improved through traditional exercises, but an occasional student finds it very difficult to change technique to a more relaxed posture. Some such students do extremely well when the usual constructs and abstractions of the studio are supplemented by visual feedback. The student can watch his or her vocal folds and tongue base during singing and eliminate the hyperfunction and tongue retraction. While such situations do not occur often, it is useful for the voice teacher to know that such assistance is available for special cases. In a great many more cases, students and teachers find visual inspection of the larynx and pharynx during singing interesting and useful, although not essential.

Vocal fold vibration can be assessed by several means, as discussed above. The most common and best is strobovideolaryngoscopy. It allows detection of scars, small masses, subtle neurologic weaknesses, and other problems that may be heard in the voice as hoarseness, breathiness, or weakness. It is invaluable for a singing teacher to have such information so that the teacher and student know whether the vocal problems they are hearing are merely training deficits or are the result of a physical problem that requires special training methods.

Phonatory Ability

Objective measures of phonatory ability are easily and readily available. Maximum phonation time is measured using a stopwatch, as discussed in chapter 8, along with physiological frequency range and musical frequency range, which can be measured at the piano. These and other tests of phonatory ability should theoretically improve during vocal training, except for physiologic frequency range (which probably remains about the same). The student or patient is instructed to sustain the vowel [a] for as long as possible on deep inspiration, vocalizing at a comfortable frequency and intensity. Ideally, the frequency (pitch) and intensity are controlled using inexpensive equipment that can be purchased at a local radio electronics store. Physiological frequency range of phonation disregards qual-

ity and measures the lowest and highest notes that can be produced. Musical frequency range of phonation measures the lowest and highest musically acceptable notes. Such tests can be performed into a high quality tape recorder and sent to a laboratory for formal analysis, including spectrographic analysis. Frequency limits of vocal registers may also be measured, as well as several other parameters. Combinations of tests of phonatory ability allow measures of glottal efficiency that may be valuable and should theoretically improve during vocal training.

Aerodynamic Measures

Aerodynamic tests may be especially valuable to the professional voice user and teacher. In some singers and actors, lung capacity may be substantially less than expected. It is especially important to identify such vocalists and optimize their pulmonary function through aerobic exercise and other means. In other singers and actors, initially good lung function gets progressively worse during singing or other exercise. Such singers may have unrecognized asthma induced by the exercise of performance. It is essential to identify such singers and treat them, or they will usually develop the same kinds of hyperfunctional voice abuse problems seen in people with poor support technique, even if they are well trained.

In addition to measures of lung function, airflow can be measured across the vocal folds. This provides a good measure of glottal efficiency and an objective way to identify voices that are excessively breathy, pressed, or well adjusted. These parameters should also improve during training, and this should be especially noticeable with many beginning students.

Acoustic Analysis

The best acoustic analyzers are still the human ear and brain. Unfortunately, they are still not very good at quantifying the information they perceive, and we cannot communicate it accurately. Acoustic analysis equipment is expensive and not needed very frequently in routine voice teaching. However, since most of the tests performed require only a good quality tape recording, they are always at a singing teacher's disposal. It is sometimes useful to document progress in vocal stability, vibrato regularity, pitch accuracy, or development of desirable harmonics (the singer's formant). In nonvoice majors required to study singing, visual feedback instruments are available to assist students in learning to match pitches.

Laryngeal Electromyography and Psychoacoustic Evaluation

Laryngeal electromyography and formal psychoacoustic evaluation have newly appreciated, great applicability in routine voice teaching. The principles of psychoacoustics may provide useful guidance for school faculty juries judging singers, actors, and other speakers. Traditionally, such juries are composed of people with differences in opinion, taste, and sometimes personality, and the biases inevitably introduced in such situations are very difficult to identify and negate. Most music and acting schools handle this problem simply by trying to have enough people on each jury to have such problems "even out." However, study of formal techniques of psychoacoustic evaluation would probably lead to improvements in the jury system. Laryngeal EMG is discussed in chapters 8 and 15.

Discussion of Studio Applications

Currently available techniques for looking at, analyzing, and documenting voice function have been used successfully by physicians and a few farsighted voice teachers. They are not substitutes for good studio teaching technique but rather are extra tools in the teacher's armamentarium. As such, it behooves the modern voice teacher to become familiar with available technology that may enhance teaching efficiency and consistency.

There are also other reasons why singing and acting teachers should be familiar with and concerned about objective voice assessment. Political and legal developments over the past several years have made it clear that voice teachers are eventually (and probably soon) going to have to introduce the same kind of peer review and quality control practiced in other professions such as medicine and speech-language pathology. At present, most teachers and music schools rely on very little beyond personal opinion to define good singing, healthy singing, successful training progress, or even a "good voice." In modern times, such subjective vagaries may be insufficient for the individual voice teacher and especially for the music school trying to assess voice teachers and select an optimal voice faculty. Objective voice analysis may help. Not only can it define parameters and progress for individual students, but it can also help teachers in self-assessment and improvement and music schools in faculty assessment. Any good teacher is eager to identify his or her strengths and weaknesses, so the introduction of objective assessment should be viewed as a blessing by most high quality people in the profession. For example, consider a school with four voice faculty members each of whom is assigned 15 freshmen. Each freshman can be recorded on high-quality audio- and videotape singing standardized scales and an audition aria and can undergo comprehensive objective voice analysis. Such recordings can be repeated at the end of the first and second semesters, and annually (or more often) thereafter. Assume further that in each studio there are four new students with the same technical problems: tongue retraction, ineffective support, poor soft singing, and slight tremolo. Then assume that these problems disappear within the first year in students of three of the teachers, but the problems shown by students of the fourth teacher get worse, and two or three students of that teacher who didn't have those problems initially develop them. Objective voice assessments detect such patterns early, document them in a clear, scientific fashion that eliminates the perceived personal persecution with which such information is often greeted, and allows the teacher, students, and administration to make appropriate adjustments before significant (and possibly compensable) harm is done to the students.

Clearly, objective voice assessment has been helpful to laryngologists and can be a valuable adjunct to the individual singing and acting teacher. Moreover, it may provide our first real means to define good, healthy singing, acting, and teaching and to help promulgate high standards of practice among those who choose to call themselves "voice teachers."

Summary

Instrumentation used by physicians and speech-language pathologists for objective voice assessment may also be valuable to singing teachers and voice trainers. The ability to assess and quantify vocal function augments traditional teaching by providing new methods of feedback, and enhanced ability to track and assess outcome.

Review Questions

1. Instruments for voice analysis do not replace traditional training, but may enhance it by providing new techniques to help identify specific problem areas and ensure steady progress.
   a. true
   b. false

2. Voice quantification requires complex, expensive equipment.
   a. true
   b. false

3. Measures of phonatory ability include all of the following except:
   a. maximum phonation time
   b. strobovideolaryngoscopy
   c. physiologic frequency range
   d. musical frequency range
   e. intensity range

4. Aerodynamic measures are physiologically constant and will not improve during the course of voice training.
   a. true
   b. false

5. Flexible fiberoptic laryngoscopy may be useful as a biofeedback tool for selected voice students.
   a. true
   b. false

29

Choral Pedagogy

Brenda J. Smith and Robert Thayer Sataloff

In most countries, choir participation starts in childhood. Most elementary schools and nearly all junior high schools and high schools have choral activities. Children's choirs are common in several religious musical traditions, and membership in such groups may occur even before a child is old enough to enter elementary school (age 5 or 6). Millions of adults sing in religious, university, community, theater, and other choruses. The choral experience is enormously influential in shaping our approach to singing and in establishing healthy or unhealthy vocal practices. Consequently, from a public health standpoint, choral conductors are in an extremely important position. They are able to influence large groups of singers, often working with more people in one evening than a singing teacher (who teaches one-on-one) sees in a week. Choral conductors have the opportunity and obligation to educate their singers and establish healthy singing practices; and they are in an ideal position to recognize vocal problems early and suggest medical referral. Therefore, it is important for choral conductors to be well educated regarding vocal health, pedagogy, and science. Unfortunately, a high percentage do not have such education. It is also important for otolaryngologists and other healthcare providers to be familiar with choral conducting, including its techniques, responsibilities, and common shortcomings, in order to be able to evaluate choral singer patients knowledgeably.

Vocal pedagogy applied to choral music is a rather new area of interest. Most people assume that choral conductors know something about singing, but this is often not the case. Most choral conductors are organists or instrumental conductors with little personal singing background and no knowledge of vocal pedagogy. For decades, such choral conductors have transferred techniques used in orchestral conducting to communicate musical information to singers. This process is inadequate, since choral organizations are not based on instrumental prototypes. Unlike the case of instrumental players, choral singers are rarely equipped through years of technical training in the use and care of their singing "instrument." Many choral singers have little or no experience in the written codes of music. Most singers join a choral ensemble because of an interest in the music to be sung, a love of singing, and a desire to share the choral experience with others. At the outset, the singers expect to be taught the skills needed to perform the music at hand. Blending the talents and training of professionals and amateurs in the corporate act of singing, the choral conductor must be prepared to amalgamate vocal pedagogy with conducting techniques to achieve choral musical goals. Acting as the vocal authority for the choir, the choral conductor is expected to speak to the vocal technical demands of the music as well as to respond to questions regarding vocal health and medical care. Choral conductors certainly must not exceed the limits of their expertise; but the responsibilities of conducting a choir demand that the conductor acquire sufficient education in vocal pedagogy and establish a referral network of professionals who can provide choral singers with accurate answers and appropriate guidance.

Recognizing that most choral singers rehearse and perform under conductors who are not vocally knowledgeable and use an instrumental approach to the voice, physicians should not be surprised to encounter vocal fatigue, hoarseness, nodules, hemorrhages, and other problems resulting from vocal abuse during choral activities. Indeed, such occurrences are disturbingly common. However, they are not necessary. Enthusiasm is just beginning for the development of an academic discipline of choral pedagogy to provide practical, appropriate vocal education for conductors who wish to work optimally with choral singers. There are many approaches to training choral conductors and to training choirs to sing in a healthy fashion. This chapter describes one systematic, healthy vocal approach to choral music as an example. It is not intended to imply that this is the only (or even the best) way to integrate healthy singing into the choral experience, but rather to provide the reader with an example, including specific insights into how this goal may be reached.

Voice Building for Choirs

In *Ethics*, Aristotle stated "it is by the practical experience of life and conduct that the truth is really tested, since it is there that the final decision lies. We must therefore examine the conclusions we have advanced by bringing them to the test of the facts of life."[1(pvii)] In the choral rehearsal, the science and practice of vocal pedagogy and medicine mingle, allowing choral singers to learn artful, healthy singing. During their long association with choirs all over the world, Drs Wilhelm Ehmann and Frauke Haasemann developed a method of choral pedagogy known as "Voice Building for Choirs." Wilhelm Ehmann, founder and director of the Church Music Institute of Westphalia in Herford, Germany, was internationally recognized for his work as conductor of the professional vocal ensemble, the Westfaelische Kantorei. With his assistant, Frauke Haasemann, Ehmann created this pedagogical method to encourage the application of vocal technical skills to choral singing. His book, *Choral Directing*,[2] continues to be a standard reference text for choral conductors. The method engages choral singers in vocal tasks drawn from daily life. By applying such activities as yawning, sighing, whimpering, and calling to the production of singing sounds, healthy vocal habits can be achieved. The process builds the singing instrument while promoting confidence and self-esteem in the singer. The basic skills are also beneficial to the speaking voice, improving pitch control, volume, and stamina.

The Basics

In Ehmann and Haasemann's pedagogical approach, four elements form the vocal technical foundation for choral singing. These elements are: relaxation, posture, breathing, and resonance. All of these elements must be addressed at the beginning of each rehearsal to ensure the best vocal results for each singer. It is advisable to adhere to the order given above, moving from simple to complex concepts and tasks.

Relaxation

Relaxation is the first step toward good choral singing. In most cases, the choral singer comes to the rehearsal from another segment of life. Conflicting thoughts and occupations must be dismissed, and bodily tensions alleviated. Each rehearsal should begin with a thorough routine, addressing and monitoring the relaxation of all major muscle groups. Relaxation is encouraged by any activity that increases the flow of blood to a given area, through manipulation, exercise, or flex and release patterns. Special attentions should be given to the upper arms, shoulders, neck, and head, locations commonly fraught with muscular distress.

Sighing is one of the body's boldest acts of relaxation, releasing unwanted air and tension. Since singing may be thought of as a sustained sigh, this final step toward relaxation is actually a leap toward the establishment of a healthy singing instrument. To sigh freely a body must be supple and coordinated. In the act of sighing, the singer becomes reacquainted with the neurolinguistic signals that govern the singing act. The sound of a choral sigh indicates to the conductor the state of the ensemble—body, mind, and spirit. The choral rehearsal presents the opportunity for a corporate act of relaxation devoid of self-consciousness or overt anxiety. Many choral singers view the choral rehearsal as a regular appointment with body awareness and coordination.

Posture

Proper body alignment is crucial to the singing instrument. Unless the forces of gravity work to the advantage of the vocal mechanism, compensation will occur through tension and fatigue throughout the singer's body. In construct, the aspects of posture include body weight centered on the metatarsal heads, knees unlocked, spinal column "anchored," scapulae and clavicles suspended at the nape of the neck, head balanced on the spine. The skeleton should be thought of as the scaffolding from which the body hangs, thereby freeing all muscle groups for movement.

Posture for singing is simply good and proper posture. It is immediately applicable to life. The choral rehearsal affords the chance for each singer to establish and practice good postural habits and to witness proper alignment in others. After rehearsal, most choral singers report a refreshment of mood and energy, a surge of power generated in part from natural posture practices.

Breathing

When the body is relaxed and properly aligned, breathing for singing is easily achieved. To encourage freedom in the abdominal region, the conductor may ask the choir to perform the rhythms of a familiar tune on f, s, $\int$, or $t\int$. Panting like a puppy or yawning are equally effective.

Exhalation is taught first, creating the physical need for a thorough inhalation of air. The choral conductor serves as the model for the choir, demonstrating a tall, open, and expectant body attitude. The singers respond by exhaling and inhaling steadily and gently. Exercises of various types can be used to increase spontaneity and fluidity. It is essential that the conductor invite singers to expel any unused air between exercises. At the conclusion of this portion of rehearsal preparation, the conductor should ask the choir to sigh, combining the elements of relaxation and posture with breath management.

Breathing is considered the universal source of stress relief and a particularly effective source of vocal stress relief. Most speech-language pathologists, singing voice specialists, and vocal coaches center their work with voice users around the establishment of organized, predictable, deep breathing regimens. The choral rehearsal abounds in chances to reinforce breathing habits as a part of the warm-up activity, as an aspect of musical style study, and as an act of relaxation between segments of the musical assignment. Correct choral singing enhances the capacity and technique of the singer, and contributes not only to vocal health but also to the sense of overall well-being that is so prized among devoted choral singers.

Resonance

The singing tone is complex. To achieve a beautiful vocal sound, the vocal tract coordinates power, oscillators, resonators, and articulators. Exercises sung on lip trills (br or r) help choral singers master the coordinated skills. The sensation of forward or facial resonance can also be felt when patterns are sung on l, η, $\eth$, v, or z. Vowels are included with these resonant consonants to move the singers toward true vocal communication. The flow of vowel and melody, text and tone can be challenging. In his discussion of the coordination of technique and communication, Richard Miller wrote:

Some of the results of neurologic events in respiration and in speech and song can be sensed while others cannot. When we establish essential coordination for singing, we cannot separate out those aspects over which we have control from the large number that are the result of reflex responses over which we have no conscious control. Therefore, almost all of the process of coordination that produces successful singing must be incorporated into a psychological attitude that includes both controllable and noncontrollable events.[3(p198)]

The psychological attitude desired is based on the memory of muscles and sensations. Choral singers cannot rely on the sound of their voices to dictate or prescribe vocal technical changes. Instead, the choir must be allowed to feel the coordination of mind, body, and tone. Acting as a musical curator, the choral conductor identifies the sensations the singers should encourage, sensations that create unified choral tone. A collective memory of beautifully resonated choral sounds emerges through the repetitive process known as choir rehearsal. Choral singers may also apply the sensations of singing to acquire more resonant and ringing speaking voices.

Once the four basic elements of relaxation, posture, breathing, and resonance have united as a vocal technical foundation, the choral conductor anticipates the vocal problems in the repertoire at hand. Using a similar pedagogical process, matters of legato and nonlegato singing, coloratura and *martellato* singing, diction and dynamics, and range and registration can also be addressed. *Martellato* is a style of singing used mostly in the music of the Baroque period. It could be defined literally as "hammering on the legato," a technique involving a diaphragmatic pulsation pattern accentuating connected, legato singing. The result is a singing style imitative of instrumental articulation.

Healthy Conducting Habits

Textbooks which imply that a clear conducting pattern permits the conductor access to a choir or orchestra are shortsighted. An established choral technique is necessary to a choral conductor, but the conductor should not forget that the hands are useless if they do not speak to the needs of the singer. Therefore, the conductor's movements indicate the vocal language the singers will translate into well-formed sounds.[4(p24)]

The pedagogical method of Voice Building for Choirs trains choral conductors to develop a vocabulary of images separate from the vocal technical terminology used by studio voice teachers. The language of the choral voice builder is consonant with common experiences of daily life that evoke healthy vocal production. In some communities, the conductor asks the singers to imitate the sounds made by farm animals. In other places, the whimpering of infants, the sighing of tired adults, or the cooing of doves might be more useful. The method encourages a fanciful approach to a healthy vocal experience, an experience completely applicable to complicated musical tasks. Minimizing the use of scientific terms is appropriate and effective with most choral groups, although it is highly desirable for the choral conductor to be familiar with them and to know the scientific basis and intent of each exercise or maneuver.

The gestures of the conductor must express the physical as well as the musical demands of the music. Of greatest significance is the breath gesture. Beginning singers are taught that the character of their breath becomes the character of their singing. Tension in the inhalation process creates tightness throughout the vocal tract and respiratory system. A shallow breath may elevate the larynx. A vigorous breath can instill stiffness. The choral conductor, through the power of suggestion, communicates the spirit and energy of the music by presenting a perfect posture and an appropriate breath gesture. By example, the conductor invites the choir to prepare and to sing in a coordinated, cooperative fashion.

The rhythmic gestures of conducting must assist good vocal habits. Conducting patterns should not generally be placed below the rib cage, if singers are to remain buoyant and open to breath and breath support. When directing fast passages, the conductor's patterns should never become frantic or tense. Any tightening of the conductor's upper arms or shoulders will cause similar tension in the bodies of the singers. Music to be sung at an extremely fast tempo must be learned slowly and carefully, allowing the tempo to increase as the singers become comfortable with every note and nuance. This also permits time to develop healthy singing habits even in rapid, challenging passages. A choir trained in this manner can rely on the rhythmic energy of the music to establish the tempo, setting the conductor free to shape climaxes and cadences. Surprising or strenuous conducting patterns hamper easy, coordinated vocal tone, and may cause strained and potentially unhealthy singing.

Voice Building for Choirs is a choral pedagogical approach centered on the humanity of the singing instrument. Human beings respond spontaneously to tone of voice, choice of word, body language. A choral conductor must analyze every exercise, every phrase of the music to ensure the success of his or her vocabulary and vocal and physical gestures.

Choral Music and Healthy Voices

Choral conductors become the authority on vocal music and vocal health for their choirs, and often on many other aspects of life. It may not be a role the con-

ductor wishes to play, but it is one that naturally goes with the choral territory. Conductors should schedule short private sessions with each member of the choir on a regular basis, using the time to confirm basic vocal technique, detect obvious physical health problems, and monitor vocal progress. Our bodies are our instruments, instruments requiring adjustment and tune-up. Furthermore, all of our lives have seasons, good and bad. The pressures of daily life can interfere with healthy singing habits, limiting the powers of concentration and coordination. Through personal knowledge of individual circumstances, the conductor has a chance to arrange the artistic expectations of the music to fit the physical and spiritual potential of the choir.

Brief evaluations of individual choral singers can lead to helpful referrals, either to private voice instructors or professional medical services. In the words of Howard Swan,

It is almost a certainty that as choral directors learn to know their singers better, special vocal problems will become evident. These may include: breathiness in the tone, a nasal tone production, tremolo versus a normal vibrato, and the necessity to modify vowel sounds. However, positive results might be heard in the development of a full bodied tone, the extension of range and the establishment of registers in each voice.[5(p98)]

It is absolutely necessary for a choral conductor to have a friendly and active rapport with the professional vocal resources of his or her community. Choral singers will present disorders of many types. In most cases, the choral conductor serves as the first diagnostician (recognizing that something is wrong) and as the most trusted referral agent. The conductor is obligated to be knowledgeable enough to deserve such trust.

Conclusion

Physicians and other healthcare providers need to understand the nature and habits of the choirs in their communities, and the styles and backgrounds of choral conductors. If a healthcare provider has not had the experience of singing in a choir, joining a choral group is recommended highly. Participation as a choir member provides experiences and insights that cannot be achieved in any other way. The best choral conductors know as much about music and singing as physicians know about medicine, and the educational pathway should go in both directions! Healthcare providers should make every effort to make contact with all the conductors in their communities, to provide educational services for conductors and their choirs and to enhance the evolution of choral pedagogy and the tradition of safe, healthy choral singing.

Summary

Choirs involve more singers than any other musical activity. Choral singing begins in childhood in most schools and is part of many religious traditions. Many choral conductors are instrumentalists without training in voice. Vocal pedagogy has not generally been applied to choral singing. Techniques exist to ensure healthy choral singing and to simultaneously enhance individual voices and the collective choral sound. Expert, healthy conducting technique is important to choral vocal health.

Review Questions

1. The largest number of singers participate in:
   a. pop music
   b. opera
   c. recital
   d. choirs
   e. musical theater

2. Most choral conductors are familiar with vocal anatomy, physiology, and technique.
   a. true
   b. false

3. In Ehmann and Haasemann's pedagogical approach, which of the following form(s) the technical foundation for choral singing?

   a. relaxation
   b. posture
   c. breathing
   d. resonance
   e. all of the above

4. Martellato singing involves complete interruptions of a tone or scale.
   a. true
   b. false

5. A conductor's personal breathing pattern during rehearsal and performance is not significant.
   a. true
   b. false

6. Choral conductors can function perfectly well in isolation and need not be an integral part of the community voice care team.
   a. true
   b. false

References

1. Aristotle. *Ethics*. X. viii.
2. Ehmann W, Wiebe G, trans. *Choral Directing*. Minneapolis, Minn: Augsburg Publishing House; 1968.
3. Miller R. *The Structure of Singing*. New York, NY: Schirmer Books; 1986:198.
4. Ehmann W, Haasemann F. *Voice Building for Choirs*. Smith B, trans. Chapel Hill, NC: Hinshaw Music; 1980:24.
5. Swan H, cited in Fowler C, ed. *Conscience of a Profession: Howard Swan*. Chapel Hill, NC: Hinshaw Music; 1987:98.

30

The Role of the Acting-Voice Trainer in Medical Care of Professional Voice Users

Sharon L. Freed, Bonnie N. Raphael, and Robert Thayer Sataloff

Acting-voice trainers are also called voice coaches, drama voice teachers, and vocal consultants. Traditionally, these professionals are closely associated with the theatre. Their skills may be useful on the medical voice team not only to restore a voice recovering from injury, but also to strengthen and develop the voice in ways that help prevent future injury.

This chapter is written to acquaint physicians, speech-language pathologists, singing voice specialists, and acting-voice trainers with many of the special issues that must be considered when they join a medical voice team.

An Overview of Acting-Voice Training for Noninjured Speakers

It is important for all members of the medical voice team to understand the teachings of acting-voice trainers and the various approaches they may use in the training process. This chapter is not intended as a comprehensive review of the profession, but rather as an overview to help the other team members understand the training and background of acting-voice trainers. Raphael has presented a similar overview in previous literature.[1] Such understanding is helpful in clarifying the value of their participation on the medical voice team.

Because voice training involves behavior modification, acting-voice trainers have developed a variety of approaches that may be used for the education of any individual. In addition to having particular vocal agendas, different people find themselves more receptive to one mode of learning than another and to one style of presentation than another. Certain speakers, for example, do best when information is auditory. Systems based on listening to a model and then making the necessary adjustments in their own sound are helpful to auditory learners. Other speakers succeed when they can obtain information visually, by observing a particular facial posture or shoulder relaxation technique and then duplicating it as well as they can while observing themselves in a mirror. Still other speakers respond most quickly when the information they receive is kinesthetic, when they can learn by being either physically touched or told what they might experience in their own breathing or postural or facial muscles and then seeing whether they can voluntarily produce the desired kinesthetic sensations.

Obviously, there is no such thing as a learning mode that is purely auditory or visual or kinesthetic; virtually all behavioral modification techniques involve stimulation and information provided in all three modes, but one or another might be more prominent and therefore more useful to a particular individual or more compatible with the style of a particular teacher. Similarly, certain voice patients or students might be more comfortable working with a teacher or coach on an individual basis while others are more comfortable as a member of a workshop or a small class. Some speakers do best with a speech-language pathologist specializing in voice rehabilitation. If the voice is free of medical problems (eg, vocal nodules or polyps, contact ulcers, vocal trauma or paralysis, chronic laryngitis), most voice patients or students can be helped by one of the four basic types of training common among acting-voice trainers, as described in this chapter: Traditional, Skinner, Linklater, or Lessac.

Traditional Approaches and Education of Acting-Voice Trainers

It is important for physicians and other healthcare professionals to understand approaches to acting-voice training, the contributions of the trainer on the medical voice team, and the possible training biases and approaches of actors who seek our care as patients. Individual acting-voice trainers have various educational, training, and practical experiences that influence their techniques. Those traditionally trained, for example, may have completed undergraduate and graduate-level courses in communication and speech education, public speaking, or oral interpretation, and perhaps in the anatomy and physiology of speech and phonetics. Typically, their training has included education in basic anatomy and function of the voice mechanism, techniques fostering the elimination of stage fright, the development of a warm-up routine, the acquisition of techniques for better breathing and development of individual vocal dynamics (ie, pitch, rate, loudness, and quality), and the elimination of subclinical problems common to many speakers, such as hypernasality, insufficient loudness, mumbling, mono-tony, poor phrasing, excessive speed, and insufficient consonant articulation. Their training also frequently includes some performance experience.

Some traditional acting-voice trainers may encourage selected patients or students to pursue the same kinds of didactic introductory education the trainers received themselves. Some voice patients and students do well with this approach, preferring introductory courses in colleges or conservatories for acquiring enough basic information and skills both to speak and perform more effectively. Advocates of traditional approaches enjoy the straightforward, easily understandable presentation of basic information and skills and feel that, by the end of a good introductory course, they know how to continue to build vocal technique by working on their own. However, the more demanding a professional voice user's vocal challenges, the more likely it is that he or she will need additional supervised training and development. This can be provided by acting-voice trainers who offer individual instruction in the skills discussed above. Critics of some traditional approaches find them too academic or cerebral, and deficient in getting knowledge and skills beyond the "brain" and down to the "gut" where they are needed to express and control the emotional content of speech.

The Work of Edith Skinner

Edith Skinner, one of the most famous students of the noted Australian phonetician William Tilly, came to the United States to teach his work in the early part of this century. After learning the International Phonetic Alphabet and techniques of sound transcription, Skinner applied them to the speech training of actors, teaching for a great many years at Carnegie-Mellon University and then at Juilliard, training a considerable number of actors and teachers to use what she called good American speech. In her work, a carefully defined and prescribed series of rules for pronunciation is applied to speaking, reading, and acting by students who have been taught the International Phonetic Alphabet and phonetic transcription. After intensive articulation drill practice, these pronunciation standards are then applied to a wide variety of materials in performance until they become habitual.

Proponents of Skinner's work observe that many judgments are made about people on the basis of how they speak and that acquiring "good American speech" will help those who wish to sound more cultured or better educated. Several sounds acquired through this training also carry more easily in large performance spaces and are more easily understood by listeners from different parts of the United States or those for whom English is a second language. The resulting speech patterns have proven extremely useful for performances of the works of Shakespeare, other classical plays, and plays in translation, as well. For example, when producing classical plays, directors often choose to identify royalty or upper class characters by having them use a pronunciation pattern similar to standard British, and then take servants or others toward something like Cockney—a bit ludicrous when you recall that *Romeo and Juliet* is set in Italy and *Hamlet* in Denmark. Subtle but effective class distinctions might be achieved in a manner that is far less obtrusive or foreign to American audiences by the juxtaposition of "good American speech" with general American speech instead. In addition, acquisition of a fairly standard sound provides the actor with an effective base for stage dialects with results that are consistent across all members of a given cast. Finally, advocates say that, by teaching consistent and optimal placement of individual speech sounds, Skinner's approach improves resonation, projection, and healthy vocal production in general. Skinner's approach can be reviewed in her manual *Speak with Distinction*.[2]

Critics note that what is identified as good American speech is not a neutral American accent but rather a somewhat affected sound, based on a Southern British model rather than on native American speech, and also based on Skinner's race and cultural standard. They feel it eradicates or undervalues the great diversity of speech patterns characteristic of different areas and cultures present in this country and is more relevant to an older generation of American stage and film actors. Nonetheless, Skinner's work produces speakers with beautifully precise speech and excellent "ears."

The Linklater Method

Kristin Linklater was trained as an actress at the London Academy of Music and Dramatic Art in England. She received her voice and speech training under the eminent master teacher Iris Warren, whom she later assisted. In 1963, she introduced Iris Warren's work to this country by training a select number of US and Canadian teachers and coaches for an extended period of time. She continues teaching and coaching actors throughout the world.

Linklater's work is based on the premise that each of us has a beautifully functioning, natural voice with which many of us interfere (because of insidious tension and habitual inhibition) as we attempt to communicate our thoughts and feelings. Her approach, as best described in her book, *Freeing the Natural Voice*,[3] involves a process of freeing the vocal channel from habitual physical and psychological impediments that may prevent the voice from emerging in its most expressive, unadulterated form.

Linklater's method begins with and never abandons a connection with breath and impulse to speak from deep within the body. Exercises deal with allowing the free passage of this breath, especially when dealing with emotionally charged material; freeing up the vocal channel via loosening the shoulders, neck, jaw, tongue, and lips; with developing greater vocal range through contact with and exploration of a series of resonators; and immersing oneself in the intricacies, subtleties, implications, and layers of the language itself, of the text being spoken. Physical, psychological, and cultural blocks to full connection with text are confronted and worked through in both individual and group coaching sessions.

Linklater has trained a great number of teachers, directors, actors, and public speakers through a month-long intensive workshop which she taught for several years at Shakespeare & Company, the courses she now teaches to undergraduates at Emerson College in Boston, and the private workshops she continues to offer in the Boston area and elsewhere. She has written two excellent texts that are widely used and available.[3,4] In addition to training a number of people who base their own teachings on her work, she has intensively trained and certified a select number of

teachers whom she feels are most qualified to pass on the essence of her technique and philosophy. A voice patient seeking to undertake Linklater work should inquire of any potential teacher about the exact nature and extent of his or her training and qualifications.

Critics of Linklater's work describe it as a long and too psychologically oriented warm-up process that shortchanges both attention to clear articulation and development of the actor's ability to characterize vocally; they say those trained solely in Linklater work may be capable of very fine and compelling acting, but only in their own personae.

The Lessac System

Arthur Lessac began his own training as a singer at the Eastman School of Music in Rochester, New York. As his interest in the workings of the human voice developed, he supplemented his musical training with formal study in the anatomy and physiology of the voice and then, later on, in the workings of the human body in general. He began to develop his system of behavior modification in a search for something organically American rather than derived or adapted from late 19th and early 20th century British acting schools. He has been investigating, experimenting, and evolving a detailed system for the use and training of the human voice for at least 40 years. During the past 20 years or so, he has expanded his consideration of the actor's body, as well.

Lessac's system is based on the proposition that the speaker must eliminate all anesthetic-deadening habits in his or her communicative behavior and replace them with an ongoing state of habitual awareness. *Awareness*, according to Lessac, is a matter of being present and conscious on a moment-to-moment basis as one breathes, produces voice, and speaks. Instead of seeking to imitate or duplicate any other models, each speaker uses kinesthetic awareness to rediscover and enjoy his or her own sounds that are both aesthetically pleasing and based on natural behavior.

Lessac approaches voice through the acquisition of three complementary vocal actions. In using structural action, the speaker rediscovers the ability of the natural forward structure of the face and oral cavity to produce vowels that are rich, full, and free of restricting habitual tensions. In tonal action, the speaker becomes aware of and learns to produce buzzing and ringing vibrations on the hard palate and up into the top front quarter of the skull to focus the tone so that it will project effortlessly and protect the speaker from any vocal injury or discomfort, even when speaking in inhospitable vocal environments or when using the voice in potentially harmful ways (eg, screaming). In using consonant action, the speaker treats each of the consonants as a musical instrument, learning to taste its particular identifying vibrations, explore its range, communicate emotional feelings and connections through it, and then incorporates these new found awarenesses into spoken language.

By leading with one vocal action or another, the actor learns to utilize different vocal and dramatic colors, interpretations, or readings of dramatic material and to adapt effortlessly to different playing spaces. By learning to explore while performing memorized materials, the actor learns to be in the present moment and to allow the performance to be a discovery rather than a reproduction of what has been rehearsed in a particular way or habituated through repeated performance.

Advocates of Lessac's system cite its ability to heal and strengthen voices that have suffered from hyperfunction and strain and its ability to produce speech sounds that are clear, communicative, and beautiful in actors who do not respond well to traditional articulation exercises and drill sheets. Some critics are put off by Lessac's untraditional terminology. Others observe that, until students fully understand and internalize their training, they may look and sound forced or uncomfortable as they speak and that, when taught incompletely or incorrectly, the system might produce a way of speaking that is self-conscious or even pretentious. They feel, contrary to Lessac's best intentions for his work, that a little learning can be a dangerous thing when it comes to the acquisition of the vocal actions. Nonetheless, actors who have mastered its basics have a system for vocal developments that can serve their needs for the rest of their lives. Lessac's system and philosophy are described in detail in his two books, *The Use and Training of the Human Voice*[5] and *Body Wisdom: The Use and Training of the Human Body*.[6]

Other Options

There are several other excellent approaches to training that actors may encounter in their training. Several excellent voice and speech teachers base their work on the writings and teachings of three highly reputed coaches in England: Cicely Berry,[7,8] Clifford Turner,[9] and Patsy Rodenburg.[10,11] Other actors and speakers

who feel that limitations or restrictions in their voices are physically based have benefitted greatly from work with an Alexander teacher,[*] a Feldenkrais practitioner,[†] or a physical therapist.

Physicians should also be aware of other areas of expertise that are common among voice trainers. Some speech-language pathologists and many acting-voice trainers also specialize in accent reduction or elimination. Through a process of auditory training and articulation practice, foreign or regional accents can be reduced significantly in many cases. However, speakers of English as a second language and even those with heavy American regional accents must be willing to make a long-term commitment if significant and permanent accent reduction or elimination is to be achieved. These issues may be of considerable importance to some professional voice users. Moreover, untrained attempts at accent reduction can be vocally taxing in some people, as can speaking a foreign language. In such situations, the right acting-voice trainer or speech-language pathologist can improve vocal technique and safety while simultaneously reducing accent.

Some voice patients and clients either really enjoy singing or have always wanted to learn to sing and discover a very strong connection between singing training and significant development of many facets of the speaking voice, including breath control, projection, resonation, range, and phrasing. Those techniques were discussed in preceding chapters.

Considerable additional information about voice and speech training techniques has been published by the Voice and Speech Trainers Association (VASTA). VASTA has also prepared an extensively annotated bibliography of books and articles on voice production and speech training, text analysis, dialect, body awareness training, speech science, and singing.[‡]

Acting-Voice Training for Injured Voices

As important as a wide repertoire of training techniques is for those who teach speakers who fall into the "normal" category, mastery of many approaches is even more critical for acting-voice trainers who work either in a medical setting or as a consultant to a

---

[*]Certified Alexander Teachers can be located through the North American Society of Teachers of Alexander Technique (NASTAT), 8710 Delgany Ave #2, Playa del Rey, CA 90293; telephone (310)827-8106.

[†]Qualified Feldenkrais practitioners can be located through the Feldenkrais Guild, 706 Ellsworth St, PO Box 489, Albany, OR 97321-0143; telephone (503)926-0981 or (800)775-2118.

[‡]For membership information, contact Barry Kur, Past President, Voice and Speech Trainers Association (VASTA), Dept of Theatre, 103 Arts Bldg, Pennsylvania State University, University Park, PA 16802; telephone (814)865-7586. For an extensive annotated bibliography of books and articles on voice production and speech training, text analysis, dialect, body awareness training, speech science, and singing, contact VASTA Bibliography, University of Utah, Theatre Department, 206 PAB, Salt Lake City, UT 84112.

medical team. The acting-voice trainer might be called on to deal with patients who are under the simultaneous care of the laryngologist, speech-language pathologist, and/or singing voice specialist. Some patients will have relatively mild vocal problems such as muscular tension dysphonia, while others may be recovering from nodules, hemorrhages, vocal fold surgery, cancer, or other organic conditions. In this setting, the acting-voice trainer must understand the disease process, the medical implications of a diagnosis, the team's overall therapeutic plan and goals, and the patient's limitations and potential. The acting-voice trainer must individualize the training plan, taking all of these factors into account. Approaching such complex problems requires an acquaintance with all of the techniques mentioned earlier in this chapter, as well as with methods used by speech-language pathologists and singing voice specialists, plus the ability to integrate these otherwise diverse approaches into a unified sequence.

Education for the Acting-Voice Trainer in a Medical Setting

First, the acting-voice trainer working in a medical office must be an expertly trained, experienced voice trainer. Ideally, he or she should also have performance experience. However, this training and experience must be supplemented with additional knowledge.

Many of the special educational requirements for acting-voice trainers who work in medical settings are the same as those discussed in chapter 27, the Singing Voice Specialist. Unfortunately, there are no organized academic programs to prepare acting-voice trainers to work with injured voices. Consequently, unless the voice trainer is willing to complete a master's program and certification in speech-language pathology (an ideal, but long route), it will be necessary to acquire training through selected courses, observation, and apprenticeships with well-established voice teams. Similarly, all of the recommendations for singing voice specialists who wish to work with injured voices apply. The acting-voice trainer needs indepth knowledge of anatomy, physiology, neurogenic voice disorders, phonetics, voice science, and laboratory instrumentation and its interpretation. He or she must spend time with an otolaryngologist, becoming familiar with the style and substance of medical practice. This process includes observation of office-based patient care, strobovideolaryngoscopy and its interpretation, surgery, and medical report writing. The acting-voice trainer also needs to observe and study the new techniques of voice therapy employed by speech-language pathologists (see

chapter 23, Voice Therapy). In addition, singing lessons are helpful and should be supplemented by observation of a singing voice specialist in a medical setting. The knowledge acquired in these approaches is invaluable in allowing the acting-voice trainer to clearly understand the function of everyone on the medical voice team and to integrate his or her training plan into the team's overall vision for each individual patient.

Assessment

As a member of the medical voice team, the acting-voice trainer must learn to perform and report a systematic assessment. Each member of the team provides a written summary of the initial encounter with a patient. Although writing such reports is routine for physicians and speech-language pathologists, it is not customary among acting-voice trainers or singing voice specialists. Chapter 27, The Singing Voice Specialist, details the assessment process and report format developed for high performance singing voice analysis. It has been used as a model in developing practices for the acting-voice trainer. A sample report can be found in appendix IV. In general, the initial evaluation approach proceeds as follows.

History

The acting-voice training session in the medical setting begins with a thorough case history of the patient. This history partially duplicates the one taken by the physician and is summarized in appendix IIb. The acting-voice trainer also obtains additional history to pinpoint the activities, habits, and behaviors in the daily life of the professional voice user that may cause or aggravate voice problems. Special attention is paid to the number of hours in a day of professional voice use, the type of performance space used by the patient (auditorium, classroom, indoor, outdoor), audience size, use of amplification, environmental factors (background noise, dust, smoke), and other issues, as discussed in chapter 7. Special attention must be paid to simultaneous employment (the "day job") that actors frequently maintain for economic stability. Many such second occupations (such as waiting tables) are vocally abusive. The acting-voice trainer is also interested in the patient's level of stress and tension, both overall and occupation-specific. Additionally, information is obtained about how the patient prepares for a professional speaking engagement or performance.

The acting-voice trainer further questions the patient about any prior voice or speech training. Surprisingly, many highly successful professional voice users (even actors) have had no voice training at all. If a patient has had some training, this can be useful in designing an effective training program. For example, if a patient has had some positive experience with Linklater training, exercises can be given during the session using the principles of this approach as a foundation for further training.

The acting-voice trainer also inquires about the patient's goals. In some cases, patients are committed to training their voices to become more efficient and powerful, whereas others are satisfied with their present voices and only want techniques to ease their discomfort.

During this portion of the evaluation, the acting-voice trainer is not only getting valuable information about the patient's vocal use; he or she is also listening to how the professional voice user is using his or her voice during conversational speech. This helps the acting-voice trainer evaluate and assess the strengths and weaknesses of the patient's vocal function.

Evaluation

The next section of the assessment consists of evaluating technical proficiency in the patient's conversational and performance voice. The patient is asked to read a passage of a dramatic monologue or present a portion of a lecture or speech that he or she frequently gives. The presentation is audio- or videotape recorded both for documenting later progress and as a teaching tool. During this time, the patient is evaluated for alignment, body tension, breath support, relaxation and isolation of the articulators, forward placement, and overall presentation style.

Alignment. The acting-voice trainer pays close attention to the alignment of the patient's body during the initial session. The head should be balanced on a lengthened and released neck and spine. The shoulders should be relaxed, open, and wide. The hips are balanced over the knees, the knees easily released forward over the toes. Special focus is given to the patient's head, neck, and torso relationship. Poor alignment in these areas can create tension and inefficiency, which can contribute to voice problems.

Body Tension. The patient is closely observed to see whether tension in the body is adversely affecting the voice. The acting-voice trainer looks for specific areas of body tension such as facial tension, clenched jaw, retracted tongue, lifted shoulders, locked knees, contracted buttocks, contracted abdomen, extrinsic neck muscle tension, arms held at sides, or clenched fists. It is also noted if body tension is getting in the way of the performer's overall communication.

Breath Support. As in initial singing and speech sessions, the acting-voice trainer looks for relaxed abdominal breathing. Although many patients are highly trained professionals, even the most well-trained professional voice user can lose efficient breath support when struggling with a voice injury.

Relaxation and Isolation of Articulators. It is essential for the professional voice user to be able to both relax and separate the function of the individual articulators. The more one articulator can move without dragging the others along with it, the more relaxed the overall articulation can be. The acting-voice trainer must assess whether the patient is using only what is necessary to create the sound and allowing everything else to stay relaxed. Specifically, the trainer looks for tension in the jaw, tongue, and lips, and the ability of the tongue and lips to function separately from the jaw.

Forward Placement. When the voice is well placed, it is easy to project in large spaces without strain. The voice is taking advantage of its own amplifier. Professional voice users with vocal injuries, because of poor technique or counterproductive muscle compensation, usually attempt to project by pushing from the throat instead of connecting the breath through to the resonating chambers.

Evaluation, Summary, and Treatment Plan

After the initial evaluation is completed, the acting-voice trainer discusses his or her analysis with the laryngologist, and then with the patient. Technical deficiencies are explained and recommendations to improve them are made. Goals are specifically defined. The patient is informed of the need for outside practice in order for sessions to be effective. Exercises are then taught to the patient, and the patient is given his or her first limited opportunity to address vocal problems using these techniques. Ideally, selected exercises will help the patient feel and/or sound better, thus encouraging compliance. Sessions are tape-recorded for ease of home practice, and a practice schedule is assigned. Arrangements for follow-up sessions are made. In addition, if the patient is an actor, the acting-voice trainer is usually the best person on the team to maintain contact with the actor's coaches, teachers, and directors if the patient plans to continue working with the team during or after treatment. Coordinated arrangements must involve not only diverse aspects of medical intervention, but also all other aspects of the patient's vocal life.

Treatment

After the assessment and establishment of a treatment plan, the plan is communicated to the other members of the medical voice team. When all team activities have been coordinated and all components of the plan are compatible and symbiotic, the acting-voice trainer proceeds with "treatment" or training, under medical supervision. This portion of the habilitation or rehabilitation process may begin immediately or be delayed until the patient has worked with the speech-language pathologist and/or singing voice specialist. In people who have had significant vocal injuries or recent surgery, acting-voice training may be delayed, but it often continues after therapy with the speech-language pathologist has been completed.

We have already noted the importance of individualizing approaches and having access to and knowledge of all available techniques from various disciplines. However, we wish to emphasize a few important differences from the work with which most voice trainers are familiar. First, the rate of progress is often different. In the theater, voice coaches are routinely under pressure to prepare performers almost instantaneously for imminent stage obligations. In theater schools, voice trainers may have 2 to 4 years during which to accomplish vocal goals with their students. In the medical setting, the rate of progress is determined by the condition of the weakest part of the system (such as the edge of a recently injured vocal fold). In patients who have sustained a vocal injury, the healing and overall rehabilitation process, as determined by the laryngologist, establish the speed at which vocal advances can be made safely. It is essential for the acting-voice trainer to understand the vocal fold and vocal tract condition of each individual. If inappropriate exercises are used, or if appropriate exercises are used too vigorously in an effort to speed progress, vocal injury may result. Such occurrences are potentially disastrous and must be avoided through proper training, communication, and pacing of training. At the same time, however, many patients are impatient. So progress must be made as quickly and safely as voice use allows. Making judgments about which approaches and exercises to use when, how vigorously, and for how long at each practice session can be difficult. That is one of the principal reasons why acting-voice trainers need extra education and close team collaboration in the medical setting.

Second, the acting-voice trainer must be acutely aware and suspicious of any voice deterioration, however subtle. People who have had vocal fold injuries frequently have fragile vocal folds. As much as voice trainers try to protect the voices of experienced actors, the acting profession challenges and taxes voices, as discussed in chapter 7; and acting-voice trainers are accustomed to helping actors rise to the challenge and overcome their vocal limitations. Although this goal applies to patients as well, it must be pursued with much greater caution. When acting-voice trainers hear a healthy actor develop a bit of voice fatigue or slight hoarseness, they commonly teach him or her how to relax and work through it. With a patient, especially early in the training process, this is generally not appropriate. Instead, we need to stop, allow the voice several minutes to return to baseline, and request medical examination (looking at the vocal folds) if it does not.

Third, the acting-voice trainer must be prepared to work toward goals that may be different from those acting-voice trainers are accustomed to in theatrical professionals. Many patients developed their vocal injuries by straining to achieve a preconceived sound. Such straining leads to muscular tension dysphonia, which can be associated with vocal nodules, cysts, hemorrhages, and other problems. If the vocal folds have been injured, auditory memory and feedback may not be the best guides for the recovering patient or his or her acting-voice trainer. Rather, like other members of the medical voice team, the acting-voice trainer must be prepared to work toward comfortable, technically correct, and safe vocal production, in some cases ignoring breathiness, hoarseness, and other vocal qualities that no one considers desirable. However, hyperfunctional efforts to eliminate them are even less desirable! The acting-voice trainer must help the patient to work with the sound achieved when technique is correct, and enhance that voice through the use of interpretation, expression, pitch, and rhythm variability, and the many other components of speech that are so important in training actors. Providing non-stage speakers with these skills allows them to fulfill their communication needs using components of speech that do not tax the vocal folds, and it gives them specific tools and skills under their conscious control which they may call upon when they need to express themselves in routine or extraordinary circumstances. Mastering these aspects of the craft of dramatic speaking gives them controlled alternatives to the brute force usually invoked by untrained patients with vocal injuries who do whatever they can to try to sound better, frequently to their own vocal detriment.

Exercises

Numerous exercises may be used in voice training. Those listed below are intended as examples of techniques found useful for many patients. The list is not intended to be complete, nor does it imply that these exercises are suitable in all cases. They are presented to provide the reader with better insights into some of the approaches commonly used by acting-voice trainers.

The Warm-up

Initial sessions with a professional voice user usually begin with some type of body warm-up. These exercises help the patient develop a kinesthetic awareness of his or her body in space, as well as an awareness of the muscles used in voice and speech production. This kind of awareness is useful in retraining muscles to work more efficiently. The warm-up also helps to strengthen and condition these muscles. The exercises should become a part of the professional voice user's daily routine and preperformance preparation. This not only helps the voice to function more efficiently, but can allow the speaker to appear more relaxed and focused in performance.

The specific warm-up exercises recommended vary depending on the individual patient's needs, but usually include exercises for general relaxation and energizing, breathing and alignment, stretching and releasing the upper body, energizing the articulators, and voice placement. Some specific examples of these exercises can be found in chapter 24.

Relaxation

When patients have excessive tension that contributes to voice difficulties, actor relaxation techniques may help them cope with life and occupational stressors, or stress related to the voice injury. Some of these techniques include progressive relaxation and imaging, modified yoga positions for stretching and releasing larger muscle groups, range of motion exercises to stretch and release specific areas of tension such as the jaw and tongue, and gentle shaking either to release tension or energize different areas of the body. Additionally, relaxation work as part of a team session can be useful in speeding the recovery process. During a singing session, for example, the acting-voice trainer can work physically with the patient by releasing specific areas of tension while the patient is doing vocal exercises with the singing voice specialist. Something as simple as placing a hand on the patient's shoulders as a reminder to keep the shoulders relaxed while inhaling or gently manipulating the head and neck to keep the extrinsic muscles released while singing often is enough to help patients kinesthetically understand the process of making sound with less effort.

The Articulation Warm-up

For patients with extreme jaw and tongue tension, a series of exercises to warm up the articulators is often useful. These exercises train patients to release tension in the jaw and tongue and develop strength and dexterity in the tongue and lips so that the voice is produced with much less effort. The following exercises are based on work condensed from and adapted by Ralph Zito from Edith Skinner's *Speak with Distinction*.[2] Ralph Zito is on the faculty of the Theatre School at the Juilliard School in New York City.

The Preparation

1. The exercises always begin with gentle stretching. The patient is asked to sit forward on the edge of a chair and let his or her spine lengthen up toward the ceiling. Keeping this length, the chin drops toward the chest to give the back of the neck a gentle stretch. With each outgoing breath, the weight of the head releases the back of the neck a little more. The patient then uses the hands to gently lift the head back into an upright position. This trains the neck muscles to use minimal effort while in motion.

2. The head is then released over the right side with the right ear directly over the right shoulder. The patient is encouraged to do this exercise without collapsing the spine so that the torso remains upright and aligned. The patient is then asked to breathe easily in and out, and imagine that with each exhalation the muscles along the side of the neck are softening, and the space between the left ear and shoulder is increasing. The head then rolls across the chest to the left side and the exercise is repeated on the opposite side. The head is again lifted back in place with the hands.

3. Next, the patient is asked to wiggle the muscles of the face, brow, and head for a minute or so as if mosquitos were landing on the face and he or she had no hands to brush them away. The patient is then asked to squeeze the face into a tiny ball and then stretch it wide open while the jaw drops and the tongue stretches out of the mouth. This is repeated a few times and then the patient is asked to blow out across the lips (like a horse) a few times. The patient is asked to observe how the face feels after the exercise to encourage developing a keener kinesthetic awareness of the muscles of articulation.

4. While maintaining the upward energy of the spine, the heels of the hands are brought up to the sides of the head, and in one easy motion the jaw is gently massaged open. The jaw is allowed to hang open

for a few moments while the patient checks the position of the tongue (ideally, resting at the bottom of the mouth with the tongue tip placed behind the lower front teeth), and breathes. A mirror is used to facilitate the patient's awareness of any jaw or tongue tension that may cause the jaw to close or the tongue to retract. The patient is then asked to tilt the head forward and slide the tip of the tongue forward over the lower lip and continue to breathe. With each outgoing breath, the patient uses gravity to increase the ability of the tongue to stretch up and out of the throat. The head then lifts by uncurling from the back of the neck, and the tongue slowly slides back into the mouth with the tip of the tongue remaining behind the lower front teeth.

The Lips

The next series of exercises is designed to help the patient learn to relax and energize the lips. They also train the patient to isolate the lips from the jaw so the lips can spread without having to close the jaw, and the jaw can open without losing the rounding of the lips.

1. First, with the jaw closed gently, the lips are pursed as far forward as possible and then spread into a smile as wide as possible, keeping the lips together. The goal is to do the exercise as slowly and smoothly as possible. This is repeated 10 times.
2. The exercise is now done with the jaw slightly open and the lips slightly parted throughout the exercise. The patient imagines sipping soda through a straw. The patient is reminded that it is important not to close the jaw as he or she smiles. A mirror is used to monitor this.
3. The sequence is repeated once again with the lips and jaw even more open and the lips moving forward into a wide oval. The patient is given the image of the face of a choir boy to use as a model. The lips are then spread into an open grin while the jaw remains still. It is helpful to have the patient place a finger on his or her chin to monitor any movement of the jaw.
4. Another exercise that is helpful for isolating and relaxing the lips and jaw is repeating *wee-wee-wee-wee-wee-wee*. The patient is trained to make these sounds lightly and easily and with minimal tension and lateralization. The patient then repeats *waw-waw-waw-waw-waw-waw*. The patient is made aware of the necessity to keep the lips rounded over the open jaw so that the sound does not become "wah." Finally the two sounds are spoken alternately (*wee-waw-wee-waw*) keeping the jaw still for the first sound and the lips rounded for the second.

The Tongue

The goals of these exercises are to increase the overall relaxation and dexterity of the tongue, to isolate the tongue from the lips and the jaw, to develop control of the tip of the tongue, and to isolate the parts of the tongue from each other.

1. With the jaw slightly open, the patient is asked to stick the tip of the tongue straight out. It is then moved slowly left and right as slowly and smoothly as possible without moving the jaw. This is repeated several times. The patient continues to use a mirror to monitor the movement. Next the tongue tip moves from the upper lip down to the lower lip, again working as slowly and smoothly as possible. These movements are then combined so that the tongue moves left, right, up, and down.
2. The patient then makes a big circle clockwise with the tip of the tongue as if the tongue is a paint brush and the patient is an artist painting a circle on the air in front of him. Reverse directions so that the movement is counterclockwise. The patient is asked to observe which parts of the movement are difficult and which parts are easy.
3. With the jaw quite open, the tongue tip moves from gum ridge down to the lower front teeth several times, as if the patient were silently saying *la-la-la*. The tongue should move straight up and down as smoothly and steadily as possible. The mirror is used to make sure the jaw remains still. The patient then releases the tongue and blows out across the lips.
4. With the jaw remaining open, the back of the tongue moves up to the soft palate and down for the sound *gah-gah-gah*. The jaw stays relaxed, and the tip of the tongue remains resting behind the lower front teeth.

It is important to do this work in short increments of time, as tension can be created by working so specifically on individual articulators. In between each of these exercises, it is helpful to do some of the stretching and shaking exercises mentioned previously.

Efficacy of the Acting-Voice Trainer in a Medical Office

We believe that the acting-voice trainer is an extremely valuable part of the medical voice team. In addition to individual sessions, many voice training sessions have been held jointly with a singing voice specialist, speech-language pathologist, or both working simultaneously with the acting-voice trainer. The concurrent use of more traditional medical approaches and acting-voice training (both voice and body techniques) has facilitated compliance and carryover and expedited recovery. In addition, the acting-voice trainer has been invaluable for advanced training in patients whom we formerly would have discharged from therapy. Although speech-language pathologists and singing voice specialists do address high-performance speaking voice needs, the added dimension of the professional acting-voice trainer has contributed enormously to our ability to carry our patients further toward reaching optimal speaking performance. In future years, we anticipate the addition of acting-voice trainers to other medical teams and the development of educational programs to make it easier for acting-voice trainers to provide more knowledgeable intervention in patients with vocal injuries.

Summary

Acting-voice trainers are drama voice teachers with additional training and experience in care of patients with voice disorders. An acting-voice trainer must be educated in numerous techniques and experienced in working with healthy actors. The acting-voice trainer must also have special knowledge of vocal anatomy, physiology, and medical care. Acting-voice trainers work in collaboration with laryngologists, speech-language pathologists, and singing-voice specialists.

Review Questions

1. Classic approaches to training the voices of actors include those of:
   a. Edith Skinner
   b. Kristin Linklater
   c. Arthur Lessack
   d. all of the above
   e. none of the above

2. The premise that each of us has a beautifully functioning, natural voice with which many of us interfere is fundamental to the approach of:

   a. Edith Skinner
   b. Kristin Linklater
   c. Arthur Lessack
   d. all of the above
   e. none of the above

3. Elimination of all anesthetic habits, and replacing them with an ongoing state of habitual awareness, are central to the approach of:
   a. Edith Skinner
   b. Kristin Linklater
   c. Arthur Lessack
   d. all of the above
   e. none of the above

4. In working with injured voices, it is optimal for the acting-voice trainer to have complete mastery of one approach to voice training and to apply it skillfully to all patients with voice disorders.
   a. true
   b. false

5. A carefully defined and prescribed series of rules for pronunciation is central to the approach of:
   a. Edith Skinner
   b. Kristin Linklater
   c. Arthur Lessack
   d. all of the above
   e. none of the above

References

1. Raphael BN. A Consumer's Guide to Voice and Speech Training. *N Engl Theatre J.* 1994;5:101–114.
2. Skinner E, Mansell L, ed. *Speak with Distinction.* New York, NY: Applause Theatre Book Publishers; 1990.
3. Linklater K. *Freeing the Natural Voice.* New York, NY: Drama Book Specialists; 1976.
4. Linklater K. *Freeing Shakespeare's Voice.* New York, NY: Theatre Communications Group; 1992.
5. Lessac A. *The Use and Training of the Human Voice.* 2d. ed. Mountain View, Calif: Mayfield; 1967.
6. Lessac A. *Body Wisdom: The Use and Training of the Human Body.* Claremont, Calif: Arthur Lessac; 1978.
7. Berry C. *Voice and the Actor.* London: Harrap; 1973.
8. Berry C. *The Actor and His Text.* London: Harrap; 1987.
9. Turner JC: *Voice and Speech in the Theatre.* 3rd ed. London: Pitman; 1977.
10. Rodenburg P. *The Right to Speak.* London: Methuen Drama; 1992.
11. Rodenburg P. *The Need for Words.* London: Methuen Drama; 1993.

31

Exercise Physiology: Perspective for Vocal Training

Carole M. Schneider, Keith Saxon, and Carolyn A. Dennehy

Aristotle wrote that "the animal that moves makes its change of position by pressing against that which is beneath it."[1] The study of movement in animals, as Aristotle pointed out, is characterized by two distinct concepts: the physical interaction that exists between the organism and the environment, and the skillful way organisms organize and carry out the physical interaction (pressing). Therefore, if we accept that movement is the result of the interaction between biological systems and the environment, we can study these concepts to learn how to improve human performance.

The study of human body functions, commonly referred to as *physiology*, emphasizes the cause and effect associated with specific mechanisms. Based on numerous scientific investigations, a large body of specialized information is gradually accumulated and generalized explanations of the results are formulated. Over time these explanations are tested and eventually distilled into principles that can be applied with consistent results.

Physiological principles associated with human activity have been extensively studied. These principles have been integrated into the science of exercise physiology and summated into training principles that can be applied across a spectrum of individuals from patients requiring rehabilitative services to elite athletes preparing for Olympic-caliber competition. It is, therefore, reasonable to assume that these basic tenets for physical training and conditioning could be applied to any type of activity involving movement, including vocal performance. Presently, there has been little research conducted that reports the benefits of exercise training on non-sport-related activities. However, a book published by Saxon and Schneider[2] has introduced the principles of exercise physiology and applied these concepts to vocal training.

The enhancement of any physical performance is directly related to the level of fitness and conditioning of the performer. Improvement in physical performance can range from drastic alterations in the untrained to acute refinement of highly developed skills in the trained individual. Overall physical conditioning of the heart, lungs, and skeletal muscles during regular prescriptive exercise can have a profound effect on the performance levels of anyone along this continuum and can serve to protect individuals against injury and disease. Vocal performers can expect to benefit from general and specific physical conditioning in this regard.

Any activity that involves working muscles can be enhanced by regularly and consistently applying the principles of muscle training and conditioning. Vocal performance is no exception. Sound is the result of complex and dynamic interactions between various muscles and the physical environment. The better the muscles are conditioned to work as independent structures and in synergistic fashion, the better they will perform. The resulting effects of muscle activity, for example, sound production, will be enhanced. When vocal performers apply a technique to improve sound quality, they may not be utilizing the best physiological principles to train the musculature involved in producing sound. However, specific and individualized muscle training may result in better overall sound quality, greater range, and sustainable phrases, as well as improve the general fitness level of the performer and increase his or her resistance to injury and disease.[2]

Improvement in physical fitness or condition leads to increased performance capacity, particularly as it pertains to the cardio-respiratory and skeletal muscle systems. Exercise physiology is based on a relatively simple premise that suggests that the more efficient these systems are, the higher the level of physical fitness and work capacity. Increasing heart and lung capacity to deliver more oxygen to working muscles and requiring less energy to perform the task allows physical activity to be extended for longer periods of time. Since these systems are essential contributors to voice production, performance quality, and endurance, training and maintaining them are important for vocalists. Furthermore, continuous refinement and maintenance of a desired level of conditioning implies that training and conditioning is a dynamic and specific process.

General Principles of Training

Training for an athletic competition involves the application of four basic principles to elicit a training effect: overload, specificity, individuality, and reversibility. Training for a vocal performance should incorporate the same training principles to produce a training effect in the musculature and energy systems utilized in vocal production.

Overload Principle

The *overload principle* states that physiological adaptations will occur in the working muscles with the appropriate stimuli. Appropriate stimuli include workloads that are greater than workloads encountered in daily life. Christensen[3] found that regular training at a constant workload gradually lowered the heart rate and produced a training effect such as an improvement of the oxygen-carrying capacity of the cardiovascular system. Additional training at the same workload did not change the heart rate response. When training involved a heavier workload, the heart rate response was even lower than the original heart rate. Adaptation occurs at a given workload. To develop further physical fitness, the training must incorporate an additional overload. Overload can be varied by manipulating the components of training as specified by the American College of Sports Medicine.[4] These training components are frequency of exercise, duration of exercise, intensity of exercise, type (mode) of exercise, and exercise progression.

The application of training overload must be gradual. Intense training should be interspersed with easy workouts (decreasing exercise intensity and/or duration). There are limited data on the laryngeal musculature regarding loading and unloading specific muscles. A correlation has been found with high pitch and high intensity and high load on the cricothyroid and

thyroid arytenoid muscles.[2,5] Additionally, sufficient rest should be given to the sport athlete or vocal performer to allow for adequate recovery.[6] Sport athletes overload by using periodization cycles, which helps prevent overtraining. Periodization has several cycles throughout the year. The *load cycle* is the building of the training program during the off-season or noncompetitive season. The *recovery cycle* is active rest (low intensity, short duration) and separates the load cycle and the competitive season. Recovery periods are essential to allow for physiological adaptations to occur. The *peak cycle* develops maximum muscular conditioning and skill enhancement. The *conditioning cycle* is active rest for a few months following the strenuous competitive season.

Manipulation of these factors during vocal training will enhance vocal performance and may reduce the incidence of injury. Skilled teachers are applying some of these concepts in the studio when interspersing vocal exercises with rest. Varying rehearsal to multiple short sessions or extended long sessions also illustrates the application of the overload principle.

Specificity Principle

The training program must be appropriate for the activity or performance. There are two basic types of specificity: *metabolic specificity* and *skill specificity*. Metabolic specificity requires that the training program overload the energy (metabolic) system that supports the activity. The energy system rate and capacity must meet the demands of the activity or performance. McArdle[7] found that the cardiovascular and respiratory training responses were most pronounced when training stressed the specific muscle groups involved in the chosen activity. Such local skeletal muscle metabolic adaptation contributes to the improvement of fitness and performance.

Skill specificity means training the muscle groups and movement patterns (neuromuscular) involved in the activity of interest. In other words, training programs should contain activities closely related to the actual performance skills. To develop the vocal skill of attaining and sustaining a pitch at high volume, the muscles should be strengthened using intense contractions of short duration while increasing the frequency of practice sessions. To develop the voice for prolonged singing, the muscles should be strengthened using low intensity contractions for long durations.[2]

Individuality Principle

The physiological responses to training vary between individuals. Similar training routines will not produce exactly the same physiological benefits to all athletes. The skilled voice teacher does not recommend the same training program to all students in the studio. Training is optimized when individual needs and capacities are addressed. The resulting effects are enhancement of performance for all skill levels.

Reversibility Principle

The majority of physiological benefits from training are lost within a short period of time when training is discontinued. The length of time is variable depending on the physiological parameter in question. The loss of the benefits of training can vary from several weeks to several months.[8] Saltin and Rowell[9] found that inactivity decreased physiological function 1% per day. Most physiological benefits of training are probably completely lost after 4 to 8 weeks of inactivity. These studies demonstrated that pulmonary ventilation and oxygen uptake were greatly affected by detraining. Since these are essential physiological components utilized during vocal performance, the reversibility principle may indicate that absolute voice rest is not recommended except in specific cases, such as after injury or surgery.

The Exercise Prescription

The American College of Sports Medicine[4] has established components that must be included in the exercise prescription (training program) that will produce a training effect. The components include frequency of exercise, duration of exercise, intensity of exercise, type (mode) of exercise, and exercise progression. The same components can be used in the studio or voice therapist's office to elicit desired changes in vocal quality.

Frequency of Exercise

Exercising three times per week has been established as the optimal frequency to produce a training effect. However, this time course is dependent on the intensity of the activity being performed. Research comparing the results of sport-specific training of comparable workloads 2 days per week, 3 days per week, and 5 days per week showed that training effects occurred with programs of 3 or more days per week.[10,11] Frequency of training, however, is dependent on the individual's initial fitness level. The lower the initial fitness level, the greater the conditioning effect even with a 2-day per week program. Training six or seven times per week provides minimal fitness improvement and increases the risk of overuse injury.[12] Exer-

cise with short duration and low intensity requires more frequent training to produce beneficial physiological effects.

Duration of Exercise

The duration of training is directly related to the improvement of physical fitness.[13,14] The American College of Sports Medicine[4] has recommended that each exercise session be at least 20 minutes in duration with continuous exercise if the exercise intensity is low (50 to 75% of maximal heart rate reserve). If the exercise intensity is high (above 75% of maximal heart rate reserve: maximal heart rate minus resting heart rate times exercise intensity plus resting heart rate), the exercise duration is decreased. Training the energy and muscular systems required for specific vocal effects at comparable durations should enhance singing performance.

Intensity of Exercise

The maintenance of vocal efficiency may depend on the intensity of the training sessions, in addition to the frequency and duration of the training sessions. An important component of physical training is exercise intensity. Physiological changes from training occur primarily from intensity overload. Subjective evaluation from the performer can help determine if the training workload is too easy or too hard, but it cannot identify an optimal training intensity. Heart rate has a linear relationship with exercise intensity. For example, as the exercise intensity increases, heart rate increases. Because of this relationship and the ease of assessing heart rate, the most common method developed to determine the appropriate exercise intensity is heart rate. The exercise intensity should be strenuous enough to get the heart rate between 60% and 90% of the performer's heart rate reserve. The heart rate can be determined immediately after the activity by counting the pulse.

The determination of blood lactic acid (lactate) is another objective measure of exercise intensity. Lactate levels can be measured using a small drop of blood from the finger. Multiple blood samples can be collected to determine the blood lactate profile of the performer during the exercise or activity. These values are then plotted and a blood lactate profile curve is produced. The point at which there is a sudden rise in blood lactate is called the onset of blood lactic acid (OBLA). The goal of the training sessions is to have OBLA occur later and later during the exercise training workout. The occurrence of OBLA at a higher exercise intensity means that the performer is able to work longer before lactic acid accumulates in the blood, thus increasing the body's utilization and tolerance of blood lactic acid and delaying muscle fatigue.[15] The application of intensity of training may be useful during singing, especially in the laboratory setting where heart rate and blood lactic acid can be easily collected. Additionally, heart rate and lactic acid could be monitored during performance to judge the intensity of work while singing.[16]

Exercise intensity can also be determined using the measurement of oxygen consumption. The capacity of the cardiorespiratory system is limited. The maximal amount of oxygen that can be utilized by the working muscles is called *maximal oxygen consumption*. The maximal amount of oxygen the muscles can consume is dependent on an increased respiration and increased cardiac output (heart rate times stroke volume). The maximal amount of oxygen an individual can utilize in this manner can be measured in a laboratory setting. Oxygen consumption is linearly related to exercise intensity and heart rate. The greater the exercise intensity, the higher the amount of oxygen utilized. The greater the capacity of oxygen consumption, the more physically fit the individual. A more fit person can perform work with less energy demand, and therefore less oxygen demand. Thus, training a singer to become more physically fit would enhance the singer's ability to perform at a lower energy demand and, thus, perform longer or with less stress on the physiological systems involved.

The final determinant of exercise intensity is ratings of perceived exertion (RPE).[17] The scale is a numeric qualifier for individuals to rate their own perception of the physical work demands. This scale ranges from 6 to 20. The RPE scale was developed to correspond to heart rate by adding a zero to the RPE value (eg, an RPE of 12 equals 120 bpm).[18] With practice an individual can learn to associate a heart rate response to an RPE value. Once this occurs, a performer can use the RPE value instead of monitoring the heart rate to determine the appropriate exercise intensity for a conditioning effect.

Type (Mode) of Exercise

The type of training modality should be specific to the activity. Training to acquire a particular skill should be consistent and directly designed to influence a particular effect. In addition to the practice of singing, exercises specific to the energy systems and muscles used during singing need to be incorporated.

Exercise Progression

The greatest physiological improvements in fitness are seen within the first 6 to 8 weeks of the training program. Further improvements require that the cardiorespiratory system and the muscular system continue to be overloaded by adjusting the duration and intensity of the exercise program to meet the new level of physical fitness. Exercise progression should be slow and gradual to avoid the incidence of injury. In regards to vocal performers, the present level of vocal conditioning would determine the stages of vocal training. The components (ie, intensity, duration) of the exercise training program do not change but the degree of progression is specific to the conditioning level of the vocal performer.

Phases of the Exercise Routine

The exercise workout for athletic performance or vocal performance should consist of a *warm-up*, a *conditioning phase*, and a *cool-down*. The function of the warm-up is to increase blood flow to the working muscles and increase the muscle temperature. This decreases the chance of muscle injury.[6] The warm-up activity should gradually intensify to prepare the muscles for the more demanding conditioning phase. The length of the warm-up should be 10 to 15 minutes.[19]

The conditioning phase should include activity at a predetermined exercise prescription, varying the frequency, duration, and intensity of the work. The conditioning phase should be specifically designed to produce the desired effects and should be adjusted as adaptations occur.

The cool-down incorporates the same activity used in the conditioning phase but at a much lower intensity. The reduced intensity facilitates venous blood flow back to the heart and avoids blood pooling in the arms and legs. Continuous movement during the cool-down prevents dizziness and the possibility of fainting.[20]

Application to Vocal Performance

Singing involves the whole body, the vocal and facial areas, the abdomen, chest, and the legs. Therefore, the muscles and energy systems utilized during performance need to be trained. The principles used for the development of a training effect in the systems involved in sport training can be applied to training the physiological systems involved with vocal performance.[2]

One example, to illustrate the point, is the requirement of proper posture for sound production. The development of proper body alignment involves correct body posture. Correct body posture involves an appropriate balance between the agonist and antagonist muscles involved with maintaining appropriate positioning of the upper thorax. Henderson[21] recommends pulling the shoulders straight back until the shoulder blades feel as if they are touching. Repeating this frequently will assist in establishing the correct postural position for the head and shoulders.

A better procedure for establishing correct posture would be to do an analysis of the muscles involved in maintaining desired posture and then develop an exercise prescription (type, frequency, duration, intensity, and progression) that involves training the muscles used to maintain the appropriate balance for enhanced posture, which would result in more effective use of the energy needed to perform.

Saxon and Schneider[2] have published a reference textbook for vocal performers. The text includes an analysis of the muscles and energy systems involved during vocal performance. The goal is to enhance vocal performance incorporating the established training principles from the area of exercise physiology.

Summary

Principles of exercise physiology have been successfully applied to Olympic and other athletic training. The vocal apparatus includes a system of muscles that are athletically used. These muscles essentially function the same way as muscles elsewhere in the body. Principles of muscles and exercise physiology are applicable to voice training.

Review Questions

1. Any activity that involves working muscles can be enhanced by regularly and consistently applying principles of muscle training and conditioning, including vocal performance.
   a. true
   b. false

2. The basic principles to elicit a training effect include all of the following except:
   a. overload
   b. specificity
   c. individuality
   d. repeatability
   e. reversibility

3. Physiological adaptations will occur in working muscles given stimuli that are greater than workloads encountered in daily life. This is an expression of the principle of:
   a. overload
   b. specificity
   c. individuality
   d. repeatability
   e. reversibility

4. Training muscle groups and movement patterns involved in the activity of interest is an example of:
   a. metabolic specificity
   b. skill specificity
   c. individuality principle
   d. repeatability
   e. reversibility

5. The optimal exercise frequency to obtain a training effect is:
   a. 1 day per week
   b. 2 days per week
   c. 3 days per week
   d. 6 days per week
   e. 7 days per week

References

1. Artistotle, Forster ES, trans. *Progression of Animals*. Cambridge, Mass: Harvard University Press; 1968:489
2. Saxon KG, Schneider CM. *Vocal Exercise Physiology*. San Diego, Calif: Singular Publishing Group, Inc; 1995.
3. Christensen EA, as cited in Astrand I, Astrand PO, Christensen EA, Hedman R. Intermittent muscular work. *Acta Physiol Scand*. 1960;48:448–453.
4. American College of Sports Medicine. Position statement on the recommended quantity and quality of exercise for developing and maintaining fitness in healthy adults. *Med Sci Sports*. 1978;10:vii–x.
5. Shipp T, McGlone RE. Laryngeal dynamics associated with voice frequency change. *J Speech Hearing Res*. 1971;14:761–768.
6. Brooks GA, Fahey TD. *Exercise Physiology: Human Bioenergetics and Its Applications*. New York, NY: Macmillan Publishing Company; 1985.
7. McArdle WD. Specificity of run training on VO_2 max and heart rate changes during running and swimming. *Med Sci Sports*. 1978;10:16.
8. Cureton TK, Phillips EE. Physical fitness changes in middle-aged men attributable to equal eight-week periods of training, non-training and retraining. *J Sports Med Phys Fitness*. 1964;4:1–7.
9. Saltin B, Rowell LB. Functional adaptations to physical activity and inactivity. *Fed Proc*. 1980;39:1506.
10. Pollock ML, Cureton TK, Greninger L. Effects of frequency of training on working capacity, cardiovascular function, and body composition of adult men. *Med Sci Sports*. 1969;1:70–74.
11. Pollock ML, Tiffany J, Gettman L, Janeway R, Lofland H. Effect of frequency of training on serum lipids, cardiovascular function, and body composition. In: Franks BD, ed. *Exercise and Fitness*. Chicago, Ill: Athletic Institute; 1969;161–178.

12. Pollock ML, Wilmore JH. *Exercise in Health and Disease.* 2nd ed. Philadelphia, PA: WB Saunders Company; 1990.

13. Milesis CA, Pollock ML, Bah MD, Ayres JJ, Ward A, Linnerud AC. Effects of different durations of training on cardiorespiratory function, body composition and serum lipids. *Res Q.* 1976;47:716–725.

14. Sharkey BJ. Intensity and duration of training and the development of cardiorespiratory endurance. *Med Sci Sports.* 1970; 2:197–202.

15. Brooks GA, Fahey TD. *Fundamentals of Human Performance.* New York, NY: Macmillan Publishing Company; 1987.

16. Saxon KG, Michel JF, Schneider CM. The singer as athlete: lessons from applied and exercise physiology. *Care of the Professional Voice, The Voice Foundation's 20th Symposium*; June, 1991; Philadelphia, Pa.

17. Birk TJ, Birk CA. Use of ratings of perceived exertion for exercise prescription. *Sports Med.* 1987;4:1–8.

18. Borg GV, Linderholm H. Perceived exertion and pulse rate during graded exercise in various age groups. *Acta Med Scand.* 1967;472 (suppl):194–206.

19. Heyward VH. *Advanced Fitness Assessment and Exercise Prescription.* Champaign, Ill: Human Kinetics; 1991.

20. Bowers RW, Fox EL. *Sports Physiology.* Dubuque, Ia: Wm C Brown Publishers; 1992.

21. Henderson LB. *How to Train Singers.* New York, NY: Parker Publishing; 1979.

Glossary

This glossary has been developed from the author's experience and also from a review of glossaries developed by Johan Sundberg (personal communication, June 1995), Ingo Titze (*Principles of Voice Production*, Englewood, NJ: Prentice-Hall, 1994:330–338), and other sources. It is difficult to credit appropriately contributions to glossaries or dictionaries of general terms, as each new glossary builds on prior works. The author is indebted to colleagues whose previous efforts have contributed to the compilation of this glossary.

AAO–HNS: American Academy of Otolaryngology—Head and Neck Surgery

AIDS: Acquired Immune Deficiency Syndrome

abduct: To move apart, separate

abduction quotient: The ratio of the glottal half-width at the vocal processes to the amplitude of vibration of the vocal fold

abscess: Collection of pus

absolute jitter (Jita): A discrete measure of very short term (cycle-to-cycle) variation of the pitch periods expressed in microseconds. This parameter is dependent on the fundamental frequency of the voicing sample. Therefore, normative data differ significantly for men and women. Higher pitch results in lower Jita

absolute voice rest: Total silence of the phonatory system

acceleration: The rate of change of velocity with respect to time (measured in millimeters per square second mm/s^2)

acoustic power: The physical measure of the amount of energy produced and radiated into the air per second (measured in watts)

acoustical zero decibels: 0.0002 microbar

actin: A protein molecule that reacts with myosin to form an actinomysin, the contractile part of a myofilament in muscle

acting voice trainer: (1) *See* **Voice Coach**; (2) A professional with extra training who may work with injured voices as part of a medical voice team in an effort to optimize speaking voice performance

Adam's apple: Prominence of the thyroid cartilage, primarily in males

adduct: To bring together, approximate

affricate: Combination of plosive and fricative

allergy: Bodily response to foreign substances or organisms

alto: (*See* **Contralto**)

AMA: American Medical Association

amplitude: Maximum excursion of an undulating signal from the equilibrium; the amplitude of a sound wave is related to the perceived loudness; mostly it is expressed as a logarithmic, comparative level measure using the decibel (dB) unit

amplitude perturbation quotient (APQ): A relative evaluation of short term (cycle-to-cycle) variation of peak-to-peak amplitude expressed in percent. This measure uses a smoothing factor of 11 periods

amplitude spectrum: A display of relative amplitude versus frequency of the sinusoidal components of a waveform

amplitude to length ratio: The ratio of vibrational amplitude at the center of the vocal fold to the length of the vocal fold

amplitude tremor: Regular (periodic) long-term amplitude variation (an element of vibrato)

amplitude tremor frequency (Fatr): This measure is expressed in Hz and shows the frequency of the most intensive low-frequency amplitude-modulating component in the specified amplitude-tremor analysis range

amplitude tremor intensity index (ATRI): The average ratio of the amplitude of the most intensive low-frequency amplitude modulating component (amplitude tremor) to the total amplitude of the analyzed sample. The algorithm for tremor analysis determines the strongest periodic amplitude modulation of the voice. This measure is expressed in percent

anabolic steroids: Primarily male hormones, increase muscle mass and may cause irreversible, masculinization of the voice. Anabolic steroids help cells convert simple substances into more complex substances, especially into living matter

anisotropic: Property of a material that produces different strains when identical stresses are applied in different directions

antagonist (muscle): An opposing muscle

anterior: Toward the front

anterior commissure: The junction of the vocal folds in the front of the larynx

antibiotic: Drug used to combat infection (bodily invasion by a living organism such as a bacteria or virus). Most antibiotics have action specifically against bacteria

anticoagulant: Blood thinner

antinodes: The "peaks" in a standing wave pattern

antihistamine: Drug to combat allergic response

aperiodic: Irregular behavior that has no definite period, is usually either chaotic or random

aperiodicity: The absence of periodicity; no portion of the waveform repeats exactly

aphonia: The absence of vocal fold vibration; this term is commonly used to describe people who have "lost their voice" after vocal fold injury. In most cases, such patients have very poor vibration, rather than no vibration; and they typically have a harsh, nearly whispered voice

appendix of the ventricle of Morgagni: A cecal pouch of mucous membrane connected by a narrow opening with the anterior aspect of the ventricle. It sits between the ventricular fold in the inner surface of the thyroid cartilage. In some cases, it may extend as far as the cranial border of the thyroid cartilage, or higher. It contains the openings of 60–70 mucous glands, and it is enclosed in a fibrous capsule, which is continuous with the ventricular ligament. Also, called *appendix ventriculi laryngis*, and *laryngeal saccule*

aria: Song, especially in the context of an opera

arthritis: Inflammation of joints in the body

articulation: Shaping of vocal tract by positioning of its mobile walls such as lips, lower jaw, tongue body and tip, velum, epiglottis, pharyngeal sidewalls, and larynx

arytenoid cartilages: Paired, ladle-shaped cartilages to which the vocal folds are attached

arytenoid dislocation: A condition frequently causing vocal fold immobility or hypomobility due to separation of the arytenoid cartilage from its joint and normal position atop the cricoid cartilage

ASHA: American Speech-Language-Hearing Association

aspirate: Speech sound characterized by breathiness

aspirate attack: Initiation of phonation preceded by air, producing /h/

aspiration: (1) In speech, the sound made by turbulent airflow preceding or following vocal fold vibration, as in /ha/. (2) In medicine, refers to breathing into the lungs substances that do not belong there such as food, water, or stomach contents following reflux. Aspiration may lead to infections such as pneumonia, commonly referred to as *aspiration pneumonia*

asthma: Obstructive pulmonary (lung) disease associated with bronchospasm, and difficulty expiring air

atmospheric pressure: The absolute pressure exerted by the atmosphere, usually measured in millimeters of mercury (mmHg)

atresia: Failure of development. In the case of the larynx, this may result in fusion or congenital webbing of the vocal folds, or failure of development of the trachea

atrophy: Loss or wasting of tissue. Muscle atrophy occurs, for example, in an arm that is immobilized in a cast for many weeks

attractor: A geometric figure in state space to which all trajectories in its vicinity are drawn. The four types of attractors are (1) *point*, (2) *limit cycle*, (3) *toroidal*, and (4) *strange*. A point trajector draws all trajectories to a single point. An example is a pendulum moving toward rest. A limit cycle is characteristic of periodic motion. A toroidal attractor represents quasiperiodic motion (often considered a subset of periodic motion). A strange attractor is associated with chaotic motion

bands: Range of adjacent parameter values; a frequency band is an ensemble of adjacent frequencies

band pass filter: Filter that allows frequencies only within a certain frequency range to pass

baritone: The most common male vocal range. Higher than bass and lower than tenor. Singer's formant around 2600 Hz

basement membrane: Anatomic structure immediately beneath the epithelium

bass: (*See* **Basso**)

bass baritone: In between bass and baritone. Not as heavy as basso profundo, but typically with greater flexibility. Must be able to sing at least as high as F_4. Also known as *basso contante* and *basso guisto*. Baritones with bass quality are also called *basse taille*

basso: Lowest male voice. Singers formant around 2300–2400 Hz

basso profundo: Deep bass. The lowest and heaviest of the bass voices. Can sing at least as low as D_2 with full voice. Singer's formant around 2200–2300 Hz. Also known as *contra-basso*

bel canto: Literally means "beautiful singing." Refers to a method and philosophical approach to singing voice production

benign tumors: Tumors that are not able to metastasize or spread to distant sites

Bernoulli's principle: If the energy in a confined fluid stream is constant, an increase in particle velocity must be accompanied by a decrease in pressure against the wall

bifurcation: A sudden qualitative change in the behavior of a system. In chaos, for example, a small change in the initial parameters of a stable (predominantly linear) system may cause oscillation between two different states as the non-linear aspects of the system become manifest. This transition is a bifurcation

bilateral: On both sides

bilateral vocal fold paralysis: Loss of the ability to move both vocal folds caused by neurologic dysfunction

biomechanics: The study of the mechanics of biological tissue

bleat: Fast vibrato, like the bleating of a sheep

body: With regard to the vocal fold, the vocalis muscle

Boyle's law: In a soft-walled enclosure and at a constant temperature, pressure and volume are inversely related

bravura: Brilliant, elaborate, showy execution of musical or dramatic material

breathy phonation: Phonation characterized by a lack of vocal fold closure; this causes air leakage (excessive airflow) during the quasi-closed phase, and this produces turbulence that is heard as noise mixed in the voice

bronchitis: Inflammation of the bronchial tubes in the lungs

bronchospasm: Forceful closing of the distal airways in the lungs

bruxism: Grinding of the teeth

bulimia: Self-induced vomiting to control weight

butterfly effect: Refers to the notion that in chaotic (nonlinear dynamics) systems a minuscule change in initial condition may have profound effects on the behavior of the system. For example, a butterfly flapping its wings in Hong Kong may change the weather in New York

cancer: An abnormality in which cells no longer respond to the signals that control replication and growth. This results in uncontrolled growth and tumor formation, and may result in spread of tumor to distant locations (metastasis)

carrier: (1) In physics, a waveform (typically a sinusoid) whose frequency or amplitude is modulated by a signal. (2) In medicine, a person who is colonized by an organism (typically bacteria such as streptococcus or pneumococcus), but who has no symptoms or adverse effects from the presence of the organism. Nevertheless, that carrier is able to transmit the organism to other people in whom it does cause a symptomatic infection

cartilage of Wrisberg: Cartilage attached in the mobile portion of each aryepiglottic fold

cartilage of Santorini: Small cartilage flexibly attached near the apex of the arytenoid, in the region of the opening of the esophagus

castrato: Male singer castrated at around age 7 or 8, so as to retain alto or soprano vocal range

category: Voice type classified according to pitch range and voice quality; the most frequently used categories are bass, baritone, tenor, alto, mezzosoprano, and soprano, but many other subdivisions of these exists

caudal: Toward the tail

chaos: A qualitative description of a dynamic system that seems unpredictable, but actually has a "hidden" order. Also a mathematical field that studies fractal geometry and non-linear dynamics

chaotic behavior: Distinct from random or periodic behavior. A chaotic system *looks* disorganized or random but is actually deterministic, although aperiodic. It has sensitive dependence on initial condition, has definite form, and is bounded to a relatively narrow range (unable to go off into infinity)

chest voice: Heavy registration with excessive resonance in the lower formants

cochlea: Inner ear organ of hearing

coefficient of amplitude variation (vAm): This measure, expressed in percent, computes the relative standard deviation of the peak-to-peak amplitude. It increases regardless of the type of amplitude variation

coefficient of fundamental frequency variation (vFo): This measure, expressed in percent, computes the relative standard deviation of the fundamental frequency. It is the ratio of the standard deviation of the period-to-period variation to the average fundamental frequency

coloratura: In common usage, refers to the highest of the female voices, with range well above C_6. May use more whistle tone than other female voices. In fact, coloratura actually refers to a style of florid, agile, complex singing that may apply to any voice classification. For example, the bass runs in Händel's *Messiah* require coloratura technique

complex sound: A combination of sinusoidal waveforms superimposed upon each other. May be complex periodic sound (such as musical instruments) or complex aperiodic sound (such as random street noise)

complex tone: Tone composed of a series of simultaneously sounding partials

component frequency: mathematically, a sinusoid; perceptually, a pure tone. Also called a *partial*

compression: A deformation of a body that decreases its entire volume. An increase in density

concert pitch: Also known as *international concert pitch*. The standard of tuning A_4. Reference pitch has changed substantially over the last 200–300 years

condensation: An increase in density

constructive interference: The interference of two or more waves such that enhancement occurs

contact ulcer: A lesion with mucosal disruption most commonly on the vocal processes or medial surfaces of the arytenoids. Caused most commonly by gastroesophageal reflux laryngitis and/or muscular tension dysphonia

contrabasso: (*See* **Bassoprofundo**)

contraction: A decrease in length

contralto: Lowest of the female voices. Able to sing F_3 below middle C, as well as the entire treble staff. Singer's formant at around 2800–2900 Hz

conus elasticus: Fibroelastic membrane extending inferiorly from the vocal folds to the anterior superior border of the cricoid cartilage. Also called the *cricovocal ligament*. Composed primarily of yellow elastic tissue. Anteriorly, it attaches to the minor aspect of the thyroid cartilage. Posteriorly, it attaches to the vocal process of the arytenoids

convergent: With regard to glottal shape, the glottis narrows from bottom to top

corner vowels: (ɑ), (i), and (u); vowels at the corners of a vowel triangle; they necessitate extreme placements of the tongue.

corticosteroid: Potent substances produced by the adrenal cortex (excluding sex hormones of adrenal origin) in response to the release of adrenocorticotropic hormone from the pituitary gland, or related substances. Glucocorticoids influence carbohydrate, fat, and protein metabolism. Mineralocorticoids help regular electrolyte and water balance. Some corticosteroids have both effects to varying degrees. Corticosteroids may also be given as medications for various effects, including anti-inflammatory, antineoplastic, immune suppressive, and ACTH secretion suppressive effects, as well as for hormone replacement therapy

countertenor: Male voice that is primarily falsetto, singing in the contralto range. Most countertenors are also able to sing in the baritone or tenor range. Countertenors are also known as *contraltino* or *contratenor*

cover: (1) In medicine, with regard to the vocal fold, the epithelium and superficial layer of lamina propria. (2) In music, an alteration in technique that changes the resonance characteristics of a sung sound, generally darkening the sound

cranial nerves: Twelve paired nerves responsible for smell, taste, eye movement, vision, facial sensation, chewing muscles, facial motion, salivary gland and lacrimal (tear) gland secretions, hearing, balance, pharyngeal and laryngeal sensation, vocal fold motion, gastric acid secretion, shoulder motion, tongue motion, and related functions

creaky voice: The perceptual result of subharmonic or chaotic patterns in the glottal waveform. According to IR Titze, if a subharmonic is below about 70 Hz, creaky voice may be perceived as pulse register (vocal fry)

crescendo: To get gradually louder

cricoid cartilage: A solid ring of cartilage located below and behind the thyroid cartilage

cricothyroid muscle: An intrinsic laryngeal muscle that is used primarily to control pitch (paired)

crossover frequency: The fundamental frequency for which there is an equal probability for perception of two adjacent registers

cycle: A 360° rotation; same as a *period* in periodic motion.

cysts: Fluid-filled lesions

damp: To diminish, or attenuate an oscillation

decibel: One tenth of a bel. The decibel is a unit of comparison between a reference and another point. It has no absolute value. Although decibels are used to measure sound, they are also used (with different references) to measure heat, light, and other physical phenomena. For sound pressure, the reference is .0002 microbar (millionths of one barometric pressure). In the past, this has also been referred to as 0.0002 dyne/cm^2, and by other terms

decrescendo: (*See* **Diminuendo**)

deformation: The result of stress applied to any surface of a deformable continuous medium. Elongation, compression, contraction, and shear are examples

dehydration: Fluid deprivation. This may alter the amount and viscosity of vocal fold lubrication and the properties of the vocal fold tissues themselves

destructive interference: The interference of two or more waves such that full or partial cancellation occurs

diaphragm: A large, dome-shaped muscle at the bottom of the rib cage that separates the lungs from the viscera. It is the primary muscle of inspiration and may be co-activated during singing

diminuendo: To get gradually softer

displacement: The distance between two points in space, including the direction from one point to the other

displacement flow: Air in the glottis that is squeezed out when the vocal folds come together

diuretic: A drug to decrease circulating body fluid generally by excretion through the kidneys

divergent: With regard to the vocal folds, the glottis widens from bottom to top

dizziness: A feeling of imbalance

dorsal: Toward the back

dramatic soprano: Soprano with powerful, rich voice suitable for dramatic, heavily orchestrated operatic roles. Sings at least to C_6

dramatic tenor: Tenor with heavy voice, often with a suggestion of baritone quality. Suitable for dramatic roles that are heavily orchestrated. Also referred to as *tenora robusto*, and *helden tenor*. The word helden tenor (literally "heroic" tenor) is used typically for tenors who sing Wagnerian operatic roles

dynamics: (1) In physics, a branch of mechanics that deals with the study of forces that accelerate object(s). (2) In music, it refers to changes in the loudness of musical performance

dysmenorrhea: Painful menstrual cramps

dyspepsia: Epigastric discomfort, especially following meals; impairment of the power or function of digestion

dysphonia plica ventricularis: Phonation using false vocal fold vibration rather than true vocal fold vibration. Most commonly associated with severe muscular tension dysphonia Occasionally may be an appropriate compensation for profound true vocal fold dysfunction

edema: Excessive accumulation of fluid in tissues, or "swelling"

elastic recoil pressure: The alveolar pressure derived from extended (strained) tissue in the lungs, ribcage, and the entire thorax after inspiration (measured in Pascals)

electroglottograph (EGG): Recording of electrical conductance of vocal fold contact area versus time; EGG waveforms have been frequently used for the purpose of plotting voice source analysis

electromyograph (EMG): Recording of the electric potentials in a muscle, which are generated by the neural system and which control its degree of contraction; if rectified and smoothed the EMG is closely related to the muscular force exerted by the muscle

elongation: An increase in length

endocrine: Relating to hormones and the organs that produce them

endometriosis: A disorder in which endometrial tissue is present in abnormal locations. Typically causes excessively painful menstrual periods (dysmenorrhea) and infertility

epiglottis: Cartilage that covers over the larynx during swallowing

epithelium: The covering, or most superficial layer, of body surfaces

esophagus: Tube leading from the bottom of the pharynx to the stomach; swallowed food is transported through this structure

expansion: A deformation of a body such that the entire volume increases

extrinsic muscles of the larynx: The strap muscles in the neck, responsible for adjusting laryngeal height and for stabilizing the larynx

Fach (German): Literally, job specialty. It is used to indicate voice classification. For example, lyric soprano and dramatic soprano are different Fachs

false vocal folds: Folds of tissue located slightly higher than and parallel to the vocal folds in the larynx

falsetto: High, light register, applied primarily to men's voices singing in the soprano or alto range. Can also be applied to women's voices

fibroblasts: Cells responsible in part for the formation of scar in response to tissue injury

fibrosis: Generally refers to a component of scar caused by cross-linking of fibers during a reactive or a reparative process

flow: The volume of fluid passing through a given cross-section of a tube or duct per second; also called volume velocity (measured in liters per second)

flow glottogram (FLOGG): Recording of the transglottal airflow versus time, ie, of the sound of the voice source. Generally obtained form inverse filtering, it is the acoustical representation of the voice source

flow resistance: The ratio of pressure to flow

fluid: A substance that is either a liquid or a gas

fluid mechanics: The study of motion or deformation of liquids and gases

flutter: Modulation in the 10–12 Hz range

F_0: Fundamental frequency

F_0–**tremor frequency (Fftr):** This measure is expressed in Hz and shows the frequency of the most intensive low-frequency F_0 modulating component in the specified F_0 tremor analysis range

F_0–**tremor intensity index (FTRI):** The average ratio of the frequency magnitude of the most intensive low-frequency modulating component (F_0 tremor) to the total frequency magnitude of the analyzed sample. The algorithm for tremor analysis determines the strongest periodic frequency modulation of the voice. This measure is expressed in percent

force: A push or pull; the physical quantity imparted to an object to change its momentum

forced oscillation: Oscillation imposed on a system by an external source

formant: Vocal tract resonance; the formant frequencies are tuned by the vocal tract shape and determine much of the vocal quality

formant tuning: A boosting of vocal intensity when F_0 or one if its harmonics coincides exactly with a formant frequency

functional residual capacity (FRC): Lung volume at which the elastic inspiratory forces equal the elastic expiratory forces; in spontaneous quiet breathing exhalation stops at FRC

fractal: A geometric figure in which an identical pattern or motif repeats itself over and over on an ever-diminishing scale. Self-similarity is an essential characteristic

fractal dimension: Fractal dimensions are measures of fractal objects that can be used to determine how alike or different the objects are. Box counting algorithms and mass-radius measurement are two common approaches to determining fractal dimension. The fractal dimension represents the way a set of points fills a given area of space. It may be defined as the slope of the function relating the number of points contained in a given radius (or its magnification) to the radius itself. For example, an object can be assessed under many magnifications. The coast of Britain can be measured, for example, with a meter stick or a millimeter stick, but the latter will yield a larger measure. As magnification is increased (smaller measuring sticks), a point will be reached at which small changes in magnification no longer significantly affect length. That is, a plot of coastline length versus magnification reaches a plateau. That plateau corresponds to fractal dimension. The more irregular the figure (eg coastline), the more complex and the more space it occupies, hence, the higher its fractal dimension. A perfect line has a fractal dimension of 1. A figure that fills a plane has a fractal dimension of 2. Fractal dimension cannot be used alone to determine the presence or absence of chaotic behavior

frequency analysis: Same as spectrum analysis

frequency tremor: A periodic (regular) pitch modulation of the voice (an element of vibrato)

fricative: A speech sound, generally a consonant, produced by a constriction of the vocal tract, particularly by directing the airstream against a hard surface, producing noisy air turbulence. Examples include s produced with the teeth, s produced with the lower lip and upper incisors, and th produced with the tongue tip and upper incisors

frontal (or coronal) plane: An anatomical plane that divides the body into anterior and posterior portions; across the crown of the head

functional voice disorder: An abnormality in voice sound and function in the absence of an anatomic or physiologic organic abnormality

fundamental: Lowest partial of a spectrum, the frequency of which normally corresponds to the pitch perceived.

fundamental frequency (F_0): The lowest frequency in a periodic waveform; also called the first harmonic frequency

gas: A substance that preserves neither shape nor volume when acted upon by forces, but adapts readily to the size and shape of its container

gastric: Pertaining to the stomach

gastric juice: The contents of the stomach, ordinarily including a high concentration of hydrochloric acid.

gastroesophageal reflux (GER): The passage of gastric juice in a retrograde fashion from the stomach into the esophagus. These fluids may reach the level of the larynx or oral cavity, and may be aspirated into the lungs

gastroesophageal reflux disease (GERD): A disorder including symptoms and/or signs caused by reflux of gastric juice into the esophagus and elsewhere. Heartburn is one of the most common symptoms of GERD. (*See* also **Laryngopharyngeal Reflux**)

glissando: A "slide" including all possible pitches between the initial and final pitch sounded. Similar to portamento and slur

globus: Sensation of a lump in the throat

glottal chink: Opening in the glottis during vocal fold adduction, most commonly posteriorly. It may be a normal variant in some cases

glottal resistance: Ratio between transglottal airflow and subglottal pressure; mainly reflects the degree of glottal adduction

glottal stop (or click): A transient sound caused by the sudden onset or offset of phonation

glottis: Space between the vocal folds. (*See* also **Rima Glottitis**)

glottis vocalis: The portion of the glottis in the region of the membranous portions of the vocal folds

glottis respiratoria: The portion of the glottis posteriorly in the region of the cartilaginous portions of the vocal folds

grace days: Refers to a former contractual arrangement, especially in European Opera Houses, in which women were permitted to refrain from singing during the premenstrual and early menstrual portions of their cycles, at their discretion

granuloma: A raised lesion generally covered with mucosa, most commonly in the region of the vocal process or medial surface of the arytenoid. Often caused by reflux and/or muscle tension dysphonia

halitosis: Bad breath

harmonic: A frequency that is an integer multiple of a given fundamental. Harmonics of a fundamental are equally spaced in frequency. Partial in a spectrum in which the frequency of each partial equals n times the fundamental frequency, n being the number of the harmonic

harsh glottal attack: Initiating phonation of a word or sound with a glottal plosive

hemorrhage: Rupture of a blood vessel. This may occur in a vocal fold

high pass filter: Filter which only allows frequencies above a certain cutoff frequency to pass; the cutoff is generally not abrupt but, rather, gentle and is given in terms of a roll-off value, eg, 24 dB/octave

histogram: Graph showing the occurrence of a parameter value; thus, a fundamental frequency histogram shows the occurrence of different fundamental frequency values, eg, in fluent speech or in a song

Hooke's law: Stress in proportion to strain; or, in simpler form, force is proportional to elongation

hormones: Substances produced within the body that affect or control various organs and bodily functions

hyoid bone: A horseshoe-shaped bone known as the "tongue bone." It is attached to muscles of the tongue and related structures, and to the larynx and related structures

hyperfunction: Excessive muscle effort for example, pressed voice, muscular tension dysphonia

hypofunction: Low muscular effort, for example, soft breathy voice

hypernasal: Excessive nasal resonance

hyponasal: Deficient nasal resonance

in vivo: In the living body

impotence: The inability to accomplish penile erection

in vitro: Outside the living body, for example, an excised larynx

incompressibility: Property of a substance that conserves volume in a deformation

inertia: Sluggishness; a property of resisting a change in momentum

inferior: Below

infertility: The inability to accomplish pregnancy

infraglottic: Below the level of the glottis (space between the vocal folds). This region includes the trachea, thorax, and related structures

infrahyoid muscle group: A collection of extrinsic muscles including the sternohyoid, sternothyroid, omohyoid, and thyroid muscles

intensity: A measure of power per unit area. With respect to sound, it generally correlates with perceived loudness

interarytenoid muscle: An intrinsic laryngeal muscle that connects the two arytenoid cartilages

intercostal muscles: Muscles between the ribs

interval: The difference between two pitches, expressed in terms of musical scale

intrinsic laryngeal muscles: muscles within the larynx responsible for abduction, adduction, and longitudinal tension of the vocal folds

intrinsic pitch of vowels: Refers to the fact that in normal speech certain vowels tend to be produced with a significantly higher or lower pitch than other vowels

inverse filtering: Method used for recovering the transglottal airflow during phonation; the technique implies that the voice is fed through a computer filter that compensates for the resonance effects of the supraglottic vocal tract, especially the lowest formants

inverse square law: Sound intensity is inversely proportional to the square of the distance from the sound source

isometric: Constant muscle length during contraction

iteration: In mathematics, the repetitive process of substituting the solution to an equation back into the same equation to obtain the next solution

jitter: Irregularity in the period of time of vocal fold vibrations; cycle-to-cycle variation in fundamental frequency; jitter is often perceived as hoarseness

jitter percent (Jitt): A relative measure of very short term (cycle-to-cycle) variation of the pitch periods expressed in percent. The influence of the average fundamental frequency is significantly reduced. This parameter is very sensitive to pitch variations

juvenile papillomatosis: A disease of children characterized by the clustering of many papillomas (small blisterlike growths) over the vocal folds and elsewhere in the larynx and trachea. Papillomatosis may also occur in adults, in which case the adjective *juvenile* is not used. The disease is caused by human papilloma virus

keratosis: A buildup of keratin (a tough, fibrous protein) on the surface of the vocal folds

kinematics: The study of movement as a consequence of known or assumed forces

kinetic energy: The energy of matter in motion (measured in joules)

lag: A difference in time between one point and another

lamina propria: With reference to the larynx, the tissue layers below the epithelium. In adult humans, the lamina propria consists of superficial, intermediate, and deep layers

laminar: Smooth or layered; in fluid mechanics, indicating parallel flow lines

laryngeal saccule: (*See* **Appendix of the Ventricle of Morgagni**)

laryngeal sinus: (*See* **Ventricle of Morgagni**)

laryngeal ventricle: Cavity formed by the gap between the true and false vocal folds

laryngeal web: An abnormal tissue connection attaching the vocal folds to each other

laryngectomy: Removal of the larynx. It may be total, or it may be a "conservation laryngectomy," in which a portion of the larynx is preserved

laryngitis: Inflammation of laryngeal tissues

laryngitis sicca: Dry voice

laryngocele: An enlargement of the ventricular space between the false folds and the true folds

laryngologist: Physician specializing in disorders of the larynx and voice, in most countries. In some areas of Europe, the laryngologist is primarily responsible for surgery, while diagnosis is performed by phoniatricians

laryngopharyngeal reflux (LPR): A form of gastroesophageal reflux disease in which gastric juice affects the larynx and adjacent structures. Commonly associated with hoarseness, frequent throat clearing, granulomas, and other laryngeal problems, even in the absence of heartburn

laryngomalacia: A condition in which the laryngeal cartilages are excessively soft and may collapse in response to inspiratory pressures, obstructing the airway

laryngospasm: Sudden, forceful, and abnormal closing of the vocal folds

larynx: The body organ in the neck that includes the vocal folds. The "voice box"

larynx height: Vertical position of the larynx; mostly measured in relation to the rest position

larynx tube: Cavity formed by the vocal folds and the arytenoid, epiglottis, and thyroid cartilages and the structures joining them

laser: An acronym for *light amplification by stimulated emission of radiation*. A surgical tool using light energy to vaporize or cauterize tissue

lateral: Toward the side (away from the center).

lateral cricoarytenoid muscle: Intrinsic laryngeal muscle that adducts the vocal folds through forward rocking and rotation of the arytenoids (paired)

lesion: In medicine, a nonspecific term that may be used for nearly any structural abnormality

legato: Smooth, connected

leukoplakia: A white plaque. Typically, this occurs on mucous membranes, including the vocal folds

level: Logarithmic and comparative measure of sound intensity; the unit is normally dB

lied: Song, particularly art song

lift: A transition point along a pitch scale where vocal production becomes easier

linear system: A system in which the relation between input and output varies in a constant, or linear, fashion

liquid: A substance that assumes the shape of its container, but preserves its volume

loft: A suggested term for the highest (loftiest) register; usually referred to as *falsetto voice*

logistic map: A simple quadratic equation that exhibits chaotic behavior under special initial conditions and parameters. It is the simplest chaotic system

Lombard effect: Modification of vocal loudness in response to auditory input. For example, the tendency to speak louder in the presence of background noise

long-term average spectrum (LTAS): Graph showing a long-time average of the sound intensity in various frequency bands; the appearance of an LTAS is strongly dependent on the filters used

longitudinal: Along the length of a structure

longitudinal tension: With reference to the larynx, stretching the vocal folds

loudness: The amount of sound perceived by a listener; a perceptual quantity that can only be assessed with an auditory system. Loudness corresponds to intensity, and to the amplitude of a sound wave

low pass filter: Filter which allows only frequencies below a certain frequency to pass; the cutoff is generally not at all abrupt but gentle and is given in terms of a roll-off value, eg, 24 dB/octave

lung volume: Volume contained in the subglottic air system; after a maximum inhalation following a maximum exhalation the lung volume equals the vital capacity

lyric soprano: Soprano with flexible, light vocal quality, but one who does not sing as high as a coloratura soprano

lyric tenor: Tenor with a light, high flexible voice

malignant tumor: Tumors that have the potential to metastasize, or spread to different sites. They also have the potential to invade, destroy, and replace adjacent tissues. However, benign tumors may have the capacity for substantial local destruction, as well

Mandelbrot's set: A series of two equations containing real and imaginary components that, when iterated and plotted on a two-dimensional graph, depict a very complex and classic fractal pattern

marcato: Each note accented

marking: Using the voice gently (typically during rehearsals) to avoid injury or fatigue

mechanical equilibrium: The state in which all forces acting on a body cancel each other out, leaving a zero net force in all directions

mechanics: The study of objects in motion and the forces that produce the motion

medial (or mesial): Toward the center (midline or midplane).

menopause: Cessation of menstrual cycles and menstruation. Associated with physiologic infertility

menstrual cycle: The normal, cyclical variation of hormones in adult females of child-bearing age, and bodily responses caused by those hormonal variations

menstrual period: The first part of the menstrual cycle, associated with endometrial shedding and vaginal bleeding

messa di voce: Traditional exercise in Italian singing tradition consisting of a long prolonged crescendo and diminuendo on a sustained tone

metastasis: Spread of tumor to locations other than the primary tumor site

mezza voce: Literally means "half voice." In practice, means singing softly, but with proper support

mezzo soprano: Literally means "half soprano." This is a common female range, higher than contralto but lower than soprano

middle (or mixed): A mixture of qualities from various voice registers, cultivated in order to allow consistent quality throughout the frequency range

middle C: C_4 on the piano keyboard, with an international concert pitch frequency of 261.6 Hz

modulation: Periodic variation of a signal property; for example, as vibrato corresponds to a regular variation of fundamental frequency, it can be regarded as a modulation of that signal property

motor: Having to do with motion. For example, motor nerves allow structures to move

motor unit: A group of muscle fibers and the single motor nerve that activates the fibers

mucocele: A benign lesion filled with liquid mucous

mucosa: The covering of the surfaces of the respiratory tract, including the oral cavity and nasal cavities, as well as the pharynx, larynx, and lower airways. Mucosa also exits elsewhere, such as on the lining of the vagina

mucosal tear: With reference to the vocal folds, disruption of the surface of the vocal fold. Usually caused by trauma

mucosal wave: Undulation along the vocal fold surface travelling in the direction of the airflow

modulation: The systematic change of a cyclic parameter, such as amplitude or frequency

momentum: Mass times velocity; a quantity that determines the potential force that an object can impart to another object by collision

muscle fascicles: Groups of muscle fibers enclosed by a sheath of connective tissue

muscle fibers: A long, thin cell; the basic unit of a muscle that is excited by a nerve ending

muscle tension dysphonia: Also called muscular tension dysphonia. A form of voice abuse characterized by excessive muscular effort, and usually by pressed phonation. A form of voice misuse

mutational dysphonia: A voice disorder. Most typically, it is characterized by persistent falsetto voice after puberty in a male. More generally, it is used to refer to voice with characteristics of the opposite gender

myasthenia gravis: A neuromuscular junction disease associated with fatigue

myoelastic-aerodynamic theory of phonation: The currently accepted mechanism of vocal fold physiology. Compressed air exerts pressure on the undersurface of the closed vocal folds. The pressure overcomes adductory forces, causing the vocal folds to open. The elasticity of the displaced tissues (along with the Bernoulli effect) causes the vocal folds to snap shut, resulting in sound.

myofibril: A subdivision of a muscle fiber; composed of a number of myofilaments

myofilament: A microstructure of periodically arranged actin and myosin molecules; a subdivision of a myofibril

myosin: A protein molecule that reacts with actin to form actinomycin, the contractile part of a myofilament

NATS: National Association of Teachers of Singing

nasal tract: Air cavity system of the nose

natural oscillation: Oscillation without imposed driving forces

neoplasm: Abnormal growth. May be benign or malignant

nervous system: Organs of the body including the brain, spinal cord, and nerves. Responsible for motion, sensation, thought, and control of various other bodily functions

neurotologist: Otolaryngologist specializing in disorders of the ear and ear-brain interface (including the skull base), particularly hearing loss, dizziness, tinnitus, and facial nerve dysfunction

nodes: The "valleys" in a standing wave pattern

nodules: Benign growths on the surface of the vocal folds. Usually paired and fairly symmetric. They are generally caused by chronic, forceful vocal fold contact (voice abuse)

noise: Unwanted sound

noise-to-harmonic ratio (NHR): A general evaluation of noise percent in the signal and includes jitter, shimmer, and turbulent noise

nonlinear dynamics: (*See also* **Chaos** and **Chaotic Behavior**) The mathematical study of aperiodic, deterministic systems that are not random and cannot be described accurately by linear equations. The study of nonlinear systems whose state changes with time

nonlinear system: Any system in which the output is disproportionate to the input

objective assessment: Demonstrable, reproducible, usually quantifiable evaluation, generally relying on instrumentation or other assessment techniques that do not involve primarily opinion, as opposed to subjective assessment

octave: Interval between two pitches with frequencies in the ratio of 2:1

olfaction: The sense of smell, mediated by the first cranial nerve

open quotient: The ratio of the time the glottis is open to the length of the entire vibratory cycle

oral contraceptive: Birth control pill

organic disorder: A disorder due to structural malfunction, malformation, or injury, as opposed to psychogenic disorders

organic voice disorder: Disorder for which a specific anatomic or physiologic cause can be identified, as opposed to psychogenic or functional voice disorders

origin: The beginning point of a muscle and related soft tissue or of another structure (eg, blood vessel)

oscillation: Repeated movement, back and forth

oscillator: With regard to the larynx, the vibrator that is responsible for the sound source, specifically the vocal folds

ossicle: Middle ear bone

ossify: To become bony

ostium: Opening

otolaryngologist: Ear, nose, and throat physician

otologist: Otolaryngologist specializing in disorders of the ear

overtone: Partial above the fundamental in a spectrum

ovulation: The middle of the menstrual cycle, associated with release of an ovum (egg), and the period of fertility

papillomas: Small benign epithelial tumors that may appear randomly or in clusters on the vocal folds, larynx, and trachea and elsewhere in the body. Believed to be caused by various types of human papillomavirus (HPV), some of which are associated with malignancy

parietal pleura: The outermost of two membranes surrounding the lungs

partial: Sinusoid that is part of a complex tone; in voiced sounds, the partials are harmonic implying that the frequency of the nth partial equals n times the fundamental frequency

particle: A finite mass with zero dimensions, located at a single point in space

pascal (Pa): International standard unit of pressure; one newton (N) per meter squared (m^2)

Pascal's law: Pressure is transmitted rapidly and uniformly throughout an enclosed fluid at rest

pass band: A band of frequencies minimally affected by a filter

passaggio (Italian): The break between vocal registers

period: (1) In physics, the time interval between repeating events; shortest pattern repeated in a regular undulation; a graph showing the period is called waveform. (2) In medicine, the time during the menstrual cycle associated with bleeding and shedding of the endometrial lining

period doubling: One form of bifurcation in which a system that originally had x period states now has 2x periodic states, with a change having occurred in response to a change in parameter or initial condition.

period time: In physics, duration of a period

periodic behavior: Repeating over and over again over a finite time interval. Periodic behavior is governed by an underlying deterministic process

peristalsis: Successive contractions of musculature, which cause a bolus of food to pass through the alimentary tract

perturbation: Minor change from predicted behavior, slight disturbance

pharynx: The region above the larynx, below the velum, and posterior to the oral cavity

phase: (1) The manner in which molecules are arranged in a material (gas, liquid, or solid); (2) the angular separation between two events on periodic waveforms

phase plane plot: Representation of a dynamic system in state space

phase space: A space created by two or more independent dynamic variables, such as positions and velocities, utilized to plot the trajectory of a moving object

phase spectrum: A display of the relative phases versus frequency of the components of a waveform

phonation: Sound generation by means of vocal fold vibrations

phonetics: The study of speech sounds

phonetogram: Recording of highest and lowest sound pressure level versus fundamental frequency that a voice can produce; phonetograms are often used for describing the status of voice function in patients. Also called *voice range profile*

phoniatrician: A physician specializing in diagnosis and nonsurgical treatment of voice disorders. This specialty does not exist in American medical training, where the phoniatrician's activities are accomplished as a team by the laryngologist (responsible for diagnosis and surgical treatment when needed) and speech-language pathologist (responsible for behavioral voice therapy)

phrenic nerve: The nerve that controls the diaphragm. Responsible for inspiration. Composed primarily of fibers from the third, fourth, and fifth cervical roots

pitch: Perceived tone quality corresponding to its fundamental frequency

pitch matching: Experiment in which subjects are asked to produce the pitch of a reference tone

pitch period perturbation quotient (PPQ): A relative evaluation of short term (cycle-to-cycle) variation of the pitch periods expressed in percent

pleural space: The fluid-filled space between the parietal and visceral pleura

plosive: A consonant produced by creating complete blockage of airflow, followed by the buildup of air pressure, which is then suddenly released, producing a consonant sound

Poincaré section: A graphical technique to reveal a discernable pattern in a phase plane plot that does not have an apparent pattern. There are two kinds of Poincaré sections

polyp: A sessile or pedunculated growth. Usually unilateral and benign, but the term is descriptive and does not imply a histological diagnosis

posterior: Toward the back

posterior cricoarytenoid muscle: An intrinsic laryngeal muscle that is the primary abductor of the vocal folds (paired)

power: The rate of delivery (or expenditure) of energy (measured in watts)

power source: The expiratory system including the muscles of the abdomen, back, thorax, and the lungs. Responsible for producing a vector of force that results in efficient creation and control of subglottal pressure

prechaotic behavior: Predictable behavior prior to the onset of chaotic behavior. One example is period doubling

pressed phonation: Type of phonation characterized by small airflow, high adductory force, and high subglottal pressure. Not an efficient form of voice production. Often associated with voice abuse, and common in patients with lesions such as nodules

pressure: Force per unit area

prima donna: Literally means "first lady." Refers to the soprano soloist, especially the lead singer in an opera

primo passaggio: "The first passage"; the first register change perceived in a voice as pitch is raised from low to high

psychogenic: Caused by psychological factors, rather than physical dysfunction. Psychogenic disorders may result in physical dysfunction or structural injury

pulmonary system: The breathing apparatus including the lungs and related airways

pulse register: The extreme low end of the phonatory range. Also known as *vocal fry* and *Strohbass*, characterized by a pattern of short glottal waves alternating with larger and longer ones, and with a long closed phase

pure tone: Sinusoid. The simplest tone. Produced electronically. In nature, even pure-sounding tones like bird songs are complex

pyrotechnics: Special effects involving combustion and explosion, used to produce dramatic visual displays (similar to fireworks), indoors or outdoors

pyriform sinus: Pouch or cavity constituting the lower end of the pharynx located to the side and partially to the back of the larynx. There are two, paired pyriform sinuses in the normal individual

pyrosis: Heartburn

quadrangular membrane: Elastic membrane extending from the sides of the epiglottic cartilage to the corniculate and arytenoid cartilages. Mucosa covered. Forms the aryepiglottic fold and the wall between the pyriform sinus and larynx

quasiperiodic: A behavior that has at least two frequencies in which the phases are related by an irrational number

radian: The angular measure obtained when the arc along the circumference of the circle is equal to the radius

radian frequency: The number of radians per second covered in circular or sinusoidal motion

random behavior: Action that never repeats itself and is inherently unpredictable

rarefaction: A decrease in density

reflux: (*See* **Gastroesophageal Reflux** and **Laryngopharyngeal Reflux**)

reflux laryngitis: Inflammation of the larynx due to irritation from gastric juice

refractive eye surgery: Surgery to correct visual acuity

registers: Weakly defined term for vocal qualities; often, register refers to a series of adjacent tones on the scale that sound similar and seem to be generated by the same type of vocal fold vibrations and vocal tract adjustments. Examples of register are vocal fry, modal, and falsetto; but numerous other terms are also used

Reinke's space: The superficial layer of the lamina propria

relative average perturbation (RAP): A relative evaluation of short-term (cycle-to-cycle) variation of the pitch periods expressed in percent

relative voice rest: Restricted, cautious voice use

resonance: Peak occurring at certain frequencies (resonance frequencies) in the vibration amplitude in a system that possesses compliance, inertia and reflection; resonance occurs when the input and the reflected energy vibrate in phase; the resonances in the vocal tract are called *formants*

resonator: With regard to the voice, refers primarily to the supraglottic vocal tract, which is responsible for timbre and projection

restoring force: A force that brings an object back to a stable equilibrium position

return map: Similar to phase plane plot, but analyzed data must be digital. This graphic technique represents the relationship between a point and any subsequent point in a time series

rhinorrhea: Nasal discharge; runny nose

rima glottitis: The space between the vocal folds. Also known as the glottis

rostral: Toward the mouth (beak)

roll-off: Characteristics of filters specifying their ability to shut off frequencies outside the pass band; for example, if a low pass filter is set to 2 kHz and has a roll-off of 24 dB/octave, it will alternate a 4 kHz tone by 24 dB and a 8 kHz tone by 48 dB

sagittal: An anatomic plane that divides the body into left and right sides

sarcoplasmic reticulum: Connective tissue enveloping groups of muscle fibers

scalar: A quantity that scales, or adjusts size; a single number

second passaggio: "The second passage"; the second register change perceived in a voice

semicircular canal: Inner ear organ of balance

sensory: Having to do with the feeling or detection of other nonmotor input. For example, nerves responsible for touch, proprioception (position in space), hearing, and so on

shimmer: Cycle-to-cycle variability in amplitude

shimmer percent: Is the same as shimmer dB but expressed in percent instead of dB. Both are relative evaluations of the same type of amplitude perturbation but they use different measures for this result: either percent or dB

simple harmonic motion: Sinusoidal motion; the smoothest back and forth motion possible

simple tone: (*See* **Pure Tone**)

singer's formant: A high spectrum peak occurring between about 2.3 and 3.5 kHz in voiced sounds in Western opera and concert singing. This acoustic phenomenon is associated with "ring" in a voice, and with the voices ability to project over background noise such as a choir or an orchestra. A similar phenomenon may be seen in speaking voices, especially in actors. It is known as the *speaker's formant*

singing teacher: Professional who teaches singing technique (as opposed to Voice Coach).

singing voice specialist: A singing teacher with additional training, and specialization in working with injured voices, in conjunction with a medical voice team

sinus of Morgagni: Often confused with ventricle of Morgagni. Actually, the sinus of Morgagni is not in the larynx. It is formed by the superior fibers of the superior pharyngeal constrictor as they curve below the levator veli palatini and the eustachian tube. The space between the upper border of the muscle and the base of the skull is known as the sinus of Morgagni, and is closed by the pharyngeal aponeurosis

sinusitis: Infection of the paranasal sinus cavities

sinusoid: A graph representing the sine or cosine of a constantly increasing angle; in mechanics, the smoothest and simplest back-and-forth movement, characterized by a single frequency, an amplitude, and a phase; tone arising from sinusoidal sound pressure variations

sinusoidal motion: The projection of circular motion (in a plane) at constant speed onto one axis in the plane

smoothed amplitude perturbation quotient (sAPQ): A relative evaluation of long-term variation of the peak-to-peak amplitude within the analyzed voice sample, expressed in percent

smoothed pitch perturbation quotient (sPPQ): A relative evaluation of long-term variation of the pitch period within the analyzed voice sample expressed in percent

soft glottal attack: Gentle glottal approximation, often obtained using an imaginary /h/

soft phonation index (SPI): A measure of the ratio of lower frequency harmonic energy to higher frequency harmonic energy. If the SPI is low, then the spectral analysis will show well-defined higher formants

solid: A substance that maintains its shape, independent of the shape of its container

soprano acuto: High soprano

soprano assoluto: A soprano who is able to sing all soprano roles and classifications

sound level: Logarithmic, comparative measure of the intensity of a signal; the unit is dB

sound pressure level (SPL): Measure of the intensity of a sound, ordinarily in dB relative to 0.0002 microbar (millionths of 1 atmosphere pressure)

sound propagation: The process of imparting a pressure or density disturbance to adjacent parts of a continuous medium, creating new disturbances at points farther away from the initial disturbance

source-filter theory: A theory that assumes the time-varying glottal airflow to be the primary sound source and the vocal tract to be an acoustic filter of the glottal source

source spectrum: Spectrum of the voice source

spasmodic dysphonia: A focal dystonia involving the larynx. May be of adductor, abductor, or mixed type. Adductor spasmodic dysphonia is characterized by strain-strangled interruptions in phonation. Abductor spasmodic dysphonia is characterized by breathy interruptions

speaker's formant: (*See* **Singer's Formant**)

special sensory nerves: Nerves responsible for hearing, vision, taste, and smell

spectrum: Ensemble of simultaneously sounding sinusoidal partials constituting a complex tone; a display of relative magnitudes or phases of the component frequencies of a waveform

spectrum analysis: Analysis of a signal showing its partials

speech-language pathologist: A trained, medically affiliated professional who may be skilled in remediation of problems of the speaking voice, swallowing, articulation, language development, and other conditions

speed: The rate of change of distance with time; the magnitude of velocity

spinto: Literally means *pushed* or *thrust*. Usually applies to tenors or sopranos with lighter voice than dramatic singers, but with aspects of particular dramatic excitement in their vocal quality. Enrico Caruso was an example

spirometer: A device for measuring airflow

stable equilibrium: A unique state to which a system with a restoring force will return after it has been displaced from rest

staccato: Each note accented and separated

standard deviation: The square root of the variance

standing wave: A wave that appears to be standing still; it occurs when waves with the same frequency (and wavelength) moving in opposite directions interfere with each other

state space: In abstract mathematics, the area in which a behavior occurs

stent: A device used for shape, support, and maintenance of patency during healing after surgery or injury

steroid: Steroids are potent substances produced by the body. They may also be consumed as medications. (*See* **Anabolic Steroids, Corticosteroids**)

stochastic: Random from a statistical, mathematical point of view

stop band: A band of frequencies rejected by a filter; it is the low region in a filter spectrum

strain: Deformation relative to a rest dimension, including direction (eg, elongation per unit length)

strain rate: The rate of change of strain with respect to time

stress: Force per unit area, including the direction in which the force is applied to the area

stroboscopy: A technique that uses interrupted light to simulate slow motion. (*See* also **Strobovideolaryngoscopy**)

strobovideolaryngoscopy: Evaluation of the vocal folds utilizing simulated slow motion for detailed evaluation of vocal fold motion

Strohbass (German): "Straw bass"; another term for *pulse register* or *vocal fry*

subglottal: Below the glottis

subglottal pressure: Air pressure in the airway immediately below the level of the vocal folds. The unit most commonly used is centimeters of water. That distance in centimeters that a given pressure would raise a column of water in a tube

subglottic: The region immediately below the level of the vocal folds

subharmonic: A frequency obtained by *dividing* a fundamental frequency by an integer greater than 0

subjective assessment: Evaluation that depends on perception and opinion, rather than independently reproducible quantifiable measures, as opposed to objective assessment

sulcus vocalis: A longitudinal groove, usually on the medial surface of the vocal fold

superior: above

support: Commonly used to refer to the power source of the voice. It includes the mechanism responsible for creating a vector force that results in efficient subglottic pressure. This includes the muscles of the abdomen and back, as well as the thorax and lungs; primarily the expiratory system

supraglottal: Above the glottis, or level of the vocal folds

supraglottic: (1) Above the level of the vocal folds. This region includes the resonance system of the vocal tract, including the pharynx, oral cavity, nose, and related structures. (2) Posterior commissure. A misnomer. Used to describe the posterior aspect of the larynx (interarytenoid area), which is opposite the anterior commissure. However, there is actually no commissure on the posterior aspect of the larynx

suprahyoid muscle group: One of the two extrinsic muscle groups. Includes the stylohyoid muscle, anterior and posterior bellies of the digastric muscle, geniohyoid, hyoglossus, and mylohyoid muscles

temporal gap transition: The transition from a continuous sound to a series of pulses in the perception of vocal registers

temporomandibular joint: The jaw joint; a synovial joint between the mandibular condyle and skull anterior to the ear canal

tenor: Highest of the male voices, except countertenors. Must be able to sing to C_5. Singer's formant is around 2800 Hz

tenore serio: Dramatic tenor

testosterone: The hormone responsible for development of male sexual characteristics, including laryngeal growth

thoracic: Pertaining to the chest

thorax: The part of the body between the neck and abdomen

thyroarytenoid muscle: An intrinsic laryngeal muscle that comprises the bulk of the vocal fold (paired). The medial belly constitutes the body of the vocal fold

thyroid cartilage: The largest laryngeal cartilage. It is open posteriorly and is made up of two plates (thyroid laminae) joined anteriorly at the midline. In males, there is a prominence superiorly known as the "Adam's Apple"

tidal volume: The amount of air breathed in and out during respiration (measured in liters)

timbre: The quality of a sound. Associated with complexity, or the number, nature, and interaction of overtones

tonsil: A mass of lymphoid tissue located near the junction of the oral cavity and pharynx (paired)

tonsillitis: Inflammation of the tonsil

tracheal stenosis: Narrowing in the trachea. May be congenital or acquired

tracheoesophageal fistula: A connection between the trachea and esophagus. May be congenital or acquired

trajectory: In chaos, the representation of the behavior of a system in state space over a finite, brief period of time. For example, one cycle on a phase plane plot

transglottal flow: Air that is forced through the glottis by a transglottal pressure

transition: With regard to the vocal fold, the intermediate and deep layers of lamina propria (vocal ligament)

transverse: Refers to an anatomic plane that divides the body across. Also used to refer to a direction perpendicular to a given structure or phenomenon such as a muscle fiber or airflow

tremor: A modulation in activity

tremolo: An aesthetically displeasing, excessively wide vibrato. The term is also used in music to refer to an ornament used by composers and performers

trill: In early music (Renaissance) where it referred to an ornament that involved repetition of the same note. That ornament is now referred to as a *trillo*

trillo: Originally a trill, but in recent pedagogy a rapid repetition of the same note, which usually includes repeated voice onset and offset

tumor: A mass or growth

turbulence: Irregular movement of air, fluid, or other substance, which causes a hissing sound. White water is a typical example of turbulence

tympanic membrane: Ear drum

unilateral vocal fold paralysis: Immobility of one vocal fold, due to neurological dysfunction

unstable equilibrium: The state in which a disturbance of a mechanical system will cause a drift away from a rest position

variability: The amount of change, or ability to change

variance: The mean squared difference from the average value in a data set

vector: A quantity made up of two or more independent items of information, always grouped together

velar: Relating to the velum or palate

velocity: The rate of change of displacement with respect to time (measured in meters per second, with the appropriate direction)

velopharyngeal insufficiency: Escape of air, liquid or food from the oropharynx into the nasopharynx or nose at times when the nasopharynx should be closed by approximation of the soft palate and pharyngeal tissues

velum: A general term that means *veil* or *covering*. With regard to the vocal tract, refers to the region of the soft palate and adjacent nasopharynx that closes together under normal circumstances during swallowing and phonation of certain sounds

ventral: Toward the belly

ventricle of Morgagni: Also known as *laryngeal sinus*, and *ventriculus laryngis*. The ventricle is a fusiform pouch bounded by the margin of the vocal folds, the edge of the free crescentic margin of the false vocal fold (ventricular fold), and the mucous membrane between them that forms the pouch. Anteriorly, a narrowing opening leads from the ventricle to the appendix of the ventricle of Morgagni

ventricular folds: The "false vocal folds," situated above the true vocal folds

ventricular ligament: A narrow band of fibrous tissue that extends from the angle of the thyroid cartilage below the epiglottis to the arytenoid cartilage just above the vocal process. It is contained within the false vocal fold. The caudal border of the ventricular ligament forms a free crescentic margin, which constitutes the upper border of the ventricle of Morgagni

ventricular phonation: (*See* **Dysphonia Plica Ventricularis**)

vertical phase difference: With reference to the vocal folds, refers to the asynchrony between the lower and upper surfaces of the vibratory margin of the vocal fold during phonation

vertigo: Sensation of rotary motion. A form of dizziness

vibrato: In classical singing, vibrato is a periodic modulation of the frequency of phonation. Its regularity increases with training. The rate of vibrato (number of modulations per second) is usually in the range of 5–6 per second. Vibrato rates over 7–8 per second are aesthetically displeasing to most people, and sound "nervous." The extent of vibrato (amount of variation above and below the center frequency) is usually one or two semitones. Vibrato extending less than ±0.5 semitone are rarely seen in singers although they are encountered in wind instrument playing. Vibrato rates greater than two semitones are usually aesthetically unacceptable, and are typical of elderly singers in poor artistic vocal condition, in whom the excessively wide vibrato extent is often combined with excessively slow rate

viscera: The internal organs of the body, particularly the contents of the abdomen

visceral pleura: The innermost of two membranes surrounding the lungs

viscoelastic material: A material that exhibits characteristics of both elastic solids and viscous liquids. The vocal fold is an example

viscosity: Property of a liquid associated with its resistance to deformation. Associated with the "thickness" of a liquid

vital capacity: The maximum volume of air that can be exchanged by the lungs with the outside; it includes the expiratory reserve volume, tidal volume, and inspiratory reserve volume (measured in liters)

vocal cord: Old term for vocal fold

vocal fold (or cord) stripping: A surgical technique, no longer considered acceptable practice under most circumstances, in which the vocal fold is grasped with a forceps, and the surface layers are ripped off

vocal fold stiffness: The ratio of the effective restoring force (in the medial-lateral direction) to the displacement (in the same direction)

vocal folds: A paired system of tissue layers in the larynx that can oscillate to produce sound

vocal fry: A register with perceived temporal gaps; also known as *pulse register* and Strohbass. (*See* **Pulse Register**)

vocal ligament: Intermediate and deep layers of the lamina propria. Also forms the superior end of the conus elasticus

vocal tract: Resonator system constituted by the larynx, the pharynx and the mouth cavity

vocalis muscle: The medial belly of the thyroarytenoid muscle

voce coperta: "Covered registration"

voce mista: Mixed voice (also voix mixed)

voce di petto: Chest voice

voce sgangherata: "White" voice. Literally means immoderate or unattractive. Lacks strength in the lower partials

voce di testa: Head voice

voce piena: Full voice

voice abuse: Use of the voice in specific activities that are deleterious to vocal health, such as screaming

voice box: (*See* **Larynx**)

voice coach: (1) In singing, a professional who works with singers, teaching repertoire, language pronunciation, and other artistic components of performance (as opposed to a singing teacher, who teaches technique); (2) The term voice coach is also used by acting-voice teachers who specialize in vocal, bodily, and interpretive techniques to enhance dramatic performance

voice misuse: Habitual phonation using phonatory techniques that are not optimal and then result in vocal strain. For example, speaking with inadequate support, excessive neck muscle tension, and suboptimal resonance. Muscular Tension Dysphonia is a form of voice misuse

voice range profile: (*See* **Phonetogram**)

voice rest: (*See* **Absolute Voice Rest, Relative Voice Rest**)

voice source: Sound generated by the pulsating transglottal airflow; the sound is generated when the vocal fold vibrations chop the airstream into a pulsating airflow

voice turbulence index (VTI): A measure of the relative energy level of high frequency noise

volume: "Amount of sound," best measured in terms of acoustic power or intensity

vortex theory: Holds that eddys, or areas of organized turbulence, are produced as air flows through the larynx and vocal tract

waveform: A plot of any variable (eg, pressure, flow, or displacement) changing as time progresses along the horizontal axis; also known as a time-series

wavefront: The initial disturbance in a propagating wave

wavelength: The linear distance between any point on one vibratory cycle and a corresponding point of the next vibratory cycle

whisper: Sound created by turbulent glottal airflow in the absence of vocal fold vibration

whistle register: The highest of all registers (in pitch). It is observed only in females, extending the pitch range beyond F_6

wobble: A slow, irregular vibrato. Aesthetically unsatisfactory. Sometimes referred to as a *tremolo*. May have a rate of less than 4 oscillations per second, and an extent of greater than ±2 semitones

xerostomia: Dry mouth

Young's modulus: The ratio between magnitudes of stress and strain

Appendix I
International Phonetic Alphabet

	English	Italian	Latin	French	German
Vowels					
[i]	meet, key	chi	Filio	qui, cygne	liebe, ihn, wir
[e]	—	—	—	parlé, nez, parler, parlerai	Seele, geben, Weh
[I]	mitt, hit	—	—	—	mit, sitzen
[e²]	chaotic	vero	—	—	Tränen
[ɛ]	bed	bello	requiem	belle, avait, mai, tête seine	Bett, hätte
[ɛ̃]	—	—	—	sein, pain, fin, faim, thym	—
[a]	—	—	—	voilà la salade	—
[ɑ]	father	alma	mala	âme	Vater, Mahler
[ɑ̃]	—	—	—	enfant, champ, Jean, paon	—
[ɔ]	jaw	morte	Domine	sortir, aura	Dorn
[o²]	rowing	nome, dolce	—	—	—
[U]	foot	—	—	—	Mutter
[o]	—	—	—	rose, ôter, pot, beau, faut, écho	Rose, tot, froh
[õ]	—	—	—	fond, ombre	—
[u]	moon	luna	unum	fou	Uhr, Buch, tun
[y]	—	—	—	tu, flûte, eût	früh, Tür
[y]	—	—	—	—	Glück
[ø]	—	—	—	peu, berceuse	schön
[œ]	—	—	—	coeur, fleur	können
[œ̃]	—	—	—	parfum, défunt	—
[ə]	Rita, oven	—	—	je, faisant, parlent (forward–use lips)	lieben
[ɛ̃]	—	—	—	—	Liebe
[æ]	cat	—	—	—	—
[ɜ]	first	—	—	—	—
[ʌ]	cup	—	—	—	—
Consonants: Fricatives					
[f]	father, physic	fuori	fecit	fou, phare	Vater, Phantasie
[v]	visit	vecchio, Wanda	vestrum	vent, wagon	Weg
[ʃ]	shine (bright)	lascia (Bright)	sciote	charme (dark)	schön, Stadt Spass (dark)
[ʒ]	Asia (bright)	—	—	je, givre (dark)	—
[s]	simple, receive	seno, questo	salutare	soixante, cent, leçon, jasmin	essen, Fenster, Haus

	English	Italian	Latin	French	German
[Z]	roses, zoo	rosa, sdegno	—	rose, azure	Seele, unser, Rose
[T]	three	—	—	—	—
[D]	this	vado	—	—	—
[?]	human	—	—	—	ich, recht
[x]	—	—	—	—	Nacht, doch, such
[h]	house, who	—	—	—	Haus, lebhaft

Consonants: Nasals

	English	Italian	Latin	French	German
[m]	mother	mamma	mortuus	maman	Mutter, nahm
[n]	nose	naso	nescio	nez	nein, Nase (dental)
[>]	onion	ognuno	agnus	oignon, agneau	—
[N]	ring, thank	sangue, anche	—	—	Ring, Dank

Consonants: Lateral and trilled

	English	Italian	Latin	French	German
[l]	liquid	largo, alto	alleluia	large, fatal	links, alte, also
[:]	milk	—	—	—	—
[r]	three	rosa, orrore	rex	roucoule	Retter, irre

Consonants: Affricates

	English	Italian	Latin	French	German
[ʃ]	cheer, pitch	cielo, cenere	cibo, coelo caeca	—	plätschert
[ʤ]	joy, George	gioia, gemo	pange, regina	—	—
[ts]	cats	zio, senza	gratias, justitia	—	Zimmer, Spitz
[ʣ]	leads	azzuro, bonzo	azymis	—	—

Consonants: Plosives

	English	Italian	Latin	French	German
[p]	pepper (explosive)	papa (dry)	peccata (dry)	papa, absent (dry)	Paar, lieb (explosive)
[b]	bow	bada	beata	bas	Bett
[t]	tent (sharp, alveolar)	tutto (dry, dental)	terra, catholicam (dry, dental)	tantot (dry, dental Palatalized before [l][y] [j][ ]) tire, tu tiens, tuer	Tante, Grund, Thau (sharp, alveolar)
[d]	dead (alveolar)	doppio (dental)	Domine (dental)	dindon (dental; palatalized before [i] [y] [j] [ ]) dire, dure, Dieu, réduit	decken (alveolar)
[k]	cat, chorus, quick (explosive)	come, ecco, chioma, che, questo (dry)	credo, bracchio (dry) mihi	comment, qui, choeur (dry, except before [i] [y] [j] [ ])	Kunst, Qual, chor, Tag (explosive)
[g]	give	gamba, grande, gonfia	gaudebit	gauche, grande	geben, General

Glides, diphthongs, and triphthongs

	English	Italian	Latin	French	German
[j]	yes (no buzz)	ieri (no buzz)	ejus (no buzz)	bien, moyen	Jahr
[w]	west	guarda	qui, linguis	oui	—
[ ]	—	—	—	nuit	—
[ʎ]	lute	gl'ochhi	—	—	—
[ʌːi]	mine, high	mai	Laicus	—	—
[ʌːI]	mine, high	—	—	—	mein, Hain
[aj]	—	—	—	corail	—

	English	Italian	Latin	French	German
[ɛːi]	say, mate	sei	mei	—	—
[ɛːl]	say, mate	—	—	—	—
[ɛĵ]	—	—	—	soleil	—
[œj]	—	—	—	denuil	—
[uj]	—	—	—	fenouil	—
[oːu]	grow	—	—	—	—
[ɔːi]	boy	poi	—	—	—
[ɔːl]	boy	—	—	—	—
[ɔːy]	—	—	—	—	treu, träumen
[ʌːu]	cow	aura	laudamus	—	—
[ʌːU]	cow	—	—	—	Tau
[ʌːo]	—	—	—	—	Tau
[ɛː ◁]	air	—	—	—	—
[ɪː◁]	ear	—	—	—	—
[ɔː◁]	ore	—	—	—	—
[Uː◁]	sure	—	—	—	—
[ʌːi◁]	fire	—	—	—	—
[ʌːu◁]	our	—	—	—	—
[ɔːy◁]	—	—	—	—	Feuer

Modified from Moriarty J. *Diction*. Boston, Ma: EC Schirmer; 1975:257–263, with permission.

Appendix IIa

PATIENT HISTORY: SINGERS
Robert Thayer Sataloff, M.D., D.M.A.
1721 Pine Street
Philadelphia, PA 19103

NAME _____ AGE _____ SEX _____ RACE _____
HEIGHT _____ WEIGHT _____ DATE _____
VOICE CATEGORY: _____ soprano _____ mezzo-soprano _____ alto
_____ tenor _____ baritone _____ bass

(If you are not currently having a voice problem, please skip to Question #3.)

PLEASE CHECK OR CIRCLE CORRECT ANSWERS

1. How long have you had your present voice problem?

    Who noticed it?

    [self, family, voice teacher, critics, everyone, other _____]

    Do you know what caused it?   Yes _____   No _____

    If yes, what?

    Did it come on slowly or suddenly?   Slowly _____   Suddenly _____
    Is it getting: Worse: _____ , Better _____ , Same _____

2. Which symptoms do you have? (Please check all that apply.)
    _____ Hoarseness (coarse or scratchy sound)
    _____ Fatigue (voice tires or changes quality after singing for a short period of time)
    _____ Volume disturbance (trouble singing)   softly _____   loudly _____
    _____ Loss of range (high _____   low _____)
    _____ Change in classification (example: voice lowered from soprano to mezzo)
    _____ Prolonged warm-up time (over ½ hr to warm up voice)
    _____ Breathiness
    _____ Tickling or choking sensation while singing
    _____ Pain in throat while singing
    _____ Other: (Please specify)_____
    _____
    _____

3. Do you have an important performance soon?   Yes _____   No _____
    Date(s): _____

4. What is the current status of your singing career?

   Professional _____   Amateur _____

5. What are your long-term career goals in singing?
   [   ] Premiere operatic career
   [   ] Premiere pop music career
   [   ] Active avocation
   [   ] Classical
   [   ] Pop
   [   ] Other (_____)
   [   ] Amateur performance (choral or solo)
   [   ] Amateur singing for own pleasure

6. Have you had voice training?   Yes _____   No _____
   At what age did you begin?

7. Have there been periods of months or years without lessons in that time?   Yes _____   No _____

8. How long have you studied with your present teacher?

   Teacher's name:
   Teacher's address:

   Teacher's telephone number:

9. Please list previous teachers and years during which you studied with them.

10. Have you ever had training for your speaking voice?   Yes _____   No _____
    Acting voice lessons?   Yes _____   No _____
    How many years?
    Speech therapy?   Yes _____   No _____
    How many months?

11. Do you have a job in addition to singing?   Yes _____   No _____

    If yes, does it involve extensive voice use?   Yes _____   No _____

    If yes, what is it? [actor, announcer (television/radio/sports arena), athletic instructor, attorney, clergy, politician, physician, salesperson, stockbroker, teacher, telephone operator or receptionist, waiter, waitress, secretary, other _____]

12. In your performance work, in addition to singing, are you frequently
    required to speak?   Yes _____   No _____
    dance?   Yes _____   No _____

13. How many years did you sing actively before beginning voice lessons initially?

14. What types of music do you sing? (Check all that apply.)
    _____ Classical   _____ Show
    _____ Nightclub   _____ Rock
    _____ Other: (Please specify.) _____

    _____

15. Do you regularly sing in a sitting position (such as from behind a piano or drum set)?
    Yes _____ No _____

16. Do you sing outdoors or in large halls, or with orchestras? (Circle which one.)   Yes _____   No _____

17. If you perform with electrical instruments or outdoors, do you use monitor speakers? (Circle which one).
    Yes _____ No _____

    If yes, can you hear them?   Yes _____   No _____

18. Do you play a musical instrument(s)?   Yes _____   No _____
    If yes, please check all that apply:
    _____ Keyboard (piano, organ, harpsichord, other _____)
    _____ Violin, viola
    _____ Cello
    _____ Bass
    _____ Plucked strings (guitar, harp, other _____)
    _____ Brass
    _____ Wind with single reed
    _____ Wind with double reed
    _____ Flute, piccolo
    _____ Percussion
    _____ Bagpipe
    _____ Accordion
    _____ Other: (Please specify)._____

19. How often do you practice?
    Scales: [daily, few times weekly, once a week, rarely, never]

    If you practice scales, do you do them all at once, or do you divide them up over the course of a day?
    [all at once, two or three sittings]

    On days when you do scales, how long do you practice them?
    [15 ,30,45,60,75 ,90,105,120, more] minutes

    Songs: [daily, few times weekly, once a week, rarely, never]

    How many hours per day?
    [½,1,1½,2,2½,3,more]

Do you warm up your voice before you sing?   Yes _____   No _____

Do you warm down your voice when you finish singing?   Yes _____   No _____

20. How much are you singing at present (total including practice time) (average hours per day)?

Rehearsal: _____

Performance: _____

21. Please check all that apply to you:

_____ Voice worse in the morning

_____ Voice worse later in the day, after it has been used

_____ Sing performances or rehearsals in the morning

_____ Speak extensively (e.g. , teacher, clergy, attorney, telephone work)

_____ Cheerleader

_____ Speak extensively backstage or at postperformance parties

_____ Choral conductor

_____ Frequently clear your throat

_____ Frequent sore throat

_____ Jaw joint problems

_____ Bitter or acid taste, or bad breath first thing in the morning

_____ Frequent "heartburn" or hiatal hernia

_____ Frequent yelling or loud talking

_____ Frequent whispering

_____ Chronic fatigue (insomnia)

_____ Work around extreme dryness

_____ Frequent exercise (weight lifting, aerobics)

_____ Frequently thirsty, dehydrated

_____ Hoarseness first thing in the morning

_____ Chest cough

_____ Eat late at night

_____ Ever used antacids

_____ Under particular stress at present (personal or professional)

_____ Frequent bad breath

_____ Live, work, or perform around smoke or fumes

_____ Traveled recently: When: _____

                                            Where: _____

Eat any of the following before singing?

_____ Chocolate   _____ Coffee

_____ Alcohol   _____ Milk or ice cream

_____ Nuts   _____ Spiced foods

Other: (Please specify.)

_____ Any specific vocal technical difficulties? [trouble singing soft, trouble singing loud, poor pitch control, support problems, problems at register transitions, other] Describe other:

_____ Any problems with your singing voice recently prior to the onset of the problem that brought you here? [hoarseness, breathiness, fatigue, loss of range, voice breaks, pain singing, other] Describe other:

_____ Any voice problems in the past that required a visit to a physician? If yes, please describe problem(s) and treatment(s): [laryngitis, nodules, polyps, hemorrhage, cancer, other] Describe other:

22. Your family doctor's name, address, and telephone number

23. Your laryngologist's name, address, and telephone number:

24. Recent cold?   Yes _____   No _____

25. Current cold?   Yes _____   No _____

26. Have you been exposed to any of the following chemicals frequently (or recently) at home or at work? (Check all that apply.)

_____ Carbon monoxide	_____ Arsenic
_____ Mercury	_____ Aniline dyes
_____ Insecticides	_____ Industrial solvents (benzene, etc.)
_____ Lead	_____ Stage smoke

27. Have you been evaluated by an allergist?   Yes _____   No _____

    If yes, what allergies do you have:
    [none, dust, mold, trees, cats, dogs, foods, other]
    (Medication allergies are covered elsewhere in this history form.)
    If yes, give name and address of allergist:

28. How many packs of cigarettes do you smoke per day?

    Smoking history
    _____ Never
    _____ Quit. When? _____
    _____ Smoked about _____ packs per day for _____ years.
    _____ Smoke _____ packs per day. Have smoked for _____ years.

29. Do you work or live in a smoky environment?   Yes _____   No _____

30. How much alcohol do you drink? [none, rarely, a few times per week, daily]
    If daily, or few times per week, on the average, how much do you consume? [1,2,3,4,5,6,7,8,9,10, more] glasses per [day, week] of [beer, wine, liquor].

    Did you formerly drink more heavily?   Yes _____   No _____

31. How many cups of coffee, tea, cola, or other caffeine-containing drinks do you drink per day?

32. List other recreational drugs you use [marijuana, cocaine, amphetamines, barbiturates, heroin, other]:

33. Have you noticed any of the following? (Check all that apply)
    _____ Hypersensitivity to heat or cold
    _____ Excessive sweating
    _____ Change in weight: gained/lost _____ lb in _____
                        weeks/ _____ months
    _____ Change in skin or hair
    _____ Palpitation (fluttering) of the heart
    _____ Emotional lability (swings of mood)
    _____ Double vision
    _____ Numbness of the face or extremities
    _____ Tingling around the mouth or face
    _____ Blurred vision or blindness
    _____ Weakness or paralysis of the face
    _____ Clumsiness in arms or legs
    _____ Confusion or loss of consciousness
    _____ Difficulty with speech
    _____ Difficulty with swallowing
    _____ Seizure (epileptic fit)
    _____ Pain in the neck or shoulder
    _____ Shaking or tremors
    _____ Memory change
    _____ Personality change

    For females:

    Are you pregnant?   Yes _____   No _____
    Are your menstrual periods regular?   Yes _____   No _____
    Have you undergone hysterectomy?   Yes _____   No _____
    Were your ovaries removed?   Yes _____   No _____
    At what age did you reach puberty?   Yes _____   No _____
    Have you gone through menopause?   Yes _____   No _____
    If yes, when?

34. Have you ever consulted a psychologist or psychiatrist?   Yes _____   No _____

    Are you currently under treatment?   Yes _____   No _____

35. Have you injured your head or neck (whiplash, etc.)?   Yes _____   No _____

36. Describe any serious accidents related to this visit.
    None _____

37. Are you involved in legal action involving problems with your voice?   Yes _____   No _____

38. List names of spouse and children:

39. Brief summary of ear, nose, and throat (ENT) problems, some of which may not be related to your present complaint.

PLEASE CHECK ALL THAT APPLY

_____ Hearing loss	_____ Ear pain
_____ Ear noises	_____ Facial pain
_____ Dizziness	_____ Stiff neck
_____ Facial paralysis	_____ Lump in neck
_____ Nasal obstruction	_____ Lump in face or head
_____ Nasal deformity	_____ Trouble swallowing
_____ Mouth sores	_____ Excess eye skin
_____ Jaw joint problem	_____ Excess facial skin
_____ Eye problem	
_____ Other: (Please specify.)	

40. Do you have or have you ever had:

_____ Diabetes	_____ Seizures
_____ Hypoglycemia	_____ Psychiatric therapy
_____ Thyroid problems	_____ Frequent bad headaches
_____ Syphilis	_____ Ulcers
_____ Gonorrhea	_____ Kidney disease
_____ Herpes	_____ Urinary problems
_____ Cold sores (fever blisters)	_____ Arthritis or skeletal problems
_____ High blood pressure	_____ Cleft palate
_____ Severe low blood pressure	_____ Asthma
_____ Intravenous antibiotics or diuretics	_____ Lung or breathing problems
_____ Heart attack	_____ Unexplained weight loss
_____ Angina irregular heartbeat	_____ Cancer of (_____)
_____ Other heart problems	_____ Other tumor (_____)
_____ Rheumatic fever	_____ Blood transfusions
_____ Tuberculosis	_____ Hepatitis
_____ Glaucoma	_____ AIDS
_____ Multiple sclerosis	_____ Meningitis
_____ Other illnesses: (Please specify.)	

41. Do any blood relatives have:

_____ Diabetes	_____ Cancer
_____ Hypoglycemia	_____ Heart disease
_____ Other major medical problems such as those above. Please specify:	

42. Describe serious accidents unless directly related to your doctor's visit here.

_____ None
_____ Occurred with head injury, loss of consciousness, or whiplash
_____ Occurred without head injury, loss of consciousness, or whiplash
         Describe:

43. List all current medications and doses (include birth control pills and vitamins).

44. Medication allergies

_____ None   _____ Novocaine
_____ Penicillin   _____ Iodine
_____ Sulfa   _____ Codeine
_____ Tetracycline   _____ Adhesive tape
_____ Erythromycin   _____ Aspirin
_____ Keflex/Ceclor/Ceftin   _____ X-ray dyes
_____ Other: (Please specify.)

45. List operations

_____ Tonsillectomy (age _____)
_____ Appendectomy (age _____)
_____ Adenoidectomy (age _____)
_____ Heart surgery (age _____)
_____ Other: (Please specify.)

46. List toxic drugs or chemicals to which you have been exposed:

_____ Lead
_____ Streptomycin, neomycin, kanamycin
_____ Mercury
_____ Other: (Please specify.)

47. Have you had x-ray *treatments* to your head or neck (including treatments for acne or ear problems as a child, treatments for cancer, etc.)?

Yes _____   No _____

48. Describe serious health problems of your spouse or children.

_____ None

Appendix IIb

PATIENT HISTORY: PROFESSIONAL VOICE USERS
Robert Thayer Sataloff, M.D., D.M.A.
1721 Pine Street
Philadelphia, PA 19103

NAME _____ AGE _____ SEX _____ RACE _____

HEIGHT _____ WEIGHT _____ DATE _____

1. How long have you had your present voice problem? _____

   Who noticed it?

   Do you know what caused it? Yes _____   No _____
   If so, what?

   Did it come on slowly or suddenly? Slowly _____   Suddenly _____

   Is it getting: Worse _____, Better _____, Same _____

2. Which symptoms do you have? (Please check all that apply.)
   _____ Hoarseness (coarse or scratchy sound)
   _____ Fatigue (voice tires or changes quality after speaking for a short period of time)
   _____ Volume disturbance (trouble speaking)   softly _____   loudly _____
   _____ Loss of range (high _____, low _____)
   _____ Prolonged warm-up time (over ½ hr to warm up voice)
   _____ Breathiness
   _____ Tickling or choking sensation while speaking
   _____ Pain in throat while speaking
   _____ Other: (Please specify.)_____
   _____
   _____

3. Have you ever had training for your speaking voice?
        Yes _____   No _____

4. Have there been periods of months or years without lessons in that time? Yes _____   No _____

391

5. How long have you studied with your present teacher?
   Teacher's name: _____
   Teacher's address: _____
   Teacher's telephone number:_____

6. Please list previous teachers and years during which you studied with them:

7. Have you ever had training for your singing voice? Yes _____ No _____
   If so, list teachers and years of study:

8. In what capacity do you use your voice professionally?
   _____ Actor
   _____ Announcer (television/radio/sports arena)
   _____ Attorney
   _____ Clergy
   _____ Politician
   _____ Salesperson
   _____ Teacher
   _____ Telephone operator or receptionist
   _____ Other: (Please specify.)

9. Do you have an important performance soon?   Yes _____ No _____
   Date(s): _____

10. Do you do regular voice exercises?   Yes _____ No _____
    If yes, describe:

11. Do you play a musical instrument?   Yes _____ No _____
    If yes, please check all that apply:
    _____ Keyboard (piano, organ, harpischord, other _____)
    _____ Violin, Viola
    _____ Cello
    _____ Bass
    _____ Plucked strings (guitar, harp, other _____)
    _____ Brass
    _____ Wind with single reed
    _____ Wind with double reed
    _____ Flute, piccolo
    _____ Percussion
    _____ Bagpipe
    _____ Accordion
    _____ Other: (Please specify.) _____

12. Do you warm up your voice before practice or performance?   Yes _____   No _____

    Do you warm down after using it?   Yes _____   No _____

13. How much are you speaking at present (average hours per day)?
    _____ Rehearsal   _____ Performance   _____ Other

14. Please check all that apply to you:
    _____ Voice worse in the morning
    _____ Voice worse later in the day, after it has been used
    _____ Sing performances or rehearsals in the morning
    _____ Speak extensively (e.g. , teacher, clergy, attorney, telephone work)
    _____ Cheerleader
    _____ Speak extensively backstage or at postperformance parties
    _____ Choral conductor
    _____ Frequently clear your throat
    _____ Frequent sore throat
    _____ Jaw joint problems
    _____ Bitter or acid taste; bad breath or hoarseness first thing in the morning
    _____ Frequent "heartburn" or hiatal hernia
    _____ Frequent yelling or loud talking
    _____ Frequent whispering
    _____ Chronic fatigue (insomnia)
    _____ Work around extreme dryness
    _____ Frequent exercise (weight lifting, aerobics)
    _____ Frequently thirsty, dehydrated
    _____ Hoarseness first thing in the morning
    _____ Chest cough
    _____ Eat late at night
    _____ Ever used antacids
    _____ Under particular stress at present (personal or professional)
    _____ Frequent bad breath
    _____ Live, work, or perform around smoke or fumes
    _____ Traveled recently: When:_____
                          Where: _____

15. Your family doctor's name, address, and telephone number:

16. Your laryngologist's name, address, and telephone number:

17. Recent cold?   Yes _____   No _____

18. Current cold?   Yes _____   No _____

19. Have you been evaluated by an allergist?   Yes _____ No _____
    If yes, what allergies do you have:
    [none, dust, mold, trees, cats, dogs, foods, other, _____]
    (Medication allergies are covered elsewhere in this history form.)
    If yes, give name and address of allergist:

20. How many packs of cigarettes do you smoke per day?
    Smoking history
    _____ Never
    _____ Quit. When? _____
    _____ Smoked about ____ packs per day for ____ years.
    _____ Smoke ____ packs per day. Have smoked for ____ years.

21. Do you work or live in a smoky environment?   Yes _____ No _____

22. How much alcohol do you drink? [none, rarely, a few times per week, daily] If daily, or few times per week,
    on the average, how much do you consume? [1, 2, 3, 4, 5, 6, 7, 8, 9, 10, more] glasses per [day, week] of [beer,
    wine, liquor]

    Did you formerly drink more heavily?   Yes _____ No _____

23. How many cups of coffee, tea, cola, or other caffeine-containing drinks do you drink per day?

24. List other recreational drugs you use [marijuana, cocaine, amphetamines, barbiturates, heroin, other _____
    _____]

25. Have you noticed any of the following? (Check all that apply)
    _____ Hypersensitivity to heat or cold
    _____ Excessive sweating
    _____ Change in weight: gained/lost _____ lb in _____
                         weeks/ _____ months
    _____ Change in your voice
    _____ Change in skin or hair
    _____ Palpitation (fluttering) of the heart
    _____ Emotional lability (swings of mood)
    _____ Double vision
    _____ Numbness of the face or extremities
    _____ Tingling around the mouth or face
    _____ Blurred vision or blindness
    _____ Weakness or paralysis of the face
    _____ Clumsiness in arms or legs
    _____ Confusion or loss of consciousness
    _____ Difficulty with speech
    _____ Difficulty with swallowing

_____ Seizure (epileptic fit)
_____ Pain in the neck or shoulder
_____ Shaking or tremors
_____ Memory change
_____ Personality change

For females:

Are you pregnant?	Yes _____	No _____
Are your menstrual periods regular?	Yes _____	No _____
Have you undergone hysterectomy?	Yes _____	No _____
Were your ovaries removed?	Yes _____	No _____
At what age did you reach puberty?	_____	
Have you gone through menopause?	Yes _____	No _____

26. Have you ever consulted a psychologist or psychiatrist?

    Yes _____   No _____

    Are you currently under treatment?   Yes _____   No _____

27. Have you injured your head or neck (whiplash, etc.)?

    Yes _____   No _____

28. Describe any serious accidents related to this visit.

    None _____

29. Are you involved in legal action involving problems with your voice?

    Yes _____   No _____

30. List names of spouse and children:

31. Brief summary of ear, nose, and throat (ENT) problems, some of which may not be related to your present complaint.

_____ Hearing loss	_____ Ear pain
_____ Ear noises	_____ Facial pain
_____ Dizziness	_____ Stiff neck
_____ Facial paralysis	_____ Lump in neck
_____ Nasal obstruction	_____ Lump in face or head
_____ Nasal deformity	_____ Trouble swallowing
_____ Nose bleeds	_____ Trouble breathing
_____ Mouth sores	_____ Excess eye skin
_____ Excess facial skin	_____ Eye problem
_____ Jaw joint problem	
_____ Other (Please specify.)	

32. Do you have or have you ever had:

_____ Diabetes
_____ Hypoglycemia
_____ Thyroid problems
_____ Syphilis
_____ Gonorrhea
_____ Herpes
_____ Cold sores (fever blisters)
_____ High blood pressure
_____ Severe low blood pressure
_____ Intravenous antibiotics or diuretics
_____ Heart attack
_____ Angina
_____ Irregular heartbeat
_____ Other heart problems
_____ Rheumatic fever
_____ Tuberculosis
_____ Glaucoma
_____ Multiple sclerosis
_____ Other illnesses: (Please specify.)

_____ Seizures
_____ Psychiatric therapy
_____ Frequent bad headaches
_____ Ulcers
_____ Kidney disease
_____ Urinary problems
_____ Arthritis or skeletal problems
_____ Cleft palate
_____ Asthma
_____ Lung or breathing problems
_____ Unexplained weight loss
_____ Cancer of (_____)
_____ Other tumor (_____)
_____ Blood transfusions
_____ Hepatitis
_____ AIDS
_____ Meningitis

33. Do any blood relatives have:

_____ Diabetes
_____ Hypoglycemia
_____ Other major medical problems such as those above. Please specify:

_____ Cancer
_____ Heart disease

34. Describe serious accidents *unless* directly related to your doctor's visit here.

_____ None
_____ Occurred with head injury, loss of consciousness, or whiplash
_____ Occurred without head injury, loss of consciousness, or whiplash
Describe:

35. List all current medications and doses (include birth control pills and vitamins).

36. Medication allergies

_____ None
_____ Penicillin
_____ Sulfa

_____ Novocaine
_____ Iodine
_____ Codeine

_____ Tetracycline   _____ Adhesive tape
_____ Erythromycin   _____ Aspirin
_____ Keflex/Ceclor/Ceftin   _____ X-ray dyes
_____ Other: (Please specify.)

37. List operations:
    _____ Tonsillectomy   _____ Appendectomy
          (age _____)   (age _____)
    _____ Appendectomy   _____ Heart surgery
          (age _____)   (age _____)
    Other: (Please specify.)

38. List toxic drugs or chemicals to which you have been exposed:
    _____ Lead   _____ Streptomycin, Neomycin, Kanamycin
    _____ Mercury   _____ Other: (Please list.)

39. Have you had x-ray _treatments_ to your head or neck (including treatments for acne or ear problems as a child), treatments for cancer, etc.?
    Yes _____   No _____

40. Describe serious health problems of your spouse or children.
    _____ None

Appendix III
Checklist of Vocal Abuse for Teachers

Please circle the following statements if they are appropriate to you. Please add any additional items that may be special in your life or setting.

Vocal Abuse/Misuse Items

1. Talking too much
2. Talking too loudly
3. Talking too rapidly
4. Talking while moving vigorously
5. Talking while lifting, bending or moving arms
6. Taking the "teacher's voice" out of the classroom
7. Shouting and yelling excessively to distant people
8. Talking over classroom, cafeteria, barroom noise
9. Inappropriate use of the telephone
10. Inappropriate emphasis on vowel onset words
11. Jerky revisions of phrases and sentences
12. Use of fillers, Uh-huh, OK, and Uhm, etc.
13. Singing or talking in the car
14. Inadequate sleep or rest
15. Excessive talking at sports events
16. Exposure to dust
17. Exposure to fumes from cleaning products
18. Exposure to primary or secondary tobacco smoke
19. Exposure to dry air
20. Poor acoustics in the classroom
21. Poor ventilation in the classroom
22. Lack of hydration (don't drink enough water)
23. Use of cough drops with menthol, mint, or anesthetics
24. Alcohol
25. Smoking
26. Caffeine (coffee, tea, carbonated beverages, chocolate)
27. Spicy foods
28. Acidic foods
29. Dairy products
30. Over the counter decongestants and antihistamines
31. Cough medicines
32. Aspirin/Ibuprofen
33. Mouthwash
34. Mints
35. Asthma inhalers
36. Poor breath support
37. Excessive chest breathing
38. Too big a breath
39. Too small a breath
40. Abrupt voice onset
41. Excessive tension in voice or throat
42. Too high or low a pitch to the voice
43. Too closed or tense jaw
44. High tongue position and tongue tension
45. Reduced use of tongue in forming words with jaw substitution
46. Poor tone focus, voice "in throat"
47. Facial tension
48. Poor posture, bent from waist
49. Neck tension
50. Speaking with jaw thrust or constriction
51. Unresolved stress

Other_____

_____

_____

_____

_____

_____

_____

Appendix IVa
Laryngologist's Report

JOSEPH SATALOFF, M.D., D. Sc.
ROBERT T. SATALOFF, M.D., D.M.A.
JOSEPH R. SPIEGEL, M.D.
1721 PINE STREET
PHILADELPHIA, PA 19103

(215) 545-3322
T.D.D. (215) 985-4080
FAX (215) 790-1192

OTOLOGY/NEUROTOLOGY
OCCUPATIONAL HEARING LOSS
PROFESSIONAL VOICE CARE

OTOLARYNGOLOGY/ALLERGY
HEAD AND NECK SURGERY
FACIAL PLASTIC SURGERY

April 27, 1995

Dear Doctor:

I had the pleasure of seeing your cousin, John Doe, in the office today. Mr. Doe describes increased hoarseness and voice fatigue over the past six months. He has had increased vocal demands over the past 1½ years, and he feels as though his voice is "worn out." He works as a trainer and presenter in the computer industry. He travels extensively around the United States and Canada, and he lectures for approximately eight hours per day, four days per week. He describes his speaking as very fast-paced, before sizable crowds (generally one hundred people or more), and he is usually the only speaker. He offers little time for questions and answers. He occasionally uses a microphone when presenting, but he does not perceive any benefit for his voice when using it. He has no avocational voice use. He reports having a lifelong problem with "talking too loud." He does not live with any individuals who are hard of hearing. His only other complaints are of excessive dryness, not only in the membranes of the mouth and throat, but also dry skin. He has occasional hayfever allergies and uses Sudafed, as needed. He denies a history of asthma. He has had no training for his voice. He is on no medications and has no medication allergies.

Otoscopic examination was normal. Examination of the nose, oral cavity, and oropharynx was normal. Laryngeal examination was performed by strobovideolaryngoscopy. Enclosed please find a videotape and copy of the examination for your review. There was marked reflux laryngitis and a slight decrease in the function of the right superior laryngeal nerve. There was also a moderate degree of muscular tension dysphonia. Reports from the members of my voice team are enclosed.

I have started Mr. Doe on an antireflux protocol. I have referred him to Dr. Steven Mandel for laryngeal EMG and to Dr. John Cohn for evaluation of his decreased pulmonary function. I will keep you advised of the results of their evaluation. Thank you again for your referral.

With best regards.

Very truly yours,

Robert Thayer Sataloff, M.D., D.M.A.
Professor of Otolaryngology
Thomas Jefferson University

RTS/jpo

Enclosures

Appendix IVb
Strobovideolaryngoscopy Report

JOSEPH SATALOFF, M.D., D. Sc.
ROBERT T. SATALOFF, M.D., D.M.A.
JOSEPH R. SPIEGEL, M.D.
1721 PINE STREET
PHILADELPHIA, PA 19103

(215) 545-3322
T.D.D. (215) 985-4080
FAX (215) 790-1192

OTOLOGY/NEUROTOLOGY
OCCUPATIONAL HEARING LOSS
PROFESSIONAL VOICE CARE

OTOLARYNGOLOGY/ALLERGY
HEAD AND NECK SURGERY
FACIAL PLASTIC SURGERY

REPORT OF OPERATION: John Doe

April 27, 1995

PREOPERATIVE DIAGNOSIS:

1. Dysphonia
2. Hoarseness
3. Voice fatigue

POSTOPERATIVE DIAGNOSIS:

1. Severe reflux laryngitis
2. Probable right superior laryngeal nerve paresis
3. Muscular tension dysphonia
4. Mild right vocal fold stiffness
5. Congenital asymptomatic sulcus vocalis

PROCEDURE:

Laryngoscopy with magnification, strobovideolaryngoscopy, and voice analysis including synchronized electroglottography

SURGEON:

Robert Thayer Sataloff, M.D., D.M.A.

The patient was taken to the special procedure room and prepared in the usual fashion. Topical anesthesia was used. In addition to the rigid laryngoscope, flexible laryngoscopy was included to permit dynamic voice assessment. The laryngoscope was inserted and suspended from the video system for magnification and documentation. Initial examination was performed using continuous light. The voice was hoarse, low in pitch, and used excessive vocal fry. There was supraglottic hyperfunctional activity with decrease in anterior/posterior diameter during phonation at the patient's habitual pitch. The appearance of the patient's supraglottic architecture did not improve significantly with voluntary increase in pitch. Abduction and adduction initially appeared normal on the right and was normal on the left. However, after repetitive maneuvers and slight fatigue, there was a distinct right vocal fold lag suggesting mild right superior laryngeal paresis. Laryngeal

Page 2
April 27, 1995
Operative Report (cont'd)
Robert Thayer Sataloff, M.D., D. M. A.
re: John Doe

EMG will be needed for confirmation. Increase in longitudinal tension tested by glissando initially appeared normal bilaterally. However, later in the examination after fatigue had occurred, there was slight decrease on the right with a minimal height disparity (left higher than right). Initially, there was no laryngeal dysdiadochokinesis; but later in the examination, there was irregular motion with right slowing.

The arytenoids were severely erythematous in color with posterior cobblestoning. True vocal fold color was normal under continuous light. However, under stroboscopic light, there was a slight pink hue to the vibratory margin of the right vocal fold. The right vocal fold margin was also slightly stiff. This appearance suggested previous injury, possibly resolved submucosal hemorrhage. This degree of stiffness should not significantly affect his voice for his purposes. There was also a small sulcus vocalis below the vibratory margin on the right. There were no vocal fold masses.

The procedure was continued using stroboscopic light. Observations were made at several frequencies and intensities. Vibrations were asymmetric in amplitude and fairly asymmetric in phase. Periodicity was regular. Glottic closure was incomplete. Incomplete glottic closure occurred as a posterior chink and occasionally as a tiny anterior glottic chink. Amplitude of the right vocal fold was slightly decreased. Amplitude of the left vocal fold was normal. Wave form of the right vocal fold was normal. Wave form of the left vocal fold was normal. There were no adynamic segments.

Simultaneous, synchronized electroglottography was performed in conjunction with strobovideolaryngoscopy. The electroglottograph revealed peak skewing. Synchronized electroglottography was also used to assess periodicity. The procedure was concluded without complication.

[signature]

Robert Thayer Sataloff, M.D., D.M.A.
Professor of Otolaryngology
Thomas Jefferson University

RTS/jpo

Appendix IVc
Objective Voice Analysis

JOSEPH SATALOFF, M.D., D. Sc.
ROBERT T. SATALOFF, M.D., D.M.A.
JOSEPH R. SPIEGEL, M.D.
1721 PINE STREET
PHILADELPHIA, PA 19103

(215) 545-3322
T.D.D. (215) 985-4080
FAX (215) 790-1192

OTOLOGY/NEUROTOLOGY
OCCUPATIONAL HEARING LOSS
PROFESSIONAL VOICE CARE

OTOLARYNGOLOGY/ALLERGY
HEAD AND NECK SURGERY
FACIAL PLASTIC SURGERY

OBJECTIVE VOICE MEASURES

NAME: John Doe   DOB: 03/22/68   AGE: 27
DATE: 04/27/95   HEIGHT: 71   WEIGHT: 180
DIAGNOSIS: reflux, SLNp, r/o myasthenia gravis, muscle tension dysphonia

RESULTS   NORMATIVE DATA

                            Age Norms:
Conversational SFF: 121   Male: 119.5 Hz
Conversational dB: 88
Reading SFF: 129
Reading dB: 88
Percent Voiced: 93.8   Marvin Williams reading passage: 94.5–100%
FRP: 48 semitones   Female: 36 semitones
(72.7–1229 Hz)   (Range 80.1–674.6 Hz)
Musical: 45 semitones
(83.3–1148 Hz)

Acoustic Measures Obtained from Spoken Prolonged /A/ vowel

			THRESHOLDS
Average Fundamental Frequency:	123.685	F_0	139
Absolute Jitter (Jita)	33.252	us	83.2 us
Jitter Percent (Jitt)	0.411	%	1.04%
Relative Average Perturbation (RAP)	0.219	%	0.68%
Pitch Perturbation Quotient (PPQ)	0.234	%	0.84%
Smoothed PPQ (sPPQ)	1.027	%	1.02%
Fundamental Frequency Variation (vF0)	1.354	%	1.10%
Shimmer in dB (ShdB)	0.158	dB	0.35 dB
Shimmer Percent (Shim)	1.789	%	3.81%

(continued)

Page 2
April 27, 1995
Operative Report (cont'd)
Robert Thayer Sataloff, M.D., D. M. A.
re: John Doe

			THRESHOLDS
Amplitude Perturbation Quotient (APQ)	1.535	%	3.07%
Smoothed APQ (sAPQ)	4.433	%	4.23%
Peak Amplitude Variation (vAm)	15.627	%	8.20%
Noise to Harmonic Ratio (NHR)	0.131		0.19
Voice Turbulence Index (VTI)	0.0240.061		
Soft Phonation Index (SPI)	19.58714.12		
F0 Tremor Intensity Index (FTRI)	0.743	%	0.95%
Ampl. Tremor Intensity Index (ATRI)	(N/A)	%	4.37%
Degree of Voice Breaks (SDV)	0.000	%	1.00%
Degree of Sub-harmonics (DSH)	0.000	%	1.00%
Degree of Voiceless (DUV)	0.000	%	1.00
Number of Voice Breaks (NVB)	0		0.90
Number of Sub-harmonic segments (NSH)	0		0.90
Number of Unvoiced segments (NUV)	0		0.90
Numberof Segments Computed (SEG)	87		
Total Pitch Periods Detected (PER)	338		

ACOUSTIC PROFILE (SPOKEN) /A/

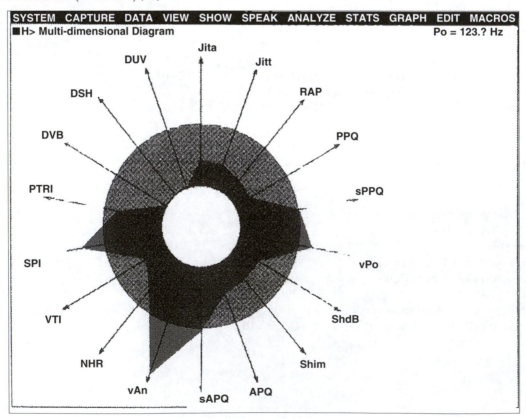

Page 3
April 27, 1995
OBJECTIVE VOICE ANALYSIS: John Doe

AERODYNAMIC/GLOTTAL EFFICIENCY MEASURES

RESULTS	NORMATIVE DATA
MPT: 27.25 sec	Male: 34.6 sec
	(confidence limits 30.2–39.4)
MFR: 142.626 mL/sec	Male: 119 mL/sec
	(confidence limits 96–141)
s/z ratio: 1.570	1.0 (confidence limits 0.8–1.299)
Inverse Filtered Wave	
AC Flow: 910	234 mL/sec (193–461)
Min. Flow: 85	101 mL/sec (101–152)
EGG QuasiOpen: .59	.55–.65 Normal Range
32.6% Closing Slope:	No current norms

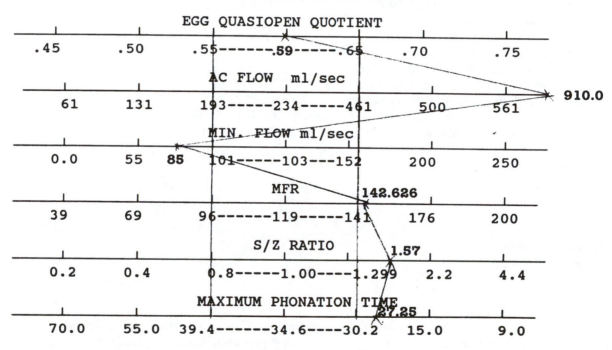

GLOTTAL EFFICIENCY PROFILE

Page 4
April 27, 1995
OBJECTIVE VOICE ANALYSIS: John Doe

ADDITIONAL OBJECTIVE MEASURES

VIBRATO MEASURES — no measurable vibrato/tremor detected

LONG-TERM AVERAGE

Long-term averaging revealed proportional energy in the following frequency bands:

> 0000–1000 Hz 51.9%
> 1000–3500 Hz 23.7%
> 3500–5000 Hz 13.1%
> 5000–8000 Hz 11.3%
>
> A print-out is attached

PULMONARY FUNCTION TESTING:
Normative data: (Knudson)
FEV 1.0: 4.12 liters (88% of predicted)
FVC: 5.39 liters (96% of predicted)
FEF 25–75: 3.48 liters (70% of predicted)
COPD Index: 8 (LOW)   Lung Age: 36
3/3 matches.   Screening Spirometry within normal limits
BORDERLINE SIGNIFICANT CHANGE POST BRONCHODILATION
FVC   +2%   FEV 1.0   +7%   FEF 25–75   +19%

Reinhardt J. Heuer, Ph.D.
Voice Technologist

Recording/Analysis Equipment:
7½" Nagra (E) reel to reel tape recorder, Beyer Dynamic (M88N-c) microphone at a distance of 15 cm., Kay Elemetrics DSP Sona-Graph (5500), Kay Elemetrics Laryngograph, Kay Elemetrics Visi-Pitch (SE 6095), CSL Model 4300, Kay MDVP 4305, Voice Identification PM Analyzer, Tamarac Presto Spiro Sense Spirometry System. The recording room met or exceeded the ANSI S3.1 (1977) standards.

Page 5
OBJECTIVE VOICE ANALYSIS: John Doe

<u>SPECTROGRAPHIC ANALYSIS</u>
<u>KAY ELEMETRICS</u>
<u>DSP SONA-GRAPH 5500</u>

POWER SPECTRUM (TOP) AND NARROW BAND SPECTRUM (BOTTOM) FOR /ʌ/:

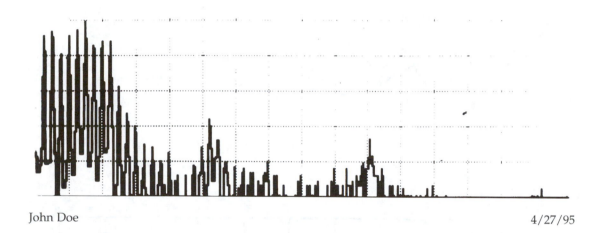

John Doe   4/27/95

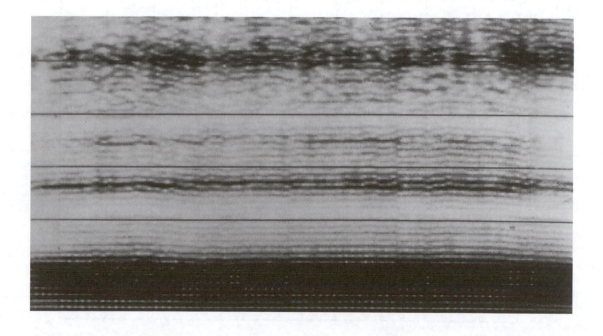

Page 6
OBJECTIVE VOICE ANALYSIS: John Doe

LONG TERM AVERAGE (MARVIN WILLIAMS PASSAGE)

EGG AND INVERSE FILTERED GLOTTAL WAVE ON /A/

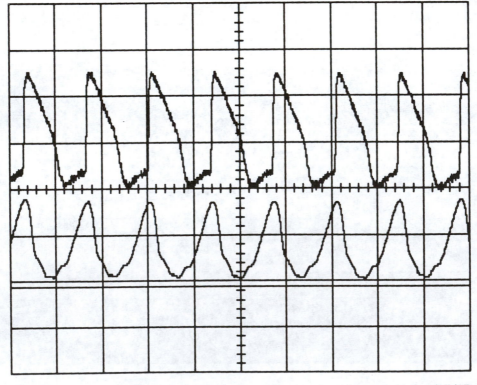

John Doe   4/27/95

TAMARAC SYSTEMS PRESTO

04/27/95   73%   09:46:31

NAME: John Doe _____

ID# 172-54-0029   AGE: 27
HEIGHT: 5' 11"   WEIGHT: 180 lbs.
RACE: 100%   SEX: MALE

THIS PATIENT IS A NON-SMOKER

_____

SPIROMETRY RESULTS

	ACT	PRED	%PR	POST
FVC	5.39	5.63	96	5.48
FEV1	4.12	4.69	88	4.40
FEV1/FVC%	76%	83%	92	80%
FEF25-75%	3.48	4.94	70	4.12
FEFmax	7.91	10.01	79	8.23
FEV3	5.26	5.35	98	5.42
FEF25%	7.80	9.31	84	8.23
FEF50%	4.28	6.64	64*	5.13
FEF75%	1.52	3.47	44*	1.91
MMET	0.78	0.57	136	0.66
FIVC	5.52	5.63	98	5.63
FIF50	6.89	6.64	104	8.51
FIFmax	7.07	6.64	106	8.81
BEST FVC	5.39	5.63	96	5.48
BEST FEV1	4.12	4.69	88	4.42

BTPS factor = 1.0979   VER 1.9
Last calibration: 04/27/95
Normals from Knudson 1983.

BASE FVC: 3 TRIES   3 MATCHES

POST-BD FVC: 3 TRIES   3 MATCHES

BASELINE TEST QUALITY:
Maneuver stopped too suddenly.

POST-BD TEST QUALITY:
Maneuver has a hesitating start.
Uneven exhalation. (Cough?)

SPIROMETRY WITHIN NORMAL LIMITS

* NO SIGNIFICANT CHANGE POST-BD

FVC	FEV1	FEV1/FVC%	FEF25-75%
+2%	+7%	+5%	+19%

COPD risk index: 8 (LOW)
Patient's lung age is 36 years.

Technician: StⁱF _____

*NOTE: Although this change is within computer
       norms, it may be significant in a
       professional voice user.

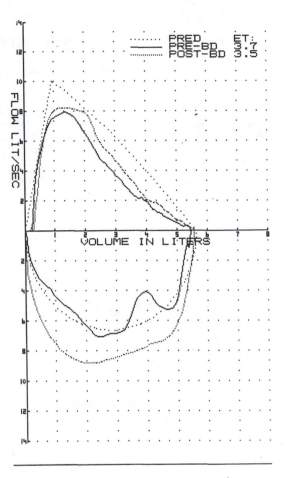

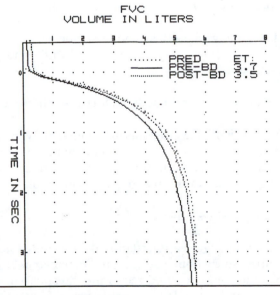

NEUROLOGY AND NEUROPHYSIOLOGY ASSOCIATES, P.C.

Steven Mandel, M.D.
Clinical Professor of Neurology
Jefferson Medical College
Neuromuscular Diseases

Ramon Mañon-Espaillat, M.D.
Clinical Associate Professor of Neurology
Jefferson Medical College
Epilepsy and Sleep Disorders

Brian Kelly, M.D.
Instructor of Neurology
Jefferson Medical College
Clinical Neurophysiology

May 4, 1995

Robert Sataloff, M.D.
1721 Pine Street
Philadelphia, PA 19103

Reference: John Doe
                Evaluation Date: 4/27/95

Dear Dr. Sataloff:

DIAGNOSIS: Superior Laryngeal Nerve Paresis

HISTORY: I had the pleasure of seeing John Doe in the office on April 27, 1995 for a neurological consultation and electrodiagnostic studies.

He is a 27-year old gentleman who has had chief complaints of losing his voice intermittently over a period of six months. He denies any other medical problems. He is a public speaker. He said his major problem is voice deformity. He speaks eight hours a day.

He has no allergies. He takes no medicine. He does not drink alcohol excessively. He does not smoke cigarettes. He is not receiving any therapy. In 1987 and 1989 he had heartburn. He has frequent sore throats. He has back pain.

Review of systems and family history are otherwise unremarkable.

EXAMINATION: He is a pleasant gentleman who appears to have no specific tenderness that I could appreciate to his neck or back area. The cranial nerves are normal. Motor examination, reflexes, coordination, and sensation are all within normal limits. No evidence of cranial or carotid bruits was noted. Graphesthesia, astereognosis, localization and extinction are all normal.

Electrodiagnostic studies were performed.

EMG: Accessory nerve stimulation demonstrated normal latency and amplitude response, with repetitive stimulation study demonstrating no incremental or decremental response. Needle EMG examination demonstrated 40% reduced recruitment response from the right superior laryngeal cricothyroid muscle. The remainder of the needle EMG study was within normal limits.

Sheridan building • 125 South Ninth Street • Philadelphia, PA 19107

1925 South Broad Street • Philadelphia, PA 19148

151 Fries Mill road • Suite 102 • Turnersville, NJ 08012

Phone: (215) 574-0075   Fax: (215) 627-8208   NJ Phone: (609) 228-0006

IMPRESSION: This is a 27-year old gentleman with a history of voice difficulties. His complaints and elec-trodiagnostic studies are most consistent with the diagnosis of superior laryngeal nerve paresis. There is a 40% reduced recruitment response from right cricothyroid muscle. The remainder of the EMG study, includ-ing neuromuscular junction testing was normal.

The above electrical studies are consistent with a right superior laryngeal nerve paresis with a 40% reduced recruitment response.

I hope this information is helpful to you.

Thank you for asking me to see this nice gentleman.

Sincerely,

Steven Mandel, M.D.

SM/cgs

Appendix IVd
Speech-Language Pathologist's Report

JOSEPH SATALOFF, M.D., D. Sc.
ROBERT T. SATALOFF, M.D., D.M.A.
JOSEPH R. SPIEGEL, M.D.
1721 PINE STREET
PHILADELPHIA, PA 19103

OTOLOGY/NEUROTOLOGY
OCCUPATIONAL HEARING LOSS
PROFESSIONAL VOICE CARE

(215) 545-3322
T.D.D. (215) 985-4080
FAX (215) 790-1192

OTOLARYNGOLOGY/ALLERGY
HEAD AND NECK SURGERY
FACIAL PLASTIC SURGERY

INITIAL VOICE EVALUATION

PATIENT: John Doe

DATE OF EVALUATION: 4/27/95

ADDRESS: x xxxx xxxxxxxxx xxxx
xxxxxxxxxxxxxxxxxx

DATE OF BIRTH: xx/xx/xx

AGE: xx

(H) (xxx) xxx-xxxx
(W) (xxx) xxx-xxxx

HISTORY

The above named patient has been experiencing vocal difficulty over the past 6–8 months. His voice has gotten progressively worse over that time period, with complaints of hoarseness, pain in his throat (particularly in the morning), and a feeling that he needs to force his voice as the evening goes on. Mr. Doe was examined on this date of evaluation by Dr. Robert T. Sataloff who diagnosed gastroesophageal reflux and a superior laryngeal nerve paresis.

Mr. Doe is an excessive voice user. For the past 1½ years he has been doing software training, speaking 8 hours/day, 3–4 days/week. He has had no previous speech or voice therapy, nor has he had any training for his speaking voice. His job requires a significant amount of air travel. Although Mr. Doe has done no singing or acting either professionally or avocationally, he has done and enjoyed doing stand-up comedy. The patient smoked "very, very, very little" approximately 10 years ago. He partakes in alcohol which includes approximately 15-20 drinks/week (social). Mr. Doe has cut down his caffeine intake significantly. He was drinking up to ½ gallon of caffeinated soda and coffee, daily. He now drinks 1–2 cups of coffee/day. The patient admits to yelling and loud talking. He exercises with regularity which includes some lifting. The breathing technique he uses in lifting was demonstrated and deemed correct. It seems that the patient's systemic hydration is adequate. He drinks at least 8 glasses of water/day. He complains of environmental dryness complicated by his air travel. He admittedly does not get adequate rest and sleep. He denies being under stress or tension.

Page 2
April 27, 1995
Initial Voice Evaluation (cont'd)
Rhonda K. Rulnick, M.A., CCC-SLP
re: John Doe

Mr. Doe describes his general medical health as "good." His history is negative for heart problems, high blood pressure, frequent bouts of pneumonia or bronchitis, post-nasal drip, allergies or asthma, frequent bouts of indigestion, or any neurogenic symptomatology. His only complaint is that of frequent sore throats. Mr. Doe has not sustained any head or neck injury and is currently on no medications.

EXAMINATION

Mr. Doe presents with a voice/speech pattern that could be best described as excessive in loudness and rate, harsh, and predominated by glottal fry. Articulation was judged to be within normal limits. "Hard" or "constricted" glottal attacks were excessive in both conversational speech and in reading (30% of the vowel initiated words in a reading passage were judged to be "hard" or "constricted."). The patient seemed to prefer a thoracic pattern of breath support. He was able to prolong the /ʌ/ for 27.25 seconds, the unvoiced /s/ for 27.03 seconds, and the voiced /z/ for 19.72 seconds. This yielded an s/z ratio of 1.37. Habitual pitch was judged to be low. However, pitch range was found to be generally within normal limits. Mandibular excursion during speech production was slightly limited with concomitant jaw and facial tension noted. The patient also tended to retract and tense his tongue while speaking. The patient's vocal placement was judged to be "back/pharyngeal." A slight regional nasal resonance was perceived.

A cursory examination of the oral/facial mechanism revealed all structures (including the face, lips, tongue, jaw, and velum) to be intact for symmetry, strength, range of motion, speed of movement, and coordination. Mr. Doe admits to some TMJ symptomatology. He is "supposed to wear a night guard" because he "gnashes his teeth at night." The patient denies any difficulty with swallowing.

TRIAL THERAPY

A number of therapy techniques were demonstrated and instructed during the course of the evaluation session. The patient responded exceptionally well to techniques of abdominal/diaphragmatic breath support, vocal placement suggestions including slight vowel elongation, and easy onset/linking of vowel initiated words. All techniques were effective in eliciting both an improved vocal quality, as well as a purported sense of ease in vocal production. Tongue stretching/relaxation exercises were not particularly helpful.

ASSESSMENT/RECOMMENDATIONS

Mr. Doe presents with a preliminary diagnosis of gastroesophageal reflux, a superior laryngeal nerve paresis, and is to be evaluated to rule-out myasthenia gravis. The voice with which he presents can be consistent with any of those diagnoses. It cannot be determined, however, to what extent his vocal complaints are related to the underlying etiology. Whenever there is a change in either the anatomy or physiology of the vocal mechanism, it is common for the individual to inadvertently and unconsciously attempt to compensate for the problem in some way. This compensation is usually in the direction of exerting more "push" and strain on the voice as opposed to "easing up" on the voice. This seems to be the case with Mr. Doe. The techniques demonstrated within this session, geared toward generalized "easing up" of the voice, were highly successful and thus support the notion that the patient has tended to overcompensate in the wrong direction.

Page 3
April 27, 1995
Initial Voice Evaluation (cont'd)
Rhonda K. Rulnick, M.A., CCC-SLP
re: John Doe

On the basis of his positive response to the trial therapy and on his purported motivation to improve, Mr. Doe presents an excellent prognosis for improving the manner in which he uses his voice, which should result in a concomitant change in his vocal quality. It is recommended that Mr. Doe undergo a course of voice therapy for approximately 4–6 sessions toward the following specific goals:

1. Eliminate vocal abuse and promote good vocal hygiene.

2. Establish a consistent pattern of abdominal/diaphragmatic breath support in all speaking situations.

3. Eliminate "hard" or "constricted" vowel initiation.

4. Encourage a slower rate of speech.

5. Promote a more oral/forward place of vocal focus.

6. Promote generalized relaxation of the head, neck, and upper torso.

Respectfully submitted,

Rhonda K. Rulnick, M.A., CCC-SLP
Speech-Language Pathologist

RKR/jpo

Appendix IVe
Singing Voice Specialist's Report

JOSEPH SATALOFF, M.D., D. Sc.
ROBERT T. SATALOFF, M.D., D.M.A.
JOSEPH R. SPIEGEL, M.D.
1721 PINE STREET
PHILADELPHIA, PA 19103

(215) 545-3322
T.D.D. (215) 985-4080
FAX (215) 790-1192

OTOLOGY/NEUROTOLOGY
OCCUPATIONAL HEARING LOSS
PROFESSIONAL VOICE CARE

OTOLARYNGOLOGY/ALLERGY
HEAD AND NECK SURGERY
FACIAL PLASTIC SURGERY

VOCAL STRESS ASSESSMENT

Name: John Doe
Date of Evaluation: 04/27/95

Mr. Doe is a 27-year-old trainer and presenter of software who came to this office for a complete voice evaluation. Mr. Doe complains of voice difficulties which have persisted for the past six months, characterized by pain in the throat in the mornings, hoarseness in the morning and evening, vocal fatigue and decreased stamina with speaking. He reports that his voice problems are worsening with time. A complete laryngeal examination was completed today by Dr. Robert T. Sataloff, revealing neuromuscular inconsistencies, reflux laryngitis, possible myasthenia gravis, right superior laryngeal nerve paresis and muscle tension dysphonia.

Medications: Mr. Doe is not taking any medications regularly at this time; however, he reports taking Sudafed for allergies and Tylenol for pain.

Allergies: Hayfever

Vocal Hygiene: Mr. Doe reports that he used to drink 6-8 cups of caffeinated beverages a day, but has reduced his consumption to 1-2 cups a day. He drinks at least 8 glasses of water a day, and approximately 15 alcoholic beverages a week. He does not smoke or use tobacco products. He sleeps 7 hours a night, which does not feel sufficient to Mr. Doe. He reports that his job is stressful, and that he has stress regarding getting married next month, but does not feel stressed. Mr. Doe describes his voice use as "speaking constantly." He estimates that he speaks 10-11 hours a day. He utilizes a microphone when giving presentations most of the time; however, he admits that he has a hard time modifying his loudness so that it is not too loud. He feels he is generally a loud talker, and admits to yelling. He reports that he carries a lot of tension in his shoulders and neck, and feels the tension has a direct effect on his voice.

This session began with a comprehensive discussion of the patient's vocal and medical histories. The focus of this session was to evaluate Mr. Doe's vocal technique and identify areas that need to be addressed for a more healthy and efficient vocal production.

Page 2
April 27, 1995
Voice Stress Assessment (cont'd)
Kate A. Emerich, B.M., M.S., CCC-SLP
re: John Doe

During the initial singing evaluation, Mr. Doe demonstrated the following technical deficiencies: facial, neck, and shoulder tension, tongue and jaw tension, thoracic breathing, insufficient breath support, throat tension, decreased airflow, decreased oral resonance, frequent glottal fry, and posterior tone placement. He presented with a generally pressed vocal production. His approximate range was B♭2-C#5.

Vocal Exercises: Abdominal breathing was explained and demonstrated, and Mr. Doe was given abdominal exercises to elicit abdominal breathing and support. S-words and phrases were used to stimulate abdominal involvement in speaking, but also to promote increased airflow and energy in the sound. Exercises to open the throat, eg, sighs, were implemented to relax the pharynx and allow for greater ease of vocalizations.

Impressions: Mr. Doe is an intelligent and motivated patient who demonstrated the ability to modify his manner of breathing to include abdominal muscle involvement. He also was able to increase his airflow to eliminate the glottal fry. He would benefit from voice therapy to promote continuous voicing and airflow, eliminate vocally abusive behaviors, improve abdominal breathing and support, decrease excessive extrinsic laryngeal muscle tension, increase oral resonance, eliminate glottal fry, promote frontal tone focus, and follow closely with vocal hygiene and reflux regimens in order to achieve a more functional voice, and prevent the development of vocal pathologies common with Mr. Doe's current manner of speaking. He should be followed.

Thank you for allowing me to participate in his care.

Sincerely,

Kate A. Emerich, B.M., M.S., CCC-SLP
Speech-Language Pathologist
Singing Voice Specialist

Appendix IVf
Acting Voice Specialist's Report

JOSEPH SATALOFF, M.D., D. Sc.
ROBERT T. SATALOFF, M.D., D.M.A.
JOSEPH R. SPIEGEL, M.D.
1721 PINE STREET
PHILADELPHIA, PA 19103

(215) 545-3322
T.D.D. (215) 985-4080
FAX (215) 790-1192

OTOLOGY/NEUROTOLOGY
OCCUPATIONAL HEARING LOSS
PROFESSIONAL VOICE CARE

OTOLARYNGOLOGY/ALLERGY
HEAD AND NECK SURGERY
FACIAL PLASTIC SURGERY

PERFORMANCE VOICE ASSESSMENT

Name: John Doe
Date of Evaluation: 4/27/95

Joe Doe is a 27-year-old software trainer and salesperson who came to this office with complaints of hoarseness and pain in his throat. He has been having voice difficulties for the past 6 months. He reports that his voice is hoarse in the morning, gets better as the day progresses, but then becomes hoarse and fatigued in the evening. Mr. Doe was given a complete laryngeal examination by Dr. Robert T. Sataloff who diagnosed reflux laryngitis, right vocal fold weakness, and possible myasthenia gravis.

Joe Doe is a professional voice user who reports using his voice professionally approximately 8 hrs during his work day. He makes presentations to both small and large groups of people. These groups range in size from approximately 10 people (with no amplification) to 70 people (with amplification). He reports making no adjustments in singing or speaking training for his voice, although he reports taking one semester of Voice for Theatre in college. The course dealt primarily with posture, meditation, and some voice production. However, Mr. Doe reports coming away with little comprehension of the material in the course. Mr. Doe does not do any vocal preparation for his speaking engagements.

Mr. Doe reports drinking 1–2 cups of caffeinated beverages per day and 2–3 quarts of water each day. He reports drinking approximately 1–2 alcoholic beverages per day. He does not smoke. He is not taking any medications at this time, although he does take Sudafed for his hayfever. He feels his stress level at work is not high. Traveling, however; which is a large part of his job, is very stressful for him. He also reports he is getting married in May which may account for some higher stress levels. The patient does not exercise.

Mr. Doe demonstrated the following technical deficiencies: thoracic breathing, extrinsic neck muscle tension, jaw and posterior tongue tension, tongue tip weakness and frequent glottal fry.

421

Page 2
April 27, 1995
Performance Voice Assessment (cont'd)
Sharon Freed, M.F.A.
re: John Doe

The session began with a discussion of the importance of a daily voice and body warm-up and cool-down for the professional voice user. Mr. Doe was given a 10-minute warm-up on a cassette tape for practice which included exercises for spine and neck stretching, upper body alignment and relaxation, jaw massage, loosening of facial muscles, and articulation warm-ups. Breath support was also discussed as a source of power for him as a speaker. Exercises for increasing breath support was given in both seated and supine positions.

Mr. Doe is an intelligent and compliant patient. Because of the intensity of the speaking requirements demanded by his job, he would greatly benefit from continued high performance voice sessions.

Thank you for allowing me to participate in his care.

Sincerely,

Sharon Freed, M.F.A.
Acting-Voice Trainer

Appendix Va
Outline for Daily Practice

I. Warm-up and cool-down routine

  A. Stretch/relaxation exercises:

    1. Head/neck range of motion

    2. Shoulder rolls and shrugs

    3. Facial massage

    4. Tongue stretch

  B. Vocalises (which are provided by the singing specialist)

  C. Speaking exercises:

    1. Easy speech breathing exercises: "Candle blowing," /s/, /ʃ/, /h/-/ʌ/, /m/, /ʌ/

    2. Oral resonance warm up: "ng-ah"

    3. Connected speech: Counting

    4. Monitoring sites of tension: /f-v/, /s-z/, /T-D/, /S-dʒ/

    5. Bridging exercises:

      a. sliding block scale for /m/

      b. spoken "vocalises"

      c. Lip trills

    6. Quiet breathing exercise

II. Additional daily practice:

The target areas are addressed systematically.

A. Breath control and support

B. Phrasing

C. Easy onset and blending techniques

D. Oral resonance

E. Tone focus and vocal placement

    F. Loudness/projection

    G. Speaking rate, rhythm, and intonation

III. Carryover practice:

    A. Application of specific goals in ongoing speech

    B. Transition from structured to spontaneous

    C. Stress management strategies

Appendix Vb
Sample Phrases

THREE SYLLABLES IN LENGTH

Put it on.

Tell me how.

Walk around.

Did you know?

Juicy peach.

Yes and no.

Do you know?

Crunchy apple.

Put them down.

What's your name?

Come over here.

Not right now.

Time to go.

Close your eyes.

Fine report.

Read the book.

Who is it?

Pick it up.

Take a nap.

Good evening.

FIVE SYLLABLES IN LENGTH

Where are they going?

The concert was great.

Turn off the iron.

FOUR SYLLABLES IN LENGTH

Pleased to meet you

You'd like it there.

The sun was bright.

Fill it up, please.

How much is it?

He knows the way

The train was late.

Maybe later.

Cream and sugar.

Bread and butter.

Salt and pepper

Toast and butter.

Pie and coffee.

Needle and thread.

Turkey and cheese.

Nice to meet you.

That's fine for now.

Don't tease the dog.

Beth arrived late.

This is enough.

SIX SYLLABLES IN LENGTH

That's a good idea.

Ted wants to come along.

Put everything away.

FIVE SYLLABLES IN LENGTH
(continued)

The book was stolen.

Tip the waiter well.

When is he finished?

Flowers need water.

Will she be here soon?

The oven is on.

The tea is steeping.

Yes, that's fine with me.

The phone is ringing.

Play the clarinet.

Let's consider it.

They enjoyed the song.

SEVEN AND EIGHT SYLLABLES IN LENGTH

The weather in August is hot.

I love sleeping late on Sundays.

What time can you come for dinner?

We will probably start at six.

The top of this jar is stuck.

Would you help me open it, please?

I can't remember the number.

Please give it to me again.

What shall we have for dessert?

Pie and ice cream sound delicious.

What are you doing after work?

Be careful not to go too fast.

The snowfall was light that year.

Our guests will arrive at nine.

They ate breakfast at the diner.

SIX SYLLABLES IN LENGTH
(continued)

He can phone us later.

She bought it somewhere else.

Leave the window open.

Place it down carefully.

Come over and see us.

The children were playing.

The fire alarm rang.

The switch is over there.

Let me know when he calls.

They moved to the mountains.

The spectators were pleased.

The puppy is playful.

NINE AND TEN SYLLABLES IN LENGTH

Lisa bought some vegetables for dinner.

He wears a 16 and a half collar.

I will be happy to meet with you.

They all went skiing for the holiday.

The bakery smells simply delicious.

There are four bedrooms on the top floor.

After the rain, the air smelled earthy.

Have you been to the theater lately?

Summer at the seashore is popular.

TEN, ELEVEN, AND TWELVE SYLLABLES IN LENGTH

City buses are often crowded and noisy.

He avoided making eye contact while riding on the bus.

Don't forget to turn off the lights and lock the door.

Oh no, I think I left my keys inside.

We usually go boating each summer.

The car was badly damaged by the crash.

Fortunately, there were no injuries.

Sally loves to go swimming in the lake.

She was reminded not to go too far.

Distilled water tastes much better than tap.

Appendix Vc
Frontal Placement Words

till	town	teal
tot	test	tips
lash	style	still
tall	team	hall
ten	mile	Bill
leash	swell	toad
much	lot	tell
tie	tip	net
latch	least	leap
dial	bell	top
smile	loft	loud
snowfall	town hall	distill
livid	low tide	windmill
tinfoil	vowel	man-made

Appendix Vd
H/Vowel Minimal-Pairs

had-add	hall-all	hold-old
head-Ed	hit-it	home-ohm
hone-own	ho-oh	his-is
hay-ay	hat-at	hand-and
hear-ear	hitch-itch	hi-I

Appendix Ve
Vowel-Initiated Words

LONG VOWELS IN ENGLISH

/ʌ/	/o²/	/ʌːI/	/i̯/
odd	oath	aisle	eat
octet	oat	eye	east
object	oak	ice	each
obtuse	old	idle	eek
octopus	oboe	I've	eager
operate	okay	Irish	Ethan
otter	only	iota	enough
obligate	overt	item	even

SHORT VOWELS IN ENGLISH

/˘/	/ɛ/	/I/	/ʌ̠/
as	end	in	up
at	ever	is	ugh
ask	effort	if	ugly
after	educate	ill	uplift
apple	elephant	id	upset
attitude	enemy	image	utmost
avenue	elegant	issue	under
accident	envy	inactive	unlock
accent	entertain	indent	usher

Appendix Vf
Phrases for Blending

fall over	go into	put upon
leave on	the only	lose it
see it	the other	win it
do it	not even	that's enough
put on	not any	leave open
down under	cold as	one of
not old	the ice	she's ill
look at	he's ill	then add
the end	yes and	so it
high up	one at	Sue is

Appendix Vg
Phrases to Practice Easy Onset and Blending

Elliot ate an apple and allowed Andrew another.

Each and every avenue is open at eight o'clock.

Over on Aston Avenue is an open air amphitheater.

I am in agreement in every aspect of our association.

Alan's attitude is overly obnoxious.

In April, Addie always attends an extravaganza in Arizona.

Alice openly acknowledges an aversion to avocados.

Exercise is an important and energizing activity.

Amanda is in Alabama at an annual event.

It is eleven o'clock already, and all of us are anxiously awaiting Ellen's arrival.

Eliminating additives is advisable.

Is Emily afraid of an eerie effigy?

Eddie is outdoors on an icy evening.

Actually, I am aware of all the errors in Adam's arithmetic assignment.

Every evening in autumn our area orchestra attempts to entertain an uninterested audience of adolescents.

Appendix Vh
Homographs

refuse-refuse

compound-compound

converse-converse

console-console

project-project

contrast-contrast

content-content

commune-commune

minute-minute

object-object

Appendix Vi
Open-Vowel Words

/ʌ/	/ˇ/	/ʌːI/	/ʌu/
top	map	tie	power
hot	match	reply	town
pocket	hot	side	found
deposit	flag	fire	coward
probable	sad	line	tower
knock	bag	fine	without
shot	cash	confide	house
doctor	cast	tired	how
father	happen	height	loud
garage	mash	rhyme	flower

Appendix Vj
Reading Passages

A classic passage including all the speech sounds of English.

The Rainbow Passage

When the sunlight strikes raindrops in the air, they act like a prism and form a rainbow. The rainbow is a division of white light into many beautiful colors. These take the shape of a long round arch, with its path high above, and its two ends apparently beyond the horizon. There is, according to legend, a boiling pot of gold at one end. People look but no one ever finds it. When a man looks for something beyond his reach, his friends say he is looking for the pot of gold at the end of the rainbow.

An all voiced passage.

Marvin Williams

Marvin Williams is only nine. Marvin lives with his mother on Monroe Avenue in Vernon Valley. Marvin loves all movies, even eerie ones with evil villains in them. Whenever a new movie is in the area, Marvin is usually an early arrival. Nearly every evening Marvin is in row one, along the aisle.

A general purpose passage useful for evaluating hard glottal attack, phrasing, and nasal resonance.

Towne-Heuer Vocal Analysis Reading Passage

If I take a trip this August, I will probably go to Austria. Or I could go to Italy. All of the places of Europe are easy to get to by air, rail, ship or auto. Everybody I have talked to says he would like to go to Europe also.

Every year there are varieties of festivals or fairs at a lot of places. All sorts of activities, such as foods to eat, sights to see occur. Oh, I love to eat ices seated outdoors! The people of each area are reported to like us . . . the people of the U.S.A. It is said that that is true except for Paris.

Aid is easy to get because the officials are helpful. Aid is always available if troubles arise. It helps to have with you a list of offices or officials to call if you do require aid. If you are lost, you will always be helped to locate your route or hotel. The local police will assist you, if they are able to speak as you do. Otherwise a phrase book is useful.

I have had to have help of this sort each trip abroad. However, it was always easy to locate. Happily. I hope, less help will be required this trip. Last trip every hotel was occupied. I had to ask everywhere for flats. Two earlier trips were hard because of heat or lack of heat at hotels.

On second thought, I may want to travel in autumn instead of in August. Many countries can be expensive in the summer months and much less so in autumn. November and December can make fine months for entertainment in many European countries. There may be concerts and musical events more often than during the summer. Milan, Rome, and Hamburg, not to mention Berlin, Vienna, and Madrid are most often mentioned for music.

Most of my friends and I wouldn't miss the chance to try the exciting, interesting, and appetizing menus at most continental restaurants. In many European countries food is inexpensive and interestingly prepared. Servings may be small but meals are taken more often so that there is no need to go hungry.

Maritime countries make many meals of seafood, such as mussels, clams, shrimp, flounder, and salmon or herring. Planning and making your own meals cannot be done even in most small, inexpensive hotels. One must eat in the dining room or in restaurants. Much fun can be had meeting the local natives during mealtimes. Many of them can tell you where to find amusing and interesting shops and sights not mentioned in tour manuals.

Suggested Reading List

(See also "Suggested Readings" and "References" listed in individual chapters).

1. Abitbol J. *Atlas of Laser Voice Surgery*. San Diego, Calif: Singular Publishing Group, Inc; 1994.

2. Andrea M, Dias O. *Atlas of Rigid and Contact Endoscopy in Microlaryngeal Surgery*. Philadelphia, Pa: Lippincott-Raven; 1995.

3. Andrews ML. *Voice Therapy for Children*. San Diego, Calif: Singular Publishing Group, Inc; 1991.

4. Andrews ML. *Manual of Voice Treatment*. San Diego, Calif: Singular Publishing Group, Inc; 1994.

5. Appleman DR. *The Science of Vocal Pedagogy*. Bloomington, Ind: Indiana University Press; 1967.

6. Aronson AE. *Clinical Voice Disorders*, 2nd ed. New York, NY: Thieme Medical Publishers, Inc; 1985.

7. *ASHA*. American Speech-Language Hearing Association. Rockville, Md 20852. (journal)

8. Baer T, Sasaki C. *Laryngeal Function in Phonation and Respiration*. San Diego, Calif: Singular Publishing Group, Inc; 1994.

9. Baken RJ. *Clinical Measurement of Speech and Voice*. Boston, Mass: College Hill Press; 1987.

10. Baken RJ, Daniloff RG. *Readings in Clinical Spectrography of Speech*. San Diego, Calif: Singular Publishing Group, Inc; 1991.

11. Benjamin B. *Diagnostic Laryngoscopy*. Philadelphia, Pa: WB Saunders; 1990.

12. Benninger MS, Jacobson BH, Johnson AF. *Vocal Arts Medicine*. New York, NY: Thieme Medical Publishers, Inc; 1994.

13. Blitzer A, Brin MF, Sasaki CT, Fahn S, Harris KS. *Neurologic Disorders of the Larynx*. New York, NY: Thieme Medical Publishers, Inc; 1992.

14. Boone DR. *Is Your Voice Telling on You? How to Find and Use Your Natural Voice*. 2 ed. San Diego, Calif: Singular Publishing Group, Inc; 1997.

15. Borden G, Harris K. *The Speech Primer*. Baltimore, Md: Williams and Wilkins; 1980.

16. Brodnitz F. *Keep Your Voice Healthy*. Boston, Mass: College-Hill Press; 1988.

17. Bunch M. *Dynamics of the Singing Voice. Disorders of Human Communication 6*. New York, NY: Springer-Verlag; 1982.

18. Butcher P, Elias A, Raven R. *Psychogenic Voice Disorders and Cognitive-Behavior Therapy*. San Diego, Calif: Singular Publishing Group, Inc; 1994.

19. Case JL. *Clinical Management of Voice Disorders*. San Diego, Calif: Singular Publishing Group, Inc; 1991.

20. Castell DO: *The Esophagus*. 2nd ed. Boston, Mass: Little Brown and Co; 1995.

21. Colton R, Casper J. *Understanding Voice Problems*. Baltimore, Md: Williams & Wilkins; 1990.

22. Crelin EF. *The Human Vocal Tract*. New York, NY: Vantage Press; 1987.

23. Critchley M, Henson RA. *Music and The Brain*. London: William Heinemann Medical Books Limited; 1977.

24. Dedo HH. *Surgery of the Larynx and Trachea*. Philadelphia, Pa: BC Decker; 1990.

25. Dejonckere PH. *Vibrato*. San Diego, Calif: Singular Publishing Group, Inc; 1988.

26. Doyle PC. *Foundations of Voice and Speech Rehabilitation Following Laryngeal Cancer*. San Diego, Calif: Singular Publishing Group, Inc; 1994.

27. Ford CN, Bless DM. *Phonosurgery: Assessment and Surgical Management*. New York, NY: Raven Press; 1992.

28. Fried M. *The Larynx, A Multidisciplinary Approach*. Boston, Mass: College-Hill Press; 1988.

29. Gould WJ, Lawrence VL. *Surgical Care of Voice Disorders. Disorders of Human Communication 8*. New York, NY: Springer-Verlag; 1984.

30. Gould WJ, Sataloff RT, Spiegel JR. *Voice Surgery*. St. Louis, Mo: CV Mosby; 1993.

31. Green MCL, Mathieson L. *The Voice and Its Disorders*. San Diego, Calif: Singular Publishing Group, Inc; 1994.

32. Jackson C, Jackson CL. *Diseases and Injuries of the Larynx*. New York, NY: Macmillan & Co; 1942.

33. Hirano M. *Clinical Examination of the Voice. Disorders of Human Communication 5*. New York, NY: Springer-Verlag; 1981.

34. Hirano M, Sato K. *Histological Color Atlas of the Human Larynx*. San Diego, Calif: Singular Publishing Group, Inc; 1993.

35. Hirano M, Bless DM. *Videostroboscopic Examination of the Larynx*. San Diego, Calif: Singular Publishing Group, Inc; 1993.

36. Hixon T. *Respiratory Function in Speech and Song*. Boston, Mass: College-Hill Press; 1988.

37. Hollien H. *The Acoustics of Crime*. New York, NY: Plenum Publishing; 1990.

38. Isshiki N. *Phonosurgery—Theory and Practice*. New York, NY: Springer-Verlag; 1989.

39. *Journal of Voice*. Raven Press, 1185 Avenue of the Americas, New York, 10036. (quarterly publication)

40. Kahane JC, Folkins JF. *Atlas of Speech and Hearing Anatomy*. Columbus, Oh: Charles E. Merrill Publishing Co; 1984.

41. Karnell MP. *Videoendoscopy*. San Diego, Calif: Singular Publishing Group, Inc; 1994.

42. Koschkee DL. *Voice Care in the Medical Setting*. San Diego, Calif: Singular Publishing Group, Inc; 1995.

43. Kotby MN. *The Accent Method of Voice Therapy*. San Diego, Calif: Singular Publishing Group, Inc; 1994.

44. Laukkanen A. *On Speaking Voice Exercises*. Tampere: University of Tampere; 1995.

45. Lindestadt P. *Electromyographic and Laryngoscopic Studies of Normal and Disturbed Voice Function*. Stockholm, Sweden: Huddinge University; 1994.

46. Linthicum FH Jr, Schwartzman JA. *An Atlas of Micropathology of the Temporal Bone*. San Diego, Calif: Singular Publishing Group, Inc; 1994.

47. Ludlow CL, Cooper JA. *Genetic Aspects of Speech and Language Disorders*. New York, NY: Academic Press; 1983.

48. Mandel S, Sataloff RT, Schapiro S. *Minor Head Trauma: Assessment, Management and Rehabilitation*. New York, NY: Springer-Verlag; 1993.

49. *Medical Problems of Performing Artists*. Philadelphia, Pa: Hanley & Belfus. (journal)

50. Moriarty J. *Diction*. Boston, Mass: EC Schirmer Music Company; 1975.

51. Morrison M, Rammage L, Nicol H, Pullan B, May P, Salkeld L. *The Management of Voice Disorders*. San Diego, Calif: Singular Publishing Group, Inc; 1994.

52. *The Journal of Singing*. Oberlin, Ohio: National Association of Teachers of Singing. (a bimonthly publication)

53. Orlikoff RF, Baken RJ. *Clinical Voice and Speech Measurement*. San Diego, Calif: Singular Publishing Group, Inc; 1993.

54. Peacher G. *Speak to Win*. New York, NY: Bell Publishing; 1985.

55. Pickett JS. *The Sounds of Speech Communication*. Baltimore, Md: University Park Press; 1980.

56. Prater RJ, Swift RW. *Manual of Voice Therapy*. San Diego, Calif: Singular Publishing Group, Inc; 1984.

57. Proctor TF. *Breathing, Speech and Songs*. New York, NY: Springer-Verlag; 1980.

58. Rubin J, Sataloff RT, Korovin G, Gould WJ. *The Diagnosis and Treatment of Voice Disorders*. New York, NY: Igaku-Shoin Medical Publishers, Inc; 1995.

59. Sataloff J, Sataloff RT, Vassallo LA. *Hearing Loss*. Philadelphia, PA: JB Lippincott; 1980.

60. Sataloff RT, Sataloff J. *Occupational Hearing Loss*. New York, NY: Marcel Dekker; 1987.

61. Sataloff RT, Brandfonbrener A, Lederman R. *Textbook of Performing Arts Medicine*. New York, NY: Raven Press; 1991.

62. Sataloff RT. *Embryology and Anomalies of the Facial Nerve*, New York, NY: Raven Press; 1991.

63. Sataloff RT. *Professional Voice: The Science and Art of Clinical Care*. New York, NY: Raven Press; 1991.

64. Sataloff RT, Titze IR. *Vocal Health and Science*. Jacksonville, Fla: The National Association of Teachers of Singing; 1991.

65. Sataloff RT. The Human Voice. *Sci Am*. 1992;267(6):108-115.

66. Sataloff RT, Sataloff J. *Occupational Hearing Loss*. 2nd ed. New York, NY: Marcel Dekker; 1993.

67. Sataloff RT, Sataloff J. *Hearing Loss*. 3rd ed. New York, NY: Marcel Dekker; 1993.

68. Sataloff J, Sataloff RT. *Occupational Hearing Loss: Source Readings*. San Diego, Calif: Singular Publishing Group, Inc; in preparation.

69. Sataloff RT, Hawkshaw M. *Chaos in Medicine: Source Readings*. San Diego, Calif: Singular Publishing Group, Inc; 1998.

70. Saxon KG, Schneider CM. *Vocal Exercise Physiology*. San Diego, Calif: Singular Publishing Group, Inc; 1994.

71. Stemple J, Gerdman BK. *Clinical Voice Pathology*. San Diego, Calif: Singular Publishing Group, Inc; 1994.

72. Sundberg J. *The Science of the Singing Voice*. DeKalb, Ill: Northern Illinois Press; 1987.

73. Titze IR. *Principles of Voice Production*. Inglewood Cliffs, NJ: Prentice Hall; 1994.

74. Tucker H. *The Larynx*. 2nd ed. New York, NY: Thieme Medical Publishers Inc; 1993.

75. Tucker H. *Surgery for Phonatory Disorders*. New York, NY: Churchhill Livingstone; 1981.

76. Vennard W. *Singing: The Mechanism and the Technic*. New York: Carl Frisher, Inc; 1967.

77. Zemlin WR. *Speech and Hearing Science: Anatomy and Physiology*. Englewood Cliffs, NJ: Prentice-Hall; 1988.

Vocal Fold Physiology Series

Under the auspices of The Voice Foundation, 1721 Pine Street, Philadelphia, Pennsylvania.

1. Baer T, Sasaki C, Harris KS. *Laryngeal Function in Phonation and Respiration.* San Diego, Calif: College-Hill Press; 1991.
2. Bless DM, Abbs H. *Vocal Fold Physiology: Contemporary Research and Clinical Issues.* San Diego, Calif: College-Hill Press; 1983.
3. Fujimura O. *Vocal Physiology: Voice Production, Mechanisms, and Functions.* San Diego, Ca: Singular Publishing Group, Inc; 1988.
4. Fujimura O, Hirano M. *Vocal Fold Physiology: Voice Quality Control.* San Diego, Ca: Singular Publishing Group, Inc; 1994.
5. Gauffin J. Hammarberg B. *Vocal Fold Physiology: Acoustic, Perceptual, and Physiological Aspects of Voice Mechanisms.* San Diego, Calif: Singular Publishing Group, Inc; 1991.
6. Hirano M, Kirchner JA, Bless DM. *Neurolaryngology: Recent Advances.* San Diego, Ca: Singular Publishing Group, 1991.
7. Kirchner JA. *Vocal Fold Histopathology.* San Diego, Calif: College-Hill Press; 1986.
8. Stevens KN, Hirano M. *Vocal Fold Physiology.* Tokyo: Tokyo University Press; 1981.
9. Sundberg J. *The Science of Musical Sounds.* New York, NY: Academic Press; 1991.
10. Ternström S. Acoustics, *Require an Orchestra.* Stockholm, Sweden: Royal Swedish Academy of Music; 1986.
11. Titze RI, Scherer RC. *Vocal Fold Physiology: Biomechanics, Acoustics and Phonatory Control.* Denver, Co: Denver Center for the Performing Arts; 1983.
12. Titze IR. Vocal *Fold Physiology: Frontiers in Basic Science.* San Diego, Calif: Singular Publishng Group, Inc; 1993.
13. Utterback AS. *Broadcast Voice Handbook.* Chicago, Ill: Bonus Books; 1995.

I

Index